MAY 16

D1709431

Sports
LEADERSHIP

Sports
LEADERSHIP

A Reference Guide

Mark Dodds & James T. Reese, Editors

MISSION BELL MEDIA

FIRST EDITION

Library of Congress Preassigned Control Number
2015937810

ISBN 978-0-9907300-1-9

MISSION BELL MEDIA

Rolf A. Janke, CEO
Leah Watson, Director of Marketing
Sara Tauber, Editorial Manager

Produced by Golson Media

Contents

List of Articles

Reader's Guide

Contributor List

Albrecht Rick
Grand Valley State University
Robert E. Baker
George Mason University
Daniel R. Bartlett
Syracuse University
Jordan R. Bass
University of Kansas
Genevieve F. E. Birren
State University of New York, Cortland
Lawrence Brady
State University of New York, Cortland
Chelsea Brehm
Grand Valley State University
Kerri Cebula
Kutzown University
Jeff Coleman
United States Military Academy
Raymond J. Cotrufo
State University of New York, Cortland
Chris Croft
University of Southern Mississippi
Brian Crow
Slippery Rock University
Christi DeWaele
Winthrop University
Heather L. Dichter
Ithaca College
Mark Dodds
*State University of New York,
  Cortland*

Janis K. Doleschal
Marquette University
Craig Esherick
George Mason University
Annemarie Farrell
Ithaca College
Ted Fay
State University of New York, Cortland
Eric W. Forsyth
Bemidji State University
Michael Fox
Independent Scholar
Jarret Gartin
Independent Scholar
Todd A. Gilson
Northern Illinois University
Elizabeth A. Gregg
University of North Florida
Peter Han
*State University of New York,
  Cortland*
Maylon Hanold
Seattle University
Robin Hardin
Independent Scholar
Lana L. Huberty
Concordia University
Jennifer Kane
University of North Florida
Timothy B. Kellison
University of North Florida

Christopher M. Keshock
University of South Alabama

Jordan Kobritz
State University of New York, Cortland

Bill Kte'pi
Independent Scholar

Julie D. Lanzillo
Neumann University

Amber Lattner
Independent Scholar

Jason W. Lee
University of North Florida

Jeffrey F. Levine
University of Louisville

Robert Lyons, Jr.
Queens University of Charlotte

Rachel M. Madsen
Niagara University

Tara Q. Mahoney
State University of New York, Cortland

Christie Marshall
Independent Scholar

Paul M. McInerny
Marquette University

Kasia A. Michalska
Independent Scholar

Kristen Misutka
Gannon University

Dana Munk
Grand Valley State University

Mark S. Nagel
University of South Carolina

Eileen Narcotta-Welp
University of Iowa

G. K. Nwosu
University of Nevada Las Vegas

Brandon Orr
University of Missouri

Molly Ott
Arizona State University

Alexander Parry
Independent Scholar

Jon Welty Peachey
University of Illinois at Urbana-Champaign

Ted B. Peetz
Belmont University

Adam G. Pfleegor
Mississippi State University

Brenda G. Pitts
Georgia State University

Katherine M. Polasek
State University of New York, Cortland

Rocco P. Porreca
Independent Scholar

Alessandro Porrovecchio
University of Lille

Steve Portenga
iPerformance Consultants

James T. Reese
Drexel University

Brian Richardson
State University of New York, Cortland

Lisa Rufer
Virginia Commonwealth University

Claire Schaeperkoetter
University of Kansas

Kristi Schoepfer-Bochicchio
Winthrop University

James A. Schwabach
Independent Scholar

Eric C. Schwarz
Victoria University

Matt Seyfried
State University of New York, Cortland

Sari Shepphird
Independent Scholar

Matthew J. Slater
Staffordshire University

Mark Slavich
Virginia Commonwealth University

Kirsty Spence
Brock University
Ellen J. Staurowsky
Drexel University
Mila C. Su
State University of New York, Plattsburgh
Kristi Sweeney
University of North Florida
Cem Tinaz
Okan University

Tracy A. Traschler
State University of New York, Cortland
George Vazenios
State University of New York, Cortland
Ryan Vooris
Indiana University
Charles H. Wilson, Jr.
Georgia Southern University
Pamela J. Wojnar
American Public University

About the Editors

Mark Dodds is an associate professor teaching sport marketing and sport law at the State University of New York, College at Cortland. He holds a J.D. from Marquette University Law School (MULS), a M.B.A. from Robert Morris University, and a B.S. in Marketing Management from Syracuse University. While at MULS, he earned a Sport Law Certificate from the National Sport Law Institute. His research area is focused on legal issues in sport business, international sport, sponsorship activation, and legal issues with internships. He has published articles in journals such as the *Journal of Brand Strategy, Journal of Sponsorship*; *Marquette Sports Law Review*; *Case Studies in Sport Management*; *Journal of Physical Education, Recreation and Dance*; *Journal of Sponsorship*; *International Journal of Sport Management and Marketing*; and *College Athletics and the Law*. He coedited the award-winning *Encyclopedia of Sports Management and Marketing* and a special motorsports issue of *International Journal of Sport Management and Marketing*.

James T. Reese, Ed.D., is an associate professor in the Sport Management program at Drexel University in Philadelphia, Pennsylvania. Reese is completing his 16th year teaching sport management in higher education. His 2013 edited textbook, *Ticket Operations and Sales Management in Sport,* is the first sport management text to address the field of ticket operations. Reese was the vice president of IFSA/USA (International Federation of Strength Athletes) from 2002 to 2003. Prior to that, he worked as a ticketing administrator for the Denver Broncos, assisting in the ticket planning of Super Bowls XXXII and XXXIII. Reese began his career in the sport industry as an assistant tennis coach and facility management assistant at Georgia Southern University, where he earned his master's degree in Sport Management, and as an assistant tennis coach and facility management assistant at the University of Northern Colorado, where he earned his doctorate in Sport Administration. Reese conducts research in the areas of ticket operations, ticket sales, ticketing-related legal issues in intercollegiate and professional sport, ethical issues related to sport, and facility and event management.

Introduction

Sport has become a vital component in the lives of many people. For a select few participants, sport can be a vehicle for wealth and fame. For others, sport is an opportunity to compete against other athletes. For some people, it is their employment. Many people watch sport and root for their favorite players and team.

But what does it take to win? Obviously talent and hard work are important factors. But many commentators, athletes, and fans attribute "leadership" to athletes and teams who win consistently. This guide will define "leadership" within many different contexts: athletic performance, motivation, and sport business, to name a few.

Leadership can be defined within a specific person. In this setting, leadership is analyzed via personality traits and behaviors. This book seeks to explain why some players and coaches such as Michael Jordan, Michael Phelps, John Wooden, Mike Krzyzewski, and Vince Lombardi achieved more individual and team success than others. Sport administrators and owners, such as David Stern, Bill Veeck, Robert Kraft, and Peter Ueberroth, are also good examples of executives who had a significant positive impact in their respective sports.

This concise reference guide provides academic support for practitioners, faculty members, and students. The entries cover a wide range of topics. Some of the topics overlap but all are designed to provide a leadership perspective on issues impacting the global reach of sport. Topics are categorized under the umbrellas of the following headings:

Leadership Among Athletes discusses topics like the development of leadership skills, self-motivation, leadership on the field and in the locker room, and how the media portrays athletes.

Leadership in Sports Organizations addresses issues such as creating an organizational vision, organizational behavior and culture, the use and influence of social media, officiating, the impact of amateur sport governing bodies, and leadership in emerging sports.

Leadership in Coaching and Managing focuses on topics such as coaching philosophy, coaching athletes with special needs, communication issues, legal responsibilities, and team building.

Ethics in Sport Leadership includes topics such as bulling/hazing, drug use in sports, health and injury issues in sports, and sexual harassment among players.

Leadership in Sport Business covers business-based topics such as entrepreneurship, the impact of professional sport governing bodies, the economics of sports, ticket sales, sponsorship sales, and issues of equal pay for women in the sport workplace.

Leadership in Sports Education looks at how leadership is infused into sport organizations, sport-based curricula, and community programs. A few of the topics include community engagement for sports teams, leadership models in sports, sport in society, sport as a force for social good, and the unionization of college athletes.

In summary, all topics will address the tangible and intangible inherent leadership qualities required to successfully participate or manage in sport or sport-related organizations. Leadership may come in many forms but it is an essential element in the success of sports teams, front offices, governing bodies, reform organizations, and in the classroom.

Mark Dodds and James T. Reese
Editors

Chronology

1876: Albert August Pope establishes the first bicycle factory in Hartford, Connecticut; Pope made an arrangement with the Weed Sewing Machine Company to build 50 bicycles, which he then sold.

1878: Frederick Winthrop Thayer, captain of the Harvard University baseball team, receives a patent for his design of a catcher's mask.

1878: The first bicycle club in the United States, the Boston Bicycle Club, is established in Boston, Massachusetts; George B. Woodward serves as the first president.

1879: Thomas L. Rankin constructs the first indoor ice skating rink in the United States in Madison Square Garden in New York City.

1883: The first African American to play Major League Baseball, Moses Fleetwood Walker, begins his career as a catcher with Toledo; the team originally plays for the Northwestern League and joins the American Association in 1884.

1883: Bob Rogers becomes the first professional sports trainer in the United States; he worked for the New York Athletic Club, following a previous position with the London Athletic Club.

1884: Women compete in the Wimbledon tennis championships for the first time; Maud Watson wins the singles titles in 1884 and 1885.

1888: Photo finishes are used to determine the winners of horse races at a track in Plainfield, New Jersey; the technology will not be adopted for human races for several decades.

1889: Amos Alonzo Stagg, football coach at Yale University, invents the tackling dummy by adapting a gym mat for the purpose.

1890s to 1930: Female baseball teams such as the New York Bloomer Girls, the All Star Ranger Girls, and the Baltimore Black Sox Colored Girls barnstorm across the United States, providing some of the first opportunities for women to compete in professional sports.

1892: Dr. James Naismith, a physical education instructor in Springfield, Massachusetts, invents basketball, with the first game played at the Springfield YMCA on January 20.

1895: Annie Smith Peak becomes the first woman to climb the Matterhorn; she later (1902) helps found the American Alpine Club.

1895: Robert Jeffries Roberts invents the medicine ball while working for the Boston YMCA;

medicine balls are weighted balls still used in physical training.

1896: The first modern Olympic Games are held in Athens, Greece, with 14 countries participating. Female athletes are not allowed to take part, but one woman, Melpomene, unofficially runs the same marathon course as the men.

1899: Charles Minthorn Murphy becomes the first person to maintain a speed of 60 miles per hour on a bicycle; known as "Mile-a-Minute Murphy" for this feat, Murphy achieved it by following a train on a specially prepared track, thus avoiding having to spend energy overcoming wind resistance.

1900: In the second modern Olympic Games, held in France as part of the Exposition Universelle, women are allowed to compete for the first time in tennis, golf, and croquet. Margaret Abbot becomes the first American woman to win a gold medal. Her medal was awarded in golf.

1906: The Intercollegiate Athletic Association, a forerunner of the National Collegiate Athletic Association (NCAA), is founded in order to create uniform standards to make football safer; in the previous year, 18 players at the college level died and over 100 were injured playing the game.

1908: The University of Pittsburgh becomes the first school to supply its football team with uniforms with large numerals to help officials and fans identify the players.

1910: Annette Kellerman, an Australian swimmer, is arrested for swimming in Boston in a swimsuit that reveals her legs.

1912: At the Olympic Games in Stockholm, countries from five continents participate for the first time. The Stockholm Olympics also make use of up-to-date modern technology, including photo finishes.

1912: Jim Thorpe wins gold medals in the pentathlon and decathlon at the Stockholm Summer Olympic Games, only to see his medals revoked on charges that he had violated the Olympic rules regarding amateur status; the medals were restored to his family in 1982.

1917: Charlotte Epstein founds the Women's Swimming Association of New York and rents a pool so female swimmers will have a place to train.

1919: Johnny Loftus becomes the first jockey to win the Triple Crown, riding Sir Barton to victory in the Kentucky Derby, the Preakness, and the Belmont Stakes.

1920: The first Olympic Games following the conclusion of World War I are held in Belgium; doves are released as a symbol of peace and the Olympic flag is used for the first time.

1920: Kenesaw Mountain Landis becomes the first commissioner of baseball; originally appointed to a seven-year term, he is re-elected three times and still holds the office at the time of his death in 1944.

1920: Suzanne Lenglen shocks the tennis world by competing in the Summer Olympics in a short skirt and sleeveless blouse; she also won two gold medals and one bronze.

1921: The Jeux Olympiques Feminine du Monde (World Female Olympic Games) are organized by a group of French women. Women at these games compete in sports such as track and field and basketball; the games are also held in 1922 and 1923.

1926: The American swimmer Gertrude Ederle becomes the first woman to swim the English Channel; she also cuts two hours off the previous best finishing time.

1927: The goalie face mask is introduced to ice hockey by Elizabeth Graham, who plays ice hockey at the collegiate level in New York City; it is not adopted by a National Hockey League (NHL) player until 1959, when Jacques Plante of the Montreal Canadiens begins wearing a face mask in games.

1928: The Olympic flame is symbolically incorporated into the Summer Olympic Games in Amsterdam; this Olympics also marks the beginning of the tradition of the Greek team entering the stadium first for the Opening Ceremony, and the host nation entering last.

1929: The Powder Puff Derby, the first transcontinental air race for women, is held. Fifteen women complete in the 2,350-mile race, which is won by Louise McPhetridge Thaden.

1929: John Garnet Carter constructs the first miniature golf course in Chattanooga, Tennessee. Carter patents the name *Tom Thumb* for his course design, which includes obstacles and hazards and is played with only a putter.

1929: The Carnegie Foundation for the Advancement of Education issues a report decrying the commercial and vested interests it sees as having an undue influence in collegiate athletics, and suggests that college administrators should take measures to reduce this influence.

1930: Golfer Bobby Jones is selected as the first recipient of the James E. Sullivan Memorial Trophy for the best amateur athlete of the year.

1932: Mildred "Babe" Didrikson wins the Amateur Athletic Union (AAU) team track championship single-handedly, setting four world records in the process.

1934: Robert Royce builds the first rope ski tow, using manila rope and a system of pulleys attached to a tractor, in Woodstock, Vermont.

1936: At the Summer Olympics in Berlin, Adolf Hitler's efforts to use sport to demonstrate the superiority of the "Aryan" race is defeated by the accomplishment of athletes such as the African American Jesse Owens, who won four medals in track and field.

1936: Sally Stearns becomes the first woman to act as coxswain for a men's varsity rowing team, leading the Rollins College Shell against Marietta College on May 27.

1936: The All American Red Heads Basketball team, composed of all women, is founded; the Red Heads barnstorm the United States for five decades, playing men's teams and winning most of their games.

1936: An electrical scoring system that automatically records touches is used during epee events in fencing, an early example of using technology to score an event rather than relying on human judgment.

1937: The Nissen Trampoline Company, founded by George P. and Paul F. Nissen, produces the first commercially produced trampoline.

1938: American Don Budge becomes the first tennis player to win the Grand Slam of tennis, winning the Australian Open, French Open, Wimbledon, and U.S. Open singles titles in the same year.

1941: Eddie Robinson begins coaching football at Grambling State University; he will continue to coach at Grambling until 1997, retiring with 408 wins (the most among Division I coaches) and a winning percentage of 0.707.

1946: Mary Garber begins her career as a sportswriter at the *Winston-Salem Journal*; she is believed to be the first female to hold a position as a staff sportswriter on a daily newspaper in the United States.

1947: Jackie Robinson becomes the first African American to play Major League Baseball in the modern era, playing for the Los Angeles Dodgers. Robinson was selected as Rookie of the Year in 1947, and two years later was selected Most Valuable Player in the National League.

1948: The National Collegiate Athletic Association (NCAA) enacts a Sanity Code intended to stem abuses in college recruiting and creates the Constitutional Compliance Committee to investigate violations; the committee is ineffective because the only penalty it can impose is expulsion, which is too severe for most violations.

1950: Mildred "Babe" Didrickson is selected as the Associated Press "Woman Athlete of the Half Century" for her achievements in many sports, including basketball, baseball, track and field, and golf.

1950: Charles Henry Cooper becomes the first African American to play in the National Basketball Association (NBA); Cooper is drafted by the Boston Celtics in April and plays his first game in November.

1950: Kathryn Johnston becomes the first girl to play in Little League Baseball, playing for the King's Dairy team in Corning, New York.

1953: The American tennis player Maureen Connolly becomes the first woman to win the Grand Slam, winning all the slam tournaments (Australian Open, Wimbledon, French Open, and U.S. Open) in a single year.

1954: Mal Whitfield, a middle distance runner for the Los Angeles Athletic Club, becomes the first African American to win the James E. Sullivan Memorial Trophy as the nation's outstanding amateur athlete.

1954: British runner Roger Bannister becomes the first person to run a mile in less than four minutes; Bannister accomplished this feat while also working full time as a physician.

1954: John Kundla, coach of the Minneapolis Lakers, becomes the first coach to win five National Basketball Association (NBA) titles (in 1949, 1950, 1952, 1953, and 1954). His record will later be equaled by Pat Riley in 2006 and Gregg Popovich in 2014, and surpassed by Red Auerbach and Phil Jackson.

1956: American tennis player Althea Gibson wins the French Open, becoming the first African American to win a Grand Slam singles title; the following year, she wins Wimbledon and the U.S. Open.

1957: Timing touch pads, developed by a physics professor at the University of Michigan, are used in swim meets, recording more accurate times and reducing the number of officials needed on the pool deck during races.

1958: Willie O'Ree becomes the first African American to play in the National Hockey League, playing for the Boston Bruins.

1960: At the Rome Summer Olympics, for the first time the Paralympics and Olympics are held in the same city and at the same time. At the same Olympics, sprinter Wilma Rudolph becomes the first American woman to win three Olympic gold medals in track and field.

1961: Ernie Davis, a halfback for Syracuse University, becomes the first African American to win the Heisman Trophy for the best collegiate football player.

1962: John O'Neill becomes the first African American coach in Major League Baseball, working for the Chicago Cubs.

1966: The Texas Western College basketball team, coached by Don Haskins, is the first to win the NCAA title while starting five African American players.

1968: At the Summer Olympics, held in Mexico City, American sprinters John Carlos and Tommie Smith perform a Black Power salute (raised, clenched gloved fists) on the medal stand. The Mexico City Olympics are also notable for the use of fully automatic timing in several sports, including track and field.

1969: Curt Flood, an outfielder for the St. Louis Cardinals, refuses to be traded to the Philadelphia Phillies, and thus challenges baseball's reserve clause, which prevented him from negotiating with other teams until a year after the expiration of his contract. Baseball at that time was operating under an exemption to antitrust law, on the grounds that if players were able to negotiate freely (as is now possible under free agency), the league would be unable to preserve competitive balance.

1969: Bill Russell, center and later coach of the Boston Celtics, wins his 11th NBA championship, a record that still stands today.

1972: Women's sports in the United States receive a tremendous boost from Title IX of the Education Amendments of 1972, which specify that women must have equal opportunities in educational programs and activities receiving federal funding; one significant consequence is a major expansion of high school and collegiate sports for girls and women.

1972: Dick Wilmarth of Red Devil, Alaska, wins the inaugural Iditarod sled dog race. The Iditarod covers about 1,200 miles through central Alaska, from Anchorage to Nome; it follows a trail previously used to transport mail and supplies, most famously diphtheria anti-toxin in 1925.

1972: Bobby Fischer becomes the first American to win the World Chess Championship, defeating Boris Spassky of the Soviet Union in a series of matches held in Reykjavik, Iceland.

1973: Tennis player Billie Jean King wins the "battle of the sexes" match against Bobby Riggs; the match is televised nationally and does much to bring support to the cause of women's sports.

1974: Frank Robinson become the first African American in Major League Baseball who works as both a player and manager for the Cleveland Indians.

1975: Junko Tabei, leading an all-female Japanese expedition, becomes the first woman to reach the summit of Mt. Everest.

1977: Janet Guthrie becomes the first woman to drive in the Indianapolis 500; she also qualifies in 1978 and 1979.

1978: Ann Meyers, formerly a collegiate star at UCLA, becomes the first woman to sign an NBA contract, winning a tryout with the Indiana Pacers.

1978: A U.S. District Court, responding to a lawsuit filed by Melissa Ludtke of *Sports Illustrated*, rules that male and female reporters must have equal opportunity to interview athletes, including access to them in the locker room.

1980: The Cyclops computer system is first used in tennis at the Wimbledon championship; the system uses infrared beams to make line calls, that is, determining whether a shot landed in play or outside the court.

1984: Billie Jean King becomes the first woman to head a professional sports league, becoming commissioner of World Team Tennis.

1986: Anita DeFrantz becomes the first African American and first American woman to serve on the International Olympic Committee; she was formerly a rower and captained the American women's eight to a bronze medal at the 1976 Montreal Olympics.

1986: Greg LeMond becomes the first American to win the Tour de France, a multistate bicycle race that is the most prestigious event in the sport.

1987: Jackie Joyner-Kersee, a track and field athlete, becomes the first woman featured on the cover of a nonswimsuit edition of *Sports Illustrated*.

1992: Manon Rhéaume becomes the first woman to play in an NHL preseason game, playing goalie for the Tampa Bay Lightning in a game against the St. Louis Blues.

1993: Julie Krone becomes the first woman jockey to win a Triple Crown race, winning the Belmont Stakes riding Colonial Affair.

1994: The first all-female team is formed to compete in the America's Cup, a prestigious sailing race.

1994: Tiger Woods wins the U.S. Amateur Gold Championship at age 18, making him the youngest person to win the event. Woods, of African American and Asian ancestry, goes on to become one of golf's greatest champions and the first African American to enjoy that level of success in golf.

1997: The French sailor Catherine Chabaud becomes the first woman to sail nonstop around the world, completing the trip in 140 days.

2005: Ed Viesturs becomes the first person to climb all of the world's mountain peaks higher than 8,000 meters; he began in 1989 with Kangchenjunga and finished in 2005 with Annapurna.

2008: Women ski jumpers from five countries file a lawsuit with the British Columbia Supreme Court, charging that failing to include ski jumping as a women's event in the 2010 Vancouver Olympic Games constitutes gender discrimination. Although the suit is unsuccessful, the International Olympic Committee later decides to include women's ski jumping in the 2014 Winter Olympics in Sochi, Russia.

2009: Ed O'Bannon, a basketball player at UCLA, files a lawsuit challenging the National Collegiate Athletic Association's (NCAA) use of the images of student-athletes for commercial purposes, and argues that the athletes are entitled to compensation in exchange for the use of their images.

2010: Phil Jackson wins his 11th National Basketball Association (NBA) championship as a coach, breaking Boston Celtics coach Red Auerbach's previous record of 10; Jackson won six championships coaching the Chicago Bull, and five coaching the Los Angeles Lakers.

2012: Pat Summit, the women's basketball coach at the University of Tennessee, retires. Her coaching record includes eight national championships, appearances in all 32 National Collegiate Athletic Association (NCAA) championship tournaments (the only team to achieve this honor), and 1,098 wins.

2012: At the Summer Olympics in London, Kimberly Rhode, a skeet shooter, becomes the first American to win a medal in an individual

sport in five consecutive Olympics: gold in 1996, bronze in 2000, gold in 2004, silver in 2008, and gold in 2012.

2012: FIFA, the international governing body for soccer, approves the use of goal-line technology to determine whether a goal has actually been scored; two systems are approved, one using a magnetic field and the other relying on high-speed cameras.

2012: John Gagliardi retires as head football coach at St. John's University in Minnesota; during his years as head coach at Carroll College (Montana) and St. Johns, he won 489 games, the most of any college football coach, and amassed a winning percentage of 0.775.

2014: A group of top international women's soccer players, led by American Abby Wambach, sues FIFA, the international governing body for soccer, for scheduling games in the upcoming Women's World Cup on artificial turf; men's international games are always played on natural grass, as specified in the rules of soccer.

2014: Diana Nyad becomes the first person to swim from Cuba to Miami without using a shark cage; Nyad, age 60, had failed in several previous attempts to complete the swim.

2014: Durrell Chamorro, a former football placekicker at Colorado State, files a class-action suit in federal court on behalf of Division I football players who have been damaged by the National Collegiate Athletic Association's (NCAA) ban on multiyear scholarships (a ban since reversed).

2014: Samantha Sackos, a former soccer player for the University of Houston, files a lawsuit against the National Collegiate Athletic Association's (NCAA), claiming that student-athletes should be considered employees and are thus entitled to payment at least as high as the federal minimum wage.

2015: Geno Auriemma leads the University of Connecticut Huskies to its 10th National Collegiate Athletic Association's (NCAA) Women's Basketball Championship. With this championship, Auriemma ties the legendary coach John Wooden in NCAA basketball championships.

2015: After serving a year-long suspension for performance-enhancing drug use, New York Yankee Alex Rodriguez hit his 660th career home run. This home run tied him with Willie Mays for fourth place on Major League Baseball's (MBL) all-time list. This milestone qualified Rodriguez for a $6 million bonus that the Yankees have decided not to pay.

2015: The National Football League's (NFL) "Deflategate" investigation found it "more probable than not" that Super Bowl champions the New England Patriots deliberately released air pressure from game-approved footballs. Some quarterbacks prefer footballs with low air pressure to gain a better grip on the ball. The investigation confirmed that 11 out of 12 footballs used in the American Football Conference (AFC) Championship were under the required inflation level.

2015: Floyd Mayweather defeated Manny Pacquiao in a unanimous decision for the World Boxing Association (WBA), World Boxing Council (WBC), and World Boxing Organization (WBO) welterweight boxing titles. Mayweather earned more than $178 million while Pacquiao took home over $122 million from the highly anticipated fight.

Academic Programs in Sport Leadership

Sport leadership, sport administration, sport management, and even athletics administration are terms that seem to be used interchangeably. As a clarification, the term *sport* is used to indicate the entirety of the range of venues as well as all types of sports. Sport management evolved in the mid-1960s, as with many other sport-focused disciplines such as sport medicine, sport history, and literature of sport, to establish an academic presence as the profession moved away from its physical education roots.

Challenges in the Field

As sport management (including all variant names such as sport leadership) programs continue to grow and evolve, the changes in society have caused an increased consideration of forming a common understanding of theories in sport management; defining and discussing sport leadership; and discussing and addressing issues of race, ethnicity, sexual orientation, gender issues, and disabilities issues. Administrative courses in sport programs are revised to better meet the changes in the sport environment.

The business world has produced a wide range of leadership books and resources based on the profiles of successful chief executive officers (CEOs) or their biographies, company histories, or results of management techniques within the nonprofit framework. These examples are not so different from the sport world, where books and resources on coach, owner,

and player profiles or biographies; institutions or team histories; or the adoption of various business strategies help to inform the context of leadership.

Leadership is expected in sport at every level from team captains to membership on a national governing body. While there are a few individuals who seem to have many qualities implicit in leadership expectations, most individuals need to be taught how to become leaders through mentoring, self-discovery, and educational programming. There is an overabundance of research in the area of psychology, sociology, and business on this topic. Just as there are many personality tests, leadership qualification surveys, and career development assessments, so are there different types of leaders and a wide range of leadership traits. In sport management programs, there is an expectation that leadership will be addressed in at least one academic course and this course is heavily reliant on the business world's view of leadership and management.

In 2014 three faculty members, Drs. John Borland (Springfield College), Gregory M. Kane (Eastern Connecticut State University), and Laura J. Burton (University of Connecticut), were so troubled with the absence of leadership discussions within the context of the academic sport environment, that they created a textbook titled *Sport Leadership in the 21st Century*. The contributors to this very practical resource provide detailed overviews on the topic, case studies, questions for discussion, and references. The framework of the textbook allows for critical exploration of leadership in sport as it relates to expectations in the Commission on Sport Management Accreditation (COSMA) program. While a limited number of programs are accredited, the rigorous process supports common standards and expectations to structure programs and resources, such as library materials, to support the research requirements.

Sport Management Academic Programs

Undergraduates and graduate students in sport management programs are often required to participate in internships or other experiential learning opportunities. Internships may be coordinated by the institution, or arranged by the student and approved by the department, and can be voluntary or paid. The important feature of these experiences is that students have an opportunity to explore which parts of a sport organization they might want to work within.

Undergraduate degree programs in sport management introduce students to the vast range of opportunities in sport and sport related jobs from marketing, sporting events manager, to coaching. Recreation and leisure activities may be included in this overview. With over 300 institutions in the United States offering bachelor of arts (BA) or bachelor of science (BS) degrees, the programs range in course offerings and requirements. It is important to understand that the expectations and opportunities will vary at each institution and employment outcomes are usually entry-level. For undergraduates who may not have the option of a sport management major or are not interested in pursuing an undergraduate degree in sport management, opportunities to volunteer or pursue classes or activities related to areas in sport should not be discouraged. Many times minors and subject-focused research within a degree can be developed in preparation for a master's degree, especially within business school programs.

Graduate degree programs at the master's level tend to be a master's of science (MS) and may include writing a thesis and completing a master's exams. For many the master's degree might be their terminal degree, as continuing for a doctorate is not required in the business sector of sport management. Graduate degrees usually prepare students to focus on a field such as academic athletic administration, marketing and events management, or recreational services management, to mention a few options. This type of advanced degree may be obtained while the student is already working in an area of sport or prior to attaining a job in sport.

While there are limited doctorate programs in sport management, sport leadership, or athletic administration in the United States and abroad, within them an individual who earns this level of degree can generally expect a position of teaching or administration in academia. There is usually a requirement for candidacy exams and the creation of a dissertation that will concentrate on a sport-focused topic or area of interest. With the limitation in a sport management Ph.D., many in the sport world who have their doctorates have earned them through other departments ranging from business, education, communications, psychology, and health.

While the North American Society for Sport Management (NASSM) provides a listing of all programs with sport management degree offerings, another challenge is accessing sport management, sport administration, or sport leadership concentrations, or minors that exist. Although many programs are offered on campus, there are numerous online and hybrid degrees available. There may be stand-alone programs or centers on sport management; most of the time the programs will be a major within a larger department or college in some variant of sport science including and not limited to health and physical education, kinesiology, recreation, human movement, and exercise science. There are other institutions where the sport management major may be within departments or colleges of business, communications, or education.

In conclusion, sport management education is a varied and constantly changing academic landscape that requires careful pursuit at any degree level. Examination of programs needs to incorporate course requirements, career objectives, and job placement ratios. Each of the above-named organizations can aid in the academic review but each individual should carefully evaluate all the options and the cost-benefit analysis of the education pursuit relative to long-term occupancy.

Mila C. Su

See Also: Athletic Directors; Comparative Models of Sports Leadership; Gender and Sports Leadership; Leadership in Recreational Sports Organizations;

Leadership Models in Sports; Race/Ethnicity and Sports Leadership; Research Methods in Sports Leadership; Risk Management Process; Women's Leadership in Sport.

Further Readings

Chen, Steve, et al. "Professional Expectations of Sport Management Students as Related to Academic Curricular Alignment Support and Preparation." *Universal Journal of Sport Management*, v.1/3 (2013).

Mathner, Robert P. and Christina L. Martin. "Sport Management Graduate and Undergraduate Students' Perception of Career Expectations in Sport Management." *Sport Management Education Journal*, v.6/1 (2012).

Miller, John and Todd Siedler, eds. *A Practical Guide to Sport Management Internships.* Durham, NC: Carolina Academic Press, 2010.

Yiamouyiannis, Athena, et al. "Sport Management Education: Accreditation, Accountability and Direct Learning Outcome Assessments." *Sport Management Education Journal*, v.7/1 (2013).

Amateur Sports

For those interested in amateur sport participation, there is a wide range of opportunities for involvement. Categorically speaking, this discussion of amateur sport will be broken down into three primary levels of involvement: youth sport (ages 0–18), amateur sport participation during college years, and adult amateur sport.

Youth Amateur Sport

According to the National Council of Youth Sports (NCYS), there are more than 60 million youth between 0 and 18 years of age that participate in organized youth sport in the United States. Approximately 66 percent of these participants are male, while 34 percent are female. Formal involvement in youth sport is not just restricted to the youth participants; there are over 7 million adults that are part of the youth sport experience, either as coaches, officials, or administrators of youth sport organizations. In further discussing the arc of a youth sport participant throughout childhood, it should be

A women's rugby union game for the 2013 women's European qualification tournament between Italy and Spain. (Wikimedia Commons/Carlos Delgado).

noted that 75 percent of youth sport participants are participating in some formal organized sport involvement on a year-round basis.

Recreational Youth Sport

There tends to be a typical youth sport funneling process that occurs between the onset of introduction to sport and the end of the high school years. At an informal level, many youths are introduced to a particular sport by playing in an unorganized fashion with family, friends in the neighborhood, or peers on the playground. For the first foray into organized youth sport, many youth begin their amateur sport careers with the more popular team sports of basketball, soccer, football, and baseball/softball. This initial formalized participation usually happens at the recreational level in local leagues organized by three different categories of organizations: local parks and recreation departments, national youth sport organizations, and religiously affiliated organizations. Examples of national youth sport organizations include the National Alliance for Youth Sports (NAYS), the National Council of Youth Sports (NCYS), U.S. Youth Soccer, Pop Warner Football, and Little League Baseball. Several more prominent, religiously affiliated youth sport organizations are Upward Bound, the Catholic Youth Organization (CYO), and Maccabi U.S.A. Through these early years of introduction to and participation in youth sport, the funneling process begins. That is, there is a thinning-out process of sorts. Presumably, not all children who play informal sports with their families and peers end up participating in youth sport in formalized recreational leagues.

Competitive Youth Sport

If and when recreational sport participants show an increased interest in the sport, have a superior skill level, or are encouraged by parents, they have an option of participating in competitive youth sports. Similar to the drop-off that occurs between informal sport participants and recreational league participation, there is also a thinning-out process that occurs between recreational and competitive youth sports. Simply put, not all youth sport participants are talented enough or have the financial resources to play on competitive teams that inherently are more competitive and cost more money. Relatedly, statistics show that over 70 percent of youth sport participants drop out of youth programs between initial participation and high school.

Competitive youth sport participants are typically involved on a team that is a member of a national organization such as the Amateur Athletic Union (AAU), the club level, or a part of an independent team. Although there are other national organizations, the AAU serves as the most prominent national organizer of competitive youth sports. The AAU is a multisport organization that sponsors and organizes officially sanctioned tournaments and competitions across the United States. The national organization is broken down into geographically based regions. Ultimately, winners of regional competitions and tournaments then go on to compete for AAU national championships. Individual teams pay for membership in the AAU in order to have voting rights in AAU Sport Committee Meetings and to compete against other AAU members and teams. The AAU organizes competitions for more than 20 sports that range from the more traditional team sport of basketball to the more individualized, obscure sports of trampoline tumbling and baton twirling. There are more than 650,000 official AAU participants.

Many teams that are members of the AAU or other large competitive organizations have a loose association with five to 10 other teams at a club level. That is, teams across different age ranges and competitiveness levels all operate under the auspices of a parent organization. Individuals have to pay membership dues to

be part of the club, but the club can build its reputation by having more teams that compete in tournaments. A team may not have interest across age levels in order to form multiple teams to make up a club; or individuals associated with the team may not want to pay membership dues to be part of a club. An alternative for that team would be to operate as an independent team. As such, the team would not have to pay membership dues, but may have a harder time building up the overall reputation of the team.

High School Amateur Sports

When entering the high school years, most youth sport participants have had experience either in recreational sport or competitive sport. Again, funneling occurs, as not all youths who participated in recreational or competitive youth sports will try out or be selected for high school teams. Officially state-sponsored sport organizations (such as KSHSAA, the Kansas State High School Activities Association) sponsor sports affiliated directly with the high school. For these official state-sponsored sport organizations at the high school level, public high schools, private high schools, and preparatory schools all have an opportunity to be a part of the statewide organization. The truly competitive high school athletes will continue participating in organized events (such as those sponsored by the AAU) when the official high school season is not going on. For example, high-school-aged basketball players may play on the high school team during the official winter high school basketball season and will also play for their competitive club teams during the spring, summer, and fall.

While youth sport is typically categorized as organized sport participation for youths between the ages of 0 and 18, sport involvement during the college years also makes up an additional and dynamic facet of amateur sport. Participation can occur at the varsity, club, and intramural level.

Competitive Intercollegiate Sport

Of the 60 million youth sport participants, a very small number of high school athletes go on to play competitive sports at the officially sponsored collegiate level. The most well-known governing body for intercollegiate athletics is the National Collegiate Athletic Association (NCAA). The NCAA has over

500,000 student-athletes that participate across the Division I, Division II, and Division III levels at more than 1,000 colleges and universities. Other intercollegiate athletic governing bodies include the National Junior College Athletic Association (NJCAA) and the National Association of Intercollegiate Athletics (NAIA). Each of the aforementioned governing bodies governs national championships for more than 20 different sports. Athletes that participate in sport at the competitive intercollegiate level typically participate in only one sport. That is, outside of the official season, they continue training year-round for their one sport specialty.

Club Sport and Intramural Sports

Club sports serve as an opportunity for sport participation that is a step below the NCAA, NJCAA, or the NAIA. Club sport teams at colleges and universities compete against club teams from other colleges and universities, but these clubs are not typically governed by a national organization. Additionally, while NCAA-member athletic departments may have upward of 200 employees and annual expenditures of $100 million, club teams are usually organized by the students themselves and receive little if any financial assistance from the university in order to participate in club sport competitions.

Intramural sports are sporting leagues and competitions between students within one institution that can range from semester-long basketball leagues to one-day kickball tournaments. Frequently, the leagues are operated by the student recreation center. Undergraduate or graduate students organize their own teams and participate in events organized by the student recreation staff. The focus of many operators of intramural leagues at a particular university is to encourage participation and an active lifestyle.

Adult Amateur Sport

As noted by the NCAA, less than 2 percent of college student-athletes will become professional athletes after their eligibility has expired. For these athletes, and those who do not play sports in college, a bevy of sport options are available. Both organized and organic sport participation options exist and are becoming increasingly popular all across the

United States. From impromptu pick-up basketball games at the local gym to sponsored national slow-pitch softball tournaments, amateur sport options are plentiful.

Individual-Level Adult Sport

Two popular individual amateur sports fit underneath the sport for fitness umbrella: running and cycling. In its annual State of the Sport report, Running U.S.A. found participation in recreational running had increased by 2.5 percent from 2012 to 2013. In all, over 29 million athletes professed to running or jogging on at least 50 days in 2013. Further, apparel companies reported over $3 billion in sales solely from running shoes. This increase in population can at least be partially attributed to the increase in organized amateur races, ranging from one-mile fun runs to 5-kilometer (and longer) benefit competitions. According to *U.S. News & World Report*, The Color Run organizers expected to have over 1 million individuals compete in 2013, spanning 120 U.S. cities and 30 countries. Even runs with unique themes, such as the zombie-themed Run for Your Lives and Rock 'n' Roll Run featuring bands, operate dozens of races annually.

As with running, competitive amateur cycling is also gaining momentum. The Sports & Fitness Industry Association noted that the number of people who reported road cycling 26 or more times rose to 21.4 million in 2013. Further, U.S.A. Cycling noted that cyclo-cross (varied-terrain obstacle-course-style cycling) participation has soared by more than 300 percent since 2005. Similarly, direct retail sales of bicycles, parts, and accessories topped $5.8 billion in 2013. Americans over 7 years of age rode a bicycle at least five times. Amateur cycling tours, such as the Midwest Flyover Omnium Race Series, have emerged across the United States and give amateur cyclists an organized outlet in which to compete.

Tennis and golf also retain a stronghold in the adult amateur sport landscape. The United States Tennis Association (USTA) stated that over 28 million people played tennis in 2012, a 4 percent increase. Tennis participation ranges from playing recreationally with friends at a public park to USTA-governed leagues with district, region, state, and national tournaments. Another racquet sport, racquetball, had just under 4 million participants in 2013. While golf participation has leveled off in the last five years, over 6 million Americans between 18 and 34 years old played a round of golf in 2013. Wide ranges of options exist for amateur golfers; over 10,000 public or municipal courses are open in the United States, with just under 4,000 private course options available.

Team Level Adult Sport

Team sports are also a prominent aspect of the adult amateur sport landscape. Impromptu games and structured leagues give participants an opportunity to continue playing sports they competed in during their younger years or acquire new skills in their adult years. Adult leagues for sports like basketball, slow-pitch softball, and kickball have become commonplace in communities across the United States. Corporations, churches, and community organizations often host or sponsor leagues and teams as part of their marketing, branding, and community relations efforts.

The Sports & Fitness Industry Association estimates that over 4 million adults participated in slow-pitch softball leagues in 2013. While rules vary by league and competition level, slow-pitch softball differs from fast-pitch in a few ways. First, an additional defender is allowed. Teams typically place an extra outfielder, often called a rover, between the traditional left and center fielder. Additionally, coed or mixed leagues often mandate different softball sizes for each gender and impose rules on the number of each gender that must hit and play the field. Finally, a limit of the amount of home runs that can be hit is often enacted to make competitions more competitive and interactive.

Adult kickball leagues are also penetrating the amateur sport market. The World Adult Kickball Association (WAKA), the largest governing body for kickball, was named one of the fastest-growing private companies by *Inc. Magazine*. The president of the Utah WAKA chapter described the appeal of kickball as a combination of "recess and . . . beers." Much like the game played on playgrounds across the world, the rules and scoring are similar to baseball and softball. The obvious difference is players kick a large, air-filled ball and can be tagged out before reaching the base with a direct hit from the ball. Additionally, typically fielders cannot come closer than the imaginary line between first and third base until the ball is kicked. As with slow-pitch softball, one of the main benefits associated with amateur kickball is the social interaction among the competitors.

Arguably, the fasting-growing adult amateur sport is pickleball. Pickleball is described as a mix of table tennis, badminton, and tennis. Two-on-two matches are played on a tennis court reduced to 44 feet by 20 feet and requires only wooden pickleball paddles and a wiffle-style pickleball. The growth can widely be attributed to the ease, accessibility, and "kindness to joints and bones" of the game for the growing, and more active, senior population. Players typically have to move only one or two steps to hit the ball and the serve must be underhand. Peter Kilborn of the *New York Times* notes that the U.S.A. Pickleball Association has tripled its membership in the last three years and has become so popular that competitive tournaments with classifications all the way to "85 years and up" have sprouted up across the country.

Conclusion

In all, a litany of amateur sport options exist in the U.S. sporting culture. Youth sport participation can be the last time a child plays a sport but can also serve as a gateway to the college and adult participation options. Within the current sporting culture, the popularity of amateur sport at all levels is only increasing and will continue to serve the wants and needs of individuals of all ages and activity levels.

Claire Schaeperkoetter
Jordan R. Bass

See Also: High School Sports; Intercollegiate Sports; National Association of Intercollegiate Athletics; (NAIA); National Collegiate Athletic Association (NCAA); National Federation of State High School Associations; Sport-Based Youth Development.

Further Readings

A.A.U. The Official Home Of The Amateur Athletic Union. "FAQs." http://www.aausports.org/FAQs (Accessed October 2014).

Kurtzleben, Danielle. "Up and Running: The Rise of the Themed Road Race." http://www.usnews.com/news/articles/2013/06/20/how-tough-mudder-the-color-run-and-the-rock-n-roll-marathon-are-leading-a-new-pack-of-themed-races (Accessed October 2014).

Levy, Allan M. *Sports Injury Handbook: Professional Advice for Amateur Athletes.* Hoboken, NJ: Wiley, 1993.

N.C.A.A. "About the NCAA." http://www.ncaa.org/about (Accessed October 2014).

Poppinga, Brady. *Amateur Sports: The Business of Developing the Character of the Youth Through Competition.* New York: Amazon Digital Services, 2014.

U.S.T.A. "Adult Tennis." http://www.usta.com/Adult-Tennis/?intloc=headernav (Accessed October 2014).

William, Frederick. *History of American Amateur Athletics.* Philadelphia: HandPress Publishing, 2014.

Athletics Director

An athletics director, often abbreviated as AD within the sporting community, is an administrator working within a college or university—and in some cases within larger high schools or middle schools—to coordinate athletics programs, coaching, and overall organization. The responsibilities of an AD also include, but are not limited to, the supervision and coordination of athletic events, the management of department budgets, revenue planning and fund-raising, acting as sports conference liaisons, and maintaining strong working relationships with the National Collegiate Athletic Association (NCAA). ADs are also, at least theoretically, in charge of coaches working for the institution. However, there is some debate as to how much impact they realistically have.

Athletics Directors and "Control" of Coaches

In theory at least, as coordinator of athletics for the institution, ADs have control over the actions of coaches, and are in principle allowed to have a say in their appointment, actions, and dismissal. However, it is often observed that most coaches are much better paid than directors, with many having a greater degree of fame or popularity through television channels, radio stations, and their own blogs or Web sites. If a coach has established a strong reputation and a winning record, then even in cases of severe misconduct the AD may find it difficult to have this coach either disciplined or removed. In fact, some coaches have enough connections to threaten an AD's employment. Notably, though, this complex situation is not seen as a good enough reason or excuse for ADs not doing their job in holding coaches accountable to pre-established guidelines and performance models. So much is this the case that if a coach is found to have carried out a severe misconduct that could create negative publicity or if a team has seriously underperformed for the institution, then both the coach and the director will often have to step down or resign.

Past Versus Present

In previous years, it was much more common to see coaches or head coaches occupying the AD role part time alongside their coaching commitments. This practice was more common in the south, with notable coaches such as Bear Bryant of Alabama, Shug Jordan of Auburn, and Vince Dooley of Georgia all serving as prime examples. The world of sports, however, moves forward at a fast pace and it has increasingly became impractical and unviable for coaches to hold these joint roles. The last coach to hold the joint role was Derek Dooley (Vince Dooley's son) who worked as AD for Louisiana Tech until 2009. The main reason that such joint roles survived as long as they did is that most ADs were typically nominal roles designed to give coaches extra pay, prestige, and the knowledge that the institution was not going to be supervising them in any regular or serious capacity. The main duties and administration of the AD were often simply delegated to an assistant director.

Gradually, though, the viability of these dual-role practices has been called into question, and the reality of working with multimillion-dollar athletics budgets in today's world has meant that ADs are increasingly no longer from coaching backgrounds. Instead, many ADs are now drawn from financial, business and managerial educations. Two examples include Michigan's hiring of Domino's Pizza chief executive officer David Brandon, as well as USC's hiring of Pat Haden direct from the private sector. It seems, in some ways, backwards to hire ADs with no coaching and often no playing experience of athletics or collegiate sport, but with the increasing demands for directors to act as marketers, promoters, fund-raisers, and contact points for big business sponsorship, a strong background in business management is fast becoming an expectation of the role.

Divisional Differences

The differences in the role of an AD vary depending on the unique nature and characteristics of each division. Most of the available information, especially in the press, is centered around Division I sports, which can be misleading in numerous ways. For example, this media focus overlooks the fact that Division III is the largest within athletics, holding 439 of the NCAA's 1,076 member schools. From an AD's perspective, some of the biggest differences stem from this focus, or lack thereof, of media attention. A Division I AD, for instance, is operating in an extremely well-funded sector, with top teams having literally millions or tens of millions of dollars to look after.

A Division III AD, on the other hand, will be dealing with a much smaller budget (disproportionately so). In this sense, then, Division I ADs could be seen to have greater pressure in regard to financial responsibility, though it is worth considering that the budgetary limitations placed on Division III directors create a separate sphere of challenges and pressures. Another important contrast between divisional responsibilities is that Division I ADs have to manage complex sponsorship deals, heightened media involvement, bigger-name coaches, and an overall atmosphere built up around big money sport. The expectation is not just that of winning, but of winning fast. The potential for earnings and renown is greater in this setting, but so is the potential for very public downfall. In Division III, on the other hand, the expectation of success is driven more by institutional and personal standards than by large corporate deals. The responsibilities of Directors and coaches in these teams, rather than including pleasing sponsors and satisfying business expectations, is often less obvious and slightly more diverse, often branching out into areas that, in bigger clubs, would have been dealt with by secondary administration staff.

Pay

In 2013, the average salary for an AD was $88,000, and there are expectations that this will rise over the next few years. There is also a growing tendency among institutions toward paying top-performing ADs extremely well; not quite to the point of rivalling top-performing coaches, but still rather impressive. Jeremy Foley of Florida, for instance, is paid an estimated $1,881,995 each year, while Tom Jurich of Louisville earns even more with an estimated $2,154,779. Director David Williams of Vanderbilt tops the table, though, commanding an impressive salary of $3,239,678, which was earned not only through his role as athletic director but through his joint role(s) as vice chancellor of university affairs and tenured professor of law.

It has been noted, however, that such inflated individual salaries within the sport, especially at the Division I level, have skewed perceptions and data regarding the average salary, and that aspiring or unproven ADs will most likely have to accept much more modest compensation packages as they build a name and reputation for themselves within the field.

Alexander Parry

See Also: Creating an Organizational Vision; Intercollegiate Sports; Organizational Leadership; Team Building.

Further Readings

Cross, Michael. "How to Become an Athletic Director (A Six-Part Series)." http://www.nacwaa.org/sites/default/files/images/How%20to%20Be%20an%20AD_Ultimate%20Sports%20Insider.pdf (Accessed November 2014).

Education Portal. "Athletic Director Job Description." http://educationportal.com/articles/Athletic_Director_Job_Description_and_Information_for_Students_Considering_a_Career_as_an_Athletic_Director.html (Accessed October 2014).

Gaines, Cork. "The 20 Highest-Paid Athletic Directors in College Sports." http://www.businessinsider.com/the-20-highest-paid-athletic-directors-in-college-sports-2013-3?op=1&ir=t (Accessed November 2014).

Schrotenboer, Brent. "Downsizing: Some College Execs Prefer Division III." http://usatoday30.usatoday.com/sports/college/story/2012/09/24/some-division-i-college-administrators-pull-out-of-the-big-time-for-a-happier-life/57838352/1 (Accessed November 2014).

B

Behavioral Leadership Theory

Behavioral leadership theory marks an important shift in thinking about leadership because it focuses on what leaders do instead of who they are. Behavioral leadership theory came about as a response to trait leadership theory. While trait theory is concerned with describing attributes of leaders, behavioral leadership theory focuses on what leaders do to be effective. The Ohio State and Michigan studies were the first to explore leader behaviors. These concurrent but independent studies during the 1950s and 1960s identified two similar broad categories of leader behavior: a focus on relationships and a focus on tasks.

Building on these studies, Robert Blake and Jane Mouton developed and refined what is perhaps the most widely used model of leadership behavior, the Leadership Grid. It is also based on two dimensions that align with the prior studies: concern for people and concern for results. While behavioral leadership theories marked a shift in thinking about leadership and leadership development, the model can be difficult to apply directly because it does not take into account unique circumstances. For this reason, situational leadership theories emerged, expanding upon behavioral approaches. Despite the fact that behavioral leadership theories have some limitations, their influence is pervasive in contemporary leadership theories; that is, leader behaviors are the focus on some level in almost every current leadership theory.

Researchers at Ohio State found that employees described two distinct types of leader behaviors: consideration and initiating structure. Consideration is the category of behaviors that have to do with relationships. These behaviors reflect the level of concern leaders have for subordinates. Consideration is being attentive to subordinates' well-being and creating a strong sense of camaraderie. Behaviors that promote friendliness, trust, and respect are ranked high in consideration. Initiating structure is the term used to describe behaviors that are essential to carrying out organizational tasks. They include organizing, planning, and clarifying roles of both leaders and subordinates. Leaders whose initiating structure behaviors result in high performance are considered high in that category. While it was thought that leaders exhibiting high consideration and high initiating structure would be the most effective, this was not the case because the model did not take into account unique organizational situations.

The Michigan studies similarly concluded that leader behaviors could be grouped into two distinct categories: employee orientation and production orientation. Employee-orientation behaviors are aimed at improving human relations within organizations. They consist of showing interest in employees, supporting them personally, and valuing who they are and what they can contribute. Production-orientation behaviors resemble initiating structure in that they are aimed at getting organizational work done. Overseeing technical aspects, implementing structures, and coordination make up production behaviors. One important finding from these studies is that being high in either employee orientation or production orientation results in high productivity; however, being high in production orientation often creates dissatisfied employees, high turnover rates, and absenteeism. These studies suggest that providing a socially and emotionally supportive environment for employees is equally as important as planning and organizing the work.

The Leadership Grid model builds on these early behavioral models, but expands the types of behaviors that are included in each of these categories in order to capture leader behaviors more comprehensively. Based on two factors, concern for people and concern for results, the Leadership Grid identifies five primary leadership (formerly management) styles: impoverished, authority-compliance, middle-of-the-road, country club, and team. Impoverished leaders do the minimum and come across as indifferent. They have little concern for deadlines or the welfare of subordinates. They count on seniority and avoid egregious mistakes in order to keep their jobs.

An authority-compliance leader is focused on getting tasks accomplished with little concern for the well-being of subordinates. This style is dictatorial and relies on clear rules and policies. This style is often very effective in the short term, but results in a high turnover rate and dissatisfied employees. Leaders who exemplify middle-of-the-road behaviors avoid conflict and compromise. This style brings forth mediocre performance and satisfied, but not necessarily fulfilled, employees. The country club leader pays attention to the social and emotional needs of employees but gives little guidance regarding the work to be done. This style assumes that with encouragement, people will be self-motivated and work hard on their own. However, without clear expectations and goals, production is average. Within this model, team leaders are considered the most effective because they are high on both personal engagement and achievement. Team leader behaviors include developing trust, gaining respect, empowering people, and establishing clear objectives so that people are committed to organizational goals. Because this model is relatively easy to understand and somewhat more detailed than the prior models upon which it is built, it is a very practical model. As a result, organizational development consultants throughout the world find it one of the most useful tools for leader development.

One advantage of the broad categories articulated in behavioral leadership theories is that they can be applied to all organizational situations. Regardless of level or organization, every leader is engaged in both relationship and task behaviors. The frameworks are easy to understand and remember. The primary disadvantages are that its usefulness is at a conceptual level only, and it does not take into account unique aspects of different organizational contexts. Nevertheless, behavioral leadership theory marks a turn toward understanding what leaders do. Such thinking has had a profound effect on subsequent leadership theories.

Maylon Hanold

See Also: Situational Leadership Theory; Trait Leadership Theory; Transformational Leadership Theory.

Further Readings
Blake, Robert R., and Anne A. McCanse. *Leadership Dilemmas—Grid Solutions*. Houston: Gulf Publishing, 1991.

Judge, Timothy A., Ronald F. Piccolo, and Remus Ilies. "The Forgotten Ones? The Validity of Consideration and Initiating Structure in Leadership Research." *Journal of Applied Psychology*, v.89/1 (2004).

Northouse, Peter G. *Leadership: Theory and Practice*. Thousand Oaks, CA: Sage, 2010.

Brand Management and Leadership

A brand is a name, term, design, symbol, or feature that identifies one sport product or service as being different from another. A brand can identify a single sport product or service (Manchester City FC, Nike), or a group of sport products or services (Barclays English Premier League, ESPN). Branding is what the consumer thinks of, positively or negatively, when they see or hear the name of a sport organization or business. By defining the brand, a foundation is created for all other components of the sport organization to build on. In order for a brand to be managed properly, there needs to be quality leadership. Leadership is the process of guiding and inspiring people. Since leadership is not a straightforward process, as people have different preferences in the way they want to be led, the way in which people manage brands will also differ. Therefore, leaders will utilize different styles of leadership based on the situation at hand and will work to position and differentiate a sport product or service from others in the marketplace by creating unique branding strategies.

Mario Gotze, top German soccer player, sporting an Adidas brand logo on his jersey. (Flickr)

From the organizational side of brand management, brands that are well managed by astute sport business leaders allow for quality communication to consumers. By defining the brand, a foundation is created for all other components of the sport organization to build on. As such, this becomes a key concept in marketing, where the goal is to provide products and services that meet the needs and wants of consumers. By communicating the brand equity to consumers through appropriate communication channels, businesses can expand their brand awareness, which in turn should result in creating competitive advantages and increase revenue streams into the organization. The communication process associated with brand management involves the organization understanding consumer behavior in terms of attitudes, learning processes, motivations, and perceptions—and how best to entice the consumer to learn and experience the brand. Information gathered through market research, the analysis of internal reports, and the collection of information through an appropriate decision support system helps build a picture of consumers and how to engage them with a brand.

All of this information can then be gathered into a sport marketing plan to allow the brand manager to create a personality for a brand that can exude anything, including innovation, creativity, energy, and sophistication, to name a few. Through the marketing plan, the brand manager can build a process for forecasting the market climate and position the brand to influence consumers in terms of product characteristics and appearance, packaging, pricing, placement, and distribution methods, and promotional interactions. This process should build relationships with chosen target markets as defined by the research, and hence lead the process of guiding the way in which the targeted sport consumers react to the personality of the brand. The resulting interaction with the brand—ranging from using associated products advertising services to identifying themselves as being brand loyal—will determine if the brand will be successful.

Beyond organizational leadership driving brand management, there is also the promotional side of leadership that plays a key role in enticing consumers to purchase brands. Opinion leadership is one of the most widely used methods by brand managers to build brand equity, brand loyalty, and brand commitment. Opinion leadership is the process by which a brand manager implements a process of informally influencing the consumption action or attitudes of consumers. The main reason that opinion leadership is an effective tool for brand managers is that the consumer views the source of the information as being credible. Typically, the opinion leader is held in high esteem by those that accept their opinions. Opinion leadership seeks to pass marketing messages about the sport marketer to as many people as possible, creating the potential for exponential growth in the sports brand's influence, as well as exposure to the associated sport product and services.

Ultimately, sport brand managers look at four key determinants of success: (1) Did the marketing program influence sport consumers to commit to the brand, (2) Did brand management via promotional efforts stimulate sport consumer purchases, (3) Was the spread of information about the sport brand via word of mouth and social media accomplished in an effective and controlled manner, and (4) Was there a creation of a secondary level of opinion leaders to further promote the sport brand.

There are three major categories of opinion leaders associated with sports brands. The first is through brand sponsorship and endorsements. Professional athletes, actors or actresses, and other popular and prominent people in society can influence consumers to associate themselves with a brand and their associated products and services. Brand endorsements tend to be stronger than brand sponsorships simply because sponsorships are when a brand seeks to become affiliated with a prominent individual to secure the right to market their association, while an endorsement involves the spokesperson describing their personal association with the brand.

The second is reference groups, which is a group of two or more people making up a unit that a sport consumer identifies with, and hence probably shares similar attitudes, values, and beliefs. When a sport consumer identifies their self as a part of a reference group, they usually conform to the norms (attitudes, values, and beliefs) of that reference group—which often extends to the brands they consume. The sport brand manager often targets elements of the reference group to spread the word about a sport brand and its associated products and services. This provides a vehicle to inform all members of the reference group about the sport brand and legitimizes the decision to use the same sport brand as the rest of the group. Opinion leaders within reference groups may take on various roles. Some people are considered influencers because their views carry weight in the final decision of utilizing a specific brand; while others are considered deciders, as they assume the responsibility for choosing the characteristics of the brands they use and execute the decision with regard to the brand.

The final category is that of early adopters. The adoption process involves the various levels of consumers who associate themselves with a sport brand. Early adopters are usually the leaders in social settings, which allows them to influence the remainder of the marketplace through their integration with their sphere of influence. As a result of the respect they have earned in the social setting, when these individuals adopt a brand, they tend to be most influential over other people, who then follow in their footsteps, which results in them being the ideal opinion leader to promote a brand.

Ultimately, there is an influential relationship between brand management and leadership. The brand expresses the uniqueness of associated products and services, while the leadership process seeks to influence consumers to purchase products and services. The overarching goal is that the integration of brand management and leadership will lead to enhancing brand equity, as well as increasing brand loyalty and commitment, to maximize revenue and increase brand awareness.

Eric C. Schwarz

See Also: Comparative Models of Sports Leadership; Identification With Sports Teams; Leadership Models in Sports; Organizational Leadership.

Further Readings

Larson, Deanne. "Global Brand Management—Nike's Global Brand." *ISM Journal of International Business*, v.1/3 (2011).

Ind, Nicholas, and Rune Bjerke. "The Concept of Participatory Marketing Orientation." *Journal of Brand Management*, v.15/2 (2007).

Parent, Milena, and Benoit Séguin. "Towards a Model of Brand Creation for International Large-Scale Sporting Events." *Journal of Sport Management*, v.22/5 (2008).

Bullying and Hazing

Individuals involved in sport are typically part of a team; as such, they rely on their teammates for support, encouragement, and leadership. The incidences of bullying and hazing in a sport context undermine these necessary team attributes, resulting in senior or veteran players often treating their opponents more respectfully than their own underclass or rookie teammates. Bullying and hazing activities are counter to most sport organizations' stated goals of creating a culture of team-first accountability and respect for one another. Hazing, however, is often more than harmless pranks and silly games; since 1970, at least one person each year has died on a college campus as a result of a hazing incident, and often as a member of an athletic team.

Hazing and bullying, while pervasive in sport, are often misunderstood and incidents are consequently underreported. Though the most insidious examples often make headlines and engender the public's temporary outrage, a great number of activities that meet the definitions of hazing and bullying occur daily in locker rooms across high school, college, and professional sport contexts. The issue of hazing and bullying in athletics therefore continues to be a problematic one for all stakeholders affected, including student-athletes, coaches, administrators, parents, professional athletes, team owners, and fans.

Definitions

Most experts agree on a commonly accepted definition of bullying to be unwanted, aggressive behavior among school-aged children that involves a real or perceived power imbalance. The behavior is repeated, or has the potential to be repeated over time. Bullying includes actions such as making threats, spreading rumors, attacking someone physically or verbally, and excluding someone from a group on purpose. Bullying is not limited, however, to middle and high school-aged students.

While many definitions of hazing exist, such definitions must be understood together to fully appreciate the breadth and depth of hazing activities, punishment, and prevention. Compiling data from N. A. Hoover and N. J. Pollard from the past decade leads to a definition of hazing as any activity expected of someone joining a group that humiliates, degrades, abuses, or endangers, regardless of the person's willingness to participate. Karen Savoy, of Mothers Against School Hazing (MASH), adds that hazing is a broad term encompassing any action or activity that does not contribute to the positive development of a person. While this enhancement to the definition is critical to accurately describing the harmful effects hazing has on an individual, the terminology is vague, thus making this definition difficult to use in legal proceedings.

Often in a sport setting, hazing is considered a rite of passage in which rookie players (i.e., new team members), are often faced with the "transition" of joining the team as a player and being "accepted" on the team as a viable member. Further, such sport participation is viewed as a special occasion and thus is often accompanied by rituals marking entry into the setting. In addition, an individual's need to belong to a group and to maintain positive, lasting, and meaningful relationships can make them more susceptible to pressures placed on them by senior team members. This need to belong is true of athletes,

particularly in team sports, where involvement is a key motivator for one's participation. Involvement and the need to belong can make participation in initiation rites seemingly normal and accepted.

Some researchers define hazing by its degree of severity or impact on victims— characterizing "little h" hazing as that which both satisfies the definitions above but which may or may not result in physical or emotional harm, and "Big H" Hazing as that which produces measurable physical or emotional harm to its victims. The progression of hazing from little "h" to big "H" is often when serious injuries occur. Brian Crow and Eric MacIntosh proposed a new definition of hazing in athletics that recognizes that coaches, not athletes, determine whether a player (hazed or not) remains on a team. They define hazing as:

> Any potentially humiliating, degrading, abusive, or dangerous activity expected of a junior-ranking athlete by a more senior teammate, which does not contribute to either athlete's positive development, but is required to be 'accepted' as part of a team, regardless of the junior-ranking athlete's willingness to participate. This includes, but is not limited to, any activity, no matter how traditional or seemingly benign, that sets apart or alienates any teammate based on class, number of years on the team, or athletic ability.

To compare, bullying and hazing are similar in that demeaning, degrading, and often harmful actions from people in positions of power impact someone in a position of lesser power. Bullying differs from hazing in that the abusive behavior is not enacted to ensure or maintain one's spot on a team or as part of a group. For hazing to have occurred, there must be an element of initiation or continued membership on a team or within a group. School administrators, team owners, coaches, student-athletes, professional athletes, lawyers, and other constituents often struggle to determine if hazing has occurred and whether or not a crime was committed, even though 44 states currently have antihazing statutes.

Many times, athletes charged with hazing rationalize their activities as traditions or claim that their creative initiation rites do not fall within a list of prohibited behaviors addressed by their advisers or coaches. The most perplexing part of the argument that hazing is traditional is that no group with any historical relevance ever was founded on the principle of harming or degrading its members. In fact, hazing, as part of tradition, severely damages the organization's reputation and often overshadows the positive activities associated with being part of an athletic team.

Hazing exploits the basic human desire to belong to a group, yet underclassmen and rookies regularly subject themselves to this behavior, oftentimes fully aware of the impending danger and risks. They fully believe that surviving these initiation activities ensures a bonding experience like no other. This belief in fact strengthens the subversive culture of hazing; it is talked about under one's breath and is mentioned only in passing to those outside the organization. But why do the current members of the group insist on escalating the severity and intensity of initiation rites such that they cross over into hazing? When current members endured hazing as rookies, pledges, or freshmen themselves, they were powerless. Now, as veterans or upperclassmen, they are in a position of power and see nothing wrong with even more deeply dividing the group by status or into a caste system. Since they allowed themselves to be hazed, they fully expect to engage in such activities with those next in line. Further, each individual who commits to hazing is generally empowered by a cohort of contemporaries who boisterously encourage the behavior.

Prevalence and Sport Examples
Hazing and bullying occur in all sectors and aspects of life, from athletics to bands, from religious groups to Greek life in colleges and universities. Study findings point to the likelihood of men being more likely than women to be the victim of hazing in their college sports program and to also haze others in the program, whereas women are more likely to say that forced consumption of alcohol was involved in rookie hazing on their teams. Further, hazing behavior seems to build upon past actions, where victims then become perpetrators. Hazing perpetuates a vicious cycle, where older members try to restore their own dignity, which they themselves lost as victims of hazing incidents, thereby recruiting new members to behave subserviently.

Examples that illustrate the prevalence of hazing and bullying in sport are found easily with little more than a Google search or a review of the local newspaper. In the fall of 2014, no fewer than a dozen high school and college teams made national headlines for hazing and abusive behavior of teammates. Several of these incidents resulted in the suspension or expulsion of athletes, the termination of entire coaching staffs, the cancellation of games or entire seasons, and in some cases the arrests of student-athletes. Scholars maintain that the awareness and prevention of athletic hazing and bullying is perhaps 10 to 15 years behind the programs that Greek systems (i.e., fraternities and sororities) have developed. While dozens of examples of hazing exist, a small yet representative sample of incidents follow:

High School
E. J. Allen and M. Madden found that approximately 50 percent of high school students have been exposed to hazing (based on the researchers' definition), yet only 16 percent felt the initiation they experienced was hazing. The researchers contend that high school students are willing to accept humiliation and endangerment to be part of a group, and are more prepared to experience hazing in college than to properly construct a term paper.

The football team at a New Jersey high school had its 2014 season cancelled and seven of its upperclassmen arrested for hazing and sexually assaulting

In the world of high school football, there have been many hazing allegations. These incidents soon become criminal investigations and can result in student suspensions, as well as dismissal of head coaches and athletic directors. (Wikimedia Commons)

underclass teammates. The entire coach staff was suspended as well. Student-athletes in the girls' soccer programs at high schools in Illinois and Connecticut, in 2012 and 2009 respectively, were engaged in hazing activities that injured underclassmen teammates and jeopardized continuing eligibility.

College

While university hazing is often aligned with fraternities and sororities, sport team hazing continues to remain in the public eye. In September 2012, veteran team members of the State University of New York Geneseo women's volleyball team hazed 11 freshman members at an off-campus party. One freshman was discovered face down and nearly dead in a yard with blood-alcohol content of 0.266 (i.e., more than three times the legal limit). In 2014, two separate women's soccer programs, at New Mexico State University and Clemson University, saw parts of their season forfeited and criminal charges filed amid team hazing allegations.

Professional

In 2013, an offensive lineman for the Miami Dolphins stepped away from the team following months of nonstop verbal and physical harassment and bullying from teammates and an athletic trainer. Following strong encouragement from the team, the National Football League (NFL) hired an independent investigator to determine the breadth and depth of the harassment. This unprecedented step granted the investigative team unparalleled access to an NFL team locker room, and exposed a systematic and hierarchical culture of harassment, bullying, and racial slurs. Many current and former NFL players justified the activities as common and necessary to build a brotherhood, with several even blaming the victim for violating the locker room code by speaking out.

Hank Nuwer, the foremost authority on hazing, suggests that the flippant manner by which members of local and national media cover hazing incidents that occur in professional North American sport may "ripple down" and lead to incidents of hazing in high school and college athletic settings. These same media members, who vilify and castigate student athletes involved in hazing, conversely make lighthearted or humorous comments about

professional athletes acting the same way. Research into media coverage of hazing has shown that young athletes can be impacted by observing the media coverage of ostensibly "harmless" activities, including challenges occurring on "reality" television and hazing in professional sports.

In perhaps the most incongruous example of media "approval" of hazing, A. Footer wrote an article for Major League Baseball's official Web site, titled "Rookies Face Hazy Days of Spring." Part of the story included guidelines for new professionals:

> Most young players know their roles during Spring Training. The rules are simple. Don't talk too much. Keep your head down. Work hard. And when your veteran teammates pick on you, you must take it. And for good measure, it doesn't hurt to pretend you're enjoying it.

To perhaps acknowledge the disrespectful tone of the article, Major League Baseball placed a disclaimer at the bottom of the webpage stating the story was not subject to its approval to most likely protect Major League Baseball or any of its clubs. This is one simple illustration of a larger and more complex problem in sport that seemingly propagates the notion that hazing is acceptable in some circumstances.

Legal Concerns

More and more student-athletes have faced criminal charges for hazing and bullying in a sport context. Forty-four states currently have some form of anti-hazing statute; yet these vary greatly in terms of defining hazing, penalties imposed, and enforcement. Coaches and athletic administrators must make their athletes aware of the potential criminal charges they could face if involved in hazing or bullying activities. Coaches and administrators can also be held vicariously responsible if athletes are accused of hazing or bullying. Oftentimes, they face civil lawsuits, generally but not exclusively based on the lack of adequate and proper supervision. Other types of negligence lawsuits can fall under the doctrine of in loco parentis (in place of the parents), which establishes a reasonable standard of care for school personnel responsible for the welfare of students. Ultimately, state courts have not established a clear precedent in deciding athletic hazing cases, and there has yet to be a federal statute passed. Most experts recommend that coaches, athletic administrators, and school supervisory personnel consult with an attorney to fully understand and comprehend the implications of hazing in their state.

Brian Crow
Kirsty Spence

See Also: Coaching Teenagers; Coaching Youth; Locker Room Leadership; Managing Conflicts; Sexual Harassment Among Players.

Further Readings

Bryce, Darren W. *Hazing 101: How We Did It and Why We Did It*. New York: CreateSpace, 2010.

Crow, R. B. and E. W. Macintosh. "Conceptualizing a Meaningful Definition of Hazing in Sport." *European Sport Management Quarterly*, v.9/4 (2009).

Lipkins, S. *Preventing Hazing: How Teachers, Parents, and Coaches Can Stop the Violence, Harassment, and Humiliation*. Hoboken, NJ: Jossey-Bass, 2006.

Lundeen, Richard. *Hazing: Rituals of Bondage*. New York: CreateSpace, 2013.

Nuwer, Hank. *The Hazing Reader*. Indianapolis: Indiana University Press, 2004.

C

Captains

Captain is a ambiguous word or title—it can be taken to mean several different things—however, by and large the term always refers to a person with leadership responsibility as a leader. In the world of sports, captains are members of a team composed of athletes in the same peer group. The interesting or variable part of the captain title is in the establishment and execution of the role.

Philosophy

There is a general understanding that the role of the captain is to be a leader. The amount of power, influence, and authority the captain has is in direct relation to the coaches' philosophy. Coaches can view the captain position as an outspoken leader of a team who is free to address the players without provocation from the coaching staff, or in the case of professional sports teams, ownership, and executives. In this scenario, the captains have been given the authority to proactively address the team issues and concerns based on one's own opinion and observations.

The strategy is to give just enough direction to protect the athletes/captains from overstepping their authority, but for the most part the philosophy is "let it be." In some instances, the captains are viewed as communicators tasked with delivering the message set forth by the coaching staff. The captains are simply the "messenger" without any real decision-making power other than to discuss situations and circumstances with the coaches before a decision is made by the coach. This type of leadership lacks empowerment, which can lead to resentment and hostility directed at the captains because they are viewed as simply the mouthpiece for the coach with no real value as far as the players are concerned. This type of model has decreased significantly over the last two decades to the point where it has virtually disappeared. It may make more sense to not have captains then to have captains that have no power to affect decision making.

The most prevalent model is one in which coaches and captains work as a management team, much like a business model. There is always going to be a boss at the end of the day to deal with questions, concerns, issues, behavior, and so forth. However, when the model or philosophy is working, the team operates like a very well-managed business.

Methodology

There are various methods in which captains are chosen, appointed, or elected. The methodology will come down from the coaching staff and the execution of the process is usually left in the hands of the players. In some cases, the coach will select a captain based on his or her own feeling or philosophy. Perhaps it is the maturity level of the team, or the coach wants to avoid a popularity contest that will lead to a lack of leadership and quite possibly resentment among the teammates. Even in cases like these, the coach may appoint one captain and then allow the team to elect the other captain or captains. At the professional level, it is commonplace for management to name a captain if the team feels the need to have one. This is in large part because players come and go throughout the actual season as well as in the off-season. Therefore, having consistency can be difficult. In football, it is standard practice to have a captain for each unit on the team, whether it be offense, defense, or special teams. And since the units really do operate as separate departments, it does not necessarily make sense for the offensive unit to have equal say in who is going to be the defensive captain.

Voting by the players is by far the most utilized method with regard to electing captains. How the votes are measured is actually secondary as to how the candidates are selected. Deciding on candidates can take on many forms including the strategy of not having candidates. Everyone on the team is eligible to become captain with nothing more than having to actually accept the candidacy. Another method used is having players nominated by the coach, either a player or players, and then conducting a vote to elect the captain(s). Self-nomination is a process that has been met with great success based on coaches' feedback and discussions. This shows the sense of leadership and confidence that the player possesses. There are also ways to modify the traditional vote of one person, one vote. Using a weighted vote is an effective way to give added power to certain players, for instance, having the seniors' vote count as four votes, the juniors' vote as three votes, the sophomores' vote as two votes, and the first year players' vote as one vote.

Training

To best serve the athletes and the teams, coaches and members of the organization are beginning to invest in formal captain training, similar to what one sees when they become a manager in business. Without proper training for captains, they will struggle to address team situations in the media, they will have a tough time controlling social media, and they will have to stay one step ahead of the pack in order to prevent such things as hazing.

Roles

The role of the captain is multifaceted and varies from program to program and team to team. As discussed, the philosophy/culture of the team will determine what the actual role of the captain is. As the athletes get older, the issues and circumstances will become more complex based not only on team rules but also on actual legal rules. At the high school level, the role of the captain will be limited based simply on the circumstances. In professional sports, there is only so much power a captain can have on their teammates once the athletes leave their training facility or stadium. The athletes are adults; therefore, it is hard to tell another adult how to lead their life away from the field or court. The captain can exercise power and direction on all team matters, especially in the locker room, where the athletes feel like they are in a sanctuary, as long as the direction given has a direct impact on the team and the team's performance.

College athletics is a different environment altogether. To be a captain at the collegiate level can be a daunting task. In college, the athletes are brought together from different backgrounds and geographic locations. The athlete did not grow up with their teammates, and they don't know the other players until they actually arrive on campus, and then every year a new group of new students joins the team, and the cycle continues. Social media and technology in general has made the world smaller, yet until one actually meets another person there is no way of knowing what the person is truly like.

Conclusion and Challenges

The role of the captain is an important part of any team or organization. If the philosophy of a team, school, or organization is to have captains, then it is incumbent on the leadership team of coaches, executives, and administrators to appropriately train the captains to handle the role. Training needs to be dynamic and proactive. Student-athletes today are dealing with issues and challenges that did not exist as recently as last year, not to mention 10 years ago. The ability for athletes to haze and get hazed through social media, the challenge to keep team issues inside the locker room walls, the exposure athletes receive whether they desire it or not, and the temptations that lie in wait for athletes is always going to be a threat. Asking an individual to work with and manage his or her peers is daunting enough; asking them to do it without proper training and support is irresponsible.

Lawrence Brady

See Also: Amateur Sports; Communication; Leadership Skills for Coaches (Amateur Sport); Leadership Skills for Coaches (Professional Sport); Team Building.

Further Readings
Dearing, J. "Follow the Leader: Beyond Captain Selection." *Coaching Volleyball,* v.29/5 (2012).
Greenwell, T. C., et al. "Peer Leadership and Ethical Conduct: Team Captains' Perceptions of NCAA Athletic Conference Code of Ethics." *Journal of Issues in Intercollegiate Athletics,* v.6 (2013).
Janssen, Jeff. *The Team Captain's Leadership Manual.* New York: Open Library, 2003.
Watson, L. "The Team Captain." *BC Coach's Perspective* (2011).

Cheating in Sports

By definition, to cheat is to break a given set of rules or codes in order to gain an advantage. Within sport, most rules are clearly defined and written in rule books, which are understood to constitute appropriate behavior and actions both during training and in competition. Notably, however, not all rules are written or formerly organized, and certain rules or codes of conduct exist more out of a pre-established, and often unspoken, code of ethics. In this sense, cheating can be classified as a subjective process. Moreover, although cheating is often linked only to individuals—particularly players—the use of rule breaking in order to gain advantage is seen in teams, coaches, and even organizations at varying levels.

Types of Individual Cheating
The use of performance-enhancing drugs is one of the best-known forms of cheating within the sports world. Various compounds have been used throughout history to improve performance at activities, though it is in the last century that big business has developed around them. Increasingly intelligent pharmacology involved in doping has led to a metaphorical arms race with testing laboratories and the World Anti-Doping Agency (WADA). Another common form of cheating is to alter or tamper with the equipment to be used within the competition. Some examples of this include putting Vaseline

on baseballs or corking a baseball bat in order to hit further. A recent high-profile example of tampering occurred in 2012, when U.S. speed skater Simon Cho, allegedly under the orders of his coach, damaged the skates of his Canadian rival Olivier Jean.

Then there are cases of cheating during game-play via the deliberate breaking of the pre-established rules of the sport. This can include, but is certainly not limited to, faking a foul or injury, covert personal fouls like grabbing a soccer player's shirt (when the referee is not looking), and inflicting pain on or taunting an opponent. Within each sport there will be hundreds of in-game rules, and so the potential for deliberately breaking or exploiting these rules during gameplay is extremely large.

Organizational and Institutional Cheating
Cheating as arranged by organizations is usually more sophisticated, and thus harder to trace, than is cheating at an individual level. Basic examples include the use of bribery, blackmail, and deceit to secure favorable decisions with regard to player sanctions, transfers, game rights, or events. More recently, there has been controversy over the 2022 World Cup being awarded to Qatar, with accusations of bribery prompting a full investigation and report by the Federation Internationale de Football Association (FIFA). The report cleared Qatar of bribery charges, although the efficacy and reliability of the report itself have now been called into question.

Cheating and misconduct can also take place as part of an unspoken but essentially official team operating procedure. In the National Football League (NFL), for example, performance based bonuses for on-field actions are classed as illegal because they are seen to circumvent player salary caps and encourage nonsporting behaviour. Regardless of the ban, an underground culture of "locker room" pools between players still exists, with an estimated 30 to 40 percent of NFL players being involved in a bounty scheme of some sort. In 2012, however, the Federal Bureau of Investigation (FBI) looked into claims that a bounty scheme was actually being organized by the club and coaches of the New Orleans Saints. The investigation uncovered systematic and highly organized bounties for tackling or aiming to injure key players in their opponent's lineup. The scandal, dubbed Bountygate, led to some of the strictest punishments seen within the NFL. Senior Defensive Coordinator Gregg Williams was suspended indefinitely, (although this was overturned the next year), Head Coach Sean Payton was suspended for the whole 2012 season, and the Saints as an organization had to forfeit their second round draft selections for 2012 and 2013 as well as pay a $500,000 fine.

Last, corporate espionage is largely considered a form of cheating within the world of sports, in that it involves the deliberate acquisition of private information for the benefit of another party. A famous example of this within sports is the 2007 NFL videotaping controversy, in which the New England Patriots were found to have videotaped the New York Jets' defensive coaches' signals. The scandal ended with Patriots Head Coach Bill Belichick admitting to using videotaping as far back as 2000. He was subsequently fined $500,000, the maximum amount any coach can be fined and the most any coach has ever been fined. On top of this, the Patriots as an organization were fined $250,000 and lost their original first round selection in the 2008 draft.

Sports Betting and Match-Fixing

Sports betting can be a complicated matter, but it is completely possible to bet on sports without breaking any rules and without cheating. This is due to the fact that sports betting regulations vary per sport, with some sports not allowing any, some allowing betting on unrelated sports and matches that one has no part in, and some sports allowing competitors to bet on themselves, but only if they bet on themselves to win.

Match-fixing, on the other hand, is a completely forbidden activity across all sports in that it undermines the entire nature and spirit of competition. Match-fixing can involve betting on oneself to lose and then throwing a game; it can also involve deliberately skewing the result of a game through poor play or, in the case of adjudication-based match-fixing, deliberately making biased decisions toward one team or competitor. An example of the latter is National Basketball Association (NBA) referee Tim Donaghy, who when investigated by the FBI in 2007 was found to have made over $30,000 from match-fixing. As it turned out, he had been battling with a gambling addiction and had debts to the mob. He

served 15 months in prison for his actions. Historically, however, match-fixing has not just been on an individual basis, and there is an example of this in the 1919 Chicago White Sox baseball controversy. In a World Series match against the Cincinnati Reds, several members of the White Sox team conspired to throw the game in order to claim major betting rewards. Unfortunately for them, word leaked about their plan, leading to a massively suspicious influx of betting in favor of the Cincinnati Reds. The result is that all bets were made void, and although not prosecuted, all of the players involved were banned from both major and minor league baseball.

Deliberate Versus Accidental

Cheating is not always deliberate, and there are multiple occasions in which cheating occurs completely by accident on the part of the competitor. This happens, and has happened, on a minor level in every football, soccer, and basketball game ever played. Numerous rules that govern how long a ball can be held, where it can be held, where players must or must not stand, and so on, are all infringed on a regular basis during the heat of competitive gameplay. It is for this reason that referees are used to control the flow of the game and to enforce gameplay rules that could accidentally be cheated during the course of that game. Accidental cheating can also occur through improper understanding of the rules, such as in junior and beginner sports competitions. In these cases, the "cheating" is done without negative intentions and is in many ways simply part of that competitor's learning process.

Intentional Fouls

Usually one would argue that deliberate fouling against the rules of the competition constitutes cheating, but there are specific examples in which this might not be the case. In most NBA games, for instance, it is common and accepted practice to foul the opposing team when nearing the end of the game in order to stop the clock and potentially regain possession. The fact that the practice is accepted and used by both sides in most games means that it is a norm of the sport, and so it would be largely incorrect to define this tactic as cheating in the broader sense of the word. Similarly, most spectators and commenters in the NFL would not call a neutral zone infraction cheating, despite the fact that it is a foul and it is aimed to give one side an advantage. The primary determinant for whether an action or a foul is classified as cheating is whether it is a widely accepted norm used by all players and teams or if it is the unique act of one player or team without the knowledge or mutual consent of opposing competitors.

Cheating and Philosophical Grey Areas

The use of performance-enhancing drugs, for instance, is now considered cheating, and some Major League Baseball (MLB) stars have been denied access to the Hall of Fame despite the fact that taking the drugs was 100 percent legal according to the rules of their competition in the period in which they competed. These competitors broke no rules and yet have still been labeled "cheaters" in this sense, one does not have to break the rules in order to cheat. Completely on the other end of this debate, if a competitor—a runner for instance— suddenly decided to cut across the athletics track, they would be intentionally breaking the rules of the race and thus disqualified for cheating. If, however, this competitor was running to save someone's life, it becomes a more complex question of whether that competitor cheated.

Enforcing Rules and Subjectivity

The rules and regulations of individual sports are decided by governing bodies, which in turn create certification courses in which people can learn how to referee that sport in the manner deemed appropriate by the governing body. These referees, also known as umpires and adjudicators, are given the responsibility of enforcing in-game rules. It is their job to remain impartial and to make decisions as objectively as possible given the evidence available to them. In bigger matches, this referee might be accompanied by an assistant referee, as well as a linesman and other adjudicators who are tasked with observing specific infractions, an example being the observation of the offside rule in soccer. The issue with this system, of course, is that in a game of multiple players, there are only a limited number of adjudicators and events can be missed and/or misread. Ultimately, the decision is made with a level of subjectivity, and it is not at all uncommon for competitors to challenge the outcome of that decision.

Sports technology has increasingly been introduced to remedy this problem. Rugby organizations introduced the use of freeze-frame footage to analyze a contested try, while tennis organizations use digital displays to capture whether a ball is "in" or "out." Soccer and now, for the first time ever, NFL referees are using wireless headsets to communicate with each other, and 2014 saw the first use of goal-line technology in an international soccer match.

Alexander Parry, Ba (Oxon)

See Also: Ethics in Sports; Legal Responsibilities for Coaches; Morality of Professional Sports; Organizational Culture; Sports Law; Sports Officiating.

Further Readings

EuroSport. "Speed Skater Tampered." https://uk.eurosport. yahoo.com/news/speedskater-tampered-rivals -skates-184817751.html(Accessed October 2014).

Hsu, L. "Ethics and Sports Rules." https://doc.rero.ch/ record/12703/files/HSU_Leo_-_C4_-_Cheating_ Deception_Foul_and_Sport_Rules.pdf (Accessed November 2014).

National Football League. "Patriots Videotaping Scandal." http://www.nfl.com/news/story/09000d5d8084899e/ article/timeline-of-events-surrounding-patriots -videotaping-scandal (Accessed October 2014).

Coaching and Sexual Abuse

The coach-athlete relationship is an important one, as coaches play an integral role not only in developing athletic skills and enhancing athletic performance but also in the growth of the athlete as a person. Sports aid in developing necessary life skills such as leadership, social success, time management, and peer relationships, and coaches play a vital role in teaching these life skills. The positive aspects of sport participation are quickly diminished and eliminated, however, when the coaching profession provides situations for sexual abuse to occur.

Public awareness of issues involving coaches and sexual abuse heightened in 2011 with the news that longtime Penn State University assistant football coach Jerry Sandusky was sexually assaulting underage boys on university property. Sandusky was eventually found guilty on 45 charges of sexual abuse and sentenced to a minimum of 30 years in prison. This incident made national headlines, but inappropriate actions involving coaches and their athletes have been an issue plaguing sport administrators for many years. U.S. swimming was rocked in 2010 when an ABC television investigation revealed numerous male coaches had lifetime bans for alleged sexual misconduct with female swimmers. U.S. gymnastics has also banned coaches for misconduct that is not in the best interests of the organization.

The amount of data available on the frequency and type of sexual abuse between coaches and athletes is sparse and inconsistent. Reports have ranged from a frequency of 2 percent to 27 percent depending on the sport and population examined. Athletes are often pressured to keep allegations private to protect the team, school, or organization, and to save everyone from public embarrassment, which results in making the reporting inconsistent.

The lack of reporting may have led to the proliferation of sexual abuse between coaches and athletes. Administrators and coaches want to protect their organization or team so they will not report coaches to avoid damaging their organization's or team's reputation. This has created an environment of secrecy and perhaps an environment of acceptability. Other reasons for not reporting include athlete embarrassment, lack of athlete understanding of sexual abuse, lack of physical evidence, lack of administrative oversight for coaches, and parental denial. There are also no physical characteristics or psychological characteristics that make coaches who sexually abuse athletes easily identifiable. Marital status, gender, age, job performance, and coaching success are not part of the equation when identifying a coach who may be sexually abusing athletes. This makes awareness of the issue that much more important.

There is no definitive definition of sexual abuse, but it can be described in two broad categories: sexual harassment and sexual assault. Sexual harassment has been defined as unwanted sexual advances, requests for sexual favors, or other verbal conduct of a sexual nature. Sexual assault takes place when physical contact is made with the intimate regions of the victim without the consent of the victim. The purpose of the physical contact involves sexual arousal or sexual gratification.

Both sexual harassment and sexual assault can involve the violation of civil rights, which also could make it a Title VII or Title IX issue. Title IX becomes part of the equation when a person believes he or she cannot continue their education free of sexual abuse as the person is being denied the right to an education. Universities and high schools must provide a safe environment for students and participants.

Although sports are thought to be a safe domain for youth, adolescent, and adult athletes, if left in the hands of an abusive coach, serious negative consequences can arise. In general, sexual abuse has been linked to an increased risk for post-traumatic stress disorder, eating disorders, anger, fear, and feelings of guilt and depression. Research on the specific consequences of sexual abuse on athletes is limited, but these negative consequences would be particularly problematic in the sporting world, especially if the athlete is engaged in high-level training.

The acceptance of girls and women in sport is increasing, but this minority population still faces some prejudice with participation. Just as girls drop out of sports, they attempt to not show their athletic prowess because they do not want to receive the stigmatized label of being a lesbian. Experiences of sexual abuse may also deter female athletes from continued participation in sport. In addition, female athletes who are sexually abused by male coaches experience traditional gender norms by being subordinated by a powerful male figure.

Conclusion

Educating athletes, parents, coaches, and administrators is a must in facing this issue. Education with athletes begins by ensuring athletes understand what sexual misconduct and abuse is. They should understand that it is wrong and unacceptable. Parents should also be aware of signs that their child may be a victim of sexual abuse, which include a reluctance to participate in the sport, sudden changes in emotional behavior, physical signs (i.e., genital injuries, bruises, scratches), and fear of closed doors. Scientists have developed a scale to measure perceptions of sexual abuse in youth sports, which can become instrumental in developing prevention policies and reporting guidelines for sport organizations.

Coaches have considerable influence over athletes, and opportunities are present for sexual abuse in a sport setting. Perhaps the most important tool for combating sexual abuse in the coach-athlete relationship is the screening of coaches at all levels by administrators.

Screening could alert administrators to potential sexual predators and prevent placing people in coaching positions where there may be a risk. Consistent education programs need to be delivered across sport organizations and teams to make administrators, coaches, and athletes aware of the issue, precautions to prevent sexual abuse, and what to do when sexual abuse is suspected. An environment also must be created where athletes feel safe to report sexual abuse. Those in leadership positions must be aware this is an issue and take all precautions to prevent sexual abuse from occurring.

Robin Hardin

See Also: Bullying/Hazing; Coaching Youth; Development of Leadership Skills; Sexual Harassment Among Players.

Further Readings

Baker T. A. III, and K. K. Byon. "Developing a Scale of Perception of Sexual Abuse in Youth Sports." *Measurement in Physical Education and Exercise Science*, v.18 (2014).

Baker, T. A., et al. "An Examination of Case Law Regarding the Liability of Recreational Youth Sport Organizations for the Pedophilic Actions of Coaches, Administrators, and Officials Based on the Theory of Respondeat Superior." *Applied Research in Coaching and Athletics Annual*, v.26 (2011).

Demers, G. "Homophobia in Sport." *Canadian Journal for Women in Coaching*, v.6/2 (2006).

Glenn, C. E. "The Legal Implications of the Sandusky Scandal." *Widener Law Journal*, v.22/3 (2013).

Hartill, M. "The Sexual Abuse of Boys in Organized Male Sports." *Men and Masculinities*, v.12 (2009).

Krebs, C. P., et al. "College Women's Experience With Physically Forced, Alcohol- or Other Drug-Enabled, and Drug-Facilitated Sexual Assault Before and Since Entering College." *Journal of American College Health*, v.57/6 (2009).

Parent, S. "Disclosure of Sexual Abuse in Sport Organizations." *Journal of Child Sexual Abuse*, v.20 (2011).

Coaching Inclusive Sport and Disability

Over much of the past half century, high schools, colleges and universities have been forced to deal with issues of social justice and inequality regarding race and gender, and now they must deal with new federal guidance focused on students with disabilities. Despite ever-increasing media coverage of the Paralympic Games, the opportunities for most athletes with a disability still remain relegated to segregated sport environments.

A prime example of this inequality can be framed in the story of Tatyana McFadden, who was forced to sue her own high school and the Maryland Public Secondary Schools Athletic Association (MPSSAA) in 2005 in order to gain access to practice with her high school track team. This occurred after she returned from the 2004 Paralympic Games in Athens, Greece as one of the youngest medalists in Paralympic Games history; she was a 16-year-old wheelchair track and field athlete. The unequal treatment and harassment that McFadden received led to a second lawsuit that culminated in the eventual landmark state legislation titled the 2008 Maryland Fitness and Athletic Equity Act for Students with Disabilities, which ultimately gave students with disabilities the same rights to fitness and varsity athletics as all Maryland high school students.

Building on the passage of this state legislation and a 2010 Government Accountability Office (GAO) that focused on health and fitness of children with disabilities, the U.S. Department of Education's Office for Civil Rights (OCR) was convinced to review and issue a "Dear Colleague" letter on January 24, 2013, clarifying elementary, secondary, and postsecondary level schools' responsibilities under the Rehabilitation Act of 1973 to provide extracurricular athletic opportunities for students with disabilities.

A June 2010 report by the GAO titled "Students with Disabilities: More Information and Guidance Could Improve Opportunities in Physical Education and Athletics" confirmed what many in the field of adaptive physical education, therapeutic recreation, and sport for individuals with disabilities already knew. The results of this national research study found that although certain federal laws help

Former Olympic gold medalist Otis Davis acts as referee at an athletic event for special needs children at Union City High School in New Jersey. Davis works as a coach, mentor, and is cofounder of the Tri-States Olympic Alumni Association, who hosted the event. (Wikimedia Commons/Luigi Novi)

ensure that students with disabilities in kindergarten through 12th grade be provided opportunities to participate in physical education and extracurricular athletics equal to their peers, the data demonstrates otherwise. The gap is particularly significant when it comes to extracurricular scholastic sports.

Many leaders in the disability sports movement often refer to the OCR guidance in the context of Title IX, the landmark legislation that transformed sport for girls and women in the United States. Making such a comparison is understandable given that Section 504 of the Rehabilitation Act of 1973 was constructed almost word for word to Title IX of the Educational Reform Act of 1972 with the exception of the words *must* and *should*, which allowed educational institutions to opt out of their responsibilities under the law. The "Dear Colleague" Letter of 2013 was an effort to reinterpret the Rehab Act and bring it more in line with the context and meaning of Title IX.

In addition to the provision of equal access to opportunities in mainstream sports, the "Dear Colleague" Letter further clarifies that institutions should expand opportunities for students with disabilities such as adding additional adapted events within existing individual sport competitions (e.g., wheelchair track and field events, wheelchair tennis, para-rowing events), Nordic and alpine sit-ski events) or sponsoring new adaptive team sports (e.g., wheelchair basketball, sled hockey, sitting

volleyball, goal ball) for students with disabilities who cannot otherwise participate in mainstream intercollegiate sports, which is often due to sensory or mobility-related issues. Explicit in the Americans with Disabilities Act of 1990 was a test to determine whether or not a reasonable accommodation is based on the underlying principle of an athlete with a disability is "otherwise qualified," meaning that they possess the requisite skills and training related to a given sport.

Recently, a number of state high school athletic associations, including the National Collegiate Athletic Association through its Office of Inclusion in conjunction with the Eastern College Athletic Conference (ECAC), have endorsed a more comprehensive, inclusive sport strategy that is intended to provide greater athletic opportunities for student-athletes with varying disabilities. This inclusion is based on four articulated inclusion principles that provide guidance for a range of reasonable accommodations for athletes to be able to participate in existing league, regional, state, or national championships by the adding of new adaptive events, as well as through the development of new scholastic and intercollegiate leagues and championships for new adaptive team sports (e.g., wheelchair basketball and ice sled hockey).

- *Inclusion Principle #1*: Inclusion of athletes with a disability in existing teams, competitions and Championships without any sport-specific accommodations required.
- *Inclusion Principle #2*: Inclusion of athletes with a disability in existing teams, competitions and Championships with reasonable sport-specific accommodations provided.
- *Inclusion Principle #3*: Inclusion of athletes with a disability through the addition of specific adaptive events in existing competitions and Championships.
- *Inclusion Principle #4*: Inclusion of athletes with and without a disability through the creation of specific adaptive team sports that participate in new leagues, competitions, and championships.

It is recommended that sport leaders, sport administrators, coaches, athletes, and their advocates become familiar with other landmark legislation, treaties, and court actions that have been used to support changes at all levels of sport in order to foster greater participation and inclusion of athletes with disabilities.

Similar to Title IX, the "Dear Colleague" letter is intended to ensure equal opportunity for participation by students with disabilities to the fullest extent possible in mainstream scholastic and intercollegiate sport by requiring educational institutions to provide reasonable accommodations upon the request of a student with a disability. Accommodations may include the modification of existing policies, practices, or specific sport competition rules. This guidance is expected to have a far-reaching impact on sport at all levels of sport beyond just the scholastic and intercollegiate sport at which it was targeted.

Ted Fay

See Also: Amateur Sports; Captains; Coaching Philosophy for College Athletics; Coaching Youth; Discrimination in Sports; Health Issues in Sports; Organizational Leadership; Positive Discipline.

Further Readings
Brittain, I. *The Paralympics Games Explained*. London: Routledge, 2010.
DePauw, K. P. and S. J. Gavron. *Disability Sport*. Champaign, IL: Human Kinetics, 2005.
Fay, T. G. and E. A. Wolff. "Disability in Sport in the Twenty-First Century." *Boston University International Law Journal*, v.27 (2009).
Hollonbeck v. U.S. Olympic Committee. 513 F.3d 1191. 1194-96 (10th Cir. 2008).
Lackowski, T. "Athletes With a Disability in School Sports:." *Boston University International Law Journal*. v.27/2 (2009).
McFadden v. Cousin, No. AMD 06-648 (D. Md. Apr. 17, 2006).
Office for Civil Rights. "Dear Colleague Letter." January 24, 2013. http://www2.ed.gov/about/offices/list/ocr/docs/dcl-factsheet-201301-504.html (Accessed March 2015).
PGA Tour, Inc. v. Martin, 532 U.S 661, 666-67 (2001).
Pistorius v. International Amateur Athletics Federation, CAS 2008/A/1480, at 7-8 (May 16, 2008).

Coaching for Character

As many adults can attest, some of the most influential people in their lives were coaches they had when they played youth or high school sports. Like their parents and schoolteachers, sports coaches are in a unique position to influence their athletes and to teach values that can help to create great parents, great citizens, and great leaders. Teachers and coaches are also in a position to do the exact opposite: to teach bad habits that can cause problems for their young, impressionable athletes and others that might be harmed by this antisocial behavior. Character development during youth and high school athletic participation should be part of the bargain in all sports programs that recreation departments, nonprofit organizations, physical education programs, and school athletic departments manage.

It is important to state what "coaching for character" is not. It is not religious education or an attempt by one group of coaches, adults, and sports administrators to indoctrinate youth. Coaching for character is an attempt to teach values that athletes can learn and apply in their daily lives to make them better neighbors and their communities better places to live. Coaching for character programs have been used at the collegiate level, too. The National Association of Intercollegiate Athletics (NAIA) uses this concept to market its schools and its governance organization. The NAIA program is called Champions of Character and it has a component directed at coaches but also at administrators, parents, and the student-athletes at NAIA schools. The NAIA has developed an outreach program for high school and youth athletes and coaches that can be used by member schools and their athletes that participate in community-relations projects.

Like the aforementioned NAIA program, an effective coaching for character program starts with a commitment from the sports organization to implement such a program across all parts of the organization. A clear mission statement, outlining exactly what this program will teach and how and who will teach these lessons, is an important first step. Countless community enhancing values can be learned through participation in athletics. Administrators, coaches, athletes, and parents of these athletes should be the target market for this informational campaign. When volunteers are interviewed for coaching positions within the organization, it should be made perfectly clear to those interested in coaching in the program, that coaching for character will be part of their duties. The values that the coaching for character program will focus on should be a product of consultation with the major stakeholders of the sports organization.

Values of the Game

The selection of the values to emphasize in a coaching for character program can focus on a few prominent goals or the program could put together a list values to become part of the sports program offered to the group of athletes that are playing for the organization, league, or team. Some of the values that are common to intentional programs like this are respect, responsibility, self-discipline, teamwork, physical fitness, sportsmanship, integrity, courage, friendship, commitment, time management, selflessness, perseverance, leadership, enthusiasm, determination, patience, poise, tolerance, toughness, creativity, empathy, joy, proper nutrition, concentration, self-confidence, healthy habits, and work ethic. Most character education programs focus on a manageable number of these values and build a campaign that is unique to their organization.

For sport organizations that sponsor multiple leagues of team sports like soccer, basketball, football, baseball, softball, and lacrosse, teaching the athletes how to work together as a team is a great place to center the coaching for character program. Working together as a team makes the sports experience fun for all involved and is also a life lesson that translates into a skill valued by many employers around the world. Emphasizing to the team the value of playing together as a team is also a chance to talk about sacrifice, humility, and unselfish behavior. Youth teams that exhibit teamwork are great examples for the parents, brothers, and sisters that come to the games and support their family members.

Some sport organizations sponsor only individual sports like gymnastics, golf, swimming, tennis, or track and field. Great athletes in sports like these have become great through long hours of solitary practice and a tremendous amount of self-discipline. College students need self-discipline to manage their lives on their own on a college campus.

Employers like to hire college graduates that have demonstrated self-discipline.

Teach and Define

Once the organization or team has decided what values will be emphasized, it then must clearly define and teach these values to the athletes in the organization. Teamwork involves team members subsuming their egos for the good of the team and it involves convincing those within and outside the circle of the team that the team is paramount to the individual. There will be countless examples in the world of sports that coaches can point to that the players can learn from; there are great examples of teamwork and unselfish behavior in all of the major professional leagues in the United States. Unfortunately, there are also some examples of selfish, egocentric behavior. These examples can also be used as a teaching tool for a coaching for character program. Coaches should define what is considered selfish behavior and also give examples of unselfish acts, both on the field of play and outside the boundaries of athletics.

Another part of this program is to reward and praise behavior that exemplifies teamwork or sacrifice on the part of an athlete. For example, one strategy would be praising the player who has exhibited this behavior in front of everyone; explain why that player's behavior exemplified an important tenet of the character education program; encourage others on the team to follow the example of that player; and be certain that the example is accurate.

Walk the Walk

In any coaching for character program, a major component of the program will be the coaches and administrators modeling the behavior they expect to see in their athletes. Coaches must exhibit respect for each other and respect for parents and game officials if they are going to build a program teaching the value of respect. Leading by example is a great teacher; coaches are one set of role models that young people look to for direction.

Evaluation

At the end of each season, the organization should examine how successful its commitment to coaching for character was, seeking feedback from all of the stakeholders involved. Each part of the program should be evaluated: modeling behavior, the promotion of the coaching for character program to all stakeholders and the local community, the impact the coaches had in teaching these values, and most important, feedback from the athletes should be examined.

Craig Esherick

See Also: Cheating in Sports; Ethics in Sports; Coaching Philosophy for College Athletics; Sport-Based Youth Development.

Further Readings
Character Education Partnership. http://www.character .org (Accessed October 2014).

Clifford, C., and R. Fiezell. *Coaching for Character: Reclaiming the Principles of Sportsmanship.* Champaign, IL: Human Kinetics, 1997.

Power, F. C., et al. "The Sport Behavior of Youth, Parents and Coaches." http://www.kintera.org/atf/cf/%7BD9E D2C0A-D259-4C2F-8CEC-AA29F7595F40%7D/ JRCE_RESEARCH.PDF (Accessed October 2014).

Watz, M. "An Historical Analysis of Character Education." *Journal of Inquiry and Action in Education* v.4/2 (2005).

Coaching Philosophy for College Athletics

Coaching philosophy is the basic foundation of objectives and principles that every coach has, regardless of whether they coach in the youth, the scholastic, the intercollegiate, or the professional level. It is the basis that molds future and ongoing decisions by coaches within every program. It is vital to have a coaching philosophy to initiate the coaching process of a team or program. This gives everyone, including the head coach, assistant coaches, players, and support staff, a sense of direction moving forward through the season. However, it is important to remember that coaching philosophies are ever changing and will evolve and continually develop through positive experiences, negative experiences, and the influences from the world and technology.

A coaching philosophy is a statement by the head coach of their coaching values and approach to their coaching opportunity. It clarifies the role as coach and extends into detail about player development and winning. It outlines the major objectives of the program and includes guiding principles and tactics for accomplishing the desired objectives. It defines to others what the program's objectives are and the plan of attack. It is normally based on past experiences as a possible player or coach, and includes a coach's knowledge, values, and beliefs. What is truly important to a head coach is that what he or she values will be translated to his or her players on a daily level.

Dictated By Coaching Levels
Coaching philosophy is often dictated by the level of coaching, since there are various goals coinciding with every level. For example, a youth coach is commonly more committed to teaching the fundamentals of the specific sport, explaining the game rules, and promoting playing opportunity and sportsmanship among all the athletes. As the coaching level increases, normally the commitment and expectations of winning increase as well. On the scholastic level, many of the youth sport level characteristics exist but competition increases greatly. On the intercollegiate athletics level, there is a tremendous pressure of winning and becoming champions due to the enormous amount of financial windfall, especially with the college football playoff system and the National Collegiate Athletic Association (NCAA) Tournament "March Madness" with college basketball. However, at the same time, there does exist the development of student-athletes academically, athletically, and socially. On the professional level, there is a total commitment to winning and organizations are operated like a business. With the absence of academics, coaches and players operate in a total athletic environment and are focusing on improving the team.

Goal of Winning Versus Process of Championship-Level Program
In a coaching philosophy, there is basically one question the coach must initially answer: Does the coach want to make winning the ultimate goal and have every decision predicated upon the concept of the ends justifying the means, or does the coach want to build a championship-level program that

is committed to development and improvement of the player academically, athletically, and socially? In the latter system, the means justifies the ends. This question must be answered initially and every forthcoming decision should reflect back to this answer.

Many high-level intercollegiate institutions like Duke, Stanford, Northwestern, and Vanderbilt are committed to both academic and athletic excellence for their student-athletes. Encouraging and advancing learning is the primary goal. These programs provide an equitable athletic experience within a nurturing environment for all participants. The educational experiences extend beyond the classroom to include a rich assortment of interaction for the purpose of enrichment and empowerment.

For example, Duke's basketball program, led by Coach Mike Krzyweski (also known as Coach K), is committed to a championship-level program in all aspects. This has been Coach K's direction since he initially became head coach at Duke in 1980. Consequently, he has developed a total program committed to his student-athletes to ensure that they develop academically, athletically, and socially.

U.S. Naval Academy football team head coach Paul Johnson sends a player into the game with the team's next play. College athletic coaching philosophy is normally based on past experiences as a player or coach, and includes a coach's knowledge, values, and beliefs. (U.S. Navy/Damon J. Moritz)

Obviously, he has encountered many student-athletes who have developed and prospered in the NBA. However, he has had far more student-athletes develop as productive citizens off the basketball court. In contrast, there are certainly other college basketball programs that have exhibited a win-it-all mentality. There has been some success on the basketball court, but Duke has also encountered tremendously low graduation rates and a multitude of off-the-court problems that have dominated the media.

Alabama football has encountered tremendous success with Nick Saban at the helm. Coach Saban has implemented a total student-athlete development program including football, academics, life skills, nutrition, and personal development. Saban is constantly discussing the process of getting better and improving over winning. He encourages his players to focus on one play at a time, while he instructs his teams to focus on one game at a time. His system aims to make each individual on the team better daily and thus the overall team becomes better throughout the season. He strives for mastery of perfection on the football field but is constantly attempting to develop his players.

Teams Mirror Their Head Coaches

Almost all teams take on the personality of the head coach and these traits are exemplified on the playing field. Successful coaches emphasize what is important to them. In these programs, players are constantly hearing these buzzwords and it becomes ingrained in them to attempt to be successful in these areas. For example, if a head football coach is very concerned about limiting the number of penalties in a football game and this is constantly reinforced to players, then there is a great chance that the football team will have very few penalties. What is emphasized constantly to players from the coach becomes very important to players, as they want to please their head coach and also believe that his focus will lead them to success.

Developing A Coaching Philosophy

Most coaches develop their coaching philosophy from their previous experiences. First, it is usually developed from playing a specific sport. These experiences as a player, both positive and negative, are usually used as a gauge of how the coach wants to shape his or her coaching philosophy. However, previous playing experience is not necessary to coach and to develop a coaching philosophy, although most coaches have encountered some experience playing the specific sport in the past at least on the youth or scholastic level. Other coaches have had success in intercollegiate athletics and the professional ranks. This success on a higher level tends to enable coaches to have more credibility from the start from their players.

Coaching today is very challenging and stressful. There are enormous interchangeable parts to gauge as well as the increased media and fan attention from social media. Coaches initially need to have a strong coaching philosophy in place to provide the core of the program in order to return to making more in-depth decisions throughout the season. For example, a coach that is focused on development of the program will have more views than a coach that is focused solely on winning. In a situation where the star point guard in a college basketball program misses extensive classes, a coach that is focused on development of the program will more than likely discipline the student-athlete by suspending him or her for a game. This is in line with the coach's philosophy of development and doing the right things both on and off the playing field. However, a coach that is focused on winning will probably overlook the class absences and play the point guard with the intention of winning the game at all costs. While neither decision is right or wrong, it is important that coaches align these specific decisions to the basic core of the coaching philosophy principles. This allows coaches the opportunity to return to their philosophy in order to make specific decisions. It is very important that coaches maintain consistency in decisions like this, as players are watching to see how certain situations are handled by the coaching staff. A coach's decision on how to handle this situation is an outward show of their coaching philosophy and emphasizes to the players how situations will be handled. This will greatly affect possible future decisions by student-athletes in the program.

Incorporating Coaching Philosophy
Coaches need to begin to incorporate their coaching philosophy during the first team meeting of the year. This ensures that all assistant coaches, players, and support staff understand the coach's expectations. This further allows the assistant coaches and support staff to begin to constantly reinforce messages each day. It is important that coaches develop positive relationships with players daily, and a great way to do this is to refer to parts of the coaching philosophy. For example, a college baseball coach could refer to the importance of academics to his baseball players and give an example of a major league star that just encountered a career-ending injury. This reminds the student-athletes that an injury could change or end their careers in the future. It also provides an excellent opportunity for the coach to show how attaining a college degree will provide a stable opportunity for a player to support him- or herself and family in the future.

Adjusting the Coaching Philosophy
The best coaches in various sports adjust their coaching philosophy through time. Coaches change strategies for various reasons. If coaching philosophies are adjusted, it is important to be absolutely certain that the change will benefit the program going forward. Players gain confidence with consistency from coaches, and when change is made, there will be adjustments from everyone within the program. However, most successful coaches have flexibility in adjusting to changing times in order to put their players in the best position to be successful.

Chris Croft

See Also: National Collegiate Athletic Association; Situational Leadership Theory; Unionization of College Athletes.

Further Readings

Liskevych, Terry. "Creating Your Coaching Philosophy." http://www.theartofcoachingvolleyball.com/creating-your-coaching-philosophy (Accessed May 2012).

Martens, Rainer. *Successful Coaching.* Champaign, IL: Human Kinetics, 2012.

Mitchell, Jeff. "Coaching Philosophy." http://coachgrowth.wordpress.com/2013/11/29/coaching-philosophy (Accessed November 2013).

Posnanski, Joe. "Alabama Coach Nick Saban Unrelenting in Pursuit of Perfection." http://www.nbcsports.com/

joe-posnanski/alabama-coach-nick-saban-unrelenting
-pursuit-perfection (Accessed November 2013).

Coaching Teenagers

The practice of coaching teenagers, also referred to as youth coaching, is one of the main branches of life coaching that is geared toward encouraging personal development in young minds as they grow through their teenage years into adulthood. It is important to do this because it provides young people with an avenue through which they can be able to release stress, tension, and anxiety and help them channel their energies toward more productive avenues in society. Coaching teenagers is not a very easy thing to do because young minds usually have much to deal with. At the same time, teenagers are also dealing and grappling with the realities of adolescence and the challenges thereof. Parents are naturally inclined to worry about the welfare of their teenage children.

While some youth coaches tend to overstep their boundaries, it is important to take note of the fact that youth coaches are not supposed to act as parents or teachers. They are not supposed to stand in as enforcement figures either. The role of the youth coach is to provide impartial and nonjudgmental support to teenagers to help them exercise their freedoms without necessarily infringing on the rights of others to exercise or enjoy theirs. The youth coach should therefore be a trustworthy individual, with whose support a young individual has a chance to be confident about what they want.

Teenagers can be troubled by many things. Troubled teenagers do require the help of professionals to get them out of the metaphorical woods and get them back on track. As sporting events are concerned, this is one of the most important times in the lives of teenagers who are involved in sports because they are able to realize their potential and live up to the expectations. The role of the coach therefore is to help individuals realize that they have the potential for greater challenges in life, and with that in mind also come to help them realize what they can be able to achieve in life if they focus their energy on becoming better sports-oriented individuals. Inasmuch as the individual is supposed to focus their energy on building their sporting ability, it is also important for the coach to make sure that the teenager gets to appreciate the sense of self-belief.

In sporting events nothing is as important as teamwork and the ability to realize and appreciate the collective effort of the team. Even in individual sporting events, the concept of a team always happens to manifest itself in one way or the other, and it is this concept that will help teenagers get through life in the future. The coach has the mandate of helping developing teenagers come to appreciate the fact that in order for them to turn out to be successful, they need to learn to work together with others, and work together for the greater goal of the team and in the long run their personal development. Teenagers that have been able to appreciate and embrace the team spirit usually turn out to be successful individuals even after they are done with sporting events.

To help teenagers deal with difficulties in sports, coaches have different ways of speaking to the teenagers. They usually try to appeal to the teenagers' innermost concerns and help them speak out about what they think and what they need in their lives. Some of the common challenges that young teenagers have to deal with in as far as sporting difficulties are concerned include accepting other individuals as part of the team and dealing with the competing spirit and the thrill of seeking out success through all means possible.

Teenagers do require someone who not only can help them set their goals in life, but also can help them work hard toward reaching the set goals.

Michael Fox

See Also: Amateur Sports; Coaching Youth; High School Sports; Minor League Baseball; Sport-Based Youth Development.

Further Readings
Martins, Rainer. *Successful Coaching*. Champaign, IL: Human Kinetics, 2012.

McRae, Barbara. *Coach Your Teen To Success: 7 Simple Steps to Transform Relationships & Enrich Lives*. New York: BookBaby, 2012.

Patton, Bill. *The Art of Coaching High School Tennis*. Tucson, AZ: Jetlaunch, 2014.

Coaching Women

During the early years of the 20th century, sport became highly organized and entrenched in U.S. society. Acceptable forms of physical activity and sport for men and women varied as a result of prescribed gender norms for men and women. Influential cultural beliefs included the notion that a woman could ruin her health by engaging in intense physical activity. A woman's reputation could be ruined by participating in unladylike behavior or activity (including sport) in public.

The first instances of women coaching women occurred primarily on college campuses and in high school physical education classes during the late 1800s. Unlike the development of men's athletics, administrators and coaches that controlled women's sport sought to prevent it from becoming highly competitive or commercialized. During the same time period that leaders in intercollegiate athletics were developing a governing body that would eventually become the National Collegiate Athletic Association (NCAA), women department leaders and coaches aligned athletics with the mission of the university. Three major differences between men's and women's athletics emerged during the early 20th century. First, women's sports were more closely supervised than men's sports. Second, unlike their male counterparts, women's coaches shunned publicity, intense training, spectators, and gate receipts. Last, women did not engage in contact sports.

When the National Amateur Athletic Federation (NAAF) set forth a platform of governance in 1923, the growth of competitive athletic opportunities for women sustained a setback. Coaches and administrators in the NAAF who oversaw sports in collegiate athletics for women believed competition would harm the female participant's reproductive organs and create masculine behavior. Consequently, noncompetitive events such as "Play Days" became the norm. Play Days were designed to provide athletic women with an outlet for participation, but were essentially social events that often concluded with ice cream socials.

Title IX and Women in Coaching

In 1972, Title IX became law and revolutionized women's sport. Title IX states "no person in the United States shall, on the basis of sex be excluded from participation in, or denied the benefits of, or be subjected to discrimination under any educational program or activity receiving federal financial assistance." Title IX's passage in 1972 mandated equal funding for women's collegiate athletics and in turn, helped expand opportunities for women's sport participation and within coaching ranks.

The rapid expansion of women's athletics necessitated the need for a unified governing body of women's athletics. As a result, the Association of Intercollegiate Athletics for Women (AIAW) was established. Developed on a student-centered educational model, coaches focused on helping young women to achieve their academic goals ahead of their athletic pursuits. Women composed the majority of individuals coaching women's intercollegiate sport. Under AIAW control, approximately 90 percent of women's intercollegiate athletic teams were coached by a woman. Similarly, 90 percent of athletic programs were administered by a female. After the NCAA assumed control of women's intercollegiate athletics during the 1981 to 1982 school year, the rates of women coaching began to decline.

Overall, Title IX was revolutionary in terms of creating participation opportunities for girls and women in sport. The number of women competing in college athletics grew from 16,000 in 1968 to over 200,000 in 2013. Unfortunately, the law has not had a positive impact for women interested in coaching. As previously mentioned, women coached 90 percent of college teams under AIAW control. In 2013, the number of women head coaches dropped to approximately 40 percent. Roughly 51 percent of unpaid coaches are currently assistant coaches of women's teams, and 57 percent of paid assistant coaches of women's teams are female. Less than 2 percent of men's teams have a woman coach.

Current State of Women in Coaching

There are a number of factors that have contributed to the underrepresentation of women in coaching. First, due to the historical trend of women being declined when they seek coaching positions, there are not enough female mentors to guide assistant coaches or athletes in the head coach professional development process. Further, research indicates that men are perceived to be more competent coaches by hiring officials. Another barrier for women who desire to coach is the phenomenon of homologous reproduction. Homologous reproduction occurs when individuals with decision making power over a hiring decision select a candidate for a job that is most similar to themselves. Because athletic directors and athletic administrators are predominately white men, it is logical that women coaches are likely to be negatively affected by homologous reproduction during job searches.

The lack of women in coaching positions is troubling for a number of reasons. Women athletes playing for a female head coach have a natural role model in that individual. Women are also in a better position to provide gender-specific advice to young athletes and help them grow and overcome challenges in a way that a male coach cannot. Data also revealed that women are more apt to pursue coaching as a career if they played for a female coach.

One of the most significant barriers for women in coaching is the challenge of balancing work and life. Coaching requires significant amounts of travel and very long days during the season. Most coaches also have to travel extensively during the summer months or in the off-season to recruit. Childbearing years coincide with the time women coaches are in the most critical developmental years in terms of their careers. Female coaches that are able to find a way to have successful careers as coaches and have children typically have a partner or other source of support at home. The University of Tennessee's legendary coach Pat Summitt, the winningest coach in intercollegiate basketball history (man or woman), managed to balance motherhood and her coaching career. Her son Tyler was a constant fixture at basketball practices and games. Not all women are so fortunate, however. Many women remain assistant coaches as a coping mechanism while others drop out of coaching altogether.

Strategies for Improvement

There are a number of strategies identified by researchers designed to increase the number of women in coaching. The further development of professional development conferences for women coaches is one such strategy. Conferences provide women with the opportunity to learn leadership skills, present networking opportunities, and allow women to learn from their peers or seasoned head coaches. For example, the Women's Basketball Coaches Association is an organization designed to help advance women in intercollegiate basketball. At its annual conference, the association offers educational programs with topics ranging from Title IX to game strategies.

Mentorship is another tactic that has proven to be effective for women interested in coaching at a high level. Mentors help guide young women interested in coaching, provide advice and tutelage on coaching techniques, and help them to understand the culture within a given sport organization. Research indicates that assistant coaches who are well supported by their boss—the head coach—experience more success than those who lack support. Due to the low number of female head coaches, there is a lack of available mentors for young coaches. Mentors frequently help their mentees to facilitate relationships with potential employers.

Over the course of history, women interested in coaching have experienced resistance, primarily due to prescribed gender norms. Women coaches also encounter numerous barriers to obtaining head coaching positions due to discriminatory hiring practices and work–life balance issues. As society and gender norms continue to evolve, it is plausible that more women will enter the coaching ranks, and stay.

Elizabeth A. Gregg

See Also: Discrimination in Sports; Gender and Sport Leadership; Women's Leadership in Sport.

Further Readings
Kerr, Gretchen. "Women in Coaching: A Descriptive Study." *Report to the Coaching Association of Canada* (2006).
Kilty, Katie. "Women in Coaching." *Sport Psychologist*, v.20/2 (2006).
Norman, Leanne. "The Challenges Facing Women Coaches and the Contributions They can Make to the Profession." *International Journal Of Coaching Science*, v.7/2 (2013)
Walker, Nefertiti A., and Trevor Bopp. "The Underrepresentation of Women in the Male-Dominated Sport Workplace: Perspectives of Female Coaches." *Journal of Workplace Rights*, v.15/1 (2010).

Coaching Youth

Coaching is not just about teaching the skills of the game, creating and analyzing plays, and determining the best strategies to use to beat an opponent. Coaching is educating the players about all aspects of the sport, and this is just one of many reasons why—although it doesn't come with a multimillion-dollar contract—coaching youth sports is the most important level of coaching.

Laying the Foundation

Everything needs a solid foundation upon which it can be built. In sports, this foundation begins with the proper footwork. If a player does not have his or her feet in the correct position, it can throw off everything else he or she is trying to do. Proper footwork is essential to succeed in sports; this supersedes catching, throwing, serving, running, or any other basic athletic skill. It is important for youth coaches to teach players proper footwork because if they are not moving correctly, they will never completely master the sport-specific skills needed to be a successful athlete.

Throwing, hitting, serving, catching, running, and other concepts are not skills people are naturally born knowing how to do correctly. Watch children throw a ball for the first time, and most, if not all, will stand facing their target with their shoulders square to that target. In that stance, they will pull either their left or right arm back and throw the ball to the target. The ball may land a few feet or a few inches in front of them, but it will not hit the target, and will have either too much or not enough loft. Ask these same children to watch professional athletes throw a ball for a while and they will start to imitate those athletes. This will result in them changing their stance so that left-handers lead with their right shoulder, and right-handers lead with their left shoulder. This small change will result in an improvement in the loft of the ball, as well as the accuracy of the throw. This is coaching, and, as previously stated, is why youth coaching is the most important level of coaching. A player who is never taught how to throw a ball correctly might simply give up because he or she is unable to reach the target, is frustrated by his/her lack of improvement, or is ridiculed by his or her friends. In life, success is

Lade Majic, Harlem Ambassadors basketball team coach and player, demonstrates proper passing techniques to children during a basketball camp sponsored by Yokosuka Morale, Welfare and Recreation Youth Sports. (U.S. Navy/Charles Oki)

built on a solid foundation. In sports, teaching footwork is the first layer of the foundation, and is then followed by teaching proper techniques for throwing, catching, hitting, serving, and other skills. The two components combined result in a sound foundation for the athlete, which ultimately leads to athletic success.

Mental Toughness

Just as the skills and fundamentals of each sport need to be taught, so does the mental side of the game. Teammates, coaches, parents, fans, opponents, and officials are all talking and yelling at different points during any sporting event. This can easily distract even the most seasoned athlete, much less a child. This is where coaching plays an important role. Coaches need to work with their players and teach them how to block out the various external stimuli and stay focused on the actual game. The only people players should listen to during a game are the coaches, officials, and teammates. Coaches need to create mentally tough players so that no matter what happens in and around the games, the players stay mentally focused on the task at hand, which is to play the game to the best of their ability.

Constructive Criticism

People have a tendency to focus on what they do not excel at, no matter the situation. When learning a new sport and all the ancillary things that go with it, focusing on what one does not excel at can make conquering the sport seem like an insurmountable task. Positive encouragement from coaches goes a long way toward making the insurmountable become just another hurdle on the path to becoming a superstar. Telling players they have done a good job when they have not only hurts the players and the team. The key is in the delivery of the assessment from the coach to the players; it needs to be done in a constructive manner.

Simply telling players they did not do something correctly, or they need to do it better, is not constructive. Coaches always need to remember that players do not intentionally do things incorrectly or without maximum effort. Players may think they are doing a drill or running a play correctly, when in reality they are not, and this is where the coaches play a critical role. Criticism is part of the process of learning something new, and there is no difference in sports. The key for coaches is to keep the criticism constructive. Players need to be able to learn from their mistakes, not just be reprimanded for them.

Being a Role Model
Coaches who yell on a constant basis are going to have players who yell too. The focus should be on coaching the players, not yelling at them, and not on all the ancillary people. Players, especially young players, tend to model their coaches' behavior. Players want to be coached and want to have fun—yelling is not fun. Children may start playing because their friends are playing, their parents sign them up, or their siblings are playing, but the youth coaches need to make it fun and encourage them to keep playing.

Pamela J. Wojnar

See Also: Coaching Philosophy for College Athletics; Coaching Teenagers; Leadership Skills for Coaches (Amateur Sport); Sport-Based Youth Development.

Further Readings
Burnett, Darrell J. "Positive Coaching: A Behavior Checklist for Youth Sport Coaches." http://assets.ngin .com/attachments/document/0020/0869/Positive _Coaching.pdf (Accessed October 2014).
DeLench, Brooke. "Ten Signs of a Good Youth Sports Coach." http://www.momsteam.com/team-parents/ coaching/general/ten-signs-of-a-good-youth-sports -coach (Accessed October 2014).
National Association for Sports and Physical Education. "101 Tips for Youth Sport Coaches." http://www.ode.state.or.us/teachlearn/subjects/pe/ naspe101tipsyouthsports.pdf (Accessed October 2014).

Command Coaching Style

Sport participation is believed to be a cornerstone in developing sportsmanship, leadership, and other positive behaviors in athletes of all ages. While there may be truth to these claims, it is also important to note that the philosophical style of a player's coach affects which of these positive outcomes are achieved. A command coaching style is one in which the coach makes all the decisions and gives all the directions with the expectation that athletes will comply. Coaches who subscribe to this style often do so because they feel that they, rather than their athletes, possess the knowledge and expertise required to coach. They also believe it is more efficient because less time is spent on decision making and that allowing athlete input undermines their credibility. While there are advantages and disadvantages associated with every coaching style, a command (authoritarian) coaching style can be a deterrent to positive outcomes of sport participation.

Disadvantages of Command Coaching Style
Command coaches may exercise authority to the point that their team operates like a dictatorship. This "my way or the highway" attitude leads the command coach to perceive questions and/or input from student-athletes as disrespectful or subordinate. The behaviors of a command coach in response to perceived opposition often include demeaning or intimidating nonverbal cues, which ultimately deter athletes from gaining greater understanding of how and why to execute a skill or strategy. This approach often stifles leadership development because athletes are denied decision-making opportunities and fear that stepping up and taking charge will be viewed as a threat to authority.

Command-style coaches typically put winning first and athlete development second. They negotiate competition under the belief that winning or "taking command" over an opponent is what matters most. To instill this attitude in their players, command coaches will often use negative discipline, such as blaming or punishing with physical exercise, to manage player behavior. A command coach believes that an athlete's performance can be improved by instilling fear about their status on the team in some way (i.e., playing time). This technique diminishes sportsmanship because team members feel they must "win at all costs" to hold a secure place on the team.

Because they feel they are experts, authoritarian coaches take a traditional approach to organizing and administrating practices. The coach sets goals, decides what skills and strategies will be taught, and then incorporates repetitive, technical drills that can be closely monitored by the coaching staff. For example, a basketball coach may set a team free-throw goal at 80 percent for the season and have the players shoot and record 100 free throws in practice each day (10 at a time with a partner). At the end of practice, any player who did not make 80 out of 100 (80 percent) runs a sprint for every missed shot over the 20 allowed. While this type of drill might be conducive to closer evaluation by coaches, it provides little instruction, is not game-like, and therefore not much fun. It also contributes to reduced focus on individual and team improvement.

Finally, the major risk associated with this style of coaching is that an athlete's internal motivation is diminished. Rather than play for the love of the sport, athletes will begin to play to earn the coach's praise and approval or to avoid demeaning verbal/nonverbal behavior. The worst case scenario is that they may start playing out of fear of losing their position or playing time. Playing out of fear takes away an athlete's ability to have fun and truly enjoy sport participation. Players become so focused on not making mistakes that they stop taking risks that lead to improvement (i.e., a tennis player will serve the ball over the net safely versus strategically). Command coaches may also experience high rates of athlete attrition because they alienate all but the highly skilled, elite athletes.

Advantages of Command Coaching Style
Despite its weaknesses, an authoritarian style can be advantageous in specific situations when incorporated in a respectful manner. First and foremost, when safety and risk of injury are involved, a command style should be used to establish rules and safety parameters. For example, an athlete who sustains a head injury during a football game should not be given the choice to go back in the game. The coach needs to take command in this situation to protect the health and safety of the athlete.

In certain stages of learning—when preparation for performance is complete and it comes to the execution phase during competition—a command style may be more desirable. For example, a coach may work democratically with the team in practice throughout the week by putting players in game-like situations and allowing them to dictate strategy, call time outs, and make substitutions, among other things. However, during competition it works much better if only the coach is providing instruction and direction. Younger and less-experienced players who are participating in a sport for the first time may need structure to keep from being overwhelmed by learning new skills, rules, and strategies. A command style enables the coach to establish safety and discipline parameters, control young players and large groups, and make effective use of limited time (i.e., "sit down with your legs crossed and hands to yourself until your turn"). It will ensure that players work toward a theme and standard of performance established by the coach.

Finally, the command style can be beneficial with larger teams such as hockey, football, and soccer when team members on the field have to work in synchronicity to run an offensive or defensive scheme. A command style can streamline decision making and increase communication to, from, and between players.

Chelsea Brehm
Dana Munk

See Also: Coaching for Character; Cooperative Coaching Style; Positive Discipline; Submissive Coaching Style.

Further Readings
Albrecht, Rick. *Coaching Myths: Fifteen Wrong Ideas in Youth Sports.* Jefferson, NC: McFarland Press, 2013.
American Sport Education Program. *Coaching Youth Track and Field.* Champaign, IL: Human Kinetics, 2008.

Calipari, John and Michael Sokolove. *Players First: Coaching From the Inside Out.* New York: Penguin Press, 2014.

Community Engagement for Sports Teams

Community engagement is the process by which a sport team interacts and connects with the target population within a specific area. Managed through the marketing department of a sport organization, and more specifically the subdepartment of community relations, community engagement is an integral part of any sports team's outreach, whether the relationship is team-initiated, league-initiated, player-initiated, or community-initiated. The main goal of community engagement and sports teams is to foster goodwill in the community and develop a long-term relationship with individuals and the community as a whole.

Reasons for Community Engagement

The main goal of any sports team is to make a profit—just as any other business. However, it is not the only goal, and the reality is that in order for a sports team to be successful in the seats, it needs to be engaged with its community. Spectators are not going to buy tickets and sponsors are not going to pay a large amount of money for marketing partnerships without there being some connection to the community. This is the foundation of the concept of corporate social responsibility, which is an organization's obligation to increase its positive impact on society as a whole while decreasing any negative impact. Sport teams attempt to accomplish this by being a quality marketing citizen, which entails adopting a strategic focus to maximize social obligations to stakeholders. In terms of community engagement, these social obligations are focused on the philanthropic efforts of sport teams.

By definition, philanthropy is defined as the social obligation an organization has to be a good corporate citizen by contributing to the improvement of the quality of life of people ranging from an individual or community to society as a whole. For sports teams, philanthropy is most often managed through the community relations department. This department works with public interest groups and the general public with initiatives that foster goodwill in the community and develop a long-term relationship with individuals and the community as a whole.

Community engagement, in multiple levels of interactions, ranges from cause-related interactions to strategic philanthropy to environmental consciousness. Cause-related interactions focus on the process of creating a relationship between a sports team and a specific social cause. These relationships can range from one-time partnership to long-term associations. Strategic philanthropy is a concept where a sports team seeks to use all of its core competencies to address the interests of its stakeholders in order to achieve both organizational and social benefits. This goes beyond cause-related interactions because it involves both financial and nonfinancial contributions. In addition, cause-related interactions focus on the direct connection with the community through specific events, whereas strategic philanthropy goes beyond and becomes engrained in the normal operations of the organizational culture.

Another area of growth within community engagement is environmental consciousness—ranging from the community environment to the natural environment. There has been a significant push in recent years to not only provide an experience with sport products and services that improves the quality of life, but also to do so while promoting a healthy environment that enhances everyone's standard of living. Hence, it has become equally important for sports teams to promote issues related to kids staying in school, saying no to drugs, and eliminating bullying as it is to educate and model behavior related to conservation, pollution reduction, and overall environmental sustainability.

Types of Community Engagement

While building brand equity and securing financial capital is an important concept to the bottom line of the sport business, there is equal importance in building social capital and creating a sense of community between the sports team and the population it serves. Social capital builds networks, engagement, and membership among individuals with similar social requirements; and a sense of community is the experiential concept that connects these relationships and dependencies. Sports teams build social capital through community relations programs in numerous ways ranging from civic engagement to creating informal social interactions through socialization, involvement, and commitment.

There are three major ways in which sports teams support community engagement: through programs initiated by the team itself, through league-wide initiatives, and in partnership with players and their foundations. It would be safe to say that the majority of teams globally have some type of community relations department focusing on community engagement. This engagement can range from simple mascot appearances at community events to more structured involvements. For example, the New England Patriots of the National Football League (NFL) were the first professional team to put in player contracts the requirement of doing 10 noncommercial public appearances in the community such as at schools, homeless shelters, and hospitals. Another even more structured example is the Boston Red Sox and their work with an organization known as the Jimmy Fund, with whom the team since 1953 has worked to raise money and awareness in the fight against cancer around the world.

League-wide initiatives are also a significant opportunity for a larger-scale community engagement across multiple communities. The NFL has had an over-40-year community relations partnership with the United Way to strengthen America's communities in a variety of programs. NBA Cares is the National Basketball Association's league-wide community outreach effort that seeks to address important social issues related to education, youth and family development, and health and wellness. The Barclay's English Premier League supports programs at clubs across the country in the areas of facilities, grassroots programming, education and skills, and sports participation.

Many individual players take it a step further, engaging in their communities either in the city they play or back in their hometown. Some of these efforts come from the desire to help in their community, while others are inspired because of a personal connection to a cause. One example of a player successfully involved in community engagement is Carlos Beltran, the winner of Major League Baseball's

Roberto Clemente Award in 2013 (in recognition of his contributions to baseball, sportsmanship, and community involvement), who through his foundation supports student-athletes near his hometown in Puerto Rico with scholarships and programs that focus on developing their talents and core values. A cause-related community engagement example is the Drew Brees Foundation. The quarterback, who was the center of the community rebirth of New Orleans after the devastation of Hurricane Katrina in 2005, created a foundation that seeks to improve the quality of life for cancer patients through care and education for the afflicted and their family. The New Orleans Saints help promote this, and the causes of other players and coaches, through their own promotional and community engagements.

Derek Jeter of the New York Yankees. Jeter created a charitable organization, Turn 2 Foundation, to help children and teens avoid drug and alcohol addiction. (Wikimedia Commons/ Chris Ptacek)

Eric C. Schwarz

See Also: Identification With Sports Teams; Sports as a Means of Developing Leaders; Team Culture.

Further Readings

Jenkins, H., and Laura James. "It's Not Just a Game: Community Work in the UK Football Industry and Approaches to Corporate Social Responsibility." http://davidcoethica.files.wordpress.com/2012/09/its-not-just-a-game1.pdf (Accessed October 2014).

Pharr, Jennifer R., and Nancy L. Lough. "Differentiation of Social Marketing and Cause-Related Marketing in U.S. Professional Sport." *Sport Marketing Quarterly*, v.21/2 (2012).

Schwarz, E. C. "Building a Sense of Community Through Sport Programming and Special Events: The Role of Sport Marketing in Contributing to Social Capital." *International Journal of Entrepreneurship and Small Business*, v.7/4 (2009).

Comparative Models of Sports Leadership

Over time, scholars have developed a long list of approaches, models, and theories to define leadership, explain leader behaviors, and identify the characteristics of effective leaders. Approaches based on situations, skills, styles, and traits provide understanding about the extent to which leadership can be developed and how it manifests in daily life. Additionally, theoretical models like contingency, leader-member exchange, and path-goal theory offer explanations for the many different ways leaders motivate and engage their followers. One challenge posed by this wealth of knowledge is that it may be difficult to see any common ground between the unique perspectives. In light of this issue, Packianathan Chelladurai proposed a multidimensional model of leadership aimed at reconciling aspects of different leadership theories and organizing them into one comprehensive, cohesive, and practical approach to understanding different styles of leadership in sport.

The multidimensional model of leadership is organized as a progression from antecedents, to leader behaviors, to consequences. Antecedents refer to the variables that precede, and likely influence, leader behaviors. These antecedents include situational characteristics (like group size and access to technology), leader characteristics (such as personality and ability), and member characteristics (including knowledge and team cohesiveness). Next, leader behaviors are classified into three types: required, preferred, and actual. Ultimately, these leader behaviors affect both the organization's bottom line and employee well-being, as illustrated by the two outcome variables included in the multidimensional model: performance and satisfaction. Implicit in the model are the assumptions that leadership is behavioral in nature, is a group process, and can have a transformational effect on followers.

Leader Behavior

While each of the model's broad categories operate interdependently, the heart of the multidimensional leadership model is the three types of leader behaviors. Required leader behaviors include all of the tasks, duties, and responsibilities a leader must perform based on the demands of the situation and of the organization's members. Take, for example, a leader who intends to hold one-on-one performance appraisal meetings with each of her or his staff members. Such a plan might be unfeasible if the organization is especially large (i.e., a situational characteristic). Required leader behaviors are not always carried out; when a leader's behaviors do not correspond with what is required by environmental and personnel demands, the organization or team will likely experience great inefficiency and dysfunction.

Situational and member characteristics also provide the foundation for preferred leader behaviors. For example, if a company is undergoing significant transformations to its management structure and operating strategies, employees may prefer the administration to be open and transparent so as to reduce apprehension toward the organizational changes. A second example is a sports organization changing the software program it uses to manage ticket sales. Some employees may already have previous experience working with the newly implemented technology, while others may have little background knowledge. Based on these individual member characteristics, the former may prefer minimal guidance from the leader, while the latter may wish to participate in an orientation about the program and receive continued guidance from the leader.

How a leader truly behaves is classified as her or his actual leader behavior. Actual leader behaviors are the products of situational characteristics, member characteristics, and leader characteristics. In particular, the influence of situational and member characteristics occurs indirectly through required leader behaviors and preferred leader behaviors, and the effects of personal—or leader—characteristics are directly reflected in the leader's actual behavior. Examples of leader characteristics include knowledge, skill, expertise, and personality, and these antecedents greatly influence how a leader will behave. Thus, whether one's actual behaviors correspond to required and preferred behaviors is largely based on the leader's own abilities and attitudes.

The extent to which required, preferred, and actual leader behaviors are congruent has important implications for an organization and its members. As illustrated in the multidimensional model of leadership, when a leader's actions are considerate of, for example, the demands of the organization and the preferences of employees, performance and satisfaction are expected to be high. On the other hand, as actual leader behaviors diverge from either (or both) of the other two leader behavior types, organizational performance and employee satisfaction are likely to suffer. Both of these outcomes have significant implications not only for the organization, but also for the long-term well-being of its employees.

Feedback

A final aspect of the multidimensional leadership model relates to feedback. Through feedback, leaders can identify sources of incongruence between required, preferred, and actual leader behaviors and make adjustments in order to optimize positive work outcomes like performance and satisfaction. Organizations can collect feedback using explicit or implicit metrics. For hard data on workplace satisfaction, a company might request that employees complete paper-and-pencil surveys or solicit their feedback during annual evaluations. Additionally, an employee's performance can be measured based on supervisor ratings and quality-control assessments. Leaders, managers, and supervisors might also sense declining morale in the workplace simply by observing how coworkers interact with one another.

While identifying inconsistencies between behaviors can be challenging enough for leaders, developing and executing an appropriate response pose its own share of problems. For example, an organization that is understaffed would benefit from hiring additional personnel, but a lack of financial resources (i.e., a situational characteristic) may make such staffing decisions impossible. Additionally, certain characteristics such as personality and emotion are generally stable traits in a person, which complicates a leader's ability to make changes when required or preferred; actual leader behaviors are incongruent in the workplace. Short of terminating existing staff members and replacing them with employees whose personalities better align with that of the leadership, leaders must find alternatives (including modifying their own behavior) to address poor performance or low morale.

The multidimensional model of leadership can be applied to many unique situations across industries.

One area within sport where it has received significant attention is coaching. Successful coaches are not just excellent tacticians; they also are able to motivate their players to work hard and perform at the highest levels. In order to be effective motivators, however, coaches must understand how their players will respond to various stimuli (i.e., member characteristics). For instance, while some individuals embrace a coach who utilizes intensity and discipline to motivate, others may respond better to a more relaxed or nurturing approach. Bobby Knight, a men's basketball coach known for his fiery disposition, was a successful leader at Indiana University (though he was not without criticism there), but his approach might have been less embraced if he was at the helm of a little-league baseball team. Additionally, it is worth noting that players on the same team may respond differently to a coach's motivational techniques. Therefore, in order to be effective, leaders must be mindful of the dynamic situational and member characteristics at play in an organization.

The hallmark of the multidimensional model of leadership is that, rather than contrasting a multitude of leadership theories and applying just one to a set of circumstances, it demonstrates that leadership behavior is a multifaceted process that is best explained when a variety of theories are compared and integrated. Through the multidimensional model, individuals can understand the dynamic factors that go into leadership development and behavior. Leaders do not operate in a vacuum; therefore, they must consider how their actions will be received by employees, the influence of whom is reflected in the model's required and preferred leader behaviors. Even when a leader is aware of employee preference for a specific style of leadership, it is not always feasible or possible to act in ways that are consistent with member characteristics. The same can be said for situational characteristics like group size or the financial resources—or lack thereof—at the organization's disposal. Finally, as explained by a number of leadership theories (e.g., trait leadership or contingency), actual leader behaviors occur as a result of a number of sometimes opposing forces, including the leader's own personality, knowledge, and expertise. The dynamics illustrated in the multidimensional model of leadership indicate that leadership behavior is a fluid process that involves not just the person at the top, but also the many different individuals and institutions impacted by a leader's decision making.

Timothy B. Kellison

See Also: Behavioral Leadership Theory; Leadership Models in Sport; Organizational Leadership; Situational Leadership Theory; Trait Leadership Theory; Transformational Leadership.

Further Readings

Chelladurai, P. *A Contingency Model of Leadership in Athletics.* Unpublished doctoral dissertation. Waterloo, Canada: University of Waterloo, 1978.
Chelladurai, P. "Leadership in Sports: A Review." *International Journal of Sport Psychology*, v.21 (1990).
Northouse, Peter. *Leadership: Theory and Practice.* Thousand Oaks, CA: Sage, 2012.

Cooperative Coaching Style

Coaches have many motivations but their primary aim should be to provide athletes with opportunities for personal, physical, and psychological growth and development. The coaching style of a leader plays an important role in determining if and how these goals are achieved because it influences how the leader communicates with, disciplines, and motivates athletes. Many variations of coaching styles exist in sports; however, a cooperative, democratic approach has come to the forefront. This transformation has occurred because it enhances athlete development, utilizes effective communication, and gives significant value to the coach–athlete relationship. This style has gained popularity among coaches, particularly in youth sports and educational athletics, because of its holistic approach. Some argue that elite professional athletes have already developed and may not benefit from the cooperative coaching style; however, the merits of this democratic approach have been noted by many successful coaches at this level.

Teaching

Cooperative style coaches recognize their responsibility to provide leadership and guide athletes toward accomplishing goals, yet know that learning to make decisions is beneficial to their athletes. Thus, athletes are given the opportunity to share decisions with the coach and their feedback is used to improve the learning environment for individuals and the team. The cooperative-style coach allows for more flexibility and variety when designing team policies, procedures, practice plans, and other tools. This creates an open learning environment of trust and mutual respect and makes each athlete feel they have something important to contribute. Athletes are empowered to take ownership of their role on the team, which fosters the development of intrinsic motivation and increased self-esteem. Athletes taught by a cooperative coach also develop enhanced problem-solving and decision-making skills that allow them to become more confident and aware of what to do in competitive situations. If athletes enjoy a heightened sense of competence and success, they are more likely to push their limits to improve performance and less likely to experience burnout.

Similarly, cooperative coaches believe that in order to enhance athlete development, it is important to provide instructional and constructive feedback on individual performances without constantly telling athletes what to do. An effective strategy used by cooperative coaches is to pose questions and provide problems for their players to try and solve. For example, during practice a volleyball coach may stop play after a blocked hit and ask player(s) to analyze the situation to help them better understand why the block occurred. This simple technique helps athletes think independently and promotes greater levels of learning from their experiences. It also creates an environment where athletes make decisions, fail, and learn from their mistakes. This increased use of questions equips athletes to solve their own problems, helps them become less coach-dependent during game experiences, and gives them a greater sense of control over their performance.

Communication

Caring relationships with the athletes are of high value to the cooperative coach and they often extend beyond sport participation. These established relationships also prove to be valuable for athletes as they continue on in their careers and many times can be lifelong. Because communication is an important element in developing these relationships, cooperative coaches demonstrate a genuine desire to get to know and understand their athletes. The environment of respect established by these relationships benefits both the player and coach, but more important the team culture on and off the court.

Cooperative style coaches also tend to have higher levels of engagement with parents and are often perceived as more approachable and accessible. This cultivates stronger parent support not only for the individual athlete but also for the entire team. Cooperative coaches establish guidelines for soliciting parent feedback while drawing clear boundaries for incorporating parent input. For example, coaches may seek postseason feedback on schedule, practice times, and team activities, but not specific advice on strategies or individual player performance.

Challenges to Cooperative Coaching Style

Because cooperative coaches share their power, a common misconception is that they have little to no control and athletes are free to do whatever they would like. This is not the case, as cooperative coaches are athlete-centered yet still coach-driven. This means that coaches put the wants and needs of the athletes above those of the team, coach, and fans. This attitude fosters what Rainer Martens, founder of the American Sport Education Program (ASEP), calls the athletes first, winning second philosophy. Cooperative style coaches believe developmental steps to success are important and place emphasis on the learning process and improvement of the individual athlete over winning.

Despite the growing popularity of this style, a cooperative coach may still witness skepticism because this style conflicts with the popular societal notion that winning is the only measurement of success. An important distinction of this coaching style is the commitment to long-term development of individuals and team. It can be difficult for coaches to adopt this style of coaching if they have not had previous exposure to it. Many coaches have been mentored in a more traditional authoritarian style and thus may feel uncomfortable giving athletes autonomy. Similarly, athletes that have never been exposed to this coaching style can misinterpret the coach's actions as laziness and/or a lack of commitment to the team.

A final challenge for cooperative style coaches is learning to balance when they direct athletes and when athletes direct themselves. A cooperative coach who operates democratically in the preparation phase of performance could struggle during competition when more coach control is needed. Finding this balance can be complex and take time but is integral to the success of a cooperative coach.

Dana Munk
Chelsea Brehm

See Also: Coaching Philosophy for College Athletics; Coaching Youth; Command Coaching Style; Positive Discipline; Submissive Coaching Style.

Further Readings
Albrecht, Rick. *Coaching Myths: Fifteen Wrong Ideas in Youth Sports.* Jefferson, NC: McFarland Press, 2013.
Lockwood, Park, and D. J. Perlman. "Enhancing the Youth Sport Experience." *Journal of Youth Sports: Youth First*, v.4/1 (2008).
Smoll, Frank, et al. "Enhancing Coach-Parent Relationships in Youth Sports: Increasing Harmony and Minimizing Hassle." *International Journal of Sports Science and Coaching*, v.6/1 (2011).

Creating an Organizational Vision

Organizational vision remains a buzz phrase in today's world of business and is largely considered an essential building block toward success. Although perhaps executed differently and more related to "coaching philosophy," having a vision in sport is also very important. This entry examines the purpose of an organizational vision in sport, describes what should be included in the vision, and provides a starting point for creating one.

Visualizing Success

An organizational vision is most simply defined as the goal a team is seeking to achieve. The most effective vision, though, is far more than a prediction of the number of wins a team wishes to achieve;

after all, winning championships is a fairly common goal. During the preseason in the National Football League, all teams share the common goal of winning the Super Bowl. But the Green Bay Packers organizational vision will somewhat differ from the Oakland Raiders. The effective organizational vision more specifically defines success, creating a crystal clear image of the values important to the team and an initial guide to appropriate processes within the team. Moreover, it provides a unifying image of the culture of a team.

An organizational vision may also be executed at many different levels, with multiple visions nested within each other. For instance, the president of a university likely has a vision for the entire institution. The athletic director may take this broader university vision and narrow it to the athletics program. Each team's coach may then have an opportunity to put his or her own stamp on the vision, and in some cases the athletes themselves have the opportunity to consider the vision of the team. If the vision at one level is incompatible with the vision at a higher level, there is a greater opportunity for friction and a less effective organization is likely to occur. For instance, an athletic director may emphasize community service as part of the greater department vision, but the coach of a team may refuse to embrace this and instead utilize a more selfish win-at-all-cost vision. While the team may win games in the short term, one may question the sustainability of divergent vision in the long term.

Some of the best examples of vision creation in athletics come from high-profile coaches. John Wooden's pyramid of success provides a detailed explanation of the building blocks toward competitive greatness. The work of Wooden and Vince Lombardi may be called "coaching philosophy," and they can be considered vision because they create a specific image of success that could be followed by the team.

When creating an organizational vision, the concepts from transformational leadership may be considered. First, the transformational leader exhibits behaviors of inspirational motivation. By definition, these behaviors call for the leader to articulate a vision that inspires a group toward a goal. This vision should be communicated with optimism and with detail that followers can clearly understand. Second, behaviors of intellectual stimulation are exhibited by the transformational leader. Not only does the leader have a great powerful vision, but he or she empowers followers to be involved in its creation, which may help the organization to buy in to the ultimate goal.

Vision Creation in Sport

The initial creation of an organizational vision may include the following steps: (1) know the team/organization, (2) define success, (3) identify values and traits, (4) define proper behaviors, and (5) attain commitment and accountability. Each of the following steps may be executed solely by a formal leader or involve an entire team, but group involvement is likely more valuable with each subsequent step.

Know the team. First, does the supervisor, administration, community, etc. have an overarching vision in which the coach or administrator must nest their vision? Also, the primary stakeholders for the organization's success must be kept in mind. Then consider the makeup of the organization including past performance, team dynamics, team leadership, cultural differences, and the unique personalities that are encompassed within the team.

Define success. Considering the information gathered as well as personal knowledge and values, the coach or administrator now has the opportunity to create a succinct statement that creates the image of success. While it may include the ultimate tangible outcome, it should optimistically describe the end state of the organization beyond wins and losses.

Identify values and traits. Each foundational box in Wooden's pyramid of success could be considered an example of a value or trait. The entire team may enter this process by brainstorming about which characteristics of great teams are used.

Define proper behaviors. In order to create a proper vision, the team must know how to act. This is done by defining the values and characteristics behaviorally. For instance, if trust is an important value to the team, behaviors that demonstrate trust should be identified and discussed.

Attain commitment and accountability. There are several creative ways to attain commitment from the group, most simply by involving the group in the process. Commitment may also be reached by documenting the process and creating posters, logos, and slogans that can serve as constant reminders. Accountability can be maintained by empowering team members to be responsible for certain values critical to the vision statement.

Conclusion

A vision is critical for a sport organization to create a vivid image of success. While wins and losses are most commonly thought of as the definition of success in sport, a proper vision should go beyond this view by defining the values deemed to be important to the organization.

Jeff Coleman

See Also: Coaching Philosophy for College Athletics; Organizational Leadership; Transformational Leadership.

Further Readings

Lombardi, Vince Jr. *What it Takes to be #1: Vince Lombardi on Leadership.* New York: McGraw-Hill, 2003.
Scott, David. *Contemporary Leadership in Sport Organizations.* Champaign, IL: Human Kinetics, 2014.
Wooden, John and Steve Jamison. *Wooden on Leadership: How to Create a Winning Organization.* New York; McGraw Hill, 2009.

Crisis Management

Crisis management has three phases: the pre-crisis plan (normally called an emergency action plan), procedures followed during the crisis, and the post-crisis mitigation and contact with the media. Together, the three phases are normally referred to as a risk management plan. Crisis management can break down if enough time and practice are not invested to ensure that the plan works.

Phase One: The Emergency Action Plan

There are three important points regarding an emergency action plan (EAP). First, every facility, practice or competitive site needs an EAP. Second, the EAP needs to be practiced on a regular basis, and a mock drill must be conducted to determine if the plan works as devised and to provide an opportunity to strengthen the weak points. Third, the EAP should include important points regarding how the media, victims, and their families should be handled following a crisis.

Phase Two: The Crisis

For purposes of this article, this author is going to offer two distinct scenarios—one, an incident involving a death of a participant at a facility; and two, an incident precipitated by weather conditions.

First, assume that a basketball tournament involving high-school-aged individuals is being conducted at a facility. The supervisors have been trained in first aid, CPR, and the use of an automatic emergency defibrillator (AED). During the third quarter of the game, a player collapses. Because this is a tournament game, an ambulance and paramedics are on-site in case of an emergency. The paramedics immediately respond and assess the victim. They decide to use an AED, but to no avail. Security personnel clear the gym of spectators, but ask that both teams and the officials remain. The paramedics decide to convey the individual to the nearest hospital, and the supervisor notifies the remaining spectators of the current status of the victim. The supervisor, with the aid of two other security personnel, then gathers about 12 witness statements from teammates, opponents, officials, and security personnel close to the point where the victim collapsed. The site supervisor notifies the executive director (ED) approximately two minutes into the collapse and the ED arrives just before the victim is being conveyed.

The second incident involves a tornado alert while a fitness facility is at its busiest time. Coaches/instructors immediately gather all of the patrons and escort them to a shelter in the basement of the building. When the tornado hits, it takes off the roof of the building, and the walls above the shelter start to collapse. Some of the debris caves in the floor above the shelter and falling debris injures approximately 10 people. Since the ED is not on site, the coaches/instructors are left to attend to the victims. While one of the supervisors grabbed a first aid kit on the way to the shelter area, the site manager neglected to check the first aid kits to ensure that they were fully stocked and neglected to place the a kit in the shelter. Only one partially stocked first aid kit is available to treat the victims of the collapsing floor. There are about 60 people in the shelter and at least five of them have first aid training. The supervisor begins to help the most severely injured, while the other trained first aid personnel use whatever items they can find to treat other victims.

Phase Three: Postcrisis Mitigation and Media Contacts

While there are public relations people that may disagree with this approach, this author's advice to anyone dealing with a crisis is to tell the truth. Having a media contact person who does not cave under pressure, is not intimidated by media personnel, and can calmly state exactly what happened and the procedures used to handle the crisis is paramount.

In the first instance, the situation was handled appropriately, but there will be questions regarding why the paramedics decided to work on the victim for 25 minutes prior to conveying the individual to a hospital. A media conference should be called and the media contact should read a prepared statement prior to answering any questions. The media person should be instructed not to offer any personal explanations or opinions. The media contact person must be able to explain the actions that were taken by the staff, the emergency action plan that was in place, and the practices that were conducted for such an emergency. Also, the media contact person must explain the decision regarding when to convey; this decision is not made by facility staff after a paramedic team is on-site. Any questions regarding their actions should be referred to the ambulance company.

In the second scenario, the on-site staff took the proper precautions to move patrons to the tornado shelter area, but the site manager did not follow established procedures regarding the first aid kits. Upon investigation, the ED also discovers that the required second quarter practice that would have uncovered the issue of the first aid kits was not conducted. Fortunately, the individuals trained in first aid adequately addressed the injured victims until the Fire Department was able to rescue the individuals trapped when the floor above them collapsed.

The media contact person should relay exactly what happened; how the coaches/instructors, with the help of other trained personnel, handled the injuries until help arrived; what the procedural shortcomings were; how they were positively addressed during the crisis; and that a further investigation will be conducted into the lack of availability of the first aid equipment. It is far superior when trying to mitigate the possible fallout of a crisis to immediately state what procedures worked and how any shortcomings were addressed. If not, someone may go to the media and the executive director of the facility will be on the defensive—a very bad place to be after a crisis has occurred. Another reason for telling the truth is that if falsehoods are stated, then there is the possibility of litigation. When the truth is told regarding the procedures used for handling the crisis, the potential for litigation is greatly reduced. On the other hand, if no procedures were in place, the potential for litigation increases. Therefore, it is paramount for the administrators of any facility, practice or competition site to address all three phases of the crisis management plan—the emergency action plan, the necessity of following proper procedures during the crisis, and the postcrisis procedures of dealing with the media and any possible questions that could come from family members of the victims.

Finally, it should be noted that during any crisis, 80 percent of the people freeze, 10 percent of the people become hysterical, and only 10 percent have the ability to maintain composure and address the situation at hand. Consequently, it is vital that an emergency action plan be put in place and practice must be undertaken so that it becomes a part of that plan.

Janis K. Doleschal

See Also: Emergency Action Plan; Legal Responsibilities for Managers and Owners; Risk Management Process.

Further Readings

Brunner, Judy M. and Dennis K. Lewis. *Safe and Secure Schools.* Thousand Oaks, CA: Corwin Press, 2009.

Ripley, Amanda. *The Unthinkable—Who Survives When Disaster Strikes and Why.* New York: Crown, 2008.

Trump, Kenneth. *Proactive School Security and Emergency Preparedness Planning.* Thousand Oaks, CA: Corwin Press, 2011.

D

Development of Leadership Skills

Leadership skills rarely develop by chance. The intentional development of effective leaders happens best with the establishment of a systematic training program that is progressive in nature and customized for the intended group. Learning happens best when aspiring leaders are exposed to good role models and receive supervision from leadership coaches. A well-crafted program, grounded in current theory and research, provides the consistency and repetition needed to consolidate the learning. Teachers and coaches understand that consistency and repetition are essential to skill building. Too many leadership programs address issues such as communication that are indifferent to both theory and practical application, resulting in such skills being taught without reference to the real issues leaders face. Many leaders struggle with communication due to lack of vision or fear of damaging collegial relationships. Teaching "communication" will do little to help prepare these leaders for true leadership challenges if not grounded in both theory and the complexities of real life.

Effective Leadership Development Programs

When structuring an effective leadership development program, it is important that it be systematic, progressive, and customized. These three principles allow for a program that moves beyond entertainment and leads to lasting behavioral change in coaches and athletes.

Systematic. Just as a leader's role is to develop strategic performance plans, a strategic plan for developing leaders should also be designed. Too many leadership programs are not deliberately planned, and thus become a collection of disjointed ideas. This makes it difficult for learners to integrate teachings into a larger mental schema of effective leadership. Transformational leadership provides a broad framework for systematic curriculum development and an internal framework for individuals to personally integrate what they are learning.

Consistency and repetition are important for the concepts to become truly ingrained in coaches' and athletes' ways of thinking and being. Couple these things with ongoing support, and the knowledge, skills, and abilities necessary to take organizations to another level become the habitual actions of the developing leaders. Therefore, programs must also include space for developing leaders to talk about their experiences with trainers. Facilitated discussions with peer leaders and one-on-one leadership coaching help stimulate different pathways to their goals and overcome the emotional hurdles that hinder putting these ideas into action.

Progressive. To be progressive simply means that the learning and practicing of leadership skills should grow more difficult throughout one's advancement in the program. The curriculum should be developmentally appropriate not only for the age of aspiring leaders, but also for time spent training and experience as a leader. The less training and experience one has, the more basic the concepts and the more support that is needed. Growth is experienced through moments of discomfort, and this progressive nature allows one to gain competence and confidence that minimizes frustration and dropout, while continuing to challenge and expand one's leadership capacity. The development and maintenance of confidence is essential for developing leaders to take the risks necessary to actually lead. Stepping out in front as a leader is challenging, and many leaders need time and support to become comfortable with these risks. Asking too much of a leader too quickly may destroy their confidence to the point that they remain safely in the pack.

Customized. Finally, customization of the program is key. It must be age-appropriate to ensure adequate cognitive, emotional, and social development. The nature of leadership differs by age, sport (individual versus team sports), and level. Athletes should be given responsibility only for what they can handle, and time for discussion and support to learn through mistakes is key.

It is important to understand that the peer leadership required of team captains creates unique challenges not typically addressed in leadership development. Athletes wearing the "C" on their chest need to find their role leading the team while maintaining relationships, or even friendships, with their teammates. Whereas many coaches do not concern themselves with being friends with the athletes, captains must constantly juggle these relationships. Additionally, although captains do have a tremendous opportunity to lead, they must do so consistent with the coach's ideals; and professional athletes are not immune to this challenge. A multiple-most valuable player (MVP) and team captain worked with one of us to devise a plan to manage differences in his leadership style with that of his coach, who was more laissez-faire with respect to details. The challenge of being both separate from and a part of their team, of being both a leader and follower, is real at every level.

When the skills of transformational leadership are systematically and developmentally customized into the overall program design, this becomes a powerful edge in behavioral learning. Such development of leadership skills allows organizations to reap the positive benefits that effective leadership has been shown to produce.

Amber Lattner
Steve Portenga

See Also: Academic Programs in Sports Leadership; Behavioral Leadership Theory; Locker Room Leadership; Organizational Leadership; Owners and Business Leadership; Race/Ethnicity and Sports Leadership.

Further Readings

Dunning, Eric. *Sport Matters: Sociological Studies of Sport, Violence, and Civilization*. New York: Routledge, 1999.

Kouzes, J. M., and B. Z. Posner. *The Leadership Challenge: How to Make Extraordinary Things Happen in Organizations*. San Francisco: Jossey-Bass, 2012.

Maxwell, J. C. *The 21 Irrefutable Laws of Leadership: Follow Them and People Will Follow You*. Nashville, TN: Thomas Nelson, 2007.

Discrimination in Sports

The goal of Olympism is to place sport at the service of the harmonious development of humankind, with a view to promoting a peaceful society concerned with the preservation of human dignity [. . .] The practice of sport is a human right. Every individual must have the possibility of practicing sport, without discrimination of any kind and in the Olympic spirit, which requires mutual understanding with a spirit of friendship, solidarity and fair play.

The previous quotes are the second and fourth fundamental principles of Olympism, in force since September 9, 2013. These principles emphasize the role of sport as an instrument that must be at the service of the harmonious development of humankind: every individual must have the possibility of practicing sport, without any kind of discrimination, when he/she wants and wherever he/she is, and sports leadership should guarantee this principle. In the Olympic chart, sports are depicted as fundamental means of education and social integration. This role should not be taken for granted: Institutionalized sports' practice has always fluctuated in the complex dichotomy between social integration and social disintegration, that is to say, between integration and discrimination.

To better understand its role and its influence on the frame of sports, it is important to focus on the concept of discrimination. In common language and in political discourse, the use of this concept tends to come into conflict with the idea of equality. Currently, the principle of nondiscrimination is singled out for many purposes. It expresses a moral requirement, calling for struggle against any kind of illegitimate discrimination (racist, sexist, homophobic, etc.). It enforces a demand for social justice, urging decision makers to look for solutions, in essence producing a growing number of compensatory forms of discrimination.

The success of this concept in contemporary political and sociological discourse, and the heterogeneity of its uses, can probably be explained by the fact that it overcomes the conceptual oppositions conventionally associated with the implementation of the principle of equality. The principle of nondiscrimination is indeed vague, devoid of any kind of normative load. It contains no substantive rules but a complex set of ethical principles, and it does not impose any specific prescription but proposes some guidelines that must be respected. It also identifies a method of control, an analysis grid of certain differences of treatment. The principle of nondiscrimination does not provide any pre-established response. It apprehends only some specific situations of discrimination that should be contextualized from time to time.

Starting from this premise, the ethical short circuit that emerges when the idea of sport—especially that which is institutionalized within the Olympic framework—collides with the idea of discrimination and becomes more important from a political, symbolic, and sociocultural point of view.

Although sport is identified primarily as a universal, neutral, and objective means of classification, based on the performance achieved through some standardized and normalized tests, its history is marked by the exclusion of certain groups of practitioners. Discrimination begins where the logic of the standardized ranking yields to some

The Rugby Football League in England has had a tradition of being inclusive and in 1997 launched an action plan to tackle racism and encourage the development of rugby leagues in Asian and black communities. In 2012, the league was awarded the Stonewall Sport Award in recognition of its work embracing inclusivity and tackling homophobia. (Wikimedia Commons)

other procedures: regulatory exclusions, self-exclusion mechanisms, or symbolic rejection as a result of ridicule, stigma, or insults. Discrimination is a process involving the distinction and identification of some differences that are then categorized. It is a sort of categorization of reality, a cognitive shortcut that every human or every group operates to understand more complex realities. Similarly, as a human product and a social construction, sport uses the procedures of distinction, identification, and categorization to establish some indisputable hierarchical verdicts. From a sociological point of view as it concerns institutionalized sports, discrimination begins when the official classification systems—the ones on which traditional sports competitions are founded—hide or produce some different systems or logics of classification.

Sports, Practitioners, and Social Movements

The Olympic Games are the clearest example of this discussion: they were initially forbidden to women and to those not squaring with the bourgeois profile of the "amateur." More generally, modern sports, developed between the 19th and 20th centuries was based on the exclusion of most parts of humanity, their practice was confined to a Western, male, and bourgeois universe. Institutionalized sports will widen their audience only in the wake of the following transformations initiated by social movements of the 20th century. The first ones were the labor movements during the 1930s. Then came the anticolonial movements, the feminist ones (with the law of wage equality approved in 1963 in the United States) and finally the homosexual ones (the Gay Liberation Front, which was established in 1969 in the United States). All these movements advanced significantly from the 1950s through the 1970s, and they all fought against some of the typical forms of discrimination: employment and status discrimination, racism, sexism, homophobia, and their derivates (misogyny, transphoby, misandry, etc.). In the United States, after resistance against a political system discriminating against black people already emerged in the 1930s, it was in 1967 that the Black Panthers defined the concept of "institutional racism." More generally, in a historical phase in which decolonization was completing, it was the persistence of the image of colonial sport that was (and currently is) still problematic.

Sexism and its Derivates

In 1921, Alice Milliat founded the Fédération Sportive Féminine Internationale (FSFI; in English, the International Women's Sports Federation), an autonomous sports federation to oversee international women's sporting events. After the refusal of the International Amateur Athletic Federation (IAAF) to include women's track and field athletics events in the Olympic Games, the FSFI decided to hold a Women's Olympic Games in 1922 in Paris. Starting from the 1920s, women's access to all Olympic sports became more and more important, although it still remains in progress today. In 1969, some riots led the U.S. gay and lesbian movements to expand based on the model of those for the rights of women and against racial segregation. Despite efforts by the Gay Liberation Front and the Black Panter Party at the turn of the 1970s, however, more than a decade passed before their requests concretized on the sports field. In 1982, Tom Waddell, decathlon finalist at the Mexico City Olympics, founded the Gay Games.

If sexism is still emerging at different levels of society, then particular gendered social relations within sport federations, the quantitative imbalance between male and female practitioners, the unequal access to some positions of responsibility, and others make sport precisely a paradigm of contemporary sexism. In fact, today women's presence in managerial positions is still modest, women's teams receive less resources than men's teams, female elite athletes are subject to an unequal treatment in the media and their salaries are significantly lower than men's, discrimination and symbolic violence against women seem to still be a dominant feature of sport cultures.

Furthermore, the bodily hierarchy established in federal sports provides a type of system that rationalizes sexism. This vision of the world is based on some data objectified by the calculation of the performances and by the domination of masculine values in most sports. Sexism also manifests in the devaluation of female athletes and in the constant injunction of being "feminine." The violation of gender order, either from an aesthetic and/or behavioral point of view, may call into question the sexual orientation of the female athlete and in some cases her biological femininity.

The Current Situation

The recent case of Caster Semenya—a South African middle-distance runner who won gold in the women's 800 meters at the 2009 World Championships with a time of 1:55.45 in the final—becomes paradigmatic of a sexism expressed at a bodily level. Much has been said about her voice and appearance: following her victory at the 2009 World Championships, it was announced that she had been subjected to gender testing. Then she was withdrawn from international competition until July 2010, when the IAAF cleared her to return to competition. This case also raised the problem of sport practice for intersex athletes, or the athletes who cannot be defined from a biomedical point of view as male or female.

Since the Gay Games, the minority protection movements are thus led to take interest in the issue of equality in sports. Their struggle was against the exclusion mechanisms that can lead to rejection, shame, and social invisibility. In their perspective, sports, despite their apparent social neutrality, are fully integrated into a system of symbolic violence that excludes nonstandard models. Erving Goffman wrote that the accesses to these claims are even stronger than the centrality of the representation of the body of the "Other" in the process of discrimination (stigmatization). However, the access to sports of these new audiences, often characterized by their own culture, will not be possible, in turn, without a transformation of space, rules, practices, and procedures. From this perspective, the fight against discrimination seems to be one of the main drivers of social evolution of sports activities.

Alessandro Porrovecchio

See Also: Bullying/Hazing; Gender and Sports Leadership; Race/Ethnicity and Sports Leadership; Sexual Harassment Among Players.

Further Readings
DeMartini, Anne. "Reverse Discrimination in Sports." *Journal of Physical Education, Recreation & Dance*, v.84/2 (February 2013).
Goffman, Erving. *Stigma: Notes on the Management of Spoiled Identity*. Englewood Cliffs, NJ: Prentice Hall, 1963.
Hargreaves, Jennifer, and Eric Anderson. *Routledge Handbook of Sport, Gender and Sexuality*. London: Routledge, 2014.
IOC. "Olympic Charter, Charter in force from September 9, 2013." http://www.olympic.org/Documents/olympic_charter_en.pdf (Accessed September 2014).
McDonagh, Eileen and Laura Pappano. *Playing With the Boys*. Oxford: Oxford University Press, 2008.

Draft System

Draft systems are designed to fairly infuse new players into a professional sports league by offering the highest pick in each round to the franchise performing the worst during the previous season, and the lowest pick in each round to the previous year's champion, with all other picks being allocated by the inverse record of each team. Though each North American professional sport league utilizes a player draft to enhance competitive balance—the concept that all teams can compete for wins over an extended period of time if they manage their franchises effectively—each has a varied number of rounds. Certain leagues have implemented distinct

rules to their draft procedures to better reflect the unique elements of each sport.

The first professional North American sport league draft was conducted by the National Football League (NFL) in 1936. University of Chicago star and first Heisman Trophy winner Jay Berwanger was selected with the initial selection. Much like other professional sports leagues that would enact their own drafts in later years, the NFL implemented its draft to allocate players to teams in order to disperse incoming talent, and, more important—given the contentious salary negotiations that had often occurred—to control salaries by limiting the negotiating power of selected players. In a sign of how different the business environment was in the 1930s versus today, Berwanger was unable to reach an agreement and never played in the NFL.

The National Basketball Association (NBA) implemented a player draft in 1947 and the National Hockey League (NHL) enacted its draft in 1963. In 1965, Major League Baseball (MLB) held its first player draft largely in response to the inefficient and expensive "bonus baby" system that had developed since 1947. Outfielder Rick Monday was the first ever MLB draft pick by the Kansas City As. It is widely believed that Monday's initial signing bonus was roughly half of the $205,000 bonus paid by the Los Angeles Angels to sign Rick Reichardt in 1964, the last predraft year. Though the June amateur player (Rule 4) draft is its most prominent, MLB actually also conducts a Rule 5 draft to disperse eligible longer-tenured minor league players throughout the league.

Until the 1990s, most professional sports leagues' drafts had many more rounds than they do today. The NBA (two rounds), NHL (seven rounds), NFL (seven rounds), and MLB (40 rounds) have all reduced their drafts considerably on insistence from the various players associations that a shorter draft provides greater opportunity for incoming players perceived to be less talented to seek their best opportunity to make a team's final roster rather than be drafted to a club that may not need their services. With a shortened draft, there is a heightened importance for franchises to not only identify "diamonds in the rough" but also convince these players to sign with their team. Despite today's much more abbreviated draft formats, it is still a long shot that any incoming drafted or undrafted player will make a professional roster, let alone sustain a long-term professional career.

Draft Requirements and Rights

Each league establishes its draft eligibility requirements. Though MLB has always included recently graduated high school players in its draft, for many years the NFL and NBA had far more restrictive eligibility rules that typically required players to wait until four years had elapsed since their high school class had graduated. The NHL had a draft system that also prevented certain players from being eligible to play despite being of legal age. There have been a variety of players who have sought refuge in the court system against restrictive draft eligibility rules. Spencer Haywood (NBA) and Ken Linseman (NHL) successfully sued their leagues to be eligible as 18-year-olds. Though there was no litigation, in 1990 the NFL changed its eligibility rules to require only three years to elapse from high school. That rule was unsuccessfully challenged by Maurice Clarett and Mike Williams in 2004. Though the NBA had permitted any 18-year-old to be eligible for the draft since Haywood's lawsuit in 1971, in 2005 the NBA and the NBA Players Association collectively bargained to change that rule to a one-year and 19-year-old eligibility requirement, sometimes referred to as "one and done" since so many basketball players spend only one year playing college basketball before entering the draft.

In addition to being willing to sacrifice certain draft rights in the collective bargaining process, players associations have also bargained for rookie wage caps that limit potential compensation for incoming players. For the current players, a restriction on rookie salaries makes economic sense, especially in a salary-cap environment in which overall player compensation is capped at a certain level. Tired of watching rookie players make more than many established veterans, in 2011 the NFL and the NFL Players Association collectively bargained for a rookie wage scale that significantly reduced incoming player salaries and allocated compensation by draft slot. In 2010, St. Louis Rams' overall first pick Sam Bradford negotiated a six-year, $78 million contract with $50 million in guaranteed money. Conversely, in 2011, under the new system, the Carolina Panthers' overall first pick Cam Newton signed a four-year, $22 million

deal. The NBA, NHL, and MLB have also established restrictive salary systems to limit the compensation of incoming players, with some of these restrictions being tied to draft position.

Though dominant players are critical to the success of any team, in baseball, football, and hockey, one dominant player does not exert as much influence on the outcome of games as in the sport of basketball. There have certainly been instances where teams in the aforementioned sports have been thankful to have a bad season result in an early draft pick, but in most cases, football, hockey, and especially baseball teams cannot expect that acquiring one dominant player through the draft will immediately change their fortunes. However, in basketball, where only five players are on the court at one time, a true superstar—even one who is only a rookie—can dramatically alter the on-court trajectory of a franchise. During the 1983 to 1984 NBA season, the Houston Rockets attracted attention from the NBA, the media, and fans as it made a series of questionable playing-time decisions, which ultimately led to it winning the first pick of the 1984 draft. With the pick, the Rockets selected center Akeem Olajuwon first, with Sam Bowie of Kentucky going second to the Portland Trailblazers, and Michael Jordan of North Carolina going third to the Chicago Bulls.

Concerned that the intentional losing of games—called tanking, by resting otherwise healthy players or other acts of on-court self-sabotage—could lead to fan disgust and diminished consumption of games in the second half of each season, the NBA announced that the 1985 draft order for the seven non-playoff teams would be determined by a draft lottery. The 1985 lottery created considerable excitement as the winner would likely select Georgetown University center Patrick Ewing. Despite having the worst record in the league, the Golden State Warriors lost the lottery and selected seventh in the 1985 draft. The New York Knicks, who had a better 1984 to 1985 record than the Warriors, won the lottery and eventually did select Ewing.

Draft Lottery Process

The NBA would eventually make numerous changes to its lottery process. In 1987, the lottery only identified the teams selecting in the first three positions. Every other team would draft according to the inverse order of its record, starting with the fourth selection. In 1990, the lottery was altered to allow the 11 teams not making the playoffs to have a number of chances related to their record. The worst team received 11 chances and the best non-playoff team received one chance. This format was changed in 1994 after the Orlando Magic won the lottery two years in a row, the second after having the best record of the nonplayoff teams. The current format provides the team with the worst record a 25 percent chance to win while the team with the best non-playoff record has a 0.5 percent chance to win.

The NHL also utilizes a lottery system for its first pick, with the nonplayoff teams having a diminishing chance at the pick based upon their final record. Only one lottery pick is made, so teams only can advance to the top pick, remain in their same position, or move back one slot.

Though the NBA Draft Lottery is designed to prevent tanking, despite the NBA's best efforts, some teams have continued to perceive their best method to attain long-term success is to lose many games in the short term in an effort to improve their lottery position. Over the last five years, many NBA fans have noted that they are often asked to pay full price for tickets to watch games where one or both of the teams may not have a vested interest in winning. Since intentional losing, even if done with a long-term franchise-enhancing goal in mind, can deter consumers, the NBA has begun to investigate changes to its player draft system. One idea in particular would be to abolish the link between previous season winning record and upcoming draft position. Instead, the NBA would institute a "wheel" where every NBA team would know its upcoming draft position over the next 30 years; or, in some variations, every team would know its wheel quadrant (such as picking at random one year from one through five, six through 10, etc.) from which its draft order would be picked at random. The potential use of the wheel would eliminate all reasons for tanking, as teams would have no incentive not to attempt to win every scheduled game.

The unique nature of sport competition, where teams compete on the field and then also cooperate off of it, often mandates systems such as player drafts to enhance the opportunity for every team to improve. Ironically, a player draft has now become a marketing and public relations activity that often attracts thousands of fans in person and millions of consumers on television and on the Internet. The NFL and NBA have been especially successful in using their respective drafts to generate attention during their off-seasons when fans often are used to not thinking about what their favorite team is doing. The importance of player drafts will continue to remain in the future, with the format for some leagues likely changing as the sport industry evolves.

Mark S. Nagel

See Also: Economics of Sports; Major League Baseball; National Basketball Association; National Football League; National Hockey League; Professional Sports.

Further Readings

Bondy, F. *Tip Off: How the 1984 Draft Changed Basketball.* Cambridge, MA: Da Capo Press, 2008.

Christl, C. *Sleepers, Busts and Franchise-Makers: The Behind-the-Scenes Story of the Pro Football Draft.* New York: Preview Publishing, 1983.

Lowe, Z. "The NBA's Possible Solution for Tanking: Good-bye to the Lottery, Hello to the Wheel." http://grantland.com/the-triangle/the-nbas-possible-solution-for-tanking-good-bye-to-the-lottery-hello-to-the-wheel (Accessed December 2013).

Drugs, Doping

Doping is, in its simplest terms, the use of performance enhancements that are considered unethical or illegal according to the rules and guidelines of a given sport or activity. Doping is banned in order to prevent health concerns and to ensure the equality of opportunity between all athletes and competitors. Despite this, doping remains a very serious, and very prevalent, part of sports, especially at a competitive level. From a competitor's perspective, the use of performance-enhancing drugs or methodologies could mean the difference between winning and losing, and potentially the difference between a mediocre and a multimillion-dollar career. From an officiating body's perspective, however, doping creates an uneven playing field, encourages potentially unhealthy lifestyle choices, and risks throwing that given sport or competition into disrepute.

The usage of performance-enhancing drugs or stimulants goes back not just hundreds but thousands of years, and across this time various substances have been developed. The most commonly talked about in the 21st century, though, are anabolic steroids. In essence, anabolic-androgenic steroids are synthetic substances based around male sex hormones such as testosterone, and although intended originally for medical usage, they were soon adopted within sport. Both studies and collated informal experience have shown that anabolic steroids can assist in the development of muscle mass, strength capacity, and recovery times, and it is this collection of effects that has led to widespread usage.

Anabolic steroids, however, are just the most visible tip of the metaphorical doping iceberg. Today's bodybuilders, for example, often cycle between multiple compounds, including, but certainly not limited to, human growth hormone. This practice is so widespread that it is now widely regarded as impossible to enter professional bodybuilding without their usage. An example of this increasing turn toward doping is Ronnie Coleman, an eight-time Mr. Olympia, who weighed in at 295 pounds at only 5 feet, 10 inches tall. For comparison, Arnold Schwarzenegger, who admitted to taking steroids and stood considerably taller at 6 feet, 2 inches, only weighed 235 pounds. Coleman's body mass index (BMI) at this weight was 42, more than double that of a genetically regular adult male.

DNP, or 2, 4 dinitrophenol, has also made its way into headlines recently as a controversial "fat burning" drug utilized both by the general public and within sport contests that require drastic weight cutting for specific weight divisions. The drug artificially stimulates the effects of cardiovascular exercise in order to burn calories, but can lead to dangerous, and potentially lethal, levels of overheating.

In endurance sports such as cycling, long-distance running, rowing, swimming, and cross-country skiing, an increasingly common drug is erythropoietin or EPO, which stimulates the increased production of red blood cells in order to improve maximal oxygen consumption (VO2 max). The drug gained popularity both due to its effectiveness and to the fact that it is harder to detect in drug tests than blood

transfusions (another way of increasing red blood cell count). It was not until 2000 that tests for EPO were developed, and it was not until 2002 that the first positive identification occurred.

Health Concerns

There are also serious health concerns associated with such drug usage. DNP, as already mentioned, can create potentially lethal levels of bodily overheating. Anabolic steroids have also been linked to liver malfunction, impotency, acne, erectile dysfunction and male pattern baldness, alongside the potential risk of infection and disease transmission through the use of injections. The use of steroids for women also carries the additional side effects of hair loss, irregular menstruation, and the development of more stereotypically masculine facial traits. The side effects and concerns become more serious with human growth hormone (HGH), which has been linked to blood cancers, hypertension, thyroid problems, stunted growth, severe headaches, loss of vision, diabetes, and crippling arthritis. Finally, the use of erythropoietin as a performance enhancer has some of the most concerning potential side effects, including risk of death, myocardial infarction (heart attack), stroke, venous thromboembolism (blood clots within veins), and tumour recurrence. Even with warnings and testing in place, erythropoietin use claimed the lives of 15 professional cyclists between 1997 and 2012.

Grey Areas

The World Anti-Doping Agency (WADA) publishes a list, available online, of every substance and variant not allowed for competition. Many substances will not change from year to year; steroidal variants are always prohibited, as are oxygen-delivery enhancers and Beta-2 agonists as well as hormonal modifiers and drug use maskers. Some categories, however, such as stimulants, are more complicated. Rather than being banned in general, they are only banned in competition, and certain stimulants are allowed in competition provided the amount in the urine does not exceed a certain level. In general, competitors will want to push as close as possible to the limits of what is permitted, but no further. In the world of natural bodybuilding competitions, for example, it is obviously illegal to use all of the compounds listed above, but it is legal to tan, to ingest foods with a high amount of sugar to improve vascularity, to exercise before a show to increase blood "pump," and to enter a state of severe dehydration to improve definition. In endurance events, while it is illegal to synthetically alter red blood cell levels, it is common practice for teams to go to high-altitude locations to become acclimatized and increase red blood cell mass. It could certainly be argued that such training methodologies greatly disadvantage competitors from poorer countries without the available funding for such types of training, and yet this advantage is allowed. Competitors, then, have to tread a very fine line between permitted and illegal training. To add another level of complication, certain foods and drink can contain compounds that closely resemble, or even loosely mimic, the effect of banned substances, meaning that competitors must be extremely aware of their diet and have a reliable and knowledgeable coach to guide them throughout the process of their training.

High-Profile Examples of Doping in Sports
There have been thousands of cases of doping across the sporting world. In the Olympics alone, there have been 119 "prosecuted" cases since 1968 against athletes or others, as in the case of the 2008 Beijing horse doping scandal. There are, however, certain high profile cases that have attracted large amounts of media attention and investigation. The 100-meter sprinter Ben Johnson, famously coached by the renowned Charles Francis, shocked the world when he set new world records consecutively in both 1987 and 1988, only to have both times disqualified and his medals rescinded. When questioned on the matter, both Johnson and his coach insisted that the use of anabolic steroids was necessary to compete at the Olympic level, a statement bolstered by the eventual news that six out of eight sprinters in that race tested positive or were implicated during their careers.

The National Football League (NFL) has also had its share of scandals, with former player and NFL coach Jim Haslett saying in a 2005 interview that at least 50 percent of the players in the 1980s were using some kind of performance-enhancing drug. To make matters worse, this announcement came only two years after the infamous 2003 BALCO scandal in which Oakland Raider's players Bill Romanowski, Tyrone Wheatley, Barrett Robbins, Chris Cooper and Dana Stubblefield were implicated.

Another recent high profile is that of the American Lance Armstrong, professional cyclist, seven-time winner of the grueling Tour de France, cancer survivor and founder of the charity Livestrong. In 2012, after retiring in 2011 and opting not to appeal his case, Armstrong was found guilty of doping and stripped of all seven of his Tour de France titles. He also received a lifetime ban from competition from all sports that run anti-doping legislation.

Although using high profile examples is useful in the sense that it demonstrates the direction of popular media attention, this can be misleading in that it places excess blame or scapegoating upon certain individuals. In most cases, these individuals are part of a team, and it is not uncommon for teams, coaches and owners to place pressure on their players to use performance-enhancing drugs. Moreover, the very fact that these high profile sportsmen felt the need to use performance-enhancing drugs can be seen as potentially indicative of the scale of abuse throughout the respective sports.

Antidoping Organizations and Their Actions
Although the International Amateur Athletic Federation (IAAF) issued their first ban on doping in 1928, the response was somewhat slow across the sporting world, with FIFA and the Union Cycliste Internationale not joining until 1966 and the

Floyd Landis, shown here at the 2006 Tour of California, was the initial winner of the 2006 Tour de France. However, he tested positive for performance-enhancing drugs, nearly three times the limit allowed by World Anti-Doping Agency rules, and was stripped of his title. (Wikimedia Commons/Michael David Murphy)

International Olympic Committee (IOC) not joining until 1967. Eventually, in 1999, the World Anti-Doping Agency (WADA) was formed, and aims to promote, organize, and monitor the fight against drugs within sport. Fundamentally, antidoping practices rely on testing in order to determine who is, or is not, using performance-enhancing drugs. These tests are usually urine samples divided into A and B samples, with the B sample used as a verification should sample A prove positive. The tests are often randomized, and athletes are given only a small degree of notice.

The main issue with testing, though, is that those being tested may attempt to cheat the system. In more outlandish cases, this has been done by submitting another person's urine for testing via a catheter or even a prosthetic penis, although generally cheating the testing system is much more of a pharmacological battle. In other words, competitors and their teams are continually trying to find new performance-enhancing drugs that are undetectable in randomized testing. The response from testing agencies is to update their testing methods, and it is common practice today for high-profile Olympic competitors to have their urine samples held for eight years to allow for future testing using new techniques. Notably, though, these updated methods in turn spark new searches for different compounds on the part of the competitors. In this sense, drug testing and regulation is a constantly evolving process.

The Future of Antidoping

More than ever before, antidoping organizations are working to prevent doping. The United Kingdom Anti-Doping Agency, for instance, is now working according to the national intelligence model (NIM) used by law enforcement agencies. This model details the best practices for investigation, retention and evaluation of information. Moreover, they are launching investigations and collecting information about performance-enhancing drug users, sellers, suppliers, transport routes and distribution networks.

Better still, the WADA is looking at methods for doping prevention, specifically by discouraging it at earlier stages in an athlete's career through education. The ALPHA program, otherwise known as the Athlete Learning Program about Health and Anti-Doping, has been developed by e-Learning experts, athletes, antidoping specialists, and antidoping social scientists. It was launched at the ADO Symposium in March 2014. Alongside this, the WADA has launched Coachtrue, a teaching platform to provide antidoping education for coaches. To supplement this, the WADA has even launched two Choose Your Own Adventure children's books titled *Track Star!* and *Always Picked Last*, in which children are allowed to make their own decisions regarding drugs and life choices without having to experience the real world consequences.

Unfortunately, the harsh reality of any antidoping activity or initiative is that it must always compete to some degree against human nature. Great athletes and sports people become so largely as a result of a desire to be the best that they can be, to win even if that means making sacrifices. For many promising and highly competitive athletes, performance-enhancing drugs offer a pathway to further success within their field, and that pathway will always have a certain appeal. Moreover, pressure from coaches, teammates, and even indirectly through sponsors and fans, can increase the temptation to use drugs to enhance ones performance. As the WADA and other organizations are increasingly beginning to realize, winning the "fight" against doping is likely to require many years of generational change and social reconditioning.

Alexander Parry, Ba (Oxon)

See Also: Ethics in Sports; Health Issues in Sports; U.S. Anti-Doping Agency; World Anti-Doping Agency.

Further Readings
Batemanaug, O. "Drugs and the Evolution of Bodybuilding." http://www.theatlantic.com/health/archive/2014/08/drugs-and-the-evolution-of-bodybuilding/375100/2 (Accessed November 2014).
Bertolino, T. "High-Profile Athlete Doping." http://www.texasbar.com/AM/Template.cfm?Section=Texas_Bar_Journal&Template=/CM/ContentDisplay.cfm&ContentID=20537 (Accessed November 2014).
Hodnik, J. "DNP: The Most Effective and Dangerous Drug for Fat Loss." http://www.vpxsports.com/article-detail/drugs/dnp-the-most-effective-and-dangerous-drug-for-fat-loss (Accessed November 2014).

E

Economics of Sports

The economic component of sports in the United States is central as the business of sports continues to evolve. In an industry that has been estimated as generating nearly $500 billion annually, an understanding of the business landscape and decisions involved with sports helps to paint a robust picture of the industry at various levels and in various contexts. Operationalized sports economics can be described as the economic aspects of sports and related decisions to realize defined and specific economic outcomes. Further, theoretical frameworks have been applied to sports economics to allow people to make sense of the landscape. These frameworks include, but are not limited to, agency theory, economic theory, and theory of the firm. A robust examination of sports economics indicates that there are three key areas that compose the field: sport consumption, the market for sports, and the business of sports.

Sport Consumption

The supply and demand aspect of sports may be considered as the foundational concept of sports economics. The law of supply and demand helps to truly understand the sports marketplace. For example, game ticket sales and premium seating, concessions, and merchandise represent revenue streams for a sport organization, but these revenues can only be realized if there is an appropriate and economically viable demand for the listed products. Sports are unique because, economically speaking, a lack of

substitution exists. If one goes to their local grocery store, they may select from any number of breakfast cereals, which generally do not differ all that much in taste, quality, and price. Otherwise stated, a number of substitutions exist which may affect Brand A, Brand B, and Brand C. One may consider sports in this manner as well. There are virtually no football operations in the United States, North America, or even the world that serve as a substitute for the National Football League (NFL). In this sense, the NFL, and several other select sport organizations, experience market power.

Demand for sports is often predicated on fan attitudes, perceptions, and identification (i.e. how strong their fandom is toward a particular sports team/organization). Fans expect that their team will share attributes in common with their competition as well as a particular level of prestige. The expectation is that these antecedents should produce winning. Ostensibly, this formula should shift the demand curve in the requisite manner. However, it is often the case that a sport organization can manipulate demand by decreasing or increasing the supply of product. For example, Team X may decide to renovate, or more appropriately, reinvent its stadium by reducing single-seat capacity, placing a greater emphasis on premium seating and suite sales. Typically, the costs to the consumer associated with these types of seating are significantly greater than single seating. Because the supply of single seating has been reduced, the requisite demand for that seating may increase, which in turn increases the ticket revenue associated with that seat. Additionally, the greater emphasis on premium and suite seating may have a similar effect on the team's revenue. As mentioned, fan attitudes and perception also play a key role in this example. Fans may be dissuaded by the costs associated with attendance due to the stadium reinvention. The quality of the participants in the game may also affect demand. To address this, a number of sports organizations have implemented a variable ticketing plan that allows for ticket pricing adjustments to fan demand. In fact, there is a spillover effect associated with filling seats, since once fans are situated in the stadium, the demand for concessions, apparel, and other related revenue-generating streams is viable.

Another key aspect of the supply/demand law in sports is rights fees associated with multimedia and television broadcasts. Rights fees themselves are a portion of the cycle that drives revenue toward sport organizations. The demand for sports programming continues to grow as evidenced by the multitude of television channels, networks, and Internet and social media platforms dedicated to such programming. In fact, in addition to national and regional broadcast agreements that major professional sports leagues forge with television networks such as ABC, CBS, ESPN, FOX, and NBC, these leagues have also established their own networks, often with an Internet presence and with access available through one's mobile device. These access points of consumption are important because as more viewers consume the programming, the access points become attractive and appropriate spaces for advertisers to promote their products. Television networks also understand this and, as the networks have the appropriate mechanisms in place to disseminate the programming, enter into partnerships with sports leagues as the exclusive broadcast rights holder.

This produces a two-way transaction: Networks provide sports leagues with millions and sometimes billions, of dollars over an extended number of years to exclusively broadcast the programming. Additionally, networks leverage their viewership with advertisers, allowing the advertisers to place their products or messages directly in front of viewers for a fee requisite to the number of viewers and the demographic composition. Through this cycle, sports leagues generate a significant amount of revenue,

networks may earn a high return on their investments, and advertisers may reach their particular audience and boost sales.

As mentioned, professional sports establish and operate their own networks typically through a multimedia division of the league. The cycle outlined above is similar, but leagues typically maintain partnerships with other larger networks and provide broadcast rights that allow access to more attractive programming. Within the last decade, the sport industry has seen a similar model percolate into the intercollegiate athletics landscape. With the growth in popularity of sports such as Division-I football in the National Collegiate Athletic Association (NCAA), major television networks are paying rights fees on par with those seen across professional sports. Additionally, many athletic conferences have established and operate their own national and regional networks, while some individual schools have established their own regional networks. To gain appropriate context as it relates to the intercollegiate athletics landscape, it should be noted that the NCAA holds agreements with numerous networks that will generate billions of dollars over the life of the agreement to be distributed, in part, to NCAA member institutions. As one can see, broadcast rights fees are a healthy revenue source and an essential piece of the economic puzzle in sports.

The demand aspect of the law of supply and demand in sports provides an appropriate scaffold to address the supply aspect in better detail. Practitioners and scholars in the sports economics area may state supply begets demand, or conversely, demand begets supply. In either case, the two are highly related. A supply-side approach complements the demand aspect and segues into the micro- and macro-decisions of the sports landscape.

The Market for Sports

In many cases, high-level professional and intercollegiate sports exist because like-minded individuals and entities have pooled resources within a particular governing body. In the United States, examples of such governing bodies in the professional ranks include Major League Baseball (MLB), Major League Soccer (MLS), the National Basketball Association (NBA), the National Football League (NFL), and the National Hockey League (NHL). The NCAA is the dominant governing body at the intercollegiate athletic level, but the National Association for Intercollegiate Athletics (NAIA) and the National Junior College Athletic Association (NJCAA) are also governing bodies in the intercollegiate athletic space.

Essentially, the role of these sports governing bodies is to provide a space where many can pool their resources and have their goals and objectives realized. In the case of the professional leagues, the "many" represent team owners. It should be noted that the term *team* is used to describe the units that compete athletically week to week—those units that help to drive gate receipts, concession dollars, and broadcast rights agreements through their accomplishments between the lines of play. As a matter of fact, professional teams are highly visible ancillary divisions of the greater business organizations that house them. The same may be said at the intercollegiate athletic level as the athletic teams that compete throughout the week are highly visible ancillary programs of the university as a whole—ones that fall in line with the mission of the university, provide a level of exposure for the university, and help to generate large sums of revenue that is untaxed due to universities' status as nonprofit organizations.

Professional leagues are large-scale operations that provide structure and mechanisms to maximize revenue and, vis-à-vis, profits for league owners. In order for this to occur, league owners pay careful attention to the parity of their leagues, team markets, league size, and governing structure. For example, a league that regularly sees a small percentage of its teams in contention for the championship everywhere may not have the same level of appeal as if a high level of parity existed over time.

However, a smaller league with fewer teams that can regularly contend is not the appropriate response to the issue of parity and economic viability. League owners have the ability to limit how many franchises (teams) will compete in the league. The complexity of this relies on market viability and revenue and cost estimates. Implicitly, a certain level of demand should exist in the given markets to positively impact total revenue. A key determinant of demand in this regard is market size. By professional sports terms, a small market is considered one with an approximate population of less than 2 million people. A market such as Milwaukee, (approximately 600,000

to a million people) may experience economically driven issues related to sport more so than a market like Los Angeles, which is exponentially larger than Milwaukee. A number of markets are left without a team over any given period because they are not seen as economically viable for the league, or because an empty market aids in increasing the profitability of the league when franchises move to or are newly granted in these markets.

A vital component to the economic viability of professional leagues is the governance structure. The principal-agent model is employed, which allows for franchise owners to collectively cede autonomy over league matters to a selected commissioner who acts on their behalf. The commissioner represents league owners as it pertains to league matters such as labor and collective bargaining agreements, television broadcast rights, and the enforcement of league-wide policies.

All of these areas may affect the demand and economic viability. Executed properly, the coalescence of each of these areas produces market power and efficiency. This is noteworthy because the business model of professional leagues essentially affords ownership with a high degree of influence over several areas that may make their league investments more or less financially successful. For example, this type of heavy influence and restriction on competition almost certainly appreciates the value of a given league and its ownership members from year to year.

Intercollegiate athletics do not operate with the same business model and autonomy as their professional counterparts, but there are certainly stark parallels. For example, parity, governing structure, markets, and size are high line-item considerations in this space as they are in the professional space, but these issues are executed much differently. To use the NCAA as an example, its highest tier, Division I, consists of 10 governing subordinate units that serve as the liaison between member institutions and the larger governing body. The smaller governing bodies, known as athletic conferences, house member institutions that resemble one another and share similar goals. Such goals may consist of competitive balance or increased revenue across the conference. Conference leadership takes an active role in realizing these goals through strategic partnerships with external stakeholders or through the process admitting new member institutions, known as conference realignment. Additionally, the NCAA as an organization, as well as individual athletic conferences, operates utilizing the principal-agent model. NCAA member institutions, led by their respective presidents, cede autonomy to an individual who presides over the organization, acting in the best interests of member institutions. At the conference level, the presidents of conference member institutions cede autonomy and select a commissioner to represent their interests. In either case, the individuals selected to oversee the NCAA and its member conferences may help to secure and diversify revenue, enforce rules, and ensure safety of participants.

These types of coordinated operations directly influence market outcomes and, from here, it can be quantified exactly how much sports markets are impacted. Many sports economists and sports marketers analyze sports markets in detail in order to make sense of data that will explain past occurrences and future decisions.

The Business of Sports

When stadiums and arenas are built, when cities are selected to host large-scale sporting events, or when the new schedule premieres highlighting the local team's home games, sport economists and sport marketers are called upon to place value in each of these instances. These economic impact analyses are important to business owners and citizens of the community, city officials, and sports organizations alike. In this sense, economic impact analyses examine the effect of sports events and activities on the economy in the area under investigation. Typically, these analyses allow business owners to understand how their businesses can be impacted, provide a forecast of new jobs created, and can also track revenue generated at the local, county, and state levels through related taxes. These impact analyses play a key role in providing a cost-benefit picture of why a community may partner with sport organizations. To explain how a community may partner with sports organizations, a description of the manner in which communities provide support is appropriate.

Some sports economists would suggest the economic impact analysis runs in lockstep with public financial support related to sports teams, facilities, and events. As outlined above, the economic impact

analysis can be used ex-ante to project effects on the given economy through sports. Often, this is an effective and acceptable manner to address public concerns about the impact of engaging in such sports enterprises and serves as the springboard to begin a dialogue about the breakdown of public and private support for these sport enterprises.

Typically, the discussion of public and private support arises when upgrades to an existing facility are needed or when the construction of a new facility is needed. Public support typically comes in the form of subsidies to the sport's organization. The community will often cede certain taxes toward the work on the facility because having the facility keeps teams and events in the community that will generate economic activity as outlined previously. In other cases, the public may issue bonds to the sport organization that are tax-exempt; in other words, loan-type financing to be paid back over a designated period with a designated interest rate. The interest rate applied is typically lower than a conventional bank-issued loan. To balance the public-private equation, the sport entity also absorbs a financial obligation, typically less than 50 percent, as the value of having the team at the facility or events associated with the facility is readily justified and quantifiable. This model may appear one-sided in favor of leagues and their teams, but community leaders are able to protect the public's investment.

A facility lease is the primary mechanism used to protect the public's investment. The lease allows the sport organization to maximize financial benefits of the facility, although the organization does not own it. This includes suite sales, concessions, parking, etc. The organization pays what amounts to rent to the city and is additionally bound to the facility for the negotiated amount of time, owing a balance and/or other negotiated fees if the lease is broken. The organization may also be required to return money previously disbursed, known as a clawback.

The preceding explanation of financial support is typically confined to the professional sports space. Note that amateur levels of sports also may experience the need for facility renovation or construction. In particular, intercollegiate athletics provide a stark contrast to what was previously outlined with their professional sports counterparts. In part because universities and their associated athletic programs operate as tax-exempt 501(c)(3) nonprofit organizations, they are able to accept charitable contributors to finance capital projects. Typically, they will engage in a donor campaign to raise large identified contributions to allocate toward large-scale projects such as stadium renovations or construction. In fact, much of the economic structure in the intercollegiate athletics space differs. Not only do donations contribute toward capital projects, but they also may contribute to operating costs and are usually attached to the procurement of season tickets or premium seating for sports such as football and men's basketball.

G. K. Nwosu

See Also: Identification With Sports Teams; Intercollegiate Sports; National Association of Intercollegiate Athletics; National Collegiate Athletic Association; Organizational Behavior; Professional Sports.

Further Readings
Fisher, Eric. "NFL Warms Up to Variable Pricing." http://www.sportsbusinessdaily.com/Journal/Issue/2014/03/10/Leagues-and-Governing-Bodies/NFL-variable-pricing.aspx (Accessed September 2014).
Fort, Rodney. *Sports Economics*. Upper Saddle River, NJ: Prentice Hall, 2010.
Noll, Roger. "Sports Economics at Fifty." http://web.stanford.edu/group/siepr/cgibin/?q=system/files/shared/pubs/papers/pdf/06-11.pdf (Accessed September 2014).
Smith, Michael. "ASU Draws on NFL Experience." http://www.sportsbusinessdaily.com/Journal/Issues/2014/08/25/Colleges/Arizona-State.aspx (Accessed August 2014).

Emergency Action Plan

No individual working in sports on any level likes to see injuries and emergencies arise, but they unfortunately do arise. Having an emergency action plan (EAP) and accident report that cover the necessary steps to be taken when an emergency arises will not only provide a way to deal with the emergency, but also will send a message that the necessary planning was in place. Knowing the plan and practicing the plan for all practice or competitive sites will ensure that the individuals responsible for addressing an emergency have the expertise to act immediately.

Creating the Plan
The simplest way to create an emergency action plan is to determine the necessary steps and then create a form that all coaches, supervisors, and others can use to personalize the plan for their particular situations. For example, if a youth team is practicing at a county park facility and is also competing at other sites, a plan should be devised for each site. If a team is playing at an away stadium, a plan should be created for an emergency situation in spite of the fact that the home school may have limited emergency personnel on site. If a cross-country team needs to conduct practice runs on rural or urban streets, a plan should be devised for possible emergencies that might arise.

Necessary Information for the Plan
The necessary information on the top of the form should include the site (practice field, basketball court, etc.) or situation (weather-related, utility outage-related, fire, etc.) and the person in charge who is responsible for seeing that the plan is properly executed.

Following the site and name should be a section designating who will call for help and the number to call for help. These two steps are crucial, especially in circumstances where there is only one coach conducting a practice. The numbers to be called can vary by city location and location inside a building. For example, if a phone is located in the pool and necessitates that a designated number must be dialed for an outside line, that information should be contained in the EAP. Relying on a cell phone inside some buildings may not be efficient, as a powerful enough cellular signal is sometimes unavailable.

Designating the address of the facility, the exact location where emergency personnel should be directed to go, and who will meet the emergency vehicle is paramount to obtaining an immediate response. If the emergency is an injury to an athlete, the EAP should designate who will render emergency first aid and who will stay with the athlete until help arrives. On the other hand, if the emergency is a

Antonio Cassano is an Italian footballer shown with an injury at the Euro 2012 finals. Emergency action plans guide the actions of the rescuers or potential rescuers of individuals with sports injuries such as these. (Wikimedia Commons/football.ua)

weather-related condition such as lightning, the EAP needs to specify where emergency shelter can be found, when individuals need to seek such shelter, and how it will be determined when it is safe to exit the shelter. Most programs, whether intended for minors or adults, require information for a contact person in case of emergency. One of the important aspects of an EAP is the determination regarding who will call the emergency contact person. This should be a responsible adult who can convey as much information as is feasible to the emergency contact regarding not only the fact that an individual has been injured or has been in an accident, but also what has been done to help the individual and to what hospital the individual has been conveyed, and, if it proves to be a necessity, following the injury/accident. If the injury occurred to a minor who had to be conveyed, then the EAP should also determine who will ride to the hospital with the minor if the parents/guardians are not on site.

Forms Regarding the Accident/Injury

Following the assessment of the accident/injury and the conveyance, if necessary, additional pieces of information should be required. The first is the accident report. Besides the normal information contained in an accident report, two additional sections of information should be required if the accident/injury occurred during a sports practice or competition and there is any chance of subsequent litigation.

First, if emergency personnel were called to the scene, the accident report should contain a section requiring the full names, badge or identification numbers, and the company the individuals responding to the scene belong to. In order to file a civil suit in most states, there is a statute of limitations of three years. Should a plaintiff wait a considerable time prior to filing a suit, the information regarding emergency responders could no longer be available. Requiring it on the accident report ensures that should it be necessary, it will be readily available.

Second, the accident report should address the format for witness statements that should include the following information: name of the individual responsible for obtaining any witness statements, followed by the actual information to be included by witnesses. The witness statements should be in writing; include the full name, date of birth, address, telephone number, and cell phone number; what the individual saw; where she or he was located in respect to the location of the accident/injury; the date and time of the occurrence; any special conditions such as reduced lighting or water on the floor; and any other information the witness feels might be relevant.

The accurately completed witness statements, the accident report and the EAP form should be kept for at least three years after the date of the incident. While the use of a well-constructed EAP will not prevent accidents or injuries from occurring in a program, it will help defend the actions of the supervisor of the activity should any questions be subsequently raised and ensure that swift action will be taken to address any emergencies that arise.

Janis K. Doleschal

See Also: Crisis Management; Health Issues in Sports; Injury; Legal Responsibilities for Coaches; Risk Management Process; Sports Law.

Further Readings

Abrams, Roger I. *Playing Tough: The World of Sports and Politics.* Lebanon, NH: Northeastern University Press, 2013.

Thornton, Patrick K. *Sports Law.* Sudbury, MA: Jones and Bartlett, 2011.

Wong, Glenn. M. *Essentials of Sports Law.* Westport, CT: Praeger, 2010.

Entrepreneurship

Entrepreneurship is the method of creating something original of value through the devotion of time and effort. The benefits of entrepreneurship are that of monetary gains and individual gratifications. Despite the perceived glory, entrepreneurs assume all of the mental, economic, and public risks associated with their endeavors. Entrepreneurs themselves seek new opportunities, they are innovative, and most important, they inspire. Entrepreneurs use their beliefs to establish and instill a culture in their organization, and they have the opportunity to give back to their communities.

The term *entrepreneur* has various meanings to different groups of people. A sports fan may view an entrepreneur as simply a team owner. A businessman may view an entrepreneur as competition, or potentially a partner. A psychologist's views of an entrepreneur may be that of extreme motivation. Regardless of the different meanings the word entrepreneur may have, one word is inherently synonymous with entrepreneur: leader.

In the world of sports, entrepreneurs are seen differently than the chief executive officers (CEOs) and presidents of nonsport businesses. In the sport industry team owners are looked at as public figures. They in their own right are celebrities at games, and the public eye is constantly watching them. In both major and minor league sports, various team owners are more recognizable than the players on the team. Due to their celebrity, the decisions made by team owners are analyzed by individuals outside of the company. This extra scrutiny and subjectivity to continual media analysis can be a burden to these entrepreneurs but it can also create the opportunity for team owners to display their leadership abilities.

The Three I's

Entrepreneurs as leaders exhibit three distinct characteristics known as the Three I's: identification, innovation, and inspiration. Entrepreneurs who display these qualities are setting themselves up to be great leaders. Entrepreneurs are regularly identifying opportunities in their industry and are searching for ways to improve or change their industry through a vision. As entrepreneurs identify new opportunities they begin to generate ideas to satisfy these opportunities. This process is achieved through innovation. Through identification and innovation comes inspiration. Entrepreneurs inspire those who are witnesses to their work. Without inspiration, the desire to dream would be nonexistent, thus eliminating the possibility of change. Inspiration in turn promotes further identification and innovation. The process is a constant cycle allowing for new ideas and new leaders to come into existence. In addition to the generation of new leaders is the opportunity for an industry to evolve. Evolution throughout history has led to growth and prosperity.

Identification

The process of identifying and evaluating opportunities is very challenging. Most opportunities for entrepreneurs do not just appear, and therefore it is up to the entrepreneur to seek out and find the opportunity. Leaders are visionaries. They are frequently dreaming and focusing on ways to invoke change and betterment.

Finding opportunities can be a result of watchfulness and/or preparedness. Entrepreneurs are constantly seeking new opportunities, and are consistently putting themselves in a position to find these opportunities. More often than not the result of a new opportunity comes from that of the consumer. Consumers regularly express their feelings and beliefs toward new products and services they would like. An entrepreneur as a leader listens to all ideas and tirelessly evaluates their potential outcomes.

Evaluating an opportunity once it is discovered can perhaps be the most thought provoking part of the entrepreneurial procedure. The evaluation process is where the entrepreneur decides whether or not the rewards will outweigh the risks, time and effort. Bill Veeck as a major league baseball owner, from the 1940s to the 1980s, exemplified the process of identifying opportunities. Throughout his storied career as an owner, Veeck never seemed afraid to take a chance to make the game of baseball better. His promotional stunts were used as a means of increasing attendance and fans of baseball. Stunts included giveaways of flowers and live animals to spectators as well as the display of fireworks during the game. One of Veeck's most famous stunts included the hiring of an actor who was less than 4 feet tall to bat during a game, thus creating a strike zone so small it would guarantee a walk. He also allowed for spectators in the stands to act as managers and tell the team whether to steal or bunt during the game.

Veeck viewed himself not as a celebrity baseball owner, but as an equal to those attending baseball games. His views allowed for his promotions to relate to those in the crowd. Many of Veeck's promotional stunts were viewed as a mockery toward the professional game, yet his idea to add the player's names to the back of their jerseys revolutionized baseball. This idea allowed for the game of professional baseball to become more recognizable with its fan base. Veeck's creative thinking identified the opportunity to increase attendance at baseball games and by him doing so he set the stage for modern day promotions at sporting events.

Innovation

Innovation is necessary for economic growth. As time moves on and technology advances, older products and industries begin to fade away. Innovations and advancements are necessary for the survival of a product or industry. With regard to sports, and sporting events, new ideas are needed to generate new fans, and to increase attendance.

Veeck's idea of placing player names on their jerseys not only identified an opportunity in the sport of baseball, but it was innovative. Great leaders are fundamentally great innovators. They are constantly thinking of new ideas to make what they do better. Innovators do not settle for what the norm is in their industry. They instead analyze their surroundings and attempt to bring an entirely new idea into fruition. Bill Veeck, as a professional baseball owner, was one of the most innovative entrepreneurs of his time. The sport of baseball has not previously experienced Veeck's level of creativeness and thinking with regards to improving the sport. Ahead of the times Veeck signed, Larry Doby, the first black baseball player to the American League. This of course was during a time of civil rights unrest. Veeck also helped to create modern day free agency with his desire to constantly shift players around on his roster. Each year resulted in multiple roster changes to help field the best possible team.

Identifying opportunities is the first step toward innovation. Leaders will analyze their current market and evaluate any potential needs. As needs are identified, they are next analyzed to determine comparative importance in their industry. Solutions are then developed through the evaluation process. Bill Veeck's innovative nature as an owner sparked an eventual revolution toward improving professional baseball. Innovations such as interleague play, newer stadiums, instant replay, and the home run derby came into existence because of Veeck's relentless industry analysis.

Successful innovators do not keep to themselves; instead they ask questions, seek thoughts, and become aware of their surroundings. Innovative leaders interact with their customer base to understand what the needs, wants, and expectations of their customers are. Mark Cuban, owner of the Dallas Mavericks, becomes a spectator during Mavericks' basketball games. He sits in the stands with other fans, waits in concession lines with those same fans, and he uses the public restroom. Cuban does this to identify and relate with his fans, but most importantly this allows him to interact with his customers.

Inspiration

Effective leadership results in inspiration. Leaders inspire members of their team through passion, honesty, care, vision, and expectation. These qualities sum up a leader who will inevitably inspire those around. Entrepreneurs as leaders are extremely passionate about what they do. If they were not passionate, they would be unable to commit the amount of time necessary to be successful. Their passion fuels excitement among others, which in return creates inspiration. Leaders are honest with themselves, and their team. Leaders are not invincible and therefore they are susceptible to mistakes. Acknowledging mistakes and seeking advice helps to earn lasting respect from those around. Teams who feel involved in decision making and feel their voices are heard will be more inclined to go the extra mile for the organization.

Leaders also create a feeling of care and encouragement toward their team. Simple acts of kindness toward team members can make the difference in how a leader is viewed. Care helps to create a sense of value that ultimately results in happiness at work. Encouragement permits individuals to think freely and pursue their own ideas. Especially during hard times, it is very important for leaders to display encouragement and affirmation.

In order for leaders to exhibit the Three I's, they must be visionaries. Effective leaders have a vision and it is important for that vision to be shared. Promoting a vision helps to create and establish an organizational culture. Finally leaders must surpass their own expectations in order to inspire those around them. Team members cannot be expected to exceed their own expectations if they do not see the same from their leader. As leaders begin to exceed what is expected of them, the rest of the organization will soon follow.

The evolution of an industry occurs because of inspiration. Individuals, through the leadership of others, become inspired to make change. Inspiration is a byproduct of care and compassion, and those who invoke change do so because of this. Innovations throughout the sports industry occur because of ones feelings toward a game. Bill Veeck cared about baseball and he did everything in his power to make the game more enjoyable for everyone. Without his passion for the game, his innovations toward improvement would not have occurred.

Establishing a Culture

Leaders define the culture of an organization. They introduce values and beliefs to an organization and help to set the stage for what type of atmosphere will be present at the workplace. Entrepreneurs as presidents or chief executive officers lead by example. Great leaders are separated from the rest of the group based on their demeanor and outlook. A strong organizational culture, created by a leader, will keep an organization intact and stable.

In order for a culture to be defined the leader must be fully committed to the values being expressed. Leaders who are perceived as hypocritical will face a continuous uphill battle against other members of the organization. Time is needed to create and establish a culture; however the amount of time needed to disband a set culture is significantly less.

Establishing a culture must be recognized by the leader. Leaders can play a dynamic role in formulating and influencing the culture. Cultures can be created by leadership through the way in which they handle certain issues, problems, or situations. Leaders as well can establish a culture by rewarding

certain behaviors and eliminating previously set consequences for other behaviors. The personal messages a leader sends to his/her team pertaining to their value to the organization can greatly influence and set in place a new culture.

Similar to that of inspiration, culture is fused through passion and belief. Leaders cannot expect a culture to form without passion and belief. A leader's belief toward a set culture will help create a sense of buy-in among the rest of the team. If a team does not buy into the proposed culture, it will be extremely difficult for the culture to be set in place.

Charitable Involvement

Entrepreneurship and leadership as a whole are much bigger than being the head of a company or industry. Entrepreneurs as leaders have the opportunity to significantly impact communities. They, as figureheads, can create a culture in which community involvement is imperative. It is important for leaders to recognize the need for community involvement, and to recognize they are in a position to make a difference.

Professional sport owners presently are significantly wealthier than the average person. Their wealth enables them to contribute to their community on a more continual basis. As a professional sports owner, Mark Cuban has made a commitment toward community and charitable contributions. The National Basketball Association (NBA) has fined Cuban around $2 million throughout his years as an owner and Cuban has matched each fine he has received with a donation to various charities. In addition to matching his NBA fines, Cuban has donated money toward helping veterans, fighting cancer, providing disaster relief, and establishing better education. Cuban's generosity displays the culture in which he has set in place with the Dallas Mavericks. Life is bigger than basketball, and as a person Cuban has used his position as a successful entrepreneur to help others in need. Cuban's generosity exemplifies what type of leader he is.

Conclusion

Opportunity is a product of leadership, but it is a necessity for entrepreneurship. Those entrepreneurs who seek opportunity are destined to find leadership. As the opportunity for leadership is presented, it is up to the individual to decide what type of leader he or she will develop into. The Three I's consisting of identification, innovation, and inspiration, are qualities performed by the best of leaders. Identification of an opportunity leads to innovation, which in return creates inspiration. The creation of inspiration leads to further identification and innovation among both leaders and followers. This continuous cycle will allow for an industry or product to evolve continuously over time.

Leaders establish a team's culture, and present an atmosphere they feel will best initiate an opportunity for success. These leaders are generous toward others, and use the position they are in to help those in need. To establish a culture, leaders must be endlessly aware of their environment. Understanding the ins and outs of a particular environment allows for one's creativity to be at its fullest. In the end, leadership is based solely on opportunity. Individuals who take advantage of the opportunities presented to themselves will be in the best position to lead others.

Rocco P. Porreca

See Also: Community Engagement for Sports Teams; Creating an Organizational Vision; Development of Leadership Skills; Leadership Models in Sports; Owners and Business Leadership.

Further Readings

Boring, S. "Leadership: Three lessons From Mark Cuban" (August 13, 2013). *SDB Creative Group.* http://sdbcreativegroup.com/lessons-in-leadership-from-mark-cuban (Accessed August 2014).

Brewster, M. "Bill Veeck: A Baseball Mastermind." *Bloomberg Businessweek* (October 26, 2004). http://www.businessweek.com/stories/2004-10-26/bill-veeck-a-baseball-mastermind (Accessed August 2014).

Corbett, W. "Bill Veeck" (2014). *Society for American Baseball Research.* http://sabr.org/bioproj/person/7b0b5f10 (Accessed August 2014).

Hisrich, R. D., M. P. Peters, and D. A. Shepherd, *Entrepreneurship,* 8th ed. New York: Irwin McGraw-Hill, 2010.

Wager, M. "Inspire Your Team." *New Zealand Management*, v.58/10 (2011).

Ethics in Sports

The increasing popularity of sport throughout the world has people tuning in to sport events in record numbers. Worldwide events such as the Olympics and FIFA's World Cup have fanatics clamoring for tickets and the casual fan glued to their television. Professional, collegiate, and amateur teams continue to grow in importance to the communities they exist in. Massive stadiums and arenas are built to hold the events and teams, and the fans come to cheer on the home team. These fans idolize the players for their incredible talents and for this the athletes are often well compensated.

As sport has risen in popularity, so too have the impacts on the societies that support it. As the earning potential of professional athletes increases, the pressure to perform to gain that employment, and maintain it, also increases. This pressure often leads to questionable behavior by the athlete. Owners want to fill their seats, fans want to watch winners, and athletes become the tools to make it happen. The actions of athletes reflect the values of society, and society reflects on the rightness or wrongness of those actions. The problems that arise at the highest levels of sport can trickle down into the lower levels over time. Such issues as the importance of winning, performance enhancing drugs (PEDs), cheating, violence, and equality of athletes are questions that continue to test the tolerance of societies.

The actions taken by the coaches and athletes are then scrutinized for their acceptability. As sport is a reflection of the society in which it exists, it also, over time, has the ability to change that society. Sport can bring about change and the acceptance of new ways. Sport has been at the forefront of changes of race, gender, and now disability. As play changes, rules are updated to take into account new actions or talents. The game is constantly evolving and the fans, owners, and players decide what is acceptable.

Winning

An oft-recited claim in sport is that the only reason one plays is to win. It is not good enough to merely win but expected that teams will bring playoff appearances and even championships to their franchise. The coach with a team that does not win will find that he or she no longer has a job. Even coaches who win will find that they have not won enough and are "shown the door." This puts a great deal of emphasis on coaches and players to win at all costs. This mentality creeps into the game until the player does not care how the sport is played, only that his or her team is ahead at the end.

For some, winning justifies the ends, and there is no guilt about how the win was achieved. A soccer player who violates the rules so seriously that the player is sent off is often praised by others because the player's actions allowed the team a chance to win. Those who support the team are thrilled at the player's brilliant play, and those rooting for the opposition hate the player and the player's brazen violation of the rules. Those who are not emotionally a part of the action are left to question the actions during the contest and its meaning for future contests. Winning has become the ultimate objective. All other concerns take a back seat to the purpose of winning. Actions are gauged as to how it helps the team win and acceptance is built on that.

Performance Enhancing Drugs (PEDs)

Athletes are looking for an edge and often turn to PEDs to gain that edge. From anabolic steroids to human growth hormone to myriad other substances, athletes are constantly on the lookout for substances that provide them with a performance edge. The question must be asked if this is a reflection of cultures that seemingly treat every imaginable human ailment with drugs, or is this a harbinger of change in sport. There is great pressure on athletes to play at their best all of the time. Athletes cut corners to improve capabilities, to rehab from injury, and to increase stamina so that they can perform night after night. In physical sports, athletes use drugs to deal with the constant pain and suffering so that they can get out on the field or court and play. While the drug may not increase their performance, it does raise the issue of PEDs, as the athlete would not be able to perform at all or at a reduced ability without the drugs.

The use of PEDs can be traced to its roots to the ancient Olympics. It seems that as long as there has been competitive sport, there has been the use of PEDs in that sport. The only change is the effectiveness of the drugs used and in the manner in which the drugs enter the body. Athletes use PEDs with the hopes that the gains are not nullified by the other's use of drugs. Even if both athletes are using, one hopes to have an advantage because the drug has a greater reaction in their system than the opposition receives. Understand that the athlete is not necessarily cutting corners to reach a greater performance. The athlete will work just as hard or harder when taking the drugs. The athlete is looking at the edge, that boost that makes them a little bit better than their opposition.

Athletes frequently use drugs to rehabilitate injury. Like surgery, they see this use as a means to return to normal play. The injury may have forced the athlete to compete at a lower performance level, one that they find hard to accept. In this case, the athlete is not seeking a competitive advantage, but a return to a level of play previously attained. From an ethical standpoint it is difficult to justify this as being significantly different than use to enhance performance. Another aspect is that the use by some athletes sends the message that if one wishes to compete at that level then the athlete must use PEDs. The athlete, because of the belief that they are being coerced into use to be competitive, in this case, justifies drug use.

While PED use is still very prevalent, the new age of technological advancement has raised concerns about the future of sport. The increasing knowledge base in the fields of nanotechnology and genetic engineering give pause to sport enthusiasts. As breakthroughs in science create stronger, healthier animals that are more resistant to disease and injury, so to will this information be used to create better athletes.

Violence

Violence and intimidation have increasingly become problematic for sport. Violence to injure or harm a player on the opposition so they cannot perform is frequently instituted by coaches to give their team a chance. Star players of the opposition are targeted, even to the point that we see National Footbal League (NFL) teams institute a bounty system for the injury and elimination of players on the opposition. In a physical sport such as football, it can be a fine line between physical play and harmful play. Athletes push the boundaries and fans cheer bone-crushing hits.

The problem is that the star players are getting hurt and missing games. The fan pays to see the best play but the numbers are reduced by the injuries. Sometimes the injuries are not known until years after the players' playing days are over. New focus on head injuries and concussions create ethical concerns about certain sports and the way those sports are played. Football and ice hockey, with their physical nature, have seen a focus on the catastrophic injuries that result from their play. Those inside the sport question the types of hits that have been prevalent in the game in recent years. Those outside the sport question the ethics of a sport that leads to the types of injuries that are being reported.

When the focus on winning becomes so great that coaches and players are willing to hurt players on the other team, the public begins to question these ethics. Coaches are reinforcing that injurious play outside of the rules is just part of the game. When purposeful actions or reckless behavior increase the likelihood that others are injured, retaliation may be the result. Again, the coaches and players justify this action as part of the game and necessary to the actual play.

Cheating

When young kids play a game, they follow the rules and do no try to take advantage of calls they did not earn; they just play the game. When coaches and adults around them begin to focus on winning, then the actions of the children begin to change. Coaches teach young athletes the essence of getting calls not otherwise available to them by flopping, acting, and by intimidation. The coach teaches that rules are to be bent and broken and that it is up to the referee or umpire to make the call. Athletes are led to believe that it is not cheating if one does not get caught. Sports are meant to be about one player's talents in a particular game versus another's talents and sports should follow the maxim of "may the best person win." Currently, athletes have to contend with trick plays, unseen violations of the rules, and strategies of teams that violate the rules for their own benefit.

It is said that in football, no action takes place without at least one violation of the rules. Every play has at least one instance of holding by an offensive player. Coaches instruct players on the art of holding so that the athletes do not get called for it. Referees will hold clinics on how to hold in the proper way. This leads the player to believe that these actions are acceptable and expected. The player then spends countless hours perfecting these talents so he gets better at holding and concludes that this is how to play football.

In baseball, one violation of the rules is the phantom tag, where the base runner is missed but the fielder acts like they put the tag on the runner. This action can lead to the runner being called out when they were actually safe. Catchers are trained by coaches to pull pitches. A pitch that is slightly out of the strike zone is made to look like a strike by sliding the glove over into the strike zone. This is to make it appear to the umpire that the pitch traveled over the plate and was caught just behind the strike zone so that the pitching team gets a call that otherwise is not theirs.

Basketball has the intentional foul and enough physical play so that it resembles football. The coaches and players have taken a no-contact sport and introduced shoving and pushing as a main staple for play under the basket. Players use their strength instead of the talents needed to be successful in the game. This slight deviation in play, when successful, leads others to follow suit. Coaches call these strategies and incorporate them into game plans. This leads to the athletes accepting these strategies as just part of the game. From a moral perspective, the earlier these strategies are incorporated into the play, the more confusion this creates about acceptable behavior in the sport and in society.

Equality of Athletes

In the United States and throughout the world, sport has helped break down racial barriers and tensions and made upward movement within society a possibility. While barriers are much lower then they once were, barriers still exist. The hiring practices of the coaches and administrators of collegiate and professional sports teams frequently come under fire. Race often becomes an issue in who is interviewed and who is hired. In some sports, policies and rules are put in place to ensure that athletes representing racial minorities are given the opportunity to interview, although this is done to ensure that more athletes from racial minorities are hired.

Minority players in some sports and countries still face racism. In European football, the breakdown of homogeneity within teams has led fans to erupt in racist ways. Even the players from non-caucasian racial backgrounds playing for the home team are not immune to the abuse of fans. While great strides have been won, there is still far to go.

Over the last 40 years, the United States has been a leader in the idea of gender equality. Since the passage of Title IX, female athletes have fought for the right to compete in sport. Women have made great strides in expanding the number and types of sport they play. Sports such as ice hockey and lacrosse have different rules for men and women, and men are allowed more physical play than women. Even basketball is called differently for men than for women, leading many to cry foul about the differences. The perception is that women are weak and cannot play similar to or with the men. The perception is also that the product of women's sport is a lesser product and not worthy of prime time viewing.

Recent battles in the equality of athletes has centered on the able-bodied athlete and the disabled athlete in direct competition. Ideas of difference are being shattered as once-thought disabled athletes are competing with and beating athletes of all abilities. Technology has given those with disabilities the ability to compete at levels that were unheard of in the recent past. As technology improves, so will the capabilities of athletes who use cutting edge technology to help them compete in sport with a disability. Now an athlete who does not have legs cannot only run but the technology can make him or her competitive. It is not far fetched to see a day when the technology will allow disabled athletes an advantage in competition over able-bodied athletes. The technology may one day become similar to drug enhancement in sport, which causes ethical questions of fairness and equity to be brought to the forefront.

College Athletics

College sports, especially football and basketball, have become big money ventures for the conferences and individual schools at the Division I level. Earnings from the conference championships, the bowls, and from the NCAA basketball tournament can be a significant portion of a school's athletic budget.

Coaches are expected to consistently field a winner in a "what-have-you-done-for-me-lately" world. The salaries paid to top coaches run several million dollars per year, which is disproportionately higher than the salaries of the university president, athletic director, or top professors.

One of the areas of concern for ethical problems arises in the highly competitive arena of recruiting. Top athletes can bring much needed attention and revenues to a program. Coaches often skirt NCAA recruiting rules to ensure the athlete enrolls at their school. The NCAA has sanctioned schools for improper benefits and payments that go to a recruit or their representative.

As the pressure to win has grown, less of an emphasis has been on the student-athlete in the academic realm. A growing list of schools have been plagued by academic scandals. Recent years have seen university scandals consisting of athletes receiving credit for bogus courses, coaches paying tutors to write papers and complete academic assignments, and athletes not attending classes. Athletes have also been caught up in more mundane scandals as cheating in courses and in taking online tests, and using others to write their papers.

Conclusion

All of these issues raise certain questions about competition and our justifications for why competition is so important. The behaviors that exist, both positive and negative, are copied and accepted by others. As behaviors that run counter to a culture become entrenched in sport, the culture decides what is acceptable. As these issues filter down in sport, we change what sport is and what sport is to become. This also changes the ethics of the individuals who play the sport, and, ultimately, the society in which the sport exists. When the focus is on winning at all costs, these types of unseemly behavior enter into the equation. Coaches have a responsibility to be moral guides in the sport realm and to teach proper action.

Brian Richardson

See Also: Cheating in Sport; Coaching for Character; Coaching Philosophy; Discrimination in Sport; Race/Ethnicity and Sport Leadership.

Further Readings

Drewe, S. B. *Why Sport? An Introduction to the Philosophy of Sport.* Toronto: Thompson Educational Publishing, 2003.

Holowchak, M. A. *Philosophy of Sport: Critical Readings, Crucial Issues.* Upper Saddle River, NJ: Pearson Education, 2002.

Kretchmar, R. S. *Practical Philosophy of Sport and Physical Activity.* Champaign, IL: Human Kinetics, 2005.

Lumpkin, A., S. K. Stoll, and J. M. Beller. *Sport Ethics: Application for Fair Play.* New York: McGraw-Hill, 2003.

Malloy, D. C., S. Ross, and D. H. Zakus. *Sport Ethics: Concepts and Cases in Sport and Recreation.* Toronto: Thompson Educational Publishing, 2003.

Morgan, J. M., K. V. Meier, and A. J. Schneider. *Ethics in Sport.* Chaimpaign, IL: Human Kinetics, 2001.

Simon, R. L. *The Ethics of Coaching Sports: Moral, Social, and Legal Issues.* Boulder, CO: Westview Press, 2013.

Simon, R. L., C. R. Torres, and P. F. Hager. *Fair Play: The Ethics of Sport*, 4th ed. Boulder, CO: Westview Press, 2004.

F–G

FIFA World Cup

Football (soccer), the most widely played and watched sport on the planet, crowns a new national team champion in both men's and women's teams via an international tournament known as the World Cup and held every four years. The International Federation of Football Asoociation (Federation Internationale de Football Association, or FIFA) organizes this international competition that attracts the attention of billions of faithful followers across the globe. The 2014 men's champion was in Germany, and the 2012 women's champion was in Japan. The 2018 men's World Cup is scheduled to be held in Russia and the 2015 women's World Cup will be held in Canada.

FIFA comprises 209 soccer (football) associations and often is referred to as the United Nations of Football. For comparison, the United Nations recognizes 195 countries. The beginning of an international football competition under FIFA's authority was in the 1908 London Olympics, with five countries participating. Since then the World Cup has evolved to generate substantial revenue for FIFA. The 2014 Brazil World Cup produced revenues of almost $4 billion in total for FIFA, primarily from television and marketing rights from corporate partners like Adidas, Sony, Visa, and Coca-Cola.

FIFA Leadership on Sport and Cultural Issues
FIFA's mission and primary objective is "to improve the game of football constantly and promote it globally in the light of its unifying, educational, cultural and humanitarian values, particularly through youth and development programs." Its second objective is to organize international football competitions while uniting and inspiring the world through its competitions and events.

Scholars and fans question the promotion of educational and humanitarian values as evidenced by FIFA's influence on the Brazilian government. Many Brazilians felt that their government was spending too much money on hosting the 2014 World Cup (e.g., building stadiums rather than improving education and living and working conditions for its citizens).

A common response to this criticism would be that the spending is an investment in the lives of the citizens. However, in South Africa, where the World Cup was hosted in 2009, the results were disappointing. The South African government was convinced that the middle- and lower-economic classes would have employment opportunities due to the World Cup, which did not happen.

Another issue involves the process to select a World Cup host country. In 1978, Argentina was ruled by a military dictatorship that by all accounts was violating its citizens' rights. This country's selection led to a boycott of the event by two of the finest players: Johan Cruyff and Paul Breitner. Similarly, the choice for the 2022 World Cup, Qatar, is marred by claims of very poor working conditions and incidents of migrant construction worker fatalities while building the new stadiums.

FIFA Organizational Structure

FIFA comprises 209 member football associations and six international football associations—AFC (Asia), CAF (Africa), CONCACAF (North America and Caribbean), CONMEBOL (South America), OFC (Oceania), and UEFA (Europe). FIFA has a congress (legislative branch), executive committee (executive branch), general secretariat (administrative body), and committees (such as member development, finance, competitions and television/marketing) to perform the tasks of the organization. The head of the organization is the president of FIFA.

History

The first FIFA president was Robert Guerin of France. He served as the president of FIFA from 1904 to 1906. Guerin was responsible for creating FIFA's Foundation Act, which is an agreement of the first statutes with representatives from the first seven country members.

1906 International Competition, Athens

- *Number of countries*: Four (Denmark and three teams from Greece/Ottoman Empire)
- *Format*: Single elimination
- *Champion*: Denmark by disqualification
- Denmark was declared champion after one of the three Greek teams forfeited at halftime of the championship match. The event had very poor attendance.

1906 to 1918 FIFA President

- Daniel Burley Woolfall, England
- President of FIFA from 1906 to 1918
- Woolfall was instrumental in creating uniform football rules on an international level, drafting a new constitution for FIFA, including a football championship at the 1908 Olympic Games, and adding FIFA members from South America and North America. Woolfall died in 1918 while serving as FIFA president.

1908 Olympic Games, London, England

- *Number of countries*: Five (Great Britain, Denmark, the Netherlands, Sweden, France)
- *Champion*: Great Britain 2–0 over Denmark
- This competition is notable because it only allowed amateur players due to Olympic rules.

1912 Olympic Games, Stockholm, Sweden

- *Number of countries*: 11 (Great Britain, Denmark, Netherlands, Finland, Hungary, Norway, Austria, Russia, Germany, Italy, and Sweden)
- *Format*: Single elimination
- *Champion*: Great Britain 4–1 over Denmark

1916 to 1921

- Olympic Games cancelled due to World War I
- There was no FIFA president from 1918 to 1921, due to the breakout of World War 1.

1920 Olympic Games, Antwerp, Belgium.

- *Number of countries*: 14 teams
- *Format*: Single elimination
- *Champion*: Belgium by default as Czechoslovakia left the field in protest.
- This is the first intercontinental tournament with the inclusion of Egypt with the European countries.

1921 to 1954 FIFA President

- Jules Rimet, France
- President of FIFA from 1921 to 1954
- Following Woolfall's death in October 1918, FIFA remained without a leader due to the activity of World War 1. From 1921, Rimet's leadership of FIFA continued its growth internationally, and financially and led to the creation of the World Cup. During his tenure, FIFA membership grew from 20 countries to 85 countries. England, Wales, and Scotland left FIFA and did not compete in a FIFA event until the 1950 World Cup.

1924 Olympic Games, Paris, France

- *Number of countries*: 22 teams
- *Format*: Single elimination
- *Champion*: Uruguay 3–0 over Switzerland
- For the first time the Americas were represented in the competition thanks to Uruguay and the United States participating. Football had become so important to the games that by some calculations it had generated almost a third of the total income for the Olympic Games. In terms of participation this would be the biggest

international football tournament until the 1982 FIFA World Cup in Spain.

1928 Olympic Games, Amsterdam
- *Number of countries*: 17 teams
- *Format*: Single elimination
- *Champion*: Uruguay 2–1 over Argentina on replay match.
- Because of its Olympic success, in 1928 FIFA voted to create a World Cup Tournament starting in 1930. This would allow the best football players including professional players to compete, which they could not do previously according to Olympic amateur rules.

1930 World Cup, Uruguay
- *Number of countries*: 13
- *Format*: Four group winners made it to semifinals
- *Champion*: Uruguay 4–2 over Argentina
- *Bronze*: United States, although a game was not actually played.
- *Top Scorer*: Guillermo Stabile, Argentina
- Uruguay was chosen to host because it was the two time official world champion based on its gold medal wins in the 1924 and 1928 Olympic Games; it was also the only country prepared to pay all travel and hotel expenses. Until two months before the event started, no teams from Europe that had signed up to participate in the event. Eventually France, Yugoslavia, Romania, and Belgium agreed to travel to South America and play.

1934 World Cup, Italy
- *Number of countries*: 16 teams
- *Format*: Single elimination
- *Champion*: Italy 2–1 over Czechoslovakia
- *Bronze*: Germany 3–2 over Austria
- *Top Scorer*: Oldrich Nejedly, Czechoslovakia
- Uruguay became the only holder of the trophy not to defend its championship because of Italy's refusal to participate in the 1930 World Cup in Uruguay. This is the first World Cup that had radio broadcasts to 12 of the competing countries. Of the 16 nations qualified, only four were non-European: United States, Brazil, Argentina, and Egypt. There were no group

stages in this World Cup, just ordinary knock-out competition and a replay if the teams were tied at the end of the game, which included a 30-minute overtime. This World Cup championship would be the first in an unprecedented string of victories for the Italians.

1938 World Cup, France
- *Number of countries*: 15 teams
- *Format*: Single elimination
- *Champion*: Italy 4–2 over Hungary
- *Bronze*: Brazil 4–2 over Sweden
- *Top Scorer*: Leonidas da Silva, Brazil
- This World Cup is notable for a few national absences. Uruguay did not compete because it did not have the funds to travel to France. Argentina boycotted the event because it was not chosen as host country. Spain did not participate due to Civil War. Germany's annexation of Austria reduced the number of finalists from 16 to 15. Given the political climate, the presence of the German and Italian teams drew antifascist demonstrations, but while the German team headed home early, Vittorio Pozzo's Azzurri repeated as champions.

1950 World Cup, Brazil
- *Number of countries*: 13 teams
- *Format*: Group stage, then knockout stage
- *Champion*: Uruguay 2–1 over Brazil
- *Bronze*: Sweden 3–1 over Spain
- *Top Scorer*: Marques Ademir, Brazil
- Brazil built the world's biggest football stadium for the 1950 finals, but lost in front of 200,000 fans in the Maracana Stadium in one of the competition's great surprises, as Uruguay upset the Brazilians by scoring the winning goal 11 minutes before the end of regulation.

1954 to 1955 FIFA President
- Rodolphe Seeldrayers, Belguim
- President of FIFA from 1954 to 1955
- The shortest tenure for a FIFA President when he died in office in 1955.

1954 World Cup, Switzerland
- *Number of countries*: 16 teams
- *Format*: Group stage, then knockout stage

- *Champion*: West Germany 3–2 over Hungary
- *Bronze*: Austria 3–1 over Uruguay
- *Top Scorer*: Sandor Kocsis, Hungary
- This was the highest-scoring World Cup with 140 goals in 26 matches (five-plus per game).

1955 to 1961 FIFA President
- Arthur Drewry, England
- President of FIFA from 1955 to 1961
- Drewry was instrumental in bringing the British countries back to FIFA.

1958 World Cup, Sweden
- *Number of countries*: 16 teams
- *Format*: Group stage, then knockout stage
- *Champion*: Brazil 5–2 over Sweden
- *Bronze*: France 6–3 over West Germany
- *Top Scorer*: Just Fontaine, France
- Pelé became the youngest player to play a World Cup finals, the youngest scorer in a World Cup final and the youngest player to win a World Cup winner's medal. This tournament is the first time the FIFA World Cup received international television coverage.

1961 to 1974 FIFA President
- Stanley Rous, England
- President of FIFA from 1961 to 1974
- Rous is credited with turning the World Cup into a worldwide television event.

1962 World Cup, Chile
- *Number of countries*: 16 teams
- *Format*: Group stage, then knockout stage
- *Champion*: Brazil 3–1 over Czechoslovakia
- *Bronze*: Chile 3–1 over Yugoslavia
- *Top Scorers*: Florian Albert, Hungary; Garrincha, Brazil; Valentin Ivanov, Soviet Union; Drazan Jerkovic, Yugoslavia; Leonel Sanchez, Chile; and Vava, Brazil
- Chile, as host nation, and Brazil, as reigning World Cup champions, were granted automatic qualification, with the remaining 14 finals places were divided among the continental confederations. The16 teams that qualified for the tournament, divided into four groups of four.

1966 World Cup, England
- *Number of countries*: 16 teams
- *Format*: Group stage, then knockout stage
- *Champion*: England 4–2 over West Germany
- *Bronze*: Portugal 2–1 over Soviet Union
- *Top Scorer*: Eusebio, Portugal
- Teams from the African continent withdrew in protest of a system FIFA had created of complicated elimination playoffs between Africa and Asia/Oceania group winners, thus not guaranteeing a single spot for an African nation in the World Cup. This World Cup had the first live, global television coverage.

1970 World Cup, Mexico
- *Number of countries*: 16 teams
- *Format*: Group stage, then knockout stage
- *Champion*: Brazil 4–1 over Italy
- *Bronze*: West Germany 1–0 over Uruguay
- *Top Scorer*: Gerd Muller, West Germany
- The first World Cup broadcast in color around the globe, as millions of fans watched Pele's Brazilian team win a third world crown.

1974 World Cup, West Germany
- *Number of countries*: 16 teams
- *Format*: Group stage, then knockout stage
- *Champion*: West Germany 2–1 over the Netherlands
- *Bronze*: Poland 1–0 over Brazil
- *Top Scorer*: Grzegorz Lato, Poland
- Dutch Total Football style of play was introduced to the world, led by charismatic Johan Cruyff, all the way to the World Cup final where it met the West German squad led by Franz Beckenbauer. The hosts managed a come-from-behind victory to claim their second World Cup in 20 years.

1974 to 1998 FIFA President
- Joao Havelange, Brazil
- President of FIFA from 1974 to 1998
- Havelange's leadership led to the creation of the Women's World Cup tournament in 1991. The men's World Cup included more teams from Asia, Africa, and North America.

1978 World Cup, Argentina

- *Number of countries*: 16 teams
- *Format*: Group stage, then knockout stage
- *Champion*: Argentina 3–1 over Netherlands
- *Bronze*: Brazil 2–1 over Italy
- *Top Scorer*: Mario Kempes, Argentina
- Perhaps the most controversial World Cup. Because of the military regime in Argentina at the time, the Netherlands' player Johan Cruyff and German star Paul Breitner refused to take part boycotting to protest Argentina's treatment of political opponents through torture and executions.
- FIFA introduced the penalty shoot-out as a means of determining the winner in knockout stages, should the match end on a draw after 120 minutes.

1982 World Cup, Spain

- *Number of countries*: 24 teams
- *Format*: Group stage, then knockout stage
- *Champion*: Italy 3–1 over West Germany
- *Bronze*: Poland 3–2 over France
- *Top Scorer*: Paolo Rossi, Italy
- Italy became world champion for the third time in 1982. The 12th FIFA World Cup was the last to feature a fully leather ball, and it invited 24 teams to the tournament rather than the traditional 16 teams. The tournament was also notable for the first-ever penalty shoot-out in a World Cup finals. West Germany beat France 5–4 on penalties after a dramatic 3–3 in the semifinals in a match often regarded as one of the best World Cup games of all time.

1986 World Cup, Mexico

- *Number of countries*: 24 teams
- *Format*: Group stage, then knockout stage
- *Champion*: Argentina 3–2 over West Germany
- *Bronze*: France 3–2 over Belgium
- *Top Scorer*: Gary Lineker, England
- Most fans remember this World Cup, as Diego Maradona's cup, both because of the "Hand of God" goal he scored against England, another goal where he dribbled through the entire English squad. Most fans consider this goal to be the best ever scored in a World Cup game.

- The two-phase group-stage format used since 1974 was now dropped and replaced by the knockout format. Now, the four best third-placed teams would join the six group winners and runners-up into the knockout stage round of 16.

1990 World Cup, Italy

- *Number of countries*: 24 teams
- *Format*: Group stage, then knockout stage
- *Champion*: West Germany 1–0 over Argentina
- *Bronze*: Italy 2–1 over England
- *Top Scorer*: Salvatore Schillaci, Italy
- This World Cup saw the African nation of Cameroon, led by 38-year-old Roger Milla, reach the quarterfinals where it narrowly lost to England. The team advanced further than any African nation had ever managed in a World Cup before.

1991 Women's World Cup, China

- *Number of countries*: 12 teams
- *Format*: Group stage, then knockout stage
- *Champion*: United States 2–1 over Norway
- *Bronze*: Sweden 4–0 over Germany
- *Top Scorer*: Michelle Akers, United States
- The inaugural Women's World Cup saw the United States become the first champions.

1994 World Cup, United States

- *Number of countries*: 24 teams
- *Format*: Group stage, then knockout stage
- *Champion*: Brazil over Italy in penalties
- *Bronze*: Sweden 4–0 over Bulgaria
- *Top Scorer*: Oleg Salenko, Russia
- The 15th World Cup was staged by the United States and drew record crowds because the games were held in American football stadiums. The U.S. tournament attracted a record total attendance of 3,587,538 spectators and a per-game average of nearly 69,000.

1995 Women's World Cup, Sweden

- *Number of countries*: 12 teams
- *Format*: Group stage, then knockout stage
- *Champion*: Norway 2–0 over Germany
- *Bronze*: United States 2-0 over China PR
- *Top Scorer*: Ann Kristin Aarones, Norway

- This event featured the first woman to referee a FIFA World Cup final, Sweden's Ingrid Jonsson.

1998– FIFA President
- Joseph (Sepp) S. Blatter, Switzerland
- President of FIFA since 1998
- Blatter has presided over a record five World Cup finals. He formed an alliance with UNICEF to increase FIFA's humanitarian role throughout the world. His tenure, however, has been plagued with rumors of bribery and corruption.

1998 World Cup, France
- *Number of countries*: 32 teams
- *Format*: Group stage, then knockout stage
- *Champion*: France 3–0 over Brazil
- *Bronze*: Croatia 2–1 over Netherlands
- *Top Scorer*: Davor Suker, Croatia
- The 16th World Cup saw an increase in the number of finalists to 32 teams for the first time. The win in the final game gave France its first World Cup title, becoming the sixth national team after Uruguay, Italy, England, West Germany, and Argentina to win the tournament on its home soil.

1999 Women's World Cup, United States
- *Number of countries*: 16 teams
- *Format*: Group stage, then knockout stage
- *Champion*: United States 0–0 (5–4 penalty shoot out) over China PR
- *Bronze*: Brazil 0–0 (5–4 penalty shoot out) over Norway
- *Top Scorer*: SISSI (Sisleide Lima de Amor), Brazil
- This event featured all 32 games broadcast live on television and a women's attendance record of 90,185 watch the final match at the Rose Bowl in Pasadena, California.

2002 World Cup, Korea/Japan
- *Number of countries*: 32 teams
- *Format*: Group stage, then knockout stage
- *Champion*: Brazil 2–0 over Germany
- *Bronze*: Turkey 3–2 over South Korea
- *Top Scorer*: Ronaldo, Brazil
- For the first time, the tournament was held in Asia, and by two countries instead of the customary single-host country. This World Cup featured teams from five continents. Brazil's captain Cafu became the first player to appear in three consecutive World Cups. It was Brazil's fifth time winning football's ultimate prize.

2003 Women's World Cup, United States
- *Number of countries*: 16 teams
- *Format*: Group stage, then knockout stage
- *Champion*: Germany 2–1 over Sweden
- *Bronze*: United States 3–1 over Canada
- *Top Scorer*: Birgit Prinz, Germany
- This tournament was moved from China due to a severe acute respiratory syndrome (SARS) outbreak. The decision to move the tournament was made in late May 2003 and the tournament began in September.

2006 World Cup, Germany
- *Number of countries*: 32 teams
- *Format*: Group stage, then knockout stage
- *Champion*: Italy over France in penalties 5–3
- *Bronze*: Germany 3–1 over Portugal
- *Top Scorer*: Miroslava Klose, Germany
- In a final game was made memorable when France's Zinedine Zidane's headbutted Italy's Marco Materazzi. Italy went on to win their fourth World Cup.

2007 Women's World Cup, China
- *Number of countries*: 16 teams
- *Champion*: Germany 2–0 over Brazil
- *Bronze*: United States 4–1 over Norway
- *Top Scorer*: Marta, Brazil
- Germany won the World Cup by not allowing a goal in six of its matches.

2010 World Cup, South Africa
- *Number of countries*: 32 teams
- *Format*: Group stage, then knockout stage
- *Champion*: Spain 1–0 over the Netherlands
- *Bronze*: Germany 3–2 over Uruguay
- *Top Scorer*: Thomas Muller, Germany
- Africa's first FIFA World Cup will be remembered as much for the spirit and smiles of the host nation as for the success of a Spanish team that achieved its own first victory at a

final World Cup game. South Africa failed to qualify in out group stage play, becoming the first host nation to bow out in the first round. Ghana was the only African nation to advance and reach the quarterfinals where it fell to Uruguay in a dramatic penalty shootout.

2011 Women's World Cup, Germany
- *Number of countries*: 16 teams
- *Format*: Group stage, then knockout stage
- *Champion*: Japan 2–2 (3–1 penalty shoot-out) over United States
- *Bronze*: Sweden 2–1 over France
- *Top Scorer*: Homare Sawa, Japan
- Over 845,711 fans attended the matches in Germany. Because of the phenomenal attendance, the Women's World Cup will increase the number of teams from 16 to 24 at the next tournament.

2014 World Cup, Brazil
- *Number of countries*: 24 teams
- *Format*: Group stage, then knockout stage
- *Champion*: Germany 1–0 over Argentina
- *Bronze*: Netherlands 3–0 over Brazil
- *Top Scorer*: James Rodriguez, Colombia
- Brazil's tournament was extraordinary in many ways, with packed stadiums, passionate crowds, upsets, and a record number of goals scored. It witnessed the first European title winner in the Americas. Some innovations that were present for the first time were the goal-line technology that helped confirm whether the ball had crossed the goal line, and the use of vanishing foam by referees to mark where the ball was to be placed for a free kick and to mark the 10-yard line for the defending team.

Future World Cup Locations
- 2015 Women's World Cup, Canada
- 2018 Men's World Cup, Russia
- 2019 Women's World Cup, in the bidding process during 2014
- 2022 Men's World Cup, Qatar

George Vazenios

See Also: Identification With Sports Teams; Ranking Teams; Team Culture.

Further Readings
FIFA. "History." http://www.fifa.com/classicfootball/history/fifa/more-associations-follow.html (Accessed September 2014).
FIFA. "1938 FIFA World Cup." http://www.funtrivia.com/en/subtopics/1938-FIFA-World-Cup-275445.html (Accessed September 2014).
Legg, Paul. "The 1954 World Cup: Triumph of a New Germany." History Today. http://www.historytoday.com/paul-legg/1954-world-cup-triumph-new-germany (Accessed October 2014).
Stevenson, Jonathan. "The Story of the 1978 World Cup." BBC.co.uk. http://www.bbc.co.uk/blogs/legacy/jonathanstevenson/2010/05/the_story_of_the_1978_world_cu.html (Accessed October 2014).
Sportsnet.ca. "2010 World Cup: Spain Finally Comes Good." http://www.sportsnet.ca/soccer/world-cup-2014/2010-world-cup-spain-finally-comes-good (Accessed September 2014).

Formula One Auto Racing

The Formula One (Formula 1, F1) Championship is the highest class of single-seat auto racing that is recognized by the international governing body of motorsports, the FIA (Federation Internationale de l'Automobile). The term *formula* refers to the unique set of rules and regulations governing the cars. All participants' cars must comply with these rules and regulations. "One" denotes the status of the championships as the highest level of motorsport race in the world. Today, the Formula One world championship is arguably the pinnacle of motor racing and the most prestigious annual motorsports event on a global scale. Nevertheless, the business of Formula One has faced and is still facing various challenges and shifts.

Origins and Current Global Reach of Formula One
The Formula One series arose from the European Grand Prix motor racing of the 1920s and 1930s. Grand Prix motor racing, in turn, originated from organized automobile racing, which began in Europe by

the end of 1890s. The major races were first brought together in the inaugural Formula One world championship in 1950. This race was held in Silverstone, United Kingdom. The first championship, which had seven rounds, included races in Britain, Monaco, Switzerland, Belgium, France, Italy, and the United States. While Europe was Formula One's traditional base, in recent years Formula One has attempted to expand beyond the traditional European and North American markets. Especially during the last decade, Formula One's scope has significantly expanded; still, almost half of each year's races are hosted in Europe. Between the years 1950 and 2000, races in Europe and North and South America always existed. Starting in 1985, races in Asia and the Middle East entered the calendar. In the 2014 season, 11 out of 19 races were held outside Europe. The respective shift has occurred as a result of the marketing strategy of Formula One. The money that flows through Formula One makes it attractive to cities that earn the rights to host Formula One events. There are several studies reporting the economic gains and other results of hosting a Formula One race.

A New Era

Bernie Ecclestone deserves most of the credit for transforming the sport into today's multibillion-dollar business. He first bought a team in 1971 and later became a member of the Formula One Constructors' Association (FOCA), which was an organization for the chassis constructors who design and build the cars that race in the FIA Formula One World Championship. Ecclestone used his position in the FOCA to leverage control over Formula One, and by the beginning of 1970s, Ecclestone had rearranged the management of Formula One's commercial rights. At that time, the circuit owners were controlling the income of the teams and negotiating with each team individually. They were paying little attention to securing commercial agreements with each of the racetracks. These agreements covered trackside advertising, gate money, hospitality and, more important, television rights. In 1978, Ecclestone became the executive of FOCA. He brought the racing teams together and offered a set sum in exchange for the exclusive rights to the teams. Television coverage and other commercial availabilities were packaged and marketed by a series of companies controlled by him.

Additionally, Ecclestone very wisely sensed Formula One's potential as a television sport. Under the patronage of Ecclestone, the championship boomed commercially, attracting bigger sponsors and larger television audiences.

Current Management Structure

Currently the Formula One Group, which consists of a group of companies, is responsible for the promotional rights of the FIA Formula One World Championship. Formula One Management (FOM) is the main operating company of the group and controls the broadcasting, organization, and promotional rights of Formula One. Bernie Ecclestone runs the company, but the Formula One Group is ultimately owned by Delta Topco, a New Jersey-based company, which is in turn owned primarily by investment companies CVC Capital Partners, Waddell & Reed, and the LBI Group. The remaining ownership is split between Ecclestone, other investment companies, and company directors. CVC Capital Partners, which is Formula One's largest shareholder, will be forced to sell its 35 percent stake in the business by July 2015 unless the majority of its investors agree otherwise.

Latest Developments

With total revenues expected to reach almost $3.3 billion in 2016, Formula One is currently one of the major sport enterprises worldwide. The sport's annual commercial rights alone produce $1.5 billion, and its top teams, backed by some of the largest global corporations, have budgets of over $400 million.

In addition to this, the Formula One culture has changed drastically since the early 2000s. Specifically, toward the end of the 2000s, Formula One headed to the dominant emerging markets such as Abu Dhabi, Malaysia, Turkey, and China. For the business of Formula One, this change has meant expanding its market reach. From the perspective of host destinations, hosting a Formula One race represents significant economic, environmental, and social impacts. But considering the high sanctions fees, which can amount to $45 million per year not including operational costs—which are covered mostly by public funds—hosting a Formula One race has become risky. In some recent cases, the hosting of a Grand Prix was unprofitable, bringing these events to an end. This situation is a clear

Nick Heidfeld and Nico Rosberg race on the street circuit in the 2008 Australian Grand Prix. The Formula One season consists of a series of races held worldwide on purpose-built circuits and public roads, and are known as Grand Prix. (Wikimedia Commons)

indication of the importance of having proper social impact assessments and full public consultation before going into the bidding process.

From the manufacturer's side, most of the Formula One teams have been incurring financial losses. Formula One teams mostly aim to break even. They intend to spend all the revenue available to them. Research indicates that Formula One teams' losses have totalled almost 320 million pounds between 2009 and 2012; in 2012, only three teams turned a profit. This environment makes it challenging for a manufacturer to stay in the business and cover the expenses alone. As a result of this, manufacturers like Honda, BMW, and Toyota withdrew from Formula One racing at the end of the 2000s. Since 2004, six car manufacturers have reduced their stakes or exited the sport entirely. Manufacturers are partnering with various companies in order to survive and focus on their core business. On the other hand, the companies buying stakes and partnering with the manufacturers evaluate their return of investments primarily by calculating their brands' on-screen exposure. For instance, between the years 2008 and 2013, Red Bull gained an estimated $1.6 billion in advertising value equivalent from Formula One. This sum alone offsets the $1.2 billion it spent on Red Bull Racing as well as on its investment in a second team, Toro Rosso.

The vast amount of Formula One teams' budgets goes to engine development and production, employee wages (teams can recruit up to 600 to 650 employees), manufacturing and research costs, and multifarious costs (traveling, catering, tests, fuel, events, etc.). The cost of competing in Formula One has increased dramatically as a result of the technological advances and safety standards of the 1990s. The teams are spending a large amount on research and development. As a result of these high costs, the FIA is almost continuously in search of new ways to cut costs.

With a long history of tradition, the business of Formula One is obligated to adapt to a changing world to fulfill the needs of its various stakeholders and remain viable. These adaptations will include innovations in racing technology as well as attempts to become more environmentally friendly. All of these strategies aim to keep Formula One races relevant and profitable in an increasingly global world.

Cem Tinaz

See Also: Brand Management and Leadership; Legal Responsibilities for Managers and Owners; NASCAR.

Further Readings

Formula1.com. "The F1 Brand-A Powerful Symbol of Excellence." http://www.formula1.com/inside_f1/f1brand.html (Accessed July 2014).

Morrison, M. "Formula One." *Autoweek*. http://www.autoweek.com/article/20110603/f1/110609963 (Accessed July 2014).

Mehrotra, K. and A. MacAskill. "Formula One Brings $650 Million Race to New Delhi After Struggles in Asia." Bloomberg News. http://www.bloomberg.com/news/2011-10-28/formula-one-brings-650-million-race-to-new-delhi-after-struggles-in-asia.html (Accessed July 2014).

Sylt, Christian. "Formula One to Get New Owner by Next Year." *The Telegraph.* http://www.telegraph .co.uk/finance/newsbysector/banksandfinance/ privateequity/10979212/Formula-One-to-get-new -owner-by-next-year.html (Accessed July 2014).

Sylt, Christian. "Revealed: Red Bull's $1.2 Billion Bet On Formula One." *Forbes.* http://www.forbes.com/sites/ csylt/2014/04/03/revealed-red-bulls-1-2-billion-bet -on-formula-one/ (Accessed July 2014).

Williamson, Martin. "A Brief History of Formula One." http://en.espnf1.com/f1/motorsport/story/3831.html (Accessed July 2014).

Gender and Sports Leadership

In order to understand gender relations in present-day sport it is first important to reflect on the past. For the past 3,000 years or so, Western cultural ideology has been grounded in patriarchy. This has enabled men to have power over women and the services they provide. In essence, patriarchal ideology defines females as inferior to males. As modern sport began to develop (in the latter period of the 19th century), it served as one of the most powerful cultural forces for reinforcing the ideology of male superiority and dominance. According to G. Sage and D. Eitzen, "organized sport created symbols, rituals, and values that preserved patriarchy and women's subordinate status in society." People celebrated the sporting achievements of men while they marginalized women into the roles of spectators and cheerleaders. Sport was seen as for males and not for females; it was created by and for men. This popular belief system enabled sport culture to become the exclusive domain of males. Today, modern sport continues to be male-dominated, male-identified, and male-centered.

Leadership Opportunities for Women

More than 40 years after the enactment of Title IX, a law which stated that "No person in the United States shall, on the basis of sex, be excluded from participation in, be denied the benefits of, or be subjected to discrimination under any education program or activity receiving Federal financial assistance", there are more female intercollegiate athletes than ever before (over 200,000). Despite the participation levels of females being at an all-time high, the representation of women in leadership positions in sport organizations remains discouraging.

According to R. Acosta and L. Carpenter, there are currently 13,963 female professionals who are employed within intercollegiate athletics. This number represents coaches, assistant coaches, sports information directors, athletic trainers, athletics administrators, and strength and conditioning coaches. To date, this is the highest number on record. Even still, upon closer examination of Acosta and Carpenter's findings one can easily begin to see the disparities in leadership opportunities. In 2014, only 43.4 percent of women's teams are coached by a female whereas 97 to 98 percent of men's teams are coached by a male. Only 22.3 percent of National Collegiate Athletic Association (NCAA) programs have athletic directors that are female (239 females serve as athletic directors in all divisions combined) whereas 77.7 percent are males. Furthermore, 11.3 percent of athletic departments have no female representation anywhere in the administration. Last, only 12.1 percent of sports information directors (SID) are female whereas 87.9 percent are males.

Similarly, the pattern of men dominating in the leadership of women's sport prevails at the professional level. Women are sparsely found in leadership positions in professional team sports. For example, in the Womens' National Basketball Association (WNBA) during the 2011 season, six of the 12 head coaches were men while 11 of the 19 assistant coaches were women. Despite the ownership and management consisting predominantly of men, women do own four of the 12 teams in the WNBA. One owner in particular, Sheila C. Johnson, is the first African American woman to be an owner of a professional sports franchise. In fact, she is an owner or partner in three professional sports franchises: the Washington Capitals (National Hockey League), the Washington Wizards (National Basketball Association), and the Washington Mystics (WNBA).

Beyond coaching and ownership, men have a powerful presence from top to bottom in most women's professional sports, while women's involvement in professional men's sports remains extremely uncommon. Women continue to be greatly underrepresented as sportswriters, sports officials, judges, commissioners, athletic trainers, racehorse trainers, and most other sports-related occupations.

The above statistics provide a small glimpse into the scarcity of female leadership opportunities. These examples appear to be the prevailing trend in sports organizations as well as in other powerful societal institutions. Numerous scholars have highlighted how women are excluded and/or underrepresented in coaching and administration throughout the world. The question then becomes, why is it so difficult for women to make it to the top? Despite the tremendous amount of social change that has taken place over the last couple of decades, sport still remains a man's world. Organizational and institutional practices that favor men and disadvantage women are still firmly in place.

Gender Inequities in Sports Leadership

According to research by I. Henry and L. Robinson, the major reasons for the underrepresentation of women in coaching and administration are as follows: (1) women are not considered for half of all coaching and administration jobs due to the mistaken belief that women cannot meet the expectations in men's sports; (2) men use well-established connections with other men in sport organizations to help them obtain jobs in both women's and men's sports; (3) job search committees are primarily composed of men who use evaluative criteria based on dominant gender ideology, which causes them to perceive female applicants as being less qualified than male applicants; (4) many women have not had the support systems and career development opportunities that many men have had; (5) women may not choose careers in coaching and administration because they know they would face challenges working in sport organizations that are male-dominated, male-identified, and male-centered (i.e., they may be judged more harshly than the men); and (6) women are more likely to experience sexual harassment, which sets them up to fail and/or discourages them from remaining in coaching and administrative jobs.

Various scholars have recommended innumerable strategies to address some of the aforementioned barriers. Some of these strategies include (but are not limited to) implementing gender-neutral hiring policies (i.e., insisting on fair and open employment practices), offering additional training/education (i.e., workshops focusing on the identification of subtle or overt discrimination), assisting with time management/support, and offering additional mentoring/networking opportunities (i.e., women's hiring networks). Unless changes are made, gender equity will never be achieved in coaching and administration. According to J. Coakley, achieving gender equity requires action by people possessing the critical awareness needed to transform gender ideology; it involves both men and women and a willingness to critically assess how sports are conducted today.

Gender and Leadership Effectiveness

Another explanation for women's underrepresentation in elite leadership positions points to the undervaluation of women's effectiveness as leaders. This explanation is supported by several theoretical perspectives including (but not limited to) lack of fit theory, role congruity theory, expectation states theory, and the think manager-think male paradigm. In essence, men may be seen as more effective leaders in male-dominated or senior leadership positions due to the masculine nature of these roles.

Discourses of masculinity (being confident, strong, assertive, and independent) are generally more valued than discourses of femininity (being warm, kind, helpful, gentle, etc.) in sports organizations. As such, women who want to succeed in an environment that celebrates masculine discourses must then embrace masculine work practices. Unfortunately, when some women express said masculinities they may then risk being accused of trying to "act like men" and fail to be taken seriously. Furthermore, this behavior (the embracing of a masculine discourse) may challenge some men's assumptions about what is acceptable behavior for women.

In order for women to become successful within sport organizations they need to learn how to negotiate both masculine and feminine discourses where appropriate. Is this the solution? S. Shaw and L. Hober propose something different. Instead of having women attempt a difficult and daunting balancing act, they assert that people need to adopt more inclusive managerial styles in order to improve individuals' experiences within sport organizations. Achieving an equitable organizational culture will not be possible if people fail to recognize the value and importance of both feminine and masculine discourses.

Katherine M. Polasek

See Also: Behavioral Leadership Theory; Comparative Models of Sports Leadership; Development of Leadership Skills; Leadership Models in Sports; Relational Model of Leadership; Transformational Leadership; Women's Leadership in Sport.

Further Readings

Acosta, R. Vivian, and Linda Carpenter. "Women in Intercollegiate Sport: A Longitudinal National Study—Thirty-Seven Year Update." http://www.acostacarpenter.org (Accessed September 2014).

Ayman, Roya, and Karen Korabik. "Leadership—Why Gender and Culture Matter." *American Psychologist,* v.65/3 (2010).

Brown, Sue, and Richard Light. "Women's Sport Leadership Styles as the Result of Interaction Between Feminine and Masculine Approaches." *Asia-Pacific Journal of Health, Sport, and Physical Education,* v.3/3 (2012).

Coakley, Jay. *Sports in Society: Issues and Controversies.* New York: McGraw-Hill Education, 2015,

Diacin, Michael, and Seung Lim. "Female Representation Within Intercollegiate Athletics Departments." *The Sport Journal* (November 21, 2012).

Henry, Ian, and Leah Robinson. "Gender Equality and Leadership in Olympic Bodies." http://www.olympic.org/Documents/Olympism_in_action/Women_and_sport/GENDER_EQUALITY_AND_LEADERSHIP_IN_OLYMPIC_BODIES.pdf (Accessed July 2014).

Hovden, Jordin. "Female Top Leaders—Prisoners of Gender? The Gendering of Leadership Discourses in Norwegian Sports Organizations." *International Journal of Sport Policy,* v.2/2 (2010).

Paustian-Underdahl, Samantha, Lisa Walker, and David Woehr. "Gender and Perceptions of Leadership Effectiveness: A Meta-Analysis of Contextual Moderators." *Journal of Applied Psychology,* v.99/6 (November 2014).

Sage, G., and D. Eitzen. *Sociology of North American Sport.* New York: Oxford University Press, 2013.

Shaw, Sally, and Lorena Hoeber. "A Strong Man is Direct and a Direct Woman is a Bitch: Gendered Discourses and Their Influences on Employment Roles in Sport Organizations." *Journal of Sport Management,* v.17 (2003).

H

Health Issues in Sports

Health issues in sports are concerns regarding the health and well-being of people practicing sports or physical activities. The safeguarding of the body, its protection against diseases, and the preservation or the improvement of its performances are what characterize common health concerns. From one era to another ideas have changed and some different paradigms concerning body and health have followed one another. Some were based on rational scientific research, trying to propose recommendations to strengthen the body through diets and everyday life hygiene, and some were purely chimerical, based on nonrational or prescientific knowledge.

In this context, the idea of managing health through physical exercise is not totally new; for example, the Scottish physician George Cheyne (1671–1743) proposed to develop health through "natural" exercises such as walking. Additionally, the importance of exercise was not unknown to Hippocrates, Galen, and Luigi Cornaro. Similarly, pharmacology, herbals, and their derivates tried to reach the same goals through the absorption of artificial or natural products. What these strategies had in common was the objective of delaying aging through diet or lifestyle.

Health Determinants and Issues in Sports

The current trend in health studies is to consider health in a dynamic rather than static perspective. In this view, health is the result of a constant interaction between the individual and his or her environment. Health conditions of both the individual and the overall population are composed of several dimensions influenced by different determinants that affect physical, mental, and psychosocial health.

Starting from this perspective, physical activities and sports practice can be considered as a particular and specific determinant that can positively or negatively affect both the individual's global health condition and that of the whole population. Sports addiction phenomena, dehydration, injuries, eating disorders, drug abuse, doping, and sports-related death are some examples of negative affection. The enhancement of the global health condition and hygiene, social integration, and education through sports are some examples of positive affection influencing both biomedical and psychosocial aspects of health. Health concerns are in fact diverse. Self-protection strategies against diseases or senescence are strongly influenced by collective cultures and health care policies that always obey the social contexts. Cultural landscapes and social contexts influence individuals, as they bring the variety of traditions, the diversity of lifestyles, the rules of the institutions, and the multiplicity of health policies. All these aspects influence both health issues in sports practice and the role of sports and physical activities in health management.

Since sport practice stimulates health conditions, the need to develop healthy and sporty lifestyles comes as a consequence. An individual's hygiene is strongly linked to the management of physical condition in order to make sure that good health becomes a constant revolving aspect. In other words, healthy regular exercises become some progress factors when they promote or improve global and/or individual health.

Physical Activity and Sports as Common Good

In Western societies, issues of public and private health are imposed on society as well as instructions. For many citizens, health benefits seem as legitimate as the ability to read and write, or the need to have electricity or (warm) water at home. In this perspective, which is currently dominant in Western societies, sports are perceived as a means of public and individual health. Because of this, sociocultural, health, and sports facilities are integrated with health, a collective heritage system that is guaranteed by policy makers. The community as a whole should benefit from the healthy benefits of sports and physical activity.

Furthermore, each citizen's behaviors differ depending on whether he or she considers himself or herself responsible for his or her health or, conversely, he or she believes that this responsibility falls to physicians, national health services, or health insurance. Based on this distinction, the strategies to improve or maintain health can differ in the following ways: (1) the citizen or the community can try to eliminate the causes and conditions of development of diseases by acting on the environment (improving housing conditions, channeling water, fighting against pollution, promoting road safety and sanitary control, encouraging health screening and health checks, and so on); and (2) personal hygiene (optimizing lifestyles, practicing sports). This is primary prevention.

Health Issues in Sports and Lifestyles

A last aspect to be considered to better understand the interaction between sports and health issues is the fact that in the 20th century, sports and health became a sort of commodity integrated within the consumption society; thus, these practices are considered as both a source of health, a common good, and a key component of lifestyles.

In Western countries, the cause of increased morbidity is to be found increasingly in lifestyles and behaviors: overeating, nervous stress, smoking, alcohol,

car accidents, and workplace injuries are among the main causes of mortality. The consumption society erased some typologies of morbidity that can still be found in developing countries, but it facilitated the development of some exogenous pathologies.

On the one hand, sports and physical activities are supposed to be used to fight against smoking, alcoholism, sociopathy, mental illness, or any kind of delinquency. Otherwise, they are supposed to promote self-care, not only by improving physical or mental performances but by introducing new health objectives. In this perspective, one must distinguish between competitive and recreational sports, since the latter are practiced outside of any organized structure. Some new needs emerged and led to a new symbolic universe related to physical activities and sports, which are now invested with the expectation of producing a new relationship with nature. The natural element makes the difference between simple health and the wholeness of life.

This means that, beyond the conventional body ailments, today the notion of health embraces all that is psychosomatic, especially all the tensions affecting everyday life and individuals' equilibrium. Having a "good" lifestyle means to be able to address these criticalities through self-control. The relationship between body and physical activities (or sports) has become more and more significant today.

Alessandro Porrovecchio

See Also: Amateur Sports; Coaching Inclusive Sport and Disability; Drugs, Doping; Injury; Preventive Discipline; Recreational Versus Competitive Sport.

Further Readings

Biddle, Stuart J. H., Kenneth R. Fox, and Stephen H. Boutcher. *Physical Activity and Psychological Well-Being.* London: Routledge, 2000.

Evans, John, Brian Davies, and Jan Wright. *Body Knowledge and Control.* London: Routledge, 2004.

Hardman, Arianne E., and David J. Stensel. *Physical Activity and Health: The Evidence Explained.* London: Routledge, 2009.

Kelly, John R., and Valeria J. Freysinger. *21st Century Leisure: Current Issues.* State College, PA: Venture Publishing, 2004.

High School Sports

During the 2012 to 2013 school year, a record 7,713,577 students participated in high school sports, up from 7,692,520 in 2011 to 2012. With the numbers of participants growing, it is vital that parents and community members understand the structure of high school sports. While many community members and parents like to think that the emphasis should be on winning, the emphasis in high school sports is on education.

Each state has a state high school athletic or activities association that is affiliated with the National Federation of State High School Associations (NFHS). The state association, a not-for-profit entity, comprises schools that become members of the association. Member schools, when joining, agree to abide by the regulations and bylaws of the state association. In addition, while schools agree to abide by the state association rules, schools may establish school rules that are more strict but not more lenient than the rules of the state association. As members of the state association, high schools compete in state tournaments, normally held in a sequential order of regional, sectional, and state, and normally schools are placed in divisions that contain other schools of comparable student populations. Some tournaments are seeded according to season records, while in other sports all member schools in a geographical area compete with no seeding involved.

Monetary proceeds of tournaments are generally shared with the teams competing at each level with the greatest amount designated for teams that advance to the state tournament level. The season regulations, eligibility rules, and bylaws vary from state to state. As a result, an infraction in one state may not be treated in a similar fashion in another state. Second, while some states operate with a committee structure that involves coaches, athletic directors, educational administrators, and the executive office, other states may not have as comprehensive a committee organizational structure. Individuals in each state should check the name, location, and structure of their state association for specific information.

Eligibility Rules

Most state associations have eligibility rules covering the following categories: participation, age, amateur status, nonschool participation, residence and transfer, physical exam, codes of conduct, and sportsmanlike behavior. For clarity, examples will follow of each type of rule. Participation rules refer to the status of students at a school. Most state associations require that athletes be full-time students at a school, and require that foreign exchange students must meet special conditions. The normal age requirement at most state associations requires that students are ineligible for competition if he/she reaches his/her 19th birthday before August of any given school year. The purpose of this rule is to prevent students who have an unfair advantage in terms of strength from playing. The rule also applies to athletes who have started high school late or who have not yet graduated.

Amateur status requires that a student competing for his/her high school must be an amateur in all sports recognized by the association. For example, if the association did not have bowling as a recognized sport, a student could be a professional bowler and still compete in other sports recognized by the association. The nonschool participation rule exists to prevent students from competing for a club team at the same time they are competing for their school team in the same sport. Residence rules require students to be residents within the boundaries of the school district or enrolled in a legal open enrollment program in order to compete for the school. The transfer rules set forth the parameters under which students can transfer and be eligible, and those situations under which students who transfer will not be declared eligible. The physical exam rule determines how often a student must undergo a physical exam to compete. Similar to this rule is the concussion rule established to determine protocol if a concussion is suspected and to hold a student out of a contest if he or she is momentarily unconscious.

The codes of conduct vary from school to school, but all include the state association rules and the school's rules to cover such incidents as the use of alcohol, tobacco, or drugs; presence at a party where alcohol is being consumed; and other behavior rules deemed important for athletes to follow. It should be noted that participation in high school sports has been deemed by numerous courts to be a privilege and not a right and that schools can hold athletes to higher standards than other students. The regulations regarding sportsmanlike behavior relate directly to the educational nature of high school sports and to functioning respectfully within society.

The 10 most popular boys' sports during the 2012 to 2013 school year were baseball, basketball, cross country, football, golf, soccer, swimming, tennis, track and field, and wrestling; and the same sports for the girls, with the exception of competitive spirit squads in place of wrestling, volleyball in place of football, and softball instead of baseball.

The National Federation of High Schools (NFHS) rules are used for most sports unless there is another set of rules historically used for the sport such as U.S. Tennis Association Rules for tennis and U.S. Golf Association rules for golf. NFHS rules are reviewed on a yearly basis with input from coaches and state associations. When changes are made, it is generally to keep the sports safer, or to clarify rules that have somehow been misconstrued. However, many times spectators apply National Football League or National Basketball League rules when watching high school contests and create problems not only for the officials but also for the coaches who are following the rules as written.

Challenges for High School Sports

One of the biggest challenges for high school sports is keeping an athletic director. Because there is no required licensing to be an athletic administrator, many individuals find that the job is so demanding regarding paperwork and hours away from home that, after two to three years, the school must find another person to fill the position. A second challenge lies in trying to find qualified individuals to fill coaching positions. There are at least two indicators that point to the problem.

First, when Title IX was enacted in 1972, schools had to create girl's and women's sports opportunities. Initially, women filled these coaching positions. But as the years progressed, the majority of girl sports on the high school level began to be coached by men. That created a smaller pool of candidates than existed prior to Title IX. Because men were no longer limited to seeking coaching positions in boys' sports, they could now apply to coach the new girls' sports that were growing at a rapid rate. Second, in the 1960s and 1970s, men were still actively involved in seeking head and assistant coaching positions, especially in football, basketball, and baseball. However, as club sports became more prolific, those same coaches began coaching club teams or their children and were no longer interested in the long hours and limited pay available to high school coaches. A third challenge, the proliferation of youth sports programs, has involved many parents as fans and spectators of their children at a much earlier age. These parents have expectations that earlier involvement of their children in summer programs, out-of-season programs, and clinics will lead to college scholarships. By the time these children and parents descend on the high school sports scene, their expectations have increased to the point where they feel they should have a say in who coaches, how that person coaches, and how much playing time their children should have, thus creating a very negative situation for the coaches and the athletic directors who must deal with these expectations. Fourth, the increasing amount of information regarding the dangers of concussions and second impact syndrome have placed a considerable amount of pressure on coaches to constantly upgrade their knowledge of safety and first aid techniques. These requirements can, at times, exist in opposition to their game philosophy regarding winning and the pressures of parents who want their children in the game no matter what.

Athletic directors and school administrators must be aware of the requirements of Title IX, Title VII, Individuals with Disabilities Education Act, Americans with Disabilities Act, and Section 504 of Federal Regulations and other nondiscrimination clauses in state statutes. Individuals interested in furthering their knowledge of the high school sports programs are encouraged to contact their state association Web site.

Janis Doleschal

See Also: Amateur Sports; Athletic Directors; Bullying/Hazing; Coaching Teenagers; Legal Responsibilities for Coaches; Sport-Based Youth Development.

Further Readings

Blackburn, Michael. *NIAAA Guide to Interscholastic Athletic Administration.* Indianapolis, IN: NIAAA, 2013.
"High School Athletics Participation Survey." http://www.cnsnews.com/sites/default/files/documents/2013-14%20NFHS%20PARTICIPATION-SURVEY.pdf (Accessed October 2014).

I

Identification With Sports Teams

> The challenge of every team is to build a feeling of oneness, of dependence on one another. Because the question is usually not how well each person performs, but how well they work together. —Vince Lombardi.

The quote above speaks to the importance of sports teams coming together to become a unified and distinct group. Indeed, creating such oneness is a great challenge and leaders play an integral role in crafting this notion of team identification. The purpose of this article is to introduce team identification and explain why it is the foundation of effective leadership, before outlining the four principles of identity leadership that can be adopted by leaders to build team identification.

Team Identification

Embracing groups or teams as defining entities of who people are rather than passive, uneventful units of individuals is crucial to fully understand the psychology of athletes. In the other words the psychology and behavior of athletes is not only a product of their personal identity (i.e., their personality), but also their team (or social) identities. This is because athletes can define themselves as individuals (i.e., "I" or "me") and as team members (i.e., "we" or "us"). Thus when athletes connect with sports

teams their thoughts and actions will be guided by their team identity opposed to their individual personality. In short, team identification reflects the extent to which an athlete feels they belong to a sports team in a significant and meaningful way, and its role in sport leadership, as Lombardi alludes to, should not be underestimated.

Leadership that understands and embraces the principles of team identification can be beneficial because when athletes feel a meaningful attachment to a team, they act consistent with the specific values associated with that team. Take a sport fan, for example; when they are in the stadium they may feel a strong identification with their team and this has ramifications in terms of their behavior. They cheer, they encourage, they hurl abuse at the opposition, they may even speak to the fellow fan sitting next to them, even though they have never met them before. This is a result of identification. In sports teams, athletes that feel a strong sense of belonging inherently aspire to think and act in the team's interests and will support, communicate, and cooperate, as well as be internally motivated to achieve for the team. Specifically, athletes' thoughts and actions will reflect the values associated with their team identification, which interestingly could be shared or in contrast to formal leaders. Nevertheless, these intrinsic motives occur because the fate of athletes' sports team is felt personally. In other words, a team success (or loss) is felt as much individually as it is at a team level. Bringing this together, leadership that is able to develop team identification and create a sense of oneness is likely to optimize team functioning (e.g., trust in one another, cooperation and communication with one another, and support of one another), which are precursors of high performance. Accordingly, in the next section, the four principles of leadership that Alex Haslam, Steve Reicher, and Michael Platow propose to develop team identification will be introduced and briefly explained. Critically, these principles are incremental and applicable for all leaders to consider and adopt.

Creating Team Identification

Now that this article has established the impact of team identification within sports teams, we turn our attention to how this sense of "oneness" can be created in leadership practice. Briefly, the four principles of identity leadership outlined by Alex Haslam and colleagues are (1) being one of "us," (2) leading for "us," (3) crafting a sense of "us," and (4) making "us" matter.

First, being one of "us" involves leaders being perceived as a team member and representing the key characteristics of their sports team. Such leadership seeks to reflect on what it means to be part of the team at present and understand what "we" seek to become. In other words, successful leaders epitomize the sports teams they lead. Such leadership is more supported by team members and leads increased perceptions of charisma; for example, a basketball coach who selects a captain that best represents the team's values rather than simply selecting the best player.

Second, leading for "us" involves leaders championing the sports team. Such leadership thinks and behaves in ways that only advance the interests of the sports team and avoids decisions or behaviors that demonstrate they are focused on themselves. Here, not only understanding and representing team values but also having knowledge of the context is important to fully appreciate what is in the team's best interest from situation to situation.

Third, crafting a sense of "us" involves leaders being entrepreneurs of identification. Such leadership is proactive and frames new ideas or a collective vision in the sports team's identification. Further, leadership may redefine and develop identification in a way that empowers team members to be involved in the process and take ownership. Novel yet consensual values may be created and act as guides for athletes when they are training and in competition. Such leadership is empathetic and uses collective language (e.g., "we" and "us") and means it. Indeed, evidence indicates that leaders who use "we" more than "I" are more endorsed by followers and potential followers.

Fourth, making "us" matter involves embedding what is important to the team in reality. Such leadership speaks to the notion that leaders must make the team vision a reality (or at least make progress toward the vision). Leadership that does not make progress toward the collective vision, as is often seen in sport, are promptly removed by team owners and new coaches are brought in. For example, such leadership may organize events, structures, and/or discussions that facilitate the achievement of the team's vision. Ultimately, such practical structures provide opportunities for "us" to achieve what we want to achieve.

In sum, leadership that focuses on sports teams' identification, through being one of "us," leading for "us," crafting a sense of "us," and making "us" matter, emphasizes the team-level and contextual factors that mobilize team members to act. This is because if team identification is created, the success and failure of the team is felt by each member individually, too, thus inspiring individual and team motivation, support, and cooperation. Such leadership can be developed and adopted to enhance team functioning and performance and is not exclusive to formal leaders (e.g., coaches); it is applicable to anyone wishing to influence or mobilize others.

Conclusion

If leadership that creates a sense of "oneness" (i.e., identification) is as crucial to optimize team functioning and performance as it appears, then leadership that draws on the four principles of identity leadership may be best placed to overcome the challenge of galvanizing the energies of the team to work in unison—achieving the ultimate shift in athletes' thinking and action from "I" and "me" to "we" and "us."

Matthew J. Slater

See Also: Creating an Organizational Vision; Development of Leadership Skills; Leadership Skills for Athletes; Organizational Leadership.

Further Readings

Haslam, Alexander, et al. *The New Psychology of Leadership: Identity, Influence and Power.* Hove, UK: Psychology Press, 2011.

Slater, Matthew, et al. "Leading for Gold: Social Identity Leadership Processes at the London 2012 Olympic Games." *Qualitative Research in Sport, Exercise, and Health*, v.7/2 (2015).

Slater, Matthew, et al. "Promoting Shared Meanings in Group Memberships: A Social Identity Approach to Leadership in Sport." *Reflective Practice: International and Multidisciplinary Perspectives*, v.15/5 (2014).

Slater, Matthew, et al. "Using Social Identities to Motivate Athletes Towards Peak Performance at the London 2012 Olympic Games: Reflecting for Rio 2016." *Reflective Practice: International and Multidisciplinary Perspectives*, v.14/5 (2013).

Injury

For sports leaders, sport injury involves more than just an athlete and a physical issue. Ethical considerations, planning, education, and communication are essential for understanding and managing injury. While injury occurrence is beyond one's control, injury management is not. Adequate preparation can increase the likelihood of successful outcomes for athlete, coach, and team.

Ethical Issues

Leader response to athlete injury should include consideration of ethical issues such as privacy, pressure to return to play, and responsibilities of providing care and compensation.

Privacy is a priority, particularly in this age of social media. Most leagues have media guidelines that must be followed so as to ensure consistency across the league regarding communication of injury information. The National Hockey League (NHL) may report simply "upper- or lower-body injury," while the National Football League (NFL) may be more specific about the nature of the injury, in accordance with NFL reporting guidelines.

Information that is shared must have the direct approval of everyone involved. The athlete's medical records and specific progress therein is protected by the Health Insurance Portability and Accountability Act (HIPPAA) privacy practices. The athlete should be made aware of and provide consent for details to be shared among the medical team or with management. At the very least, the athlete's condition and progress throughout rehabilitation and recovery, the extent of the injury, the estimated timetable for return to play, and any setbacks should be communicated clearly.

The goal of sport injury rehabilitation (SIR) programs is to heal and prepare the athlete to return to play. Interest in the athlete's speedy return is great, especially for the high-profile athlete, highly paid superstar, or Olympic athlete poised to win a medal. In an Olympic year with the games just around the corner, the pressure to return is immense. It is no longer enough to simply recover from an injury; the athlete has a deadline to meet. A coach whose team could play in the national championship needs his best athlete healthy. Applying pressure, either real or implied, is an ethical issue. Pressure applied to the athlete, or to the medical team, can do more harm than good. Clearing an athlete to play at less than 100 percent healed or ready can produce consequences that in the short term may be positive but can backfire, causing long-term injury from which the athlete may be less likely to recover.

An athlete may pressure herself due to fear of losing her position, missing the big competition, or disappointing herself, family, coach, team, and fans. The medical team should be trained to recognize such behaviors and should counsel the athlete to trust and follow protocol without rushing. Occasional reassurances from team management—the coach in particular—that the athlete is still valued and that his or her recovery has the full support of the team—can help to assuage his or her fears.

An injured youth athlete sees medical professionals through his parents' medical plan. These professionals are beholden to their patient alone and make decisions based solely in his best interest, though pressure from the athlete or parents sometimes occurs. An athletic trainer on the company payroll, however, may feel pressure to ensure the injured athlete is ready to return to play when management has decided the athlete is needed back. Team-hired physicians may feel pressure to prematurely clear the athlete for play. On-the-field decisions may be

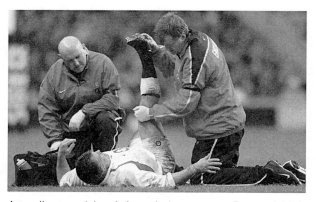

Attending to an injured player during a game at Roosevelt High School in 2013, in San Antonio, Texas. Coaches need first aid training to be able to handle administering to mild injuries that can be treated on the field. (Flickr/Stuart Seeger)

difficult—should the player who suffered a blow to the head be allowed to keep playing against the better judgment of professionals if he insists he is "fine?" If the team has guidelines in place for these situations and all personnel are required to follow them, then the choices are easy and ethically sound. Sports medicine groups, including the National Association of Athletic Trainers, developed guidelines for injury, rehabilitation, and return by which management and medical personnel agree to abide. Whichever medical professional is appointed to give final say actually has the final say and is entitled to overrule any other decisions or suggestions offered. Pressure may persist but having a structured plan makes ultimate choices easier to make. It also ensures the safety of the players and strengthens the credibility of the sport program.

Coverage for the cost of care for injured athletes varies. Youth teams or leagues are not required to provide monetary assistance. Professional athletes have access to top-notch medical professionals often employed by the team. The college level is less straightforward. According to the National Collegiate Athletic Association (NCAA) Division I manual, most university athletic departments do not have to publish their health care policies in writing, nor do many have any contractual obligation to actually treat any injuries that result from the athletes' play at that university. This is not to say assistance is never provided, though such assistance is more likely for high-profile players or if the injury is severe or

public. Additionally, there are no provisions in place to prohibit a coach from revoking a scholarship or financial aid should an athlete suffer an injury rendering them unable to perform for the team at their expected capacity. What a coach or team official at any level owes a player who suffers a career-ending injury must be considered both ethically and legally.

Preparation for the Inevitable

Injury in competitive sport is common; it is less "if" and more "when" injury will occur. Planning is key. Team management should have a structured plan for addressing the inevitable from onset of injury to return to play, and an organized multidisciplinary team of trusted medical professionals to handle and coordinate care. The care team includes the athletic trainer as typical point person, who usually has the most direct access to the player. It may also include physicians of relevant specialties, physical and massage therapists, and sport psychologists. Understanding the roles each of the professionals play ensures a level of trust and confidence in the process.

With each athlete comes a new set of experiences, as well as biological, behavioral, psychological, and psychosocial factors, all of which play a part in determining the success of the SIR program. While the greatest emphasis is typically on the physical injury and measures of recovery, the psychological aspects should not be overlooked. The athlete's mind set is immensely important to the success of the program and readiness to return to play.

Managing Injury

Educating coaches and players about proper technique, hydration, rest and recovery, recognizing signs of burnout, or overtraining can significantly reduce the incidence of injury. Proper supervision of athlete training is vital. Coaches should be trained in first aid to handle mild injuries that can be treated on the field and be trained to recognize injuries requiring removal of the athlete from play for further evaluation.

Comprehensive records of training and injury should be maintained. Injury tracking management systems and software offer features for tracking each athlete's vital statistics, medical issues, or previous injuries. The date and circumstances of injury are recorded, along with progress notes from each professional involved in his care. The data is secured, with limited access granted. Progress notes from point person to management can be sent securely, allowing dialogue between parties to be maintained on record.

Christie Marshall

See Also: Ethics in Sports; Health Issues in Sports; Legal Responsibilities for Managers and Owners.

Further Readings
Arvinen-Barrow, M. and N. Walker, eds. *The Psychology of Sport Injury and Rehabilitation*. New York: Routledge, 2013.
MomsTeam. "NATA." http://www.momsteam.com/nata (Accessed September 2014).
Salmon, Paul M. *Human Factors Methods and Sports Science: A Practical Guide*. Boca Raton, FL: CRC Press/ Taylor & Francis Group, 2010.

Intercollegiate Sports

Intercollegiate athletics have been present in American society since the mid-1800s. Around this time, students began to seek a respite from the monotony of college academics and began engaging in forms of exercise that became increasingly organized over time. The first officially recognized intercollegiate athletic competition was a men's crew regatta between Harvard University and Yale University in 1852 on New Hampshire's Lake Winnipesaukee, an event won by Harvard that signaled the start of the longest running rivalry between two college athletic programs. Since this preliminary event, athletic competition between institutions of higher learning blossomed to include other sports such as baseball, football, track and field, and others by the turn of the 20th century. All the while, debate between members of college communities about the place of athletics within the college landscape was percolating. While students and participants in athletics lauded the contributions that sport participation made to the overall development of students, academics argued that sports were simply a distraction that diverted time and attention away from students' academic pursuits.

Around this time, a slew of serious injuries and fatalities resulting from participation in football prompted a review of intercollegiate athletics in 1905 at the urging of President Theodore Roosevelt. While the review was primarily concerned with increasing the safety of participants, a move toward increased governance of college athletic competition in a general sense was undertaken as a result of these proceedings. In 1906, the Intercollegiate Athletic Association of the United States (IAAUS) was formed to oversee athletic competition at the participating universities and to establish and administer rules and regulations for each sport offered. This organization evolved into the National Collegiate Athletic Association (NCAA) in 1910, and has been the pre-eminent governing body for intercollegiate athletics ever since. During the course of the 20th century, the NCAA grew into one of the largest sport organizations in the world, with oversight over 100 athletic conferences and more than 1,000 institutions across three divisions of competition (Divisions I, II, and III).

In the sections to follow, a discussion of the governance and structure of intercollegiate athletics in the United States will be presented. This discussion will include an overview of the NCAA and similar national governing bodies of college athletics (the National Association of Intercollegiate Athletics [NAIA], the National Junior College Athletic Association [NJCAA], and others), information about the organization of championship events in college sports, and key issues surrounding intercollegiate athletics that have recently surfaced, with a look ahead to the potential future state of intercollegiate athletics resulting from these ongoing changes in the college sports landscape.

Governance Structure of Intercollegiate Athletics
Intercollegiate athletics in the United States are currently governed by a number of different umbrella organizations. The largest of these organizations, the NCAA, provides oversight for more than 1,000 institutions across three levels of competition—Division I, II, and III.

NCAA Division I. The highest level of NCAA sport, Division I (D-I), is further divided into three segments. Football Bowl Subdivision (FBS), formerly known as Division I-A, consists of all of the schools (128 in total) that offer the sport of football and offer full grants-in-aid (scholarships) to all student-athletes participating in football. In addition, D-I FBS schools are eligible to participate in a series of postseason bowl games as well as in the College Football Playoff, which is a new addition for the 2014 season. Next, the Football Championship Subdivision (FCS), formerly known as Division I-AA, consists of 124 schools and is distinguished from FBS by limitations on the number of full grants-in-aid that may be awarded to participants in football. D-I FCS schools participate in a nationwide championship tournament similar to those offered in other intercollegiate sports. Finally, 98 D-I institutions do not offer varsity football and are contained within the third category of D-I schools, known as nonfootball Division I schools.

D-I FBS greatly outshines the other two categories of D-I schools in terms of media exposure and notoriety, and is far and away the most lucrative of the NCAA levels. Men's and women's sports in D-I FBS are featured prominently on a variety of media outlets, with their regular season and championship events broadcast nationally on a yearly basis. This is especially true for the sports of football and men's and women's basketball, in addition to baseball, softball, hockey, men's lacrosse, track and field, and others with high levels of national exposure. D-I FCS sport programs also experience some media exposure, though this is greatly limited when compared with their FBS counterparts. Consequently, there is a similar divide between the revenue generated by larger FBS athletic departments and that of institutions at lower levels of Division I.

Conferences. Each level of NCAA athletics is subsequently subdivided into smaller governing bodies called conferences. The conference structure of NCAA D-I FBS, for example, consists of 10 conferences, five of which have been recently designated as the "Power Five" conferences. These conferences are the Atlantic Coast Conference (ACC), Big Ten Conference (B1G), Big 12 Conference (Big 12), Pacific-12 Conference (Pac-12), and the Southeastern Conference (SEC). In addition, the following conferences also make up the rest of FBS: the

American Athletic Conference (AAC or The American), Conference USA (C-USA), the Mid-American Conference (MAC), the Mountain West Conference (MWC), and the Sun Belt Conference (Sun Belt). Finally, a group of four schools participate on the D-I FBS level but is unaffiliated with any of the 10 conferences, which are known simply as Independents. As of 2014, these schools were the U.S. Military Academy (Army), the U.S. Naval Academy (Navy), Brigham Young University (BYU), and the University of Notre Dame. However, Notre Dame has recently joined the ACC for all sports other than football, BYU is affiliated with the MWC for sports other than football, and Navy currently has plans to join the AAC after the 2014 to 2015 academic year.

The 124-member FCS comprises of 13 athletic conferences across the United States: the Big Sky Conference, Big South Conference, the Colonial Athletic Association (CAA), Ivy League, Mid-Eastern Athletic Conference (MEAC), Missouri Valley Conference (MVC), Northeast Conference (MEC), Ohio Valley Conference, Patriot League, Pioneer League, Southern Conference, Southland Conference, and Southwestern Athletic Conference (SWAC).

NCAA Divisions II and II. Beyond Division I, there are a great number of institutions that participate in intercollegiate athletics at either the Division II or III levels. Division II is composed of 282 schools in 24 conferences. Division II schools must provide at least 10 sports (combined men's and women's) and at least four sports for each gender. D-II institutions are able to provide grants-in-aid to student-athletes but are restricted to a limited number of scholarships in each sport when compared to Division I. For instance, D-II schools offering football are only able to offer a maximum of 36 scholarships, while this number is considerably fewer for other sports. D-II athletic programs are featured far less prominently in the national sport media, with only the championship games in football, men's basketball, and women's basketball receiving coverage by a national television network.

D-III is unique when compared with other NCAA levels in that D-III schools are not able to offer athletically related grants-in-aid to student-athletes. While D-III schools often are smaller schools with limited enrollment compared with those in D-I and II, there are a number of larger schools that compete at the D-III level. Division III is made up of 449 member schools in 55 regional conferences, with a handful remaining unaffiliated with a conference (Independents). Like D-II, D-III schools must offer a minimum of 10 sports with at least four for each gender, unless they have limited (less than 1,000 students) enrollment or are a single-sex institution. Finally, there is a small grouping of schools (seven) that participate in D-III athletics for the majority of sports, but do offer one or two D-I sport programs, allowing them to offer athletic scholarships to student-athletes participating in those sports only.

Additional Governing Bodies in Intercollegiate Athletics. While the NCAA seemingly dominates the intercollegiate athletics landscape, there are additional national governing bodies of note that preside over college sports. The National Association of Intercollegiate Athletics (NAIA), for instance, is a governing body of smaller athletic programs that has been in existence since 1937 and has operated under the NAIA label since 1952. The NAIA governs 13 sports for 23 conferences with 257 member schools, and is specifically focused on developing character-building opportunities for student-athletes and on playing a role in helping students balance their athletic and academic pursuits. In addition, the National Junior College Athletic Association (NJCAA) provides oversight for two-year colleges that are state or regionally accredited institutions. Established in 1938, the NJCAA is divided into three divisions (Division I, II, and III) similar to the NCAA, but is split into 24 conferences that are designated by region. In NJCAA Division I, there are 221 member institutions, while 117 schools are members of Division II and 98 are members of Division III. The NJCAA is responsible for administering 17 sports for its 436 member institutions, though some schools are participants in one sport only (football).

Sport Seasons and NCAA Championships

The intercollegiate athletic year is divided into three seasons: fall, winter, and spring, with each sport offered contained within one of these three seasons. While each NCAA sport has its own championship structure depending upon the sport and level of competition, each of the most popular intercollegiate sports has a signature championship event that garners significant national exposure. For instance, the NCAA Division I men's and women's basketball championships, commonly referred to as the NCAA Tournament or the moniker "March Madness," is a three-week event in March and early April in which 68 men's basketball teams and 64 women's basketball teams compete in single-elimination tournaments for each, culminating in the men's and women's Final Four championship events. Baseball and softball each have a College World Series tournament that begins with regional competitions before a final double-elimination tournament to decide the champion for each sport. Men's and women's hockey compete in a 16-team and eight-team single-elimination tournament, respectively, that culminates in the Men's/Women's Frozen Four. Other team sports follow a similar model. More individualized sports such as track and field and others provide the opportunity to compete in additional types of championship meets or events.

Schools in each of the three NCAA divisions, as well as the NAIA, each compete for the National Association of Collegiate Directors of Athletics (NACDA) Learfield Director's Cup for their respective divisions. The Director's Cup is an award that honors the institution at each level with the most successful all-around performance in all qualifying college sports. Points are awarded for each school's overall finish in each qualifying sport, which are added together to reach an overall score for each institution. The top performing institution in the Director's Cup standings receives the honor of being regarded as the best overall collegiate athletics program for the academic year. For NCAA Division I, 20 sports qualify for the Director's Cup (10 men's sports and 10 women's sports), with 14 for Division II (seven each for men's and women's sports), 18 for Division III (nine for each), and 12 (six each) for the NAIA.

The Influence of Football in NCAA Division I

However, despite the equal consideration provided to the qualifying sports for awards such as the Learfield Director's Cup, NCAA D-I FBS football has long been the most influential, prominent, and lucrative intercollegiate sport. Consequently, football continues to follow a model that is unique to other NCAA sports. At the D-I FCS level, a championship tournament is held similar to other sports such as hockey. However, D-I FBS football decides its annual champion in a unique manner. For many years, teams with winning records during the season (assuming the team is otherwise eligible by the NCAA and counts no more than one win versus an FCS opponent) would qualify for one of several postseason bowl games—a major single-game event that is, in most cases, individually sponsored by a company with national brand recognition. Following the bowl games, sportswriters and coaches would independently vote for the top 25 teams, as is also customary during each week of the season, with the number-one team being declared the national champion.

In 1998, the Bowl Championship Series (BCS) was formed, in which both polls and computer models would contribute to the decision of which teams would compete in the four most prominent bowl games: the Rose Bowl in Pasadena, California; the Fiesta Bowl in Phoenix, Arizona; the Sugar Bowl in New Orleans, Louisiana; and the Orange Bowl in Miami, Florida; plus the separate BCS Championship Game. The winner of the BCS Championship Game would be declared the national champion, though there have been instances in the past in which an undefeated winner of one of the four major bowl games asserted a claim to the national championship over the winner of the BCS Championship Game.

In 2014, NCAA D-I FBS football transitioned to a hybrid bowl/tournament format to decide the national champion. While the bowl system will remain intact in the near future, the newly instituted system will involve a four-team single-elimination playoff to decide the national champion, with the four participating teams decided by a selection committee comprised primarily of major college athletic directors and notable prominent individuals within the domain of college athletics (former coaches, conference commissioners, and other dignitaries). The two tournament semifinal games and the championship game will rotate among the four existing BCS bowl sites plus the Peach Bowl and Cotton Bowl, which have historically been two of the most high-profile bowl games in college football.

The Shifting Landscape of Intercollegiate Athletics

NCAA football at the Division I level has also been a significant influence for the evolution of the intercollegiate athletics landscape that has occurred in recent years and, by many accounts, is still ongoing. Starting most recently in 2010, the desire of some NCAA D-I institutions to align with the so-called power conferences in football, along with a parallel desire by conferences to expand their memberships to include key institutions in high-profile media markets, sparked a radical movement toward conference realignment and a shift in conference membership. For instance, schools such as Texas A&M and Missouri left the Big 12 Conference to join the SEC, which is widely regarded as the premier college football conference. Rutgers, Maryland, and Nebraska each left their respective conferences to join the Big Ten Conference. Pittsburgh, and Syracuse left the traditional basketball powerhouse Big East Conference to join the ACC, which is regarded as a stronger football conference.

These and other corresponding shifts had widespread effects on all of NCAA Division I. In one of these corresponding moves, the Big East members without football programs departed the conference to form their own league, keeping the Big East name and leaving the remaining schools behind. Those remaining schools, led by Louisville, Connecticut, South Florida, and Cincinnati, joined schools from Conference USA and elsewhere to form the AAC, which began operations during the 2013 to 2014 academic year. Louisville has since departed the AAC for the ACC. Finally, in the summer of 2014, the conferences now known as the "Power Five" (SEC, Big 12, B1G, ACC, and Pac-12) won the right to determine their own policies independent of the other Division I FBS conferences, which is a ruling that is currently undergoing significant debate among institutions, the media, and fans. Thus, while conference shifts have seemingly calmed for the 2014 to 2015 year, whether this stability will last for a significant period of time remains to be seen.

Notable Current Issues in Intercollegiate Athletics and Future Directions

Two additional issues surrounding the current state of intercollegiate athletics involve the ethical and equitable treatment of its participants. Although it was not originally intended to be applied uniquely to athletics, Title IX legislation passed in 1972 is most popularly associated with athletics and guarantees equal opportunity to both men and women in "any educational program or activity receiving federal financial assistance" (Title IX of the Education Amendments, 1972). While this law has been in place for more than four decades, institutions still must work diligently to evaluate their athletic programs and to ensure that they accommodate the participatory needs of all students regardless of their gender. To do so, schools must satisfy one of three tests that demonstrates one of the following: (1) that opportunities provided to participate in athletics are substantively proportionate to the student enrollment, (2) that the institution has demonstrated a continued growth of opportunities for the underrepresented gender, or (3) that the interests and abilities of the underrepresented gender are fully accommodated with the current programs offered by the college or university. While the majority of institutions are in regular compliance with Title IX regulations, there are occasional instances in which women, in particular, are denied sufficient opportunities to participate in intercollegiate athletics.

Additionally, there has been considerable debate in recent years over whether or not college athletes should be regarded as employees and paid for their efforts. The debate has gained considerable traction with the establishment of the National College Players Association (NCPA), a union formed to serve the interests of participants in college sports. Proponents of the idea contend that college athletes expend considerable effort on behalf of their colleges and universities on the playing field, from which, in many cases, the institution obtains a significant financial benefit. Yet college athletes often struggle financially like many traditional college students do. In addition, those in support of the movement argue that grants-in-aid are not guaranteed for all four years, but rather are renewable by the institution on a year-to-year basis. One of the main contentions of supporters of unionization is that while grants-in-aid do constitute significant compensation for student-athletes in many ways, they do not cover the full cost of attendance at colleges and universities.

Detractors of this movement have argued that college athletes receiving grants-in-aid benefit significantly from their participation in athletics, since they are provided education, room, and board that may cost traditional students $100,000 or more over a four-year span, and that endeavoring to provide additional financial compensation for athletic participation would risk the end of the current concept of amateurism.

Furthermore, until 2014, college athletes had been prohibited from profiting from their names and likenesses, made possible from their participation in intercollegiate sports. The famed federal class-action suit *O'Bannon v. NCAA* (2014), shed considerable light on this issue, however, in which a federal judge ruled that college athletes could not be legally prevented from pursuing financial opportunities as they see fit. This debate was also fueled by the All Players United movement, which was started by athletes at Northwestern University who have primarily pushed for universities to provide student-athletes with the full cost of attendance, as well as long-term health insurance benefits for cases in which athletes suffer debilitating injuries during practices or competition on behalf of their colleges or universities.

These are simply two of several ongoing debates in the world of intercollegiate athletics that are likely to continue for some time. While it is difficult to predict the direction intercollegiate athletics will take in the future, given the current tumultuous state of the industry and the intensity of the debates surrounding some of the key issues presented here, it seems that college athletics are likely to continue to evolve into a framework that may not resemble the current system in the very near future.

Raymond J. Cotrufo

See Also: National Association of Intercollegiate Athletics; National Collegiate Athletic Association; Title IX; Unionization of College Athletes.

Further Readings
Bonnette, Valerie McMurtrie. *Title IX and Intercollegiate Athletics, How It All Works—In Plain English*. San Diego, CA: Good Sports, 2004.

Covell, Daniel and Carol A. Barr. *Managing Intercollegiate Athletics.* Scottsdale, AZ: Holcomb Hathaway Publishers, 2010.

Hruby, Patrick. "The End of Amateurism Is Not the End of Competitive College Sports." *The Atlantic* (August 28, 2014). http://www.theatlantic.com/entertainment/archive/2014/08/the-end-of-amateurism-not-the-end-of-college-sports/379200 (Accessed September 2014).

Learfield Sports. http://thedirectorscup.com (Accessed September 2014).

National Association of Intercollegiate Athletics (NAIA). http://www.naia.org (Accessed September 2014).

National Collegiate Athletic Association (NCAA). http://www.ncaa.org (Accessed September 2014).

National Junior College Athletic Association (NJCAA). http://www.njcaa.org (Accessed September 2014).

International Olympic Committee

The International Olympic Committee (IOC), a nongovernmental organization headquartered in Lausanne, Switzerland, is the governing body for the Olympic movement and is guided by the Olympic Charter. The IOC has more member states than the United Nations, demonstrating the importance ascribed to the Olympic Games. The IOC works with the National Olympic Committees (NOCs), international federations that govern each sport, and the organizing committees for each Olympic Games. The Summer and Winter Olympic Games have grown with enormous revenue from sponsorship and television broadcasts to become mega-events, which has also led to a major scandal and subsequent reforms.

Governance
The IOC was founded in 1894 in Paris by the Frenchman Baron Pierre de Coubertin. The first president of the IOC was Demetrius Vikelas (1894–96), whose native Greece hosted the first modern Olympic Games in 1896. Coubertin took over the presidency (1896–25), followed by the Belgian, Count Henri de Baillet-Latour (1925–42). IOC vice president J. Sigfrid Edström of Sweden kept the organization running after Baillet-Latour's death during World War II, and Edström became president at the first postwar meeting (1946–52). Avery Brundage of Chicago was the lone non-European to hold the presidency (1952–72), followed by Ireland's Lord Killanin (1972–80), Spain's Juan Antonio Samaranch (1980–01), and Belgium's Jacques Rogge (2001–13). Germany's Thomas Bach became president in 2013. IOC presidents are elected for an eight-year term and can be re-elected for four-year terms. Under Samaranch the presidential elections moved to the year following the Summer Olympics. The 1999 reforms limited reelection to one term, with a maximum of 12 years as president.

The Olympic Charter is the governing document of the IOC and has been updated several times since it was first written in 1908. The Olympic Charter covers the structure of the IOC, its relationship with the related governing bodies, the organizing of the Olympic Games, and dispute resolution procedures. A central feature of the Olympic Charter is the promotion of Olympism, the philosophy whereby sport (and particularly the Olympic movement) is used for the betterment of individuals and society along ethical lines. The charter's fourth fundamental principle states, "The practice of sport is a human right. Every individual must have the possibility of practising sport, without discrimination of any kind and in the Olympic spirit, which requires mutual understanding with a spirit of friendship, solidarity and fair play." This idea is often used to criticize the Olympic movement, including when NOCs have not included female athletes on their teams or when the host country places restrictions on various groups' rights.

Olympic Games
The modern Olympic Games were first held in 1896 in Athens, Greece. They have taken place every four years except in 1916, 1940, and 1944, when the Olympics were cancelled due to the world wars. The IOC selects the city that will host the Olympic Games. The organizers of the 1924 Paris Olympics held an International Sports Week for winter sports, which the IOC retroactively called the First Winter Olympics. During the 1920s and 1930s, countries that would host the Summer Olympics were given the opportunity to host the Winter Olympics, but if the country refused the IOC bestowed the games

to a city in another country, a process discontinued after World War II. In 1986, the IOC decided to move the Winter Olympics to the other even-numbered year to ease the pressure of having two Olympic Games in the same year and also to provide greater exposure for the Olympic movement. The last time both Olympics were held in the same year was 1992 in Albertville, France (Winter) and Barcelona, Spain (Summer). The first Winter Games not held in the same year as the Summer Olympics was in Lillehammer, Norway, in 1994.

The growth and costs of the Olympic Games has risen dramatically. The Summer Olympics have approximately 10,000 athletes and the Winter Games have about 4,500 competitors. Following the massacre of the Israeli team at the 1972 Munich Games and the 9/11 terrorist attacks in the United States, Olympic security measures have tremendously expanded and compose a huge portion of the organizing committees' budgets. The 2014 Winter Games in Sochi, Russia, cost an estimated $51 billion in part because of the massive infrastructure costs needed to transform a coastal resort into a major winter sports venue. These costs are prompting fewer bids to host the Olympics alongside greater public discussions about the escalating costs and value of hosting the Games.

Revenue

Early Olympic Games did not produce much revenue, but under Juan Antonio Samaranch the IOC established two consistent sources of revenue: broadcast rights and sponsorship. Television revenue began in 1960 when CBS paid $50,000 to broadcast 15 total hours of the Winter Olympics from Squaw Valley, California. The three major U.S. television networks (ABC, CBS, and NBC) then competed with each other to purchase the broadcast rights for the Olympic Games, providing nearly half of the total broadcast revenue which the IOC receives. In 1995, the IOC signed a $1.25 billion contract with NBC to broadcast both the 2000 Olympic Games in Sydney, Australia, and the 2002 Winter Olympics in Salt Lake City, Utah. NBC has extended this contract several times, including in May 2014 to continue this partnership through 2032. The IOC estimates 3.6 billion people worldwide watched the London 2012 Olympics via television or online.

The IOC also created The Olympic Partners Program (TOP) in the lead-up to the 1998 Olympic Games. TOP sponsors are the exclusive providers in a specific category and in return gain access to market their products with the trademarked Olympic rings. TOP sponsors sign a single contract with the IOC instead of separate contracts with each NOC, enabling them to advertise in all 204 Olympic member states. TOP has between nine and 12 companies that by the 2010s each paid approximately $100 million. Revenue from TOP is split between the Olympic Games Organizing Committees, the NOCs, and the IOC.

Reform

Following the Salt Lake City bid scandal, in which the organizers of the city's successful bid for the 2002 Winter Olympic Games had bribed many IOC members and provided them or their family members with lavish gifts and opportunities, the IOC in December 1999 passed several reforms. Changes to the bidding procedure were implemented, including limitations on IOC member visits to applicant cities. The reforms limited the total number of IOC members to 115, with 70 independent members and 15 each from the international federations, NOCs, and the athletes commission.

Concerns over the Olympic bidding process, and the large number of cities that withdrew bids for the 2022 Olympics, has prompted the IOC to consider revising the bidding process again, which Thomas

The headquarters of the International Olympic Committee (IOC) is located in Lausanne, Switzerland. The IOC was created in 1894 in Paris and today consists of 100 active members. (Wikimedia Commons)

Bach wants to make a central component of his presidency.

Heather L. Dichter

See Also: Sports Merchandising; United States Olympic Committee; World Anti-Doping Agency.

Further Readings

Barney, Robert K., et al. *Selling the Five Rings: The IOC and the Rise of the Olympic Commercialism*. Salt Lake City: University of Utah Press, 2002.

Chappelet, Jean-Loup and Brenda Kübler-Mabbott. *The International Olympic Committee and the Olympic System: The Governance of World Sport*. London: Routledge, 2008.

London 2012 Olympic Games Global Broadcast Report. http://www.olympic.org/Documents/IOC_Marketing/ Broadcasting/London_2012_Global_%20Broadcast _Report.pdf (Accessed July 2014).

Olympic Charter. http://www.olympic.org/ documents/olympic_charter_en.pdf (Accessed July 2014).

L

Ladies Professional Golf Association

Golf was one of the first sports to welcome women athletes; in the United States, the inaugural women's amateur championship was held in 1895. While golf flourished among women as an amateur endeavor, the acceptance into professional competition eventually was realized. Legally formed in 1950, the Ladies Professional Golf Association (LPGA) is one of the oldest organizations of professional women athletes. The LPGA is headquartered in Daytona Beach, Florida, and consists of two branches that touch just about every aspect of golf—the playing tour and the teaching and club professionals division.

The LPGA came to fruition in May 1949, replacing a failed earlier effort to associate. Players agreed to form the LPGA at the Eastern Open in Essex Falls, New Jersey, and immediately hired Fred Coroan, also employed by Wilson Sporting Goods, as tournament manager. The official Articles of Incorporation as a nonprofit entity were reviewed at a tournament in Wichita, Kansas, and then formally signed on October 9, 1950, in New York by players Patty Berg, Helen Dettweiler, Sally Sessions, Betty Jameson, and Helen Hicks. Also credited as charter members were Alice Bauer, Marlene Bauer Hagge, Bettye Mims Danoff, Opal Hill, Marilynn Smith, Shirley Spork, Louise Suggs, and Babe Zaharias, a multiple-sport standout and Olympic Gold-medalist. Berg served as the first LPGA president. From its beginning, the LPGA took a nondiscriminatory stance, opening membership to players of all races while scrutinizing courses for segregation policies. Althea Gibson became the first African American player on the tour in 1963. Gibson, before taking up golf, was a star tennis player winning Wimbledon twice and the U.S. Open.

Starting with 13 members, the LPGA reached 350 touring pros by its 50th anniversary in 2000, and in 2014, the LPGA comprised more than 460 players representing 27 countries. The LPGA Tour has more than 30 tournaments highlighted by five majors: U.S. Women's Open (started in 1950), Wegmans LPGA Championship (1955), Kraft-Nabisco Championship (1983), RICOH Women's British Open (2001), and the Evian Championship (2013). Marquee players through the decades such as Berg, Zaharias, Mickey Wright, Kathy Whitworth, Jan Stephensen, Nancy Lopez, Annika Sorenstam, Karrie Webb, Se Ri Pak, Michelle Wie, and many others helped drive the LPGA's popularity growth. Besides the tour events, the LPGA initiated the Solheim Cup in 1990, in which the top U.S. players take on Europe's best every two years as the women's equivalent of the Ryder Cup.

LPGA tournament prize money has grown from $50,000 in its first year to $56 million in 2014. The first televised women's golf event was the 1963 U.S. Women's Open. In 1982, the first four rounds of a tournament—celebrity Dinah Shore's tournament—were broadcast live for the first time. By 2014, more than 350 hours of women's golf tournaments were televised.

Attesting to its growth, in 2007 the LPGA acquired the Symetra Tour, which is the official developmental tour. More than 300 players compete annually from March through September with the top-10 money earners gaining membership in the LPGA for the following year. This tour is in addition to LPGA's annual qualifying school.

While many associate the LPGA with its playing tour, the teaching and club professionals division (T&CP) has more than 1,500 members—the largest organization of women golf professionals in the world—as well as its own staff. LPGA charter members Marilynn Smith and Shirley Spork started the teaching division in 1959 to promote the game as well as increase women's participation. LPGA T&CP certification is earned through a comprehensive curriculum designed for golf instructors, business managers, and coaches. The division is known for its research-based golf education. Among the many T&CP initiatives are programs to teach golf to those with physical limitations, introducing golf to urban boys and girls ages 7 to 17, junior development programs with more than 2,500 girl participants, junior clinics, and clinics for women in business. The T&CP division has its own championship golf tournament.

Since its beginning, the LPGA has advocated for its members' welfare. Early on, the association offered an insurance program, and in 1981 started a retirement benefit—the first ever deferred compensation plan for nonteam professional sports. For its first 25 years, tour players administered all facets of the LPGA. In the 1970s, tour member Jane Blalock sued the LPGA over accusations of rule infringement. The result of the settlement was the significant reorganization of the governance structure. In 1975, Ray Volpe was hired as the LPGA's first commissioner along with formation of a board of directors, relieving tour players of administrative responsibilities. The new structure led to dramatic financial expansion. Today, the LPGA board of directors consists of the commissioner, six independent directors, seven tour players (Player Executive Committee), and the president of the LPGA Teaching and Club Professionals. The board oversees a sizeable staff.

Through both LPGA divisions, charitable support has been a significant component for decades. The playing tours benefit local charities and many outreach programs serve the economically disadvantaged. The LPGA Foundation was formed in 1991 to develop and maintain junior programs, establish scholarship programs for junior golfers, provide financial assistance to those in the golf industry, and conduct research and develop educational activities related to golf instruction. The LPGA Foundation is a separately incorporated nonprofit organization but works closely with the LPGA.

The LPGA Tournament Owners Association also is a separate nonprofit that consists of the individual tour events.

Paul M. McInerny

See Also: Gender and Sports Leadership; Professional Golf Association; Professional Sports; Race/Ethnicity and Sports Leadership; Women's Leadership in Sport.

Further Readings:
Hudson, David L. *Women In Golf: The Players, the History, and the Future of the Sport.* Westport, CT: Praeger, 2008.
Kahn, Liz. *The LPGA: The Unauthorized Version, The History of the Ladies Professional Golf Association.* Menlo Park, CA: Group Fore Productions, 1996.
Ladies Professional Golf Association (LPGA). http://www.lpga.com (Accessed October 2014).
Sanson, Nanette S. *Champions of Women's Golf: Celebrating Fifty Years of the LPGA.* Naples, FL: QuailMark Books, 2000.

Leadership in Recreational Sports Organizations

Not unlike other sport administrators, recreational sports leaders are charged with many responsibilities, including creating a vision for the organization, establishing goals and developing an agenda to meet those goals, building a team, supporting and motivating personnel, and solving problems. Recreational sports leaders like city recreation managers, park rangers, and campus recreation directors also encounter a wide range of issues specific to recreation- and leisure-based services. Recreational sports organizations also afford participants a unique opportunity to develop personal leadership skills.

Recreational sports organizations provide a wide array of programs and services to their communities, which may include towns and cities, regions and states, and institutions of higher education. At the local level, municipal parks and recreation departments are responsible for developing and maintaining green spaces, waterfronts, and sports facilities; organizing special events designed to foster community wellness; and offering youth and adult sports leagues. Organizations such as the YMCA and the Amateur Athletic Union (AAU) also provide opportunities for youth to engage in sport and physical activity. State and national parks systems encourage participation in recreational activities while providing protections for the natural environment and wildlife. On college campuses, recreational and competitive sports departments deliver myriad programs to students and staff members, including personal and group fitness, aquatics, intramural sports and sport clubs, and outdoor adventure.

Leadership Characteristics

Given the large populations they serve, recreational sports organizations require leaders who can manage many challenges, including issues of funding and finance, accessibility and participation, community outreach, facility operations and management, and human resources management. Central to all recreational sports organizations is the goal of developing a lasting appreciation of sport, physical activity, and healthy living. Therefore, recreational sports programs often emerge to help fulfill societal goals such as reversing the rate of childhood obesity, creating a safe environment for leisure and play, and reducing sedentariness among seniors.

Reaching out to these special populations or the community at large requires an individual who can understand and connect with people. Successful recreational sports leaders are often proactive planners and astute money managers. Because they seek to make recreation accessible to all, leaders must identify the programs and services that best meet the diverse needs of the community, and in many cases, they do so while facing shrinking financial support from their local governments. Despite these budgetary constraints, recreational sports leaders may be charged with overseeing a wide range of activities for the community, including cycling, running, walking and hiking, group fitness, weightlifting, camping, fishing, boating, tennis, racquetball, swimming and diving, baseball and softball, indoor and outdoor soccer, basketball, football, hockey, golf, volleyball, bowling, disc golf, skateboarding, and more. In light of the many programs and services offered in recreational sports, organization leaders must consider the most effective and efficient ways to construct and maintain indoor and outdoor infrastructure.

Across all levels of recreational sports, communication skills are used by organization leaders when lobbying with policy makers and decision makers to maintain or increase funding for recreational services and facilities. Additionally, recreation professionals must make the case to the taxpaying public for maintaining or increasing public funding for parks and recreation programs and infrastructure. For example, leaders must articulate the merits of funding for public parks, local youth and elderly programs, and intercollegiate sport clubs. If budget cuts occur, they must make difficult choices such as reducing access to facilities, discontinuing programs, and laying off personnel.

In addition to interacting with public officials and the voting public, recreational sports leaders must have excellent interpersonal skills in order to manage their human resources and to provide outreach to the community at large. A central responsibility of recreational sports leaders is to recruit, select, develop, and retain personnel to manage their organizations' many programs and services. Such a wide range of offerings necessitates a diverse collection of personnel, many of whom are required to hold advanced proficiencies in sport, physical activity, coaching, officiating, maintenance and operations, or public safety. In many cases, recreational sports organizations are staffed by a combination of paid employees and community volunteers; in either case, recreational sports leaders must ensure that all personnel are sufficiently trained and committed to the mission, values, and goals of the organization.

Developing Leadership Among Employees

Staff development is a vital component of any organization, but it is especially pronounced in collegiate recreational sports departments. Because campus recreation programs are usually staffed by a large number of student employees, many recreational sports leaders have contributed to the achievement of their universities' educational missions by fostering an environment for extracurricular learning in the workplace. Techniques for promoting student leadership development include promoting students to supervisory and managerial positions, establishing student advisory councils and leadership workshops, and empowering employees to recommend new ways to expand or improve their departments' recreational offerings. The role of student employees is especially important in campus recreation, as they represent an often-diverse student population with many unique needs and interests.

For collegiate recreational sports leaders, developing the managerial skills of a student staff has its challenges. Turnover is often high, as students' work schedules are built around class time and holiday travel. Even among veteran student employees, tenure typically lasts just a few years, as graduation ultimately forces students to pursue careers outside of the university or in other fields. While employee turnover may limit the opportunity to create dedicated leadership-development strategies within a single institution, alternative initiatives exist. For instance, leadership development at all levels is a key focus of the National Intramural-Recreational Sports Association (NIRSA), a network of collegiate recreational sports departments and leaders in the United States and Canada. NIRSA has several leadership-development initiatives, including the Women's Leadership Institute and the *Recreational Sports Journal*, which publishes research related to campus recreation. Additionally, the Emerging Recreational Sports Leaders Conference provides leadership training and networking opportunities to students and young professionals, and the association annually presents William N. Wasson Student Leadership and Academic Awards to top student leaders in collegiate recreation programs across North America.

Developing Leadership Among Users

Leadership-development initiatives in campus recreational sports are not limited to employees. Intramural sports, for example, encourage participants to assemble teams, organize practices, and develop team strategies. Often, a team captain is appointed to act as a liaison between the recreational sports department and its participants. These student leaders are expected to inform their teams' players of the rules, regulations, and policies; manage team sportsmanship and player conduct; and provide suggestions for improving the quality of recreational sports programming. Similarly, sport club teams are usually managed (and sometimes formed) by an elected president, who is responsible for completing administrative tasks like maintaining certifications and collecting paperwork, overseeing a budget, and organizing travel to extramural competitions.

A subset of leadership development in recreational sports relates to using sport and physical activity as a medium through which groups and teams can develop skills that make them more cohesive, synergistic, and productive. In campus recreation, outdoor adventure programs led by trained facilitators provide settings that force teams (e.g., an athletic team, a work unit, a group of friends) to work together in order to complete challenging tasks like a high-ropes course or a weekend camping expedition. This type of experiential learning, often termed outdoor education, has been widely used around the world to develop leadership and teamwork skills among users. Popular examples of outdoor education programs include Outward Bound and the National Outdoor Leadership School. The recent rise in team-oriented, endurance-obstacle races such as Spartan Race, Tough Mudder, and Warrior Dash reflects how leadership development can occur spontaneously through participation in recreational sports. These examples suggest that recreational sports leadership may include not only administrators and student staff members but also participants.

Timothy B. Kellison

See Also: Amateur Sports; Recreational Versus Competitive Sport; Sport-Based Youth Development; Sports as a Means of Developing Leaders.

Further Readings

DeGraaf, Donald, Debra Jordan, and Kathy DeGraaf. *Programming for Parks, Recreation, and Leisure Services*. State College, PA: Venture Publishing, 2010.
Moore, Roger, and B. L. Driver. *Introduction to Outdoor Recreation: Providing and Managing Natural Resource*

Based Opportunities. State College, PA: Venture Publishing, 2005.

NIRSA. http://www.nirsa.org (Accessed September 2014).

Nunes, Christopher and Robert Baker. "A Blueprint for Effective Recreational Sport Leadership." *Recreational Sports Journal*, v.26 (2002).

Russell, Ruth. *Leadership in Recreation*. Urbana, IL: Sagamore Publishing, 2012.

Leadership Models in Sports

Most definitions of leadership, when aggregated, indicate that leadership has common defining elements. First, leadership is a behavioral occurrence related to what leaders do. By its nature, leadership involves interpersonal interaction among stakeholders such as leaders and members. In addition, leadership is directed toward influencing members' actions toward a collective goal. Directed toward these common elements, leadership theories have been characterized into three main approaches: trait, behavioral, and situational.

The early trait approaches examined the personal characteristics of the leader, focusing on who the leader is. The intent was to connect the personal qualities of individuals with success as a leader in an attempt to distinguish a set of successful leadership traits from those of unsuccessful leaders. The behavioral approaches did not examine who leaders are, but rather they examined what leaders do. Styles of leadership and dimensions of leader behavior are a central focus. While these theories distinguish among leaders' behaviors, they rarely connect the behaviors to improved performance. The behavioral approaches examine leader behavior irrespective of the circumstances. In other words, they do not account for environmental or situational differences that may impact the effectiveness of leaders' behaviors. The situational approaches associate situational factors with the effect of the aforementioned traits and behaviors of leaders on group performance. For example, a situational approach would connect the specific environmental context (i.e., antecedents) with appropriate leader behaviors and resultant consequences (i.e., performance and satisfaction). This ABC model of leadership (adapted from Robert E. Baker, 2003) is reflective of situational leadership theories that have taken into account the antecedents, behaviors, and consequences of leadership. These leadership theories, both within and outside of sport, inform current sport leadership.

Nonsport-Based Leadership Models

Antecedents include all factors that precede leadership. These precursors establish the field of play for leadership and include the motives and dispositions of stakeholders (e.g. leaders and members), general environmental circumstances (e.g. economic conditions), and specific situational characteristics (e.g. tasks at hand and resources available). Leader behaviors are impacted by antecedents. These behaviors focus on interpersonal interactions, leadership styles, interventions, and any mediating actions in the process of leadership. The consequences of leadership are the subsequent satisfaction and performance resulting from leadership activities. Consequences can themselves become the antecedents in a continuous process of leadership. As the framework to integrate leadership concepts, these ABC paradigms frame the interaction of leaders, members, organizations, and environmental dimensions.

Within the framework of antecedents, behaviors, and consequences, essential leadership theories examine leaders, members, and the environments in which they interact. The framework of situational leadership theories developed outside of sport contributes to the understanding of sport-related models. In alignment with Frederick Herzberg's maintenance and motivation factors, Abraham Maslow identified a hierarchy of needs, namely physiological, safety and security, social, self-esteem, and autonomy, that serve to motivate people.

Fred Fiedler's contingency model proposes that any leadership style, ranging from task- to people-oriented, can be effective if it is matched with the appropriate situation. Situational favorableness, or the degree to which circumstances foster leader influence, is based on leader–member relations, task structure, and position power. The better the leader–member relationship, the more favorable situation will occur. Task structure is determined by the clarity of goals, the procedural options, the ability to measure output, and the standards used for evaluation. The more structured the task, the more favorable the

A National Guard soldier compares himself to NBA legend, Michael Jordan. Many consider Jordan the greatest basketball player of all time, and he shall remain a leadership model for the game of basketball. (Flickr/Bernard Chan)

situation. Position power is the authority invested, which reflects the leader's control. The greater the position power, the more favorable the situation. Fiedler concludes that, dependent upon situational favorableness, either people-orientation or task-orientation can be influential in leadership. Task-oriented leaders are effective in circumstances that have very high or very low favorableness, whereas people-oriented leaders are more effective in moderately favorable circumstances. Fiedler's contingency model suggests that some elements of situational favorableness may be more stable than others. As such, altering the situational favorableness is possible by addressing task structure, position power, or leader-member relations.

P. Hersey, K. H. Blanchard, and D. E. Johnson offer the situational leadership model. They integrate leadership theories by integrating critical leadership concepts into a comprehensive model. Member characteristics, leader behavior, significant environmental circumstances, and dimensions such as personality, power, and motivation are considered. Among the many factors considered, the model associates member readiness with leadership style. Member readiness is based upon the constructs of willingness, confidence, commitment, ability, or knowledge and proficiency. Related to their task-oriented, directive behaviors and/or relationship-oriented, supportive behaviors, appropriate leadership styles are characterized as delegating (low-task, low-relationship behaviors), participating (low-task, high-relationship behaviors), selling (high-task, high-relationship behaviors), or telling (high-task, low-relationship behaviors). For example, in appropriate situations where members are both willing and able, leaders can

utilize a delegating style to reassign authority for decisions and execution to members. Facilitative leaders using a participating style share thoughts, seek member input, and include members in decision making if the member is able but insecure or unwilling. Consultative leaders make the decisions but explain and clarify decisions and engage members in dialogue if the members are less able but willing. Authoritative leaders give specific instruction and close supervision to members who are both unable and unwilling or insecure. Based on situational factors, aligning the appropriate leadership style to the performance readiness of members informs effective leadership.

The path-goal theory presents the leader as a facilitator whose role is to clarify the paths to individual goals and align these goals with group goals. The path-goal approach shares the fundamental premise that the situation impacts the effect of leadership, but presents the leader function as supplemental. Four categories of leader behavior are associated with the path-goall approach. Instrumental leader behavior initiates and clarifies what is expected. Supportive leader behavior reflects concern for members. Participative leader behavior involves sharing information and encouraging participation in decision making. Achievement-oriented leader behaviors involve setting challenging goals and having performance expectations. Each of these behaviors is influenced by situational factors such as the nature of the task, the composition of the group, and the goals of the group. In the path-goal approach, the group offers guidance on acceptable goals and procedures, providing direction and support to each individual member. The individual member is the central element in the path-goal process. Members set individual goals, and—with the assistance of the leader—align these goals with the group goals. The path-goal leader facilitates the identification of effective paths to individual goals for each member, which individually and collectively supports group goals, thereby fostering both individual and group success. For example, a coach should merge the goals of individual players with the goals and best interests of the team. Therefore, if each player achieves his or her personal goals, the team will succeed.

Current theories of transactional and transformational leadership focus on the interactive relationship between leaders and members in the leadership process. J. M. Burns identified two distinct approaches to leadership, transformational and transactional, focusing on the process of leadership and not on the leaders themselves. Transactional leadership is not inherently bad, but rather it is situation-dependent. If the circumstances are stable and members and leaders are satisfied with the goals, methods, and outcomes, then the transaction approach may be effective in maintaining the status quo. Transactional leaders use contingent reinforcement through promises, rewards, and punishments in order to stimulate desired member behaviors to which members comply. In contrast to transactional leadership, transformational leadership is grounded in shared vision, collective purpose, leader-member interaction, empowerment, inspiration, trust, and mutual understanding. Transformational leaders articulate the vision for the organization, persuade members of its efficacy, and inspire confidence in member proclivities. Transformational leadership exhibits interrelated facets of (1) idealized charismatic influence, (2) inspirational motivation, (3) intellectual stimulation, and (4) individualized consideration. Burns presented transactional and transformation as mutually exclusive approaches akin to D. M. McGregor's Theory X and Theory Y, wherein a fundamental belief that employees are either inherently lazy and need autocratic leadership, or inherently motivated and need participatory leadership, determines disparate leadership styles. However, effective leadership may actually reflect a combination of both transactional and transformational processes, where transactional and transformational leadership are viewed as opposite extremes on a continuum. Based on environmental circumstances, transactional and transformational leadership influences members to pursue desired goals begrudgingly, willingly, or eagerly.

Sport-Based Leadership Models

Based upon many previous leadership theories external to sport, two models specifically developed in sport are W. J. Weese's Five C Model and P. Chelladurai's Multidimensional Model of Sport Leadership. Weese identified five components of sport leaders: (1) credible character, a foundation of leadership where leaders are respected, reliable, and trustworthy; (2) compelling vision, which creates a focus on desired goals; (3) charismatic communicator, both formally and informally to inspire members; (4) contagious enthusiasm, reflected in the leader's passion and emotional intelligence; and (5) culture builder of shared values within the group that are aligned with the aforementioned vision.

A significant integration of theoretical concepts specifically developed within the context of sport and addressing multiple facets of leadership is Chelladurai's Multidimensional Model of Leadership (MML). Chelladurai isolates such antecedents as leader, member, and situational characteristics. Leader characteristics include personality, ability, and knowledge. Member characteristics include attitudes, skills, commitment, understanding, and so forth. Situational characteristics include (1) the nature of the task at hand; (2) situational norms and leader expectations; (3) organizational structure, goals and size; and (4) the nature of the group. Chelladurai distinguishes leaders' behaviors as required, preferred, and/or actual behaviors. Required behaviors are determined largely by situational elements such as organizational structure, group norms, and the task at hand. Preferred behaviors reflect what members favor in a given situation, derived from the characteristics of members and the situation. Actual behaviors are the actions taken by the leader in a situation based on leader characteristics and required and preferred behaviors. The consequences of the MML, resulting from the congruence of required, preferred, and actual behaviors, are performance and satisfaction. The concept of transformation is included as an influential element in the MML process wherein transformational leaders shape the antecedents that facilitate individual and group outcomes.

The many conceptual models of leadership each have merit, and each adds to a collective understanding of how organizations, leaders, members, and situations interface in yielding productive outcomes. When taken collectively, they also provide insights into the universal nature of leadership and the strategies effective leaders can employ.

Robert E. Baker

See Also: Behavioral Leadership Theory; Command Coaching Style; Development of Leadership Skills; Gender and Sports Leadership; Leadership Skills for Coaches (Professional Sport); Sport Leadership Academic Curriculum; Submissive Coaching Style.

Further Readings

Baker, R. E. and C. Esherick. *The Fundamentals of Sport Management.* Champaign, IL: Human Kinetics, 2013.

Baker, R. E. "Effective Strategies for Sport Leaders." Presented at the Conference of the American Alliance for Health Physical Education Recreation and Dance. Philadelphia: April 2003.

Bass, B. M. *Leadership and Performance Beyond Expectations.* New York: Free Press, 1985.

Burns, J. M. *Leadership.* New York: Harper Perennial, 1982.

Chelladurai, P. *Human Resource Management in Sport and Recreation*, 2nd ed. Champaign, IL: Human Kinetics, 2006.

Chelladurai, P. *Managing Organizations for Sport and Physical Activity*, 4th ed. Scottsdale, AZ: Holcomb-Hathaway, 2014.

Chelladurai, P., et al. "Preferred Leadership in Sports." *Canadian Journal of Applied Sport Sciences*, v.3 (1978).

Hersey, P., K. H. Blanchard, and D. E. Johnson. *Management of Organizational Behavior.* Upper Saddle River, NJ: Pearson Prentice Hall, 2008.

Herzberg, F. "One More Time: How Do You Motivate People?" *Harvard Business Review*, v.46 (1968).

House, R. J. "A Path-Goal Theory of Leader Effectiveness." *Administrative Science Quarterly*, v.16 (1971).

Maslow, A. (1943). "A Theory of Human Motivation." *Psychological Review*, v.50 (1943)

McClelland, D. C., et al. *The Achievement Motive.* New York: Appleton-Century-Crofts, 1953.

McClelland, D. C., et al. "Power is the Great Motivator." *Harvard Business Review*, v.54/2 (1976).

Weese, W. J. "Do Leadership and Organizational Culture Really Matter?" *Journal of Sport Management*, v.19 (1996).

Leadership of Emerging Sports

According to the "NCAA Sport Sponsorship and Participation Rates Report: 1981–82 to 2012–13," since the 1996 to 1997 academic year there were more championship sport teams sponsored in the National Collegiate Athletic Association (NCAA)

for women than for men. The number of women's championship sport teams sponsored in the NCAA has increased each year for the past 30 years. However, an annual analysis of the number of men's teams sponsored paints a very different picture. The number of men's championship sport teams has decreased in two of the last 10 years, but has been steadily increasing since 2003 and 2004 and was at a record high in 2012 and 2013.

In the 2012 to 2013 academic year, just as in the five years previous, the average NCAA member institution sponsored approximately 17 teams—eight for men and nine for women. The trend of sponsoring more teams for women than for men began in the 1997 to 1998 academic year. Compared to early reports from the 1981 to 1982 academic year, the average NCAA school now sponsors approximately two more women's teams and one less men's team.

Much of the shift in program offerings for men and women's programs can be attributed to Title IX, but also to the creation of the NCAA's Committee on Women's Athletics (CWA). The CWA is charged with identifying and managing the progress of emerging sports for women, as well as legislation. The emerging sports program was created in 1994 to help boost participation opportunities for women in a range of new sports. An emerging sport is a women's sport recognized by the NCAA that is intended to help schools provide more athletics opportunities for women, more sport sponsorship options for institutions, and help that sport achieve NCAA championship status.

NCAA Emerging Sport Criteria and Timeline

When the NCAA adopted the recommendations of its Gender-Equity Task Force in 1994, one of the recommendations was the creation of the list of emerging sports for women. Nine sports were on the initial list. NCAA bylaws require that emerging sports must gain championship status (minimum 40 varsity NCAA programs, in Division III only 28 programs are required) within 10 years or show steady progress toward that goal to remain on the list. Institutions are allowed to use emerging sports to help meet the NCAA minimum sports-sponsorship requirements and minimum financial aid awards. In the years since the list was created, four sports have earned championship status: women's rowing, women's ice hockey, women's water polo, and women's bowling.

Four sports have also been removed from the list for lack of growth: women's archery, women's badminton, women's synchronized swimming, and women's team handball. There are four emerging sports on the list: women's equestrian, women's rugby, women's sand volleyball, and women's triathlon.

Men's and coed sports do have a route to NCAA championship status but it is different than the emerging sport for women process. To start a men's or coed sport, 50 NCAA institutions must sponsor varsity programs. Once 50 programs are operating, a petition for adoption is submitted to the NCAA membership before competition is considered official. Not only must the criteria be met to be considered an emerging sport but the activity petitioning must also be classified as a sport. For emerging sport purposes, sport is defined as an institutional activity involving physical exertion with the purpose of competition versus other teams or individuals within a collegiate competition structure. Furthermore, sport must include regularly scheduled competitions (at least five) within a defined competitive season, and have standardized rules with a rating/scoring system ratified by official regulatory agencies and governing bodies. In 2009, when Quinnipiac University's volleyball team sued the university on the basis of Title IX for replacing its program with a co-ed cheer program, a federal judge ruled that cheer in its current state could not be classified as a sport. Two national organizations associated with cheer, U.S.A. Cheer and U.S.A. Gymnastics, worked quickly to meet the definition of sport by creating stunt and acrobatics and tumbling, respectively. Both proposals have been submitted to the CWA and currently stunt has 28 programs competing (19 Division I and nine Division II), whereas acrobatics and tumbling has 10 schools participating (three Division I, six Division II and one Division III). According to a 2014 CWA Report, although both proposals are thorough, the committee decided not to forward either proposal, and has recommended the organizations work together on a single proposal.

Criteria that must be addressed in the proposal include (1) at least 20 or more varsity teams or competitive club teams on college campuses in that sport; (2) an understanding that once classified as an emerging sport all institutions willing to sponsor the sport must abide by NCAA regulations; (3) general competition rules, suggested NCAA regulations (e.g., playing and practice season, financial aid limits, coaching limits, recruiting), and format for the sport (e.g., expected facility requirements and costs, minimum and maximum competitions). In addition to the proposal, 10 letters of commitment must be submitted. The letters must be from 10 member institutions that sponsor or intend to sponsor the sport as an emerging sport and include the signatures of the president and the athletics director of those institutions.

The Case for Triathlon and Sand Volleyball

In January 2014, the NCAA classified women's triathlon as an emerging sport, effective August 1, 2014. More than 160 colleges and universities have triathlon clubs and at least a dozen universities signed a letter of commitment. Yet when asked about the commitment, only one university said it planned to compete at the NCAA level. The CWA report includes information on presentations to the committee from representatives of U.S.A. Triathlon about reaching elite youth coaches and athletes in regard to the emerging sport status, in the hope of educating participants about the current status. Currently, there are about 1,200 collegiate triathletes competing at the national championships and athletics directors like the idea, but many cite lack of funding for their lack of commitment to the sport. U.S.A. Triathlon is helping develop parameters that could be used to include collegiate competition sections of existing events. Data from the CWA report show that the amount of female participation was a factor in its decision to add women's triathalon to the emerging sports list. The expectation is that the addition of women's triathlon will produce a significant increase in participation opportunities for women.

Sand volleyball was added to the list of emerging sports in 2010. The sport, made popular in the United States by the successful Olympic duo Misty May-Treanor and Kerri Walsh, is also aligned with a national governing body, the American Volleyball Coaches Association (AVCA). At the 2010 NCAA convention, sand volleyball survived a petition against adding the game to the emerging sports list. Athletic directors were concerned with finances of adding another sport and losing potential indoor volleyball recruits who also want to play sand volleyball. Since being added to the list, sand volleyball is the fastest growing NCAA sport and has passed the minimum 40 sponsoring institutions to request an NCAA championship. The CWA reported that the sport has met both the goals of the emerging sport for women program and that it is moving to championship status for 2016.

Leadership of emerging sports is multifaceted. It involves college and university students with a desire to participate in a varsity sport, athletic directors, already established sport organization governing bodies like U.S.A. Triathlon and AVCA, along with the NCAA and their desire to boost opportunities for women in new sports through committees like the CWA. Working together to meet the needs of all parties while completing the petitioning process is a time-consuming and arduous task, but one that serves many people well once a sport receives championship status.

Christi De Waele

See Also: Discrimination in Sports; Professional Sports; Title IX; Women's Leadership in Sport.

Further Readings

National Collegiate Athletic Association "NCAA Women's Sport Inventory." http://www.ncaa.org/sites/default/files/NCAA-WSI.pdf (Accessed October 2014).

National Collegiate Athletic Association. "Report of the NCAA Committee on Women's Athletics." http://www.ncaa.org/sites/default/files/April%202014%20CWA%20Report.pdf (Accessed October 2014).

United States of America Triathlon. "FAQs: USA Triathlon's NCAA Initiative." http://www.usatriathlon.org/news/articles/2013/2/021913-collegiate-faqs.aspx (Accessed October 2014).

Leadership Scale for Sports

The Leadership Scale for Sports (LSS) was developed by Pakianathan Chelladurai and Shoukry Saleh to determine if traditional leadership theories were applicable to sport coaches and teams, and to empirically test the Multidimensional Model of Sport Leadership's contention that the effectiveness of coaches'

behavior is dependent on their alignment with team members' preferences and situational requirements. Three unique participant samples (total N = 485) participated in the development of the LSS instrument. Forty items describing the most significant aspects of coaching behavior are divided into five subscales. These factors are identified as (1) training and instruction, (2) democratic behavior, (3) autocratic behavior, (4) social support, and (5) positive feedback. Of the 40 items, 13 items describe training and instruction, nine items describe democratic behavior, five items describe autocratic behavior, eight items describe social support, and five items describe positive feedback.

Training and instruction coaching behaviors are directed toward improving the athletes' performance and include planning, organizing, coordinating, and instructing activities relative to the skills, techniques, and tactics of the sport. Democratic behaviors reflect the degree to which the coach allows athletes to share in important decisions, such as setting group goals, practice methods, and game tactics and strategies. Autocratic behaviors reflect the coach's authority and independent decision making. Social support reflects the coach's concern for the well-being of athletes by fostering interpersonal relationships in a positive environment. Positive feedback behaviors are directed toward reinforcing athletes' positive actions, as well as recognizing and rewarding noteworthy performance. Each item in the LSS is preceded with, for example, "The coach should . . .", "prefer my coach to . . .", "My coach . . .", or "In coaching . . .", depending on the scale's purpose, which is directed toward either required leader behavior, preferred leader behavior, or actual leader behavior, respectively. Each of the 40 items in the LSS provides five Likert-scaled response categories: always, often, occasionally, seldom, and never, where "often" aligns with 75 percent of the time, "occasionally" aligns with 50 percent of the time, and "seldom" aligns with 25 percent of the time.

Chelladurai identified three main purposes for the LSS, to examine (1) athletes' preferences for leadership behaviors, (2) athletes' perceptions of coaches' leadership, and (3) coaches' perceptions of their own leadership behavior. The LSS has been utilized to investigate coaches as leaders. For example, athletes' preferences for, and perceptions of, specific coaching behaviors have been studied. Coaches' perceptions of their own leader behaviors have also been studied. Supporting the Multidimensional Model of Sport Leadership, the LSS measures (1) preferred leader behavior as it refers to athletes' favored behaviors; (2) athletes' perceptions of leader behaviors, which are akin to required leader behavior; and (3) coaches' perception of their own leader behavior as it relates to the actual behavior of the coach.

The LSS has been applied in sport settings to measure sport leadership in a variety of contexts. It also provides researchers the opportunity to investigate the relationship among leadership and a wide range of other variables, from cohesion to organizational commitment to self-efficacy. Different versions of the LSS have been used to investigate leadership in relation to other important areas in sport, for example (1) athletic maturity by P. Chelladurai and A. V. Carron in 1983, (2) coach–athlete relationships by T. Horne and A. V. Carron in 1985, (3) group cohesion by D. L. Light Shields and D. E. Gardner in 1997, (4) gender-based discrepancies in preferences (C. A. Sherman, R. R. Fuller, and H. D. Speed in 2000), and (5) cross-cultural distinctions in sport leadership (P. Chelladurai and colleagues in 1988).

J. Zhang, B. E. Jenson, and B. L. Mann revised the three versions of the LSS that address athlete preference, athlete perception, and coach self-evaluation. A number of potential problems as noted in the literature precipitated the revisions, including varied cultural influences on coaches' behaviors. Zhang et al. proposed that a careful revision of the original LSS would yield a more effective tool for measuring leadership in sport. The revision process consisted of (1) the addition of factors and items, (2) a linguistic check of the LSS, (3) determining the content validity of the LSS, (4) investigating the construct validity and internal consistency reliability of the LSS, and (5) proposing the final revision of the LSS. The revised version of the LSS maintained the same three versions, similar preceding phrases, and the same Likert-scaled response categories. Athletes (n = 696) and coaches (n = 206) were participants in the testing of the LSS, which resulted in 120 new items. The revision yielded two additional factors, which take into account the coaches' behavior directed toward (1) clarifying athlete relationships and improving group cohesion and (2) consideration of

situational factors such as time, environment, game, and group. The revision was determined to be similar in its appropriate use to the original LSS, according to J. Zhang and colleagues. Although this revised LSS is an acceptable measure of leadership in the sport context, the original LSS is still considered a valid and reliable measure of sport leadership.

The LSS is a preeminent mechanism making a significant contribution to study leadership in sport.

Robert E. Baker

See Also: Academic Programs in Sports Leadership; Behavioral Leadership Theory; Leadership Models in Sports; Research Methods in Sports Leadership.

Further Readings
Chelladurai, P. "Leadership in Sports." *International Journal of Sport Psychology*, v.21/4 (1990).
Chelladurai, P. and A. V. Carron. "Athletic Maturity and Preferred Leadership." *Journal of Sport Psychology*, v.5/4 (1983).
Chelladurai, P. and S. D. Saleh. "Dimensions of Leader Behavior in Sports: Development of a Leadership Scale." *Journal of Sport Psychology*, v.2 (1980).
Chelladurai, P., et al. "Sport Leadership in a Cross-National Setting." *Journal of Sport & Exercise Psychology*, v.10 (1988).
Horne, T. and A. V. Carron. "Compatibility to Coach-Athlete Relationships." *Journal of Sport Psychology*, v.7 (1985).
Light Sheilds, D. L., et al. "The Relationship Between Leadership Behavior and Group Cohesion in Team Sports." *Journal of Psychology Interdisciplinary and Applied*, v.131/2 (1997).
Sherman, C. A., et al. "Gender Comparisons of Preferred Coaching Behaviors in Australian Sports." *Journal of Sport Behavior*, v.23 (2000)
Zhang, J., B. E. Jensen, and B. L. Mann. "Modification and Revision of the Leadership Scale for Sport." *Journal of Sport Behavior*, v.20/1 (1997).

Leadership Skills for Athletes

A great many universities and organizations place a high level of importance on the subject of athlete leader development. Despite this, there is a comparative dearth of literary attention paid to athlete leadership versus coach leadership development. As a result, the leadership skills exhibited by coaches are expected to be the same ones that are critical to athletes. While overlap is certain, considering the role of the athlete is unique compared to the coach, it is important to specifically examine the functions and skills related to effective athlete leadership.

The Need for Athlete Leadership

General managers, athletic directors, and particularly coaches set the leadership tone for organizations, influencing athletes in numerous ways. As predicted in many theories, such as transformational leadership, it is likely that the leadership behaviors of these upper-level individuals influence how athletes lead. There is a need for athlete leaders on a team to not only emulate the vision put forth by coaches and administrators but also ensure any remaining leadership functions that may not be exhibited by coaches are fulfilled. Ultimately, the job of an athlete leader is to influence peers toward the upholding of group values and providing what is needed to help the team achieve its goals.

There are both formal and informal roles in fulfilling the leadership need of teams. Formal roles are most often held by captains, although some teams also have team leadership committees. These individuals are elected by coaches, the athletes themselves, or a combination of the two. Not surprisingly, experience and superior athletic skills are the most common characteristics that formal leaders have. Position on the field may also influence who holds formal leadership roles as these individuals may act as the "coach on the field." For instance, players who play in positions centralized on the soccer pitch are often seen as leaders and the quarterback in football as a key on-field decision maker is almost always considered an important leader.

Informal leadership, sometimes called peer leadership, refers to the leadership any athlete on a team may provide to one or more of their teammates. The captain of a team is one voice that may inspire and guide teammates toward a common goal, but he or she does not influence all team members equally. By leveraging the informal leaders on a team, the influence of the captain can then be multiplied. Moreover, as will be discussed briefly below, team processes such as cohesiveness, communication, and collective goal setting are likely enhanced if all members of a team are involved in the leader process.

A related but relatively untapped way to examine athlete leadership is through the concept of shared leadership. In this case, all athletes have equal leadership responsibility and influence on the team. This mode of leadership exemplifies the fact that no one individual can fulfill all the team's leadership needs, and instead all individuals are empowered to take part in the leadership process.

Critical Athlete Leadership Skills

Perhaps because coaches want to choose the correct leaders for their team, more research exists explaining the characteristics of athlete leaders compared to the actual leadership skills and functions of these leaders. Instead, it is generally assumed that the leadership skills important to the coach are the same for athletes. For example, the Leadership Scale for sports, created primarily to examine coach leadership, has been used with athletes with little modification. The Multifactor Leadership Questionnaire, which measures transformational leadership behavior, has likewise been used for both coaches and athletes. An examination of these leader taxonomies that are described in other sections of this article will provide an adequate summary of what general leader skills athletes may exhibit.

It is, however, important to consider which leader skills are most critical to athletes. One dichotomy to consider where coaches and athletes differ is task- versus social-related leadership skills. For instance, it may be more important that coaches have leadership skills that relate most to training and instruction while athlete leadership skills must center on group maintenance and social cohesion. One also may assume that a strict coach who demands a great deal from his players must be balanced with athlete leaders who provide a great deal of positive support through the learning process. Taken in combination, one of the most important skills an athlete leader must have is the ability to convey optimism and enthusiasm.

Perhaps the most important leadership skill unique to athletes is their actual skill in sport. This actual skill in sport may translate into a real leadership attribute: lead by example. While this may seem

One of the important leadership skills for an athlete is to lead by example. When an athlete's actions lead to a derogatory outcome, a media frenzy can result, as was the case with Tonya Harding. Harding, a U.S. figure skating champion, was involved in an incident where a fellow competitor, Nancy Kerrigan, was attacked. Harding received probation, community service, and a fine for her participation in the attack. (Wikimedia Commons/Andrew Parodi)

like an overly simplistic way to view athlete leadership, it is possible that the one way athletes can most influence their peers and help a team toward its goals is by working hard and performing well. The athlete's job is to execute motor skills to achieve some outcome. It is likely that a peer will want to follow those who are performing at a high level.

Leading by example, though, must include more than high performance. It must also include working hard at practice, living the standards of the team, and exhibiting proper values in aspects of life. Confidence, composure, focus, and communication are all aspects athletes must master in order to consistently lead by example.

Athlete Leader Development
There are many modes for leader development including experience, mentorship, and training. While it is clear to most coaches that experience is a predictor of who is a leader, it is not always known what the most important experiences that lead to "effective" leadership are. In other words, performing on a team for a longer period of time may make it more likely that an individual is a leader, but the athlete's leadership skills likely will not be optimized without some nurturing. In many cases, the only leadership development an athlete will receive is mentorship. Athletes may be given different responsibilities

or roles where they have the opportunity to make team-related decisions. Examples may be creating and maintaining locker room standards, recruiting visits, or helping new members transition to the team. Coaches then can provide consistent and appropriate feedback and reinforce positive behaviors.

Teams or individual athletes may also seek out more formal leadership development training from legitimate sport psychology consultants. These professionals may put athletes through a variety of educational experiences. Leadership skills training should be research-based and may include discussing what sport leadership is. Areas of equal importance are the development of communication skills, identification and personalization of core leader values, and the ability to apply motivational strategies. Sport psychologists may also facilitate discussions of group climate, cohesion, team coordination, and overall communication. These activities may set leaders up for success by empowering an entire team to discuss its vision and mission statement. This process may include the identification of core values of a team and a discussion of what behaviors underlie these values. Team leaders can then more easily hold members accountable to transparent expectations of the group.

Conclusion
Identifying and developing athlete leadership is a hot topic in today's world of competitive sport. Foundationally, athletes must lead by example and then according to the needs of a team be empowered to contribute leadership functions of the team. To further enhance team leadership processes, qualified sport psychology professionals may be employed.

Jeff Coleman

See Also: Captains; Development of Leadership Skills; Leadership Scale for Sports; Transformational Leadership.

Further Readings
Gould, D., et al. "Best Coaching Practices for Developing Team Captains." *The Sport Psychologist*, v.27 (2013).
Gould, D., and D. K. Voelker "Youth Sport Leadership Development: Leveraging the Sports Captaincy Experience." *Journal of Sport Psychology in Action*, v.1/14 (2010).

Loughead, T. M., J. Hardy, and M. A. Eys. "The Nature of Athlete Leadership." *Journal of Sport Behavior,* v.29 (2006).

Leadership Skills for Coaches (Amateur Sport)

Coaching amateur sports athletes, especially young people, can be a heavy responsibility for those who volunteer for this duty. Taken in their entirety, the leadership skills necessary to be an effective amateur sports coach are a unique combination of skills or traits that can be learned by the coach who wants to excel at his or her job. These skills or leadership traits are just as necessary for the superstar athlete that is retired and wants to coach her kid's soccer team as for the math teacher at the local high school that did not play baseball and was not close to a superstar athlete but has been asked to coach his middle-school-age son's team. Leadership skills and the ability to be an effective coach are not dependent on the athletic ability or sport skill possessed by the coach; great golfers do not necessarily make great golf instructors and Hall-of-Fame football players do not necessarily possess the leadership skills to become great coaches.

Communication and the Art of Listening

The single most important leadership skill for coaches is the ability to communicate with their players, their player's parents, their assistant coaches, the referees, the umpires, and the coach's supervisor. Without good communication skills, the coach cannot teach, cannot motivate, and cannot convey plays, instruction, or commands to their players.

Coaches must communicate to their players during practice, in meetings, during games, at halftime, during time-outs, after practice, during the off-season, or at an end-of-season banquet. These "communications" can be over the phone, in person, or via digital or social media methods. Each of these communications gives the athletes an indication of the coach's personality and philosophy.

In order to develop a rapport with the team, a coach must be an active listener. Each team member possesses a different set of athletic abilities, sport-specific skills, and a unique personality. Active listening also will permit the coach to learn what motivates each athlete. A leader that develops their listening skills will always have a sense of the pulse of the locker room; an active listener can anticipate problems. An active listener will also encourage team members to come to them if they sense a problem has developed with a teammate.

Expertise

A successful coach must possess a certain amount of knowledge of the sport in which the team is playing or participating as athletes. Each sport has a set of skills, each event or game has a set of tactics, and each sport has a set of rules of competition. It is essential for the coach to have a thorough understanding of skills an athlete needs to be successful, an understanding of game or event tactics to prepare the athlete or the team, and an ability to understand the rules to teach and to benefit the team.

Motivation

Leaders must be able to motivate. Coaches must motivate their athletes to train, to practice, and to compete. Motivation is not something a coach does on the day of the big game or athletic event. Coaches that have the motivational and communication skills to instill in their players a commitment to improve will see constant growth in their teams and individually down the line with each of their athletes.

Team Building

The ability to create a team atmosphere and to inspire team members to work together and be unselfish is both a difficult skill to learn and a valuable skill for sport coaches to possess. Even groups of athletes that participate in individual sports like golf or tennis can benefit from a coach who preaches and lives team building as a leadership skill. Great teams practice more efficiently, enjoy practice more, and get together outside of practice and competitions to engage in more team building. Team members motivate each other and are better able to sense when a teammate needs encouragement when this type of organizational culture has been created. Great coaches can create a team atmosphere that builds upon itself, welcomes new members, and creates lasting legacies for those that have moved on.

Decision Making

A leader of athletes has to make decisions constantly, such as who to place in the starting lineup, what player to name as team captain, when to discipline when team rules have been broken, and when to change strategy during an athletic competition. Many decisions that coaches have to make will not be well received by a few or many of the members of the team. The coach should discuss the steps that went into the making of the decision and communicate to the group why the decision is in the best interests of the team. One of the more difficult decisions coaches have to make at every level of sports is cutting the roster to a manageable or required number of athletes. When coaching young people, these decisions are traumatic for the athlete and the athlete's parents. Disciplinary problems will arise during the course of a season, every coach has had to discipline a player for a violation of team rules.

Teaching Skills and Trustworthiness

A coach is a teacher. Just because one can play a sport well, it does not make a person a good coach or a good teacher of that sport. Teaching is a leadership skill that involves several of the aforementioned skills. Communication, listening skills, and imparting motivation are part of being a good teacher. One learns the verbal or visual cues that each player best responds to when they are developing technical or tactical skill. In addition, new media can help one teach. A video of the movements a coach wants their team to emulate will help teach a new skill or team tactic.

Teams function better and athletes play harder for coaches that they trust. A team will go through losing streaks and a coach will make mistakes over the course of a season. If a team has confidence in a coach's ability to communicate, believes that the coach have the necessary expertise needed for the team, and recognizes the coach as a caring and active listener, th coach is almost all the way home. Teams and athletes also develop trust in leaders that tolerate failure. Coaches should develop the patience to encourage their team members to try new things, and teach the team to not fear failure. This will develop confidence in each athlete and also trust in the coach.

Craig Esherick

See Also: Comparative Models of Sport Leadership; Cooperative Coaching Style; Development of Leadership Skills; Team Building.

Further Readings

Baker, Robert E., and Craig Esherick. "Leadership in Sport Organizations." In *Fundamentals of Sport Management*. Champaign, IL: Human Kinetics, 2013.

Jackson, Phil, and Hugh Delehanty. *Sacred Hoops*. New York: Hyperion, 1995.

Jones, R. L., and Kieran Kingston. *An Introduction to Sports Coaching*. New York: Routledge, 2013.

Riley, Pat. *The Winner Within: A Life Plan for Team Players*. New York: G. P. Putnam's Sons, 1993.

Leadership Skills for Coaches (Professional Sport)

Leadership has been defined countless ways, but definitions in the coaching context commonly include the concept of the leader influencing his or her followers to take a specific course of action that will assist the team in reaching its goals. Coaches at every level of competition are tasked with leading their teams to reach their highest potential or peak performance. Whereas coaches at the intercollegiate, scholastic, and youth level have a more balanced, dual responsibility to both produce peak performance and also teach life lessons, the focus of professional coaches is almost entirely on producing peak performance.

Although many of the best professional coaches also teach life lessons through their sport, they are rarely recognized or rewarded for this. Along with leading their players, they must lead their staff of assistant coaches, athletic trainers, strength and conditioning coaches, and office workers, to name a few. This requires that professional coaches refine their leadership skills in order to cast their vision for the organization in the following ways: communication skills, analytical skills to create a mission statement and core values in alignment with their vision, emotional intelligence to connect with their followers, motivational ability by combining their communication and emotional intelligence skills, strategic and tactical knowledge of their sport and the ability to communicate that knowledge, and coping skills to handle the high stress of the job from both internal and external sources.

Leadership Challenges

Professional coaches share many of the same leadership challenges of coaches at other levels. For example, professional and high-level collegiate coaches must lead players who have often always been the best player on their team or in their event; players who have also often received years of adulation and praise from recruiting services, pundits, coaches, and fans. This barrage of praise can distort a player's perception of their ability in relation to the competition, making them more resistant to accepting instruction. However, professional coaches also face the unique challenge of dealing with adult players who often are initially less accepting of a coach's authority than a child or young adult might. In addition, these adult players are often still in their early 20s and have enormous amounts of money from their playing contracts. This combination of youth and money can also impact some players' decision making, which can hinder their performance or even eligibility to play. Furthermore, these players often make significantly more money than the coach, adding another twist to the traditional power structure of the person in charge being the highest paid. Finally, some professional players have succeeded on raw talent in the past and may not have the fundamental skills needed to be successful at the professional level where the competition is also immensely talented. Getting a player to accept that they may be lacking fundamental skills that will improve their performance may be a tough sell for professional coaches.

Vision, Mission, and Core Values

Whenever a coach takes over a professional team, a critical early task is to cast a vision for the organization. A vision statement is simply a big picture, best-case concept of where the organization should go, or a desired end state. In most cases, selling his or her vision is a large part of the coaching interview process and the initial press conference upon his or her hiring. Once the vision is established then the mission statement can be crafted, often with input from

team and organization members. Allowing input from others is a common technique of effective leaders to get them to buy in to the new vision. The mission statement explains how to turn the vision into reality. Both the vision and mission are supported by the organization's core values. These make up the uncompromising bedrock of the organization. Many coaches work their core values into everyday team activities to ingrain them into players and staff. All three of these components, vision, mission, and core values, are key to establishing the team culture. Communicating this new culture, through individual, small-group, and large-group interactions, is a key leadership skill of professional coaches.

Implementation

Once the direction is set through the new culture it must be constantly enforced. However, this enforcement cannot come solely from the head coach. If the head coach has effectively communicated the culture and empowered his or her followers, then it becomes everyone's job to hold each other accountable. This is a daily emphasis that can be maximized through the leadership skill of emotional intelligence. Emotional intelligence is the skill of sensing and assessing others' emotions, and also sensing, assessing, and controlling one's own emotions. While this terminology is relatively new, it is an old leadership skill of coaches. For example, suppose a coach has a player who is having an issue at home, such as an ill parent, that is distracting the player from his or her preparation, and thus negatively impacting his or her performance. It is a great leadership skill for the coach to show empathy for that situation, perhaps discussing it with the player privately or finding some other way to offer support or resources to the player. This shows the player that the coach values them as a human being and not as simply a cog in an athletic machine. This can help build a strong sense of loyalty between the player and coach, which can positively impact the player's attitude and performance.

If the coach has cast a clear and compelling vision, supported it with a succinct mission statement and core values, and intentionally connected with his or her players by demonstrating emotional intelligence, then it is much easier to motivate those players to give maximum effort in the preparation and competition of athletic events. Motivation now becomes more individualized, more personal, less canned, less disconnected, and less self-serving. The coach does not want the player's best so that the coach gets a reward. Rather, the coach wants the player's best because he or she genuinely cares for that player.

Obviously, a professional coach must also be deeply knowledgeable of the strategies and tactics of their sport. Demonstrating this knowledge, but only after establishing a relationship with players, allows the coach to build credibility and continue to grow support for their team culture. Attempting to demonstrate sport knowledge as a way to get compliance from players is a common mistake of young and/or insecure coaches. It really does not matter how much knowledge a coach has; what is important is what they have imparted to their players, and most important, what their players do with that knowledge under game pressure.

Finally, coaches must have the leadership skill of coping with stress. This is something that can be passed on to the players but also is critical for the coaches themselves. Coaches, especially at the professional level, are under high stress to win games immediately, consistently, and by a margin and in a manner that the media and fans think are appropriate. This pressure can cause some coaches to deviate from their mission and make compromises to their beliefs in pursuit of short-term wins. For example, perhaps a talented but selfish player can help win one game, but this causes more problems in the long run by creating dissension in the locker room, which hurts the performance of other players.

Coaches who are intrinsically motivated, or get their motivation from an internal desire to be the best they can be, have been shown to better cope with the high stress of the job. When players see the head coach coping well with pressure, it also gives them confidence in the coach and a role model in handling their own stress. Coaches who are extrinsically motivated, or get their motivation from external rewards like publicity, money, or fame, have been shown to not cope with stress as well. Again, this example has a large influence on their players and can negatively impact their performance.

Charles H. Wilson, Jr.

See Also: Comparative Models of Sports Leadership; Leadership Scale of Sports; Leadership Skills for Coaches (Amateur Sport); Professional Sports; Team Culture.

Further Readings

Blanchard, Ken, and Don Shula. *Everyone's a Coach*. Grand Rapids, MI: Zondervan, 1995.

Borland, John. *Sport Leadership in the 21st Century*. Burlington, MA: Jones Bartlett Learning, 2014.

Carroll, Pete. *Win Forever*. New York: Penguin, 2011.

Jones, Robin. *The Sociology of Sports Coaching*. New York: Routledge, 2011.

Ramsey, Jack. *Dr. Jack's Leadership Lessons Learned From a Lifetime in Basketball*. Hoboken, NJ: Wiley, 2004.

Riley, Pat. *The Winner Within*. New York: Berkley Books, 1993.

Woods, Ronald. "Coaching Sport." In *Social Issues in Sport*. Champaign, IL: Human Kinetics, 2011.

Legal Responsibilities for Coaches

The legal responsibilities of a coach follow the theory of negligence law. Negligence law consists of a duty, breach of that duty, the proximate causation of harm and actual harm, or damages suffered by the plaintiff. A duty is a responsibility to protect another person from an unreasonable risk of injury. The source of this duty is inherent to the relationship that exists between a coach and athlete. Therefore, a coach is legally responsible to protect his/her athletes from an unreasonable risk of injury.

A coach must provide adequate supervision. This responsibility includes the type of supervision (general or specific, depending on the nature of the activity and age of participant) and number of supervisors required, which commonly depends on the physical environment. In *Hemady v. Long Beach Unified School District* (2006), a 12-year-old student who never played golf before was hit in the head with a golf club by another student. The court held that being hit by a golf club was not inherent to the game of golf nor would having the coach liable for mitigating the risk of being hit in the head be considered a fundamental alteration of the game. Therefore, a physical education teacher may be held liable for the injury to the student by another student.

A coach must provide adequate instruction to the athlete. This requires a coach to teach fundamentals appropriate to the age and skill level of the participants. Many courts require the coaching standard to be reckless as opposed to a lesser standard of simple negligence. For instance, a 260-pound football coach picked up a 144-pound, 13-year-old player and slammed him to the ground, causing a broken arm. The court acknowledged that teaching tackling is vital to football but held that the coach's greater size and experience, his instructions, the force he used, and his prior practice of not using force to teach football technique could allow a reasonable person to find the coach acted in utter disregard for the player's safety.

A coach must provide a safe environment for games and practice. This duty requires the coach to inspect the facility and the equipment. The coach

A coaching team monitors players during a training session. Coaches and their organizations can be legally protected from litigation by having players sign waivers. These waivers state that the athlete promises not to bring a negligent lawsuit against the coach or the team. (Wikimedia Commons/Bernard Chan)

cannot use the facility or any equipment if it is in need of repair. This requirement is a limited duty where the coach does not have to protect against inherent risks of the sport. In the case of *Bukowski v. Clarkson University* (2011), the court held that a coach did not have to provide an L-screen baseball pitching shield for an indoor batting practice because a pitcher getting hit by a batted ball is inherent to the game of baseball, even in batting practice. A California appeals court ruled a horse that was "unfit to ride because of prior falls and a lack of practice" with an avid, youth equestrian competitor can be considered as equipment in its legal analysis.

A coach must evaluate players to match abilities with their competitor's abilities. This responsibility is vitally important for contact sports (e.g., wrestlers must be in the same weight class) and noncontact sports (e.g., a young, inexperienced diver should not be required to dive off a 10-meter dive tower). This duty is limited because a coach or teacher must be able to challenge athletes to improve his or her skill level. In *Kahn v. East Side Union High School District* (2003), a novice member of a swim team practiced a dive into the shallow end of a swimming pool and broke her neck. Although she was terrified of diving and had virtually no experience, her coach required her to dive in order to participate on a relay team. The court applied a reckless standard where a coach must "intentionally injure the student or engage in conduct that is reckless . . . that is totally outside the range of the ordinary activity" of coaching the sport.

A coach must evaluate injuries and perform emergency medical care when needed. A player should not be forced to practice or compete in a game unless they are physically able. In *Jessica Mercier v. Greenwich Academy, Inc., Trustees of Westminster School, Inc. and Bryan Tawney* (2013), a student basketball player was hit in the head during a game by an opposing player. She informed her coach that she felt dizzy and he sat her on the bench for five minutes, where she alleges she exhibited symptoms of a concussion. She re-entered the game and was struck in the head a second time. The court declined to apply the negligence standard, which may chill competitive play. The court would allow a reckless claim to proceed to decide if allowing an injured player who exhibits symptoms of a concussion constituted an extreme departure from ordinary care.

The failure to perform these duties at the level of a reasonable, prudent coach constitutes a breach of duty. When the breach of the duty is the proximate cause for the injury, a coach may be held liable. For instance, a coach may be liable for a player's head injury if the athlete wore an ill-fitting helmet during a game but probably not for an ankle injury. The ill-fitting helmet would need to be the proximate cause of the injury because of the duty to provide the athlete a safe environment.

Finally, there must be an actual injury. If the player wore an ill-fitting helmet but it did not cause any injury (perhaps the player never got into the game), then the coach would not have been negligent in his legal duties.

A coach has legal defenses available to him against these claims. First, if one of the negligence elements was not met, then there is no liability. For example, the breach of duty did not proximately cause the injury. In *Sanders v. Kuna Joint School District* (1994), a weightlifting teacher decided to have his class play softball instead of lifting weights without giving notice to the students. Despite a student breaking his ankle during the game, a court found no connection between the teacher not providing any softball instruction and the injury suffered by the student. Therefore, the coach was not legally liable for the injury.

Another available defense is the assumption of risk defense. For this defense to be available, the injury must be suffered due to an inherent risk to the sport and the athlete must know, understand, and appreciate that risk. A coach has no duty to protect an athlete from a risk that arises from the nature of the sport itself. Sports, especially contact sports, possess a significant potential of harm to the participants. Football players will be tackled. Runners will suffer from pulled leg muscles. Swimmers will develop sore shoulders. These injuries result from the participation in the sport itself. A sport organization can use a signed document to prove the athlete knew, understood, and appreciated the inherent risks to a sport.

Finally, many sport organizations protect themselves from potential liability arising from a coach's legal responsibilities via a signed waiver. A waiver is a contract that provides the sport activity in exchange for a promise by the athlete not to bring a negligence lawsuit. Although a waiver does not absolve a coach of his or her duty to protect the athlete from an unreasonable risk of harm, it provides a legal barrier against a potential lawsuit in many jurisdictions.

Sporting activities are inherently dangerous to participants. A coach has a legal duty to protect athletes from an unreasonable risk of harm while participation in a sporting activity.

Mark Dodds

See Also: Draft System; Economics of Sports; Legal Responsibilities for Managers and Owners; Owners and Business Leadership; Sports Law; Team Culture.

Further Readings

Epstein, Adam. *Sports Law*. Boston: Cengage Learning, 2002

Mitten, Matthew. *Sports Law & Regulation: College Edition*. Aspen, CO: Aspen Publishers, 2012.

Sharp, Linda, Anita Moorman, and Cathryn Claussen. *Sport Law: A Managerial Approach*. Scottsdale, AZ: Holcomb Hathaway, 2010.

Spengler, John R., Paul Anderson, Dan Connaughton, and Thomas Baker. *Introduction to Sport Law*. Champaign, IL: Human Kinetics, 2009.

Wong, Glenn M. *Essentials of Sports Law*. Westport, CT: Praeger, 2010.

Legal Responsibilities for Managers and Owners

Legal issues, with respect to managers and owners of professional sport leagues and individual sport player associations, primarily include contract law, labor law, federal antitrust law, and the law of private associations. The governance structure of professional leagues can create legal issues for both owners and managers included but not limited to legal structure of leagues, franchise relocation, expansion, contraction, equipment regulations, commissioner power and authority, ownership, and player safety.

Governance Structure of Professional Sport Leagues and Legal Considerations

Professional sport leagues in the United States are typically structured in a three-tier format: commissioner, board of governors and/or owners, and the league office. The players are represented through a labor union structured as a players association. Collective bargaining agreements govern the relationship between the players and league management. Collective bargaining law and federal labor laws as defined by the National Labor Relations Act require professional players (as represented by their unions) to negotiate with management a contract stipulating hours, wages, work conditions, and other terms and conditions of employment. The role of the commissioner is unique in that he/she is hired and fired by the owners, yet the commissioner has the authority to discipline owners. Commissioners make decisions that presumably weigh owner interests in the overall implications of a situation on the league's reputation.

In 2014, National Basketball Association (NBA) Commissioner Adam Silver did just that when he banned Los Angeles Clippers owner Donald Sterling for life for racial comments. Silver's authority in the Sterling case is set forth by "prejudicial and detrimental" actions as defined in the league constitution, such actions being damaging to the integrity of the league. Sterling's actions, thus, resulted in a $2.5 million fine, a lifetime ban, and a mandate to sell the team.

National Football League (NFL) Commissioner Roger Goodell has also come under recent scrutiny for initially barring Ray Rice from two games and then legthening the ban to indefinite suspension after a video surfaced of him hitting his then fiancé and now wife in an Atlantic City hotel elevator. A league commissioner's authority is constrained by the league constitution and the terms of the collective bargaining agreement. Goodell contended the subsequent suspension of Rice was within his power to "act in the best interest of the game" in an attempt to maintain the public's confidence in the league. An outside arbitrator overturned Goodell's indefinite suspension of Rice, concluding it was unfair to punish Rice twice for the same offense.

Goodell's decisions in the Rice situation appears on one account to be supported by the court's ruling in *Finley v. Kuhn* (1978). The case established that the courts should not interfere with the authority of the commissioner if he/she is acting in the best interest of the game, and if his/her actions are within the scope of his/her duty as set forth by the league's constitution and bylaws and collective bargaining agreements (CBA). The argument made by the National Football League Player's Association (NFLPA) on Rice's behalf case contests that Goodell acted outside the scope of his duty as defined by the CBA when increasing his initial two game suspension of Rice to an indefinite one. *NBA v. Artest* (2004) and *Chicago National League Ball Club v. Vincent* (1992) both established that the discretionary power of league commissioners to "act in the best interest of the game" do not supersede a league's constitution, bylaws, and bargaining agreements.

The governance structure of professional sport organizations—predominantly the "Big Four," as well as new and emerging leagues (with a team structure)—present unique challenges to the traditional application of antitrust law as applied to businesses. Historically, and in present day, the "Big Four" of professional sport leagues in the United States is made up of the National Football League (NFL), Major League Baseball (MLB), National Basketball Association (NBA), and the National Hockey League (NHL). Contrary to other sport businesses like Reebok and Under Armor, who compete for increased market share and seek to overrun their competition, professional sport leagues seek to maintain parity in an attempt to maximize the value of the competitive product and the league's revenue. This approach forces cooperative action between teams, more specifically owners, and the league to preserve financial competitiveness. Emerging leagues, like Major League Soccer (MLS) and the Women's National Basketball Association (WNBA), have constructed single-entity models in order to establish parity in large and small markets. It is this attempt to thwart economic competitive, that presents sport organizations with antitrust implications and potential violations.

Legal Precedents and Implications

The Sherman Act (15 U.S.C. §§ 1-2) prohibits concerted action (i.e., joint action between two or more parties) that unreasonably restrains trade in a relevant market. Relevant market refers to the economic market in which a business operates. Section 2 of the act prohibits predatory or exclusionary conduct that is designed to enable an organization to acquire or maintain monopoly power in a relevant market. The primary purpose of antitrust legislation is to protect the free market and provide consumers with competitive prices. Courts have established the rule of reason analysis when examining matters of antitrust as it applies to professional sport leagues. The rule of reason analysis accommodates for the economic competitive balance needed for professional leagues to prosper. Essentially, this balances the necessary need to unreasonably restrain trade or other per se violations for the "good of the collective whole," in other words, the league. In *Brown v. Pro-Football, Inc.* (1996), the Supreme Court maintained that professional sport teams must strike a balance between competition and cooperation.

Additionally, in *Fraser v. Major League Soccer* (2002), the court upheld the single-entity model of the MLS and concluded that the league was not in violation of antitrust laws by controlling player salaries. The single entity model appears to potentially limit antitrust liability (*San Francisco Seals, Ltd. v. National Hockey League*, 1974; *Fraser v. MLS*, 2002) but not eliminate it completely. The majority of courts have ruled against the single-entity defense when argued by the traditional professional sport leagues in the United States (e.g., *North American Soccer League v. National Football League*, 1982; *Los Angles Memorial Coliseum v. National Football League*, 1984; *Sullivan v. National Football League*, 1994). Yet, this model remains popular among emerging leagues primarily because it allows leagues greater control over player costs by their ability to impose salary cap restraints unilaterally.

Additional antitrust considerations for league owners and managers include: team ownership, cross-ownership (*North American Soccer League v. National Football League*, 1982), transfer of ownership (*Piazza v. Major League Baseball*, 1993; *Baseball at Trotwood, LLC v. Dayton Professional Baseball Club*, 1999), franchise relocation and territorial rights (*Los Angeles Memorial Coliseum v. National Football League* [*Raiders I*], 1984), restrictions player supply (*Philadelphia World Hockey Club, Inc. v. Philadelphia Hockey Club*, Inc., 1972), television (*United States Football League v. National Football League*, 1988), and regulation of equipment that restricts exclusivity in equipment contracts (*American Needle v. National Football League, 2009*).

Professional sport managers and owners must have knowledge of the principles of both contract and employment law. Most leagues and collective bargaining agreements require the use of standard player contracts. Historically, leagues utilized the standard player contract with a "reserve clause" to control player costs. The reserve clause withstood numerous legal challenges under contract law, and it was not until it was challenged under antitrust law that it was eliminated in *Flood v. Kuhn* (1978). *Flood v. Kuhn* (1978) established modern-day free agency, allowing players to competitively bid their services to other teams. Standard players contracts, to date, cannot contradict league collective bargaining agreements, constitutions and bylaws. Very few player contract disputes have gone to court since the introduction of collective bargaining agreements in professional sports.

Contract negotiation, structure, and remedies for breach of contract are vital to the overall financial health of a team. For example, *White v. National Football League* (2008) had considerable implications for Atlanta Falcons' owner Arthur Blank when the court ruled that the team could not recover over $16 million of bonuses paid to former and imprisoned quarterback Michael Vick. The court ruled that roster bonuses were "other salary escalators" and therefore already earned. On the contrary, *Miami Dolphins, Ltd. v. Williams* (2005) upheld an arbitration award that required Ricky Williams to repay $8.6 million paid in signing bonuses and incentives to the Dolphins after a four-game suspension for his third violation of the league's substance abuse policy.

Sport managers must understand the importance of negotiating contracts from a "worse case" perspective. This philosophy should apply to all contacts, including but not limited to coaching contracts, sponsorship, marketing, and endorsement agreements by the sport organization.

Legal implications for sport owners and managers are vast. Litigation, legislation, and collective bargaining agreements are continuously changing the legal considerations required of sport owners and managers to make sound management decisions. Successful sport managers understand that legal considerations are inherently interlaced into their managerial roles. Sport organizations that gain competitive advantage in the marketplace do so by maintaining superior businesses practices that are legally sound, thereby minimizing liability.

Kristi Sweeney

See Also: Draft System; Economics of Sports; Legal Responsibilities for Coaches; Owners and Business Leadership; Sports Law; Team Culture.

Further Readings

Epstein, Adam. *Sports Law.* Boston, MA: Cengage Learning, 2002.

Mitten, Matthew. *Sports Law & Regulation: College Edition.* Aspen, CO: Aspen Publishers, 2012.

Sharp, Linda, Anita Moorman, and Cathryn Claussen. *Sport Law: A Managerial Approach.* Scottsdale, AZ: Holcomb Hathaway, 2010.

Spengler, John R., Paul Anderson, Dan Connaughton, and Thomas Baker. *Introduction to Sport Law.* Champaign, IL: Human Kinetics, 2009.

Wong, Glenn M. *Essentials of Sports Law.* Westport, CT: Praeger, 2010.

Locker Room Leadership

While strong in-game management, motivation, and talent is vital to the success of both amateur and professional sports teams, leadership outside of the performance setting plays a significant role in creating a close-knit team or driving players apart. This is not only because individual team members who understand organizational culture exhibit behaviors more conducive to success, but also because of increased restrictions on the amount of time that coaching staffs and managers can interact with their athletes. Sports teams, which operate similarly to other business organizations, create management structures whereby coach or player appointed leaders become representatives for the entire team in meetings with coaches and ownership. Frequently, a captain is elected or assigned and becomes the authority among the players in terms of on- and off-field team culture. This is analogous to a middle manager in an office setting being responsible for aligning his or her team's performance with the goals of upper management, while also providing key bottom-up information about the state of the team.

Leaders in the locker room, who are often times veteran players, have a significant role in instilling team culture and norms to new (and often young) players. Thus, while there can be a huge benefit when a team has strong leaders, when there is poor "off-field" leadership, it can be a significant detriment to team cohesion. To combat the possibility of a weak or toxic leader, sporting organizations have begun to elect leadership councils to divide up power and leadership responsibilities. At high levels of competition, practice, preparation, and a general desire to work together are paramount to consistent success in games, and strong leaders on and off the field set the tone for the team.

Organizational Structure

It is almost exclusively the responsibility of ownership and coaches to create the roster of their team through the league draft, trades, and signing free agents. However, once the team is created, it is the captain or team leadership council that defines the team's mission and establishes expectations for the rest of the team. While these expectations may be influenced by the coaching staff, the leader in the locker room sets the tone for following the direction of the coach. Clear expectations from ownership and coaches are thus vital; but with the need for the athletes to actually carry out the desired behaviors, it is important for the team to see a peer adhering to a set of standards if they are to be compelled to follow specific rules. Like in many other business settings, peer coaching and mentoring have positive effects on team effectiveness as compared to a superior (e.g., coach, supervisor), simply telling subordinates how to behave. However, with a greater influence on team culture and behavior, peer leaders who are not positive role models can be a huge detriment to the team.

Impact of Poor Leadership

Toxic leadership outside of game situations can distract team members during play and also lead to unwanted negative publicity from the press and

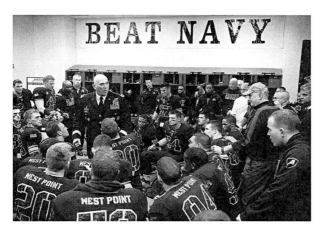

U.S. Army Chief of Staff, General Raymond T. Odierno, gives a locker room speech to the Army Black Knights football team prior to the 113th Army versus Navy football game on December 8, 2012, in Philadelphia. (U.S. Army/Teddy Wade)

fans. In the case of the 2013 Miami Dolphins football team, it was not a lack of peer influence off the field that led to divisions among team members, but rather athletes in leadership roles that abused their position of power and did not uphold organizational values. The scandal manifested when Jonathan Martin, an offensive tackle for the Dolphins, resigned from the team, citing bullying from Richie Incognito, a teammate who had been voted by the players to the team's leadership council. Incognito's on-field skills and veteran status may have made him a strong candidate for a leadership role, but it became clear that he did not instill any sense of team unity or mutual respect for teammates off the field; in addition to sending harassing texts and voicemails to Martin, Incognito created a culture of bullying among the entire offensive line, which culminated in Martin's teammates ignoring him during team meals and questioning his toughness. In most teams and organizations, Martin would be able to report this type of harassment to a superior; however, in this case, the toxic leader was the one causing the mental distress among those he was leading.

While bullying and harassment among peers in both a locker room and office setting clearly has a negative effect on team performance, it becomes much harder to address when it is a team leader driving the team apart with harassment or general disregard for upholding team values. That

is, general managers and owners put captains and team leadership councils in place in order to quell exactly the type of disputes that came up between Martin and Incognito. The team leaders are put in positions to stop any behavior that would be detrimental to the team's unity and on-field performance; and given that players are spending such a significant amount of time with one another during the season, leaders presumably have a hand on the pulse of team morale and attitude. In Incognito's case, he seemed to have a misconstrued understanding of increasing self-esteem in his teammates. Furthermore, it was clear that he hid problems from upper management because bringing up the Martin case would have only been an indictment of him. With this scandal, which is certainly not the first or last case of toxic leadership in sports, it becomes clear that experience and talent should certainly be part of the criteria for choosing team leaders. However, leaders must be held accountable for teaching ethical and supportive behavior to their teammates. The most effective leaders do this by first displaying these behaviors themselves.

Importance of Strong Leaders

It is rare that team leaders and captains are given power over playing time, game strategy, and management of the team from a strategic perspective. Thus, the impact of an influential leader is demonstrated by setting an example for teammates to follow rather than dictating orders. In many sports, the role of the leader is to be a mentor to younger players and exhibit valued behaviors. For instance, in Major League Baseball, the captain of the team is the face of the franchise and is connected to the local community and charitable organizations. It is important for both younger players and players new to the organization to see these behaviors in a long-standing member of the team who has already gained respect and trust from upper management and also from the fan base. This gives the coach and ownership a model of behavior for other players to follow, and if the behaviors are not followed, it gives the coaching staff reason to not keep specific players on the roster or discipline them accordingly.

Nowhere is leading by example more important than in major television markets such as New York. There are simply more media outlets to scrutinize an athlete both on and off the field. Derek Jeter, the former captain of the New York Yankees, and David Wright, the captain of the New York Mets, were handpicked by ownership not just for their play on the field but also because of the example they set off the field. These players purposely keep their personal lives guarded and make sure to remind younger players to not give the media headline stories from outside the field of play.

Furthermore, when the team is going through adversity on the field, the captain takes on the important role of keeping team morale high and focused on getting back on track. Conversely, when the team experiences success, the captain plays an integral part in keeping motivation high in order to stay at a high level of play.

The title of the captain and locker room leader is not bestowed on run-of-the-mill players, and typically not all teams will have a captain at a given time. The players must meet stringent qualifications while also playing for the same team for the majority of their career. With the comparatively short career lengths in other professional sports coupled with a maximum of four years with a team at the National Collegiate Athletic Association (NCAA) level, many teams have divided up the responsibilities of the team leaders and elect new leaders on a yearly basis.

Addressing Team Leadership Issues

One way in which amateur and professional sports teams have attempted to mitigate the issues that can come from a single locker room leader is the formation of a leadership team. That is, in collegiate football, the National Hockey League and the National Football League, management spreads responsibility among multiple players so that there is a checks and balances system in place in case one leader fails to uphold organizational values. Within football locker rooms at the collegiate and professional level, the sheer size of a roster tends to call for multiple leaders as opposed to a single captain. The different personalities found within a defensive line and wide receivers, for instance, require different leadership traits and tactics. A baseball roster, by contrast, with only 25 players in uniform for the majority of the season, may look for one voice in the locker room instead of multiple voices as seen in football and hockey. Assigning

important roles to multiple players can also instill a strong sense of responsibility among a larger percentage of the team. However, each leader on the leadership committee must exhibit the same organizational values and hold each player accountable for this system to work.

The recent scandal in the Miami Dolphins' locker room highlighted a lack of leadership throughout the organization, since the other players on the leadership council failed to call out Incognito's abuses. Whether via a single source of influence or multiple sources, successful teams have strong leaders in place. When there is a common understanding of acceptable behavior among team members in and out of game situations, members become more comfortable with one another and works together toward common goals. And, while strong leadership outside of the playing environment can never guarantee success, weak or abusive leadership creates divisions within a team that take the focus away from coming together to build a winning culture. In-game skill and strong leadership is crucial to success in team sports, but often it is the off-camera behaviors of team leaders that make the biggest difference in cohesion and trust.

James A. Schwabach

See Also: Bullying/Hazing; Captains; Organizational Leadership; Team Culture.

Further Readings

Bell, J. "Bell: Bullying Case Points to Leadership Void on Dolphins." *USA Today*. http://www.usatoday.com/story/sports/nfl/columnist/bell/2013/11/05/bell-richieincognito/3440153 (Accessed September 2014).

Hughes, J. "David Wright, Derek Jeter and the Role of Captains in MLB."http://bleacherreport.com/articles/1585248-david-wright-derek-jeter-and-the-role-ofcaptains-in-mlb (Accessed September 2014).

McCormack, B. "Players Say No Shortage of Leadership in Jackets' Locker Room." http://bluejackets.nhl.com/club/news.htm?id=730813 (Accessed September 2014).

Morgeson, F., D. DeRue, and E. Karam. "Leadership in Teams: A Functional Approach to Understanding Leadership Structures and Processes." *Journal of Management*, v.36 (2010).

M

Major League Baseball

Major League Baseball (MLB), founded in 1869, oversees the sport of baseball at the highest level in the United States and Canada and is the management group for Minor League Baseball (MiLB), the World Baseball Classic (WBC), and the International Baseball Federation. MLB is organized in two divisions, the American and National League, which are each composed of 15 teams. A key difference between the leagues is the use of a designated hitter (DH) by the American League. During interleague play, the DH rule is only used in American League ballparks. MLB hosts an annual All-Star game in July and competition culminates each fall in a World Series to crown the champion in a best-of-seven series. A commissioner and several vice presidents oversee all management aspects of the league. Currently, major league baseball boasts the largest attendance in the world for professional sports.

Early Years
The MLB was founded in 1858, making it the oldest of the four major professional sports leagues in the United States. Previous to this, rules were established by the New York Knickerbocker Club, with the first official baseball game being played under these rules in June 1846. The first "professional" team, the Cincinnati Red Stockings, was established by a group of investors looking to capitalize on the game's growing popularity following the Civil War. The team, which would move to Boston a year later,

joined with eight other teams on the east coast to form the National Association of Base Ball Players.

While the MLB was still in its infancy, leagues battled for supremacy and baseball began to take shape as a business. The National League had the most authority, while the American Association and Player's League attempted to gain a foothold. In 1900, the American League was founded and many star players bolted the National League in favor of the new establishment. Instead of battling each other for players and control, the National League and American League came to form the National Baseball Commission, which would soon usher in the first World Series in 1903. The National Baseball Commission formed the foundation for Major League Baseball today.

Governance and Organization
There are four components to *The Official Professional Baseball Rules Book*, the overall governing document for the league: the MLB constitution, Major League rules, Professional Baseball Agreement, and Basic Agreement.

The Major League constitution is the governing document for MLB, and was enacted in 1876. The constitution has undergone numerous changes as the organization and sport have evolved. Currently, the constitution consists of 11 articles addressing all aspects of the game and leadership, from playing rules to fiscal responsibility. The charter establishes the league administration as one commissioner, a chief operation officer, and five vice-presidents that oversee numerous departments.

Major League Rules has 33 topical areas, providing policies regarding all aspects of league governance. It articulates rules regarding the player draft, contracts, transfers, umpires, retired players, and waivers. Furthermore, it details numerous examples of misconduct such as throwing games, gifts to umpires, betting on events, violence, and player misconduct. Other areas addressed include fiduciary aspects such as gate receipts, finances, schedules, and postseason play and revenue. Last, the document addresses the balance of power between MLB and the Major League Baseball Players Association, (MLBPA) noting that the collective bargaining agreement would supersede any rule conflicts. The Professional Baseball Agreement is most commonly referred to as the collective bargaining agreement (CBA). In 1968, MLB signed the first ever CBA in professional sports. The CBA deal at the time of publication is set to expire on December 1, 2016. In addition to the Basic Agreement, the MLBPA has included both a Joint Drug Agreement and NSF-Approved (National Science Foundation) Supplements list to the CBA.

MLB Commissioner's Office

The commissioner is the chief executive officer of MLB, overseeing all aspects of management for MLB, MiLB, and other international operations. Team owners choose the commissioner by vote. The commissioner's office is structured as an independent party, acting on behalf of the best interests of the game.

Commissioners have played a key role in the development of the game as a business. Former federal judge Kenesaw Mountain Landis (1920–44) was baseball's first sole commissioner, leading the league through the Black Sox Scandal of 1919, in which several players of the Chicago White Sox threw the World Series to aid gamblers. Leadership by Happy Chandler (1945–51) led the way to integration. He was followed by Ford Frick (1951–65), who oversaw team expansion. Bowie Kuhn (1969–84) oversaw a period of great development of revenue but also much labor strife. He ushered in evening games for the World Series, which saw increased viewership. Following in Kuhn's footsteps, Peter Ueberroth (1984–89) continued to press baseball's business interests by negotiating a $1.2 billion contract with CBS, expanding playoff series, and broadening sponsorship agreements with several companies to add additional revenue streams. While attendance was increasing and teams were making profits or breaking even for the first time in years, Ueberroth's legacy was marred by several legal actions brought against the league by the MLBPA, who successfully argued CBA violation cases against the league in court.

Following Ueberroth, Bartlett Giamatti (1989) served for a short time, but his legacy is forever connected to his lifetime ban of Pete Rose for gambling. Faye Vincent (1989–92) succeeded in expansion efforts, provided leadership during the 1990 lockout, and laid the groundwork for team realignment, which would become a reality in 1994. He was removed in 1992 by a no-confidence vote of owners, who were still angry about his handling of the lockout and were concerned about falling viewership numbers. Leading his ouster was owner Bud Selig, who took over after Vincent's removal. Under Selig's leadership, MLB introduced interleague play, the development of the World Baseball Classic, additional team expansion and realignment, instant replay, and considerable new stadium development. Revenues increased dramatically under his leadership, while the luxury tax and revenue sharing system continued to attempt to address issues of competitive balance. Rob Manfred became commissioner in 2015.

MLB Advanced Media and Productions

In recent years, as more focus has shifted to media management to capture additional revenue sources, MLB Advanced Media (MLBAM) and MLB Productions were created to administer team Web sites and oversee traditional and social media. MLB is also the largest ownership group in the MLB Network.

In 2000, with the Internet becoming a greater vehicle for promotion and fan engagement, MLB clubs consolidated all Internet rights and formed MLBAM as a central unit. In an effort to develop additional revenue sources, the league began streaming online and allowing fans to purchase out-of-market games for a fee. Several years later, in 2010, MLBAM partnered with media power ESPN for video-streaming capabilities as newer technologies allowed baseball fans to access games across numerous platforms.

MLB International is the organizational arm of MLB that connects the world and U.S. troops serving abroad to games through traditional media. In addition, the World Baseball Classic (WBC) features the combinations of national teams and professional players from MLB, who represent their home country. Since the elimination of baseball as an Olympic-sponsored sport in 2005, the WBC has become the global showcase of baseball, yet is still struggling to gain widespread popularity in the United States. The event is held every four years and serves to continue the expansion of the sport and the MLB brand globally.

MLB Player's Association

The beginning of a players union dates back to 1912, when harsh treatment by owners led several key league stars to form the Fraternity of Professional Base Ball Players. While initially ignored by management, a threat from a new league seeking to use player disharmony to poach players away from MLB led baseball owners to finally recognize the fraternity and initially consent to player demands and raise salaries. This, however, did not last long. Historians attribute player dissatisfaction with management as a key reason for the Black Sox Scandal. This stain on the game cemented the role of a single commissioner following hefty lifetime bans issued by the office. Other player associations such as the National Baseball Players Association of the United States (1922) and The American Baseball Guild (1946) were established to address player issues.

The MLB Player's Association (MLBPA) was formally established in 1953, but did not make significant strides until Marvin Miller took over the organization in 1966. Two years later, Marvin oversaw the first collective bargaining agreement (CBA), raising the minimum salary and setting the table for the following CBA, which resulted in arbitration and later the first player strike. Several player stoppages would mark the last 40 years.

Today, the MLBPA is widely considered the most powerful player representation organization in professional sports; it has been a central force during the "steroid era." While initially opposed to testing, the association bowed to pressure from Congress and the public and agreed to a testing program. Notably, MLB is the only professional league of the largest established leagues in the United States to not utilize a salary cap.

MLB, Antitrust, and the Reserve Clause

Rising player salaries has been a management worry since baseball's infancy as a professional sport. In order to control the ability of players to shop their services to multiple teams, and thus drive up player salaries as result, baseball created the reserve clause. The reserve clause meant that a team held the rights to a player following the year in which the player's contract expired. This limited free agency. However, industries have not been prohibited from this type of collusion by the Sherman Antitrust Act.

In 1922, the U.S. Supreme Court ruled in *Federal Baseball Club v. National League* that baseball is not interstate commerce and therefore cannot be subject to federal antitrust law. This decision was later reaffirmed in 1953 in *Toolson v. New York Yankees* and the 1972 case *Flood v. Kuhn*, which, while upholding MLB's antitrust exemption, led the way to baseball establishing free agency.

Steroid Era

Though performance-enhancing drug use in baseball has existed for generations, the late 1980s through the end of the 2000s has been labeled the "steroid era" due to its impact on the game publically and politically. Steroids were banned in 1991, but league-wide testing did not begin until 2003. Though without testing it was tough to conclusively prove players "juiced," several admissions from Jose Canseco's autobiography to the federal investigation of the Bay Area Laboratory Co-0perative (BALCO) brought steroid use in baseball to greater public and congressional scrutiny.

Baseball's popularity surged with the marketability of power hitters and record breakers such as Mark McGwire, Sammy Sosa, and Barry Bonds. However, along with their feats came doubts about the path to their success. In 2006, U.S. Senator George Mitchell was tasked by MLB to convene a panel to investigate drug use by players. In 2007, the Mitchell report linked 89 players, including several stars, with the use of drugs and put forward 20 recommendations to bolster the current drug policy. Under new guidelines, several players have been issued lengthy suspensions and Hall of Fame voting has been impacted by player admissions.

Annemarie Farrell

See Also: Drugs, Doping; Economics of Sports; Minor League Baseball; Professional Sports.

Further Readings

Davies, Ross E. "Along Comes the Players Association: The Roots and Rise of Organized Labor in Major League Baseball." *New York University Journal of Legislation and Public Policy*, v.16 (2013).

Elfrink, Tim, and Gus Garcia-Roberts. *Blood Sport: Alex Rodriguez, Biogenesis, and the Quest to End Baseball's Steroid Era*. New York: Dutton Adult Trade, 2014.

Fero, Howard, and Rebecca Herman. *Lead Me Out to the Ballgame*. San Diego, CA: Major League Leadership Enterprises, 2014.

Gennaro, Vince. *Diamond Dollars: The Economics of Winning in Baseball*. Las Vegas, NV: CreateSpace, 2013.

Steve Bernier of the Calgary Flames and Brad Ference of the San Jose Sharks begin a fight during a game in 2006. Fighting in ice hockey is an established tradition in North America, with a history including both amateur and professional play, as well as some notable individual fights. (Flickr/Elliot Lowe)

Managing Conflicts

Conflict management or conflict resolution includes a number of methods and processes for facilitating the amicable ending of a conflict in a way that demotivates, prevents, or discourages retribution, and that, at the same time, brings about a true resolution rather than postpones the resumption of hostilities. Conflicts need not necessarily be hostile to require management and resolution. Consensus building is an approach to decision making that seeks to find a consensus among the group in order to prevent conflict and to produce decision outcomes that can be abided by even those participants who disagree with them. Though this is not always possible, in sports it may at least be an ideal.

In sports, each game or match is, in a sense, a conflict in and of itself or a conflict that has in some sense been dramatized or abstracted. This is not irrelevant to managing conflicts within the sporting world; when adrenaline is pumping and team members and staff are emotionally engaged with the abstract conflict, they may also be more inclined to conflict with each other or to let their egos or tempers get in the way when such conflicts occur. This is true even independent of the possibility that sports at a high-enough level of skill attract personality types who may be especially conflict-prone or powerful in their egos.

Conflicts occur whenever one individual objects to or attempts to prevent the actions of another individual. In sports, this may happen between one coach and the opposing coach; the coach and the staff or management; the coach and parents; the coach and athletes; the coach and a referee, umpire, or other official; the coach and fans; parents and fans; parents and their children; parents and their children's teammates; parents and referees; parents and other parents; teammates among themselves; athletes and opponents; or even within an individual him/herself.

Typical conflicts in children's sports involve a parent upset by the way their child-athlete is being coached, especially feeling that their child is spending too much time on the bench or, conversely, is being made to spend too much time at practice (at the expense of studies or household responsibilities); a coach upset by a referee or umpire's ruling; two athletes competing for the same position, or for a single spot on a team; or problems with the administration, such as the need to suspend a player from the team due to poor grades, or the inability to upgrade equipment because of budget problems. There may also be off-field conflicts with the other team, especially in the case of regional rivalries; in many towns across America, it is traditional for rival teams (or their student supporters) to pull pranks of varying severity on one another, especially in the weeks leading up to an anticipated game. Heated tempers and adolescent short fuses can easily let otherwise lighthearted pranks escalate into serious and harmful conflicts.

The experience of conflict, however, is also one of the benefits of playing sports as a young person, not only because of coaches who encourage their athletes to "leave it on the field"—that is, to use the structured and safe environment of the sporting event to work out aggressions and tensions—but because it provides practice in maintaining control during times of conflict and in building interpersonal skills in order to resolve those conflicts.

Communication occurs both verbally and nonverbally and includes both those things that are overtly stated and those things that are implied—the subtext—and likewise, those things consciously conveyed and those things unconsciously revealed. Many conflicts occur or are exacerbated because of communication issues, whether because someone has expressed him/herself poorly or because communication problems make it difficult to reach an agreement on a point of difference. Further, many attempts to resolve conflicts are spoiled by poor communication skills, which may even serve to heighten the conflict. The most obvious example is a situation in which an athlete commits a foul against an opponent on the field—intentionally or otherwise—followed by a heated exchange of words that only increases tensions rather than contains or dispels them. This is an issue not only of communication but of having the sense and mindfulness to prevent emotions—especially one's current, in-the-moment emotional state—from dictating one's response, which leads to impulsiveness and exaggerated responses. Athletes generally have an understanding of this, in that emotions must also be controlled and mindfulness mastered in order to focus on the basic tasks of sports, from taking a foul shot to pitching a curve ball. In these moments, doubt, anger, excitement, distraction, and even the pleasure of a possible win must be put aside in order for the athlete to perform at his best.

Bill Kte'pi

See Also: Coaching Youth; Crisis Management; High School Sports.

Further Readings
Coakley, J. *Sport in Society: Issues & Controversies*, 7th ed. New York: McGraw-Hill, 2015.
Miller, Saul. *Performing Under Pressure: Gaining the Mental Edge in Business and Sport*. Toronto: J. Wiley & Sons Canada, 2010.
Rainer, M. *Successful Coaching*, 4th ed. Champaign, IL: Human Kinetics, 2012.

Media Portrayals, Cable TV

Over 40 years ago, cable television forged its way onto the U.S. media landscape. In its earliest days, however, it was not known as "cable." What is now referred to as cable was originally called community antenna television, or CATV, and was developed in order to enhance the viewing experience for television consumers. Cable television, some thought, would provide reception, or at least better reception, to many homes that had previously had difficulty receiving a signal from broadcast transmitters on their home antennas. Cable providers would build receiving beacons to capture the transmitted signals and then send the images via cable to homes in topographically low-lying areas.

Eventually, cable television would morph into something more akin to what exists today, with tiers being offered by local cable outlets. The tiers would usually consist of a bundle of channels, including channels that would exclusively provide sports programming (i.e., ESPN, FOX Sports) and ultimately even sport-specific programming (i.e., The Golf Channel, NFL Network). Home Box Office, commonly referred to as HBO, was the first of cable's premium channels, making its debut in 1972. The first HBO event to be broadcast was a sporting event. In 1972, the New York Rangers hockey game was broadcast to 1,000 cable subscribers in Pennsylvania. By 1980, CNN and ESPN were also offered via cable providers. The two upstart cable channels, CNN, which provided 24-hour news coverage, and ESPN (originally called E.S.P. Network), which provided sports-related programming, both shared a precipitous introduction to the broadcast industry. Low ratings and difficulty in finding desirable programming content threatened the cable networks and hinted at possible failure. With 8,760 hours of time to fill each year on the 24-hour networks, suitable programming was a viable initial concern. The early days at ESPN were filled with sports like kickboxing, racquetball, volleyball, and Australian Rules Football—hardly the type of programming that would draw the ratings necessary for broadcast survival. It was not enough to financially sustain the cable network. Eventually, with programming contracts inked by the NCAA and the National Hockey League (NHL) in the early days—and later with Major League Baseball (MLB), the National Football League (NFL) and the National Basketball Association (NBA)—ESPN started to gain some much-needed credibility among consumers.

The "Big Three," ABC, CBS, and NBC, were all initially skeptical of the idea of a 24-hour sports network, and were, therefore, not intimidated by the prospect. The Big Three assumed that ESPN would fail. The fledgling cable industry had not yet discovered 24-hour programming opportunities, or any advertising potential, either national or local. The business proposition of cable television was based upon subscriber revenue, and at that time the cable operators were not about to pay ESPN a monthly subscriber fee for 24-hour sports. By the time the Big Three realized that ESPN (now a Disney subsidiary) was not going away, it was too late. In an effort to compete, the Big Three explored opportunities in cable television and failed, initially, by trying to run their cable companies in the same way they ran their networks. Heavily reliant on advertising for revenue at a time when cable was still new, they lost significant amounts of money in their cable ventures.

By 1982, ESPN started to reap the benefits of audience demand. Perhaps due to broadcast exclusivity contracts with professional sports leagues, in addition to the Federal Communications Commission's (FCC) Cable Television Report and Order of 1972, which, among other things, allocated satellite usage to cable companies for the broadcast of live sporting events, ESPN quickly ascended to be a cable industry leader. Today, according to the Nielson's cable channel coverage estimates, ESPN is received in nearly 98 million homes in the United States, transmitting to roughly 86 percent of the available homes with cable in the country. Sports programming is not different than other business practices with regard to

innovation. The basic economics of success in business is supply and demand—if there is demand, the business will manufacture supply. With an ever-increasing audience demand for sports programming, media companies were incentivized to quickly create the supply by offering other sports programming entities on cable television. National cable companies that currently provide sports programming include FOX Sports 1, FOX Sports 2, CBS Sports Network, and NBCSN. Specialty networks include the NFL Network, NBA TV, the NHL Network, the MLB Network, and the Golf Channel. These cable options provide sport media consumers with a variety of live events, news segments, talk shows, documentaries, and other sports-related programming.

Sports as Entertainment
The ability of sport to provide inherently conflicted, unscripted, dramatic events makes it a perfect fit for television. Sport can provide the type of content suited to television's commercial interests. It is the original reality television, where consumers can tune in to live and, therefore, watch unpredictable action. Not unaware of its potential, cable companies have packaged sporting events to take advantage of the entertainment value that sport offers to consumers. Beyond the live-game broadcast, cable has expanded its content platform to include sports journalism programs, like ESPN's *SportsCenter*, or FOX Sports' *NASCAR This Morning*. Sports movies, like *The Natural*, have been included in the programming. Sport news magazine shows, such as HBO's *Real Sports With Bryant Gumbel*, and short documentary programs, like ESPN's *30 for 30*, have been a popular addition to cable sports programming as well. While event coverage fills a great amount of the allotted programming time and space, these other sports-related (nonevent) programs vastly outnumber the amount of sport event coverage on cable television.

By the Numbers
While ESPN is not alone in the sports programming genre, it has certainly become the marketplace leader. In 2012, ESPN produced over 30,000 hours of live event and/or studio programming across media platforms. Its flagship show, *SportsCenter*, draws an average of 115 million viewers per month. However, ratings declined a bit in 2013, forcing ESPN to have

its first major layoff since 2009. Nearly 400 employees were let go, as company insiders cited the high cost of buying live rights plus a need to meet profit margins as reasons for the job eliminations. At the same time as the layoffs were announced, shares in Disney stock, the company owning an 80 percent share of ESPN, were at their highest levels.

ESPN has been aggressive over the past decade in signing, and resigning, broadcast exclusivity agreements with professional sports leagues and college conferences alike. The practice is consumer-driven, much like ESPN's decision to expand the network to include more cable channels. The ESPN "family" now includes ESPN2, ESPN3, ESPN Films, ESPNews, ESPNU, ESPN Classic, ESPN Deportes, Longhorn Network, and the SEC Network. This decision is an attempt to grab a piece of every niche in the sport broadcast marketplace, to cross cultural lines, and to offer something specialized to meet the needs of every sports fan.

While ESPN has grown, other cable networks have made an attempt to get a piece of the sometimes profitable sport television genre. TNT (Turner Network Television) has been a player on the sports broadcast scene since 1988, when it telecast its first live NBA game. Since that time, the cable network has expanded its sports programming to include NCAA Men's Basketball, NASCAR, NFL, MLB, and Professional Golf Association (PGA) events. Some of TNT's sports programming, especially NCAA basketball, gets shared with two fellow Turner stations, TruTV and TBS. USA Network is another cable television network that offers some sports programming.

In the late 1980s and early 1990s, a new type of cable sports network emerged. Regional Sports Networks, commonly referred to as RSNs, started popping up on the menu for cable subscribers around the United States. FOX Sports was among the early players in the RSN game. While the FOX Sports Network broadcasted games nationally, regional affiliates like the FOX Sports Mountain Network would air games that were thought to appeal more to a regional audience. Since that time, a great number of RSNs have been born. For example, the Buckeye Cable Sports Network (BCSN) founded in 2003, airs everything from high school, to college and professional games within the state of Ohio and southeast Michigan. BCSN even acquired the rights to broadcast

Cleveland Indians baseball games. The cable network is representative of many similar regional stations—it broadcasts local and regional sports to an audience that most likely cares more about these regional teams than they do about a team located outside the region. The business model of the RSN is built upon the principle that meeting audience demand will equate to financial success. The RSNs do not have the resources to compete on a national stage, nor do they want to. The RSN competes against larger cable and broadcast networks by providing a local flavor, something they should be able to do better than ESPN.

The Influence of Cable on Sport

The amount of revenue that cable companies generate for sport leagues and conferences undoubtedly wields influence across sport entities. From NCAA conference realignments to league expansions by major professional sport organizations, the effort to attract the most lucrative broadcast bid has had a dramatic effect on the sport landscape. The effect is far-reaching, as it has driven up the values of sport franchises, caused teams to switch to larger media markets, and elevated salaries for players and coaches. As the landscape of sport evolves, so evolves media.

In an effort to combat cable television's encroachment into the networks' longtime stranglehold on sport event broadcasting, network television executives have gotten resourceful and, in some cases, have even acted in collusion to beat out cable in bidding wars for sports exclusivity. For example, in 1999, NBC and FOX experimented with a shared broadcast exclusivity agreement for NASCAR. The four-year deal would give NBC and FOX shared rights to live NASCAR event coverage for the years 2000 to 2004. In the first year, 2000, NBC would televise the first race of the season, the Daytona 500, and every other race from that point on (every odd-numbered race in sequence on the schedule) for the duration of the season. FOX, on the other hand, would televise every even-numbered race for the entire season. In the second year of the deal, the two networks would alternate, allowing FOX to broadcast the Daytona 500 and every odd-numbered race, while NBC televised the even-numbered races. The third year was exactly the same as the first and the fourth year the same as the second. Over the course of four years, given no changes in the NASCAR schedule over those four years, the two networks covered the same exact number, as well as location, of events. This agreement was a direct reaction to cable's intrusion into live event coverage. The networks, NBC and FOX, beat out other television bids, shared the expense, and retained the exclusivity agreement. It was one win for network television but a venture that failed to suppress the growth of televised sport on cable.

Given the proliferation of sports media coverage on a regional and national scale by cable entities, the impact on athletes has been profound. The natural evolution of cable has led to the creation of numerous regional sports networks, all of whom compete with other broadcast media to fill programming allotments. As a result, many smaller, traditionally less popular, sports and teams have been given valuable air time, broadcast exposure that had previously been reserved for bigger, more popular, sports, and teams. With an increase in exposure, the pool of potential professional athletes is saturated with college athletes from smaller programs, to whom the dream of playing professionally has become more than a pipe dream. The regional cable exposure can quickly ascend to a national level. On November 15, 2014, for example, the State University of New York at Cortland played rival Ithaca College in their annual football matchup, where the two Division III schools compete for a trophy dubbed "the Cortaca Jug." The game, broadcast on the local Time Warner cable station, and produced by the Cortland Regional Sports Network, came down to a final play— a botched game-tying field goal attempt that quickly turned into a game-winning touchdown throw, propelling underdog Cortland to victory. The final play was rebroadcast in highlights 16 times over the next 24 hours by ESPN's *SportsCenter* to a national audience. While the Division III athletes from the highlights most likely do not have realistic aspirations of playing professionally, the media portrayed them as they would any other player from a bigger, more widely recognized program. The growth and expansion of cable has provided an opportunity for traditionally underexposed athletes to gain publicity. As cable television moves into new frontiers, more athletes must learn to navigate the public landscape in a fashion that benefits them, their teams, and leagues.

Matt Seyfried

See Also: Media Portrayals, Print; Media Portrayals, Radio; Media Portrayals, Women.

Further Readings

Deninger, Dennis. *Sports on Television: The How and Why Behind What You See.* New York: Routledge, 2012.

Meisenheimer, Mark. *No Pants Required: A Behind-the-Scenes Look at Television Sports Broadcasting.* Tucson, AZ: Wheatmark, 2008.

Michaels, Al, and L. Jon Wertheim. *You Can't Make This Up.* New York: William Morrow, 2014.

O'Neill, Terry. *The Game Behind the Game: High Pressure, High Stakes in Television Sports.* New York: HarperCollins, 1989.

Owens, Jim. *Television Sports Production.* New York: Focal Press, 2006.

Media Portrayals, Print

A sportswriter can have a tremendous impact on the way people view a sporting event or an athlete. Grantland Rice penned perhaps the most famous column in sports history when he wrote about Notre Dame's "Four Horseman" backfield after a 1924 game against Army at the Polo Grounds in New York City. Rice's soaring rhetoric, colorful metaphors, and heroic prose made the game sound as if it was the most epic clash in football history despite the game's rather mundane final score of 13–7. Rice is still known today as the Dean of Amercan Sports Writing.

Other writers such as Ring Lardner, Damon Runyon, Red Smith, Jim Murray, Frank Deford, and Wendell Smith wrote eloquently about the sports they followed and set the standard for generations of print journalists. Lardner and Runyon were contemporaries of Rice during the 1920s, a time period commonly known as the golden age of American sportswriting. Both writers focused primarily on baseball, but expanded their writing to short stories, novels, and stage plays later in their careers. Murray, whose career spanned five decades, won the National Sportswriter of the Year Award 14 times, including 12 in a row. Murray was known as the master of the punch line who could say in 10 words what a regular writer would take 20 to tell. Red

Smith, who devoted himself to a precise use of the English language, wrote about all major U.S. sports, first for the *New York Herald Tribune* and later for the *New York Times*. Deford has written in-depth long-form pieces for *Sports Illustrated* since 1963. He is a six-time recipient of the National Sportswriter of the Year Award and has published 18 books.

Few print journalists have changed the sport they covered through their leadership and advocacy. As a sportswriter for the *Pittsburgh Courier,* Wendell Smith did this and a great deal more. Smith was instrumental in helping Jackie Robinson break baseball's color line and helped to frame how the print media of the day portrayed Robinson. While being honored at the California state house in 2013, Robinson's widow Rachel remarked, "Wendell Smith was an amazing source of support. There are aspects of that early period that I don't know if we could have lived through without Wendell." Smith's story is one of relentless advocacy for a cause and demonstrates how the sports print media in American can be a leader for a just cause. Smith was arguably the reason that Jackie Robinson become the first black man to play in the major leagues.

After graduating from West Virginia State College at Charleston, Smith joined the *Pittsburgh Courier,* an influential national newspaper that was the most read African American paper in the first half of the 20th century. Smith joined the paper in 1937 and one year later became its sports editor.

Smith used his position as sports editor to campaign tirelessly for the integration of baseball. Smith was obsessed with fighting the racial injustices he saw. He used his columns in the *Courier* to stress the need for integration and call upon baseball executives to fully realize baseball's claim as the national pastime. In Pittsburgh, he had a firsthand look at some of the best black baseball players in the country. The city supported two of America's most popular Negro League teams, the Pittsburgh Crawfords and the Homestead Grays. Future Hall of Famer Josh Gibson, who was known for his majestic home runs and was commonly referred to as the "black Babe Ruth" starred for the Crawfords and later the Grays during Smith's time in Pittsburgh. The Grays played at Forbes Field, the same field that the Pittsburgh Pirates played in. Smith saw them routinely fill the stadium with paying customers. He knew

that black players were capable of playing in the major leagues.

Within Major League Baseball (MLB), there existed a gentleman's agreement between the 16 team owners that none of the owners would sign a black player. By 1945, this agreement had existed without interruption for over half a century. The agreement was supported in part by the commissioner of MLB, a former federal judge named Kenesaw Mountain Landis. African Americans resorted to organizing their own baseball leagues. The Negro Leagues existed in various forms starting in the 1880s. By 1920, organized leagues covered much of the United States. In 1924, the Negro League World Series was held for the first time between teams from the Negro National League and the Eastern Colored League. Negro league teams regularly challenged and often won exhibition games with MLB teams. As the legend of Negro League players such as Satchel Paige and Josh Gibson grew, Negro League teams began to sell out MLB ballparks for exhibition games of their own.

Leading the Charge for Change
Commissioner Landis died in 1944. As his replacement the owners choose Albert "Happy" Chandler, a U.S. Senator from Kentucky. In the spring of 1945 Wendell Smith and another prominent African American sportswriter, Rick Roberts, meet with new commissioner to find out his stance on blacks playing in MLB. Chandler reportedly told the two men, "If a black boy can make it on Okinawa and Guadalcanal, hell, he can make it in baseball."

That same spring, Smith arranged a tryout in Boston for Negro League players. The Boston Red Sox said they would try out the players if Smith would find them. Smith chose three players for the tryout: Jackie Robinson, Sam Jethroe, and Marvin Williams. Reports of the players' performances were sterling, but there was a deeper truth. The Red Sox had only called the tryout to appease local black leaders who had pressured the club to integrate and to assuage the concerns of a local council member. The tryout was a sham; there was little chance the Red Sox would actually sign any black player. In fact, when the Red Sox signed Pumpsie Green in 1959, they were the last MLB team to add a black player to their roster.

The Boston Red Sox had brought Robinson in for a tryout that was more publicly stunt than legitimate talent assessment. Nevertheless, Robinson's talent display that day stuck with Smith, and when he later learned that Branch Rickey was considering signing the first black player to an MLB roster, he personally traveled to Brooklyn to visit with him. During that meeting, Smith recommended to Rickey that Robinson possessed the talent and the temperament to be the first black player in MLB. Rickey commissioned his scouts to evaluate Robinson. After getting positive reports from them, he met with Robinson and offered him a contract with Brooklyn's minor league team for 1946. He asked Smith to travel with Robinson during 1946 and then again in 1947, when Robinson joined the Dodgers.

Robinson's Chronicler

Smith's role as arguably the most prominent chronicler of Robinson's 1947 rookie season helped to define how many people understood Jackie Robinson. As a print reporter for a national newspaper in the days before television, Wendell Smith had tremendous influence over public opinion. Smith took care to portray Robinson as a nonviolent man who had great respect for the game. It helped that Robinson's behavior reinforced this portrayal. Where other writers might have commented only on Robinson's baseball performance, Smith took the time to comment on his demeanor. He understood the importance of humanizing Robinson to his readers. There was a great deal at stake for both Smith and Robinson. If Robinson played poorly or came across badly in the press, it might harm the chances of future African Americans to play in the big leagues. Part of Smith's approach in portraying Robinson to America centered on Robinson writing columns about his experiences with the Brooklyn Dodgers. These columns were ghostwritten by Smith but relied heavily on Robinson's input. Smith also used his own columns to urge black fans of Robinson to avoid confrontations with white fans. Smith understood how important appearances were for this great experiment.

As Robinson traveled the country during his first year with the Dodgers, Smith traveled with him as his roommate. From every ballpark in the National League, Smith chronicled the accomplishments of Robinson on his road to winning the 1947 National League Rookie of the Year Award. Prominent print journalists, such as Dick Young of the *New York Daily News*, befriended Smith and regularly relied on him for information about Robinson. Smith was also careful to create a narrative that was appealing to baseball executives following Robinson's rookie campaign. His 1947 columns often make mention of the large crowds that came out to see Robinson. The message was clear: black baseball fans were willing to fill MLB stadiums to watch black baseball players. Smith followed Robinson during all of 1947, culminating in the Dodgers trip to the World Series.

Conclusion

Smith's role as the chronicler of Robinson's rookie season earned him enormous praise and recognition. After the 1947 season, the *Chicago Herald-American* hired him as their first African American sportswriter. Smith continued to write elegantly about baseball, boxing, and racial injustice for the next two decades. In 1964, he became a sportscaster for WGN in Chicago, where in 1969 he was named Sportscaster of the Year. He also served as the president of the Chicago Press Club. When Jackie Robinson died of a heart attack in October 1972, Smith wrote his obituary. It was the final story Smith ever wrote. One month after Robinson's passing, the man who helped shepherd him into the major leagues died of pancreatic cancer at age 58. The Baseball Hall of Fame posthumously recognized Wendell Smith's contributions by awarding him their highest award for journalists during their 1994 induction ceremony.

Ryan Vooris

See Also: Discrimination in Sports; Major League Baseball; Race/Ethnicity and Sports Leadership.

Further Readings

Eig, Jonathon. *Opening Day: The Story of Jackie Robinson's First Season*. New York: Simon & Schuster, 2007.

Harvey, Antonio. "Jackie Robinson's Wife Remembers 'Great' Black Sports Reporter." *The Sacramento Observer* (September 16, 2013). http://sacobserver .com/2013/09/jackie-robinsons-wife-remembers -great-black-sports-reporter (Accessed August 2014).

Peterson, Robert. *Only the Ball was White*. New York; Oxford University Press, 1970.

Robinson, Jackie, and Wendell Smith. *My Own Story: As Told by Jackie Robinson to Wendell Smith*. New York: Greenberg, 1948.

Media Portrayals, Radio

Sports is one of the most popular forms of entertainment around the globe, and sports fans inherently want to know more about the figures and personalities that interest them. Just by turning their televisions on, hundreds of options are available to satisfy viewers. Prior to the invention of TV, however, there was only radio. Sports radio programming not only provided information but also inspired personal connections not previously possible. Athletes became more than just names and team members, and personal stories and quotes were shared. The court of personal opinion could now debate an athlete's actions, appeal, and credibility. How an athlete is portrayed on radio impacts credibility and appeal, as well as marketability. Savvy use of radio media by sport leaders and athletes can promote a positive and successful image and reputation.

The Beginnings of Sports Radio

While difficult to consider in the current technology-driven world, there was a time when there was no television. Radio became an important mode of information dissemination. As interest in sports grew, so, too, did the desire to receive the latest scores, news, and interest stories. Thus, sports broadcasts were born. In a time before live broadcasting was even possible, early sports radio broadcasts were simply announcements of sports scores after the fact. The first World Series scores to be broadcast in this manner were courtesy of an experimental radio station called WWJ in Detroit, Michigan, in 1920. Once commercial radio emerged that same year, more stations joined, now providing play-by-play re-creations of sports events based on phoned-in reports from individuals in attendance. These re-creations were what drew people to their radios in rapt attention, enabling a personal connection to be made to the sport, team, fellow fans, and announcers they could not otherwise "see." Early

pioneers of sports broadcasting managed to do the impossible: to bring sports directly to the fans, no matter where they lived, and to do so in such a way as to captivate audiences for generations to come. A number of announcers became household names as their voices were welcomed into millions of homes. Mel Allen's phrase "How about that!" was repeated by baseball fans everywhere. President Ronald Reagan began his media career announcing University of Iowa football games in 1932. Bob Costas, famed television sportscaster, began his career announcing games at KMOX-AM in St. Louis.

The growing demand for "you are there" sports experiences and the desire for discussion and debate about sports, teams, and athletes ensured a bright future for sports radio even as other technology emerged. More than 700 stations now carry sports radio in the United States, and sports radio was counted among the two radio formats to see the biggest growth between 2000 and 2012.

Athletes on the Radio

Few radio listeners who heard Lou Gehrig's impassioned ". . . today I consider myself the luckiest man on the face of Earth" speech would ever forget it. The impression these words gave of what kind of person Gehrig was could not have been created by anyone but the man himself. Radio has enabled athletes to share parts of themselves with a great number of people. Fans learn their heroes are more than just athletes. Famed slugger Babe Ruth, for example, was interviewed on radio during a day of quail hunting.

Being an athlete with a media presence comes with many benefits, but it also comes with a great deal of scrutiny. Many athletes have a "love–hate" relationship with the media for this reason. Additionally, radio is an entertainment medium that often thrives on the dramatic in order to engage and intrigue listeners, while controversial hosts promoting "hot button" topics are common. Yet while station owners and broadcasters may have their own ratings and success in mind, those being interviewed can certainly be central in influencing the way they are portrayed. For good or bad, comments made on the radio may be long remembered. Who can forget Miami Heat guard Tim Hardaway's radio comments about how he would deal with a gay teammate, or the interview when Clinton Portis was pulled over for speeding while on the air. On the other hand, poised leaders such as Derek Jeter, Joe Montana, Phil Mickelson, and Mia Hamm who are skilled and consistent during interviews will long be regarded as athletes who deliberately, and successfully, elevated their image though positive media portrayals.

Implications for Sport Leaders

Even a snapshot view of sports radio makes it clear how important this media format is to the field of athletics. From broadcasting rights, to driving merchandise and ticket sales, to increased exposure and visibility, sports radio offers athletes, coaches, and athletic staff the chance to shape their public image. Radio also affords unique opportunities to stay "visible" in the public eye while often allowing for more prepared, structured, and tested remarks. A sports leader with media savvy can use radio's reach to promote his or her own or the team's image and reputation, and build successful relationships with the fan base locally, nationally, and even internationally.

A key facet of sports leadership involves honing the media skills necessary to best represent oneself, one's team, athletic staff, sponsor, or philanthropic foundation. In today's culture of sports entertainment, acquiring tools that make for a positive and successful media portrayal on radio should be thought of as an indispensable part of athletic career development.

Sari Shepphird
Christie Marshall

See Also: Brand Management and Leadership; Media Portrayals, Cable TV; Media Portrayals, Print; Sports Merchandising.

Further Readings

Covil, Eric C. "Radio and its Impact on the Sports World." http://www.americansportscastersonline.com/radiohistory.html (Accessed December 2014).

Favorito, Joe. *Sports Publicity: A Practical Approach.* New York: Routledge, 2013.

Houlihan, Barrie. *Sport and Society: A Student Introduction.* London: Sage, 2008.

Insideradio.com. "Changes Among Radio's Top-billing Formats." http://www.insideradio.com/article.asp?id=2710554&spid=32060#.VC2eSFdceSo (Accessed September 2014).

Media Portrayals, Women

Media both shape and reflect the ideas, beliefs, and values of a society. Television and cable networks, magazines, newspapers, and Web sites and blogs produce representations or texts imbued with meaning. These representations construct common-sense notions about particular groups in society. Sport is one such cultural institution that produces and reproduces conceptions about gender, as it is considered a site of masculine preservation. In the United States, women are considered men's cultural opposite; thus, women who participate in sport challenge cultural norms. Over the last 30 years, sportswomen have become an accepted part of U.S. sporting life, but these athletes are still subject to media representations that reinforce ideologies of natural gender differences and female inferiority and serve as a site for the reproduction of traditional gender roles.

Media portrayals of women are rooted in the historical. Sport scholars have described historical moments when existing gender roles began to shift. One particular historical moment was the convergence of the final days of the Victorian era and the establishment of the Industrial Age. The rise in leisure time, growth of communication technology, and an increase in education and literacy propelled sport into the forefront of American consciousness. Sport, through the Muscular Christianity movement, was considered good for the mind, body, and soul; however, only the minds, bodies, and souls of men benefitted from sport. The massive organization and development of youth, amateur, and professional leagues at the turn of the 20th century declared sport solely as male space. In the century since, it has been difficult for women to claim an equitable place in the increasingly institutionalized space of sport because men continue to assert sport as exclusively male. Sport became and remains a cultural space where gender relations produce, reestablish, and preserve the logic of male power in society.

In the early 20th century, science and media constructed the common-sense notions about gender and sexuality. Science linked the separate concepts of gender and sexuality while mediated commercial leisure pursuits promoted heterosexual dating and traditional gender roles as the norm. Female athletes have and continue to resist against the notion of sport as solely a masculine preserve. The 1920s gave rise to the "New Woman," who was active, political, and independent, and demanded access and entrance to previously exclusive male institutions such as higher education, religion, the business world, and sport. The New Woman rode bicycles; drove motorcycles; and played tennis, golf, swimming, field hockey, basketball and baseball. Her disruption of the status quo and female physicality produced new awe-inspiring ideas about women's strength, endurance, and power. Yet, these characteristics also instilled fear, panic, and alarm over the female athlete's voluntary violation of traditional notions of femininity. Resisting traditional femininity raised questions about a female athletes' sexuality. Female athletes who demonstrated a proclivity for sports were considered "muscle molls"—a mannish, muscular woman—connoting failed heterosexuality. This cultural anxiety over the meaning and performance of female sexuality and femininity has and continues to influence contemporary biases of sporting women.

Billie Jean King won 39 Grand Slam titles in her professional tennis career. In 1973 she won the Battle of the Sexes tennis match against Bobby Riggs, a highly publicized match. (Wikimedia Commons/ KingEnterprises)

In 1972, the U.S. government passed the publically acclaimed feminist legislative mandate, Title IX. This federal law grants girls and women equal access to educational and athletic opportunities. Millions of women have reaped the benefits of Title IX through increased access to both education and sport. Beneath the structural success of female participation in sport lingers a subtle ideological form of control—media representations. Although there are rare moments of respectful coverage of women, female athletes continue to be controlled in patriarchal cultures through images and narratives about their bodies. Simply, sport is a medium in which women are controlled through ideological processes.

Specifically, the underrepresentation of women athletes in the media generates the notion of "symbolic annihilation"—the absence of representation. In 2013, the amount of television coverage of women sport was the lowest ever recorded. Even with the presence of two professional leagues, the Women's National Basketball Association and the National Women's Soccer League, media coverage of women's sport had declined. A longitudinal study examined *Sports Illustrated* and found that 89.9 percent of feature articles were about male athletes or men's sports while only 9.7 percent were on female athletes or women's sports. The overall lack of media coverage of women conveys a message to audiences that sport continues to be by, for, and about men.

Female athletes are often trivialized. Trivialization is a major process through which hegemonic masculinity in sport is maintained. Men are the "real" athletes, while all women are seen as inferior. When women are included in mainstream media frames, the coverage reproduces narrow, stereotypical representations of female athleticism that draw upon sexist or racist ideologies. Women athletes are either infantilized as "girls" or "young women" or undercut with objectifying comments about their physical attractiveness and private lives. Narratives and images of black female athletes are often confined to stereotypes about the angry black woman, the jezebel, or link their athleticism to animality.

The heterosexualization of female athletes is used to reinforce traditional notions of heterosexuality and femininity. Through the lens of male heterosexual desire, women athletes are described and depicted in media narratives and images as sexual objects. Much like the muscle molls of the 1920s, this media portrayal is underpinned by unfounded fears of homophobia—the irrational fear of people who love those of the same sex. Narratives about female athletes often partially focus on their roles as a girlfriend, wife, and/or mother, rather than their athletic expertise on the field. The effective result is an apology for the women's violation of gender norms. Further, media uses satire to poke fun at the stereotypes of women athletes as unnatural women and unfeminine, disallowing any acceptance by the status quo. These media representations undercut the possibilities of physical activity as a liberating activity for women.

Eileen Narcotta-Welp

See Also: Gender and Sports Leadership; Sociology of Sport; Title IX; Women's Leadership in Sport.

Further Readings:
Cahn, Susan. *Coming On Strong: Gender and Sexuality in Twentieth-Century Women's Sport.* Cambridge, MA: Harvard University Press, 1994.
Cooky, Cheryl, et al. "Women Play Sport, But Not on TV: A Longitudinal Study of Televised News Media." *Communication & Sport*, v.1 (2003).
Lumpkin, Angela. "Female Representation in Feature Articles Published by *Sports Illustrated* in the 1990s." *Women in Sport & Physical Activity Journal*, v.18 (2009).

Minor League Baseball

Professional baseball in the United States is divided into two levels, Major League Baseball (MLB), which is the highest level at which the game is played, and Minor League Baseball (MiLB), where players gain experience and develop their skills in the hope of someday playing at the MLB level. There are two types of MiLB, so-called organized or affiliated baseball, where most teams are independently owned but affiliate—enter into a player development contract (PDC)—with a MLB team, and independent baseball, where teams have no affiliation with MLB. In organized baseball, all the on-field personnel—players, managers, coaches, and trainers—of a MiLB team are employed by and are under contract to a MLB team. In independent ball, the MiLB team employs everyone involved with the team including on-field personnel. Affiliated MiLB has an oversight organization now known as Minor League Baseball. In independent ball, each league has its own structure, but unlike affiliated ball, there is no central oversight organization for all independent leagues and teams. This entry will be limited to a discussion of affiliated baseball. References to MiLB will be to Minor League Baseball in general and to the governing organization that oversees all affiliated minor leagues and teams.

Formation of the National Association of Professional Baseball Leagues
In 1900 the Western League decided to change its name to the American League and proceeded to compete with the older and more established National League for players. At that time there was no distinction between Major and Minor leagues; there were only leagues with teams in larger cities, mostly in the American and National Leagues, and leagues with teams in smaller cities. A group of eight league presidents, led by Eastern League President Patrick T. Powers, was concerned that the battle between the National and American Leagues could pose a threat to their existence. The group met in Chicago on September 5, 1901, and agreed to form the National Association of Professional Baseball Leagues, referred to thereafter as the NA for short until it formally changed its name to Minor League Baseball (MiLB) in 1999.

MiLB History
From 1901 to 1931 the vast majority of NA teams were independently owned, signing and paying their own players, some of whom they sold to MLB teams for a fee to generate additional revenue. In 1931, Branch Rickey, who was then the general manager of the St. Louis Cardinals, began affiliating with and in some cases purchased NA teams in order to provide a guaranteed source of players for the MLB team. Other MLB teams adopted Rickey's model and before long affiliated MiLB teams outnumbered independent teams. By 1949, known as the peak of the post-World War II MiLB boom, the NA consisted of 438 teams in 59 leagues. That figure dwindled steadily over the next 14 years, attributable in part to the national television broadcast of MLB games, MLB expansion, and the rising popularity of other sports, to only 15 leagues, all in the United States and Canada. In 1963, MiLB and MLB agreed to enter into the Professional Baseball Agreement (PBA) that expanded the parties' relationship by increasing affiliation agreements (PDCs), purchasing MiLB teams, sharing affiliations among MLB teams, and creating co-op arrangements

where MLB teams provided a number of on-field personnel but also allowed MiLB teams to include their own players on the roster. In exchange for accepting these additional financial subsidies from the very group the NA was created to protect itself from, MiLB agreed to a reorganization that resulted in the classification system that exists today.

For most of the first half of the 20th century, MiLB was divided into six classifications, three levels of A—AAA, AA, and A—along with B, C, and D. Currently, MiLB consists of 19 leagues that include a total of 243 member clubs in cities and towns across the United States, Canada, Mexico, the Dominican Republic, and Venezuela. The current classification system divides leagues into one of five classes, Triple-A (AAA), Double-A (AA), Class A (which includes two levels, Class A Advanced and Class A, also referred to as High A and Low A, respectively), Short Season (sometimes referred to as Class A, although a lower level of ball than Class A), and Rookie. The top three classifications are designated as full season leagues where teams begin play on the Thursday after the MLB season opens, while the other two classifications play a short season, with games beginning after the annual MLB Rule 4 draft in June for college eligible and high school players. Rookie level is further subdivided into Rookie Advanced, where teams operate similarly to the other classifications, playing before fans in ballparks around the country; Complex Based Rookie, where teams play at MLB spring training complexes in Florida and Arizona primarily for the benefit of team personnel and scouts—there is no admission charge and few fans in attendance beyond family and friends; and International Summer leagues located in the Dominican Republic and Venezuela, where teams are owned and operated by MLB teams. Each league has a president and operates under its own governing documents.

MiLB Leadership in the Modern Era

Mike Moore was elected the 10th president of the NA in 1991. He had pledged to reorganize the NA, which had historically been operated more like a dictatorship with virtually absolute power vested in the president. In January 1992 he convened a constitutional convention that rewrote the National Association Agreement (NAA), a document signed by the 14 leagues and drafted by the Powers-led convention

in 1901. It spelled out the relationship between the NA and its member leagues. The NAA had been essentially unchanged for 90 years. Moore's goal was to convert the NA to more of a corporate or business structure. The NA under Moore's 16-year leadership experienced phenomenal growth. He established a partnership between the Professional Baseball Promotion Corporation, an NA subsidiary, and Major League Baseball Properties to oversee the licensing of MiLB merchandise. From a few million dollars when Moore took office, annual merchandise sales now exceed $50 million. The promotion corporation also began national marketing in 1993, providing a central office that allows national sponsors to work with any number of Minor League teams on a local level or in a national program. The program has paid more than $34 million in sponsorships to member clubs since its inception. Another subsidiary created by Moore, Professional Baseball Umpire Corp., operates and maintains the umpire development program for the 16 domestic leagues and provides umpires for MLB under the PBA. Attendance in MiLB exploded, reaching an all-time record of 43,263,740 in 2008, due in part to the construction of over 100 new ballparks.

Pat O'Conner, who was chief operating officer under Moore for 15 years, became MiLBs 11th president in January 2008. He was re-elected to a second four-year term in December 2011. Under O'Conner's leadership, the PBA with MLB was extended through the 2020 season; a new five-year collective bargaining agreement was executed with the Association of Minor League Umpires through 2016; two Class A leagues were reorganized; MiLB Internet rights were bundled; the first diversity initiative was instituted; an industry-wide health care program was offered; and a Green Team initiative was undertaken to make MiLB teams and stadiums more ecofriendly and cost-effective.

Conclusion

MiLB has become a big business that requires expert leadership. Team budgets can exceed $5 million and franchises have sold for $35 million, suggesting why sport management (SPM) programs have proliferated and why courses in leadership should be included in the SPM curriculum.

Jordan Kobritz

See Also: Draft System; Major League Baseball; Professional Sports.

Further Readings

Borland, John F., Gregory M. Kane, and Laura J. Burton. *Sport Leadership in the 21st Century*. Burlington, MA: Jones & Bartlett Learning, 2015.

Hayhurst, Dick. "An Inside Look Into the Harsh Conditions of Minor League Baseball." http://bleacherreport.com/articles/2062307-an-inside-look-into-the-harsh-conditions-of-minor-league-baseball (Accessed July 2014).

Johnson, Lloyd, and Miles Wolff. *Encyclopedia of Minor League Baseball*, 3rd ed. Durham, NC: Baseball America, 2007.

Minor League Baseball. "History." http://www.baseball-reference.com/minors (Accessed August 2014).

Models of Athlete Development

While certain people are genetically predisposed toward athletic talent, innate physical and psychological attributes alone are insufficient to produce long-term sports success. Models of athlete development, constructed from studies of world-class competitors, offer insight into cultivating sports talent, as well as how to support athletes across their careers. Most developmental models suggest athletes advance through three stages en route to elite levels, and they are especially physically, socially, and psychologically vulnerable when transitioning stages. These models underscore the importance of practice and interpersonal relationships in supporting athlete development, although the specific nature of these influences varies by developmental stage.

Models of Talent Development

The introduction to playing a sport, described as the initiation or sampling stage, typically occurs between ages 6 and 13. Participation during this period is fun, playful, and not typically guided by achievement-focused goals. During the initiation stage, engaging in "deliberate play" contributes to the development of sport interest and talent. Deliberative play describes casual activities such as pickup basketball or street hockey. Though guided by rules similar to those used in formal competition, deliberative play also maximizes participants' immediate enjoyment, interest, and engagement. Athletes often play several different sports during this phase. Research suggests early diversification, rather than immediate specialization in a single sport, prevents future burnout and overtraining injuries. Siblings and friends often encourage young athletes' interest. Parents provide material (e.g., purchasing equipment, paying fees, providing transportation) as well as interpersonal support. They also instill sports-related values such as discipline, high standards, and leading an active lifestyle.

Typically in middle to late adolescence, during a period described as the development or specializing stage, athletes become more serious about sport. Though it remains a source of personal enjoyment, the focus shifts to improving skills, achieving goals, and competitive success. Athletes in this phase dedicate more time to practice than during initiation. Deliberative play is less frequent; instead, research emphasizes the value of "deliberative practice." These activities are directly relevant to skill improvement, concentrate on improving performance, and require intense cognitive and physical effort. Practice and competitive experiences also help athletes hone the mental attributes critical for sport success. In contrast to choices made during the initiation phase, athletes begin to sacrifice other personal and extracurricular priorities. Also, while those in the prior stage often participate in several sports, at some point during development, most opt to focus on a single one.

During the investment stage, which typically aligns with late high school and college/university, sport takes primacy in athletes' lives and is a central aspect of individual identity. Athletes spend between 15 and 40 hours per week practicing, though the number of hours is less important than the quality of practice activities. Regimens typically encompass mental and tactical training in addition to deliberate practice, technical skill enhancement, and general physical/strength conditioning. Coaches become prominent influences, offering technical advice, feedback on technique, goal-setting, encouragement, and emotional assistance. Teammates also are important, challenging one another to improve as well as providing interpersonal support. Though not as actively involved in day-to-day sports-related activities, parents contribute to an athlete's ongoing development by offering unconditional support, showing interest in performance, offering emotional assistance especially through training or competitive setbacks, and providing material resources.

Many athletes encounter adversity at some point during the development or investment stages, either sport-related (e.g., injury, loss of a starting role, problematic coach relationship) or personal (e.g., loss of a family member, parents' divorce, difficulties in school). Navigating such difficulties sharpens coping skills and promotes a sense of resiliency, important traits for long-term success at elite levels.

Characterized by expert mastery (e.g., professional, Olympic levels), the final period of development is variously labeled as the perfection, culmination, or maintenance stage. Research suggests that approximately 10 years of sustained deliberative practice results in achieving such proficiency. Athletes are typically between ages 18 to 21 when entering this stage, which then lasts from five to 15 years. In addition to deliberative practice, strength training, and mental preparation at levels similar to the investment years, attention to long- and short-term recovery is also emphasized. Nutritionists, exercise physiologists, and sports psychologists often become valuable resources in addition to coaches, teammates, and families. Finally, during the discontinuation stage or recreational years, athletes cease competing at top levels of their sport. They may return to deliberate play; however the emphasis is on fitness, health, and enjoyment over winning.

Models of Career Transitions

Athlete development should be considered not only from the vantage point of nurturing talent, but also in terms of how to support individuals as they navigate changes across their athletic careers. Key transition points can be when athletes first join organized sport, from junior to senior levels, from amateur to professional, or from elite to retirement.

When athletes are unprepared for a transition, they may experience psychological, psychosocial, academic, or vocational difficulties. Negative consequences can include decline in performance, injury, overtraining, depression, substance abuse, criminal behavior, eating disorders, and even attempted suicide. Former Washington State University and National Football League (NFL) quarterback Ryan Leaf exemplifies an athlete with such challenges. A Heisman Trophy finalist, Leaf was the second pick in the 1998 NFL Draft. Despite his intercollegiate success, Leaf immediately struggled with the transition to professional football, exhibiting poor on-field performance, strained relationships with teammates, coaches, and management, and mishandled media and fan attention. After retiring at age 26, Leaf attempted to pursue a college coaching job and sports journalism opportunities. This transition was also difficult; Leaf was convicted of burglary and drug charges in 2009 and again in 2012.

Career transition models emphasize the importance of proactive interventions to help athletes plan for the next stage of their careers, develop coping skills, and prevent transition-related crises. Many sports governing bodies have developed programs to prepare elite athletes for retirement. For example, since 1991, the National Collegiate Athletic Association (NCAA) CHAMPS Life Skills program has supported college athletes' academic, career, civic, and personal development. Member institutions organize workshops, speakers, and other resources aimed at cultivating skills transferable to a post-college career, managing the effects of on an individual's athletic identity, and ensuring a long-term social support system. Approximately 20 percent of athletes experience psychological, psychosocial, academic, or vocational difficulties when terminating the most advanced stage reached in sport. Sports psychologists can assist athletes analyze adjustment issues and construct an action plan. A network of family and friends, in addition to relationships developed through sport, is especially beneficial for former athletes coping with transition-related crises.

Molly Ott

See Also: Captains; Sport-Based Youth Development; Sports as a Means of Developing Leaders.

Further Readings

Alfermann, Dorothee, and Natalia Stambulova. "Career Transitions and Career Termination." In *Handbook of Sport Psychology*, 3ed., Gerald Tenenbaum and Robert Eklund, eds. Hoboken, NJ: John Wiley & Sons, 2007.

Bloom, Benjamin, ed. *Developing Talent in Young People.* New York: Ballantine Books, 1985.

Côté, Jean, et al. "Practice and Play in the Development of Sport Expertise." In *Handbook of Sport Psychology*, 3ed., Gerald Tenenbaum and Robert Eklund, eds. Hoboken, NJ: John Wiley & Sons, 2007.

Morality of Professional Sports

Sport is often promoted to uphold and develop values in its participants, namely that of character. However, when sport adopts winning as its sole purpose, values and principles suffer, none greater than character. The basic mechanism for upholding a system of values, merits, or principles within any entity is a constitution. Aristotle held that all institutions composing a given culture should also be subject to the constitution of that culture.

This tenet helps to expand the discussion regarding the place that professional sport holds within a culture. Sport represents a constitution holding influence over its competitors, just as a constitution within government holds influences over its constituents. Aristotle spoke of how tension can rise as individuals struggle to uphold personal constitutions in the midst of government constitutions; tension between being a good person and a good citizen. This is witnessed through the dilemma of a father out of work, compelled to steal food (bad citizenry) in order to provide for his starving children (good person). One's personal navigation within these constitutions provides the framework for the formation of one's character.

As such there is an obligation of sport, through its status as a cultural institution, to impart a positive influence over one's character. It is important to note a particular distinction in character that often leads to a fallacy about the merits of sport: the distinction between social character and moral character. The coronation of sport as promotional of leadership and character is misrepresentative of the full effect of sport participation on athletes' "moral" character. Understanding the link between achievement motivation and moral function provides a lens for considering the impact of sport. At all levels, the predominance of winning and superior performance over others is growing as the primary constitution within sport, nowhere greater than at the professional level. The emphasis placed upon winning without consideration for the moral identity of athletes prevents those participating in sport to consider it as a moral domain in and of itself. This negates the values society ascribes sport to embody.

Narratives on the Purpose of Sport

There are two prevailing narratives about the purpose of sport, based on the Greek models for sport, which supported the educational aims of respective cultures. The Athenian Model is rooted in the concept of Arête: excellence of mind, body, and soul. Physical training was seen as a cultural program supportive of the pursuit of Arête. The argument is often made that the focus within amateur sport for the development of mind, body, and soul through the pursuit of competitive excellence parallels the Athenian Model of educating individuals through physical means. Conversely, the Spartan Model of sport is rooted in excellence through victory, representative of the aim of Sparta's educational program: militaristic supremacy. The manner in which one achieves excellence within this model is by outperforming all others. The parallel seen here is in the current system of professional sport where the desired end is winning. Therefore, sport under this model supports educating individuals on all the tenets of physical means. Utilizing these two models as a comparison for amateur versus professional sport is a misunderstanding of Greek culture strongly linked to Pierre de Coubertine's revival of the modern Olympiad.

The Greek language has no support for the word *amateur* and therefore Greek models of sport would not be delineated as such. Considering the appeal made to the gods through sport, there is no viability for Greek athletes to consider themselves "amateur." Often the purposes driving sport are separated between amateur and professional based upon the level of sport, with youth, secondary, and collegiate catalogued under amateur. Accompanying this separation is an acceptance for an emphasis placed upon winning within the professional ranks, while remaining secondary at the amateur ranks. This is a critical note to be made when arguing for the regard for athletes' moral function and moral identity within professional sport as it commissions professional sport and amateur sport alike to promote moral character.

Indices of Character

Critiquing the claim that sport promotes character and leadership revolves around the distinction between social and moral character. Before heralding sport, it is first important to consider the traits of social and moral character and how the emphasis placed upon winning impacts both. Work ethic, discipline, persistence, perseverance, resiliency, dedication, commitment, and passion: all can be identified as traits of social character. And sport, most certainly, can be championed as a strong facilitator of each. However, these elements do not represent the moral domain. Instead they are more representative of social character and citizenship within sport, meaning abiding by what it takes to be a great athlete. Moral character is not externally attached to a system of rules or laws, like those present in sport; instead it is an internalized matter rooted in the assessment by an individual of what is right and just. Moreover, beyond the discernment of what is right and just, moral character is most readily demonstrated in the ability to act upon that which is right. As such, an individual's moral character is demonstrated through one's moral willpower (volition), which is a process of moral reasoning and moral functioning.

The tension represented between social character and moral character within sport lies in the reality that one could be highly disciplined for the sake of their sport while disregarding certain moral constitutions. Social character is to a great player what moral character is to a great person. The two receive their identity from the end they support: one being winning and superiority and the other action in accordance with values. Social character can easily stop with sport because sport provides an incentive to athletes to act in accordance with these elements. Moral character's only incentive is regard for doing what is right in accordance with one's self-identity as a moral being. The distinction between these two is a powerful insight for why so many athletes face volumes of troubles off the field, despite being model "citizens" on the field. Social character for the sake of athletic performance does not translate off the field for values-based actions. Athletic willpower does not necessarily correlate with moral willpower. These principles speak to the compelling reasons for enhancing athletes' self-awareness as moral beings and understanding what impacts actions have on one's moral character.

Moral Function and Game Reasoning

The assessment of what is right can differ on any number of systems and influences. In accepting whatever system brings one to the discernment of what is right or wrong, the greater focus is on the qualifier within moral will, absent of contingencies or conditions. The long-held viewpoint for an individual's moral reasoning held that an individual's moral function and reasoning remains constant regardless of context and situations. Investigating the impact of context on moral reasoning has since proven that the influence of context and situation indeed holds considerable influence. Sport has proven to be one domain of context and situation with impressionable impact upon moral reasoning and moral function. An athlete who may not regularly endorse intentionally injuring another person and an athlete who may not regularly endorse cheating; will both justify doing such acts within sport, especially when coupled with the belief it may lead to victory or when such acts are encouraged or endorsed by their coaches.

Achievement Motivation's Impact Upon Moral Function

Because moral function has been proven to not remain constant across situation and condition, the conclusion can be made that sport influences the manner in which individuals develop morally, impacting the development of their moral identity and moral willpower. As constitutions represent influence upon one's values and values are shown to influence one's behavior, then the constitutions within sport influence athletes' behavior. The strongest of these constitutions is winning and its relationship with another contextual variable: achievement motivation. Achievement motivation in a most elementary presentation involves two orientations: task and ego. Task orientation is synonymous with task mastery and process orientation. The criterion of success within this motivational framework is for one to master the skill sets associated with a given task. In this a football player, a defensive back for example, is driven by the quest to master, to the maximum of his ability, each phase of the position: stance, footwork, hand positioning, ball skills, coverage responsibilities, tackling, block destruction, etc. Conversely, ego orientation adopts a criterion of success of outperforming others through superior performance; that is, winning. This involves a normative framework wherein one is measuring capacity and ability by comparing him/herself to the levels of others. Individuals within achievement motivation are not one or the other; instead they are more a profile of both at the same time. This is of considerable importance related to moral functioning, as the general relationship follows a pattern that athletes high in ego orientation report lower moral function indices.

Self-determination theory also provides an intriguing lens for the dialogue surrounding moral function in sport and achievement motivation. The strongest relationship to be promoted within sport is what self-determination theory regards as autonomous and internal regulation of behavior, leading to self-determined behavior. Self-determined behavior reports highly with prosocial behavior representative of strong social and moral character. Within a sporting context, autonomy affords for an athlete to have ownership over his/her actions. Internal regulation of behavior affords for the athlete to have self-determined behavior that is not subject to external demands like reward or fear of punishment. In a sporting context reward can easily be regarded as synonymous with winning, while punishment is synonymous with losing. This construct follows the above relationship with moral function and moral reasoning, which provides a critical insight into the impact of sport upon moral identity.

Sport's Constitutions
Because the function of a constitution is to compel individuals to act in accordance with the values they hold, winning as the primary constitution within sport compels athletes to act in accordance. This presents the possibility of a predominantly ego-oriented achievement motivation, winning and outperforming others as a criterion of success, while decreasing the emphasis upon moral character. Moreover, winning as the primary constitution

does not allow for self-regulated behavior, representing potential negative ramifications on one's moral functioning.

To see sport in light of its Greek origins is to consider it at all levels as an educational tool within a given society. The viewpoint of sport as educational then promotes the coaches as teachers, resulting in an obligation on behalf of coaches to present sport as a moral domain influential upon athletes' moral identity. As the understanding of the link between achievement motivation and moral function comes to light, coupled with the understanding of both as contextual, a power of sport becomes evident: the power to influence one's perception of their own moral identity.

Understanding the distinction between social character and moral character sheds light as to how sports' most disciplined athletes can be its poorest ambassadors for model behavior and citizenship off the field. Sport represents a domain where athletes reason for behaviors consistent with its constitutions of winning, glory, and pride. While these behaviors are heralded for the victories they produce, they have also been shown to negatively impact one's moral function. The considerations within this article present a position for professional sport to hold regard for moral identity and to understand the distinction in form and function between social character and moral character, and the impact of sport upon both.

Brandon Orr

See Also: Cheating in Sports; Managing Conflicts; U.S. Anti-Doping Agency.

Further Readings
Bredemeier, B., and D. L. Shields. "Divergence in Moral Reasoning About Sport and Life." *Sociology of Sport Journal*, v.1 (1984).
Bredemeier, B., and D. L. Shields. "Moral Growth Among Athletes and Non-Athletes: A Comparative Analysis." *Journal of Genetic Psychology*, v.147 (1986).
Broadie, S., and C. J. Rowe. *Nicomachean Ethics*. Oxford, UK: Oxford University Press, 2002.
Kavussanu, M. "Motivational Predictors of Prosocial and Antisocial Behavior in Football." *Journal of Sport Sciences*, v.24 (2006).

N

NASCAR

The National Association for Stock Car Auto Racing (NASCAR) was founded in 1947 by Bill France, Sr., in Daytona Beach, Florida. France saw the need to organize and standardize the loosely based stock car industry. NASCAR is the governing body that among other things levies sanctions, develops marketing campaigns, negotiates network television deals, develops fan initiatives, and executes company strategy. Currently, NASCAR oversees three major racing series: the Sprint Cup Series, the Nationwide Series, and the Camping World Truck Series. Over 175 teams (i.e., the Penske team and the Joe Gibbs Racing team) and a multitude of drivers are under the purview of NASCAR. Since 1947, NASCAR has seen tremendous growth both monetarily and in popularity.

As of 2014, NASCAR sanctioned 1,200 races in 30 states at over 100 tracks, and its races are broadcast in 150 languages in over 20 countries. Moreover, more Fortune 500 companies sponsor NASCAR events and drivers than in any other professional sport in America. Multinational companies such as UPS, McDonald's, Home Depot, Coca-Cola, and Sprint pay anywhere from $20 million to sponsor a NASCAR team driver to $100 million annually to sponsor a NASCAR-sanctioned event. In terms of company valuation, NASCAR peaked prerecession (2006) at $2 billion and is currently valued at $1.2 billion. This is the aggregate amount of the NASCAR team values. NASCAR generates $3 billion annually from racetrack revenues, ticket sales, merchandise sales, television broadcast rights, and corporate sponsorships.

NASCAR: The Organization

NASCAR's mission statement indicates that NASCAR is committed to ensuring that the sport better reflects America's composition. Its mission is to engage females and people of diverse ethnic and racial backgrounds in all facets of the NASCAR industry. Currently, NASCAR is fulfilling its mission by enacting several programs and initiatives that support various ethnic and women's groups. From a leadership perspective, it makes sense to attract all types of fans to grow a business. NASCAR's original fan base were white males who lived in the south. Society has changed and the NASCAR leaders have taken notice. The sport has welcomed, developed, and recruited drivers from various demographic backgrounds. Female driver Danica Patrick is one of the sport's most notable, successful, and controversial figures. Max Siegel, an African American lawyer, entrepreneur, and multicultural activist, is the owner of Rev Racing, which is a company developed and designed to increase minority involvement in NASCAR and the motorsport industry as a whole. Siegel's company "was founded in 2009 and has fielded cars for many minority drivers notably Sergio Pena, Darrell Wallace, Jr., and Kyle Larson." NASCAR in association with Rev Racing launched its Drive for Diversity program in 2004. This program is specifically designed to recruit and train minorities who are interested in becoming drivers, pit-crew members, and even shop employees.

NASCAR is highly structured and highly formalized. From an organizational standpoint, the concepts of complexity, effectiveness, efficiency and strategy have to be more than conceptualized; they have to be executed. The motorsport industry has grown exponentially. As a result, NASCAR's organizational structure has changed tremendously since its inception in 1947. This has resulted in vertical complexity in that there is a chief executive officer and numerous vice presidents and directors or layers of leadership. The leadership challenge in this respect is to make sure that the lines of communication are standardize and formalized. With the proliferation of business units NASCAR has grown horizontally. For example, NASCAR includes units such as marketing, media relations, corporate sponsorships, and the NASCAR Foundation. There is also spatial complexity that refers to the number of geographical locations in which the company operates. Spatial complexity can be seen in the number of cities in which NASCAR has offices. The NASCAR company operates offices in eight cities across the United States. Races are conducted in Europe on the NASCAR Whelen Euro Series, Canada in the Canadian Tire Series, and in the Mexico Toyota Series. With this type of geographical or spatial complexity, the leadership in NASCAR has to standardize its processes and the means by which it conducts business. Operating in a spatially complex environment means that companies have to be familiar with the customs and norms of those environments. And in the case of operating in other countries, NASCAR officials have to be well versed in understanding language barriers, monetary policies, and various social and political policies.

Strategy refers to a company's ability to plan its activities in an effort to reach its goals. NASCAR's strategy is in synch with its mission statement. It realizes that there are great growth opportunities within various demographics. This growth strategy calls for NASCAR to develop various initiatives such as the Drive for Diversity program and the NASCAR Foundation, which raises money for children in need. The growth strategy that NASCAR has adopted also requires the company to develop strategic relationships and partnerships with minority groups and sponsors. Developing and cultivating these partnerships and initiatives, allows NASCAR to introduce its sport and brand to new and diverse audiences with the intent of developing new and loyal NASCAR fans for the future.

The Uniqueness of NASCAR

The inherent uniqueness of NASCAR lends itself to interesting and complex leadership challenges. Unlike other professional team sports, NASCAR racetracks are neutral sites for all its teams and drivers. A National Football League (NFL) team will play half of its games in its own stadium and as a result will have the proverbial "home field" advantage. There is no home team advantage in NASCAR. Each NASCAR team must ship its cars and staff to racetracks all across the country to compete. Team leaders and NASCAR senior management have to ensure that each of the tracks (which are independently owned) abides by the NASCAR rules and regulations. In addition, each state and city that NASCAR races in has to be evaluated to make sure they are not in violation of that state and city's laws and/or ordinances. NASCAR leaders must be well versed in communicating their plans and strategy with numerous racetrack owners, and city and state officials in order to execute each race.

Another unique aspect of NASCAR is its fan base. NASCAR fans have been deemed by many as the world's most loyal fan base. NASCAR fans have a tendency to align themselves with a driver. Once they do, NASCAR fans follow and root for their driver just like a baseball fan will cheer and root for his favorite team. When one considers the fact that NASCAR races occur all across the nation, then the fan that wishes to see and support their favorite driver has to travel to multiple cities. NASCAR fans will travel an average of up to 150 miles to attend a racing event. Compare that to an average football fan, who travels on average of 25 miles to attend a game. The challenge for NASCAR leaders is to ensure that their drivers are constantly connecting and bonding with their respective fan base. Since the drivers are the "main" attraction at each race, it is imperative that drivers conduct themselves professionally on and off the track. It is also necessary that drivers engage with fans via social media and conduct guest appearances at NASCAR- or sponsor-related events. Furthermore, a NASCAR race can be very dangerous event, with cars reaching speeds of 200 miles per hour. To this end, driver safety is paramount. A driver who is hurt or behaves in an unprofessional manner can ruin or taint the image of NASCAR. As a result, fans may lose interest in a race or a series. Waning fan interest can result in lower fan attendance and a decrease in revenue.

NASCAR is truly concerned about its image and is dedicated to its loyal fan base. A distinct aspect of NASCAR as it relates to its fans is its official NASCAR Fan Council. The Fan Council allows fans to offer their opinions regarding any aspect of the NASCAR business. Fans can weigh in on issues such as their tailgating experience, their race day experience, rules and regulations, driver etiquette, and even television announcers. NASCAR leaders use fan information to improve the overall NASCAR experience and to enhance their brand image and brand awareness.

NASCAR: Driven to Profit

For decades sponsors have benefitted NASCAR financially and sustained the company, its teams, and its drivers. Sponsors utilize NASCAR to create awareness for their company's brands. Research indicates that close to 70 percent of NASCAR fans purchase the products and/or services of the companies that sponsor NASCAR drivers, teams, and races. Sponsors pay millions of dollars per year to sponsor NASCAR events. Sprint paid NASCAR $750 million for 10 years for the Sprint Cup Series naming rights, which is NASCAR's signature event. This deal is set to expire in 2016. Cable network giant Comcast paid an estimated $200 million to become a title NASCAR sponsor. This megadeal is set to expire in 2024. NASCAR teams can profit as well. The top most valuable NASCAR teams generate anywhere from $50 million to $120 million annually. In terms of team value, some NASCAR teams, such as Joe Gibb's Racing and Hendrick Motorsports, are valued between $170 million and $350 million.

Probably the most notable and lucrative means of NASCAR revenue is via the television networks. In 1999, NASCAR negotiated a $2.4 billion and with FOX, TNT, and NBC. By 2005, NASCAR had signed an eight-year $4.5 billion network deal with ESPN, TNT, and FOX. In 2013, NASCAR landed a jaw-dropping $8.2 billion deal with NBC and FOX.

These deals will ensure that NASCAR drivers (who can make up to $30 million per year), teams, and track owners are supported financially for years to come. A by-product of television profitability is the fact that NASCAR can continue to fund and grow its business. The end result is to continue to attract new fans and retain loyal ones.

Robert Lyons, Jr.

See Also: Brand Management and Leadership; Formula One Auto Racing; Sports Merchandising.

Further Readings

Latford, Bob. *50 Years of NASCAR*. London: Carlton Books, 2000.
Poole, David. *Tim Richmond: The Fast Life and Remarkable Times of NASCAR's Top Gun*. Champaign, IL: Sports Publishing, 2005.
Waltrip, Michael, and Ellis Henican. *In the Blink of an Eye: Dale, Daytona and the Day That Changed Everything*. New York: Hachette Books, 2011.

National Association of Intercollegiate Athletics

The National Association of Intercollegiate Athletics (NAIA) is the governing body for more than 250 college and university athletic programs in the United States and Canada. Founded in 1937 and headquartered in Kansas City, Missouri, the NAIA focuses its efforts on smaller educational institutions. Each year more than 60,000 student-athletes compete in 13 sports and 23 national championships. Similar to the National Collegiate Athletic Association (NCAA) Division I and Division II institutions, student-athletes who compete in the NAIA are eligible for athletic scholarships. In fact, NAIA member institutions provide over $450 million in athletic scholarships annually.

The NAIA evolved out of the National College Basketball Tournament, which was started by James Naismith, the inventor of the game of basketball. The tournament has since become the longest-running event in college basketball. The organization was so tied to basketball and the tournament that it was originally called the National Association of Intercollegiate Basketball (NAIB). In addition to hosting this historic event, the NAIA has long been an innovative leader in college athletics. The organization is known as "the association of firsts" for being the first collegiate athletic association to invite historically black institutions into its membership, as well as being the first to sponsor both men's and women's championships. In 1952, the organization changed its name to the National Association of Intercollegiate Athletics to properly reflect the wide range of sports the association was now overseeing. The NAIA sponsors the following sports for women: basketball, cross-country, golf, indoor and outdoor track and field, soccer, softball, tennis, and volleyball. Men's sponsored sports include baseball, basketball, cross-country, football, golf, indoor and outdoor track, soccer, tennis, and wrestling. In 1986, the NAIA Council of Presidents moved from an advisory to a governance role. The organization subscribes to the democratic principle of each member institution receiving one vote and the privilege of any member to initiate legislation by using the appropriate channels.

Champions of Character Initiative

The NAIA is dedicated to character-driven intercollegiate athletics and consistently strives to positively develop the culture of sports. In 2000, the association reaffirmed this stance by creating the Champions of Character initiative. Using a set of five core values (integrity, respect, responsibility, sportsmanship, and servant leadership) the program seeks to create an environment where all participants and spectators are committed to the true spirit of competition.

One of the Champions of Character core values is integrity. The NAIA defines integrity as internal traits that guide behavior. Oftentimes in sport, athletes are confronted with ethical dilemmas where a person's integrity may be challenged. For example, a golfer might be in a situation where they need to call a penalty on themselves even when their opponent would otherwise not have noticed the infraction.

Treating individuals in the way one would want to be treated is displaying the NAIA's core value of respect. Respecting the cultural diversity of a team or an opponent is one example of how athletes implement this core value. The Champions of

Character program offers training for student-athlete and professional development for coaches and staff to place values such as respect at the forefront of their lives.

The NAIA lists responsibility as the social force that binds someone to the good of the team. Along with the other core values included in the Champions of Character program, responsibility is about understanding how an individual's actions impact those around him. For instance, if an athlete on a team performs poorly in the classroom and becomes ineligible, it shows a lack of individual and team responsibility by the player.

The idea of sportsmanship is at the heart of the NAIA's Champion of Character program. The organization displays sportsmanship by following the rules, spirit, and etiquette of competition. The NAIA places high value on gestures as simple as a postgame handshake.

The final core value of the Champions of Character program is servant leadership. The idea of servant leadership is to have student-athletes serve the greater good while still focusing on the team's mission and purpose. Servant leadership raises the expectations of the student-athletes by holding them accountable for themselves and the success and growth of those around them. A strong team is usually centered on the best interests of all its members, not just the star player.

The Champions of Character initiative and NAIA's Live 5 program aims to teach student-athletes, coaches, and spectators how to extend these core values into every aspect of their lives. The Live 5 program provides short, interactive courses for student-athletes and coaches. Upon completion of the coursework involved within the Live 5 program, schools are eligible to receive Five Star Institution awards, which recognize a member institution's commitment to the NAIA's core values.

Eligibility

In 2010, the NAIA established its Eligibility Center to help potential collegiate athletes know if they qualify academically to participate within the association. The NAIA Eligibility Center is not the same as the NCAA's Clearinghouse since the academic standards for participating in the two organizations differ slightly. NAIA eligibility rules are simple and well defined. A potential athlete looking to play at an NAIA school must meet two of three criteria after high school graduation: 2.0 grade point average (GPA) on a 4.0 scale, an 18 ACT or 860 Critical Reading and Math SAT, and graduate in the top 50 percent of their class. If any two of these criteria are met a student would be eligible to compete in their freshman year. Once initial eligibility is established a minimum course requirement per semester and grade point average must be maintained in order to compete.

Although the organization encourages member institutions to have the broadest possible student involvement with their athletics programs, the quality of competition remains at a very high level. The NAIA has produced many notable coaches and athletes including basketball legends John Wooden, who got his first collegiate coaching job in the NAIA, and seven-time NBA All-Star Scottie Pippen. More recently, NAIA student-athletes have participated at the 2012 Olympic Games and 37 players were selected in the 2014 Major League Baseball Draft.

The NAIA has been an organization that has provided a structure where student-athletes can thrive both academically and athletically. From its humble beginnings of organizing a basketball tournament to having member institutions across North America, the NAIA is dedicated to promoting and upholding the best aspects of college athletics.

Ted B. Peetz

See Also: Amateur Sports; Coaching for Character; Intercollegiate Sports; National Collegiate Athletic Association.

Further Readings
Duderstadt, James J. *Intercollegiate Athletics and the American University: A University President's Perspective.* Ann Arbor: University of Michigan Press, 2003.
National Association of Intercollegiate Athletics. "About the NAIA." http://www.naia.org/ViewArticle.dbml ?DB_OEM_ID=27900&ATCLID=205323019 (Accessed September 2014).
Wilson, John R. M. *The History of the National Association of Intercollegiate Athletics: Competition-Tradition-Character.* Monterey, CA: Coaches Choice, 2005.

National Association of Sports Commissions

In 2011, over $7.6 billion was generated from travel connected to sporting events and destinations in the United States. Major league sports teams from leagues like the National Football League and National Basketball Association travel throughout their seasons, requiring luxury accommodations, charter flights and buses, and shipping of equipment, among other things. College athletes ranging from elite National Collegiate Athletic Association (NCAA) Division I programs to junior colleges travel to competitions, also needing of transportation, lodging, and meals. Leisure travelers who plan vacations around attending a game in another city or state, visiting a sports-themed destination like the Baseball Hall of Fame or Pebble Beach Golf Links, contribute to the local economies when they visit. The youth sports market has contributed, with parents planning family vacations around sporting events. The National Association of Sports Commissions (NASC) was founded in 1992 with its mission to serve as the primary communication outlet to connect the key stakeholders of the immense sports event travel industry.

Key Stakeholders
The revenue that is generated as a result of these activities comes primarily in the form of hotel lodging, all forms of transportation, tickets, participation fees, meals, concessions, and other related purchases. For many economies, this is a significant source of their revenue, and as a result, the NASC was founded to give various groups the ability to connect and grow the industry as a whole.

Historically, the task of attracting sports-related travel to a specific destination was the responsibility of the local convention and visitors bureau (CVB). However, due to the increasing importance of sport-specific travel and the significant revenue potential for any region, there are approximately 110 Sports Commissions across the United States that exist for the purpose of attracting these visitors and bringing the events themselves to the local community, not just the participants and spectators. These sports commissions represent major

Dedicated football fans wearing raingear. The National Association of Sports Commissions is an association in the sport tourism industry. Sport tourism refers to travel involved to either observe or participate in a sporting event. (Flickr/John Martinez Pavliga)

cities as well as small communities all seeking to gain their share of this market.

Event owners are the groups that organize and promote sports-related events and frequently move their event location from year to year. These groups can range in size and impact from the United States Olympic Committee, which seeks out international cities to host these global games, to small youth tournaments that may seek out a town that can offer sufficient field or court space for a weekend event. The sports commissions and CVBs regularly work in concert to attract these events to their local area due to the economic impact they can impart to the local economy through out-of-town visitors spending money in hotels, restaurants, and stores.

Facility owners are the entities that own the locations where these events take place. They are the stadiums, sports complexes, and arenas that host events throughout the year and generate revenue through rental fees, concession sales, and admission charges. Facility owners can also include small governmental agencies (parks and recreation departments) looking to attract appropriate events to their municipal recreation centers and parks to help supplement the local tax base.

The tourism and hospitality sectors are important constituents to the sports travel industry. Within the domain of hospitality are the lodging outlets and event planning. Tourism can include places like museums, halls of fame and historic

sports facilities that all serve as destinations sought by a segment of the sports traveling population. Event planning organizations can serve a critical role with larger sports events by assisting with details such as volunteer recruitment and management, hospitality functions for visitors, and tours. When travelers go to a sport facility, event, or destination, all of these stakeholders have the potential to benefit from the money that is spent by these groups and individuals while visiting their local area.

NASC Services

In an effort to support this industry, the NASC has developed several services that seek to help bridge these stakeholders and create opportunities for the industry to continue to grow. The flagship event hosted by the NASC is the annual Sports Event Symposium. Attendees come from all of the key stakeholder groups for the purpose of networking, education, and sharing best practices. The symposium can be viewed by event owners as a one-stop source for meeting with representatives from numerous locations in an effort to determine the best area to host an event. Event holders are provided with free exhibit space and registration in an attempt to create an event that can maximize the business opportunities for all stakeholders. For facilities and sports commissions, the symposium provides these organizations the opportunity to showcase all of the amenities that their sites have to offer to those groups and individuals looking to bring an event or tour to their area.

The NASC Web site is a valuable portal with updated contact information for all member groups (event owners and vendors), allowing these stakeholders to connect virtually and digitally. With well-constructed search engines, it is a dynamic resource that serves as an excellent research and education tool. For all stakeholder groups there are Webinars that address industry-specific issues such as event sponsorship, contracts, event volunteer management, event security, economic impact calculations, and creating sustainable sports events. The NASC is also involved in regular research on the sports travel industry. It seeks to provide an annual review on the status of its organization and the segments of the industry that it represents.

Julie D. Lanzillo

See Also: Economics of Sports; High School Sports; Intercollegiate Sports.

Further Readings

The Big Business of Sports Tourism: http://www.sports commissions.org/Portals/sportscommissions/Docu ments/NASC_140814.pdf (Accessed September 2014).

Cronin, Mie, and David Mayall, eds. *Sporting Nationalism: Identity, Ethnicity, Immigration, and Assimilation.* Portland, OR: F. Cass, 1998.

Schumacher, Donald G. "Report on the Sports Travel Industry." https://www.sportscommissions.org/ Portals/sportscommissions/Documents/About/ NASC%20Sports%20Travel%20Industry%20 Whitepaper.pdf (Accessed September 2014).

National Basketball Association

The National Basketball Association (NBA) is one of the most popular and financially lucrative professional sports leagues in the world. The league's current popularity and financial growth was seen in the NBA's October 2014 announcement of a new nine-year, $24 billion television and media rights deal with ESPN and Turner Sports. The NBA currently consists of 30 men's basketball teams, 29 of which are located in the United States and one in Canada. However, the league has made a concerted effort to expand its global footprint through numerous outreach efforts, including basketball camps, coaching clinics, memorabilia tours, and exhibition games between NBA teams throughout the world. This investment in international basketball has been returned through an influx of talented international players and coaches into the NBA, as well as financial returns through increased internationally licensed merchandise sales. In fact, according to the NBA's "Beyond the Arc," its 2014 to 2015 opening night rosters showcased a record 82 international players from 36 countries and territories. The NBA's story is one of a remarkable rise to prominence from among several competing professional leagues, poor facilities, and low revenues into a global marketing behemoth and cultural force.

History

In order to appreciate the NBA's current prominent position in sports, it is helpful to understand the history of the game and professional basketball leagues. James A. Naismith invented basketball in Springfield, Massachusetts in the winter of 1891 as a way to keep college students interested in winter month physical education classes, despite limited equipment and space. Naismith used the resources he had available, including a soccer ball and two peach baskets, to create a global phenomenon. Those peach baskets gave the game its name. Basketball spread quickly to all levels, from youth to amateur to professional. Evidence of basketball's early global popularity is seen in the fact that it was chosen as a demonstration sport in the 1904 Olympics, and the International Basketball Federation (FIBA) was formed in Switzerland in 1932. U.S. colleges and universities began their wildly popular postseason basketball tournaments, now known as March Madness, with the National Invitational Tournament (NIT) in 1938 and the National Collegiate Athletic Association Tournament (NCAA) in 1939.

As with many North American professional sports in the first half of the 20th century, professional basketball struggled to find footing in an American culture dominated by professional baseball. Early professional basketball leagues rapidly expanded and contracted, and were often accused of plundering the top players and/or teams of rival leagues. However, in 1949, two of the leagues that had previously been jockeying for position merged to form the NBA. The Basketball Association of America (BAA), which was founded in 1946, and the National Basketball League (NBL), which was founded in 1937, came together to form one stronger league with 17 teams stretching from Boston to Denver. This was a significant turning point and provided a level of stability that had previously been elusive. Yet, roughly 20 years later, the NBA would face another challenge from the upstart American Basketball Association (ABA), which was founded in 1967. The ABA was known for its fast pace of play; its red, white, and blue ball; and its innovative game promotions that challenged the NBA's status quo. Many elite level players chose to sign with the ABA rather than with the NBA. However, the ABA threat was thwarted when the two leagues reached a financial agreement and the NBA added four ABA teams to its fold in 1976. This increased the NBA's league roster at the time to 22 teams.

Turning Point

The NBA's attendance and television ratings were slipping by the late 1970s. Some have argued that this down period in NBA history was due to a new focus on isolating superstar players, making basketball less of a team game. Ironically, many credit the addition of two new superstars, the Boston Celtics' Larry Bird and the Los Angeles Lakers' Earvin "Magic" Johnson, with reviving the league and preparing it for the exponential growth that was to follow during their careers. Bird's and Johnson's spearheaded a league revival that coincided with the growth of satellite television. This new medium was a great way to showcase their teams, as either Bird or Johnson's teams won eight of the 10 championships in the 1980s. In 1979, the desperate league also added the three-point line, which many smaller professional leagues had experimented with over the years, to add excitement to the game.

However, the 1984 arrival of Chicago Bulls' rookie Michael Jordan would take the league to another level. Considered by many to be the greatest basketball player of all time, Jordan utilized his basketball ability to create a marketing wave for a diverse array of products, including Nike, Gatorade, McDonald's, and Hanes. The intense fan and sponsor interest that Jordan inspired was good for the entire league, which the NBA rode to ever-higher league-wide revenues. Jordan's Bulls teams delivered six championships in just eight seasons in the 1990s. This was a period of dominance not seen since the Celtics dynasty of the 1960s. Bird, Johnson, and Jordan also combined to compete on the 1992 U.S.A. Olympic Men's Basketball "Dream Team," which won the Gold Medal in Barcelona, Spain. This highly publicized run to the gold medal sparked heightened global interest in basketball. The Dream Team was the first U.S. team to use professional players in the Olympics and is widely considered the greatest team of all time. The Dream Team's popularity inspired the world to improve basketball development, and by 2004, Team U.S.A. was no longer the gold medalist. Though Team U.S.A. won the 2008 and 2012 gold medals, they were hard-fought games—not the enormous blowouts of the Dream Team.

Current Structure

The NBA last expanded in 2004 by adding the Charlotte Bobcats, which are now known as the Hornets. Some have predicted that an upcoming lucrative television and media rights contract, set to take effect in 2017, could encourage the NBA to expand further in the near future. However, the NBA is currently made up of two conferences of 15 teams. Each conference, the Western and Eastern Conferences, contains three divisions of five teams each.

The three Western Conference divisions are the Northwest, Pacific, and Southwest Divisions. The Northwest Division includes the Denver Nuggets, the Minnesota Timberwolves, the Oklahoma City Thunder, the Portland Trail Blazers, and the Utah Jazz. The Pacific Division includes the Golden State Warriors, the Los Angeles Clippers, the Los Angeles Lakers, the Phoenix Suns, and the Sacramento Kings. The Southwest Division includes the Dallas Mavericks, Houston Rockets, Memphis Grizzlies, New Orleans Pelicans, and San Antonio Spurs.

The three Eastern Conference divisions are the Atlantic, Central, and Southeast Divisions. The Atlantic Division includes the Boston Celtics, the Brooklyn Nets, the New York Knicks, the Philadelphia 76ers, and the Toronto Raptors. The Central Division includes the Chicago Bulls, the Cleveland Cavaliers, the Detroit Pistons, the Indiana Pacers, and the Milwaukee Bucks. The Southeast Division includes the Atlanta Hawks, the Charlotte Hornets, the Miami Heat, the Orlando Magic, and the Washington Wizards.

The NBA Playoffs consist of the eight teams in each conference with the best win-loss records being seeded from one to eight. They then play a best-of-seven series to advance until the conference champions meet in the NBA Finals. The winner of the NBA Finals earns the Larry O'Brien Championship Trophy, which is named for the NBA's commissioner from 1975 to 1984. Each series in the NBA Playoffs is played in a 2-2-1-1-1 format, with the higher seeded team earning home court advantage. For example, in the first round, the number eight seed plays the number one seed. The number one seed then hosts the first two games and games five and seven, if needed. The number eight seed hosts games three and four, and game six, if needed.

Team roster sizes and player salaries are determined by the current collective bargaining agreement (CBA), which is set to expire in 2017. NBA teams must dress at least eight players for every game and can carry a maximum of 13 players on their active roster. These players are paid under a soft salary cap system that allows for many exceptions to exceed the cap, which is determined by a percentage of league revenue. According to ESPN, the highest paid player in the 2014 to 2015 season was the Los Angeles Lakers' Kobe Bryant, who commands a salary of $23.5 million per year, while 12 players make the league minimum of $507,336. These figures are expected to rise significantly under the upcoming television and media rights deal.

Players are acquired by a combination of the annual NBA Draft, where teams select players, and through free agency, where eligible players select teams. Like the salary cap, the NBA Draft is intended to encourage competitive balance in the league. The draft consists of two rounds of player selections and has become a media event in its own right. Draft order is based on the previous year's standings, with teams that have poor win-loss records getting higher draft picks in general. The draft lottery system was intended to prevent "tanking" or intentional losing to get a higher draft pick. It does not guarantee the worst team the highest pick, but rather gives that team the best chance at the number one pick though a weighted lottery system. However, teams can trade draft picks to move up or down in the draft. Any player not selected in the draft is eligible to sign as a free agent with any team. Whether a player is eligible for free agency or not depends on the terms of its contract under the existing CBA.

League Leadership

Adam Silver became the fifth NBA commissioner in 2014, succeeding David Stern, who oversaw massive growth in his 30-year tenure as commissioner. Stern led the league through expansion to the current 30-team roster, instituted the draft lottery system, created the Women's National Basketball Association, (WNBA) and the NBA Developmental League (NBDL), established NBA offices in numerous foreign countries, and dramatically increased revenues.

New commissioner Silver has already faced significant challenges in his tenure, requiring crisis management skills under public scrutiny. For example, Commissioner Silver led the forced sale of the Los Angeles Clippers due to owner Donald Sterling's offensive remarks in violation of league policies. The Clippers later sold for a record $2 billion in 2014 to former Microsoft Chief Executive Officer Steve Ballmer, a reflection of the ever-increasing value of NBA franchises. Silver's organizational vision is seen in the innovative terms included in the television and media rights deal announced in October 2014.

The deal features new potential revenue streams aimed primarily at millennials, who are not cable television or satellite television subscribers, by creating a new, fee-based, Internet service to deliver live games. This new strategy is reflective of the NBA's long-standing tradition of adopting its product to the fans. Other examples of NBA innovation include adopting the 24-second shot clock—in sharp contrast to the slow-down college game at the time—implementing the three-point line, which was later adopted by college, high school, and international basketball; and adjusting the game rules to take some of the physical play out of the game in attempts to increase scoring and fan enjoyment.

Charles H. Wilson, Jr.

See Also: Comparative Models of Sports Leadership; Crisis Management; Draft System; Owners and Business Leadership; Professional Sports.

Further Readings
National Basketball Association. "Beyond the Arc." http://www.nba.com (Accessed October 2014).
Neft, David S., et al. *The Sports Encyclopedia of Pro Basketball.* New York: Grosset & Dunlap, 1975.
Noverr, Douglass and Lawrence Ziewacz. *The Games They Played: Sports in American History, 1865-1980.* Lanham, MD: Taylor Trade Publications, 1983.
Sandomir, R. "ESPN Will Stream Out-of-Market Games on Web as Part of NBA Deal." *New York Times* (October 7, 2014). http://www.nytimes.com/2014/10/07/sports/basketball/espn-will-stream-out-of-market-games-on-web-as-part-of-nba-deal-.html?_r=0 (Accessed October 2014).

National Collegiate Athletic Association

The National Collegiate Athletic Association (NCAA) is a nonprofit organization that governs the athletic operations of over 1,200 member colleges and universities in the United States. The primary purpose of the NCAA is to protect the academic and athletic interests of the approximately 444,000 college-level student-athletes. The national office, run since 2010 by president Mark Emmert, designates specific committees to accomplish governance tasks in academics, championships, fairness and integrity, health and safety, and rules violations. Representatives from the member colleges and universities (e.g., presidents, faculty, and athletic department personnel) serve on committees to create legislation in order to accomplish the governance tasks and ensure the proper administration of rules to protect and benefit all of the student-athletes who compete in NCAA sports.

The NCAA was formed out of a need for more stringent controls within college athletics. As college sports became more popular in the cultural landscape, the value placed on athletic success increased. Individuals at institutions of higher education were stretching the limits of acceptable practices to gain a competitive edge against other institutions. Ineligible athletes, nonstudents with exceptional athletic abilities, were recruited to compete on behalf of the institutions. One of the earliest documented incidences of the use of an ineligible athlete was in the 1800s. The Harvard University rowing team competed with a coxswain who was not a student of the university. In order to help control the issues of burgeoning professionalism inherent with increasing commercialization of sport, oversight of the programs shifted from the student to the faculty. Throughout the 20th century, governance duties shifted again to conferences and ultimately resulted in the creation of a national governing body.

American football is one sport that has been in the national spotlight since its inception. In the early 20th century, the number of deaths and injuries in college football was brought to the attention of President Theodore Roosevelt. The associated publicity brought about swift action. The president helped create the first national governing body for collegiate sports to help ensure safety of the competitors and to help prevent sport-related injuries and deaths. The group was initially named the Intercollegiate Athletic Association (IAA) and later renamed to the NCAA. Throughout the 20th century, the visage of the NCAA continued to evolve and divide to cover issues relevant to the membership. With the advent of Title IX of the Education Amendment Acts of 1972, women were granted more opportunities to compete in sports at the collegiate level. The movement gained both strength and speed over the next decade. In 1983, the NCAA usurped the governing body for women's collegiate sports—the Association for Intercollegiate Athletics for Women (AIAW).

In spite of all the changes within the structure and governance duties, the fundamental purpose remained one of providing amateur athletic opportunities for college students to compete. As the college sports landscape continued to evolve with the times, the voting members approved the reclassification of three divisions to better handle emerging competitive differences. In 1973, the NCAA reclassified schools into three major divisions: Division I, Division II, and Division III.

Classification of NCAA Division

Over 350 schools have achieved the NCAA Division I classification through an extensive application and review process and subsequent acceptance into the organization. Two-thirds of the institutions are

The National Collegiate Athletic Association (NCAA) organizes athletic programs at many universities in the United States and Canada. For every sanctioned sport, the organization awards trophies, like those shown won by various UCLA teams. (Wikimedia Commons)

public, while one-third of the institutions are private. Division I is the only division with subdivisions that only apply to football. Initially, the subdivisions were known as I-A and I-AA. Colleges and universities with football programs competing in bowl games are now classified into the Football Bowl Subdivision (FBS), formerly Division I-A. Those with football programs that compete in a championship tournament are members of the Football Championship Series (FCS), formerly Division I-AA. Both of these subdivisions have a competitive focus based upon garnering competitive success at the national level. The FBS institutions have the ability to offer full athletic scholarships to a number of athletes; however, not all athletes receive athletic scholarships. The FCS also offers athletic full scholarships but typically relies on partial athletic scholarships.

Division II is the smallest division within the NCAA classification system. Fewer than 300 schools participate in Division II athletics. These institutions mostly make use of partial athletic scholarships to recruit student-athletes. Regional competition and success is emphasized. The competitive focus is on balancing the pursuit of athletic competitive success with classroom success and the development of the student-athlete to contribute positively with service to society.

Division III is the largest of the three divisions with 444 member institutions. Division III institutions offer no athletic scholarships and compete with a variety of competitive foci. There have been talks at recent NCAA national conventions to further divide Division III to provide more competitive championship opportunities and allow for institutions to realign with each other based upon similar athletic and academic philosophies. Institutions not under the umbrella of the NCAA can apply for membership and may be granted a provisional membership until full status is awarded. Thus, the number of competing institutions is fluid and open to change along with the number of sports sponsored at each institution.

Sport Sponsorship

The NCAA officially sponsors 23 championship experiences for 89 sports. Both men's and women's sports are represented in these championships. Not all institutions sponsor all sports. Member institutions choose which sports to fund based upon the interests and abilities of the students at the institution. Division I institutions are required to offer a minimum of 14 sports (seven men's and seven women's, or six men's and eight women's) with at least two being team sports for each gender. Division II institutions have to sponsor a minimum of five sports for men and five for women, or four for men and six for women. Similarly, Division III institutions have to sponsor a minimum of five and five with two team sports in each gender. Sport sponsorship primarily comes under fire when gender equity issues arise.

Sports that are not officially sponsored by the NCAA that help achieve gender equity are classified as "emerging sports for women." Sport programs are added in this manner to provide more competitive opportunities for the historically underrepresented sex. In order for a sport to maintain the emerging sport for women status, the sport must gain championship status within 10 years or show adequate progress toward championship status. The sport of women's rugby, for example, has been classified as an emerging sport, which allows athletic departments to allocate funds to the program and count the participants toward the total for gender equity compliance.

Amateur Athletes or Professional Athletes?

In 2010, the NCAA signed a contract with CBS and Turner Sports for $11 billion over 14 years to broadcast the Division I men's basketball championship. The NCAA reallocates approximately $740 million back to the member institutions to fund the championship experiences for the student-athletes in all three divisions. While NCAA athletics have been relatively recession-proof, expenses for supporting programs annually, with and without football, have increased across all divisions. Athletic victories are perceived to help produce additional revenue streams for institutions that can be channeled back to the institutions to help fund the programs. The cycle of spending is one in which very few institutions profit. Recent statistics revealed that only 20 Division I schools competing in the FBS reported positive net revenues.

Still, with the flood of money exchanging hands in college sports, student-athletes have not seen a cut of the profits. Under current legislation, student-athletes cannot receive extra benefits or compensation for competing and/or certain displays of athletic ability. Yet, many have been at risk of falling less under the classification of "amateur athlete" and more under the classification of "professional athlete." In the revenue-generating sports of men's football and men's basketball, the issue is most apparent and the dividing line is most fragile. In the interest of preserving the tenets of NCAA amateur athletics, the NCAA board has used its purview to close loopholes and regulate practices that force the pendulum to swing toward professional sports and compensation of student-athletes.

Two strong opinions exist in the matter of compensation to student-athletes. Opponents of the current structure argue that the NCAA and athletic staff at the colleges and universities are profiting unfairly on the athletic ability of the student-athletes. Supporters of the current structure believe that the scholarships received by the student-athletes in question are compensation enough. In one of the more public trials related to compensation to student-athletes, Ed O'Bannon, the primary plaintiff and a former collegiate basketball student-athlete, sued the NCAA in an antitrust lawsuit. The video game manufacturer Electronic Arts licensed the NCAA brand to be used in the creation of its basketball and football video games, and the plaintiffs argued that the defendants profited off their image, name, and likeness (NILs) without the explicit permission of the student-athletes. Specifically, the NCAA prohibited them from earning money from the sales of the product in which they were featured. The courts have ruled in favor of the plaintiffs, determining the amateurism rationale is a violation of the rights of the student-athletes as a group. This ruling, along with the announcement of Division I restructuring, further weakens the hard line the NCAA struggles to maintain between amateurism and professionalism.

In the summer of 2014, landmark legislation was announced by the NCAA, again altering the Division I landscape. The 65 institutions with teams in the five power conferences (PAC-12, Southeastern Conference, Atlantic Coast Conference, Big Ten, and Big-12) were officially given more autonomy in decision making within the organizational structure on the board. The shift in structure and representation gave the schools more power to make changes without approval from the entire NCAA membership. The new structure could result in immediate votes to change scholarship values and athletic stipends for the student-athletes who compete for the power conference institutions, particularly for football student-athletes. Historically, such attempts were blocked by the majority of the decision makers, many of whom represented institutions without the financial resources of institutions in the power conferences. Such autonomy is expected to open the gates for further compensation for student-athletes and, many predict, a possible secession by the power conference institutions.

Academics: Student-Athlete Eligibility

Another issue frequently under scrutiny, related to amateurism/professionalism, is student-athlete eligibility. The question has been posed as to whether high-profile student-athletes are at college for an education or just to compete in athletics. Current legislation stipulates that rising college student-athletes desiring to play a sport for an NCAA member institution offering athletic-based scholarships (Division I and Division II) must meet a minimum high school academic requirement in grade point average (GPA) and Standardized Achievement Test (SAT) scores. GPA is calculated on completed core courses in English, math, natural/physical science, and social science. The scores are submitted to the NCAA Clearinghouse, and the Eligibility Center determines freshman eligibility based upon a sliding scale of the two components. At the Division III level, student-athletes are not required to go through the clearinghouse, and eligibility is determined in conjunction with the standards for the general student body.

Once enrolled at an institution, the student-athletes must complete a certain number of credit hours a year and maintain a minimum GPA to remain eligible to compete in sports. The GPAs of Division I student-athletes are sent to the NCAA as part of an initiative to ensure progress toward the college degree. The GPA report card is called the Annual Progress Report (APR). With the average self-reported time spent on athletic-related activities hovering between 30 and 45 hours per week, the APR was implemented in an effort to make sure academics were not neglected. Still, balancing athletics and academics has been a challenge for some. For example, former student-athletes of the University of North Carolina men's basketball team have admitted to registering for fake classes and turning in term papers written by other individuals to remain eligible to play. Such academic scandals highlight the concern with regard to whether the student-athletes actually receive an education at the institution for which they compete.

Division II representatives broached the topic of progress toward a college degree by approving the Path to Graduation package in early 2014. The package includes stipulations for initial academic standards for eligibility, continuing minimum GPA requirements, and course completion requirements. Unlike Division I and Division II, Division III members have not yet approved a division-wide mandate for academic progress toward a degree, but institutions set and maintain their own initial and continuing eligibility standards.

Safety: Concussion Legislation

Another major issue at the forefront of recent legislation is concussion management. With the advent of new findings on the severity and permanence of mental and physical health issues related to concussions, the NCAA has implemented new legislation to mandate specific protocols in an effort to protect student-athletes. Athletic trainers and staffs have become increasingly educated about concussion signs, symptoms, and care. Return-to-play protocols have become more stringent to ensure the student-athletes adequately recover from the episode before being introduced into a situation in which a subsequent concussion could be sustained. A recent $75 million settlement was awarded to former college football student-athletes by the NCAA, members of which accused the organization of ignoring the concussion issue. The health consequences are still being studied at all levels of athletic competition and changes to practices and policies for NCAA sports can be expected as more research on concussions is published.

Other Associations

While one of the most publicly visible organizations with oversight in athletic competition in U.S. colleges and universities, the NCAA is not the only organization to govern intercollegiate athletics. In addition, the National Association of Intercollegiate Athletics (NAIA) is a governing body that parallels the NCAA in intent but with different rules and regulations for operation. Junior colleges (two-year colleges and universities) have their own organization to which institutions can belong called the National Junior College Athletic Association (NJCAA), and a number of institutions choose to remain entirely independent of national affiliation entirely.

Conclusion

The NCAA is a governing body made of member institutions set on preserving the founding tenets of amateur athletic competition at colleges and universities. Individuals at the member institutions work with NCAA employees to try to preserve the integrity and philosophy of amateur college athletics. The mission was, and continues to be, to provide positive experiences for all 444,000 student-athletes who wear the banner of their institution.

Tracy A. Trachsler

See Also: Intercollegiate Sports; National Association of Intercollegiate Athletics; Title IX.

Further Readings

Barrett, Paul M. "New Evidence of Academic Fraud at UNC." *Business Week* (June 6, 2014). http://www.businessweek.com/articles/2014-06-06/new-evidence-of-academic-fraud-at-unc (Accessed July 2014).

Berkowitz, Steve, Jodi Upton, and Erik Brady. "Most NCAA Division I Athletic Departments Take Subsidies." *USA Today* (May 7, 2013). http://www.usatoday.com/story/sports/college/2013/05/07/ncaa-finances-subsidies/2142443 (Accessed July 2014).

Farrey, Tom. "Ed O'Bannon: Ruling is Tip of the Iceberg." ESPN. http://espn.go.com/espn/otl/story/_/id/11332816/ed-obannon-says-antitrust-ruling-only-beginning-change (Accessed August 2014).

Smith, Rodney K. "A Brief History of the National Collegiate Athletic Association's Role in Regulating Intercollegiate Athletics." *Marquette Sports Law Review*, v.11 (2000).

Vaughan, Kevin. "NCAA Agrees to Settle Concussion Lawsuits, Impose New Guidelines." FOX Sports. http://www.foxsports.com/college-football/story/ncaa-agrees-to-settle-concussion-lawsuits-impose-new-guidelines-072914 (Accessed July 2014).

National Federation of State High School Associations

The National Federation of State High School Associations (NFHS) is a not-for-profit organization composed of state activity and athletic associations from all 50 states and the District of Columbia. These state organizations manage and govern high school athletic competition, hold state championships, and provide opportunities for high school students to compete against other high schools in activities like theater, debate, forensics, creative writing, and dance. Each state high school athletic/activity association determines eligibility for these competitions.

These associations determine academic requirements, establish rules relative to amateur status, publish eligibility rules relative to transfer students, and establish length of playing and practice seasons for each sport and activity. A few examples of these state organizations are the Illinois High School Association (IHSA), the Virginia High School League (VHSL), the Texas University Interscholastic League (UIL) and the California Interscholastic Federation (CIF). The national federation is a clearinghouse for the rules of competition for many high school sports and activities. The NFHS does not determine eligibility for these competitions; this determination is left to the individual states and their high school administrators.

High school athletics competition was originally the province of the students, in a very similar way to the beginning of intercollegiate competition. Teachers, coaches, and administrators did not get involved until later in the development of high school athletics, physical education departments, and interscholastic competition. Early high school athletic competitions and organizations were modeled after private boarding schools in England, like Eton and Harrow. By the early 20th century, most schools had access to playing fields, and many had indoor gymnasiums and formal associations that were being organized to manage high school athletic competition. The first statewide association was formed in Georgia in 1904. The first multistate high school athletic association was formed in 1920 and called itself the Midwest Federation of State High School Athletic Associations (MFSHSAA). This association was composed of sport administrators from Iowa, Illinois, Indiana, Wisconsin, and Michigan. This group was joined by many more state athletic associations, and it decided to change its name to the NFHS in 1923. The word *athletic* was dropped from the name of the organization when high school activities (e.g., drama, theater, and debate) and their administration were added to state associations, portfolios around the United States, sometime in the 1970s. There are over 19,000 high schools in the United States today and more than 11 million students participate in after-school activities and athletics.

The NFHS headquarters is located in Indianapolis, Indiana, and is next door to the largest college governance organization, the National Collegiate Athletic Association (NCAA). The NFHS is governed by an executive director and a board of directors. The professionals that fill these positions are high school administrators from around the country, primarily former athletic directors and coaches. The board of directors represents all eight of the NFHS defined regions along with at-large members, the acting president, and the president-elect. The NFHS has established many committees that have helped to update the rules that govern sports competitions at the high school level and to help conduct the business of the federation. There are rules committees for basketball, football, baseball, softball, cross-country, wrestling, and golf. There are separate boys' and girls' rules committees for the sport of lacrosse. There are separate committees to develop the rules for gymnastics boys' and girls' high school competition as well. There is a sport medicine committee, an athletic director's advisory committee, a board of directors' committee, and a publications' committee. Each of the popular high school activities like music, speech, debate, and theater has committees to design and improve the rules of competition.

The Indianapolis office has a full-time staff that is managed by the NFHS's executive director; on the executive staff is a general counsel, chief finance officer, and a chief operating officer. There are directors and managers of publications, communications, marketing, officials' education, coaches' education, and sports medicine and development. The NFHS has affiliate members that contribute greatly to the administration of high school athletics at the local, state, and national level. One organization that is an affiliate is the National Interscholastic Athletic Administrators Association (NIAAA); this group is composed of athletic directors and directors of student activities. The NFHS Coaches Association, the NFHS Officials' Association, the NFHS Music Association Directors, and the NFHS Spirit Association are also valuable affiliate members.

As part of the NFHS's longtime responsibility for the rules of each NFHS sanctioned sport, an updated rule book is published each year for all high school sports competition. The federation also publishes case books that further help to explain the rules to the athletes and coaches. Manuals are published by the NFHS for the referees, officials, umpires, and judges involved in high school sports games, events, and competitions. The NFHS publishes the official scorebook for each sport, PowerPoints to explain the rules, a book of diagrams to help explain the dimensions of each playing field or surface, and statistician manuals for each sport. Official records for high school competitions are kept by the NFHS and these records are updated and published each year. The magazine *High School Today* is published by the federation digitally online and also as a print product. In this magazine one can find articles about fund-raising, tips on how to develop teamwork for the high school coach, ideas on how to productively use social media, and discussions about legal topics that a high school athletic director might have to deal with in their role as the head of a high school athletic department.

The NFHS convenes important meetings over the course of the year to conduct the business of the federation and to bring together leaders from the state high school athletic and activity associations around the country. These meetings serve as a valuable networking opportunity for both administrators from NFHS and the 51 members from the states and the District of Columbia. They can compare notes on issues like athletic department budgets, marketing, eligibility, issues with social media, new innovations in the construction of indoor and outdoor athletic facilities, and event management. The rules committees for each sport meet annually to discuss current issues particular to the playing, coaching, or officiating of their respective sport. They evaluate the past season and determine whether the rule book needs updating.

In its role as an information source for high school athletics, the NFHS has developed a Web site called NFHSLearn. Visitors to this site can take courses on first aid, health, and safety. Coaches can take courses on the fundamentals of coaching and a series of online courses for the NFHS National Certification Program. The NFHS provides an online NCAA eligibility video for those coaches, parents, and athletes that are interested in college athletics. The NFHS has also established a YouTube-like site for high school sports and activities like drama productions, pep rallies, chorus performances, marching band, and dance competitions.

The federation has partnered with the company PlayOn Sports to aggregate all of this content in one place: the NFHS Network (www.nfhsnetwork.com). More than half of the states in the United States are participating in this NFHS-sponsored partnership. An additional benefit for high schools around the country is the experience given to high school students to produce sports shows, game productions, and other videos of their classmates for the NFHS Network. This partnership is helping to produce future journalists, broadcasters, and producers. There are links to live and on-demand content on the site. There is also an iPhone and Android app for this new network.

Craig Esherick

See Also: Academic Programs in Sports Leadership; Amateur Sports; Athletic Directors; Coaching Teenagers; Coaching Youth; High School Sports; Sport-Based Youth Development.

Further Readings
Hums, M., and J. C. MacLean. *Governance and Policy in Sport Organizations*. Scottsdale, AZ: Holcomb Hathaway Publishers, 2013.
Illinois High School Association. http://www.ihsa.org (Accessed January 2015).
National Federation of State High School Associations. http://www.nfsh.org (Accessed January 2015).
Virginia High School League. http://www.vhsl.org (Accessed January 2015).
Whisenant, W. A., and E. W. Forsyth. "Interscholastic Athletics." In *Contemporary Sport Management*. Champaign, IL: Human Kinetics, 2011.

National Football League

The National Football League (NFL) is the most popular and profitable of the major professional sport leagues in North America, having surpassed Major League Baseball (MLB) as "America's pastime." The league's annual revenues surpassed $9 billion in 2013 with franchise values up 23 percent from the previous year, the largest year-over-year increase since 1999. The league's television popularity has led to record high media rights fees that bolster the rising revenues and franchise values. The Super Bowl, the NFL's championship game, has become an unrecognized holiday in the United States and the most-watched sporting television event annually. The chief executive officer of the NFL, commissioner Roger Goodell, projects the league's annual revenues will reach $25 billion by 2027.

The NFL was the first U.S. professional football league, founded in 1920 as the American Professional Football Association (APFA). The league became known as the NFL in 1922. The league emerged as an alliance of professional football teams primarily throughout the midwest, with the exception of two New York-based clubs. In the early years, the league fluctuated between eight and 22 teams before reorganizing into its modern-day form with fixed franchise limits in 1933. This modern-day form consisted of 10 teams located in major metropolitan areas with the exception of the Green Bay Packers. Today, the NFL consists of 32 teams equally divided between the National Football Conference (NFC) and the American Football Conference (AFC). Currently, both conferences are composed of North, South, East, and West Divisions, with four teams each.

The NFL tackled competition from the following rival leagues of significance: All-American Football League (AAFC), 1946 to 1949; American Football League (AFL), 1960 to 1969; World Football League (WFL), 1974 to 1975; and the United States Football League (USFL), 1983 to 1987. The NFL's first viable competitor, the AAFC, would bring the Cleveland Browns, Baltimore Colts, and the San Francisco 49ers to the NFL. Yet, the league's most notable rival was the American Football League (AFL). The AFL capitalized on both the growing popularity of professional football and the NFL's failure to expand into viable and emerging U.S. markets. The AFL would present the greatest challenges to the NFL until the two merged in 1970. Additional rival leagues would be founded but none with the ability to thwart the NFL.

Leadership

In the league's formative years, numerous individuals would serve in the role of president of the league. Jim Thorpe, star running back, served as the league's first president. Joseph Carr quickly succeeded Thorpe in 1921. During Carr's 18-year tenure, he introduced a standard player contract and established league rules prohibiting college players from signing with professional teams until after graduation. By 1925, the emergence of former college stars, like Red Grange, into the league boosted the league's play and attendance. NBC aired the first radio broadcast on Thanksgiving Day 1934 featuring the Lions and Bears, a game that remains a modern-day holiday staple.

Carr was influential in establishing both the league's credibility and public trust. More important, Carr recognized that the viability of the league hinged on franchise location and stability. He moved teams to major metropolitan areas, emulating MLB, and successfully recruited wealthy owners. By 1937, Carr had successfully carried out his plan with NFL teams in nine of 10 major league cities, the only exception being the Green Bay Packers.

In 1941, Elmer Layden would become the NFL's first commissioner following changes to the league's constitution. His tenure would last just five years and his successor, Bert Bell (1946–59), would best be remembered for coining the phrase "Any given Sunday" and the NFL's merger with the AAFC, the integration of the NFL, and the first televised champion and regular season games. Bell's era was also marked by some of the league's most notable talents from Cleveland Brown's legendary running back Jim Brown to the Baltimore Colts' player Johnny Unitas. Unitas is most remembered for leading his team to a sudden death overtime victory in the league's championship game, often called "the greatest game ever played."

The Rozelle Era

Former Los Angeles Rams general manager Alvin Ray "Pete" Rozelle became the league's fourth commissioner, and the first in the era of television in 1960. Rozelle is credited for making the league one of the world's best. Media rights and revenues became essential to the growth of the league during his tenure. He was an influential supporter of the 1961 Sports Broadcast Act, which provided antitrust exemption to the four professional sport leagues for shared media rights. Rozelle implemented the "league think" policy wherein media rights were equally divided among all franchises. Rozelle's "league think" remains an integral component of the NFL's economic business model and continued financial success.

In 1961, the league extended television and radio broadcast rights to NBC. The following year, the NFL signed an exclusive rights deal with CBS. During this time, the NFL was facing its greatest challenge in the AFL led by Lamar Hunt. Hunt would later become the owner of the NFL's Kansas City Chiefs. The AFL proved a direct threat to the NFL when it signed a five-year contract with NBC, providing it with a national platform to grow its brand. While the AFL struggled to draw large audiences, it continued to challenge the NFL's popularity. The remaining part of the 1960s would bring significant changes to the league including a merger with the AFL, continued expansion, and the first Super Bowl.

The NFL saw continued expansion throughout the 1970s. The NFL's American Football Conference (AFC) was created in 1970 when Baltimore, Cleveland, and Pittsburgh joined forces with the existing AFL teams. In that same year, the Kansas City Chiefs won the Super Bowl and *Monday Night Football* made its national debut. By 1977, Rozelle had established a 16-game regular season schedule and negotiated the largest media rights package to date. Rozelle had secured national broadcasts for every regular season and postseason game and is credited with the expansion of the NFL brand to multiple media outlets.

Rozelle's final decade as commissioner was wrought with labor tension and yet another rival league challenger, the United States Football League (USFL). The league's first work stoppage lasted 52 days and cost the NFL half of the 1982 regular season. In 1983, the NFL faced yet another antitrust challenge when the USFL claimed the NFL was unjustly prohibiting it from obtaining national

television media rights. The NFL was found in violation of antitrust laws in 1986. This did not deter it or its debut on ESPN a year later. ESPN's NFL broadcasts quickly made the record books, drawing record viewership. In 1989, Rozelle resigned and was replaced by Paul Tagliabue.

Under Commissioner Tagliabue, the NFL would expand from 28 to 32 teams with expansion franchises awarded to Charlotte (1993), Jacksonville (1995), Cleveland (1999), and Houston (2002). The league also saw significant movement of franchises during this decade with Los Angeles losing both its franchises to relocation. In 1995, the Rams relocated to St. Louis and the Raiders returned to Oakland. Additionally, the Houston Oilers relocated to Tennessee and changed their name to the Titans in 1997. This move served as the catalyst for the league awarding Houston an expansion franchise in 2001, when the Texans replaced the former Oilers.

That same year, the league cancelled a week of games following the terrorist attacks of 9/11. This also marked the first season the Super Bowl was moved to February. Tagliabue resigned in 2006 and was replaced by present-day Commissioner Roger Goodell.

Goodell's rise within the ranks of the NFL began as an administrative intern in the league office in 1982. In 2001, he was appointed the NFL's chief operating officer (COO). He remained in this role until 2006, when he succeeded Tagliabue as commissioner. Goodell's first season as commissioner was a historic one for the NFL. The NFL became the first of all professional leagues to establish a Web presence; the Super Bowl featured two African American head coaches for the first time; and Brett Favre and Tom Brady set new record-breaking marks. The league continued to be the leader in technology and began fully streaming games online in 2008.

Goodell's early years were historic in other ways as well. The league established a level of notoriety associated with the high frequency of player arrests, which have occurred at a rate of more than one arrest per week since 2006 when Goodell assumed the helm of the league's office. His inaugural year brought 47 player arrests, with the Cincinnati Bengals accounting for nearly one out of every four, spawning the NFL's Personal Conduct Policy. Other notable events include Michael Vick's dog fighting activities, Plaxico Burress's self-inflicted gunshot, and the New Orleans' "Bountygate" scandal. The Goodell era has seen off-season (February to June) crimes increase by 60 percent since the policy's implementation. Most recently, the NFL has come under heavy public criticism surrounding issues of player-related violence, most specifically domestic violence.

Goodell's power, specifically as it relates to the review and discipline of player conduct, is the broadest of any of the four professional league commissioners. Scrutiny of his authority increased in 2012 with the exposure of the New Orleans Saints "Bountygate" scandal. A league investigation exposed the Saints' "pay-for-hit squad" initiated by then Defensive Coordinator Gregg Williams and several players. The league's probe revealed that 22 of 27 defensive players participating in a bounty system were rewarded for inflicting injuries on opposing players. Goodell imposed historic team penalties, including the suspension of management and coaching personnel; a $500,000 franchise fine; loss of draft picks; and the suspension of four Saints' players he deemed to have participated in the program, contributed large sums of money to the pool, and exhibited leadership roles within the team. The four players' initial appeals were rejected by Goodell but would later be vacated by process of the league's collective bargaining agreement. The bounty scandal marked the beginning of a series of challenges to the league's existing system of disciplinary review.

Such challenges continued when the league and the commissioner came under heavy public criticism surrounding issues of player-inflicted violence—most notably, the case of former Baltimore Raven Ray Rice. In February 2014, Rice assaulted his then fiancée in an Atlantic City hotel and was initially suspended for two games by Goodell in what the commissioner defended as a punishment that was "consistent with other cases." After much criticism, Goodell introduced a new player (domestic) violence policy delineating tougher penalties, including: a six-game suspension for first time offenders and a lifetime ban for the second offense (with the opportunity for reinstatement after one year). Goodell noted, "I didn't get it right. Simply put we must do better," a statement he also addressed to owners in a memo stating, "despite our

The Chicago Bears play the Green Bay Packers in Green Bay, Wisconsin, the Bears winning the game 27–20. The National Football League is the largest professional football league in the United States. (Wikimedia Commons/Paul Cutler)

best efforts we fall short of our goals. We clearly did so in response to a recent incident of domestic violence." Days after the new policy was introduced, the Rice domestic violence video aired publicly and Goodell quickly rendered an indefinite suspension of Rice. Goodell cited the video as new evidence that revealed a different account of the event than Rice had previously told in June 2014. The National Football League Players Association (NFLPA), on Rice's behalf, appealed the indefinite suspension. A federal judge reversed the suspension on the following grounds: Rice did not mislead the commissioner in his account of the incident. Therefore, the video was "not new evidence," and the commissioner acted in an arbitrary manner when he issued the second penalty on Rice.

Shortly after the Rice ruling, the NFLPA filed a federal suit on behalf of Minnesota Vikings' running back Adrian Peterson, arguing that the league-appointed arbitrator's ruling to uphold his season-long suspension was a violation of the collective bargaining agreement. Peterson plead no contest to a domestic violence misdemeanor charge involving his 4-year old son in November 2014, yet maintains the league agreed to let him return to play after the case was resolved. The Peterson case challenges a multitude of factors but most significantly the league's approval of new personal conduct policy provisions without negotiations with the players. The Rice precedent and pending Peterson lawsuit appear to be setting the stage for new limits to the commissioner's scope of power to initial disciplinary action, which may no longer provide Goodell the role of "judge, jury, and executioner," according to Michael McCann of the Sports Law Blog.

More damaging to the league's long-term future than the often short-lived public relations crisis over player behavior is the league's duty to mitigate risks detrimental to the health and safety of its employees. Under Goodell, the league has faced mounting concerns related to concussions and traumatic brain injuries resulting from the sport. In 2007, the NFL formalized new concussion protocols and Goodell later defended them in House Judiciary Committee hearings in 2009 and 2010. In 2013, the NFL agreed to pay $765 million to former NFL players now suffering from health issues as results of head injuries. The players claimed the league was negligent in its duty to enact league-wide concussion guidelines and "fraudulently concealed the long-term effects of concussions." The settlement agreement would later be revised and would remove any specified cap amount, obligating the league to compensate any qualifying, retired player with neurocognitive conditions. This will continue to be an area of concern for the league.

It is without question that Goodell's tenure has seen the largest revenue growth of all former NFL commissioners but not without challenges. He is credited for his work with NFL owners and the NFLPA in ending the longest work stoppage in league history and the first since 1987. The new collective bargaining agreement (CBA) established a revenue sharing split wherein the owners will receive approximately 52 percent and the players 48 percent of annual league revenues. Under the new agreement, owners will no longer be allowed to deduct certain expenses as cost credits from shared revenues, thus providing a greater portion of annual revenues to the players. This is a significant amount given annual league revenue was approximately $9 billion in 2010 and is projected to be in excess of $20 billion by the end of the decade. The new CBA runs through 2020 and expects that team salary caps will increase significantly over the 10-year agreement in large part due to growing media revenue.

The following season, the NFL Referees Association and the league failed to finalize a new collective bargaining agreement by the start of the 2012 to 2013 season and were forced to use replacement officials. Goodell took substantial criticism for the inexperience of the replacement officials, and the NFLPA ordered the NFL owners to end the labor dispute, citing player health and safety concerns.

The NFL's popularity is near market saturation at 72 percent of U.S. adult men. The NFL continues to focus its efforts on growing its market share both globally and at home. For example, the NFL hosts annual games in London. The league appears mindful of the integral role women play in the future growth of the NFL both financially and culturally. It is widely documented that women make up 45 percent of the NFL's fan base, providing evidence that there remains substantial room for growth in the female market at home. Women have substantial influence on spending on products that are thought to be traditionally masculine, including sport products. The female consumer base is both a dynamic and economic force on the NFL in today's market.

Kristi Sweeney

See Also: Formula One Auto Racing; Ladies Professional Golf Association; Major League Baseball; NASCAR; National Basketball Association; National Hockey League; Professional Golf Association; World Tennis.

Further Readings

Bennett, Tom. *The Pro Style: The Complete Guide to Understanding National Football League Strategy.* Upper Saddle River, NJ: Prentice Hall, 1976.

Buckley, James, and Jim Gigliotti. *The Treasures of the National Football League.* London: Carlton Books, 2011.

Crepeau, Richard C. *NFL Football: A History of America's New National Pastime.* Champaign: University of Illinois Press, 2014.

Dunnavant, Keith. *America's Quarterback: Bart Starr and the Rise of the National Football League.* London: St. Martin's Press, 2012.

National Football League. *The First 50 Years: The Story of the National Football League 1920–1969.* New York: Simon & Schuster, 1969.

Schultz, Brad. *The NFL, Year One: The 1970 Season and the Dawn of Modern Football*. London: Potomac Books, 2013.

National Hockey League

The National Hockey League (NHL) is one of the four premiere sport leagues in North America. The league is composed of 30 teams, with 23 in the United States and seven in Canada. Complementing the fact that roughly a quarter of its teams are located in Canada, a large number of its players come from outside of North America—most notably European countries including Russia, Sweden, Finland, and the Czech Republic. In an era when U.S. sport leagues are striving to globalize their markets, the NHL has a unique advantage as the most diverse league in North America.

History

The NHL began in 1917 following the demise of the National Hockey Association (NHA). Starting with just four Canadian teams, the league initially experienced a series of ups and downs, with teams being added and dismissed. It took until 1942 for the NHL to finally stabilize with what is now known as the "original six"—Montreal, Toronto, Boston, Chicago, New York, and Detroit. Six more teams were added in 1967 to double the league's size to 12, and the expansion continued over the next decade with a total of 21 teams included by the end of the 1970s. The final wave of addition occurred in the 1990s as the league dipped into the southern and western United States, putting teams in San Jose, Tampa Bay, Miami, and Anaheim. A number of teams also relocated during the 1980s and 1990s, which allowed cities like Atlanta and Dallas to receive franchises.

League Structure

The NHL is governed at the top by a commissioner whose primary job is to supervise and direct the league. The current commissioner of the league is Gary Bettman, who has served in this role since 1993. Apart from the commissioner, the league has a board of governors, which establishes and upholds league policies. Individually, each NHL team has an owner, general manager, head coach, and several assistant coaches. Numerous other positions exist within each team, ranging from scouts to medical staff to ticket sales representatives.

From 2013 to 2014, the NHL fulfilled a long-awaited realignment plan that decreased the number of divisions from six to four and moved several teams into more geographically sensible divisions. The Eastern Conference composes of the Atlantic and Metropolitan divisions, both with eight teams. The Central and Pacific divisions compose the Western Conference, which have seven teams per division.

Season Format

An NHL season consists of 82 games, with 41 played at home and 41 on the road. The season spans from early October to mid-April. At the conclusion of the regular season, eight teams from each conference reach the postseason—the top three teams from each division, plus the two teams from each conference with the highest point totals. These teams are seeded one through eight in each conference, with the division winners earning the top two spots and the remaining teams being seeded according to points earned during the regular season.

The playoff format features three seven-game series for each conference. Each series alternates two games at the home arena of the higher seed, two at the lower-seeded team, and the final three (if necessary) alternating back and forth. At the conclusion of the first three rounds, the winners of the Eastern Conference and Western Conference meet in the Stanley Cup Final. The final is set up the same as the previous rounds, with the winner being determined the Stanley Cup champion.

Game Rules

An NHL game is 60 minutes in duration, divided into three 20-minute periods with an 18-minute intermission between each period. A goal is recorded each time one of the teams shoots the puck into the opposing team's goal. At the end of regulation, the team with more goals is declared the winning team and this team earns three points in the league standings. If the teams are tied at the end of regulation, both teams earn one league point, and the teams play an additional five-minute overtime period. Unlike regulation, each team is only allowed four skaters in addition to its goaltender. The first team to score a goal during the overtime period is declared the winner. If neither team scores a goal during the overtime period, the game is determined by a shoot-out. The winner, determined in either overtime or the shoot-out, earns an additional league point, for a total of two points. For the shoot-out, each team selects three players to each take a shot. Each team alternates shots until the conclusion of the six shots, or until the outcome is numerically decided. If the teams have scored an equal number of shots, the shoot-out continues in a shot-by-shot format, until one team makes a shot and the other does not.

During playoff games, the conclusion of games is decided in a different manner. If the score is tied at the end of regulation, the teams enter a "sudden death" period, in which the first team to score a goal is declared the winner. If neither team scores after 20 minutes of play, the teams break for another intermission. This process continues until a team scores a goal.

Each team is composed of 20 players: 18 skaters and two goaltenders. During gameplay, each team is allowed five skaters and one goaltender on the ice at one time. The five skaters include two defensemen, a right wing and left wing player, and a center. Substitution of players occurs both during play and following stoppages. These substitutions are referred to as "line changes" as teams substitute several players at a time.

Penalties

Every NHL game features four officials—two referees and two linesmen. The linesmen are responsible for making sure the teams are onside, as well as other related penalties, while the referees are charged with calling other types of penalties. The NHL has numerous rules and consequently a wide range of penalties. Rule violations including offside and icing, in which a team illegally shoots the puck to the other end of the ice, are enforced with relatively insignificant penalties, such as a team being awarded a face-off in its attacking or offensive zone. Other penalties, including slashing, boarding, charging, holding, and hooking, are termed minor penalties and carry a two-minute penalty. This results in the player committing the offense having to sit out for two minutes in a penalty box. The game is played with five skaters against four skaters for the duration of the two minutes. This period of time is called a "power play" for the team who did not commit the penalty and a "penalty kill" for the team committing the infraction. If the team on the power play scores a goal before the two-minute penalty expires, the penalty is released upon the goal.

More serious penalties are called "major penalties" and encompass a five-minute removal from the action for the penalized player. In most serious offenses, a player may be assessed a match penalty in which the player is forced to sit out the duration of the game. These penalties are most commonly assessed when a player deliberately attempts to injure another player.

A source of constant disagreement among many players, coaches, media, and fans is fighting. While fighting is technically not allowed, the league sees it as part of the game. Penalties for fighting range in degree from a major, five-minute penalty to a match penalty, or perhaps suspensions depending on the type and severity of fighting.

Playing Surface

The size of the playing surface is 200 feet long and 85 feet wide. A red line bisects the ice in the middle of the rink, and two blue lines on both sides of the red line segment the ice into three sections. These three divisions of the ice are referred to as the defending zone, the neutral zone, and the attacking zone. The goals, which measure 6 feet wide and 4 feet tall, are located 11 feet from each end of the ice. Each team's goaltender is charged with defending his team's goal and not allowing the opposing team to score. Various other lines and regions are found along the ice, most notably five red circles. These circles are home to face-offs that pit one player from each team against each other to determine which team gets possession of the puck at the start of each period and after play stoppages throughout the game.

League Concerns

Over the course of the last several decades, the NHL has faced several issues. The most serious cause of concern among the NHL and its fans has been its labor disputes. Since 1992, there have been four work stoppages. The longest of the four took place during 2004 to 2005, which saw the entire season canceled. With league popularity already declining, many people inside and outside the game wondered if the league could ever fully recover from the damage it created with the lockout. However, attendance and television ratings showed that fans did return—at least for the most part.

Less than a decade later, though, the league halted again. The 2012 to 2013 season was cut down from 82 to 48 games, and the All-Star Game and popular Winter Classic—an annual game held outdoors—were canceled.

Apart from labor issues, the other significant issue the league has faced is player safety. Numerous players have suffered concussions and other serious injuries as a result of the physical contact of the sport. The most notable case is that of Pittsburgh Penguin captain Sidney Crosby, who many people consider the best player in the league. He has missed more than 100 games over the last three seasons due to concussions and similar injuries. As a result, the league has instituted a number of rule changes to help protect players and has increased the severity of penalties to players who cause injuries.

Popularity

Despite the lockouts and safety concerns, the NHL has seen a great increase in popularity over the last several seasons. The league is still behind the other major professional leagues with respect to popularity, but it is safe to say it has found its niche in North America.

One constant factor that is known among all sport fans is the trophy the league awards to its champion. The Stanley Cup has been awarded since 1907, even before the NHL existed, making it the oldest trophy in sports. The trophy, made of silver, stands just under 3 feet tall and weighs 34 pounds. Among the many traditions associated with the cup is that every champion player's name is engraved on the trophy. Another modern-day tradition calls for each player to spend one day with the trophy however they choose.

The NHL has been a mainstay on television in both Canada and the United States for many years. Most notably in Canada, the league was featured on Canadian Broadcasting Corporation's (CBC)

Hockey Night in Canada, which began in 1952. In the United States, the league has been televised on various networks including ESPN, FOX, and most recently NBC. In recent years, the league has signed two long-term lucrative television contracts, guaranteeing the league a place in front of viewers in both countries while also bringing in significant revenue that will help the league to continue to prosper.

Following many years of constant stability, the NHL has undergone tremendous change over the last several decades. The league has seen several waves of expansion that have placed teams throughout the United States in addition to its traditional locations in the United States and Canada. Meanwhile, labor dysfunction has severely impaired the league at times, damaging its reputation. With a recent surge in popularity, though, in combination with two large television contracts, the league has given itself an opportunity to be very successful for many years.

Mark Slavich

See Also: Economics of Sports; Health Issues in Sports; Professional Sports; Ranking Teams.

Further Readings
Allen, Kevin. "NHL Lands $5.2 Billion for Canada TV Rights." *USA Today* (November 26, 2013). http://www.usatoday.com/story/sports/nhl/2013/11/26/nhl-tv-canada-rights-rogers-sportsnet-tsn/3746859 (Accessed September 2014).

Hiebert, Tim. "Detailed History of NHL Expansion and Realignment." http://www.sportingcharts.com/articles/nhl/detailed-history-of-nhl-expansion-and-realignment.aspx (Accessed September 2014).

Hockey Hall of Fame. "Engraving Facts, Firsts, and Faux Pas." http://www.hhof.com/htmlsilverware/silver_stFFFs.shtml (Accessed September 2014).

McIndoe, Sean. "Everything You Know Is Wrong: Original Six Edition." http://grantland.com/the-triangle/original-six-toronto (Accessed September 2014).

National Hockey League. "National Hockey League Official Rules 2013-2014." http://www.nhl.com/nhl/en/v3/ext/pdfs/2013-14rulebook-update.pdf (Accessed September 2014).

National Interscholastic Athletic Administrators Association

The National Interscholastic Athletic Administrators Association (NIAAA), a partner of the National Federation of State High School Associations (NFHS), was founded in 1977 and has become the national governing body for high school athletic administrators from around the country and abroad. The NIAAA has just under 10,000 members, and a working budget of approximately $2 million, has become accredited by the North Central Association (NCA), offers a curriculum of 38 courses within its leadership training institute, and has established a thriving professional certification program that offers four distinct certification levels. The NIAAA is dedicated to the professional development of secondary school athletic administrators and shares a number of initiatives relative to interscholastic sport today. This article will provide a closer look into the NIAAA's professional development program, its leadership-training institute, its collaboration with state associations, and its commitment to strategic alliances with like-minded education-based agencies.

Professional Development Program

The professional development program, also known as the certification program, brings a better connection between the athletic administrator's training and preparation for the complexity of this position in which she/he will engage. The NIAAA developed four certification levels dedicated to the athletic administrator's professional development: a registered athletic administrator (RAA), a registered middle school athletic administrator (RMAA), a certified athletic administrator (CAA), and a certified master athletic administrator (CMAA). Each distinct certification level comes with its own completion guidelines toward self-improvement in serving his or her school, community, and the athletic administrator profession.

Leadership Training Institute

The NIAAA's leadership training institute currently offers a curriculum comprising 38 courses with a focus on (1) foundational concepts, (2) operations and management concepts, and (3) leadership concepts. Foundational courses primarily focus on legal issues such as employment law, Title IX, sexual harassment, hazing, and risk management. In addition, philosophy, professional development, and budgeting and finance strategies are also covered in the foundational courses. Operation and management courses cover topics such as management, marketing, technology use, field and equipment management, and contest management. Issues related to sport medicine, concussion assessment, strength and conditioning, and field safety are also addressed. Leadership courses address topics such as administrative issues, personnel issues, assessment issues, as well as character issues of student athletes, coaches, and parents. Behavioral issues such as challenging personalities, sporting conduct, and mentoring techniques are also covered.

Collaboration With State Associations

Various committees exist under the organizational structure of the NIAAA. Any member of the NIAAA may submit an application to serve on a committee of his/her choice. The various committees and their charge include the following:

- *Accreditation*: Maintaining logistics and communication regarding accreditation issues.
- *Awards*: Overseeing nomination awards that are presented during the national conference.
- *Certification*: Evaluating and revising the certification program guidelines.
- *Coaches Education*: Assist in promoting the coaches education program offered by the NFHS.
- *Conference Advisory*: Responsible for assisting in planning the national conference.
- *Endowment*: Seeking out philanthropic opportunities that will increase the endowment's value.
- *Sports Turf*: Providing advice with respect to sport turf maintenance and safety concerns.
- *National Emergency Network*: Assisting the membership in medical and vehicular emergencies and national disasters.
- *Leadership Training Institute*: Administering the professional development program,

developing and revising curriculum, and creating the training of faculty that will teach courses.

- *Credentials*: Soliciting state delegates for elective and legislative actions of the association.
- *Hall of Fame*: Selecting candidates to be honored for their service to the profession.
- *Publication*: Seeks out relevant articles of interest for athletic administrators.
- *Retired*: Aiding the NIAAA due to retired members' knowledge and expertise.

Strategic Alliance With Education-Based Agencies

Some of the many alliances the NIAAA has developed a relationship with over the years include: ACS Athletics, which develops athletic event management software; the NFHS Learning Center, which offers coaching certifications; the National Athletic Trainers Association, which was created to provide quality health care for student-athletes; the Sports Turf Management Association, regarding sport field safety and management; and the NFHS, which is an overseer of state high school associations. The NIAAA and the NFHS have been cooperatively producing public service announcements for respective state associations. The main themes of these public service announcements have been advocating the value of students participating in interscholastic sport programs; student participants exhibiting good sportsmanship toward one another, their coaches, and administrators; and encouraging listeners to become advocates and supporters themselves within their respective local districts. The campaign has been going strong and is likely to continue in the years to come.

Athletic administrators have the most complex, multifaceted position in the interscholastic sport arena, and often receive the least appreciation for their commitment to the betterment of their sport programs and youth participants. Interscholastic, education-based athletic programs would not be the profession it is today if it were not for the leadership efforts of the NIAAA and the athletic administrators who oversee these programs.

Eric W. Forsyth

See Also: Amateur Sports; Athletic Directors; High School Sports; National Federation of State High School Associations; and Youth Sport Leadership.

Further Readings

Blackburn, M., E. Forsyth, J. Olson, and B. Whitehead. *NIAAA's Guide to Interscholastic Athletic Administration*. Champaign, IL: Human Kinetics, 2013.

National Interscholastic Athletic Administrators Association (NIAAA). "Leadership Curriculum." http://www.niaaa.org/niaaa-programs/leadership -training-institute/leadership-training-course -descriptions (Accessed October 2014).

National Interscholastic Athletic Administrators Association (NIAAA). "Leadership Training Institute." http://www.niaaa.org/niaaa-programs/leadership -training-institute (Accessed October 2014).

National Interscholastic Athletic Administrators Association (NIAAA). "Partners and Affiliates." http://www.niaaa.org/about-the-niaaa/partners -affiliates (Accessed October 2014).

Whisenant, W., E. Forsyth, and T. Martin. "Interscholastic Sports." In *Contemporary Sport Management*, 5th ed., P. M. Pedersen, et al, eds. Champaign, IL: Human Kinetics, 2014.

Organizational Behavior

Organizational behavior can be described as a field that strives to make sense of the people who compose an organization. In this sense, it provides a microperspective that can readily and easily be applied to different disciplines. As one applies organizational behavior to the sports industry, one can better understand the cogs that make the industry as dynamic as it is today.

Sports organizations are unique entities. They can often be described as the bodies that govern organized sports activities, the teams that compete in said activities, or the manufacturers and distributors that produce equipment and goods central to the industry. In this respect, sport organizations cater to both participants and spectators.

Based on this brief sampling of sports organizations, one can see how the organizations within the same industry differ, but stark parallels exist. For example, those inputs that compose each sport organization are typically steeped in the social and historical culture of the greater industry permeating into each organization and the goal-directed nature of each organization. Often, these goals are interrelated within the industry and across the boundaries that partition each subcategory. Sport organizations are often described as living organisms, likely because of their ability to adapt to each other, the environment, and internal or external regulations. Other descriptions include that of the organization as a machine or as a political system. This type of dynamism underscores the importance of the people who drive these organizations.

With clearly defined goals, the individuals within the organizations can chart and measure progress toward the attainment of said goals or their effectiveness. A method analogous with this type of approach places emphasis on outputs and not necessarily inputs. For example, the stated goal may focus on increased sales revenue in a given fiscal quarter relative to another data point the organization has tracked. Conversely, an approach that focuses on the inputs in order to realize the same goal may emphasize ticket sales and attendance, or how to best exploit the market in relation to those inputs. An approach that aligns well with the organizational behavior lens focuses squarely on the individuals who manage the inputs in order to produce outputs.

For example, the scouting department of a professional sports team is charged with evaluating talent to potentially add to the team's roster in the hopes that the talent (i.e., players) will execute the functions necessary to achieve organizational goals. Those individuals in the scouting department would be expected to have a high acumen for player evaluation and player projections in order to be effective in their positions. With this stated, there are a number of key stakeholders affiliated with a sports organization both internally and externally. Organizations strive to assign a level of importance to each stakeholder because the value extracted from each influences the effectiveness of the organization.

An integral part of any organization is its ability to adapt and evolve within its industry. It is often a coordinated strategy spearheaded by leadership and executed by members of the organization that allows the organization to remain relevant in a dynamic space. Strategies can be birthed from an organization's core values and mission statement, an analysis of the market and the organization's place in that market, strategies at the business operations and corporate levels, and the structure of the organization. Strategies may be planned, explicit long-term efforts, or may develop more organically in response to competition or changes in the landscape. For example, in the intercollegiate athletics space, many individual institutions have deliberately enacted changes to their athletic conference affiliation in order to exploit real or perceived benefits. However, through this realignment process, many institutions have been forced to react to these changes, producing somewhat emergent realignment strategies.

Often the outcomes of these strategies, whether planned or organic, produce growth, stability, or allow an organization to protect its share in the market. Additionally, organizations may realize a competitive advantage due to simple production efficiency, specialization, or catering to niche markets. Both strategy and structure are key components of organizational behavior. Both can be maximized when organizations combine resources, ideas, and objectives. When organizations are able to collaborate in the manner outlined above, they are able to strategically position themselves to economic benefit. This allows for cross-promotion of goods and services as well as decreased costs associated with doing business. Consider a strategic alliance between a leading beer manufacturer and a popular professional sports league. The beer manufacturer is not inherently a sports organization but a strategic alliance with the professional sports league may be beneficial as both likely share a similar target demographic. The beer manufacturer may leverage this relationship to effectively promote its product tied with the brand of the professional sports league, likely reducing costs if the manufacturer were to try to promote its product without the alliance in place. The sports league can now reach its audience in spaces it is unlikely to reach on its own and is likely to receive lucrative and dedicated revenue through the alliance.

In professional sports, scouts are charged with watching athletes play their sport and determining whether their skills are what the scout's organization needs in order to achieve organizational goals. These baseball scouts are watching players at a game at Turner Field in 2008. (Wikimedia Commons/Chris J. Nelson)

The above is just one example of collaboration involving parties in different industries. Organizations in the same industry collaborate in the same manner. In these instances organizational learning, efficiency, trust, and mutual dependence are staples of the relationship. The relationship can be fully maximized if there is congruency among inputs, capabilities, values, and cultures among the involved partners, although these areas are not necessarily requisites to evaluate these alliances. In fact, conditions exist that more accurately and effectively characterize various forms alliances. Regardless, the collaboration should allow all parties involved to achieve the highest level of competitive advantage possible.

G. K. Nwosu

See Also: Creating an Organizational Vision; Economics of Sports; Intercollegiate Sports; Organizational Culture; Professional Sports.

Further Readings
Child, John, and David Faulkner. *Strategies of Cooperation: Managing Alliances, Networks, and Joint Ventures.* New York: Oxford University Press, 1998.
Kinicki, Angelo, and Robert Kreitner. *Organizational Behavior: Key Concepts, Skills, and Best Practices.* New York: McGraw-Hill/Irwin, 2008.

Slack, Trevor, and Milena Parent. *Understanding Sport Organizations: The Application of Organization Theory.* Champaign, IL: Human Kinetics, 2006.

Organizational Culture

Organizational culture has become a popular topic for researchers and academics in recent years. However, there has been little consensus on a precise and widely accepted definition of the term. It is generally understood that culture represents the values and beliefs that are evident in the dynamics of how a company or organization operates, the accepted behaviors of the organization's members, and the meaning that is attached to those actions. Quite simply, it is often referred to as "the way things are done" and has a significant impact on the organization's dynamics, operations, and interactions with its personnel, clients, and various other stakeholders. Culture can be intentionally established by leaders or develop over time with no clear plan for how it may evolve and unfold. Regardless, each organization has one, and it can be healthy or dysfunctional. While a strong, healthy organizational culture will not ensure organizational success, a toxic one can most certainly stifle it.

Popular Researchers and Models

There are general understandings among researchers about what organizational culture means but there are also a wide variety of popular models that have been developed, each with its own unique attributes. Geert Hofstede developed a Theory of Cultural Dimensions in the 1980s. His work ultimately grew to include six dimensions, which attempt to explain how culture itself ultimately impacts the values of the members of an organization and how these values then shape member behavior.

Daniel Denison created a model of four dimensions that he believed collectively describes organizational culture: mission, adaptability, involvement, and consistency. His line of research has established a strong correlation between organizational culture and robust business performance objectives as measured through profitability, customer satisfaction, growth, and innovation.

In a different approach, Terrence Deal and Allan Kennedy proposed a model of organizational culture that was founded on six distinct cultural elements: history, values and beliefs, rituals and ceremonies, stories, heroic figures, and the cultural network. By studying these components, Deal and Kennedy concluded that organizations fall into one of four distinct types of cultural patterns, no one of which is best. Instead, knowing which one exists within an organization allows the leadership to make decisions that best impact the stakeholders.

Gerry Johnson established an interlocking network of elements that jointly work to describe, as well as influence, organizational culture. Johnson's web model allows organizations to analyze the current culture, identify values to maintain or discard, and align those decisions with strategic organizational goals.

Perhaps the most well-known authority on organizational culture is Edgar Schein. In congruence with the discord on a universally accepted definition of the term, Schein claimed that organizational culture is the most difficult attribute to modify, as its foundation is so deeply rooted, even after key people responsible for its development have left the organization. The development of his model on organizational culture spanned three decades and evolved into the establishment of three distinct levels in organizational cultures: artifacts and behaviors, espoused values, and assumptions, which are increasingly less visible to the outside observer. Because of this theory that the values and assumptions are at the root, unseen level, they are pervasive, entrenched, and generally unspoken. Therefore, they create an arduous challenge for any sport management leader wishing to invoke cultural change in an organization.

Benefits of a Healthy Organizational Culture

Much like the actual definition of organizational culture, there is no best or healthiest culture. Generally understood, a culture is at its optimal level when the organization is performing well on established, measurable dimensions related to its position in the market. This can mean a team is winning games, employee turnover is low, productivity and profits are high, and potential employees are seeking opportunities with the organization. When leadership establishes a clear vision, provides equal opportunity, values innovation and learning, and embraces honest and open communication, employee morale is generally high, and as a result, performance and engagement are strong.

Robert Cooke established a set of norms related to what he coined "constructive cultures." In this environment, Cooke maintained that communication is the foundation. He claimed that when employees feel a sense of appreciation from leadership for their ideas and opinions, they are more empowered and feel more motivated in their work.

Organizational Culture and Leadership

Researchers have determined that culture can be established by those in formal leadership positions within an organization as long as a strong vision is established, efforts to drive the culture are clear, and the leader has the necessary respect of and influence on its stakeholders. It is also understood that informal organizational leaders, those with positions of influence throughout an organization, can impact the emergence of subcultures. Simply having the title of leader is not a prerequisite for influence among other organizational stakeholders.

The actions, values, and priorities of leaders help establish the cultural agenda for any organization. The pre-existing culture of an organization, conversely, has an impact on the role of its leadership. The two are intertwined and one cannot operate without the influence of the other in some capacity.

Organizational Culture Change

As Schein noted, organizational culture is the most difficult attribute to change. Yet, organizational cultures regularly require modification. The people in an organization are responsible for the resultant culture. Whether it was an intentional leadership initiative, or simply a culture that evolved over time, the people in the organization established the priorities in terms of values, behaviors, and beliefs. It is a difficult task for a leader to modify culture, especially when the culture is one that is well entrenched, even if it is toxic and dysfunctional.

Culture change requires commitment. It demands that the leader or a group with substantial influence decides that change is necessary, establishes a clear vision of what that change must look like, and then begins to act in accordance with that new direction. If these changes reflect a measurable and discernable positive result and there are rewards for that change, the policy or vision has an excellent chance of being sustainable. Buy-in from those with influence, whether formal or informal leaders in the organization, is required.

For change to be effective, a sport management leader has to demonstrate that innovation and creativity are encouraged and embraced. The type of leader someone may be is critical in this process. An authoritative leader that emphasizes immediate results and instills a sense of fear or the use of punishment may not be the most effective change agent. It has been suggested that leaders with a transformational style are the most skilled at creating real change in an organization.

Organizational Culture Fit

For sports management leaders, the idea of hiring for culture fit is becoming increasing popular. The concept behind this general organizational movement is that culture is something that cannot be taught. Finding employees that share the same values as the organization is thought to contribute to better employee engagement and retention. In addition, there are training and learning curves with each new hire, and if the belief systems are in alignment between organization and individual, the training is more effective and the employee is more likely to be highly effective in their new role.

Sport management leaders must also consider culture fit in the areas surrounding athlete recruitment, player drafts, free agent signings, and mergers and acquisitions. Many athletes with high performing skill sets have simply not thrived in some environments and have excelled in others. This may be attributed to poor organizational culture fit.

Julie D. Lanzillo

See Also: Creating an Organizational Vision; Leadership in Recreational Sports Organizations; Organizational Behavior; Organizational Leadership.

Further Readings
Balthazard, P., R. Cooke, and R. Potter. "Dysfunctional Culture, Dysfunctional Organization: Capturing the Behavioral Norms That Form Organizational Culture

and Drive Performance." *Journal of Managerial Psychology*, v.21/8 (2006).

Deal, T., and A. Kennedy. *Corporate Cultures: The Rites and Rituals of Corporate Life*. New York: Perseus Books, 2000.

Denison, D. *Corporate Culture and Organizational Effectiveness*. New York: John Wiley & Sons, 1990.

Frontiera, J. "Leadership and Organizational Culture Transformation in Professional Sport." *Journal of Leadership & Organizational Studies*, v.17/1 (2010).

Hofstede, G., G. Jan Hofstede, and M. Minkov. *Cultures and Organizations: Software of the Mind*, 3rd ed. New York: McGraw-Hill, 2010.

Johnson, G., R. Whittington, and R. Scholes. *Fundamentals of Strategy*. Upper Saddle River, NJ: Prentice Hall, 2012.

Kotter, J. *Leading Change*. Cambridge, MA: Harvard Business School Press, 1996.

Schein, E. *Organizational Culture and Leadership*, 4th ed. New York: Jossey-Bass, 2010.

Organizational Leadership

Often when thinking about leadership the idea of the great man comes to mind: Leaders such as Abraham Lincoln, Winston Churchill, or Martin Luther King, Jr., exemplify the idea of a great leader. When considering why each leader is great, traits such as intelligence, compassion, bravery, and perseverance quickly come to mind and are used to identify how each became a great leader. However, the situation that each was in also could have created the optimal environment for a great leader to emerge; essentially, these men may have simply been in the right place at the right time. The dispute between traits making the leader, and the situation making the leader, begins the complex study of organizational leadership. This disparity has made defining organizational leadership difficult, and it has laid the groundwork for many explorations into what constitutes a leader worth remembering. From these beginnings, the study of organizational leadership has presented many theories to describe what makes a leader; leader-member exchange, path-goal theory, authentic leadership, and servant leadership are just a few of the theories that have been developed to explain organizational leadership. Additionally, examining poor leadership presents another dimension to leadership by providing nonexamples of leadership. Followers are also an integral part of leadership because without followers, leadership does not exist, which again will help determine the type of leadership that exists in an organization. Finally, leaders who develop networks, foster communication, and are able to see the big picture help to set up organizations for success.

Leadership Theories

The classical theories of leadership have provided a framework for today's research. These theories are the result of the studies of great scholars, each having contributed something exceptional to the field. When studying the classical theories, many questions are raised as to how the theories can be improved, how to make them more applicable, and how to increase their validity. Based on these questions, the field started with the examination of traits and moved onto studying behaviors, both universally and contingently. The advent of trait research opened up doors for other important studies about leaders and created important ideas that are still studied today. The Normative Decision Making Model, Path Goal Theory, and the Situational Leadership Theory bring into focus the situation of leadership, thus providing another way to examine leadership. The classical theories, in some ways, can be interconnected and used to support one another. Although the interconnected ideas have not been tested or validated, they help a novice more fully develop an understanding of the classical leadership theories and enable future research to occur.

The neoclassical theories of leadership have built upon the questions stemming from the classical theories of leadership. Using these classical ideas as a solid base, the theorists of the neoclassical theories expand the traditional framework and its dimensions to include human behavior and the building of relationships. With these added dimensions, the field of leadership becomes more complex, allowing for the phenomenon of leadership to be explained and described. The examination of the relationships begins in Leader-Member Exchange Theory, and then those relationships are fostered and transformed through Transactional and Transformational

Leadership Theory. Finally, an organization is transformed through Charismatic Leadership Theory.

Classical and neoclassical leadership theories provide a foundation of constructs and ideas to consider as researchers form new, contemporary theories. Contemporary leadership theories have been developed during a time when leaders lack integrity, make poor judgments, and are often driven by selfish reasons. The neoclassical theories added the dimensions of human behavior and relationships to the trait-based and situational theories. Contemporary leadership theories include these dimensions of human behavior and relationships, while adding relational behavior and a cognitive aspect. Servant leadership offers a way for leaders to serve the people of the organization, as opposed to serving themselves. Authentic leadership is developed around the idea that the leader is his true self, and therefore, he gains the respect of his followers. Finally, the idea of shared leadership is based around a group of people sharing the leadership role and different leaders arise when needed.

Traits and Situations of Leadership

Examining the process of becoming a leader is important when developing a theory of leadership. When a person enters an organization, he may be on the track for a leadership position and the current leaders may groom him. On the other hand, he may have no interest in a leadership position, but regardless, he ends up in a formal leadership position. During this time, qualities may have been developed in order to promote him to a leadership position. The traits that a leader espouses become important to know and to examine because these traits may influence how the leader came to be in a position of power. The process of becoming a leader is important, but it is not the only aspect of leadership that would be important to describe when examining leadership. Two leaders who have the same traits may be placed into different situations where one has long term success and the other is forced out quickly. The situation will often dictate the success or failure of a leader.

Followers and Leadership

In order to be a leader, one must have followers, and a theory of leadership should integrate the influence of the followers. Once in a leadership position, the selection of those who work under the leader is important. Thus, focusing on the process of the selection of the people who work for the leader becomes important. The leader may choose people who always agree with him and inflate his ego. On the other hand, the leader may choose people who will engage him in debate so that the leader is always kept on his toes. Again, the traits of the leader and the situation that the leader is in can influence how a leader chooses those who work directly under him. Additionally, people may be chosen for strategic purposes. For example, the connections a person has in the organization or outside an organization may make him a strategic choice for the leader.

Often the leader does not have a choice in those that work for him, so examining the relationships that develop between the leader and his followers

Peyton Manning, quarterback for the Denver Broncos, is a five-time league MVP. He started his own charity, the Peyback Foundation, to help disadvantaged kids, as well as volunteering assistance in the wake of Hurricane Katrina and making donations to St. Vincent's Hospital in Indianapolis, Indiana. (Wikimedia Commons)

is important. When entering an organization, it is a leader's responsibility to develop relationships with the people despite the resistance he may encounter. Often, the relationships that are developed or that are not developed will change the path that the leader is on. This selection also speaks volumes about a leader; a leader who is able to see the larger picture, or the whole system, may have a greater chance of fostering the right type of relationships in order to promote the success of the organization. Regardless of the relationships developed, the followers are important in the success of the leader.

Poor Leadership and Informal Leadership

Another aspect that a leadership theory should examine is poor leadership. It may seem unproductive to focus on poor leadership, when what organizations want is effective leadership but focusing on poor leadership will provide examples to enhance the study of leadership and the development of leaders. In an era with corruption and self-serving leaders, examining what happened to different leaders may provide nonexamples of leadership. Conversely, these leaders may share commonalities with successful leaders, but something in the situation caused the leader to fail or become corrupt. Poor leadership will also provide insight into organizational problems, relationship issues, and other problems that a leader may face.

When a poor leader is in charge, organizations need to compensate for such leadership. One way that organizations may compensate is through the emergence of informal leadership within the organization. Throughout most organizations, an informal leadership structure exists that is either working to help the formal leadership or working against the formal leadership. Examining the informal structure will provide insight into both the organization and the leader. At times, the informal leadership can be so powerful that it contributes to the poor leadership in the organization. On the other hand, the informal leadership could be what is keeping the organization running despite the poor leadership that exists within the organization.

Networking and Communication in Leadership

When thinking about a leader, it seems necessary that he has developed a solid network in order to disseminate information and to assist in accomplishing the goals of the organization. However, before that person becomes a leader, he may have that network already developed, allowing him to become the person who leads the organization. On the other hand, as a result of becoming the leader the person may develop the appropriate networks. Also, if a potential leader has developed the right network connections, he may not need to have the most appropriate leadership skills to run the organization. This may be an asset because if he can sell himself as the best leader, he may be placed in a position of power and have the followers support him. The development of a network would be another useful topic when developing theories of leadership. In addition to creating a network, a leader is responsible for setting up a system of communication that allows the necessary information to flow from person to person. The communication process is important for a leader and the information that he is trying to convey.

A leader should be willing to communicate both the good and the bad news to his or her organization. Presenting the good news is generally not a difficult task; however, presenting bad news can be difficult. The leader of an organization should be a person who can skillfully present bad news to the followers regardless of the reaction; it is simply part of the job. A leader who finds success hopefully is willing to complete the difficult tasks. In addition, when speaking in front of a large group, the way information is presented is important. A leader has to consider the audience to whom he is speaking and plan accordingly. This will help establish a healthy working relationship because the lines of communication will be open.

The Big Picture

One of the responsibilities of a leader is to see the big picture when it comes to the organization. Although this may seem like an easy task, seeing the bigger picture, or the long-term goal, is often completely forgotten once the day-to-day activities of leadership become overwhelming. A leader who is able to see the entire forest instead of focusing on the individual trees will be able to find the success for which he is looking. The ability to do both is often difficult because it requires a solid vision, continuous learning and improvement, dedication, learning from failure, and the ability to change. All of these aspects of leadership need to be faced head-on in order to help move the organization in the direction of success.

Conclusion

The study of organizational leadership is as interesting as it is complex. Without an agreed-upon definition of leadership, or an agreed-upon way to examine leadership, the study of leadership often raises questions rather than providing answers. Each of the leadership theories from classical to contemporary has provided insight into what a leader should be and how leadership works. And as each person in the field or in a related field examines leaders and leadership in an organization, the field is one step closer to defining leadership and determining what exactly makes a successful leader.

Kristen Misutka

See Also: Leadership Models in Sports; Situational Leadership Theory; Team Building; Trait Leadership Theory; Transformational Leadership.

Further Readings
Bass, B. M., and B. J. Avolio. "Transformational Leadership: A Response to Critiques." In *Leadership Theory and Research: Perspectives and Directions*, M. M. Chemers and R. Ayman, eds. New York: Academic Press, 1993.
Bono, J. E., and M. H. Anderson. "The Advice and Influence Networks of Transformational Leaders." *Journal of Applied Psychology*, v.90/66 (2005).
Pearce, C. L., and H. P. Sims, Jr. "Vertical Versus Shared Leadership as Predictors of Effectiveness of Change Management Teams." *Group Dynamics: Theory, Research, and Practice*, v.6/2 (2003).
Seers, A. "Better Leadership Through Chemistry: Toward a Model of Emergent Shared Team Leadership." *Advances in Interdisciplinary Studies of Work Teams*, v.3 (1996).
Sendjaya, S., J. C. Sarros, and J. C. Santora. "Defining and Measuring Servant Leadership Behavior in Organizations." *Journal of Management Studies*, v.45/2 (2008).
Yammarino, F. J., S. D. Dionne, J. U. Chun, and F. Dansereau. "Leadership and Levels of Analysis: A State-of-the-Science Review." *Leadership Quarterly*, v.16 (2005).

Owners and Business Leadership

Leadership is defined as the process of guiding and directing a group through a process of influence. Business leadership of a sport organization adds the aspect of encouraging, motivating, and inspiring employees to engage in actions resulting in the accomplishment of the goals and objectives for the sport organization, which in turn should attain the organizational vision articulated in its strategic plan. Owners play a significant role in business leadership of sport organizations, ranging from day-to-day operations to brand management. There are numerous leadership theories and methodologies employed by sport business owners to attain the vision for their organization—some implemented successfully, while others unsuccessfully and requiring organizational change. This entry will focus on the various leadership theories, approaches, and styles utilized in sport business ownership, with examples of owners who have successfully implemented their brand of leadership within their sport organization to help meet its strategic vision.

Leadership Basics

Managers manage tasks—leaders lead people. Sport owners implement the process of business management across the operation of their organization—because without people they cannot run their organization. The leadership function is directly connected to the human resource management function in an organization, as human resources are assets that often work more effectively by being influenced and inspired rather than by being told what to do. In turn, the evolution of implementing human capital management philosophies into leadership of sport business organizations is crucial to the successful attainment of strategic visions ranging from profit to championships and many points in between.

Leadership is the process of guiding and inspiring people. Leadership is not straightforward, as people have different preferences in the way in which they want to be lead, and leaders will utilize different styles of leadership based on the situation at hand. Generally there are three basic styles of leadership: autocratic, democratic, and laissez-faire.

Autocratic leadership is a more dictatorial style of leadership where the owner tells employees what to do and limits discussion about alternative courses of action. While this does not promote a sense of teamwork in the organization, it is an important style to utilize when time is limited, there is a lack of skill or knowledge among the human resources, or when new groups of people have not worked together in the past.

Democratic leadership is a participative style of leadership when ownership wants employees to be involved with the decision-making and problem-solving processes for the sport business. This style of leadership recognizes the importance of teamwork, takes into account the individual skills and knowledge of employees, and is most effective when there is time to make decisions and ownership empowers and motivates employees.

Laissez-faire, or hands-off leadership, is where the owner defers decision making and problem solving to employees because of their extensive experience, skill, and knowledge about a given process. This is an especially powerful style of leadership with longtime employees who are familiar with the routines and services within an organization or if an owner is more of a silent partner in the business.

Approaches to Leadership

There are two approaches to business leadership utilized by sport owners. The first is a contingency approach, sometimes also referred to as a situational approach. This approach theorizes that the most effective style of leadership is dependent on factors relating to employees' and the work environment itself. The two contingency theories of leadership that are most often utilized in sport business are the path-goal theory of leadership and the situational leadership model. The path-goal theory was developed by Robert House when he was a student at Ohio State University in 1971. His theory focuses on how leaders influence employee perceptions of work and self-development goals, as well as the paths to goal attainment. The model explains what effect directive, supportive, participative, and achievement-oriented leader behavior will have on employee satisfaction and productivity. The situational leadership model, developed and modified by Paul Hersey and Kenneth Blanchard in the 1970s and 1980s, focuses on assisting leaders in selecting their leadership styles based on the readiness of employees in terms of task behavior and relationship behavior. The situational variable between the task and relationship behavior and leadership effectiveness is the workers' maturity level in terms of their technical ability and level of self-confidence, resulting in either the leader having to define roles and telling employees what to do; the leader being supportive and providing employees with instructions; the leader and employees sharing in the decision-making process; or the leader providing little instruction, direction, or personal support to employees because they have the skills and behavior to be self-directive.

While the first approach is more of a transactional style of leadership, focused on the management operations of a sport business, the second approach utilized by sport owners is a transformational approach to business leadership, often referred to as charismatic leadership. This approach is most often used when leaders need to continuously make changes in their organizations to address the evolving and highly competitive global nature of the sport business world. Transformational leaders go beyond exchanges with employees to achieve a set of goals; they develop new visions for the sport organization and inspire followers to attain these new visions. Transformational leaders have the ability to lead by example, clearly communicate a positive vision of the future, support and encourage staff development, treat employees as individuals, provide encouragement and recognition to employees, empower employees by fostering trust and involvement in decisions, and encourage innovative thinking. These leaders generally exude charisma to inspire others to be highly competent.

Sport Owners and Their Brand of Business Leadership

Sport owners that can incorporate multiple approaches and styles of leadership possess the ability to drive change for their sport organizations. However, that change can be positive or negative. Using two such owners in the National Football League (NFL) as examples—Robert Kraft of the New England Patriots and Jerry Jones of the Dallas Cowboys—both owners are among the richest in professional sports today and own the top-two valued NFL franchises. But while the valuation of the franchises have increased—both positives from a business ownership standpoint—the success on the field since the turn of the century is divergent. The New England Patriots have won their division 12 out of 13 years (2001–14) and been to the Super Bowl eight times—winning five. In contrast, the Dallas Cowboys through 2014 had only been to the playoffs five times since the turn of the millennium, finished first in their division twice, and won only two playoff games since 1996. This brings up the question if there is more involved in sport ownership and business leadership than just increasing the value of the organization, which for most businesses would be enough. Does the additional factor of good business leadership need to extend to success on the field to judge success? Can an owner in sport be a good transformational leader from the business side but a poor transactional leader when managing people?

In the case of Robert Kraft, it could be argued as a result of the business and team success of the New England Patriots that he is a good business leader on both ends. He employs all aspects of contingency leadership—autocratic, democratic, and laissez-faire—when appropriate. He can be decisive when needed, but for the most part he allows his employees (such as head coach Bill Belichick) to run their operations. This is an owner who supported his coach when he wanted to leave a quarterback on the bench who was being paid $10 million per year (Drew Bledsoe) when he returned from injury because his backup quarterback (Tom Brady) was playing better. This is also an owner that people want to go play for—there are numerous examples over the years of players who have wanted to join the Patriots because of the positive organizational culture.

On the other hand, Jerry Jones can be viewed as a poor situational leader because he tends to default to being an autocratic leader. Jones is in control of everything—as president, general manager, and owner. Any time he has ceded control to others, he has very quickly taken back the reins. He has been noted to subscribe to a "now-or-never" approach to management. Jones appears to want his influence on everything, including the play on the field, and he can often be seen on the sidelines during games. He has a habit of often switching coaches, players, and management and wants what many have seen as too much input on everything from trades to draft picks. The results on the field have been poor. However, as noted earlier, nobody can fault him for his business success on the transformational side, having recently moved into the number-one-most valuable franchise in the NFL list; and in 2009 he opened the currently named AT&T Stadium—a sport palace holding more than 100,000 that has hosted a wide range of events from NFL games to college football championships, international soccer matches, the National Basketball Association (NBA) All-Star Weekend, and the 2014 National Collegiate Athletic Association (NCAA) Basketball Final Four.

Eric C. Schwarz

See Also: Comparative Models of Sports Leadership; Creating an Organizational Vision; Leadership Models in Sports; Organizational Leadership.

Further Readings
Chelladurai, Packianathan. *Human Resource Management in Sport and Recreation.* Champaign, IL: Human Kinetics, 2006.

Frontiera, Joe. "Leadership and Organizational Culture Transformation in Professional Sport." *Journal of Leadership and Organizational Studies*, v17/1 (2010).

Scott, David. *Contemporary Leadership in Sport Organizations.* Champaign, IL: Human Kinetics, 2014.

Tesone, Dana V., et al. "The Human Capital Factor: Strategies for Dealing With Performance Challenges in Business and Sport Management." *Journal of Applied Management and Entrepreneurship*, v9/3 (2004).

Wolfe, Richard, et al. "Moneyball: A Business Perspective." *International Journal of Sport Finance*, v2/4 (2007).

P

Positive Discipline

Most people are inclined to think of discipline as just another term for punishment. In reality, however, to administer discipline simply means to provide guidance and instruction in order to help someone adhere to a certain standard of behavior—to do things in their proper or prescribed manner. It often helps to remember that the words *discipline* and *disciple* (a student or follower who accepts and acts in accordance with a certain set of teachings) share a common origin in the Latin word for teaching or instruction. These behavioral ideals can be imposed and guided from within (i.e., self-discipline) or by others (e.g., parents, coaches, teachers, supervisors) and can be fostered through coercion (negative discipline) or encouragement (positive discipline).

Instruction and teaching in sport has traditionally been associated with coercive training techniques. It is almost impossible, for example, to think of a coach administering athletic, performance-related discipline without automatically visualizing stereotypical images of command-style coaches intimidating, threatening, and criticizing their athletes for every behavioral or performance infraction. For decades, the so-called disciplinarian styles of iconic coaching figures such as Bobby Knight (college basketball), Vince Lombardi (pro football), and Woody Hayes (college football) served as the definitive model of discipline for generations of coaches in every sport and at every level. In recent years, however, there has been a noticeable change in coaching

and training techniques. Command-and-control style coaches are slowly being replaced by coaches committed to disciplining their athletes in a more respectful, calm, and positive manner.

Problems With Negative Discipline

The recent movement away from punishment—and toward more positive forms of discipline—is largely due to a better understanding of the unintended negative consequences that often accompany coaches' attempts to impose learning by force on their athletes. Undermining the effectiveness of punishment is the fact that although short-term compliance can sometimes be achieved, it often comes at a heavy price. Negative discipline essentially relies on changing behavior by creating a learning environment so uncomfortable, unpleasant, and unfriendly that learners are willing to comply with almost any demand simply to avoid additional physical or psychological pain. One problem with punitive discipline is that it can induce a fear of failure and reduce risk-taking in learners as they attempt to avoid making punishable mistakes. In addition, negative discipline can decrease confidence and motivation, foster rebellion and resistance, and serve as a model for a team culture that emphasizes heavy doses of blame, shame, and pain until the desired behavior is achieved.

Cooperation, Caring, and Compassion Versus Coercion, Control, and Confrontation

The idea of modifying behavior through the use of positive discipline has its roots in the theories of early-20th-century psychiatrists Alfred Adler and Rudolf Dreikurs, but has been recently popularized by a series of books written by Jane Nelsen and colleagues in their effort to help school teachers effectively manage disruptive behaviors in the classroom. This general concept of teaching through cooperation and compassion, rather than coercion and control, is now finding its way into related instructional settings such as parenting and, most relevant to the current discussion, sport coaching. At the core of positive discipline is the basic assumption that creating a learning environment of mutual respect, rather than confrontation, between teacher (coach) and learner (athlete) will encourage and empower learners to accept personal responsibility for their own behavior.

Neither Punitive nor Permissive

Advocates of positive discipline understand that their learners—simply because they are in the process of learning—are going to make behavioral and performance errors (there would be no need for teachers if learners never made mistakes). These inevitable mistakes, however, are not seen as unbearable problems or personal flaws that need to be eliminated through punishment but rather as perfect opportunities to help learners improve their future behavior through nurturing, encouragement, and respect.

Despite their reluctance to resort to any form of punishment, it would be inaccurate to think practitioners of positive discipline choose to ignore or tolerate inappropriate behaviors. In fact, they view both punishment and permissiveness as alternate ways of disrespecting their learners. Because of this, the principle of error correction through firmness and kindness has become a central feature of positive discipline. A lack of kindness is seen as disrespectful to the learner (athlete), whereas a lack of firmness is disrespectful for both the teacher (coach) and the importance of the situation. Authoritarian, command-style coaching rarely lacks sufficient firmness but is often disrespectful to the athlete. On the other hand, a submissive style of coaching may actually be deficient in terms of both firmness and kindness as a passive, detached, and overly permissive coach squanders opportunities to help athletes improve performance and learn valuable life lessons.

Positive Solutions Versus Negative Sanctions

Still another important element of positive discipline involves preventing behaviors that might require future disciplinary action from happening in the first place. Therefore, positive discipline focuses on understanding and addressing the underlying reason an inappropriate behavior has occurred rather than merely forcing the behavior to stop. A good example of how positive discipline can strike an appropriate balance between firmness and kindness can be seen in cooperative-style coaching where the coach and athlete, by means of mutual respect and collaboration, share in decision making designed to improve the technical, tactical, and life skills of all members of the team. By providing structure and positive guidance without dictating specific conduct or demanding absolute compliance, the cooperative-style coach allows the athlete to practice the valuable life skills of making decisions and taking responsibility for the outcomes of these decisions.

One positive discipline technique that allows even young and inexperienced athletes to become personally involved in the decision-making process is to provide them with a range of acceptable options or structured choices. This strategy ensures that when the learner arrives at a decision, it will be appropriate, while still allowing them to take an active role in determining their own fate. An example of how this technique might be used can be seen in the way coaches typically choose to organize their practices.

Rutgers University head football coach Greg Schiano greets wide receiver Kyle Murphy during pregame warm-ups before a game against Howard University. Positive discipline and a genuine concern and respect for the athletes play a large role in sports discipline. (Wikimedia Commons)

Supposing an athletic team performed poorly during its last competition. Most coaches are apt to arrive at the next practice with a detailed agenda of the exact performance areas that need to be corrected. The coach often begins by telling the team where he or she thinks change is needed and describing how the team will work on making these changes. This approach can be contrasted to a more cooperative shared decision-making model, where the coach begins the practice by first asking the athletes, rather than telling them, about their game performance. The coach can ask what they think they did well and in what areas do they feel they need to improve. In all likelihood, the athletes' assessments of their performance will be very similar to that held by the coach. If important weaknesses in the performance are overlooked, the coach can offer these after the athletes are finished expressing their views. The important distinction between these two approaches is whether the coach or the athletes take the lead in determining the team's activities. After the performance areas to be addressed are jointly established, the athletes can be asked to prioritize the skills they would like to work on first. It typically does not matter which area of skill development comes first, so why not turn that decision over to the athletes? Allowing the athletes to control what, when, and how skills are practiced gives them the opportunity to contribute to team decisions. Because they are encouraged to become involved in their own learning, they generally take ownership—and responsibility—for their actions and are more likely to do everything in their power to make it a success.

Addressing Performance Errors: The "Feedback Sandwich"

Reducing the likelihood that performance errors will be repeated in the future is the stock and trade of the coaching profession. However, the methods used to alter these behaviors are entirely up to the coach. It is not unusual, for example, to see coaches who have somehow arrived at the conclusion that performance errors need to be corrected through the use of harsh criticism, personal attacks, and forced physical activity (e.g., running or push-ups). Another, more positive, approach to behavior change can be seen in what is commonly referred to as the "feedback sandwich." Instead of trying to intimidate and bully a bad performance out of an athlete, the feedback sandwich challenges coaches to resist the natural temptation to react negatively to a mistake by (1) focusing on what was right about the performance, (2) providing future-oriented instruction, and (3) offering sincere encouragement and support prior to the next attempt.

More often than not, the learner is keenly aware that the performance was incorrect. What they often do not know is why it happened. When a mistake occurs, they tend to feel frustrated, embarrassed, humiliated, angry, and demoralized. These negative feelings only increase the chances that another unwanted behavior or performance will happen in the future. The last thing athletes needs at this point is for a coach to publicly ridicule them for their mistake. What they often do need, however, is a compassionate and caring coach to remind them of what they have done correctly. After all, most of the performance was probably fine. Only one or two small—and correctable—problems made it appear to be all wrong. This positive approach motivates the otherwise discouraged athlete to continue trying to improve. The key to this improvement requires the athlete to recognize how things can be done differently next time (there is no way to turn back the clock and correct a previous error). Instead of lecturing the learner on what to do, the positive discipline approach suggests the athlete be asked to consider, for themselves, the best ways to address the situation. If no solution is apparent, the coach can offer his or her own suggestions. Finally, it is important to convey that the coach has real confidence that the athlete can make the necessary changes.

No longer is a "spare the rod and spoil the child" attitude seen as the most effective way to improve athletic performance. Positive discipline techniques such as providing feedback sandwiches and structured choices, along with a genuine concern and respect for the emotional needs of the learner, are quickly becoming "the next big thing" in sports discipline.

Rick Albrecht

See Also: Command Coaching Style; Cooperative Coaching Style; Preventive Discipline; Submissive Coaching Style; Team Culture.

Further Readings

Albrecht, Rick. *Coaching Myths: Fifteen Wrong Ideas in Youth Sports.* Jefferson, NC: McFarland, 2013.

Nelsen, Jane. *Positive Discipline.* New York: Ballantine Books. 2006.

Nelsen, Jane, Lynn Lott, and H. Stephen Glenn. *Positive Discipline in the Classroom*, 3rd ed. Roseville, CA: Prima Publishing, 2000.

Preventive Discipline

Efforts to mitigate individual conduct problems have always been a concern for athletic administrators. Similar to societal issues such as violence, substance abuse, and cheating, sport regulators must also contend with these same misfortunes. This is especially true in a technology-enhanced world where athlete miscues are uploaded to social media instantaneously. Lewd acts committed by athletes, poor sportsmanship, and a blatant disregard of governing body guidelines, fostered by a win-at-all-costs mentality, have prompted the need for disciplinary structure. In an attempt to mitigate ill-advised actions by sport stakeholders and encourage proper conduct by those associated with sport programs, proactive measures are often executed. One mechanism, a preventive discipline approach, has been utilized to educate sports participants about what is considered right and wrong behavior. Since sport leaders are responsible for shaping character and temperance among athletes, front-end loading becomes a significant means to eradicate improprieties in comparison to reactionary measures when things go awry. While a multitude of issues may surface at various sport levels, preventive discipline measures in the form of bylaws, policies, and team rules become relevant and allow sport leaders to influence individuals from acting irresponsibly. Moreover, when disciplinary punishments for ill-advised acts are known, applied equitably, and valued by those obligated to follow rules, they may serve as a deterrent to thwart unwarranted actions.

Discipline

Often mired in the nature of sport programs and goal attainment is the lack of understanding toward the means in which sport parties are to reach goals, and confusion may exist relative to what constitutes proper behavior along the way. In an attempt then to direct sports constituents, leadership becomes more about educating followers relative to what is expected of them and how they are to behave to operate more efficiently. Adding to this, leaders are inherently responsible during the managerial function of planning to avoid discipline-related problems utilizing preventive discipline. Preventive discipline can be accomplished through setting conditions and enacted positional power.

Power

Discipline problems both on and off the field can be prevented through the use of power that requires anticipation of group behavior and redirection. Power used to influence behavior is the ability to get someone else to do something an individual wants or make things happen the way the individual wants. Ostensibly, leaders, by nature of their supervisory status (positional power), can activate legitimate, coercive, and reward power to get followers to accomplish tasks the right way. Of these, coercive power or threat of punishment to influence others to behave appropriately is traditionally used in sport by international governing bodies, groups advocating the advancement of a particular sport, and at the team level.

Bylaws, Policies, and Rules

Behavior conditions at the professional sport level may have different concerns in comparison to children competing in community recreation sports. Typically, bylaws delineate the rights and responsibilities of member teams and provide a mechanism for dealing with violations. Policies are general statements that guide decision making, and procedures are the steps followed to make sure policies are not broken. A rule is a statement that either prescribes or prohibits action by specifying what an individual may or may not do in a specific situation. Within each of these jurisdictions punishments are assigned and amended to coincide with the compelling nuances surfacing in sport. For example, in the sport of football, concussions resulting from head–to-head contact have recently been highly publicized. At the professional and intercollegiate levels, targeting rules are now more fully explained and the penalties enforced for such infractions carry more extreme punishments. These penalties include ejecting players who target and contact defenseless players above the shoulders. A recent rule in football means that discipline for those players flagged for violations will mirror the penalty for fighting. These amendments concur with preventive discipline measures to deter players from contact that may result in severe injuries, further supported by stiffer penalties.

Maintaining Discipline and Punishments

Sometimes the adage of "the best defense is a good offense" is not only applicable for competition but also to deter sport participants from misbehaving and the potential development of moral callousness. To build a solid defense three types of rules in the form of constitutive rules, proscriptive rules, and sportsmanship rules are developed to standardize play, prevent harm, and regulate behavior. Constitutive rules guide play within a particular contest to equalize competition, eligibility of players, and what actions are permissible during games. Game officials monitor rules of the sport with fouls and penalties assessed to players during competition to prevent these types of actions from continuing. Proscriptive rules forbid specific actions such as overly aggressive behavior or bench-clearing brawls and are punishable by fines or suspensions from governing bodies. The last type of rule relates to sportsmanship. Sportsmanship rules are created to prevent ethically questionable behavior; namely, a blatant disregard toward game officials when a questionable foul is called during a contest or not shaking the hand of an opponent after a loss. Examples given of good and bad sportsmanship are necessary since sport participants receive mixed messages, and the win-at-all costs mentality clouds participant judgment.

Many discipline problems could be avoided if coaches anticipated the occurrences of misbehavior and developed team rules to deal with them. Most often athletes want clearly defined limits and structure for how they should behave. Therefore, coaches can adopt a two-step plan that includes defining team rules and enforcing team rules. Creating a list of the desirable and undesirable behaviors that exist at different sport levels aides in creating team rules. At the youth-participant level, safety concerns are paramount, therefore protective equipment rules are critical. At the professional sport level, where social media exposure is prominent, rules have been initiated prohibiting derogatory comments about the team and players. Each of these rules must be explicit in type and context so players and coaches fully understand it.

The second component or rules enforcement is done so recurrences become less likely. Punishments are only effective when meaningful to players. Legendary coach John Wooden suggested physical punishment for rules violations did little to prevent misbehavior, while game playing time was more highly valued, so punishments stripping contest minutes from those breaking team rules were employed. Careful attention should also be given toward the severity of punishments. Zero-tolerance applications are reserved for more heinous acts that carry criminal allegations, whereas poor sportsmanship behavior may trigger a point-accumulation model. The latter is more readily used at the scholastic level to allow sport participants an opportunity to learn from mistakes without discontinuation of sport participation altogether.

Christopher M. Keshock

See Also: Cheating in Sports; Ethics in Sports; Positive Discipline.

Further Readings

Borland, J. F., G. M. Kane, and L. J. Burton. *Sport Leadership in the 21st Century*. Burlington, MA: Jones & Bartlett, 2014.

Hums, M. A., and J. C. MacLean. *Governance and Policy in Sport Organizations*. Scottsdale, AZ: Holcomb Hathaway Publishers, 2009.

Lumpkin, A., S. K. Stoll, and J. M. Beller. *Sport Ethics: Applications for Fair Play*, 3rd ed. New York: McGraw-Hill, 2003.

Wooden, J. R., and J. Tobin. *They Call Me Coach*. New York: McGraw-Hill, 2004.

Professional Golf Association

Golf is the only sport that has been played in another world—*Apollo* astronaut Alan Shepard, took a golf club and golf balls on a trip to the moon and hit two golf shots that went "miles and miles and miles." Golf is an old sport most likely originating around 100 B.C.E. from a Roman game called paganica—a game that involved participants using a bent stick to hit a stuffed ball covered in leather. Golf could also have evolved from other similar games using a stick or a club and a ball that were played in China during the first centuries. However, the game as it is known today is traced to Scotland in the 1400s. Since that time the game and its equipment have seen numerous changes, evolving into the game that exists today.

The first known rules of today's game were written in 1744. In that first version, there were merely 13 rules. In today's game, there are still few rules but the number has increased to 27 or 32, depending on two different versions with numerous addenda; but they are still very close to the original, with detailed additions and changes where greater clarification has been needed. The rules today have been the domain of the Royal and Ancient Golf Club of Saint Andrews, the governing body of golf around the world with the exception of the United States and Mexico. The rule book, titled simply *Rules of Golf*, is published by the Royal and Ancient Golf Club, referred to as R&A. The rule book for the United States and Mexico is titled *Rules of Golf and the Rules of Amateur Status 2012–2015*, and was written by the United States Golf Association in conjunction with R&A. The central rule of golf is found on the R&A rule book's cover, although it is not one of the written rules: "Play the ball as it lies, play the course as you find it, and if you cannot do either, do what is fair. But to do what is fair, you need to know the Rules of Golf."

Golf Participation

Golf is a popular sport that is played in many parts of the world. Growth in participation increased every decade since its invention until recent years. In recent decades, growth in participation has declined in the United States, while increasing in a few parts of the world. Golf reached a peak in the United States in 2000 when 29.8 million golf participants played a record 518 million rounds, according to J. Reitman. It has been declining ever since. In 2013, 3.7 million participants took up the game, but 4.1 million left the game, for a net loss of 400,000. At the same time, the number of women golfers

increased by 260,000 while the number of men golfers decreased by 650,000.

While its popularity was growing, a number of countries around the world built golf courses to capitalize on the growth. The United States leads this list as the country with the most golf courses per capita with around 50 percent of all known courses. It is believed that the first golf club in the United States was the Chicago Golf club in Wheaton, Illinois, which opened in 1893. The first U.S. governing body of golf began in 1894. Some of the countries with the most golf courses per capita include the United States with 17,672 courses, the United Kingdom with 2.752 courses, Japan with 2,442 courses, Canada with 2,300 courses, Australia with 1,500, Germany with 684, France with 559, China with 500, Sweden with 480, South Africa with 450, and all others with 5,773 courses, for a total of over 35,000 golf courses around the world in 2008. However, in 2006 in the United States, due to the economic recession, more courses closed than opened for the first time since 1946. This has occurred every year; in 2014, 14 new courses opened while 157 courses closed.

Golf as an Olympic Sport

Golf was first offered in the Olympics at the 1900 Olympic Games in Paris and in the 1904 Olympic Games in St. Louis, Missouri. In the 1900 Olympics there were 22 golfers, of which 10 were women and 12 were men, from four nations: France, United States, Great Britain, and Greece. In 1904 women did not participate and only men competed in golf. The sport was offered at subsequent Olympics but there were no interested golfers. Golf has not been an official Olympic sport since then. However, golf will be an official Olympic sport again for the 2016 Olympic Games in Brazil.

Golf as a U.S. University Sport

College sports are a unique phenomenon in the United States. Golf is an official college sport that started for men in 1897 and for women in 1941. It probably started earlier for women but records are more scarce. Playing college golf is considered to be a great stepping stone for golfers who want to eventually be professional golfers. Many college golfers have gone on to be professional golfers. Some notable players include Stacy Lewis, Bubba Watson, Lorena Ochoa, and Randy Fowler.

Amateur and Professional Golf

The vast majority of sport participants are amateurs—those who participate in sports activities for enjoyment without pay or other remuneration—and compose the largest segment of the sport business industry, according to B. G. Pitts and D. K. Stotla. Professional sports are derived from amateur sports. In professional sports, those who participate are remunerated in some form for their participation.

Golf began as most sports do: participation was a leisurely pastime activity for fun and entertainment. The first golf association to operate in the United States was the Amateur Golf Association of the United States in 1894. Amateurs competed in national amateur championship tournaments. As a result of two tournament champions in particular—William G. Lawrence at the Newport (Rhode Island) Golf Club and Laurence B. Stoddard at St. Andrews Golf Club—the runner-up in both events, C. B. Macdonald, called for the formation of a governing body to organize and supervise a universally recognized national championship. As a result, the Amateur Golf Association of the United States was founded on December 22, 1894. This organization is today called the United States Golf Association.

The first official amateur championships were held the following year in 1895—the first men's and women's "U.S. Amateur Championship" at Newport Golf Club. The first U.S. Open for professionals was held the next day at the same club. Further, a U.S. Women's Amateur Championship was held at the Meadow Brook Club in Hempstead, New York, in 1895.

In the history of golf, the word *professional* was originally used to denote those who worked at the golf club, especially those who taught the game of golf to the members. It is still used in that way today, although it has expanded to include professional golfers—those who earn money to play the game.

Most likely, the first "professional" golf tournament was held in 1860 in Scotland at the Prestwick Club, according to R. Cavendish. Eight professionals competed in this tournament. As was typical with many sports, golf's first professional prizes did not include money; rather they involved other types of

awards. For this first professionals-only golf tournament, the prize was a red leather belt with silver clasps. Men's professional golf in the United States started in 1895 at the first U.S. Open held in Newport, Rhode Island. This tournament was played with nine professional golfers and one amateur. Most golf was being played in warm weather states, and those are the primary states that held the first professional tournaments.

Sam Snead was an American professional golfer who won a record 82 PGA Tour events during his career. He was known for having a so-called perfect swing. He achieved the PGA Tour Lifetime Achievement Award in 1998. (Wikimedia Commons/ ABC Television)

Women's professional golf was played by several women in the late 1800s and early 1900s, although an organization started later. Helen Hicks was the first woman to become a professional golfer in 1934—she was also one of the first women to sign an endorsement contract with a sporting goods company, the Wilson-Western Sporting Goods Company, to promote its products.

The first known women's professional golf organization in the United States was started in 1950 with the launch of the Ladies Professional Golf Association (LPGA). Although women have always played golf at most golf clubs, some golf clubs were built for and opened only to women golfers. The first known women's golf club opened in 1876 alongside St. Andrews in Scotland and was called the Ladies Club of St. Andrew's. In fact, Mary Queen of Scots (1542–87) loved to play golf and is credited for coining the word *caddie* from the "cadets" who were her assistants. She so loved golf that she was often criticized for playing too much. The first women's-only golf club in the United States was opened in 1893—the Shinnecock Hills Golf Club on Long Island, New York.

Golf Associations

Golf business is a large and diverse industry. There are organizations for every type of job and career associated with golf, such as the golf course manager/

executive, the caddie, the turf manager, golf club and equipment manufacturers, and the golf clothing and shoe industry. A few examples include the Golf Course Superintendents Association of America, the National Golf Course Owners Association, and the Association of Golf Merchandisers. Additionally, there are organizations that span the diversity of gender, age, profession, and handicap or skill level. Examples include the Executive Women's Golf Association, the American Seniors Golf Association, and the First Tee (junior golf association).

There are several professional golf organizations, ranging from local and state associations to international golf organizations. Some of these include the National Golf Federation, the United States Golf Association (USGA), International Golf Federation (IGF), American Junior Golf Association (AJGA), and the Professional Golf Association of America (PGA). The Professional Golf Association of America, commonly called the PGA, claims to be the world's largest sports organization with over 27,000 members.

Professional Golf Tours

A professional league in golf is called a professional tour. To earn money as a professional golfer, the golfer must qualify for and join one of the tours. There are more than 20 professional golf tours for men and women in the United States and each is run by a different organization. Each one has members—the golfers—who earn money and other rewards in a variety of ways by playing in tournaments. The top tours for women are the LPGA Tour and the Ladies European Tour. The top tours for men are the PGA Tour and the European Tour.

Professional Golfers Association: The PGA Tour

The origin of the professional men's golf association in the United States is traced to a wealthy business owner who built a resort, the Buckwood Inn, with an 18-hole golf course near Shawnee on Delaware, Pennsylvania, where in 1912 a group of professional golfers gathered and played golf before having a discussion about starting an official professional organization. The original name for professional golf for men was the Professional Golf Association of America, founded in 1916. The first PGA of America tournament was held in 1916 but was not held again until 1919 due to World War I. The tournament was open to both professional and amateur players. In 1981, the name was officially changed to the Tournament Players Association (TPA) Tour, and later changed again to its current name, the Professional Golfers Association Tour, now known as the PGA Tour.

Ladies Professional Golf Association: The LPGA Tour

The first women's professional golf organization was started in 1944, although women played professional golf at tournaments in the 1800s and early 1900s. The first known woman to turn pro was Helen Hicks in 1934. The first professional organization was the Women's Professional Golf Association (WPGA). Some of the early players were world legends of the game: Babe Didrikson Zaharias, Patty Berg, and Louise Suggs. Although the WPGA folded in 1949, the stage was set for women's professional golf. In 1950, 13 women gathered and founded the Ladies Professional Golf Association (LPGA). The LPGA is the primary organizer of women's professional golf tournaments in the United States. The LPGA has grown from an American-focused professional tour organization to an international association with professional golfers and tours around the world. Among its many accomplishments, the LPGA includes the LPGA Tour, the LPGA Teaching and Club Professionals, the LPGA Foundation, the LPGA-USGA Girls Golf program, the Symetra Tour, and the FUTURES Tour.

Brenda G. Pitts

See Also: Amateur Sports; Gender and Sports Leadership; Ladies Professional Golf Association.

Further Readings

Berkley, N. "Important Events in Women's Golf." http://www.nancyberkley.com/774892.html (Accessed November 2014).

Cavendish, R. "The First Professional Golf Tournament." *History Today*, v.60/10 (2010). http://www.historytoday.com/richard-cavendish/first-professional-golf-tournament (Accessed November 2014).

Pitts, B. G., and D. K. Stotlar. *Fundamentals of Sport Marketing*. Morgantown, WV: Fitness Information Technology Publishers, 2013.

Scottish Golf History. "Rules of Golf – 1744." http://www
.scottishgolfhistory.org/origin-of-golf-terms/rules-of
-golf (Accessed November 2014).

Professional Sports

A major distinguishing aspect of professional sports is the payment of players who play in organized contests against other professional athletes. While there are a multitude of amateur athletes and sporting organizations, professional sports hold the distinction of having a written rule book and providing economic benefits to players. Moreover, while many professional athletes enjoy their job, there is a distinct difference between the attitudes and training regimens of recreational and professional athletes. The proliferation of professional sports in modern society has been marked by an explosion in worldwide participation, popularity, and diversity in professional sports organizations. While games and contests have been around for millennia, the idea of the professional athlete (an athlete who plays at the highest level within their sport and receives payment for playing) is a more modern development. The Industrial Revolution was a turning point in the world of sport, as it brought about increased leisure that opened the door to increased participation in activities not directly related to the production of goods. Further advancing the popularity of professional sports was the expansion of radio and television, which gave access to millions more fans across the globe.

With the potential to make millions of dollars as a professional athlete, there are, however, growing controversies as to when an elite athlete can begin to call himself or herself a professional athlete and receive payment for their sporting talents. Also, while the proliferation of professional sporting organizations began in industrialized nations, the growth of the middle class in developing countries has had a large impact on the popularity of a variety of sports, and with this increased popularity throughout the world, female professional sports organizations have seen increased success as well. All in all, with strong encouragement within modern society to stay active, the increased media coverage, and the promise of economic prosperity, modern sport will continue to grow in popularity throughout the world.

History

Throughout history the spectacle of human physical triumphs and competition has been highly valued. From horse races, to the Olympics in ancient Greece, to the first recorded wagers on boxing matches, there has always been a place in society for those wishing to showcase their physical abilities and those wanting to witness the physical prowess of others. However, up until the industrialized era, sporting contests were unregulated, had simple rules, and generally not remembered long after the event. In modern sports, and more specifically in professional sports, on the other hand, detailed rules and records along with a much higher regional, national, and international following have been created as methods of comparing performances and giving viewers the ability to interrupt game situations.

The biggest push toward professional sports occurred in the 1850s during the Industrial Revolution in America. Before the urbanization of the United States, the majority of work done in the country occurred on farmland where there was little time for leisure activities. Furthermore, the heavily ingrained religious culture throughout the country framed sports and most leisure activities as blasphemous and unwelcome in society. However, with the increase in factory work and the development of much larger communities in urban settings, more and more citizens found themselves with an increased amount of leisure time. Thus, physical activity and competition developed a better reputation as wholesome and character-building activities. Sports also served as a way to define class structure in modern, heavily populated cities.

Cities also proved to be a major factor in the rise of professional sports because of the amount of spectators that had access to sporting events. As urban populations grew exponentially in the late 19th century, entrepreneurs looked to capitalize on the increased leisure time by providing permanent venues for specific sporting events. The first sporting venues, such as horse racing tracks, were created to provide a central location to gamble on the events. Gambling also occurred during prize fights, which were early, loosely regulated boxing matches. However gambling was frowned upon if not illegal in most states and only a small percentage of the population could afford to gamble on horses, while an even smaller percentage could stomach the brutality of bare-knuckle boxing matches. It would not be until a sport that stood for morality and strong character while also appealing to all socioeconomic classes that professional sport would begin to grow to the levels seen today.

Baseball offered something for everyone at the turn of the 20th century. For one thing, baseball provided a clear and written rule book that all new players and teams could follow and be coached on. This consensus allowed for stronger competition and rivalries to be formed between teams of neighboring towns and cities, since all teams were playing by the same rules. Second, ticket prices to watch the best players were much cheaper than other sporting events and even the lowest class of citizens could afford to occasionally attend games. Baseball clubs also preached the idea of hard work and dedication to practice, thereby providing hope to the lower- and middle-class citizens that they, too, could reach the professional ranks. Additionally, with more and more people eager to watch the best of the best, players were able to demand compensation for playing and winning. While baseball's rules, fan base, and code of conduct helped it stand out in early professional sport, the rise of mass communication led baseball and professional sport as a whole into the next era.

Sports Media and Rise in Popularity

The growth of mass media in modern society and the growth of professional sports have enjoyed a mutually beneficial relationship over the last century. As the Industrial Revolution took hold in America, the media benefited from guaranteed content and exciting story lines that readers, listeners, and, later on, viewers were excited to learn about, while professional sports were able to reach countless more potential fans with the proliferation of media outlets throughout the world. Media coverage of sports, understandably, followed the attitudes and values of the public, and the media being led by the will of the people has continued to this day.

In the mid-1800s, newspapers and magazines began to recognize the value in the coverage of sport. With decreased costs of printing and a more concentrated readership helped by urbanization, newspaper publishers began to earn large profits from advertising and circulation of dedicated sports magazines. However, the content was limited to horse racing and various other "high-class" contests, leaving out more brutal sports such as boxing until later in the 19th century. It was not until after the Civil War that sports such as boxing and the new sport of baseball began to be covered more by the media. Several early sportswriters and entrepreneurs sought to standardize (and print) the rules of baseball and encourage professional leagues to form in order to grow a fan base and sell more papers. By the 1920s, the growth in popularity of baseball, boxing, and college football led to daily sports pages and segments in most media outlets. With this greater coverage of sports and specific athletes, fans began to be drawn to the spectacle of large crowds and stadiums to see the "heroes" they had read about in the papers. This brought in even greater profits for both the sports teams and the media outlets that covered them, which increased the desire of children to dream about becoming a professional athlete. The increased use of radio broadcasting proved to be another boom for professional sports.

During the 1920s, when professional sporting contests (mostly baseball and prize fights) continued to garner more and more followers, access to radio broadcasts in American households grew dramatically as well. This access instilled a familiarity with professional athletes, since fans could hear about their favorite teams and players on a daily basis and connect to the action immediately. Gradually, live sporting events, both at the physical venue and over the radio waves, were able to be hyped and marketed before the games were even played. A prize fight could be advertised weeks in advance, people knew when the intercity rival was coming to town to play their hometown baseball team, and fans became more knowledgeable about the rules, players, and teams in professional sport. Additionally, advertisers began to market products and services during radio broadcasts since they knew many potential consumers were tuning in. This strategy continued to be implemented throughout the Golden Age of Radio, but the visibility of professional athletes really took hold when fans began to see their sports heroes on television.

While radio continued to be a major factor in the increased popularity of professional sports, the onset of household television brought business revenues to a new level. In the 1960s, the National Football League (NFL) began airing games on TV, which led not only to lucrative television contracts but also to increased merchandising opportunities for cities and team owners. Suddenly, cities that had no professional sports team pushed for a football team that could visually showcase the city. Advertisers also jumped at the opportunity to pitch their products to huge audiences from across the country. Other sports followed the lead of the NFL, and by the late 1960s the major professional sports organizations including baseball, hockey, and basketball all had major television contracts. Professional athletes also enjoyed lucrative sponsorship opportunities by filming commercials for products that would be shown during games on television. This ability to make money outside of playing the sport itself further separated professional athletes from the college and amateur ranks. A professional athlete was someone who was putting significant time and effort into their sport in order to both win and make a large amount of money both on and off the field. An amateur, on the other hand, may possess the skill to compete at the professional level but choose to play for the love of the sport or as a means to receive a college education. However, in recent years, this line between amateur and professional sports has been significantly blurred.

Growing Controversy in Collegiate Sport

Throughout the 19th and 20th centuries, professional sports were able to gain acceptance into mainstream America because of the heavy emphasis on morality, clean living, and teamwork. However, as athletes' salaries and endorsement deals grew exponentially in the second half of the 20th century, many fans began to worry that money would corrupt the young athletes and take their minds off of gaining a college education. The idea of competing in sport for the love of the game while earning an education became a rallying point for many sports fans and more importantly for the National Collegiate Athletic Association (NCAA). The NCAA put a premium on the amateur status of college athletes and prohibited anyone on a collegiate sports team from receiving money or special gifts from the college or

business seeking to use the athletes as spokespeople. However, for similar reasons that the popularity of professional sports grew so rapidly throughout the 20th century (media, strict code of conduct, etc.), colleges, universities, and the NCAA have enjoyed enormous revenue gains in the past few decades. This has led some to question whether high-performing college athletes are really amateurs at all.

In 2014, a judge ruled in favor of the ability of student-athletes on the football team at Northwestern University to unionize and collectively bargain. Previously, only professionals (athlete or otherwise) were allowed to unionize and negotiate for better compensation. The judge's ruling has brought up controversy, since collegiate athletes may now be viewed as professionals who are compensated for providing a service to an employer. The judge cited significant time commitments by the players and scholarships provided to players by the school as being equivalent to any other employee–employer relationship. With this ruling, it seems that while the NCAA and its member schools have attempted to promote academics and amateurism over sport and getting paid to devote one's life to sport, professionalism continues to infiltrate all levels of sport.

Current Trends

With continued increases in the access to mass media throughout the world, many professional sports organizations that are relatively new have been able to gain a large following throughout the world. During the early days of the 20th century baseball, horse racing, and boxing dominated the sports pages and radio airwaves. By the time TV was embedded in industrialized nations, professional football slowly overtook other sports as the most lucrative professional sport. However, as more and more countries have modernized with their own industrial revolutions, the popularity of certain sports worldwide has changed dramatically. With the world as a whole still experiencing a rise of the middle-class population, more and more people are gravitating to leisure activities that include both playing and watching sports.

Interestingly, despite the popularity of the National Football League in the United States, football is only the 10th most popular sport in the world in terms of the approximate number of fans and professional leagues. Outside the United States and Canada, football has a growing but negligible following. In fact, of the top three most popular sports in the United States (football, basketball, and baseball), none of them are in the top-five most popular sports worldwide. Both tennis and golf rank higher in popularity on a world scale, partially because of the increased success of female professional sports organizations. As sports in general have increased in popularity throughout the world, more opportunities have been given to female professional athletes, with tennis even offering equal prize money to both male and female athletes. Additionally, with the growth of the middle class in China and India, professional table tennis, field hockey, and cricket organizations all enjoy much larger worldwide fan bases than any organization founded in the United States, although athletes' salaries in U.S. professional sports leagues are generally well above those of athletes playing in leagues in other countries. Professional soccer players, however, do get paid at levels that rival the top athletes in the United States.

Soccer is the number-one sport in the world in terms of fans and participants and easily beats out all other sports in worldwide popularity by more than a billion people. The structure of both national and international soccer leagues creates a climate of intercity and international rivalry not seen since the turn of the 20th century with the first professional sports leagues. The World Cup, which occurs every four years, brings about a sense of nationalism among competing countries and allows professional athletes to take the world stage. While the Olympics offer athletes a similar performance scenario, many countries lack the resources and climate that would lend themselves to the development of top-level Olympic athletes. Soccer, on the other hand, can be played essentially anywhere with little equipment, thus lending itself to worldwide popularity. It is clear that professional sports will continue to gain followers as TV and Internet access in developing nations grows, and the current professional sports leagues will prosper along with new leagues, up-and-coming sports, and even better athletes.

James A. Schwabach

See Also: Amateur Sports; Economics of Sports; Recreational Versus Competitive Sport; Unionization of College Athletes.

Further Readings

Barak, E. "Top 10 Most Popular Sports in the World in 2014." http://www.top10zen.com/most-popular-sports-1584 (Accessed September 2014).

Polsson, K. "Chronology of Sports." http://worldtimeline.info/sports (Accessed September 2014).

Riess, S. *Sport in Industrial America, 1850–1920.* Hoboken, NJ: Wiley-Blackwell, 2013.

Vint, P. "Explaining What the Northwestern College Football Union Decision Means" (2014). http://www.sbnation.com/college-football/2014/3/27/5551014/college-football-playersunion-northwestern-nlrb (Accessed September 2014).

Wenner, L. *Media, Sports, and Society.* Thousand Oaks, CA: Sage, 1989.

R

Race/Ethnicity and Sports Leadership

Race and ethnicity are often used interchangeably; however, the two terms are very different. Race refers to the physical characteristics of a person; that is, skin color, hair color, color of eyes, and even facial bone structure. The term *ethnicity*, on the other hand, can refer to, among other things, a person's customs, beliefs, and language. By understanding the distinction between race and ethnicity, people can begin to have more meaningful and purposeful dialogue. Those who are in leadership positions in sport must understand these terms in an ever-increasing multicultural and diverse world. It will take a very informed and practical leader to navigate all of the cultural norms and beliefs in order to create a welcoming sport environment.

To lead a sport team is a monumental task. One has to be able to deal with both internal and external constituents and balance their needs. The sport leader needs to be able to address the concerns of all constituents and make decisions regarding these concerns in a rational and prudent matter. Constituents come from various backgrounds and experiences, which makes the sport leader's job even more challenging. Sport leaders must have keen analytical abilities to understand the origins of the concerns that they address. Moreover, they must be able to determine the impact of their decisions on various constituencies. In essence, the job of a sport leader is very complex when one considers all the different variables that exist. Take, for example, a sport leader who must discipline a player regarding cheating. The sport leader must determine if the player cheated; if so, what was the severity of the offense; and what punishment must be levied. The punishment must be congruent with policies and procedures. This is an oversimplified example, but the fact still remains that sport leaders must take into account multiple sources of information from multiple parties.

Diversity, Race, and Ethnicity in the National Hockey League

The National Hockey League (NHL) originated in 1917. There were five teams: the Montreal Wanderers, Montreal Canadians, Ottawa Senators, Quebec Bulldogs, and the Toronto Arenas. Since its inception the NHL has grown to 30 teams that play in both the United States and Canada. Teams are now owned by corporations or wealthy families. The value of an NHL franchise as of 2014 ranges from $175 million to $1.1 billion, with the average cost of a team being $413 million. Values of NHL franchises continue to increase. This is due in part to the leadership of the current NHL commissioner Gary Bettman. Bettman is an Ivy League-trained attorney who began his sports career with the National Basketball Association (NBA) in 1981. Bettman was primarily responsible for the marketing and legal matters of the NBA. He is also credited as being one of the architects of the modern-day salary cap that was first created by the NBA. Bettman became commissioner of the NHL in 1993 and his accomplishments are commendable. The owners of the NHL teams charged Bettman to "grow" the league. Since Bettman became commissioner the league has grown by six teams from 24 to 30. Other areas of growth can be seen in the increases of ticket sales revenue, merchandise revenue, corporate sponsorships, television revenue, and overall fan popularity. In addition, in 1998 Bettman negotiated the largest NHL television deal with both ESPN and ABC. That deal was worth $600 million for five years. The NHL also under Bettman's watch created an All-Star weekend similar to that of the NBA. In spite of all of his accomplishments, Bettman does have his detractors. Labor disputes and work stoppages have made him very unpopular with some fans, former NHL players, and current players alike. In Bettman's second year, for example, the NHL experienced a lockout. Owners wanted a salary cap and other cost-constraint measures such as a luxury tax. Bettman, on behalf of the owners, was able to strike a deal with the player's union and a rookie salary cap along with other concessions were made. However, there was another contentious strike in the 2004 to 2005 season that lead to Bettman making the most unprecedented statement in all of sports. He cancelled the entire NHL season. Another strike followed in 2012 to 2013 that erased half of the season.

In addition to labor unrest, the NHL has had to deal with other controversial matters. Race was one of those matters. In 1958, Willie O'Ree became the first black person to play for the NHL, playing for the Boston Bruins. O'Ree was born in Canada and is referred to as the "Jackie Robinson of the NHL." O'Ree broke the color barrier in hockey during a time when Jim Crow laws and segregation were still practiced in the United States. He encountered racial bigotry while playing hockey. However, O'Ree's courage and fortitude has paved the way for other minority players. After O'Ree's brief stint with the Boston Bruins, the NHL welcomed a number of black players, such as Grant Furh, J. T. Brown, and Trevor Daly, to name a few. The NHL has recognized the importance and significance that O'Ree has contributed to hockey. One initiative the NHL has created in order to introduce hockey to minority populations is NHL Diversity. Created in 1995 under Bettman's leadership, NHL Diversity seeks to expose the game of hockey to

economically and socially disadvantaged youth. The program, part of the NHL Foundation (a nonprofit branch of the NHL), has been a resounding success by introducing the game of hockey to more than 40,000 economically disadvantaged youth. Furthermore, there are 30 inner-city nonprofit youth hockey organizations that received various types of support from the NHL. In a very fitting and appropriate gesture, the NHL appointed Willie O'Ree director of youth development and hockey ambassador for NHL Diversity. Bettman and the NHL owners recognize that the game of hockey must change with the times. This means changes to technology, business models, and racial matters. As a sport that is often dubbed "the whitest sport in America," NHL leadership understands that it must cross the racial divide and begin to develop methods to attract a new type of fan from a different demographic. This takes planning that involves buy-in from owners, players, and fans. The NHL has made a great attempt to include racial and ethnic minorities in the game of hockey. Now it must develop the means to sustain its efforts.

Diversity, Race, and Ethnicity in the National Football League

The National Football League (NFL) is arguably the premier professional sport league in the United States. The NFL championship game, the Super Bowl is the most watched television show annually in America. The 2014 Super Bowl between the Seattle Seahawks and the Denver Broncos was watched by a mind-blowing 111.5 million viewers. Team values for NFL teams range from $930 million to $3.2 billion. Team values continue to escalate. Jerry Jones, the owner of the Dallas Cowboys paid $150 million for the Cowboys franchise in 1989. As of 2014, the Cowboys were the most valuable franchise in the NFL at $3.2 billion dollars. This is a 2,100 percent increase from his original purchase price. Other owners have seen dramatic increases in team values as well. The revenue that teams generate annually is also impressive. For 2013, the Cowboys generated $560 million in revenue, the New England Patriots generated $428 million, and the Washington Redskins generated $375 million. These numbers are astounding and dwarf that of teams in other leagues. The revenue that NFL teams generate is supplemented by television rights fees. These are fees that television networks pay to broadcast NFL games. Network fees have been a boon for the NFL. In 1964, the NFL garnered $14.5 million in rights fees from the CBS network. In 2014, the NFL collected a total of $4.9 billion from the likes of CBS, ESPN, FOX, and NBC. The NFL also has a revenue-sharing program whereby teams split the revenue generated from ticket sales, merchandise sales, and rights fees, to name a few. The NFL is a $9 billion business. Tickets prices for a family of four to attend an NFL game can range from $350 to upward of $4,000. That is just a ticket price that does not include the cost of parking, merchandise, and novelties and concessions. With all of the good fortune that the NFL has had over the recent years, there have been numerous controversies. Player conduct on and off the field has been a major issue for the NFL. Issues have ranged from illegal hits on the field to off-the-field antics such as beating women, illegal drug use, and other illegal activity. In addition to these matters, there is also the issue of race. The person that must respond and address all of these matters is the current NFL commissioner Roger Goodell.

Goodell's rise to commissioner is a true American story. Goodell began his NFL career as an intern in 1981 and worked his way up to commissioner by 2006. Goodell has been credited with increasing the revenue and popularity of the game. He states that his primary goal is to "protect the shied," or in other words he must protect the integrity of the game. Goodell understands that as a leader of the most popular and profitable sport in the United States, he must demand integrity from staff, owners, players, and fans. If the NFL loses its integrity or if fans and media perceive that the integrity is tainted, then league revenue and reputation will suffer tremendously. Goodell and his staff need to uphold and constantly manage and be proactive in dealing with crises. Race is an issue that the NFL leadership has managed to address very well.

In 1920, Fritz Pollard became the first African American to play professional football. He played for the Akron Pros and helped lead them to the championship game that year. The following year he was also made a player coach for the Pros. The NFL inducted Pollard into its Hall of Fame in 2005. Pollard was considered by most to be the first

African American coach in professional football. It would be another six decades before another African American coached a professional football team. In 1989, Los Angeles Raiders owner Al Davis appointed African American and former Raider legend Art Shell head coach. Shell took over the Raiders after Davis fired Mike Shanahan early in the 1989 season. To this end, the issue of race in the NFL and the hiring of minority head coaches is an issue worth addressing. The number of African American players in the NFL as

In 1947, Jackie Robinson's debut in the major leagues brought an end to almost 60 years of segregation in professional baseball. (Wikimedia Commons/ Bob Sandberg, *Look* Magazine)

of 2014 was approximately 75 percent, yet for years the number of African American coaches in the NFL was below 10 percent. To address this racial disparity among coaches, the NFL introduced the Rooney Rule in 2003.

The impetus for the rule was the threat of lawsuits from various civil rights groups. The late Pittsburgh Steelers owner Dan Rooney was the champion of this rule, hence the moniker Rooney Rule. The rule states that whenever there is a head coaching or general manager position open within the NFL, a minority candidate must be interviewed. If the rule is not adhered to, then the specific team is fined. Three years after the rule was implemented, the number of minority coaches in the NFL went from 6 percent to 22 percent. Goodell and his staff have worked diligently to create a league that is tolerant of diversity and issues that impact minority groups. Aside from the Rooney Rule, the NFL has established a Diversity Committee that is charged with reviewing and assessing the NFL's progress toward diversity. The committee was also instrumental in helping to craft the NFL's diversity statement, which is intended to show that the NFL is concerned and taking a proactive step toward ensuring racial and ethnic fairness in all its business dealings.

Diversity, Race, and Ethnicity in the National Basketball Association

The National Basketball Association (NBA) is arguably the most globally recognized and respected sport of all the four major professional sports in the United States. NBA players represent countries from all over the globe including China, Spain, Argentina, Africa, Europe, Russia, and Australia. The NBA plays games around the world and markets and promotes its players globally as well. As a matter of fact, the NBA's international footprint is very sizable indeed. There are NBA league offices in Madrid and Barcelona, Spain; Bejing, China; London; Seoul, Korea; Toronto, Canada; Mubai, India; and Hong Kong. NBA games are televised in 215 countries around the world and broadcast in 43 different languages. NBA players are some of the most recognizable professional athletes in the world. This globalization is a far cry from the NBA's humble beginnings. In 1946, the first NBA game was played between the Toronto Huskies and the New York Knickerbockers.

That year, however, there were two rival leagues: the Basketball Association of America and the National Basketball League. The two leagues merged in 1949 and became the NBA. There were 17 teams in 1949, all of which fielded white players only. As of 2014, there were 30 NBA teams that drew millions of fans. The total NBA attendance for the 2103 to 2014 season topped 18 million fans. Team values, just like in other leagues, have been on the rise as well. The value of NBA teams ranged from $405 million (Milwaukee Bucks) to $2 billion (Los Angeles Clippers). The average NBA franchise is valued at approximately $700 million. The revenue that teams have generated has increased as well. The Los Angeles Lakers generated $295 million in revenue between 2013 and 2014, followed by the New York Knicks at $287, and the Chicago Bulls at $195 million.

Every team in the NBA saw its team value rise. The Brooklyn Nets, Houston Rockets, Lakers, and Golden State Warriors saw their 2013 to 2014 season team values increase by 47 percent, 36 percent, 35 percent, and 35 percent respectively from the previous year. In another stroke of good fortune for the NBA, the league recently signed the largest television rights deal in the history of the league. The deal, which approaches $23.4 billion, grants ABC, ESPN, and TNT the rights to broadcast NBA games for the nine years beginning in the 2016 to 2017 season. That adds up to $2.66 billion over the nine-year deal. Having good fortune has not always been the case for the NBA. The golden years of the NBA can be traced back to the late 1950s and 1960s when the Boston Celtics were a dynasty and legendary players such as Wilt Chamberlain, Bill Russell, Oscar Robinson, and John Havlicek ruled the courts. The 1970s saw its fair share of raising stars such as Earl "the Pearl" Monroe, Kareem Abdul Jabbar, and Julius Erving. However, the 1970s brought with it the drug culture and the NBA athletes were not immune to this drug phenomenon. The image of the league had suffered because of drug use and attendance was starting to dwindle. Some blamed the drug use and the loss of popularity on black athletes.

The league, which for decades had black superstars, was confronted with the issue of race. Not only were fans complaining about the black players but so were sponsors. When David Stern became the executive vice president of the NBA in 1980, the league was in total disarray. Stern and then NBA Commissioner Larry O'Brien worked with the player's union to institute mandatory drug testing for players and the legendary salary cap. These measures were taken to restore the integrity and faith in the game and to allow teams to share desperately needed revenue in order to survive. Stern became commissioner in 1984. He quickly realized that racial equality in the NBA was a crucial issue and he went about establishing a culture of racial sensitivity and inclusion. The NBA for years has lead all other professional sport leagues in hiring black coaches and league personnel. In 2002 and 2012, for example, 14 of the league's 30 head coaches were black—almost 50 percent. With a black player population of approximately 78 percent, some believe the NBA has done a great job of trying to get its coaching staff to mirror the players on the court.

As a sport leader, Stern recognized the need to be proactive in seeking diversity and inclusion. This attitude must be ingrained in every facet of the NBA business strategy. With a large number of NBA fans who themselves are members of racial and ethnic minorities, it behooves the NBA to hire and promote minorities. Minorities are not only present on the court but also are represented in the NBA boardroom as high-ranking members on the teams and even as owners. Michael Jordan is the owner of the Charlotte Hornets. The previous owner of the Hornets was African American billionaire Bob Johnson. Additionally, Jordan's chief operating officer for the Hornet organization is Fred Whitfield—an African American and former attorney. Interestingly, the NBA was the first professional sport league in the United States to have a black owner. Again, diversity and racial inclusion just does not "happen." It takes leadership, and, more important, an aggressiveness and vision. The NBA has set the bar for racial and ethnic diversity and inclusion.

Diversity, Race, and Ethnicity in Major League Baseball

Major League Baseball (MLB) has been called "America's Pastime." Baseball found its way into the hearts of the American public in the late 1800s. The MLB was also at the forefront of being an organized entity. In 1903, an agreement was signed creating the National Baseball Commission. The commission was established to develop policies, rules, and regulations for baseball. In 1903 the first World Series was played and pitted the Boston Americans versus the Pittsburgh Pirates. The Americans prevailed in an eight-game series, winning five of the eight games played. Baseball has transformed tremendously since 1903.

There have been many legendary players. Early stars include Ty Cobb, Honus Wagner, Walter Johnson, and Cy Young. In the 1920s, the New York Yankees became America's darling, winning pennant after pennant. The Yankees boasted a number of legendary players during that time—none more recognized and revered than Babe Ruth. His mammoth home runs and his off-the-field antics made him the stuff of legends and helped to solidify and galvanize baseball fans everywhere. As the 1920s came to a close the 1930s saw players such as Joe DiMaggio of the Yankees and Ted Williams of the Boston Red Sox take center stage. Baseball has continued to enjoy popularity and prosperity. Unlike the NFL, NBA, and NHL, the MLB has no salary cap per se and teams can negotiate their own television rights deals. Although the MLB does not have a salary cap, it does have a revenue-sharing program that requires large-market teams, that is, teams that play in cities such as New York, Chicago, Los Angeles, and Houston, to share a portion of their revenue with small-market teams such as the Seattle Mariners and the Oakland Athletics. This revenue-sharing program is meant to allow small market teams to compete with large-market teams when it comes to bidding on desirable players. Team valuations for MLB franchises are formidable.

The New York Yankees and the Los Angeles Dodgers are valued at $2.5 billion and $2 billion respectively. The lowest valued team in the MLB is the Tampa Bay Rays, which is valued at $485 million. As in the other three professional leagues, the revenue generated by teams in MLB is impressive. Again, the New York Yankees lead the way by generating $461 million, followed by the Boston Red Sox at $357 million, the San Francisco Giants at $316 million, and the Los Angeles Dodgers at $293 million. Twenty-five of the 30 MLB teams saw their 2014 franchise values increase from the previous year. The San Francisco Giants saw their 2013 team value increase from $730 million to $1 billion in 2014. That is a 27 percent increase. Total fan attendance at MLB games for 2013 was 73.9 million. The average attendance per game during 2013 was 30,442.

It is clear that teams in the MLB are enjoying success on the field and in their bottom line. However, the MLB has had its fair share of scandals and misgivings. As far back as 1919, MLB had to deal with the legendary Black Sox scandal when players on the Chicago White Sox intentionally lost games in exchange for receiving money from notorious gangsters. Much later, the steroid scandal in the 1990s resulted in players such as St. Louis's Mark McGuire, San Francisco's Barry Bonds, and Chicago Cub's Sammy Sosa being implicated in a steroid scandal that rocked MLB. There have been numerous other scandals, but one thing that MLB can be proud of is the fact that it hired the first African American player in the history of modern sports. In 1947, Brooklyn Dodgers' general manager Branch Rickey called up Jackie Robinson to play on the Major League level. Robinson was maligned by fans, teammates, opponents, and the media. Robinson kept his poise and dignity and played in spite of the racial slurs and threats that he encountered during his early days. Robinson went on to win a pennant with the Dodgers and was eventually elected to Major League Baseball's Hall of Fame.

A close look at Robinson's arrival at MLB is a character study in tenacious leadership. Branch Rickey had to endure the pain and scorn, not only of those around him but also of those across America who were not ready for social change and racial equality. If one looks at the environment and the conditions in which Rickey had to make this tough decision, then one begins to understand and appreciate his leadership qualities. Rickey had to convince himself that he was not only making a baseball decision, but a racial decision that could have very well backfired on him and the civil rights movement. Rickey had to deal with malicious and scathing comments from other owners and MLB officials, not to mention the threats against his life and the life of his family. Additionally, Rickey's own players and coaches were not in agreement with his decision. What can be learned from Rickey is that when it comes to challenging racial and cultural prejudices and bigotry, a leader must be willing to sacrifice his own life and character. After Jackie Robinson broke the color barrier in MLB in 1947 (which predates the Civil Rights Act of 1964), other teams started to draft and play players of color such as Larry Doby, Roberto Clemente, Hank Aaron, Willie Mays, Roy Campenella, Frank Robinson, Satchel Paige, and many others. Rickey's decision to bring Jackie Robinson to the big leagues had far reaching benefits for future generations of black and Latino baseball players.

Robert Lyons

See Also: Discrimination in Sports; Identification With Sports Teams; Leadership Skills for Coaches (Professional Sport); Major League Baseball; National Basketball Association; National Football League; National Hockey League; Sociology of Sport; Team Building; Team Culture.

Further Readings

Crepeau, Richard C. *NFL Football: A History of America's New Pastime*. Urbana: University of Illinois Press, 2014.

Lewis, Michael. *Money Ball: The Art of Winning an Unfair Game*. New York: W. W. Norton, 2003.

McKinley, Michael. *Hockey: A People's History*. Toronto: McClelland & Stewart, 2006.

Pluto, Terry. *Loose Balls: The Short, Wild Life of the American Basketball Association*. New York: Simon & Schuster, 2007.

Rapersad, Arnold. *Jackie Robinson: A Biography*. New York: Ballentine Books, 1997.

Ranking Athletes

The ranking of athletes based on their athletic prowess, all-time or single-season greatness, individual or team competitive accomplishments, career success, clutch performances, and other various physical and competitive feats is a common popular media and professional endeavor across the sporting industry. The pursuit spans in importance and outcome from trivial debates concerning Michael Jordan versus LeBron James as the greatest National Basketball Association (NBA) player of all time, to the immense financial, economic, and social ramifications of scouts and organizational leaders ranking amateur athletes prior to intercollegiate recruiting or professional draft selections. Despite these conversations for fans and organizational decision makers (e.g., general managers, owners, scouts, coaches), little consensus exists for what specific combination of qualities should be included in making these assessments (e.g., remaining calm under pressure, championships won, mental toughness, athlete playing aesthetic, clutch performances, or a mastery of skills associated with their particular sport). For example, some popular media personnel and fans stipulate that in order to be considered one of the greatest players of all time in a ranking, a player must have a championship victory, while others deem this a moot point in lieu of showcasing expert sport-specific skill. Further, some professional sport organizations choose to forgo selecting players who have been in trouble with the law or lack the appearance of a cooperative and collegial teammate, while others simply select players on the basis of their on-the-field performances. No matter the end of the spectrum, ranking players in sport is an important topic of study for sport scholars.

Use by Popular Media

In 1999, ESPN undertook a venture to establish a list of the greatest athletes of the 20th century. In its multisegment series *Sportscentury*, the network personnel and popular media writers founded and created a list of the greatest athletes spanning a variety of sports (e.g., American football, soccer, baseball, horse racing, track and field, tennis, boxing, hockey, or golf) that captured the attention of many fans and sport enthusiasts. After the highly publicized release of this ranking, sport media personalities routinely included conversation and debate over the greatest players of all time within their talk shows or media programs. Much of the debate on the *Sportscentury* rankings centered on the ability to compare performances not only across decades and eras, but also across sports and even species (i.e., the inclusion of horses on the list).

Exacerbated by the growth of media presence in amateur and professional sport, the ranking of athletes continues to be a common topic of conversation on sport radio shows and television broadcasts. Within professional sport, common rankings and debates surround the greatest players of all time within a particular sport; the best player of all-time within a particular franchise, conference, or division; the most impressive single seasons; and other, often trivial comparisons. Primarily, the rankings serve as a launching point for compelling radio and television broadcasts and appear to resonate with sport fans who often carry the debate and rankings into other aspects of their daily life, such as the proverbial bar debate or work water-cooler talk.

In more serious media rankings, professional athletes are often ranked according to a myriad of statistics in order to determine who will receive post-season awards such as Most Valuable Player (MVP) at the end of a season. In amateur sport, media entities rank the top high school athletes prior to the recruitment and signing periods of intercollegiate athletics. The rankings serve as an informational source for fans to track where the best players ultimately select to play. In intercollegiate athletics, particularly football and men's basketball, popular media sources release and constantly update "Big Boards" that rank prospects prior to entering professional drafts. The ranking of amateur athletes prior to drafts has become so important to media outlets such as ESPN, FOX Sports, NBC Sports, and others that many employ experts who solely concentrate on formulating rankings on intercollegiate and amateur players (e.g., Mel Kiper and Todd McShay with ESPN). Although organizational decision makers do not rely on the expertise of the media personalities, fans become engaged with the rankings and become invested in the ranking and selection process.

Ranking of Amateur Athletes

In rankings that have far more serious economic, financial, and social ramifications than popular media discussions and debates, scouts from professional sport teams are continually evaluating amateur talent within intercollegiate and amateur sport from around the world. The management team often takes into consideration the needs of the current organization, and provides lists to organizational decision makers before the draft containing their rankings and personal suggestions. As professional athletics continue to grow as a multibillion dollar entity, the focus and scrutiny on the ranking of amateurs has similarly intensified. With initial (i.e., entry-level rookie) contracts in the National Football League (NFL) ranging from $2 million to $8 million per year, a gaffe on player evaluation and ranking could severely limit the competitiveness and financial flexibility of a franchise for the foreseeable future. In order to avoid "busts" (i.e., players that significantly fail to perform up to their athletic expectation), amateur athletes are tested physically and mentally prior to ranking their overall ability and organization fit.

Conclusion

The concept of ranking athletes either in a trivial manner or a professional pursuit is an important sporting phenomenon in both amateur and professional athletics. Whether pundits from a local sport radio show discuss their local intercollegiate quarterback's chances of winning the Heisman Trophy, or scouts spend years analyzing an athlete prior to an upcoming draft, ranking athletes serves a critical role within the sporting community. Consumers of amateur and professional sport often willingly enter into debates concerning the athletic prowess of one athlete against another. This type of colloquial exchange remains a key part of sports talk radio and sports television programming. Rankings create debate and discontent among viewers and pundits, which in turn establishes a more entertaining production. For intercollegiate programs and professional organizations, the ranking of athletes is an imperative process that is undertaken by skilled scouts and recruiters in order to acquire the best players. With the immense amount of financial, economic, and social implications stemming from these decisions, decision makers rely on rankings to help form the most appropriate decision for their organization.

Adam G. Pfleegor

See Also: Draft System; Leadership Skills for Athletes; Ranking Teams; Self-Motivation.

Further Readings
ESPN. "Top North American Athletes of the Century." *ESPN Sportscentury.* https://espn.go.com/sports century/athletes.html (Accessed December 2014).
Hibbs, D. "A Conceptual Analysis of Clutch Performances in Competitive Sports." *Journal of the Philosophy of Sport,* v.37 (2011).
Holowchak, M. A. "The 'Measure' of an Athletic Achievement: Character Versus Production, or a Forced Dichotomy in Competitive Sport." *Journal of the Philosophy of Sport,* v.38 (2011).
Kershnar, S. "Solving the MVP Problem." *Journal of Social Philosophy,* v.39 (2008).

Ranking Teams

Ranking teams serves a crucial role in sports. Differences exist at the professional, collegiate, and high school level regarding the format of these rankings. Despite these differences, the goal is the same for all—organizing teams according to merit with the eventual goal of determining a champion.

U.S. Professional Sports

In American professional sports, teams are ranked in conferences and divisions. These rankings are extremely objective, as the basis for ranking teams is clearly stated prior to each season and is consistent for all teams. Unlike collegiate sports, professional teams within divisions face the same or similar opponents throughout the season, creating an equitable system.

In the National Football League (NFL), Major League Baseball (MLB), National Basketball Association (NBA), and National Hockey League (NHL) teams are divided into two conferences or leagues. These teams are further divided into two, three, or four divisions. The NFL, MLB, and NBA each have either four or five teams in each division, while the NHL—which has just two divisions within both leagues—has either seven or eight teams.

The function of these divisions is to create a system that eventually decides which teams reach postseason play. These leagues all differ in the numbers of teams reaching their postseasons, but they select the teams similarly. At the end of each season, the teams within each division with the most wins—or points, in the case of the NHL—advance to the postseason. All of the four professional sport leagues guarantee that the winner of each division advances to the postseason, with various numbers of the next-highest teams also advancing to the playoffs.

Collegiate Sports

United States colleges and universities are divided into divisions according to school size. The National Collegiate Athletic Association (NCAA) governs play of the majority of schools, segmenting these schools into either three or four divisions, depending on the sport. Other governing bodies include the National Association of Intercollegiate Athletics (NAIA) and National Junior College Athletic Association (NJCAA). Within these organizations, schools are divided into conferences, which govern how teams are further divided as well as specific rules and regulations.

As with professional sports, college teams are ranked within each conference and division according to wins, losses, and points. However, the selection of which teams reach postseason play varies dramatically according to specific sport and conference rules. Most conferences have championship games or tournaments to decide champions at the conclusion of the regular season, and these champions automatically qualify for the national tournament. The biggest difference between professional sports and collegiate sports is how each sport's national champion is crowned. At the collegiate level, each conference crowns a conference champion, and then a separate tournament is held to determine the national champion. The playoff formats vary by sport, but in most sports committees of athletic directors and other sport personnel select which teams earn admission into the playoff based upon specific criteria. Conference and division rankings are included in this process, but are of relatively little importance, especially compared to professional sports.

Many collegiate sports also have polls that rank the highest teams, most often the top 25. These rankings mostly serve as a guide for fans. While they do aid in helping determine many sports' postseason participants, they are only part of the criteria used.

High School Sports

High school sports rank teams very similarly to professional leagues, determining the postseason participants based upon objective criteria agreed upon prior to each season. Unlike professional sports, though, the specific formats are created and governed by each individual state. Most states have fairly similar formats in segmenting their schools, dividing them into classifications based upon school populations, and helping create competitive balance. These classifications are further divided into regions and districts based upon geography, with states placing various numbers of schools within each district. At the end of each regular season, the winners of these districts—along with differing numbers of the next-highest teams—earn admission into each sport's playoff. At the conclusion of the playoff, each classification has its own state champion.

Several organizations—most notably, *USA Today*—rank several sports nationally. At the end of each season, *USA Today* will crown a school "National Champion." These champions are determined in a subjective way and primarily serve as a way to increase fan interest. They have no impact on each state's champions.

International Soccer

International soccer offers a very unique spin associated to ranking teams. In various countries around the world, soccer leagues rank teams similar to the United States' professional leagues, according to wins, losses, and draws (ties). However, since many countries have several professional soccer leagues, the leagues are put into a hierarchy

based upon prestige. At the end of each season, in addition to the league standings determining which teams are crowned champion or enter a playoff, the standings determine which teams advance to a higher league or fall to a lower league. The number of teams changing leagues varies for each country; however, the overall system remains the same and provides teams with even greater incentive for finishing at the top of their leagues. Unlike American professional leagues, the lower teams also have an incentive to not finish at the bottom of their leagues.

Mark Slavich

See Also: High School Sports; Intercollegiate Sports; Major League Baseball; National Association of Intercollegiate Athletics; National Basketball Association; National Collegiate Athletic Association; National Football League; National Hockey League.

Further Readings

Entertainment Sports Programming Network (ESPN). "2014 NCAA Men's Basketball Rankings." http://espn.go.com/mens-college-basketball/rankings (Accessed September 2014).

Major League Baseball. "Standings." http://mlb.mlb.com/mlb/standings/?tcid=mm_mlb_standings (Accessed September 2014).

National Collegiate Athletic Association (NCAA). "Football Standings." http://www.ncaa.com/standings/football/fbs (Accessed September 2014).

USA Today High School Sports. "*USA Today* Super 25 Expert Rankings." http://usatodayhss.com (Accessed September 2014).

Recreational Versus Competitive Sport

Participation in physical activity and sport is a favorite leisure time activity and/or professional pursuit for many individuals across the globe. Whether the game is a pick-up contest with few binding rules in a local community park, or a professional sporting contest involving highly paid visible athletes in front of thousands of fans in a state-of-the-art facility, sport remains an important part of culture in today's society. Due to the range of athletic endeavors, scholars have contemplated the merits of competition and the factors that differentiate competitive sport and athletic contests from their less structured recreational counterparts. To elaborate, elements such as score and time keeping; utilizing paid professional players; the type of venue the contest takes place in; the affiliation with a particular institution, conference, or league; the mind-set of participants; and the role of fun have been used in a attempt to differentiate between the two versions of athletics.

What initiated as a cursory examination that appeared to have a simple solution with a few discriminating features has morphed into a widespread debate about the merits of competition and the specific tenets that differentiate competitive athletics from recreational athletic endeavors. Simply stated, the signature difference between recreational and competitive athletics is where the participant focus is placed. For recreational participants, the process of the activity and the pleasure of participation is the end. Contrarily, in competitive sport, the end goal is outcome success.

Sport Participation Through the Years

For many youth, participation in athletics at an early age is a seminal part of childhood. At the core of youth sport participation is the understanding and hope that the activities support a recreational mindset, with fun and leisure being paramount features. At the earliest of ages, children participate in physical activity for the enjoyment of movement, camaraderie, knowledge, and social experiences. As children progress through athletic participation, more emphasis is placed on the outcome success of the activity. The shift toward a competitive style of athletics occurs at different rates and times depending on the activity in question, type of organization, coaching expertise, and the child's demeanor. However, it remains imperative that the participatory process and recreational attitude is stressed to children at the youngest ages of athletic participation.

In both high school and intercollegiate athletics a combination of recreational and competitive levels exists. Oftentimes, high schools and institutions of higher education will support intramural athletics for all students. Intramural athletics, which

In organized sports, records of performance are often kept. Recreational sports, however, like these children playing ball in Morocco, are played with the ultimate goal of having fun along with the pleasure of participation. (Wikimedia Commons/Adam Axon)

often contain participants with a vast array of skill levels, is aimed at providing an extracurricular activity focused on fun and enjoyment to the student population. Essentially, participants in intramural-type activities are focused on the enjoyment of socialization and participation, rather than solely on outcome success. On the competition side of the spectrum, students often have the opportunity to play, or try out for, school-sponsored competitive sport. With a more formalized structure including a coaching hierarchy, proper officials, contests against opponents from other schools and institutions, and regular practice sessions, school-sponsored competitive athletics is geared toward competitive success as a primary outcome goal.

Adult athletes have options to participate in a variety of both recreational and competitive athletic endeavors. For example, many adult recreation leagues exist that are sponsored by local businesses, bars, restaurants, churches, and recreation centers. Participation in these recreational leagues is focused on socialization. On the contrary, adults have the opportunity to participate in professional athletics, in which outcome success and financial stability are the end goals of the participation. Due to the immense financial, economic, and social ramifications of professional sport, it can almost always be classified as a competitive endeavor. It is important to note that the presentation of different athletic options over a life span is a stark generalization. For a cursory analysis, this may be sufficient to differentiate between the two versions of athletics. However, a more complete and genuine analysis, an examination of the participants' attitude and goals, is appropriate and necessary.

The Attitude of Participants

While many of differentiating features between recreational and competitive sport appear vague at best, perhaps the best explanation involves the attitude and goals of the direct and indirect participants. Although competitive sport can be a leisure and fun-based activity, it maintains a more direct goal of competitive or outcome success (e.g., winning, personal records). In order to accomplish this task, athletes are expected to maintain an attitude that focuses on the outcome. For recreational athletics, the participation in sport for fun and/or leisure is an end in and of itself. To elaborate, the main priority of the participant is not the acquisition of the most favorable outcome (i.e., winning), but rather to enjoy the process of participation. It is important to note that a focus on the process rather than outcome does not necessarily demean or cheapen success; rather outcome success is simply not the single most important feature for the participant. For example, if two leisure golfers set out on a Sunday afternoon to play 18 holes in a recreational fashion, the most important aspect of the endeavor is the enjoyment of participation. This could include the love of the sport/activity, the pleasure of being outdoors, and the amusement of camaraderie, yet the overall enjoyment is not solely based on outcome success. In the presented scenario, both golfers could seemingly compete in a friendly manner and strive to achieve their best, but posting the lowest score by any means necessary at the completion of the round is not the priority of either participant.

Conclusion

The distinguishing features between recreational sport and competitive sport are often more easily felt and experienced in a phenomenological manner rather than defined. For amateur athletes, the most significant distinguishing feature is the focus on the process of participation and the enjoyment of the activity rather than the outcome or competitive success. On the contrary, participants engaged in competitive athletics are focused on the end objective of winning. Last, it is important to point out that participants of recreational athletics can be competitive and desire to perform at a high level. However, winning is not the sole or most important target. In similar fashion, competitive athletes can enjoy participating in the activity and focus on fun throughout their participation, however, the primary objective is that of competitive outcome success.

Adam G. Pfleegor

See Also: Amateur Sports; Coaching Youth; High School Sports; Intercollegiate Sports; Professional Sports.

Further Readings

Coakley, J. *Sports in Society: Issues and Controversies*, 11th ed. New York: McGraw-Hill, 2014.
Hyland, D. "Competition and Friendship." *Journal of the Philosophy of Sport*, v.5 (1978).
Kretchmar, S. "A Phenomenology Of Competition." *Journal of the Philosophy of Sport*, v.41 (2014).
Torres, C. R., and P. F. Hager. "De-Emphasizing Competition In Organization Youth Sport: Misdirected Reforms and Misled Children." *Journal of the Philosophy of Sport*, v.34 (2007).

Relational Model of Leadership

While contemporary models of leadership view relationships as central to the leadership process, the Relational Model of Leadership, put forth by Susan Komives, Nance Lucas, and Timothy McMahon in 1998, was the first to make this aspect of leadership overt. This model reflects the important shift in thinking about leadership as an individual process to that which is concerned with group processes. In other words, instead of thinking about leadership as carried out by one individual in an authority position, this model assumes that leadership happens through relationships and can happen at any level. The Relational Model of Leadership consists of five related elements: purposeful, inclusive, empowering, ethical, and process-oriented. Within this framework, leadership is viewed as occurring when people come together in order to accomplish goals aimed at making a positive difference.

The Relational Model of Leadership is purposeful at its core. It is grounded in hope, shared values, and commitment to a shared vision. Goals become shared through the co-creation of that vision. All members of a group contribute to the goals rather than one leader setting the agenda. This can occur within the context of overall organizational goals. For instance, if getting more fans to games is an organizational goal, ticket sales can still collaborate on the specific vision for increasing ticket sales. The purpose of the group gains validity when it is aimed at bringing about positive change. In the case of ticket sales, improving fan experience is a positive change that also meets the goal of increasing ticket sales. The most important aspect about establishing a purpose is that it should be aimed at challenging the status quo and creating a better world in the process.

A key value of this model is inclusivity. Being inclusive means not only understanding differences but also valuing them and incorporating various viewpoints and skills in order to accomplish group goals. Inclusivity should be an active endeavor such that different views, styles, and approaches to problems are encouraged and taken seriously. For inclusivity to work well it must also include embracing different personal attributes such as gender, race, sexuality, and culture. Inclusive language means using "we" and respecting what people say by acknowledging that their views were heard and understood. Simply summarizing what people say and asking if the summary is correct is one example of inclusivity. The result of inclusivity is that multiple perspectives come to the surface, which helps a group get a more accurate picture of the obstacles and opportunities. As a result, better solutions and paths to achieving objectives are discovered. As a group moves forward in their goals, inclusiveness also means educating others outside the group about the group's vision and work.

Features of the Model

Empowering is a distinct feature of the Relationship Leadership Model. Empowering differs from delegating in that completing group goals becomes a shared activity; that is, it does not involve assigning individual tasks that contribute to group goals. In the Relational Leadership Model, empowerment arises when each group member commits in two ways. First, they must see themselves as personally responsible for the outcomes. Specific actions include anticipating what needs to be done and how they can contribute and being proactive about taking on tasks. Second, empowerment extends from the belief that everyone needs to contribute regardless of his or her current understanding of the situation or personal style of interacting with others. It means that everyone should be open to learning so that group knowledge becomes broad as well as deep. Typically, empowerment extends from group members sharing power even if the group has someone designated as the leader. The leader who has authority should imagine her/his role as working with or alongside others, not over others. Viewing power in this way requires that members are strong in self-empowerment. Self-empowerment is having confidence, believing in one's ability to make a difference and avoiding excuses for not getting involved.

Embedded in the Relational Leadership Model is the idea that all actions should be ethical. It is not simply enough to accomplish group goals; it is also important how these goals are accomplished. Ethical action means that all actions are aimed at improving the conditions of people. Furthermore, the pursuit of these actions is guided by a commitment to positive values, morality, and virtue. Positive values contribute to human dignity. Morality is about doing no harm. Virtue is about doing the right thing, at the right time, given the circumstances and people involved. The Relational Model of Leadership does not assume leadership to be a value-neutral endeavor. It explicitly states that leadership is collaborative and reliant on positive values. Viewed in conjunction with empowerment, individual ethical behavior is critical to ethical group actions. Each person must act in an ethical way on a daily basis for the group to collectively act ethically.

The last element of the model is that it is process-oriented. Being process oriented means that how a group goes about its work needs to be in the forefront of the minds of group members. This element is essential because the end goal is most often the focus in work environments, which tends to overshadow how the works gets done. This tendency frequently leads to poor working conditions, unethical behavior, and human injustices. Prioritizing process-oriented thinking counteracts this tendency in organizations. Simply put, process involves how the group is established, how it works together, how it maintains ethical behavior and inclusivity, how it makes decisions, and how it accomplishes the vision of the group. For instance, a process orientation means that establishing group norms, making plans, creating timelines, and agreeing on interim objectives should be the focus of the work. Furthermore, the process should align with the purpose of the group and contribute to accomplishing group objectives. Being process-oriented does not imply that end goals are forgotten. Rather, it requires that processes are put in place intentionally in order to achieve group goals. Part of being intentional is periodically stepping back from the daily work to assess how the process is going. It is important to honestly reflect on what is working and what needs to be changed. This applies equally to progress on fulfilling the group purpose as well as attending to the elements of inclusivity, empowerment, and ethical actions.

Conclusion

The primary assumption of the Relational Leadership Model is that leadership is essentially a collaborative activity that can be enacted anytime, anyplace by anyone. This model emphasizes collaboration over coordination. Collaboration is viewed as being more effective than competition because it alleviates fear and anxiety that individuals may experience within a work environment. This model relies on a clear purpose that is established by the group. The purpose becomes achievable when inclusivity, empowerment, and ethical thinking influence daily actions. Inclusive behaviors, empowerment, and ethical actions simultaneously shape and are shaped by the processes, which are given priority.

Maylon Hanold

See Also: Comparative Models of Sport Leadership; Leadership Models in Sports; Organizational Behavior; Organizational Culture; Team Building.

Further Readings

Komives, S., N. Lucas, and T. McMahon. *Exploring Leadership, for College Students Who Want to Make a Difference.* San Francisco: Jossey-Bass Publishers, 1998.
Roth, V., E. Goldstein, and G. Marcus. *Peer-Led Team Learning: Handbook for Team Leaders.* Upper Saddle River, NJ: Prentice Hall, 2001.
Salmon, Paul M. *Human Factors Methods and Sports Science: A Practical Guide.* Boca Raton, FL: CRC Press/Taylor & Francis Group, 2010.

Research Methods in Sports Leadership

Research methods involves the systematic process of collecting data in a predetermined manner for the purpose of deepening the understanding a specific problem, topic, or issue. Effective sports leaders may employ various research methodologies to gather the appropriate information to make data-driven decisions in their organizations. The data collected from research studies can take either a qualitative or quantitative form. Researchers will select the specific methodology based upon the research questions they wish to address, the specific problem under investigation, and the anticipated manner by which they hope to gather the desired data.

Popular Quantitative Research Methodologies in Sport Leadership

Quantitative research methods involve the collection of numerical data for the purpose of statistically analyzing the sample results, with the hope of making inferences about the population from which the sample was drawn. For researchers wishing to collect data from large groups, quantitative methodologies are preferred. Quantitative studies can help researchers determine if a relationship may exist between two or more variables, or if one variable may cause an effect in another variable. For instance, if an individual in sport leadership wants to understand if a specific promotion at a minor league baseball game has an impact on fan attendance, a survey may be given to fans at the stadium to determine their attitude about the use of certain game promotions on their decision to attend a particular game. As a result, the sport leaders may determine that families are impacted in their decision to attend a game when promotions that add value, such as postgame fireworks, are offered as part of the ticket price. Conversely, the same quantitative survey study may reveal that young, single fans are more influenced by discounts in the actual ticket prices. The collection and appropriate analysis of these data can assist the sport leaders in making critical marketing decisions relative to their organization.

Quantitative survey research is one of the most popular methodologies used in the sports leadership field. It is relatively easy to employ and provides a quick glimpse into a certain area of inquiry at one point in time. The methodology usually involves the administration of a survey or questionnaire to a large group of participants. Quantitative research may also involve the analysis of pre-existing numerical data for the purpose of exploring trends or behaviors. For instance, the same sport leader may look at the individual game attendance from a previous season, compare it to the various promotions offered on specific dates, and make conclusions about the impact these promotions may have had on ticket sales. Interpretation of this form of quantitative analysis must be employed carefully by the sport leader as it does not indicate any implication of causality between one variable and the other.

Other forms of quantitative research methods include correlational or experimental designs. Correlational studies seek to determine if a relationship exists between two or more variables. For instance, in the sport leadership setting a researcher may observe over time that high school student-athletes seem to perform better in their academic studies than their nonathlete peers. The researcher can seek to devise a quantitative study that collects data about both groups of students (athletes and nonathletes), to determine if a relationship exists between sport participation and academic achievement among high school student-athletes.

True experimental designs are the only form of research that allows for the claim that one variable actually causes another variable to occur. In the sport leadership setting this may regularly be used to test the viability of specific training methods in the sport performance environment. For instance, a researcher may seek to understand if there is a difference in the impact that one coaching method has over another in the teaching of a specific skill. The researcher would design a study where one large group is given a pre-test on the desired skills. The group is then divided, at random, into two equal groups of participants. One group would then be exposed to the first training method and the other group would be exposed to the other training method. The researcher would seek to control as many outside influences as possible and then test both groups on the same desired skill. If the results vary significantly, the researcher may begin to claim that one coaching method is better than the other. The important factor in a true experiment is the ability to control for potentially conflicting variables that could impact the final results.

Popular Qualitative Research Methodologies in Sport Leadership

Quantitative research methods entail the collection of data for a deeper understanding of the phenomena in question. Where quantitative research can yield large amounts of data from vast numbers of participants, qualitative data seek to explore the reasons "how" and "why" certain things occur, so the sample size in these studies is generally much smaller. In qualitative research, the natural environment in which something occurs is the setting for data collection. The researcher, who serves as the instrument through which the data are ultimately filtered, makes field observations.

Qualitative research can take on many different forms. In sport leadership research some of the more popular methodologies include case studies, interviews, focus groups, direct observation, field note taking, or an analysis of documents. In the qualitative approach, the researcher seeks to identify themes or trends that surface in the data. This is where the researcher becomes the instrument through which the data are collected and analyzed.

In the sport leadership academic literature, qualitative research is not as plentiful as that from the quantitative methodologies. The case study is one of the more frequently employed qualitative methods. In this scenario, the researcher will observe a single case (such as a person, organization, or team) over an extended period of time. Where the quantitative survey seeks to collect data at a single point, the case study method involves the collection of data over a sustained period of time and is geared toward a more thorough understanding of the phenomena under investigation.

Interviews are another popular method for qualitative research in sport leadership. These may be both structured or unstructured. In the structured format, the researcher has established a set of questions to be administered to the participants in the same order. In this format, the researcher has no opportunity to ask a follow-up question based on the results of the previous answer. The researcher must also be very aware of the need to be neutral and not influential in their interactions with the participant. In the unstructured interview, the interaction between the researcher and participant is paramount. These interviews are generally perceived as conversations, where the researcher can probe further into specific areas and follow the natural flow of information provided by the participant. This method allows for a stronger degree of trust based on the interpersonal skills of the researcher, which can yield a much deeper level of understanding of the topic in question.

Focus groups are another form of gathering qualitative data. In this methodology, a group of usually eight to 12 participants is gathered in a controlled environment. The sport leader may use this methodology in conducting market research. These groups are very effective for testing new ideas, gathering input on promotion effectiveness, and measuring attitudes. Ethnographic research can incorporate a variety of research methodologies for the purpose of uncovering the culture of an organization. The researcher seeks to become embedded in the culture of question to allow for minimal impact on those being studied and reduced personal bias on the interpretation. Ethnographic researchers may employ interviews, surveys, observation, and note taking as data collection methods.

Academic Journals and Conferences

As a relatively new academic discipline, both sports leadership and management have a young but quickly growing body of research literature. The North American Society for Sport Management (NASSM) was founded in the mid-1980s by a group of sport management academics. The organization's purpose is the promotion of academic research, writing, and professional development in the area of sport management, which includes sport leadership.

NASSM publishes the *Journal of Sport Management* (JSM), which published its inaugural edition in 1987. As the official journal of NASSM, JSM is regarded as the first academic journal dedicated to research in this discipline. Since 1987, the body of academic literature in the area of sport leadership has grown, prompting the need for additional outlets for research presentation and discourse.

The *Journal of Sport and Social Issues* is the official journal of Northeastern University's Center for the Study of Sport in Society. This journal is a valuable outlet for research essential to sport leaders that addresses important contemporary social issues and their relationship with the sport industry.

The *Journal of Sport Economics* and *International Journal of Sports Finance* both address key issues for sport leaders on the broad topic of sport finance. Studies and articles relate to compensation for coaches and athletes, free agency impacts on professional sport, amateurism, sport event economic impact, and stadium financing.

The *International Journal of Sports Marketing and Sponsorship* and the *International Journal of Sport Management and Marketing* both serve the sport leader with critical research on marketing topics related to strategic management, communication, emerging technologies, human resources, sponsorship, customer service, and branding.

There are an ever-growing number of sport leadership conferences around the world. Some serve the academic research or practitioner populations exclusively, but an increasing goal of many events is to provide a forum for both groups to mingle and share experiences. This attention toward integrating researchers with practitioners in sport leadership is critical toward the shared understanding of all issues that impact sport leaders.

Julie D. Lanzillo

See Also: Academic Programs in Sport Leadership; Comparative Models of Sports Leadership; Sport Leadership Academic Curriculum;.

Further Readings

Andrew, Damon P. S., Paul M. Pedersen, and Chad D. McEvoy. *Research Methods and Design in Sport Management*. Champaign, IL: Human Kinetics, 2011.

International Journal of Sport Management and Marketing. http://www.inderscience.com/jhome.php?jcode=IJSMM (Accessed October 2014)

International Journal of Sports Marketing and Sponsorship. http://www.imrpublications.com/journal-landing.aspx?volno=L&no=L (Accessed October 2014)

Journal of Sport and Social Issues. http://jss.sagepub.com (Accessed October 2014).

Journal of Sport Management. http://journals.humankinetics.com/jsm (Accessed October 2014).

Journal of Sports Economics. http://jse.sagepub.com (Accessed October 2014).

North American Society for Sport Management. http://www.nassm.com (Accessed October 2014).

Skinner, J., et al. *Research Methods for Sport Management.* New York: Taylor and Francis Group, 2014.

Risk Management Process

Service providers and other professionals in all areas of sport and recreation services must recognize the importance of risk management. The risk management process requires careful consideration of risks that exist for injury to person or property and expose the organization to financial liability or legal liability for negligence. Limiting said exposure is paramount; service providers must systematically develop a risk management plan to effectively manage identified risks within their organization. Specifically, a risk management plan must identify risks that are present, categorize (or classify) risks in terms of frequency (how likely the risk is to occur) and severity (how severe is the harm likely to be), and consider approaches to eliminate or mitigate the risks identified. Further, risk management plans must not be stagnant; as the nature of service provided or sport organization changes, so too must the risk management plan. Risk management requires routine assessment of shifting organization variables, such as funding or available personnel; adequate risk management planning requires adapting or modifying the plan when appropriate.

Risk Identification
The risk management process must begin with a comprehensive overall analysis or audit of the sport or recreation organization. Specifically, service providers and sport professionals must conduct three separate analyses: a site/facility analysis, a policy analysis, and an organization analysis. As risk can be present in any or all of these areas, a review of each is required.

A site/facility analysis assesses risks related to the facility itself. Specifically, facilities must be reviewed to determine if any of the following risks are present: (1) conditions that may result in danger to participants or spectators; (2) failure to adhere to, or implement, industry standards for equipment or facilities; (3) maintenance issues; (4) impact of environmental factors; and (5) adequate provision of necessary rules or warnings. This list is intentionally broad given the many unique variables that are present in the many different types of sport and recreation facilities. No two facilities are identical; thus, the risk identification process must be adapted to each organization individually.

A policy analysis assesses risks that result from organization policies that are in place or are lacking. Specifically, policies must be reviewed to determine if they allow for an appropriate information/documentation system, provide for competent and adequate personnel, and appropriately regulate the conduct of participants or spectators; policies lacking in any of these areas may create risk of liability. Perhaps more important is considering policies that are absent; does the organization lack policies that may mitigate risk of injury to person or property? Sport and recreation organizations are best served by using similar organizations as a basis of comparison to determine which additional policies might be needed.

Last, an organization analysis assesses risks that result from an organization's relationships to other organizations or groups. For example, does an organization's membership in a league or other governing body impose certain mandates or restrictions that impact the overall existence of risk? Oftentimes, sport and recreation organizations are bound by the policies of others; assessing this potential impact is a key component of risk identification.

Risk Categorization
Once all facility, policy, and organization risks have been identified they must be individually

categorized based on the anticipated frequency and severity of the risk. Frequency considers how likely a risk is to manifest into personal or property injury; severity considers how significant the injury (physical or financial) is likely to be once it occurs. Organizations are best served by implementing a formal categorization matrix, or scale, so that all risks can be categorized based on like criteria. There are a multitude of suggested approaches to categorize risk ranging from numerical scales to terminology such as high, medium, and low (frequency) and catastrophic, critical, moderate, and low loss (severity). Regardless of the scale used, it is important that the categorization be based on valid criteria that also consider probability, such as past incidents, injury data or statistics, and experience of the risk auditor/sport or recreation professional. If organizations have an adequate documentation system they can likely produce data themselves; however, obtaining data from outside sources is also appropriate. Factoring probability into the ultimate frequency/severity categorization is important; if risks are not categorized appropriately, the ability to adequately treat the risk through mitigation or elimination becomes compromised.

Risk Mitigation/Elimination
Once risks have been identified and categorized, sport and recreation professionals must determine how to mitigate or eliminate each individual risk. While mitigation is far more common than elimination, which is only accomplished through avoidance or discontinuance, both are viable options in this phase of the risk management process.

When risks exist that are categorized as too frequent and/or too severe, sport and recreation organizations may be best served to either avoid or discontinue the services or activity responsible for said risks. Discontinuing a risk means eliminating a service or activity that already exists, while avoidance means choosing not to engage in an overly risky endeavor ahead of time. When a sport or recreation organization considers the value of a service or activity compared to the frequency, severity, and probability of harm, it may make the most sense for the organization to eliminate the offering altogether. More commonly, however, sport and recreation organizations opt to mitigate risk. Risk mitigation is a broad concept that encompasses a significant number of potential options to reduce risk. Sport and recreation organizations are likely to use a number of mitigation strategies, or combination thereof, for any identified risk; however, there are three general actions that are used most often: (1) risk transfer, (2) risk retention, and (3) risk reduction.

Risk transfer is a mitigation technique where the risk of financial liability for personal or property injury is transferred to another individual or entity by contract or other legally binding agreement. Common transfer methods include the use of exculpatory agreements, such as waivers and releases, informed consent agreements, facility lease agreements, indemnification agreements, or the use of an independent contractor. As common as waivers and releases are in sport and recreation activities, it must be noted that the enforceability of these documents is covered by state law and there are many variances in state requirements for waiver validity. While a well-written, enforceable waiver can effectively transfer risk from the sport/recreation organization to the participant, a waiver should never be considered a "guaranteed" risk mitigation method; there are no such guarantees.

Regarding risk retention and risk reduction, both involve an organization recognizing that a risk must be retained but the frequency and/or severity can likely be reduced. There are a multitude of strategies that can be employed to reduce risk. Specifically, organizations can provide adequate training to personnel; warn participants of inherent risks associated with activities; provide adequate supervision for participants and spectators, including special populations; establish clear and thorough emergency care procedures; regularly inspect and properly maintain all equipment, property, and facilities; and maintain a systematic documentation system when physical or financial harms occur.

Regular Review
Beyond identifying, categorizing, and mitigating risk, sport and recreation organizations must implement a regular review of their risk management processes; such review is necessary due to the complex and variable nature of such organizations. Changes in personnel, services offered, policies, equipment,

participants/spectators, and revenues/expenditures can all impact an organization's exposure to risk, and these types of changes are exceptionally common in sport and recreation organizations. Creating a comprehensive risk management plan is an important step for any sport or recreation organization; however, keeping the plan as current as possible by regularly reviewing all three phases is paramount to the plan's overall effectiveness. Many organizations are satisfied after initially undertaking the risk management process and creating a plan document; however, the continuous review is as important as the initial process itself.

Kristi Schoepfer-Bochicchio

See Also: Crisis Management; Emergency Action Plan; Sports Law.

Further Readings

Ammon, Robin. Jr. "Risk Management Process." In *Law for Recreation and Sport Managers.* Dubuque, IA: Kendall Hunt, 2013.

Appenzeller, Herb. *Risk Management in Sport.* Durham, NC: Carolina Academic Press, 2005.

Spengler, J. O., D. Connaughton, and A. Pittman. *Risk Management in Sport and Recreation.* Champaign, IL: Human Kinetics, 2006.

Van der Smissen, Betty. *Legal Liability and Risk Management for Public and Private Entities.* Cincinnati, OH: Anderson Publishing, 1990.

S

Self-Motivation

Self-motivation refers to the forces that propel a person to undertake a task or strive for a certain level of excellence. Self-motivation is a key life skill, and sport leaders such as coaches, administrators, and athletes usually possess strong personal motivation for achievement. The concept is multidimensional and can include personality traits, social variables, and a person's perception of a particular situation. Sport provides an ideal platform for the examination of this topic and a substantial amount of research has been developed on self-motivation and achievement behaviors.

Intrinsic Motivation

Intrinsic motivation is a fundamental factor when discussing this concept. Intrinsic motivation refers to behaviors that are driven by internal rewards such as the satisfaction someone receives from completing a task or reaching a goal. A marathon runner, for example, may train because they enjoy running and love the sense of accomplishment they feel when they finish a race. On the other hand, a person focused on extrinsic motivators is moved to action by rewards that are more tangible in nature, such as money. Although extrinsic rewards may provide motivation in some instances a self-motivated individual, by definition, will always be driven by intrinsic returns. Interestingly, researchers have found that when external rewards are offered to someone who is already internally motivated it can actually reduce the satisfaction they get out of the activity. When this occurs it is known as overjustification. For someone who is self-motivated the intrinsic reward of engaging in the task is reward enough so when extrinsic compensations are offered a person becomes uncertain as to the true motivation and may cause performance to suffer.

Autonomy, Mastery, and Purpose

Previous research of the topic of motivation reveals that self-motivation is at the core of an individual's productivity. Traditionally, organizations have focused on extrinsic rewards, sometimes referred to as sticks and carrots, that do not engage a person's deep internal motives. However, sport leaders who emphasize the three essential elements of motivation will likely evoke stronger motivational responses. The three elements of motivation include autonomy, mastery, and purpose.

Autonomy is an individual's ability to determine their actions. Someone who is strongly motivated will likely have high autonomy in whatever they are pursuing. A sport leader who is hoping to get the most production out of a team or individual should consider allowing for a certain level of autonomy to create a simulating environment where athletes will actively seek to become involved. A sense of freedom allows the individual to decide the appropriate way to complete a task and provides them a sense of ownership over the situation. For example, a personal trainer may be more successful at getting a person to complete an exercise program if they allow for choice in activities during the workout. By offering an individual the ability to choose, the feeling of autonomy will be increased and a self-motivated individual will likely be more engaged in the activity.

Within the context of self-motivation, mastery is a person's desire for improvement in something that they feel is important. Mastery includes the element of self-confidence due to the fact that one must feel they can get better in order to stay motivated and work toward the intended result. Since mastery can sometimes be an unachievable result, in order for someone to stay motivated they need to set challenging yet achievable goals. A sport leader needs to be aware of this delicate balance when trying to evoke a strong motivational response through goal setting. It is vital to establish an environment where someone will feel competent and believe they are producing quality outcomes.

Last, purpose provides the framework for the first two elements of self-motivation. When someone feels a sense of meaningfulness they believe that what they are doing is making a difference, whether it is personally or for others. A sense of progress is gained when the effort put forth is leading to a completed task and the belief that it was done well. The stronger these intrinsic pulls are the greater likelihood a person will be self-motivated to accomplish a specific objective.

Self-Efficacy Theory

Self-Efficacy Theory has been a popular framework used to analyze sport motivation. The theory essentially states that the higher a person's confidence in successfully completing a task the more motivated they will be to work toward that end. The most powerful source for self-appraisals is from past performances. Applying this concept to sport, one could assume that a professional golfer who has won a major championship will most likely have a strong belief they can win another. Self-efficacy is a term that is oftentimes used interchangeably with self-confidence. Sport leaders can help to promote self-efficacy by using techniques such as participant modeling. For example, a gymnastics coach may use participant modeling by having a student demonstrate a particular skill to a class and provide guidance to those observing on how it is performed. In fact, self-efficacy can be improved by simply watching an activity completed successfully. This is called

vicarious experience and it aids in reducing anxiety along with raising one's confidence. It is important to note that self-efficacy is focused on a person's perception of their ability to accomplish a certain outcome, not necessarily on their actual abilities.

When supporters of a team cheer or yell positive encouragement they are engaging in verbal persuasion. Even a simple phrase such as "You can do it!" has been shown to enhance a person's self-efficacy. Ultimately one's level of self-efficacy can play a major role in their choice of activity, level of effort, and persistence.

Need Achievement Theory

One of the most influential theories on motivation is Need Achievement Theory. This theory essentially states that there are two motives that will impact whether or not a person will take on an action or a task. The two central concepts in this theory include the motive to achieve success and the motive to avoid failure. These intentions respond to cues from the environment, which are assessed with either a feeling of pride or shame. A person's response to a specific situation will then elicit acceptance or avoidance behaviors. A sport leader will most likely be someone who is viewed as a high-need achiever, in that their will to succeed is greater than their avoidance of failure. In theory, these types of people will take on more risks, select challenging tasks, and demonstrate continued improvement. In contrast, someone who is a low-need achiever would have their attention focused on the potential failure that might occur and would be less likely to be motivated to take risks or accept a challenge.

Self-motivation is a central concept within the topic of sport leadership. A sport leader will usually be self-motivated through strong intrinsic drives such as enjoyment or sense of accomplishment. A person who is in an environment where autonomy, mastery, and purpose are supported will likely feel strongly motivated to accomplish tasks or work toward an end. The topic of self-motivation is complex and although a number of theories have been developed to examine this phenomenon, researchers and practitioners continue to work to understand this fascinating subject and how it applies to sport.

Ted B. Peetz

See Also: Creating an Organizational Vision; Positive Discipline; Sport Psychology.

Further Readings

Deci, Edward. *Why We Do What We Do: Understanding Self-Motivation.* London: Penguin Books, 1995.

Dweck, Carol. *Mindset: The New Psychology of Success.* New York: Ballantine Books, 2007.

Pink, Daniel. *Drive: The Surprising Truth About What Motivates Us.* London: Penguin Books, 2011.

Sexual Harassment Among Players

Sexual harassment and sexual abuse are contentious topics that have long been a challenge in the world of sports. These involve situations where an individual exercises or expresses power over another. More often than not, women and girls are usually on the receiving end of sexual harassment rather than men and boys, but there have been cases of men and boys being sexually harassed either by female or male counterparts.

Many victims of sexual harassment end up leaving the sport they are in instead of speaking up. As a result of the fear of being undermined in sports due to this form of abuse, there have been both men and women that fail to realize their true potential. Unfortunately, there are also sports in which men and women choose to endure the attention of their oppressors either out of fear or in a bid to seek out some athletic award that might have been promised to them in return for sexual favors. This also becomes a problem in team sports because an individual without proper talent could be selected for particular sport events at the expense of individuals who are more talented, or those who have rescinded the attention of the oppressor. This leaves the team in turmoil since the other players secretly know the reason behind the surprise selections.

Low self-esteem is one of the other causes of concern for individuals that have been exposed to sexual harassment in sports. Often the challenge for these players is that even with the presence of a useful channel or protocol to follow in such events, they may be unaware of the avenues within which they can seek help. In addition, they may be coerced into believing that using these avenues will only lead to more harassment and trouble. Typically, predators in sports make victims feel and believe that they are at fault for being vulnerable, something that makes the victims unnecessarily feel guilt.

Sexual harassment in general is well orchestrated, with predators taking the time to observe and prey on those they believe to be unlikely to speak out after the crime. Even worse, some players with a leadership role over the team or over other players take advantage of their leadership position and exploit the plight of other players. According to research, most sexual abuse predators are usually men.

Basketball player Sheryl Swoopes announced she was gay in 2005, making her one of the highest-profile professional athletes to do so. Sexual harassment can play a part in an athlete's decision to keep personal information secret. (Wikimedia Commons)

Coaches and other leaders in the field are often expected to help athletes and to ensure that they are in environments where they know they can feel comfortable and welcome without being at risk of serious problems relating to how they are treated and taken care of when preparing for competition. Apart from that, there are no mechanisms in place that can help protect the athletes that are already so frightened. As a result, the abusers and the harassers only end up taking advantage of the victims and the system, and exploiting all the gaps that are available for them.

One of the worst aspects of sexual harassment among players and in sports in general is that it takes its toll on some of the victims to the point where they are no longer able to trust anyone. Some victims are so distraught that they cannot even consider the possibility of being in a healthy sexual relationship with another person. These are some of the main challenges that athletes have to go through when they are under this form of duress.

Generally, the definition of sexual harassment is as simple as an unwanted sexual attention, which is often persistent. It may therefore include any of the following:

- Threats or verbal abuse
- Comments that are sexually charged
- Lewd jokes, comments, and innuendoes that are uncalled for
- Taunting someone about their dressing, body, sexuality, or marital status
- Bullying
- Ridicule
- Homophobic or sexual graffiti

There are instances where the perpetrators will start off with intimidating remarks or invitations that are not so pleasant to the victims in a bid to test their will to overcome. For the first attempt, most victims usually just choose to ignore the perpetrators, but the perpetrators only take this ignorance as a sign that they need to keep being persistent and they will realize their goals. Most of the time, sexual harassment does not just happen all at once; it is a buildup of events and actions that occur on a gradual basis. By the time the victim realizes that they are being exploited sexually, they are in too deep, and they have a lot of mixed emotions and reactions that make it difficult to respond as they should or to report their concerns to those in authority.

Simple things, like patronizing or condescending behavior toward one another in sports, are elements of sexual frustration and harassment that prevent others from realizing their true potential in sports. There are perpetrators who take things to a greater degree and insist on physical contact, which may include pinching, kissing, or even fondling. Offensive phone calls and messages are usually a common occurrence, but it is the buildup to these conversations that can at times make the victims feel like they encouraged the perpetrators; they therefore feel so guilty that they are not able to make a formal report on the incidents.

The biggest challenge with sexual abuse is the fact that a victim is often manipulated to the point that they believe their involvement with their predators is acceptable or is an unavoidable circumstance.

Some of them even believe that this is a normal part of the training exercise and is nothing that they should worry about. The risk of sexual harassment is paramount in cases where there are different factors coming into play. These include weak organizational holds on the system, which can be exploited by the perpetrators.

A code of ethics needs to be established in all sporting circles to oversee the actions of players and to give men and women in athletics a voice to speak on their behalf. There should be mechanisms in place that will make men and women in athletics feel safe and confident in reporting anything they feel is unbecoming.

Michael Fox

See Also: Legal Responsibilities for Coaches; Morality of Professional Sports; Team Culture.

Further Readings

Brackenridge, Celia. *Spoilsports: Understanding and Preventing Sexual Exploitation in Sport* (Ethics and Sport). New York: Routledge, 2001.

Kirby, Sandra, Lorraine Greaves, and Olena Hankinsky. *The Dome of Silence: Sexual Harrassment and Abuse in Sport.* London: Zed Books, 2001.

Volkwein-Caplan, Karin and Gopal Sankaran. *Sexual Harassment in Sport: Impact, Issues and Challenges.* Berlin, Germany: Meyer & Meyer, 2002.

Situational Leadership Theory

Situational Leadership Theory, often referred to in leadership circles as SLT, is a theory used to evaluate situations and determine which leadership techniques are most applicable to any particular situation. The theory has been derived from two models called Situational Leadership Theory I and II, by Paul Hersey and Ken Blanchard, respectively. As a leadership theory, SLT provides a series of guidelines to suggest the best leadership action at any given point in a situation.

One reason the Situational Leadership Theory has been successful over the years is that it is applicable for any type of leadership (i.e., business, household, athletic) and the concepts remain independent of time.

In the late 1970s and early 1980s, Paul Hersey founded the Centers of Leadership Studies as a platform for him to develop individuals and share his leadership principles. In 1969, Hersey co-created the Situational Leadership Theory with Ken Blanchard in a publication titled *Life Cycle of Leadership Theory*. This theory is based around a simple model of four segments, each with a unique label telling (S1), selling (S2), participating (S3), and delegating (S4). Shaped like a bell curve in four sections, the curve is described by the amount of relationship behavior required (y-axis) and amount of guidance and teaching required (x-axis.) The final component is performance readiness, where S4 is highly prepared and S1 is unprepared. The model is used to serve as a reference for an individual to analyze where they stand in a situation and understand what leadership techniques to use to better the situation. Centers of Leadership Studies (CLS) courses focus on developing leaders to diagnose the situation, adapt and adjust behaviors, communicate effectively, and move toward a goal. The theory has transformed the view society has on behavioral sciences and interactive leadership in many different settings.

Though Hersey has been partially credited with the creations of the Situational Leadership Theory, his former partner, Blanchard, became much more famous for his work in writing and leadership coaching. Blanchard left CLS in 1979 to form his own leadership development center, which he called Blanchard Training and Development (later renamed to Ken Blanchard Company), with his wife Marge. In 1982, he came into the spotlight as a business leadership and self-help coach. His work in Situational Leadership Theory propelled his writing/leadership coaching career when he wrote *One Minute Manager* with Pat and Drea Zigarmi. At this point, he released the concept of Situational Leadership II, which, according to KenBlanchard.com, "acknowledged the foundation of Situational Leadership and revised the concepts based on feedback received from clients as well as the work of several leading researchers in the field of group development." CLS, via its Web site, www.situational.com, has suggested that Blanchard has not introduced anything revolutionary and, in fact, the two theories are still very similar. On his Web site, Blanchard describes the transformation as a "dramatic departure from the original Situational Leadership Theory." One way or another, Ken Blanchard has built a very strong business in the Ken Blanchard Company (KBC) and has become an internationally renowned author and an Amazon Hall of Fame (one of the top-25 best-selling) author.

Blanchard's first independent book, *The One Minute Manager,* has become one of the most widely popular self-help books of all time. The short book follows a fictional character searching for the world's greatest manager who through the process learns how great managers set goals, praise, and reprimand all in one minute. Selling over 13 million copies since publication, *The One Minute Manager* is one of the best-selling leadership books in history.

In 1985, Blanchard, along with Susan Fowler and Laurence Hawkins, published *Situational Leadership and the One Minute Manager: Increasing Effectiveness Through Situational Self Leadership,* a book that motivates and teaches individuals to analyze themselves intrinsically and use SLT principles to determine how to be more effective. The book emphasizes that "empowerment is something someone gives you, [but] Self leadership is what you do to make it work." Another key focus is on relieving "assumed constraints" on your ability. Situational Leadership Theory separates power into five separate categories (diagramed on a star fish): position power, task power, personal power, relationship power, and knowledge power. The book is often required reading for leadership classes and serves as one of the top-rated self-help books of the past 40 years.

Blanchard's other works discuss leadership theory in depth and serve as self-help books in developing skills to advance an individual's leadership in all aspects of life. Most of his works are focused around self-development and leadership principles of developing businesses and organizations; however, the Situational Leadership Theory and methods are applicable in other mediums such as sports, personal relationships, and community.

In sports, situational leadership is not a common topic, though the most successful coaches have a firm understanding whether trained in the theory or not. They understand how to react to various situations throughout a practice or game. If a player is not performing well, a good coach understands his player and knows what aspect of the model needs to be implemented to get that player back on track.

In addition to the coach understanding, a successful team will have players that understand how to interact with other players, despite their status on the team. Depending on the situation, a team with strong leadership will be able to self-reflect on what role they fill on the team at that time and adjust to fill the aspects that the team requires at that time. Just like skill sets, leadership must be practiced and honed to fit each individual. Leaders can be vocal commanders, thoughtful motivators, or soft-spoken servants of their team—each has a role to contribute.

The greatest leaders in sports are flexible enough to find solutions both by raising their teammates' performance while finding ways to improve on their contributions. As a basketball reference, Kevin Garnett is one of the best possible examples. His personality and competitiveness demands the most out of himself and his teammates. He is often barking orders and appearing extremely angry. However, underneath the bulldog persona, he can be found encouraging his players, giving them opportunities for success while adjusting his game to be versatile around those other skill sets. At various points in his career, Garnett, nicknamed "KG" or "The Big Ticket," has played every player role on the basketball court—primary scorer, number-two option, defensive stopper, defensive anchor, offensive facilitator, mentor and role model—for very successful Minnesota Timberwolves, Boston Celtics, and Brooklyn Nets teams. Through introspective analysis, he is able to understand what the team needs of him on a nightly basis, and he is able to fill these roles, while motivating and leading his teams to success. This is the definition of a situational leader—leading his team by telling, selling, participating, and delegating at all points throughout his career.

Today, prospective students of SLT can find training directly through the Center for Leadership Studies or the Ken Blanchard Company. The programs teach SLT I and II, respectively. Additionally, the theory and principles are a part of basic leadership training and can be found as a part of leadership development courses unassociated with SLT in a variety of fields including military, business, and sports. Blanchard's self-help books also serve as quality educational tools with information that has succeeded over the past 45 years and adapted to the fast, digital world that humans have created over the past 20 years.

Situational Leadership Theory is a proven platform for individuals to analyze and adapt their leadership techniques at any given point in any situation. A successful adaption requires a flexible and motivated leader, selflessly willing to adapt to the circumstances. Both SLT I and II are proven models of consistency, existing and succeeding over the course of 40 years of coaching leaders in business, sports, and community. The theory itself is a simple model that is easily transferable to any field of leadership. Whether getting formally trained in courses or just by reading Blanchard's material, understanding Situational Leadership Theory provides a leader with the mechanisms to expand their influence and achieve significant results.

Jarret Gartin

See Also: Behavioral Leadership Theory; Comparative Models of Sports Leadership; Organizational Leadership.

Further Readings

Craig, Peter, and Paul Beedle, eds. *Sport Sociology*. 2nd ed. Exeter, UK: Learning Matters, 2010.

Dunning, Eric. *Sport Matters: Sociological Studies of Sport, Violence, and Civilization*. New York: Routledge, 1999.

Green, Christopher D., and Ludy T. Benjamin, Jr., eds. *Psychology Gets in the Game: Sport, Mind, and Behavior, 1880–1960*. Lincoln: University of Nebraska Press, 2009.

Social Media, Players, and Athletes

There is no denying the popularity of social media, especially among the younger generation. As sport organizations have realized the popularity and power of social media, they have begun to imagine ways to utilize the societal phenomenon to enhance their efforts in public relations endeavors and other communication strategies, like marketing. Social media, needless to say, has had a significant impact on the sports world. The social media experience has been, and will continue to be, an interactive practice, whereby sport organizations have the ability to create positive messages for consumers, while collecting potentially important information about their fans.

Social media is a platform where people from every walk of life have the ability to communicate to, and with, millions of other people within an instant. This virtual voice for the general population serves as a relevant and important cultural barometer. Social media is for information-sharing as well as opinion-sharing. Sport organizations that have adopted a proactive approach to social media usage have benefited from the ability to quickly measure both fan discontent and satisfaction. The ability to get immediate feedback from consumers about an organization's product or service is something that traditional forms of communication lacked. The organization can act very quickly if the situation warrants a fast reaction. Public relations teams, for instance, have become adept at framing messages to subdue potential media crises, especially if the crisis is realized in its earliest stages.

The interactive nature of the social media communication is a central inducement, which creates a sense of involvement for sports fans. The fan can offer encouragement, criticism, ideas, and praise to an organization or athlete. They get a peek behind the celebrity aura and get to be "friends" with professional athletes and teams. There's a little hint of irony in that using this form of communication, where the online forum is anything but "personal," fans feel as though they have established personal relationships with the athletes through social media.

Fans tend to get the greatest amount of satisfaction from sports' best social participants—the athletes who make surprise virtual appearances on fan-driven communities. However, for the receivers of these messages, caution must be exercised, as social media functions in a sometimes duplicitous role, where the transmitter of messages through this particular medium can be inauthentic. Many professional athletes, for example, have hired social media consultants to post messages on their behalf. The athlete may only occasionally, or may never, visit the actual platform themselves. In an even less authentic situation, someone with no ties whatsoever to the professional athlete may create a page to simulate dialogue, pretending to be the athlete.

Technology

The Internet provides a quantitative database for sports enthusiasts, providing an unrivaled amount of instantly accessible information. Components of new media, like social media, have taken the world by storm, delving into not just a qualitative analysis of sport but also into the personalization of sport. New media has transformed the root of sport, amplifying the dominance of pictures and images from past methods by morphing illustrations from written words.

In the early days of the Internet, Web 1.0 delivered a mostly one-way, centralized experience. A sport organization might build a Web site and populate the site with static content. Fans would visit the site and consume the content but would very rarely have the ability to interact or have a dialogue with the organization or its athletes. Since 2007, Web 2.0 changed the way many in the public consumed media. The desktop computer has been joined by faster, more portable, and more convenient smartphones and tablets. More important, the new model offered an interactive experience for consumers. It became a participatory, conversational, and decentralized experience.

Whereas Web 2.0 allowed consumers to interact with producers of content, Web 3.0 combines semantic markups with Web services to provide the potential for applications to speak directly with each other, and for broader searches for information through simpler interfaces. Web 3.0 offers an automated reasoning system, allowing the user to search millions of databases using semantically different versions of a search query.

In sports, if one fan searches on a National Hockey League (NHL) Web site with the word *check*, in theory, they could be provided information from other sports leagues with regard to blocks, tackles, and fouls, in addition to the information on body checks in the NHL. The context of the word *check*, given the database that was searched, would cause the automated reasoning system to query similar examples across multiple platforms and channels.

Sports Marketing

Social media has been a valuable tool in the holster of the sports marketer. Agencies and brands have been creative in their attempts to digitally connect with consumers. They consider platforms like Facebook and Twitter mandatory implements in any marketing campaign. Marketers strive to provide unique content that sports fans might read and share with online followers and friends. The power of social media to track usage is an appealing concept. An agency can determine very quickly when a campaign or promotion works and does not work.

One strategy employed by digital marketers is the targeting of influencers. Fans or consumers that have a large social media following and who tend to set an agenda when it comes to chattering about a team, athlete, or sport, are targeted by marketers. Agencies have offered free tickets to games and other events, with the expectation that the influencer will post something about the experience on social media. Influencers, upon arriving, have been handed a laminate credential that told them how to access the local Wi-Fi network, what the hashtag was, and Twitter handles of celebrities that were in attendance.

One of the unique aspects of social media as a marketing tool is the fact that it can deliver more value on an investment that would otherwise have a limited shelf life. Social media conversation and sharing creates a three-part arc: anticipation leading up to the event, accounts of what happens during the event, and postevent recaps and follow-up stories. As long as consumers either do not realize, or do not care, about the commercialization of content on their phones and tablets, digital marketing through social media will continue to grow and expand.

Sport Organizations

When Minnesota Timberwolves forward Kevin Love tweeted, in June 2009, that Kevin McHale would not return as head coach of the team, it sent the Wolves' media relations team into a furor. The organization had not released the information at the time of Love's tweet. Love learned of the coach's removal when McHale called the team together in a meeting to let them know of his dismissal. Before the Wolves had a chance to formulate a message for the public, Love formulated his own. When organizations speak of the dangers of social media, the

Kevin Love misfire is an example of their concern. Many professional sports leagues toyed with the idea of banning social media use completely by athletes, coaches, administrators, and staff. Clearer heads prevailed and leagues and teams instead opted for rules governing the use of social media by all personnel, including athletes.

The National Football Leagues' (NFL) social media policy states that coaches, players, and operations personnel are restricted to use social media on game day up to 90 minutes before kickoff. The restrictions cease upon the completion of media responsibilities after the game has ended. The policy adds that updates are not permitted to be posted by the individual himself or anyone representing him during this prohibited time on his personal Twitter, Facebook, or any other social media account.

The National Basketball Association (NBA) has a similar social media policy. It states that cell phones and other communication devices cannot be used within 45 minutes of game time and until players finish media responsibilities after the games. The rules apply to coaches and all operations personnel, in addition to the athletes. However, the memo does not specify penalties. Understanding that the severity of the infraction might vary greatly in each situation, the league wanted to be able to penalize the violator appropriately in proportion to the severity of the violation. The policy also states that teams have freedom to create their own internal policies.

Athlete/Coach

Chad (Ochocinco) Johnson has become as famous for his tweets on Twitter as he was for playing football in the NFL. His reputation for flamboyance on the football field carried over into his off-the-field activities. His rants and warring on Twitter have become something of legend. In April 2011, the former Cincinnati Bengals wide receiver was named the "Most Influential Athlete on Twitter" by CNBC. Johnson, with over 3.7 million followers on Twitter, has been criticized for a number of online spats, including one with a teenage fan.

Not every athlete who uses social media has stirred up controversy, and the ensuing consternation, via the online tool. Michael Phelps, Lance Armstrong, and Danika Patrick are examples of athletes who were all quick to realize the benefits of social media. These athletes have utilized social media in appropriate ways to enhance their image, build relationships with fans, and extend the reach of sponsors. They have used Facebook, Twitter, and Instagram to become, essentially, their own media platform by creating and atomizing exclusive multimedia content, broadening their social footprint, and owning their relationship with fans. By making themselves more accessible through social media channels, the professional athlete can have authentic interactions with fans, distribute exclusive content, and contribute to their own brand beyond traditional media platforms. Some athletes, like NBA players LeBron James and Dwight Howard, have even extended an invitation to social media "friends" to meet off-line. Both Howard and James have treated hundreds of these fans to dinner at public restaurants, for example.

Journalists now view social media as a new pool in which they can fish for controversial fodder. Many athletes create stories through social media blunders that give journalists much to write about. When New York Mets pitcher Matt Harvey posted a picture on his Twitter account in April 2014, it created quite the uproar in the tri-state media. The picture was one that his mother had taken six months previous—Harvey in a hospital bed, about to go under the knife for Tommy John surgery. In a playful manner, Harvey flipped his middle finger to the camera. When the media published the picture, the Mets organization was upset and asked Harvey to remove the picture from Twitter. Harvey deleted his entire account.

While there are inherent dangers in allowing athletes to post unfiltered messages on social media, the financial benefits of a personal online presence can be very rewarding. Sponsorship opportunities are vast for those athletes who create a large, measurable social footprint. As long as the athlete provides a transparent view into their lives, their brand will become more marketable to teams, sponsors, and personal endorsers.

Former NBA All-Star Shaquille O'Neal, for example, who makes roughly $15 million per year through traditional endorsements, could make an extra $1 million to $5 million per year, thanks to his 7.7 million followers on Twitter. Athletes who use the social media approach to marketing typically pitch their corporate sponsors in one of two ways; either as per a requirement laid out in an endorsement deal or in the fast-growing pay-per-tweet market. Rather than negotiating social media activity through endorsement contracts, some athletes have opted for the much easier and faster paying process of pay-per-tweet. In pay-per-tweet (PPT) agreements, the athlete will make a one-time deal with a corporate sponsor to tweet about one of the sponsor's products or services and get paid $10,000 to $15,000 for that single endorsement. The ease of PPTs means the athlete can profit very quickly for doing nothing more than typing a few words into a Facebook status, or tweeting an idea, and avoiding endorsement deals that could take months to come to fruition.

The oversaturation of business deals into the athlete's social media presence, however, could have devastating consequences. If it is true that one of the main reasons fans enjoy following professional athletes on social media is because of the authentic nature of the communication, then it will not take long for fans to tire of not-so-subtle marketing attempts by athletes. Paid-for ads, sometimes written by corporate advertisers and tweeted in the voice of their clients, have spoiled the intimacy of some social media accounts. Professional skateboarder Tony Hawk reportedly has lost sponsorship deals because he refused to write verbatim on his Twitter account what the sponsors asked him to write. Hawk felt as though it was too scripted and lacked "heart."

Social media can be a complex minefield an athlete in today's world must navigate. Everyone from the fans to the press wants more access to players. Social media gives as much access as an athlete is willing to spare. The beauty of the social media access is that it is unfiltered; the downside of the social media access is that it is unfiltered. While new media provides a field of play for this discourse, there is nothing really new about the game. It is the same game, played under more lights, with more people watching, and more communication. In an industry that is content-driven, social media might be the best piece of equipment on the sports field.

Peter Han

See Also: Morality of Professional Sports; Sponsorship Sales; Sports Merchandising.

Further Readings

Darley, A. *Visual Digital Culture: Surface Play and Spectacle in New Media Genres.* London: Routledge, 2000.

Sandvoss, C. "Technological Evolution or Revolution? Sport Online Live Internet Commentary as Postmodern Cultural Form." *Convergence,* v.10/3 (2004).

Spanberg, E. "Connecting With Consumers." *SportsBusiness Journal,* v.15 (November 26, 2012). http://www.sportsbusinessdaily.com/Journal/Issues/2012/11/26/In-Depth/Digital-marketing.aspx (Accessed February 2015.)

Social Media, Teams

Social media is an ever-present part of society. With social media giant Facebook having well over 1 billion registered users, and other platforms such as Twitter, Instagram, and Snapchat all having hundreds of millions of users, it is not surprising that sport entities would adopt such platforms in order to reach and engage their audience. Since the emergence of social media merely a decade ago, many sport organizations have realized the power of social media and actively use these platforms to share information, build relationships, and interact with fans.

One of the unique aspects of social media is the concept of two-way communication with fans. Traditional communication platforms use one-way communication, meaning the organization crafts a message and communicates, or at, individuals. Social media has opened up a dialogue between organizations and their customers, known as two-way communication. For instance, when a sport team posts information about a promotional fireworks night after one of their games, sport consumers have the opportunity to not only consume that message but also to respond back. Sport consumers may have additional questions or opinions about the content posted, and through social media they have the ability to directly interact with the sport organization.

Many teams use social media to cultivate engagement with fans, facilitate relationship building, and disseminate content to build their brands and interact with fans via two-way interactions. Creating an online community around a team may provide the potential to increase brand loyalty and influence merchandise and ticket sales. Social media eliminates geographic boundaries and assists teams in reaching a wide audience of fans.

Technological Advances

The exponential use of smartphones by the general public has also had a direct impact on social media usage. The worldwide use of smart phones increased almost 47 percent in one year from 708 million in 2011 to almost 1.1 billion in 2012. The instant access to social media platforms through smartphones makes it easier than ever for sport fans to access information. Interestingly, in a recent study, researchers found 83 percent of sport fans will check their social media accounts while watching a game on television, and 63 percent will do so while watching a live sporting event. This phenomenon is known as the "second screen." Sport teams should be aware of the greatly increased second-screen use by fans and actively seek to engage them, whether they are watching on television or are in the stadium.

Recognizing the shift in mobile phone use, many leagues have had a call to action to increase the technological components of stadiums in order to meet the needs of fans and enhance their overall experience. Chief technology officer for the National Hockey League (NHL) Peter DelGiacco stated:

A mobile device can be used to provide fans with an enhanced experience with content on another device, such as a television. This device, known as a "second screen," can offer interactive features while the fan is watching a sports event either on television or in an actual arena. (Wikimedia Commons)

Wi-Fi at the arenas is very important to us. We look at it as true Wi-Fi or getting to a level where we can increase the fan engagement especially through an immersive mobile experience.

In turn, the National Football League (NFL) has asked all of its stadiums to provide free Wi-Fi by 2016, and Major League Baseball (MLB) and the National Basketball Association (NBA) have similar requests of their teams and venues.

Many teams have successfully used the second screen to increase the fan experience and facilitate in-game purchases. The Brooklyn Nets, for example, use a mobile application to provide fans with player bios and statistics and instant replays from multiple camera angles, so regardless of where they are sitting in the stadium, fans can have the in-game experience they want at their fingertips. The Nets also provide fans with the opportunity to purchase food and drink from their mobile device and have it delivered to their seat. In addition, they offer seat upgrades for a certain dollar amount that will decrease in price as the game goes on, giving fans a chance to modify their viewing experience mid-game.

More commonly, teams will encourage in-game social media usage and interaction throughout the game by displaying Instagram photos of individuals at the stadium on the jumbotron, or hosting trivia contests via Twitter and providing the winners with prizes delivered to their seats. The reality is, sport fans are using their mobile devices whether they are in the stadium watching the game or not. Therefore, sport teams have begun to engage fans via social media in a variety of contexts. As entertainment options increase and ticket prices rise, it is even more important for sport organizations to improve the overall experience and maximize customer satisfaction for sport fans in order to lure them away from their big screens and get them to the stadium.

Platform-Specific Usage

Facebook. Facebook currently has 1.32 billion monthly active users and 829 million daily active users, with over 81 percent of all active users outside the United States and Canada. Considering that Facebook is the most-used social media platform, many sport organizations use this platform to communicate their organizational voice. In general,

Facebook tends to be a more corporate platform for sport organizations. Many teams use Facebook to provide information to their customers and promote corporate sponsors. For example, the San Jose Sharks posted on their Facebook timeline "REMINDER: Sharks round 1 playoff tickets (games A & B) are on sale now. Get them at www.ticketmaster.com/san josesharks." Included below this message was a graphic that stated "Sharks Playoffs: Presented by El Camino Hospital—the hospital of Silicon Valley." While it may seem simple, the San Jose Sharks crafted content that achieved many goals. The Sharks were able to provide time-sensitive information to fans, use a call to action to encourage fans to purchase tickets, and incorporate both the Sharks logo and corporate sponsor logo, increasing brand loyalty for both organizations in one simple post.

Other teams have found success in hosting contests; for example, in 2012 the Tennessee Titans promoted a contest to win a trip to the NFL Draft and announce the team's draft pick. This contest encouraged fans to submit videos explaining why they were the Titans' biggest fan and should be chosen to announce the draft pick. After all of the videos were reviewed, the team chose the top-10 videos and let the Facebook community vote for the winner based on these top 10. This contest was extremely effective because it encouraged fan-created content and interaction within the Tennessee Titans Facebook community over a set time period. While this campaign was primarily run through Facebook, it was cross-promoted on other social media platforms using the consistent title of #TitansDraft. Throughout the month time period when the Titans promoted and conducted this contest, they gained over 30,000 new likes, 10,000 new Twitter followers, and were featured in local media television broadcasts and newspapers. In addition, the Titans used this contest to increase their database and gain more information from their fans to hopefully increase future ticket and merchandise sales.

Using a more unique approach, the Boston Celtics have seen great success from their Facebook application the "3-Point Play." The concept of the 3-Point Play is very simple: choose three Celtics players and make predictions of their statistics in the upcoming game. 3-Point Play participants are entered for a chance to win various prizes at each game and throughout the season. Participants are also encouraged to challenge friends in the game. One of the biggest dilemmas in social media strategy is monetization, however, the Celtics have been able to directly track over $200,000 in ticket sales directly back to fans playing the 3-Point Play.

Twitter. Twitter currently has 270 million monthly active users, and over 500 million tweets are sent each day. Currently every professional team in the Big 4 (basketball, baseball, football, and hockey) has active Twitter accounts. Considering the premise of Twitter relies on crafting messages with less than 140 characters, this platform has mainly been used by teams to share information and interact with fans. For example, the Boston Red Sox (@RedSox) live-tweeted games during their 2013 playoff run, while also including additional information such as player bios, statistics, photos, and videos.

The reply and retweet functions of Twitter also lend themself to facilitating conversations with and among fans. Many teams use this platform to engage fans in a dialogue and encourage engagement and participation in the conversation. A common technique for facilitating a conversation is question-and-answer sessions with players via Twitter, using a specific hashtag. This allows fans to gain unprecedented access to their favorite players and directly ask them questions through Twitter, once again facilitating a two-way conversation. While this is a great idea in theory, there have been multiple incidences of negativity associated with these question-and-answer Twitter interviews. For instance, Florida State used the hashtag #AskJameis to engage fans to ask preseason questions to quarterback Jameis Winston. Many of the responses they received poked fun at the quarterback and his checkered off-field behavior as opposed to the upcoming season.

Instagram. Instagram (owned by Facebook) has 200 million monthly active users with an average 60 million photos shared each day. As the primary photo-sharing social media platform, Instagram assists teams in connecting with fans through visual images and videos. Many times, that visual representation can provide fans with more of an emotional connection to their team and players and further enhance brand loyalty.

The Philadelphia Eagles have been extremely successful in leveraging the photo platform Instagram with almost 200,000 followers. The Eagles typically post photos embedded with graphics (e.g., statistics, temperature at game time) or quotes from players or coaches. The team also uses Instagram to craft promotional videos and get fans excited about upcoming games and rivalries, such as with the Dallas Cowboys. Additionally, the Boston Bruins use Instagram as a way to provide fans with unprecedented access to their players and team off the ice. Photos highlight pregame rituals, locker room scenes, and photos of the team traveling to various games across the country.

YouTube. YouTube currently has more than 1 billion unique users each month. In addition, according to Neilsen, YouTube reaches more adults in the United States between the ages of 18 and 34 than any cable network. Following along with the photo and video trend, YouTube is the most popular video-sharing social media platform. Teams can effectively use YouTube to provide fans with behind the scenes access and content not typically broadcast on television. Niche sports, such as Major League Lacrosse, have even used YouTube to live-stream full games (and seasons) that may not be broadcast on local television channels. This assists the league in creating awareness for new fans and enhanced brand loyalty for existing fans. Many leagues and teams have created their own YouTube channels and have regularly scheduled programming to engage fans. While Instagram and Vine also host videos on their platforms, YouTube continues to be a prominent social media platform.

Pinterest. With over 70 million monthly active users, some teams may not invest as much time in this platform as others. Many sport teams have a goal of expanding their demographics and reaching a wider audience, yet have trouble finding the appropriate avenue to reach the female audience. Pinterest may be the solution. Over 65 percent of all monthly active users on Pinterest are female. Some sport teams, such as the Pittsburgh Penguins, have leveraged this platform to reach the female audience. The Penguins use Pinterest to post photos of new apparel, Pittsburgh Penguin-inspired photos and drawings, and even recipes for tailgating.

Tips for Success

It is clear that social media is here to stay. Three major tips for successful team usage of social media are to (1) be present, (2) implement a defined strategy, and (3) provide unique content.

Be Present. First and foremost, teams need to have a social media presence. Not only is it necessary for sport organizations to have social media accounts, but they also need to be actively engaged in the dialogue. It is important for teams to listen and learn from their customers via social media. Additionally, sport teams should be aware of new social media platforms as they enter the ever-changing landscape. Social media is an excellent avenue to efficiently and effectively reach a global audience; however it does take time and energy to consistently engage in a dialogue with fans on various platforms.

Implement a Defined Strategy. In order to have a successful social media presence, teams must have a defined social media strategy, including goals, objectives, and evaluation metrics. Teams should plan strategy for each platform they plan to use as well as the integration of such platforms. Additionally, the social media strategy should be effectively communicated throughout the organization.

Unique Content. Teams should provide unique content on each platform within their social media strategy to encourage fan engagement across platforms. Social media aggregation and dissemination tools assist teams in compiling or scheduling the release of social media content, yet releasing the same content across multiple platforms can be redundant and discourage fan engagement. Teams should have a social media strategy and unique content for each platform that draws in fans. For instance, the Boston Celtics' brand and organizational voice remains consistent across all platforms; they provide unique content such as the 3-Point Play on Facebook, locker room interviews on their YouTube channel, and a photo with unique graphics on Instagram.

Tara Q. Mahoney

See Also: Community Engagement for Sports Teams; Social Media, Players, and Athletes; Team Culture.

Further Readings

Langer, E. "Crowning the Most Social Sports Teams in the U.S." CNBC (May 29, 2014). http://www.cnbc.com/id/101714566# (Accessed November 2014).

LePage, E. "Building a Loyal Fanbase: How Sport Organizations Use Social Media." (July 31, 2103). http://socialbusiness.hootsuite.com/rs/hootsuitemedia inc/images/3-ways-sports-organizations-use-social -media-to-increase-fan-loyalty.pdf (Accessed November 2014).

Wallace, L., et al. "Sporting Facebook: A Content Analysis of NCAA Organizational Sport Pages and Big 12 Conference Athletic Department Pages." *International Journal of Sport Communication*, v.4 (2011).

Sociology of Sport

Sociology is the study of the social life of people, groups, communities, and societies. It deals with the behavior of humans as social beings and with social rules and processes that combine (and separate) people not only as individuals but as members of a larger society. Its field of interest ranges from the analysis of short interactions between individuals (microlevel) to the study of global social processes (macrolevel). Sociology uses various methods of empirical investigation and critical analysis to develop a body of knowledge about social order and social change. Sociology is composed of many subareas. One can define sociology of sports as a subarea of sociology that focuses on sports as sociocultural phenomena. Sport is a phenomenon characterized by too many meanings and implications to be fully enclosed within a specific subdiscipline. This is maybe one of the reasons that delayed its maturation: although some pioneers can be found in the 19th century, sport sociology emerged as a specific subdiscipline only in the 1960s. The fact that sport as a sociocultural phenomenon was considered marginal, and thus not worthy of sociological interpretation, complicates its genesis.

Heinz Risse: An Almost Forgotten Precursor

Heinz Risse (1898–1989), in the 1920s, provided a first example of a possible sociological analysis of sports. In his *Soziologie des Sports* (1921) he developed a critique of sociological specialisms that, according to him, were not able to interpret phenomena characterized by too many meanings and implications to be enclosed within a specific subdiscipline. In his studies one can find some suggestive echoes of Friedrich Nietzsche (1844–1900), Max Weber (1864–1920), Werner Sombart (1863–1941), Ferdinand Tönnies (1855–1936), Oswald Spengler (1880–1936), and Karl Marx (1818–83). These multiple influences can be found in the analysis of technicalization, bureaucratization and specialization of sports; in the study of the body; the origins of sports; in the dialectics that he introduces between man and machine, popular sports, and bourgeois sports; and much more.

Even if he was not the first to analyze the body from a sociological perspective, Risse's approach is very interesting and innovative. Anticipating what the scholars of the Frankfurt School began, and Anthony Giddens later continued, Risse considered the body as a kind of crossroad between the dynamics of alienation and identity production. This was only one among many of his suggestive ideas that unfortunately sociology abandoned. Sociology "rediscovered" the body only several years later, thanks to the works of, among others, Michel Foucault (1926–84), Erving Goffman (1922–82), and then Chris Shilling and David Le Breton. Sociology of sports, in particular, rediscovered the body through the Cultural Studies approach in the works of Henning Eichberg and Pierre Bourdieu and his school.

Émile Durkheim and the Structural Functionalist Paradigm

Émile Durkheim (1858–1917) can be considered the main precursor of the structural-functionalist paradigm. The first point of reference with regard to his scientific heritage in the context of sociology of sports is probably the notion of "collective representation"; that is, the instrument through which the individual gives a symbolic shape to the power relations in force in social groups, and elaborates in the form of a symbolic universe the dominant moral codes and the social structures. Starting from Durkheim's perspective, sport can be considered a social institution: it is a system of rules; it transmits values; it helps to control, manage, and direct tensions and conflicting impulses existing in every

social group; it produces formal organizations. If one also takes into account the functionalist approach of Talcott Parsons (1902–79), sport is essentially a social subsystem that performs some specific functions and interacts with other subsystems.

Another scientific inheritance provided by Durkheim is derived from his studies of religion: sports practices can be interpreted as rituals to which both the practitioners and the spectators participate. Sports rituals can be assimilated to religious ones; sports stars can be assimilated to living totems; and the whole symbolic universe of sports is composed of rituals, taboos, and evocative allusions to the sacred. The rules and rituals of sports then generate processes of identification and integration that reinforce the values and dominant hierarchies. This approach is still quite fruitful: Robert Coles for example has approached the experience of identification experienced by football audiences with that of traditional religions; Gunther Lüschen and George Sage consider sport as a subsystem that reproduces in its own way the larger social system (and its inequalities).

Max Weber and Comprehensive Sociologies

Although he never studied sports, Max Weber opened historical and comprehensive approaches to sports sociology. One can find an important echo of Weber in some key concepts of sociology: secularization, rationalization, social action, individualization, and in the social analysis based on "ideal types." Based on his perspective, sports can be considered an integral part of that process of rationalization covering all the main forms of expression of Western culture, such as arts and leisure. In the same way, Allen Guttmann initially thought about sports as a form of rationalization of social life under the influence of the Protestant ethic. He characterized the modern physical activities and sports based on seven criteria that distinguish them from traditional games. In his view, sports and physical activities are secular, egalitarian, specialized, rational, bureaucratically organized, quantified, and in quest of records. In a second phase, based on Robert K. Merton's works (1910–2003), Guttmann modified Weber's approach to propose a vision of sports closer to the history of culture: the emergence of modern sports do not represent the triumph of capitalism or the rise of Protestantism, but rather the slow development of an empirical, experimental, and mathematical vision of the world.

Georg Simmel and Interpretative Sociologies

Some elements of particular interest in Georg Simmel's (1858–1918) formal sociology are the differentiation of social and cultural forms, the development of dualistic thinking, the analyses of human sociability, and his concern with individuality in modern metropolitan culture. His sociology bequeaths a strong influence on the paradigm of symbolic interactionism, and provides to sociology of sport at least four key themes. The first one is that of the game. The game has some fundamental characteristics: a commitment that can be total, a prevailing symbolic component, and the presence of latent odds at stake. The second theme is the concept of conflict, which offers a view diametrically opposed to the functionalist one. Simmel sees conflict as a decisive factor of social change and as the symbolic place in which the rules that govern the life of the community are processed, and thus show an intricate system of relations. The third theme lies in the perception of the growing importance that industrial societies attribute to free time and leisure. Finally, the fourth theme comes from the notions of space and city as key concepts (even in the context of a dialectic with the concepts of time and country). These two concepts will then cross modern and contemporary sociology.

Thanks to Simmel, sociological analysis has been enriched by the contributions of social psychology, symbolic interactionism and Cultural Studies on legitimating the idea of subculture. Simmel's influence on George Herbert Mead (1863–1931) and Erving Goffman has been fundamental.

Frankfurt School and Cultural Studies: The Neo-Marxist Approach

At its peak in the 1960s, when sociology of sports was taking shape, Marxist sociology was initially interested in the economic contexts in which sports developed. At the same time the neo-Marxist critiques, which can be partially framed within the Frankfurt School and Cultural Studies, were taking over.

The phrase *Frankfurt School* hides a rather heterogeneous group of scholars, such as Theodor Adorno, Max Horkheimer, Walter Benjamin, Herbert Marcuse, and Jürgen Habermas, in part influenced—as well as by Gyorgy Lukacs's vision of Marxism—by Freudian psychoanalysis and Weber's and Simmel's approaches. Starting from this theoretical framework, their criticism was addressed to the entire capitalist society, and in particular to the logic of capitalist production; thus, they considered sports as a capitalist form of exploitation of the body, without proposing a real sociology of this topic. The interaction between sports and society was analyzed starting from some categories that were considered fundamental: time, performance, the way in which the body becomes the base of the productive value of the individual, and the vision of an indefinite increase in performance. These analyzes were developed mainly (but not only) in the European context, starting with Jean-Marie Brohm, that represents the French neo-Marxist approach. Brohm, from 1967 on, calls for a critical analysis of the cultural industry and the alienation of the working classes; in his opinion the role of the sports entertainment industry is fundamental.

Starting from the rediscovery of Antonio Gramsci, another neo-Marxist approach is that of Cultural Studies, developed among some British and North American scholars during the 1970s. Compared to the Frankfurt School, Cultural Studies' use of the theoretical tools borrowed from classical Marxism was more flexible and open to various forms of hybridization. Starting from this premise, Cultural Studies proposed—and still offer today— a relational view of sport at the crossroads of culture and power. In fact, they paid special attention to the dynamics of persistence, resistance, assimilation, innovation, and anticipation of the cultural models that sport and leisure bring to light. The concepts of subculture and lifestyle (and many others) are located right at the center of the interests of Cultural Studies, and have been endorsed by many scholars, as for example Dick Hebdige and Stuart Hall. Using different approaches, Cultural Studies analyzed urban subcultures characterized by the fact that they dressed in a particular way, listened to a particular type of music, and practiced a particular sport to which was attributed a particular symbolic value (e.g., surfers, skaters, practitioners of parkour).

Norbert Elias and Civilization

Norbert Elias (1897–1990), as part of his collaboration with Eric Dunning, analyzed the transformation of physical games from the Middle Ages on. His works on civilizing processes, which are partially inspired by Durkheim, Talcott Parsons, and Robert K. Merton, led him to place the transformation of games in sports within the wider processes that changed social life. He showed the genesis of a social habitus that marks the social life of contemporary industrialized and urbanized countries.

Elias defines modern sports through the systematic comparison with game competitions in ancient Greece (e.g., pankration), wrongly perceived as their precursors. From this perspective, not only is modern sport is no longer considered a normal and consistent evolution of ancient games, but modern society is itself presented as being based on a different form of social relationship. His theory allows one to understand the progressive codification of sports and the strengthening of physical security standards.

Contemporary Sociology of Sports

From the 1960s on, the question of sport is analyzed from various perspectives by different theoretical traditions: as a social issue, as a form of entertainment; as a form of culture, as a social problem (violence, doping, discrimination), as a political issue, as a health issue, from the "gender" point of view, and as a particular aspect of some broader issues (e.g., marketing, media). Despite the slowness of its development, the sociological reflections on sports tried to highlight some aspects hitherto neglected: sport is a social activity that can be woven into everyday life and as such it plays an important role in determining the nature of social relations. For this reason, it can be analyzed as a mirror of societies' transformations, and its study can be a key to analyze changes in social interactions and collective representations.

Sociology of sport has changed along with society and culture. Today, sport is a form of institution, both international and national, that takes advantage of its global impact and its influence in subcultures. Its importance as an object of study has increased; it is a source of employment, a collective identification support, a vector of social integration and education, a health resource, a marketing tool, etc. As a result of social change, sport has progressively become an essential element of lifestyle, of social and cultural identity, an expression of everyday life, and an increasingly important element of broadcast media scheduling. It can valorize the aspects and critical issues of the just-mentioned phenomena, relating them to the broader social context.

At the present time, the sociologies of sport are trying to focus on all these aspects. Sport has become increasingly important for sociologists; in particular for those who aim to conduct research that may be applied directly to social life or that can be used by third parties, as, for example, the companies supporting or funding research.

Alessandro Porrovecchio

See Also: Comparative Models of Sports Leadership; Economics of Sports; Identification With Sports Teams; Leadership Models in Sports; Organizational Culture; Recreational Versus Competitive Sport; Research Methods in Sports Leadership; Sport Psychology; Team Culture.

Further Readings

Dunning, Eric, and Dominic Malcolm, eds. *Sport: Critical Concepts in Sociology*. New York: Routledge, 2003.

Elias, Nobert, and Eric Dunning. *Quest for Excitement: Sport and Leisure in the Civilizing Process*. Oxford, UK: Basil Blackwell, 1986.

Smith, Earl, ed. *Sociology of Sport and Social Theory*. Champaign, IL: Human Kinetics, 2010.

Yiannakis, Andrew, and Merrill Melnick, eds. *Contemporary Issues in Sociology of Sport*. Champaign, IL: Human Kinetics, 2001.

Sponsorship Sales

Sponsorship can be defined as a relationship between the sponsor and sponsored person or organization, which occurs as an investment, in cash or in kind, in an activity, person, venue, or event in return for access to the exploitable commercial potential associated with that entity. Sponsorship is a great opportunity for many companies since it enables them to reach consumers through their hearts and minds, while allowing them a valuable opportunity to promote themselves and their brands.

Since sport has proven its potential as a marketing vehicle by delivering revenue to many companies, sponsorship is currently one of the most utilized marketing strategies in sport. As a result of globalization and new media, sport is able to reach more people than ever before. Thus, media exposure, especially at global sport events like the Olympic Games or FIFA World Cup, makes sponsorship very attractive for global companies. Global sport events enable global companies to reach their customers worldwide through sponsorship deals.

Sponsorship deals enable the companies to reach their varying marketing goals. For instance, sports event sponsorship provides companies opportunities for promotional activities, such as advertising, publicity, and selling. The foremost objectives of sponsorship investments are increasing consumer awareness; increasing brand loyalty; driving retail sales; and changing, reinforcing, and improving corporate image. The effectiveness of sponsorship depends significantly on the level of congruence between the image of the sponsor and the sponsored person or organization. Thus, matching the image of the sponsored person or organization to the sponsorship will provide benefits for both parties. In addition to the above-mentioned objectives, through sponsorship deals corporations can seek to increase their product trials, improve their communication with their target market, obtain target market data, and enhance employee motivation. Through live marketing events sponsors can increase their visibility and encourage consumers to instantly experience their products.

The success of a sponsorship relationship depends on varying factors, including image fit between the entity being sponsored and the sponsor, the level of integration, target market fit, and the demographic profile of the participant or audience. Of course, economic factors are another key element in the sponsorship match. Strategic sponsorship management can lead to the creation of a long-lasting association between the sponsor and the sponsored entity. In some cases this association can continue even after the sponsor withdraws. Sponsorship management is related to both the efforts of the sponsor company and the efforts of the sponsored person or organization. Sport is inherently full of unexpected issues. The winners of the last season can be the losers of the current season. Star players can be injured or perform poorly, or in the worst scenario, they can be associated with various unethical situations. Since marketing objectives can easily be affected by performance outcomes, sponsorship contracts should include stipulations for guaranteed television ratings or other objective measures. The sponsored person or organization needs to have a high level of professionalism and stability. Sponsorship liaisons, third parties working with the sponsor and sponsored entity, minimize these associated risks.

When deciding whom to sponsor, the sponsor companies need to fully understand and affect the consumer psychographics. The psychographics include personality, values, opinions, attitudes, interests, and lifestyles of the participants or audience interested in the sponsored person or organization. If there is a logical connection between the sponsor's brand and the property, as in the case of a gas station and a car race or car racing team, fans are more likely to recall the sponsor when considering the sport event overall. Besides this natural connection, relevancy is another factor that leads to an increase in product sales. For instance, food and beverages tend to be good prospects since it is possible to increase the sales volume of these products by securing the distribution rights at the sport areas as part of the sponsorship agreement.

Sponsorship Sales: Designing the Offer and Price-Related Issues

The potential sponsor needs to be convinced that there is a good match in the demographic composition of their target market and the participants or audience interested in the sponsored entity. If there is a marketing liaison or agent between the potential sponsor and person or organization, it is that person's responsibility to present a proposal that identifies bilateral benefits, rights, and needs. There should be a unique approach for every potential sponsor and person or organization, and both need to acquire detailed information before entering the sponsorship relationship. An increasing number of companies are using online platforms to get sponsorship offers since they receive such a high number of proposals. In addition, many companies announce special criteria in order to avoid getting unsuitable offers.

When preparing a sponsorship offer, the person or the organization should pay attention to the benefits that are projected to be delivered to the sponsor. The leveraging alternatives should also be listed in the proposal in order to reach projected and extended marketing impacts. The offer should provide a clear understanding and detailed information about the sponsored person or organization. If the sponsored entity is an athlete, then more attention should be paid to the personal achievements, career goals, yearly schedule, and possible additional appearances. If an event is sponsored, then the focus should be on the historical aspects of the event, the profile of the participants, the broadcasting availabilities, and potential exposure. The sponsorship offer has to provide a clear rationale regarding the kind of benefits the sponsorship will produce for the potential sponsor and how. The offer also has to provide an understanding of the demographics and psychographics of the participants or spectators.

Additional activities, which can maximize the impact of the sponsorship, should be outlined within the offer. The potential exposure of these additional activities should also be referred to. Most of the sport entities have the availability to increase the level of exposure by adding new communication platforms, such as official newsletters and new Web sites. Individual benefits should be created for individual sponsors. This requires a partner orientation rather than a customer orientation. Partner orientation requires extensive research on the potential sponsor to ensure that a sponsorship fits within a company's existing marketing strategy. In many cases, the sponsors want to see alternatives that they can choose, which is why listing different options for the sponsor in one offer can be a competitive advantage for the seller. The long-term perspective requires an intention to develop a partnership that leads to regular renewals of the sponsorship. This long-term perspective is also the only way to create a strong connection between the sponsor and participants or audience who are interested in the sponsorship. Sponsors will likely renew their agreement if they are satisfied with the partnership.

Different types of entities can provide different types of additional availabilities. At this point, the most important and sensitive factor is the availability of performing the conditions of the contract. In many circumstances the sponsors tend to abolish their partnership because they are not able to receive the full benefits of the contract. Besides the professional perspective, which concerns the corporate objectives, not receiving the full benefits of a contract creates an issue of trust. Since the sponsored entity is the one who sells the rights to its property, the sponsors tend to act like customers, and they tend to be demanding. The sponsored person or organization will be dealing with various problems and should provide solutions in order to meet these demands.

Pricing the sponsorship is a very sensitive and important topic. When calculating the value of their sponsorship packages many sport entities consider their expenses, for example, the cost of implementing their event, or for an individual athlete, the cost of attending tournaments. There are several methods used in the sport industry for pricing sponsorship; the cost-plus method, the relative-value method and competitive market strategy are the most common. Pricing can cover the whole package available for the sponsor or it can be divided into specific options, allowing the sponsor to select the most useful. Offering several options is a good strategy to fulfill the distinct needs of the potential sponsors.

The suitability of the offer depends on the availabilities and capabilities of the sponsored person or organization. High-profile sport properties, especially global events or teams, are able to produce a high level of visibility and accessibility for the sponsors. Since the sport property has to deliver communication media to the sponsor to expand its reach, the visual and audio media should be made available to the sponsors. The sponsored person or organization can then provide the sponsor with various visibility options, including broadcast rights, on-site signage and banners, usage of official rights, usage of the logos on their products or in their advertisements, and on-site communication and promotion availabilities. Another value in sponsorship is that sponsorships enable companies to build and develop business relationships with other companies. VIP lounges and hospitality areas can be very convenient places to make new business relationships. Business-to-business relationships enable companies to use the same communication platforms collectively for the creation of cross-promotions. A win-win situation occurs when two or more sponsors promote each other via the property. Another important value, which could be delivered to the sponsors by the sponsored person or organization, is the data that are provided by research.

Activation of Sponsorships

Activation of sponsorships refers to putting the sponsorship into action. Since a banner ad alone cannot lead to sales, the sponsors need to activate (in other words, leverage) their sponsorships. Activation of sponsorships means supporting the sponsorship rights by marketing communications in order to achieve sponsorship and communications objectives. To do this, sponsors need to communicate continuously with their audiences in meaningful and effective ways. The ultimate goal of activating sponsorships is to create meaning for the fans. Activation leads to an emotion transfer from sports to the sponsor. In addition, activation adds value to the brand equity of the sponsored person or organization.

Failure to reach the objectives is unavoidable if the sponsor underestimates the investment of money and time required to activate a sponsorship. Successful activations require financial investment and integration of sponsorship across all business activity. Integration of other marketing tools into sponsorship activation will maximize the potential for consumer–product interaction. Even though the amount of additional spending for the activation of the sponsorship can vary according to the type and extent of the sponsored entity, the general rule is that the sponsor should spend an amount at least equal to the rights fee of the sponsorship. There is a direct connection between the effectiveness of a sponsorship and the degree to which sponsors are willing to leverage their rights. On the other hand, there are always limitations on the number of resources that can be utilized for sponsorship activation. The sponsors need to identify how they can utilize the available resources in an effective and efficient way to reach their objectives.

Measuring Return on Investment in Sponsorships

For successful communication in a sponsorship, sponsors must set measurable goals, then evaluate their performances using different methods, and finally review and revise their approaches. A common mistake in measuring return on investment in sponsorships is to relate this process only with the value of the media coverage provided by the sponsorship. There are numerous research methods and activities conducted by the sponsors to gain a deep understanding of the effectiveness and results of their sponsorships. It is possible to divide these methods into three main groups: quantitative research, qualitative research, and media valuations.

Quantitative research is very useful and convenient for answering closed questions such as what, who, where, when and how. It provides a numerical value that allows the researcher to measure and track different variables at different stages of sponsorship. Generally, quantitative research is survey- or questionnaire-based. The most common methods used in sport business are face-to-face interviews, using self-complete data capture systems or e-mailed questionnaires, phone interviews, and questionnaires for the whole target market to complete and return. These questionnaires should ideally take no more than 15 to 20 minutes to complete, and the researcher should design clear and consistently interpreted questions.

Qualitative research, on the other hand, can effectively be used to answer "why" questions and provides a better understanding of the consumers' attitudes, behaviors, motivations, and feelings about the sponsor and sponsored person or organization. Qualitative research can be undertaken with fewer people and allows the researcher to have deeper discussions with respondents. If qualitative research is used alongside or after the quantitative research, it can provide a better understanding of the return on investment. The most commonly used tools for completing this type of research are focus groups and in-depth interviews. Focus groups should ideally last about 90 minutes. The success of this tool depends significantly on the skill of the moderator.

Finally, many sponsor companies consider the amount of press coverage as a measure of success and do media valuation in order to understand the effects and return on investment of their sponsorship. Media coverage is calculated by looking at the sponsor's branding on TV and radio broadcasts, mentions, print branding, Internet coverage, and other kinds of displays, such as billboards. Media valuation allows companies to reach a monetary value on the free exposure through sponsorship generated by media coverage.

Each of these tools enables the sponsor to reach different kinds of information related to the success of the sponsorship. As a result, many sponsor companies are currently designing their own return on investment tools and methodologies to reach the most accurate and consistent results.

Cem Tinaz

See Also: Economics of Sports; Identification With Sports Teams; Owners and Business Leadership; Sports Merchandising.

Further Readings

Houlder, F. *Sponsorship Measurement and Evaluation: A SportBusiness Group Report.* London: Philip Savage, 2009.

Lagae, W. *Sport Sponsorship and Marketing Communications: A European Perspective.* Edinburgh, UK: Prentice Hall, 2005.

Ukman, L. *Return on Sponsorship*, 2nd ed. Chicago: International Events Group, 2004.

Sport Leadership Academic Curriculum

Sport leadership, sport administration, sport management, and even athletics administration are terms that seem to be used interchangeably. As a clarification, the term *sport* is used to indicate the entirety of the range of venues as well as all types of sports. Sport management evolved in the mid-1960s, as did many other sport-focused disciplines such as sport medicine, sport history, and literature of sport, to establish an academic presence as the profession moved away from its physical education roots. These disciplines evolved through an interdisciplinary integration of various fields to explore the role and relationship of sport in the context of the discipline. In the case of sport administration and sport management, the correlation is the business management framework within a sport organization. The sport organizations include all levels, such as recreational,

scholastic, collegiate, or professional. Positions such as athletic directors, coaches, managers, commissioners, and fitness directors are examples of sport administrators; however, commissioners and athletic directors also play the role of sport managers. A leader in sport is not automatically in a role of a sport administrator, although there is an assumption that an administrator is a leader.

Challenges in the Field

As sport management (including all variant names such as sport leadership) programs continue to grow and evolve, the changes in society have caused an increase in consideration of forming a common understanding of theories in sport management. This has led to defining and discussing sport leadership and discussing and addressing issues of race, ethnicity, sexual orientation, gender, and disabilities. Sport programs revise their administrative courses to better meet the changes in the sport environment. The business world has produced a wide range of leadership books and resources based on the profiles of successful chief executive officers or their biographies, company histories, or results of management techniques within the nonprofit framework. These examples are not so different from the sport world, where books and resources on coaches, owners, and players' profiles or biographies; institutions or team histories; or the adoption of various business strategies help to inform and understand the context of leadership.

Leadership is expected in sport at every level, from team captains to membership of a national governing body. While there are a few individuals who seem to have many qualities implicit in leadership expectations, most individuals need to be taught how to become leaders through mentoring, self-discovery, and educational programming. Just as there are many personality tests, leadership qualification surveys, and career development assessments, so are there different types of leaders and a wide range of leadership traits. In sport management programs there is an expectation that leadership will be addressed in at least one academic course, and this course is heavily reliant on the business world's view of leadership and management.

In 2014, three faculty members, Drs. John Borland (Springfield College), Gregory M. Kane (Eastern

Connecticut State University), and Laura J. Burton (University of Connecticut), were so troubled with the absence of leadership discussions within the context of the academic sport environment that they created a textbook titled *Sport Leadership in the 21st Century*. The contributors to this practical resource provide detailed overviews on the topic: case studies, questions for discussion, and references. The framework of the textbook allows for critical exploration of leadership in sport as it relates to expectations in the Commission on Sport Management Accreditation program. While a limited number of programs are accredited, the rigorous process supports common standards and expectations to structure programs and resources, such as library materials, to support the research requirements.

Selected Professional Organizations

Many sport governing bodies, coaching associations, and professional sport organizations provide educational opportunities for leadership training or certification programs for coaches, administrators, and others in the sport world. Sport management and leadership are considered to be a continuous learning and education requirement for professionals in the field.

- *Commission on Sport Management Accreditation* (COSMA). COSMA functions as an independent accreditation body for undergraduate and graduate level sport management programs.
- *National Association of Collegiate Women Athletics Administrators* (NACWAA). NACWAA provides assistance and guidance to men and women in their career interests in intercollegiate athletics through educational and networking opportunities.
- *National Interscholastic Athletic Administration Association* (NIAAA). The NIAAA offers a certificate program in conjunction with the Leadership Training Institute.
- *North American Society for Sport Management* (NASSM). NASSM is the national organization for sport managers as well as educators. NASSM has collaborated internationally, assisting other countries' development of sport management organizations and educa-

tional programs. NASSM also collaborated with the National Association for Sport and Physical Education (NASPE), a former division of the American Alliance for Health, Physical Education, Recreation and Dance (AAHPERD), to form COSMA.

- *SHAPE America*: The Society of Health and Physical Educators was formerly the American Alliance for Health, Physical Education, Recreation and Dance (AAHPERD). Standards in health, physical education, as well as leadership education in coaching and teaching are provided by this organization.

Sport Management Academic Programs

Undergraduates and graduate students in sport management programs are often required to participate in internships or other experiential learning opportunities. Internships may be coordinated by the institution, arranged by the student and approved by the department, and are voluntary or paid.

Undergraduate degree programs in sport management introduce students to the vast range of opportunities in sport and sport-related jobs, from marketing, sporting events manager, to coaching. Recreation and leisure activities may be included in this overview. With over 300 U.S. institutions offering bachelor of arts (BA) or bachelor of science (BS) degrees, the programs range in course offerings and requirements. Expectations and opportunities will vary at each institution where the program is offered and the employment outcome is usually at the entry level. For undergraduates who may not have a sport management major option or are not interested in pursing an undergraduate degree in sport management, opportunities to volunteer or pursue classes or activities related to areas in sport should not be discouraged. Many times, minors and subject-focused research within a degree can be developed in preparation for a master's degree, especially within business school programs.

Graduate degree programs at the master's level tend to be a master's of science (MS), and may include writing a thesis and completing master's exams. For many, the master's degree might be their terminal degree, as continuing for a doctorate is not required in the business sector of sport management. Graduate degrees usually prepare students to focus on a field such as academic athletic administration, marketing and events management, or recreational services management, to mention a few options. This type of advanced degree may be obtained while the student is already working in an area of sport or prior to attaining a job in sport.

While there are limited doctorate programs in sport management, sport leadership, or athletic administration in the United States and abroad, within them an individual who earns this level of degree can expect positions of teaching or administration in academia. There is usually a requirement for candidacy exams and the creation of a dissertation that will concentrate on a sport-focused topic or area of interest. With the limitation in a sport management Ph.D., many in the sport world who have their doctorates have earned them through other departments.

While NASSM provides a listing of all programs with sport management degree offerings, another challenge is accessing sport management, sport administration, or sport leadership concentrations or minors that exist. Although many programs are offered on campus, there are numerous online and hybrid degrees available. There may be standalone programs or centers on sport management, but most of the time the programs will be a major within a larger department or college in some variant of sport science, including and not limited to health and physical education, kinesiology, recreation, human movement, and exercise science.

In conclusion, sport management education is a varied and constantly changing academic landscape that requires careful pursuit at any degree level. Examination of programs needs to incorporate course requirements, career objectives, and job placement ratios. Each of the above-named organizations aid in the academic review, but each individual should carefully evaluate all the options and analyze the cost benefit of an education pursuit relative to long-term occupancy.

Mila C. Su

See Also: Athletic Directors; Comparative Models of Sports Leadership; Gender and Sports Leadership; Leadership in Recreational Sports Organizations; Leadership Models in Sports; Race/Ethnicity and Sports

Leadership; Research Methods in Sports Leadership; Risk Management Process.

Further Readings
Borland, John, et al. *Sport Leadership in the 21st Century.* Burlington, MA: Jones and Bartlett Learning, 2015.
Chen, Steve. "Professional Expectations of Sport Management Students as Related to Academic Curricular Alignment Support and Preparation." *Universal Journal of Sport Management*, v.1/3 (2013).
Dane-Staples, Emily. "Constructing a Sport Management Classroom." *Sport Management Education Journal*, v.7/1 (2013).
Doherty, Alison. "Invest in Sport Management: Value of Good Theory." *Sport Management Review*, v.16 (2013).
Nite, Calvin, and John Nathaniel Singer. "An Examination of Sport Management Doctoral Programme Research Requirements." *Educate*, v.13/2 (2013).
Schwab, Keri A. "Choosing Sport Management as a College Major." *SCHOLE: A Journal of Leisure Studies and Recreation Education*, v.28/2 (2013).
Spahr, Kendra, and Stephanie Wiegand. "Library Collections for the Support of Academic Sport Management Programs." *Journal of Business and Finance Librarianship*, v.17 (2012).

Sport Psychology

Sport psychology is the scientific study of individuals, the behaviors they exhibit based on environmental factors, and the application of knowledge acquired to enhance participants' experience. While top-level athletes use sport psychologists to augment their performance—from a cognitive perspective—sport psychologists also work with coaches and athletes at a variety of levels to maintain a healthy sport experience. Among other factors, casual exercise is used by participants to bolster motivation, artists use performances to improve group-level performance, and military personnel use aid in the transition back to civilian life. In addition, many of the principles sport psychologists cultivate in others (e.g., confidence building, leadership development, coping with setbacks) are skills that can be transferred to other domains away from the sporting experience. For instance, learning how to control one's stress level can help a job applicant in the moments before an important interview. Therefore, the understanding and application of sport psychology concepts provides individuals with the opportunity to be more self-reflective as they examine ideal behaviors that should be displayed based on the situation.

Roles of a Sport Psychologist

Sport psychologists interact with people through the combination of three main roles: teaching, research, and service. Sport psychologists who teach engage in the educational aspect of the field and instruct classes in a university setting focused on behavior change, small group processes, and social aspects of sport. Additionally, these individuals may also work with coaches or larger organizations, such as state high school athletic associations, to deliver workshops on how leadership and communication can be better facilitated among all group members. A sport psychologist who uses the primary role of research investigates how psychological constructs can impact the sport experience, and what cause-and-effect relationship may exist between these variables and behavioral outcomes. Individuals in this role may work in a university setting but can also work for a private company (e.g., Nike, Gatorade) in determining the value individuals place on a new product. Finally, sport psychologists engage in counseling, where they directly work with sport participants to produce positive outcomes. An important aspect to delivering consulting services is the training of the sport psychologist; specifically, they can be trained with an educational or clinical background. Educational sport psychologists likely have a great deal of sport experience, both as first-person participants and through educational institutions; however, they lack the qualifications to treat more severe mental diagnoses such as depression or substance abuse. In contrast, clinical sport psychologists are licensed through their respective state to provide services for correcting severe mental diagnoses, though the relevant sport experience of these consultants may be lacking compared to the background of educational sport psychologists.

History

To understand the purposes of sport psychology today, a brief examination of how the field developed is warranted. Norman Triplett, who sought to understand why individuals performed tasks more competently when other people were present, conducted some of the earliest experiments related to the field of sport psychology. In the 1920s and 1930s, the field became a recognized program of study through the work of Coleman Griffith and Franklin Henry. Griffith became a prominent researcher, establishing a research lab at the University of Illinois, producing book publications, and working with the Chicago Cubs. Meanwhile, Henry created the first graduate program in the area of psychology of physical fitness at the University of California at Berkeley, which served as a precursor to the broader field of kinesiology. After World War II, the field of sport psychology expanded rapidly as scholars began to focus on the applied aspects of the field. This paradigm shift led to the establishment of professional organizations and journal publications specific to the field of sport psychology. Today, sport psychology is an internationally recognized field of study that seeks to bridge the gap between science and practice.

Topics of Inquiry

While the field of sport psychology is a broad-based field focused on various cognitive factors that affect individuals' behaviors and performances, there are distinctive classifications in which the most notable factors can be grouped; namely, personality traits, group processes, and environmental constructs.

Personality traits focus on how one individual differs from another in a specific setting and may examine the concepts of motivation, confidence, and anxiety. Specifically, sport psychologists study how people's motivation to complete difficult tasks can be enhanced with internal motivation (i.e., engaging in the activity for pleasure), external motivation (i.e., engaging in the activity to receive a reward), or a varying combination of the two. As an example, sport participants may genuinely dislike certain aspects of sport that are required for optimal performance, such as training and conditioning. A sport psychologist can work with individuals to better understand their motivational tendencies and help them mentally overcome the challenges associated with their sport. In addition to motivation, it is also known that confidence can be a significant psychological factor that distinguishes successful athletes from nonsuccessful ones. By understanding how confidence develops and the optimal level of confidence for each individual, sport psychologists can aid participants in reaching their performance goals. Finally, when engaged in a stressful situation where the individual places a high degree of importance on a desired outcome, an increased level of anxiety is another important variable to be aware of from a mental standpoint. Whether anxiety manifests itself as negative thoughts, increased heart rate, or sweaty hands, multiple theories help explain how this concept can potentially inhibit performance.

Most sport experiences do not take place in isolation; thus, sport psychologists also study various group (or team) processes. In particular, popular constructs include group cohesion, leadership, and communication. Group cohesion consists of understanding and then applying the factors that explain why some groups stick together during tough times, while others dissolve and go their separate ways. To this end, sport psychologists note that both the degree to which group members work together toward a goal and how much individuals enjoy each others' company are important factors in assessing the level of group cohesion. Additionally, when a team has a defined leader, the behaviors displayed by the leader can affect team members' motivation, effort, and subsequent performance. For instance, the most effective leaders have a specific style they are most comfortable utilizing (and believe is most effective); however, they are not afraid to adapt specific aspects of that leadership style based on the situation at hand or the experience of the people they are leading. Furthermore, one of the ways individuals can effectively lead others is through the application of key communication principles. The great National Collegiate Athletic Association (NCAA) men's basketball coach John Wooden embodied many of these principles by always trying to give short bouts of instruction followed by modeling of the incorrect and correct behavior so his players could rectify their mistakes.

Sport psychologists also pay special attention to the environment in which participation takes place because personality traits and group processes can be impacted based upon the climate created by the coach, parents, and peers. A coach-created climate can influence the effort and enjoyment levels, as well as the motivational tendencies of individuals

depending on important aspects the coach highlights to players. As an example, a coach may decide to assign playing time based solely on skill ability—as demonstrated by outperforming others on the team. This type of climate will produce players who more often practice when hurt and cheat to demonstrate superior ability. In contrast, a coach can stress the importance of learning and developing skills over time, which will be more likely to result in players who encourage and cooperate with one another. Parents can also influence the sport climate through inherent messages they send about their child's ability and the goals of participation. By overemphasizing a child's need to improve, the child may experience a decrease in perceived competence, increased anxiety, and a general loss of satisfaction from participation in sport. Akin to coaches and parents, peers can affect the climate of sport participants by altering one's level of commitment. Specifically, the level of conflict with others on a team, how peers react to mistakes, the social interactions of team members, and the perceived equality in the opportunity to improve can all greatly impact the sport experience.

Techniques to Enhance Performance

Once a sport psychologist has a better understanding of an individual's personality, the group in which he or she belongs, and the environmental variables important to performance, the sport psychologist can devise a psychological skills training program to increase the chances of goal attainment. The end result of such a program is hopefully better self-regulation on the part of the individual so that problem identification, application of a psychological skill(s), and evaluation of its effectiveness can all take place without the aid of the sport psychologist.

Perhaps the most common psychological skill employed by athletes—at all ages and ability levels—is goal setting. Setting moderately difficult goals produces adaptive behaviors such as directing attention to important task elements, persisting in the face of failure, and developing new strategies to accomplish a task. While sport psychologists can aid individuals in devising goals, their work focuses more on effective principles one can use when developing goals. For instance, many sport participants have an end goal of winning the game (known as an outcome goal); however, because many factors in achieving that goal are uncontrollable, sport psychologists also work with participants to set various performance and process goals. The former are goals that serve as a marker of excellence, where a soccer team may set a performance goal of possessing the ball for 55 percent of the game. Process goals are the ideal behaviors one must exhibit during the performance, as tennis players should toss their serve forward into the court to gain more power. By utilizing a multiple goal-setting strategy, participants have been shown to improve both from a performance and psychological standpoint. Finally, sport psychologists can also work with group members in the development of team goals. Here, leaders are encouraged to first conduct an assessment of the group's strengths and weaknesses to make key goals more apparent. Then leaders share the developed goals with the group and encourage members to buy into the larger team goals. Last, leader and participants evaluate the progress toward goals at systematic intervals to determine their effectiveness—as well as what should be altered going forward.

Another psychological skill that can be applied to assist in the development of physical skills is imagery. Quite simply, imagery is using one's mind to recreate an environment devoid of any external stimuli. Sport psychologists teach athletes how to use imagery for a variety of purposes. Specifically, athletes can use imagery to mentally practice a physical skill, correct past mistakes, develop and execute strategies, and control emotions during a high-pressure moment. Much like a dream, individuals can either image themselves inside their own body or as a third person, observing their behavior and performance. The former allows participants to have a greater kinesthetic sense of how their body feels during the execution of a skill, while the latter incorporates more of a visual sense providing individuals the chance to observe their performance as others might see it. Therefore, because of the variety of purposes and perspectives embedded within the concept of imagery, a sport psychologist is a valuable asset in guiding individuals to ideal outcomes through the use of this psychological skill.

The last psychological skill that is vital for athletes to develop is coping. In sport, no one plays a perfect game each time they take the field; instead, participants commit errors and display incorrect behaviors that negatively affect outcomes.

Sport psychologists work with individuals to show them how to cope with impending challenges and recover quickly from past mistakes. For instance, if a participant is suffering from an extreme amount of muscle tension before a performance, relaxation can help the individual feel more at ease and confident. Additionally, athletes must be able to control negative thoughts that present themselves at the most inopportune times. The last thing a baseball pitcher wants to be thinking during the bottom of the ninth inning with his team leading by one run is how he must not allow a home run and lose the game. Through the use of self-talk, or a personal dialogue where one gives reinforcement and instructions, negative thoughts can be rendered ineffective. In the previous example, the baseball pitcher in question may employ a technique referred to as countering—where individuals use facts to refute negative thoughts—as he can remind himself that from a probability perspective, he is much more likely than the batter to succeed. There are various types of relaxation and self-talk techniques; thus, through the use of a sport psychologist, individuals can better understand which strategies will produce the best chance of success based on personality traits and environmental constraints.

Future Directions of the Field

Working as a sport psychologist (especially consulting with athletes) is a desired field for many people. While professional athletes, larger universities, and national organizations (e.g., the United States Olympic Committee) do employ full-time sport psychologists to enhance performance, these jobs are difficult to obtain because of the relatively low number of positions available. As the focus in the United States continues to shift toward health promotion for the larger population, it is expected that sport psychologists will have increased opportunities to utilize their training in these roles. Furthermore, in 2009, the U.S. military began the launch of Comprehensive Soldier Fitness training centers around the country with the goal of building holistic mental and emotional strength. Through these programs, soldiers (and their families) learn how to better apply critical thinking, self-regulation, and coping skills for the challenges military personnel face on a daily basis. Because sport psychologists have studied many of the principles emphasized in this program, it is not surprising that military personnel directly seek to hire individuals trained as sport psychologists. Thus, the field of sport psychology is constantly evolving, and through research and application individuals with a passion to assist others from a cognitive standpoint can share their talents to increase the satisfaction and performance of participants in a number of settings.

Todd A. Gilson

See Also: Sociology of Sport; Sports as a Means of Developing Leaders; Team Building; Transformational Leadership.

Further Readings

Baltzell, Amy L. *Living in the Sweet Spot: Preparing for Performance in Sport and Life.* Morgantown, WV: Fitness Information Technology, 2011.

Cox, Richard M. *Sport Psychology: Concepts and Applications.* New York: McGraw-Hill, 2012.

Roberts, Glyn C., and Darren C. Treasure. *Advances in Motivation in Sport and Exercise.* Champaign, IL: Human Kinetics, 2012.

Tharp, Ronald G., and Ronald Gallimore. "Basketball's John Wooden: What a Coach can Teach a Teacher." *Psychology Today*, v.9/8 (1976).

Williams, Jean M. *Applied Sport Psychology.* New York: McGraw-Hill, 2010.

Sport-Based Youth Development

Sport-based youth development programs are specifically designed to capitalize on the appeal of sport in order to engage youth in purposeful activities that promote positive youth development. These programs are most typically run during after-school hours when youth are, in some cases, most susceptible to risky behaviors. In most instances, sport-based youth development programs target at-risk and disadvantaged youth who lack a safe and healthy environment at home. Successful participation in a sport-based youth development program can provide at-risk youth opportunities to interact with positive adult role models who can serve a consistent and positive influence in their lives. Other programs provide athletic opportunities for children using a pay-for-play model. Each platform has the potential to provide rich learning experiences for children.

Youth Development

The Academy for Educational Development/Center for Youth Development and Policy Research defines youth development as "a process by which youth develop the personal, social, academic, and citizenship competencies necessary for adolescence and adult life based on their capacities, strengths, and formative needs." Youth development programs strive to help adolescent-age youth gain the skills they need to become competent and productive citizens within their communities. Youth are encouraged to shape their future with healthy decision making and the obtainment of positive life skills gleaned through sport participation. Typically, youth sport development programming is directed at building character and community by helping young people to learn how to become empowered. The focus of a given youth development program should be centered upon the advancement of a child's social, emotional, behavioral, and cognitive development, which is key to the prevention of risky behaviors. At-risk behavioral patterns include the use of drugs and alcohol, truancy, involvement with gangs, and teenage pregnancy. Each of these negative activities has the potential to derail a child's progress at various stages of their development. Therefore, sport development curriculum should engage youth in targeted actions that provide opportunities to build the skills and confidence young people need to break the cycle of poverty and become productive adults.

Why Sport?

The United Nations and other prevalent groups describe sport as a universal language. Regardless of a child's ethnicity, race, or socioeconomic status, sport presents a vehicle through which they can learn life skills that will allow them to thrive in numerous environments. Research in the area of youth sport has demonstrated that having fun, learning skills, and competition are the top motivations for youth sport participation. A number of studies also document several benefits from sport involvement including teamwork, positive attitude, sportsmanship, goal setting, fitness, and social and cognitive development. It has been estimated that 27.4 million children between the ages of 6 and 17 play sports in the United States on an annual basis. Sport participation and skill development are considered secondary outcomes in sport-based youth programs. Sport provides an excellent "hook" that ultimately allows for the opportunities to reach, teach, and foster positive relationships and experiences that result in youth development.

Unfortunately, there are some very specific challenges evident within youth sport that relate specifically to minority children. Participation in organized sport is becoming increasingly privatized. Private youth sport programs are typically expensive, primarily due to the prevalence of travel teams, high-priced equipment, and the access to elite training. A pay-for-play model has made sport participation for individuals in low socioeconomic situations more difficult to gain access to. Simultaneously, many states have had to eliminate school-based sport programs due to budget cuts. Students interested in competing in elementary, middle, and high school sports often have to pay an athletic fee in order to participate. As a result, African American, Hispanic, and other underprivileged youth have a much more difficult time gaining access to quality athletic programs because they are overrepresented in low socioeconomic groups. Athletic administrators must focus on young people from low-income families because they are at a greater risk for falling into negative behavioral patterns. Research related to youth sport has demonstrated that children who participate in youth sport earn higher grades, are more resistant to risk-taking behavior, have greater levels of self-esteem, and are more likely to participate in volunteer opportunities within their community. Young athletes develop meaningful bonds with their peers and are more academically inclined than their nonathletic peers.

While the benefits of youth sport are undeniable, there are certain elements that must be in place in order for a child to maximize benefits of their youth sport development experience. Below are some of the criteria necessary to ensure a quality youth sport development experience.

Components of Quality Youth Sport Development Programs

While each youth development program may differ somewhat in the way in which it addresses the objectives of the program, all youth sport development programs should have some common components. These include, but are not limited to, the following:

Mentoring. The mentor–mentee relationship provides interaction between the youth and a positive adult role model. These connections are critical because a positive, constructive type of role model is often missing in an at-risk youth's life. Consistency and continuity with the mentor is also important for the relationships with the mentor to flourish. The selected role models should be willing to spend quality and purposeful time with the youth(s).

Positive Peer Support. One of the primary risk factors adolescents face is the impact of negative peer influence. Disadvantaged youth typically lack both parental and positive peer support. It is imperative that young people are able to have opportunities to interact and engage with peers who can be a positive influence and who can serve as a sounding board for youth who are facing challenges and obstacles on a regular basis. Youth development programs should involve an aspect of peer support that provides an environment in which the child feels safe and comfortable.

Low Adult–Youth Ratio. The quality of the relationships that are formed in the youth development program can directly influence the attendance and the benefits a participant can gain. Lower adult-youth ratios can yield more sensitive and supportive relationships with regular opportunities for engagement and support. Programs that foster low adult-youth ratios are more likely to produce environments in which youth feel valued and respected and in which relationships demonstrate a sense of continuity.

Well-Trained Staff. Staff in youth development programs play a very important role in the success of the program. Staff members who receive the appropriate training are better able to assist the participants in a wide range of activities. They also recognize their role in assisting the participants in achieving personal goals as well as their responsibility to their community. Staff must be able to provide participants with a wide range of activities, including conflict resolution, the avoidance of drugs and pregnancy, the development of more positive body images, career and college readiness, tutoring, homework help, and the integration of fun and challenging sport and fitness activities.

Clear Expectations. Youth who are considered at risk are typically in homes where there is no set structure or clear boundaries. It is important that youth development programs have clear and consistent rules and that expectations for behavior are established and communicated. Consequences for breaking rules or when expectations are not met should be predictable and consistent. Staff should be firm yet caring and nurturing.

Required Time Commitment. Most effective youth development programs run for a minimum of nine months. Some programs span over a four-year time frame and end with the successful transition into a postsecondary education program. This allows for relationship building and for a safe and positive environment to be maintained over an extended period of time.

Developmentally Intentional Learning Experiences. Youth development programs should provide opportunities for participants to learn physical, intellectual, psychological, emotional, and social skills. These learning experiences should result in the development of intentional learners who are empowered by their knowledge, informed about the process of natural inquiry, and responsible for their actions. There should be a focus on critical and strategic thinking that can lead the participants to have greater self-awareness about the reasons for their learning and draw upon their knowledge to make informed decisions.

A Practical Example: The First Tee

The First Tee is an organization whose mission is to "impact the lives of young people by providing educational programs that build character, instill life-enhancing values, and promote healthy choices through the game of golf." Established in 1997, the First Tee has grown into a global youth sport organization that touches the lives of millions of children. First Tee programs are delivered in a variety of formats including after-school programs, at public and private golf courses, and community organizations (such as the YMCA).

The First Tee developed nine core values that are now integrated into all of its programming. The core values consist of respect, integrity, responsibility, courtesy, sportsmanship, judgment, confidence, honesty, and perseverance. Recognizing that sport also has the power to develop healthy lifestyle choices, the First Tee has also integrated nine healthy habits into its curriculum. Examples of healthy habits include proper diet, sound sleep practices, goal setting, the importance of developing proper study habits, and the importance of giving back to one's community. Through golf instruction, instructors are able to help young athletes to refine problem-solving skills, develop emotional maturity, create friendships with diverse populations, and acquire time management skills. A study conducted in 2006 demonstrated the power and effectiveness of programming offered by the First Tee. Participants reported higher than their peers in developmental areas such as life skills, demonstration of positive character traits, goal setting, and emotional management. This is but one example of the positive developmental outcomes available to children engaged in youth sport.

Jennifer Kane

See Also: Amateur Sports; Coaching Teenagers; Coaching Youth; High School Sports; Leadership Skills for Coaches (Amateur Sport).

Further Readings
Berlin, Richard A. "Examples of Sports-Based Youth Development Programs." *New Directions for Youth Development*, v.115 (2007).
Fuller, Rhema D. "Positive Youth Development: Minority Male Participation In A Sport-Based Afterschool Program in An Urban Environment." *Research Quarterly For Exercise & Sport*, v.84/4 (2013).
Gould, Daniel, and Dana K. Voelker. "Youth Sport Leadership Development." *Journal of Sport Psychology in Action*, v.1/1 (2010).

Whitley, Meredith A., Tanya Forneris, and Bryce Barker. "The Reality of Evaluating Community-Based Sport and Physical Activity Programs to Enhance the Development of Underserved Youth: Challenges and Potential Strategies." *Quest,* v.66/2 (2014).

Williams, James Arthur, Chris Roberts, and Robert Bosselman. "Youth Sports and the Emergence of Chameleon Leadership." *Journal of Leadership Studies,* v.5/3 (2011).

Sports as a Means of Developing Leaders

Teams and organizations rise and fall based upon the quality of their leadership. At its core, leadership is a process of influence: influence of one's self, influence of others, and influence of the environment within which one finds himself or herself. Many would argue that leadership is desperately lacking in schools, in government, in businesses, on teams, and in homes. This dearth of leadership can be attributed to the scarcity of opportunities for the intentional development of the knowledge, skills, and abilities (known as the KSAs) of effective leadership in young people's lives.

Sport as a Learning Laboratory

Fortunately, sport is a space that offers incredible potential for developing leaders and equipping them to have the type of influence needed to positively impact society. Studies have shown, however, that student-athletes do not acquire leadership or life skills by simply being a part of a team. The KSAs of leadership must be intentionally taught if athletes are to internalize the behaviors of effective leaders, and opportunities must be provided for them to practice and become proficient at using these skills.

Sport presents an opportunity to learn. Indeed, learning and coaching are an expected part of kids' sport experiences. Just as kids can systematically learn an instep pass, penalty kill, or jump serve, they can also learn how to lead. Practices and games offer a wonderful classroom within which to find occasions to give athletes responsibilities and to hold them accountable. Many teams have captain positions where young people are progressively given more opportunities to practice and develop their leadership skills. Leadership skills, like any other skill, benefit from systematic and consistent repetition, feedback, and support.

Despite the importance placed on sport, everyone recognizes that sports are not "real" life. Successes and failures on the field should not profoundly impact the athletes' identities or future well-being. As such, sports provide a marvelous place to experiment and make mistakes. Learning from mistakes is an inherent part of the typical skill development progression within sports. Athletes get feedback from coaches during practice or while debriefing after a game. Mistakes are analyzed and plans are created for minimizing them from happening in the future. This same process should be capitalized upon for leadership skill development. Instead of waiting until kids are in positions of leadership that truly matter, they should get time to experiment and practice when the consequences may not be as high. Fear of negative consequences can too easily prevent young leaders from testing new skills and ideas.

Intentionality is Critical

A systematic, comprehensive approach to developing leaders on one's team is key. Most people assume that the most skilled athlete will also emerge as the team leader. However, those selected as team captains are not always naturally equipped to truly lead.

There are not many venues where children are engaged and excited to be present as participation in a sport. Sports coaches have the ability to impact a child's future by beginning to teach effective leadership skills. (Wikimedia Commons/Michael Tedesco)

Studies in management have shown that the most skilled worker does not make a great leader without also learning leadership skills to accompany his or her technical skills. The same applies in athletics.

Just as coaches develop practice plans and game plans, they also need to develop plans to teach leadership skills. Athletes tend to learn what is taught, and consequently, coaches have a responsibility to teach skills that apply to student-athletes' lives beyond the field, track, court, or pool. Coaches must intentionally teach athletes the leadership and character skills that they desire for their athletes to embody, and then help the student-athletes understand how these skills apply to life outside of sport.

Just as physical, technical, tactical, and mental sport skills can be taught and learned, so, too, can leadership skills. Jim Kouzes and Barry Posner identified five effective practices to optimize individual and team performances: (1) encourage the heart, (2) inspire a shared vision, (3) model the way, (4) challenge the process, and (5) enable others to act. These are intangibles that coaches inherently know are important but rarely recognize as their responsibility to intentionally teach through the sport experience. Leadership skills should be deliberately taught in practice. As with important team or strategic philosophies, leadership skills need ongoing attention and reminders. Aside from consistently talking about different leadership skills throughout training sessions and the season, two additional components are needed to optimize leadership development through sport: experience and supervision.

In order to develop effective leaders, there must be opportunities for athletes to practice the skills they are learning. Depending on the nature of the sport and the season, this experiential component could take many forms. For example, teams could manage their own disciplinary process through an intrateam board process; paired individuals could be given the freedom to coordinate warm-ups; upperclassmen could be responsible for teaching underclassmen team norms, cultural standards, or mental skills; and during team meetings, players could be in charge of reviewing plays or techniques in front of the rest of their position or team. At the very minimum, ample and consistent opportunities for athletes to communicate in front of their peers should be provided, as confident, effective communication is one of the most powerful mechanisms a leader has to influence others. Many coaches complain about their athletes not taking responsibility, yet these same coaches often overcontrol their athletes, thus giving them no chance to learn how to be responsible.

Supervision over leadership development initiatives has also shown to be powerful in helping individuals consciously process the successes and challenges of leadership practices. This could be as simple as a coach who checks in with his or her athletes on a consistent basis surrounding their leadership experiences, or as elaborate as a leadership consultant who helps implement and monitor the leadership development experience for a program.

To Teach Leadership, First . . . Lead!

Coaches themselves serve as one of the most powerful training tools, and by having strong leadership as a coaching staff, the team will vicariously learn how to apply the KSAs of effective leadership on a daily basis. Eventually, sport ends in every athlete's life. The transition out of sport is often incredibly challenging for athletes, as a large part of their identity suddenly disappears. If athletes do not know what skills they possess outside of the physical, technical, or tactical elements of their sport—or how skills transfer to life outside of sport—this transition is even more difficult. Coaches must be concerned with deliberately using sport to teach important leadership lessons in a comprehensive, ever-present way; if this is done, the overall potential for societal impact of each student-athlete's life is dramatically increased. Coach leadership must be present, and from there, the coach needs to capitalize on the unique opportunity that sport provides to teach and practice effective leadership behaviors to the future leaders of the world.

Amber Lattner
Steve Portenga

See Also: Academic Programs in Sport Leadership; Behavioral Leadership Theory; Development of Leadership Skills; Leadership Skills for Athletes.

Further Readings

Borland, John F., Gregory M. Kane, and Laura J. Burton. *Sport Leadership in the 21st Century*. Burlington, MA: Jones & Bartlett Learning, 2014.

Kouzes, J. M., and B. Z. Posner. *The Student Leadership Challenge.* San Francisco: Jossey-Bass, 2008.

McGuire, Rick. *Winning Kids With Sport.* Ames, IA: Championship Productions, 2012.

Sports as a Means of Integrating Population Groups

Around the world, there are various population groups that are marginalized in society and socially excluded from community life. Many initiatives and programs attempt to help integrate and assimilate these groups into communities and society through a combination of education, the arts, and job training, for example. More recently, sport has also been targeted as a means to assist in integrating various population groups, providing a means to improve social inclusion of marginalized groups by developing social, economic, and cultural capital. Many such sport programs are in operation around the world, in both urban and rural contexts, and working with myriad marginalized populations. While many of these programs are effective in using sport to help integrate population groups, there are also some cautions regarding the efficacy of sport in achieving such integration.

Social Exclusion and Inclusion

Throughout history, many groups have been socially excluded from communities and marginalized to the edges of society. From persons suffering from homelessness or a mental or physical disability, to racial and ethnic divides, society is fraught with exclusion rather than inclusion of these individuals. An individual is socially excluded and not integrated into society if he or she is geographically resident in society, but for reasons beyond his or her control cannot participate in the normal activities of citizens in that society, and he or she would like to participate in these activities. Thus, individuals have disparate access to occupational, political, and educational opportunities, and the risk is that these individuals may then withdraw from society. In addition, sport is a symbol of broader social access, and as such, social marginalization can result

in lower participation in and access to sport. The core idea of social inclusion is social connectedness; the more connections individuals build and maintain, the better off they will be emotionally, socially, physically, economically, and culturally. Social inclusion represents a sense of belonging, acceptance, and recognition and it is explained through four interconnected dimensions: (1) spatial—the closing of social and economic distances; (2) relational—a sense of belonging and acceptance; (3) functional—the enhancement of knowledge, skills, and understanding; and (4) power—a change in one's locus of control, or the feeling one has that he or she is in control of one's life.

Why Sport?

Recently, sport has been touted as a means and catalyst for helping to reduce social exclusion and integrate various population groups. Why would sport have the ability to help in this capacity? Research has demonstrated that there are many benefits to participation in sport, including encouraging pride in one's community and enhancing a sense of collective efficacy. To be more specific, sport participation promotes social integration, active citizenship, and social justice. Considering these positive aspects of sport and its universality (every culture in the world has some form of sport or game), sport is widely regarded as a core component of integrating diverse population groups. In other words, sport can be an excellent tool for re-engaging marginalized individuals who are suffering from disadvantages into society, providing a supportive environment to encourage and assist these individuals in their social development and integration.

Sport can support not only connections between various groups and social networks but can also promote social inclusion and social mobility for marginalized individuals. Consequently, sport has the ability to develop and expand networks, eventually reducing social isolation. These social networks are helping these individuals integrate back into society by feeling a part of the community again and developing a sense of belonging and mattering. Through enhanced self-esteem and self-confidence that can result through sport participation, historically excluded individuals can begin to feel good about themselves again and take initiative to form friendships and connections with individuals perhaps different from themselves, a process that leads to the ability for them to integrate to a greater degree back into society. In other words, sport can provide a cornerstone and environment for the development of relationships within communities that can result in an increase in social capital.

Sport and Social Capital

When considering the role of sport in integrating diverse population groups, many experts point toward the ability of sport to help individuals increase their social capital. Social capital can be defined as a collective property rooted in reciprocity and the establishment of a range of formal and informal social networks. A foundation of networks fosters sturdy norms of generalized reciprocity and encourages the emergence of social trust. From a sociological point of view, social capital forms the basis of a more productive, supportive, trusting, and effective society. To put it simply, social capital plays a role as a stepping-stone for individuals to receive further access to economic (i.e., material wealth) and cultural (i.e., knowledge, education, skills) assets. Social capital can hold benefits for marginalized individuals and groups through building mutual trust and shared values.

Social capital operates through the concepts of bonding, bridging, and linking. Bonding social capital results when individuals form friendships and networks with other individuals like themselves, such as close neighbors or individuals from the same background living in the same area. Bridging social capital is the formation of relationships and networks with individuals different from oneself, such as individuals from one racial group and socioeconomic strata developing relationships with individuals from another racial group and socioeconomic strata. When these bonding and bridging relationships form, individuals build mutual trust and shared values and develop a network of support, which can facilitate integration into society. This integration can be termed linking social capital, or the leveraging of these expanded bonding and bridging networks to access a broader set of economic and cultural resources.

Participation in sport has the ability to increase bonding and bridging social capital, which then facilitates linking social capital development and subsequent social inclusion and integration of individuals and population groups marginalized in society. Scholars have demonstrated that social exclusion, derived from a lack of social capital, can be due to the lack of access to sport participation. Consequently, lower rates of sport participation are a feature of groups that possess characteristics of lower socioeconomic positioning and marginalization. Thus, sport participation can lead to some level of personal change and expansion of social capital, which will yield broader, positive social impacts and integration of those typically excluded from society.

Examples of Sport Initiatives Striving to Integrate Population Groups

There are a number of examples of programs around the world using sport as a means to help integrate population groups and combat social exclusion. For example, an event called the Homeless World Cup is held each year for teams of individuals who are homeless. More than 60 countries send national teams to this soccer tournament, which has a goal to help improve the lives of homeless individuals who are marginalized and excluded from society. Many of the players were able to restore their self-esteem through the cup experience and developed a sense of belonging through increased bonding and bridging social capital. Upon returning home, they were then able to leverage these expanded networks to gain access to resources not available before the tournament and make positive changes in their lives, such as obtaining sustainable housing, jobs, or an education. There is a comparable U.S. program called Street Soccer USA, which operates in 22 U.S. cities and uses soccer to assist homeless individuals. Volunteer coaches in the Street Soccer program play an important role in helping to transition and integrate these homeless players back into society.

In another example, Australian Rules Football is Australia's indigenous sport and one of the world's oldest organized sports. Rural football clubs have continually striven to enhance social inclusion and integration by providing opportunities for rural residents to build associations with the local community, since rural regions of Australia have been struggling with low socioeconomic disadvantages.

Participants in these rural football clubs formed dense social networks and reciprocal trust among members, which facilitated collective efficacy, or the sense that people can collaborate and achieve higher goals as a group.

Other sport-based initiatives have had success with helping immigrant population groups better integrate into communities, using sport as the catalyst to stimulate network expansion and access to resources. Adaptive sport programs targeting individuals with physical disabilities have also been effective at helping to better integrate these individuals into schools and communities. Along a similar line, sport and recreation-based programming has been initiated to help injured war veterans with transitioning back into civilian life, helping to create a sense of fulfillment and belongingness for these individuals. Other programs have also had success with addressing social exclusion of women and racial minorities through sport, establishing environments that reduce white, male dominance to model more inclusivity and promote equality. One interesting international initiative in this regard has used the sport of quidditch, based on the Harry Potter franchise books by J. K. Rowling, to promote gender equality and inclusion. Through the coed nature of the sport, which does not change the rules for female participants, male and female players have learned to overturn stereotypes about the other gender and be more inclusive outside of the playing field. Many other examples of sport's ability to address issues of integrating population groups could also be illuminated; the ones presented here are simply illustrative examples.

Cautions

While sport does have the potential to integrate population groups, there are cautions to the use of sport in this manner. One caution concerns the dark side of social capital, in that marginalized individuals can bond together without forming the requisite bridging relationships to link to external resources and integration does not take place. This danger can surface in sport programs if care is not taken to help develop and expand networks. Another problem area revolves around competition. Highly competitive sport environments can actually have the opposite effect as desired for marginalized individuals with low self-esteem and who have experienced

exclusion. If these individuals do not win or succeed through sport, their self-esteem and self-confidence can actually diminish and they can feel more ostracized than before. Thus, care must be taken in the design of sport programs to de-emphasize winning for certain population groups. Despite these cautions, if designed and managed well, sport does have the ability to serve as a viable means of integrating population groups.

Jon Welty Peachey

See Also: Coaching Inclusive Sport and Disability; Discrimination in Sports; Sociology of Sport.

Further Readings
Sherry, Emma. "(Re)engaging Marginalized Groups Through Sport: The Homeless World Cup." *International Review for the Sociology of Sport*, v.94 (2010).
Skinner, James. "Development Through Sport: Building Social Capital in Disadvantaged Communities." *Sport Management Review*, v.11 (2008).
Spaaij, Ramon. "Sport as a Vehicle for Social Mobility and Regulation of Disadvantaged Urban Youth." *International Review for the Sociology of Sport*, v.44/2 (2009).
Welty Peachey, Jon. "Sport for Social Change: Investigating the Impact of the Street Soccer USA Cup." *ICHPER-SD Journal of Research*, v.8/1 (2013).

Sports Law

Sports law refers to a collection of legal subject areas that interact with sports in some meaningful way. Although historically not considered a substantive area of law, this trend may be changing to the point of sports law actually becoming a recognized substantive body of law. One may divide sports law by legal subject area, or by a specific sport and by competitive level (i.e., amateur or professional). Because this entry refers to a vast amount of information beyond the scope of a concise reference guide, the text below is only intended to introduce the reader to critical and fundamental points of the subject. Leaders who may not have a broad background in sport management or sport law may use this entry as a general reference to learn the basics to get up to speed. Because sports leaders, just like virtually every member of society, interact with the law on a daily basis, it is critical for these individuals to understand the fundamental definitions and concepts of sports law so that he or she can navigate the increasingly complicated field of sport management and maximize the law to the practioner's advantage.

Modern History of Sports Law

Sports law's origin may reach back as far into history as that of organized sport itself. However, the modern history of sports law within the United States finds its origins rooted in professional baseball. During the 1800s, multiple professional baseball leagues competed with each other for the same talent. Lawsuits became a common avenue to force players to honor their respective contracts and/or prevent players from jumping to a new team. Each lawsuit contained an element of sports law.

As the game of baseball, along with other American professional sports leagues, have become more professionalized over the years and revenue streams have increased so has the importance of a variety of legal topics, including contracts. This increase in money has led to interesting and complicated legal issues in virtually every aspect of the law related to sports, including, but not limited to, contracts, criminal law, antitrust, labor, torts, employment law, intellectual property, agency, disability law, bankruptcy, tax, constitutional law, and the law of private associations. Most recently, U.S. sports law has focused on issues concerning the various professional sports leagues, the changing landscape of amateur sport, intellectual property rights in sport, commissioner authority challenges, and safety issues in sport specific to concussions.

Difference Between Transactional Law, Litigation, and Arbitration

The practice of law occurs in different classifications. In the realm of sports law, issues arise via three forms: transactional law, litigation, and alternative dispute resolution, which most commonly is presented in the form of arbitration. Explaining these three forms of legal practice as they apply to sport management perhaps is best done via an illustration:

John Doe is general manager of a professional football team. Doe, as representative of the organization, negotiated a contract with the team's top draft pick. That contract fully explained the rights and responsibilities for both the organization and the player. Upon reaching an agreement, the parties signed a contract. The negotiation, drafting, and signing of the contract is considered transactional law. Transactional law focuses on creating agreements with legal effect that binds the parties pursuant to their understanding at the time of execution. About halfway through his rookie season, the team's top draft pick violated an important term in the contract. This rendered the contract materially breached and unable to be performed pursuant to its terms; thus, the football team decided to file a lawsuit against the top draft pick to recover the monetary loss the franchise suffered as a result of the player's breach. The act of filing a lawsuit is considered litigation. The football team has, in effect, asked a court of competent jurisdiction to provide a remedy for the player's alleged breach, and the player is then forced to participate in the lawsuit and defend against its allegations.

Arbitration, a similar concept to litigation, may also apply to the above example. Arbitration mostly mimics the process of a lawsuit but differs in that a third party, with the consent of both parties to the dispute, is substituted for a judge and makes a decision in a similar matter a judge would based on hearing testimony and examining other forms of evidence. The main difference between litigation and arbitration is that in litigation, a defendant is being forced to appear in court, whereas a binding arbitration, in most situations, requires the consent of both parties before first commencing. The chief advantages of arbitration include costing less than and being a speedier process than litigation. Thus, although each of the three types of legal practice varies, all may apply to a sports law issue.

General Anatomy of a Lawsuit

When most people think of legal matters, their minds' may conjure up courtroom theatrics or images of lawyers engaged in heated arguments in front of a judge and/or jury where life and limb are at risk. Although sports law issues can appear in the form of criminal matters (see *State of Massachusetts v. Aaron Hernandez*), the vast majority of legal matters are civil in nature. Thus, instead of potentially sentencing a defendant to prison time, the only penalties in a civil suit involve monetary damages. In extraordinary circumstances, a court may enforce a specific action through an injunction. Because sports leaders should be familiar with the legal process, the following summarizes the anatomy of a lawsuit.

One initiates a lawsuit by filing a civil complaint with a court. A complaint is a legal document that serves several functions: (1) advises the court why it has jurisdiction to adjudicate the dispute, (2) communicates the relevant facts and circumstances that gave rise to the dispute, and (3) specifies the remedy or remedies the plaintiff is asking the court to grant. Before filing the complaint, the plaintiff must choose the proper jurisdiction and venue, both of which entail ascertaining which court will adjudicate the claim. The chief issue concerning jurisdiction is whether the defendant has sufficient connections to the geographic location where the court is physically located, so that forcing the defendant to travel to, attend proceedings, and be bound by that specific court's decision is equitable. Assuming jurisdiction is proper, a copy of the summons and complaint are then "served" upon the party or parties named in the complaint as defendant or defendants. Proper service often includes hiring a third party to actually go to the defendant's home and physically giving the defendant a copy of the summons and complaint. The purpose of being served is to put the defendant(s) on notice that a lawsuit was filed against that individual or those individuals. Prior notice is paramount because apprising someone of the allegations against them is an essential part of the requirement of providing due process.

After serving the other party, the defendant must file an answer. An answer contains the defendant's responses to the allegations contained in the complaint, as well as the general defenses to the plaintiff's claim(s). Generally, unless granted an extension by either the plaintiff or court, a defendant must respond to the complaint within a specific period of time, in most cases 20 calendar days from the date of service. The specific rules governing the time frame to respond are dictated by a jurisdiction's rules of civil procedure, which may differ by state. If a defendant fails to answer a complaint, the plaintiff may then file the paperwork necessary to obtain a default judgment against the other party and the initial lawsuit may end at that point.

If a defendant answers a complaint, the discovery stage of a lawsuit begins. During this stage, the sides exchange information relevant to the lawsuit; take depositions of material parties to the controversy; and may file motions, or written requests that the judge take action, with the court asking for a variety of relief. After the discovery stage concludes and, if necessary, a trial will then ensue. Evidence is presented and arguments concerning the law and facts are put forth in front of a judge, jury, or both. Both parties possess the right to appeal the judge's decision after the trial's conclusion.

Sports Law Fundaments: Contract Law

A contract is a generally defined as a promise or set of promises between several parties, for which the law will enforce a remedy in the event of breach. Contract law is based on the notion that it is good public policy for parties to reduce agreements to writing and the law will usually enforce what the parties agreed to, as it is not the business of a court to actually judge the contents of the agreement so long as it is not ambiguous.

A valid contract must include the elements of offer, acceptance, and consideration. Further, a contract is unenforceable if a party lacks capacity or covers an illegal topic. An offer is created when one unambiguously communicates to another an intent to be bound by a certain set of promises. A valid offer names (1) the parties to the contract, (2) the subject matter, (3) the time and place performance will take place, and (4) the price or value being exchanged. Once a valid offer is communicated, the receiving party accepts it by unequivocally consenting to the exact terms as communicated by the offering party. Both the offer and acceptance must be unambiguous. The final major element to a valid contract—consideration—is defined as a legal detriment and is met when both parties form an agreement to gain and lose something in the transaction. Quid pro quo, or "this for that," is often used to explain consideration. As long as both sides are obligated to perform under the agreement, both sacrificing and receiving a tangible benefit, consideration is met.

Once a valid contract is formed, it creates benefits and obligations that the law will enforce in the event of a breach. One side may allege a breach and the other side might object, creating the need for a court to interpret a contract's provision due to certain provisions being ambiguous. Sport managers often run into issues involving contracts because an agreement fails to define an important aspect of the agreement. Thus, this important yet undefined clause may have several interpretations. To avoid this situation, the best practices include making sure important words and/or other elements of a contract are well defined and that the duties, rights, and responsibilities for each side cannot have multiple interpretations or meanings. One important clause to define is what acts or omissions constitute a material breach of the agreement. As a corollary, it is also paramount to set out the specific remedies in the event of material breach.

Sport managers interact with and are impacted by contract law on an almost daily basis. Examples of contract law include, but are not limited to, employee contracts, facility leases, ticket agreements, new member agreements, waivers, releases, player contracts, endorsement agreements, licensing agreements, player-agent agreements, and bylaws and collective bargaining agreements. Because of its prevalence, sport management leaders must understand contract fundamentals to prevent problems from occurring during contract formation.

Sports Law Fundaments: Negligence

Negligence is conduct that falls below a specific duty of care. As a result of this breach of duty, the law punishes the offending party by awarding the aggrieved party money damages. Intent is not an element of negligence; thus, a sport manager can be found liable for negligence even though he or she had no intent of committing the offending conduct that resulted in the breach and injury.

A successful negligence claim contains the following elements: (1) creation of a duty, (2) breach of the duty, (3) causation, and (4) damages. The type of duty of care owed is dictated by the nature of the relationship between the parties. Breach of the duty of care is determined by examining whether the defendant acted reasonably under the circumstances and whether they protected the plaintiff from a foreseeable risk of harm. Such an inquiry requires that one apply the viewpoint of a "reasonably prudent person," an objective standard based on a hypothetical person's conduct under the same situation, who is framed as a "reasonably prudent person." Causation is a causal relationship directly linking the breach to the injury. Thus, if the injury never would have occurred "but for" the defendant's breach, the causation element is met. Damages simply refer to any sort of economic injury that resulted due to the defendant's breach. The entire analysis flows from the duty of care owed. Once the duty, or how the defendant should have conducted himself/herself/itself under the circumstances is established, the other elements of breach, injury, and causation fall into place.

Practioner Subset: Negligence and Vicarious Liability

Sport managers must understand the concept of vicarious liability, as it directly impacts an employer. Vicarious liability holds an employer liable and thus legally responsible for the negligent acts of its employees. A court will impute liability to the employer if the violating employee was acting within the scope of his or her employment at the time the negligent act occurred. Whether an employee was acting within the scope of his or her employment is determined by looking at the job responsibilities of the employer and whether that employee was acting in a way to advance the interests of the employer at the time the civil wrong was committed. Vicarious liability is founded under a public policy rational. Liability flows from the employer-employee relationship. The employee acts unreasonably, and the employment relationship imposes liability and responsibility on the employer.

Practioner Subset: Premise Liability

Premise liability is an umbrella term that applies negligence law to landowners and facility owners. Premise liability explores the duty of care owed to individuals who enter a facility and/or use a facility. The duty of care owed to each individual on the property varies depending on his or her legal status. A person's classification falls into one of the following categories: (1) invitee, (2) licensee, or (3) trespasser. In the case of sport management, because each designation places a different burden on a facility, sport managers must understand the characteristics that distinguish one classification from another so that he or she can recognize and apply the correct standard to each situation.

An invitee is anyone who received an invitation by the property owner to enter the premise. If an individual confers an economic benefit to the landowner as part of entering the premise—such as paying for a ticket to gain access to the property—then the person is classified as a "business invitee." The invitee classification requires the landowner to expend maximum effort in protecting the individual from foreseeable risks of harm. Sport managers thus possess a duty of care to (1) design a reasonably safe facility free from foreseeable risks of harm, (2) warn of hidden or latent dangers within the facility and on the grounds, (3) actively inspect the facility and grounds for newly discovered dangers, (4) repair any discovered conditions, and (5) render medical assistance if the need arises. Thus, the duties are very substantial.

The second classification, a licensee, is defined as someone who has the landowner's permission to be on the property, but is not providing a direct economic benefit to the facility. The duty of care owed to the licensee is less than that owed to an invitee. The facility is not required to actively inspect for dangers and is only required to protect the licensee from known foreseeable risks of harm.

The final classification under premise liability, a trespasser, is defined as any person who enters onto the property of another without the landowner's permission or knowledge. The duty owed to a trespasser is minimal; the property owner cannot take steps to make the premise less safe. One example of making the property less safe is placing some form of trap on the property to injure a trespasser. In this event, the landowner would arguably violate his or her duty of care to the trespasser. There is one major exception to the trespasser distinction: an attractive nuisance. An attractive nuisance is based on a public policy rationale that landowners possess a duty of care to child trespassers who are attracted to, and thus may not appreciate, the dangers of a dangerous condition on the property. Such a dangerous condition takes many forms, but examples often include unfenced swimming pools, open construction sites and the like. Thus, when such a condition exists on the property, the landowner possesses a higher duty of care similar to that of an invitee.

Sport management leaders working in event or facility management must understand the concepts contained in premise liability and the duties owed to the various classifications. Awareness and understanding is integral in designing risk management plans to combat potential liability. As society becomes more litigious, and sports facilities/events become more susceptible to foreseeable risks of harm, like the 2013 bombing at the Boston Marathon, knowledgeable leadership may be the difference between avoiding liability and substantial exposure.

Practitioner Subset: Participant Liability in Sport

Injuries are a common consequence of participating in sport. At times, sport managers and the facilities he or she oversees face potential liability for tortious acts committed by participants during a game or event. Generally speaking, participants who commit civil wrongs that violate the law during the course of a game are liable for the injury they cause. However, defenses exist to this liability. Sport or event participants may assume a risk of injury from foreseeable risks of harm. This assumption of risk is heightened if the sport involved is a contact sport. However, a participant's words and/or conduct determine whether he or she has assumed the natural consequences based on the nature of the activity and the other participants' reasonable conduct. Under the traditional standard used for contact sports, those participating in sporting events generally are immune from being sued for traditional negligence, excluding any incidents of intentional or reckless conduct leading to injury. Further, unless somehow negligent, the facility owner/operator shall not face liability.

Sports Law Fundaments: Intercollegiate Athletics Governance

Intercollegiate governance is overseen by the National Collegiate Athletic Association (known as the NCAA or the "Association"). The NCAA was founded in 1906 at the behest of the public to bring safety, oversight, and uniform governance to a mostly unregulated and growing field of college athletics. Currently comprised principally of member institutions from Divisions I, II and III, as well as conferences, the NCAA's current mission is to curb commercialism, promote professionalism, promote safety, and preserve the amateur principles espoused by the association. The NCAA creates and enforces the rules members must abide by in order to be members. In the event allegations of rule violations arise, the NCAA also investigates, prosecutes, and punishes offenders through quasi-legal proceedings. While these proceedings are subject to appeal, all of these events are encapsulated within the NCAA framework without the ability to appeal to outside legal authorities, potentially raising issues of lacking due process.

Historically, courts have deferred to the NCAA and supported most decisions made by members comprising the association. The key factors in evaluating deference are whether the NCAA or one of its members acted arbitrarily, capriciously, violated one of its own rules, or acted against public policy. However, as the landscape of college athletics has undergone a major shift within the last 10 years, courts are becoming increasingly less supportive of NCAA decisions (as in the case of *O'Bannon v. Nat'l Collegiate Athletic Assn. et al*). This lack of support now opens NCAA governance decisions to outside legal scrutiny from the legal system.

Professional League Governance: Power of the Commissioner

The rise of the commissioner within professional sport is attributed to the infamous Chicago Black Sox Scandal of 1919, which involved several members of the Chicago White Sox fixing the World Series after allegedly being bribed by gamblers. The appearance that the outcomes of professional baseball games can be manipulated battered the credibility of baseball, imperiling the future of the professional game. Thus, due to these drastic times, Major League Baseball (MLB) owners turned to federal judge Kenesaw Mountain Landis and appointed him the first commissioner of baseball. With Landis's sweeping powers, he was able to remedy the damage done by the Black Sox Scandal and now every major sport boasts a commissioner to oversee a variety of duties, most principally safeguarding the best interests of their respective sport.

Historically, just like the NCAA, courts defer to the actions of the commissioner so long as such support is consistent with public policy. Again, key factors in evaluating deference include evaluating whether the

commissioner acted arbitrarily, capriciously, violated one of the league's own rules, or is acting against public policy. As practitioners, one must recognize that commissioner decisions are sweepingly supported by the courts so long as such action does not fall within one of the previously mentioned exceptions. Thus, it is prudent to defer to and abide by commissioner decisions. If an issue arises, consult legal counsel.

Jeffrey F. Levine

See Also: Bullying/Hazing; Cheating in Sports; Coaching and Sexual Abuse; Crisis Management; Discrimination in Sports; Drugs; Doping; Ethics in Sports; Legal Responsibilities for Coaches; Legal Responsibilities for Managers and Owners; Risk Management Process; Sexual Harassment Among Players; Title IX.

Further Readings

Champion, Walter, Jr. *Fundamentals of Sports Law.* St. Paul, MN: Thompson West, 2013.

Davis, Tim. "What Is Sport Law?" *Marquette Sports Law Review,* v.11 (2001).

Prairie, Michael, and Timothy Garfield. *Preventative Law for Schools and Colleges.* San Diego, CA: School & College Law Press, 2004.

Sharp, Linda A., Anita M. Moorman, and Cathryn L. Claussen. *Sport Law: A Managerial Approach.* Scottsdale, AZ: Holcomb Hathaway, 2014.

Spengler, John O., et al. *Introduction to Sport Law.* Champaign, IL, Human Kinetics, 2009.

Sports Merchandising

Sports merchandising is an important and valuable asset to teams and organizations. Merchandising in simple terms is just a marketing tool used to foster growth in sales of goods. In more detail, merchandising is the planning and promotion of products to the right target market at the proper time with the correct pricing. These products create greater value for both the team and the fan. For the fan, there is a closer association with the team; for the team, these products create greater loyalty.

Licensed and branded goods are the two products most often identified as sports merchandise. Licensed products consist of apparel, gear, or other products that bear the logo of a team. Merchandise manufacturers pay a royalty fee to the teams and organizations so that they can use their name and logo on the products they sell. Royalty fees can vary depending on the product they are placing the logo onto. As cited in *Sport Marketing* (3rd ed.), royalties typically range between 4 and 20 percent on nonapparel goods and 11 and 15 percent for apparel-related products. On the other hand, branded products consist of apparel from merchandise manufacturers such as Nike and Adidas. Branded products used by athletes help to increase the sales of the manufacturer's brand as fans try to emulate their favorite athlete. Thus, a strategy for these manufacturers is to provide free products to teams to help increase branded product sales.

Trends in Sports Merchandising

A recent trend in sports merchandising is for the manufacturer to expand its current markets by reaching new target audiences: women are one of the new target customers. As Fara Warner points out, in today's economy, women make over 80 percent of all purchasing decisions, spending over $7 trillion in consumer purchases. Women also make up over 40 percent of the viewing audience of sports. On top of manufacturers making apparel that is designed to better fit women, stores are creating displays that target women. Thus, the placement of certain goods in the windows or by the front of the store is crucially important to final sale of goods.

Another trend in sports merchandising is the use of nontraditional stores. More and more organizations are using kiosks, pop-up stores, and the sale of goods at pregame events. Organizations such as the National Football League (NFL) have used this strategy when selling goods at the Super Bowl. By selling merchandise at these moveable locations, more fans are reached. In sports merchandising, this creates a higher chance of impulse purchases.

One of the past issues that sports merchandising has faced is the inability to accurately predict demand and to effectively understand visitor and purchase behavior both in-store and online. However, with many technological advances over the last few years, teams and organizations have started looking at how they can better serve their consumers. One way they are using technology is to collect data on their consumers' purchasing patterns including when, where, and how they are making purchases.

The "when" of sports merchandising is important because if organizations can figure out the apex times when products are being purchased, they can target their deals at those times. It is important to track these data as they can be analyzed to give insight into consumers' minds, thus leading to a better marketing plan and potentially higher profits. Sports merchandisers use barcodes, quick response (QR) readers, and radio-frequency-identification (RFID) chips to collect this data. Barcodes are the oldest tool for tracking data but are still effective for seeing when and at which price products were purchased. QR readers are marketing tools that allow fans to scan a code and receive offers or see promotions going on. RFID technology is a newer version of barcodes. RFID chips allow merchandisers to track not only where and when the merchandise is bought, but also its shelf life and how it has moved around. Then they use these data in real time to make timely decisions.

The "where" of sports merchandising identifies what channels consumers are using to purchase their goods—in-store or online. With a high percentage of consumers making purchases online, sports merchandisers have the opportunity to make sales at all times of the day. Some fans may not live in the city or even the country of the team that they root for, so by selling merchandise online, teams are reaching a far bigger fan base then just having physical stores. An important part of sports merchandising in online sales is making sure that the Web site is visually appealing, meaning that there are items that draw the consumer's eye.

Challenges Facing Sports Merchandisers

The usage of online sales leads to a major issue sports merchandisers are facing. While online purchases are creating huge revenue streams for teams and organizations, they are also creating difficulties. There are customers that may go into the team's store, look at a variety of items, try the apparel on, and then go onto their phones and search for the item and find it cheaper online. This is called the showroom effect. It directly affects the profit teams and organizations are making from the sale of merchandise. This also creates a second issue facing sports merchandisers.

There is a high level of competition through knockoff products—mostly apparel. With online shopping, consumers can find similar apparel offered directly from teams and manufacturers globally at cheaper prices. Some companies are creating these knockoffs with a lower quality as well as possibly changing the colors of the logo, thus changing the image the team is trying to establish as its brand. There are online retailers who are producing stunningly accurate replicas of official merchandise at a significantly lower price. A third type of knockoff competitors are companies and individuals who create knock-off apparel themselves and try to sell it at games. Organizations and manufacturers have taken legal actions, suing those who are selling products with their logos but without the proper license. Another tactic that is reducing knockoff competition is the use of kiosks and pop-up stores. By having an official selling point located where the fans are before or after games, fans are more likely to buy official gear than the knockoff version.

Conclusion

Sports merchandising, if correctly managed, can be a major revenue builder for teams and organizations. It also helps create greater value by developing stronger relationships with fans. When teams and organizations can effectively analyze the data they collect from consumers, they can overcome the issues facing sports merchandising today. These issues include competition both online and knockoffs, but more important, having the right product at the right price for their fans. In the future, sports merchandising will continue to develop as marketers try to develop more techniques to connect with their fans, especially through the use of technology.

Lisa Rufer

See Also: Brand Management and Leadership; Identification of Sports Teams; National Football League.

Further Readings

Mullin, Bernard J., et al. "Licensed and Branded Merchandise." In *Sport Marketing*, 3rd ed. Champaign, IL: Human Kinetics, 2007.
Warner, Fara. "Introduction." In *The Power of the Purse: How Smart Businesses are Adapting to the World's Most Important Consumers—Women*. Upper Saddle River, NJ: Pearson Prentice Hall, 2006.
Wyld, David C. "The Chips Are in: Enhancing Sports Through RFID Technology." *International Journal of Sports Marketing and Sponsorship*, v.9 (2008).

Sports Officiating

Sports officials are a prerequisite for nearly every sport and level, although there are a few examples where the participants themselves also act as officials and enforce the rules of the sport. However, in most modern sports, there is a specialized role of game official, whether that person, or group of people, is known as a referee, umpire, official, or some other term. The two chief tasks of sports officials are to maintain the safety of the participants and to enforce the game rules. Officiating sports is a challenging, but crucial, role in sports. Recruiting, retaining, and training qualified and competent sports officials should be a priority for those in leadership positions at every level of sport. Few jobs face the public scrutiny, and even the occasional open hostility, that sports officials face. However, the rewards of officiating are many, including the opportunity to stay involved with the sport after their competitive playing career, enabling others to play the sport they love. Sports officiating can be a fun way to volunteer in the community, a paying side job, and even a lucrative, full-time career.

The fundamental responsibilities of game officials are (1) to attempt to ensure the games are as fair as possible by enforcing the rules and any penalties that result from breaking the rules, (2) to promote and protect the safety of the participants by enforcing the rules and inspecting the playing arena, and (3) at younger levels, to assist athlete development. In order to accomplish this, sports officials must possess or build many attributes and skills.

Promoting Fairness and Sportsmanship

First, sports officials must be people of integrity. Unethical sports officials can have a great impact on the outcome of games by unjustly punishing a player or team, or by intentionally ignoring obvious violations to give one player or team an advantage.

This is an uncommon reality, but a ubiquitous accusation of upset fans. The rare instances of sports officials acting unethically, such as former National Basketball Association (NBA) official Tim Donaghy, who was sentenced to prison for his role in schemes involving his manipulating the outcomes of NBA games and passing privileged information to gamblers, only serve to heighten fan cynicism. Therefore, sports officials must not only be certain to act with integrity and call the game as they see it, but they must also avoid the appearance of impropriety or favoritism.

Sports officials must enforce the rules fairly while showing a self-confidence that does not cross into arrogance. This self-confidence should come from the knowledge that sports officials spend a great deal of time studying game rules, official positioning, and officiating mechanics. Officiating positioning and mechanics refers to such things as being in the right spot on the court or field, rotations with other sports officials, and areas of responsibility or coverage. No official can see everything, so most sports have designed their officials to have specific responsibilities and areas so that they can cover as much of the playing area as possible. Sports officials can spend years in training learning their craft at lower levels and at off-season camps and clinics.

Sports officials need to be able to think quickly under duress. Coaches, players, and fans alike scrutinize every call and non-call and can demonstratively express disagreement with the officials. A seasoned sports official is able to block out the noise and focus on their responsibility at that time. However, they must also have the personal diplomatic skills to communicate with team captains and coaches in an appropriate manner that builds respect. In addition, they must be able to anticipate potential problems and communicate with players, coaches, and/or game administrators in order to prevent larger problems in the future. Game administrators handle the fans and any crowd control issues that may arise. The sports official must communicate with the game administrator if there is a problem with a particular fan being overly unruly or threatening.

Sports officials can assist in promoting sportsmanship by always maintaining the appearance of a fair but firm enforcer of the rules who does not abuse

his or her power. This may require an official with some ties to a school or organization, such as being an alumnus or working there, to decline to officiate games involving that school or organization to avoid even the appearance of a conflict of interest. In addition, good communication skills are vital to a successful sports official. Many poor sportsmanship issues can be prevented with good communication from officials to players and coaches. The question is not whether there will be conflict during a competition, but rather how will the sports official handle it?

Promoting Safety

Sports officials are also tasked with helping to promote the safety of the participants. Examples of this responsibility include inspecting the playing area, including the playing surface and equipment, to ensure they meet the sport's requirements. This might include inspecting the bats, pads, sticks, or other equipment of a particular sport. In addition, the sports officials also enforce rules intended to promote safety that regulate the types of casts, braces, cleats, mouthpieces, and other types of protective equipment. This is often done in a pregame inspection. In addition, most sports have very stringent rules regarding bleeding players and sports officials must enforce these rules, which may include stopping a game or match and removing a player if the bleeding cannot be stopped and the wound covered. These rules are intended to protect the other participants from any blood-borne pathogens.

In addition, sports officials have a duty to enforce their league or association's rules regarding environmental hazards, such as playing field or arena conditions. Making sure that participants and spectators are protected as much as possible from potential injury is paramount. This may include clearing the spectators' stands or playing surface during inclement weather. Another example is a roof leaking onto a basketball court, making a court slippery and dangerous. A wise official would consult with the coaches and game administrator to ensure that the playing surface is dry and safe to continue playing.

Assisting Athlete Development

At younger levels, sports officials also assist athlete development by adjusting the rules enforcement to age-appropriate levels. These adjustments, which may include overlooking some minor infractions, can help athletes to learn the rules in a less punitive environment, enhancing their experience and enjoyment of the game. In these cases, the sports officials can almost act like coaches on the field or court by proactively talking to players to help them avoid violations or penalties, and helping to educate the players on the rules. This can also help establish a good first impression of sports officials for young players and lay the groundwork for a relationship of respect and mutual love of the sport, rather than an adversarial relationship based on perceived punishment from the official due to rules enforcement.

Getting Into Sports Officiating and Moving Up

Each sport has their own system for getting into sports officiating. Most require that a prospective sports official undergo some sort of training, whether it be in person or online, and pass a rules test. The new official would then begin officiating at lower levels, building their knowledge of the sport and its rules in action, learning the proper positioning and mechanics, and building self-confidence. Many sports then have off-season camps or clinics where sports officials continue to receive training and are evaluated for assignments at higher levels. Depending on the sport, this may include a progression over several years from the small college to the large college level, to professional minor leagues, and finally the highest professional league for that sport. Finding a local officials' association can also help get prospective sports officials on the right track quickly. In addition to formal training, officials' associations provide informal learning opportunities by interacting with veteran officials. It is a great place to get support and learn from those that have already been through similar game circumstances and can help new officials learn from their mistakes and avoid future ones.

Legal Considerations

Sports officials in all but the highest levels are considered independent contractors and are thus not employees of any league, conference, or association. Thus, the official will need a contract to work games, which is simply an agreement between two parties. This may include such information as what teams are competing and in what sport, when and where the competition is, the pay rate for the

competition, and how many officials are working. Some sports have smaller officiating crews for sub-varsity games than varsity games. The state association or some other governing body may determine the number of officials and pay rate.

Most officials belong to officials' associations that handle game assignments for a particular area and level of play, such as high school games or matches in a certain region of a state. These associations usually also provide training opportunities for officials both during and after the season. They may also provide personal liability and personal injury insurance for their members in conjunction with their duties as sports officials. Some sports officials rely on the income to support their families, so an injury can limit this ability to produce income. However, if they have personal injury insurance they may be able to replace this income while they are recuperating. Personal liability insurance can help protect the official in the event that a player, coach, or fan is injured during a game. Sports officials should consult with an attorney in their state to find the best protection for their particular situation. The National Association of Sports Officials is one organization that has offered insurance coverage options in the past. It is rare for an official's in-game ruling to be overturned by a court of law, but some sports allow for an appeals process through the sports governing body. However, this is also rare. Officials' judgments in the heat of action are often given greater consideration than an after-the-fact review.

Benefits and Challenges

Sports officiating can be very rewarding emotionally and, in some cases, financially. Emotionally, many officials express pride at being an integral part of the competition. They may enjoy being a part of a sport they love but can no longer compete in at a high level. Many officials express the same satisfaction that athletes share in being a part of a team, as some sports require several officials in the same event. This "team" or crew of officials can feel solidarity with each other despite the occasional hostility of coaches, players, and fans. This can lead to lifelong friendships with other sports officials who share their passion for the sport and officiating.

Similarly, many officials enjoy the pressure to get their calls right, similar to the pressure an athlete faces to perform in the game. These sports officials may relish the challenge of handling this pressure in heat or cold; rain, sleet, or snow; and large or small crowds. The increasing speed of many sports make getting the calls correct even more difficult, and several sports at the highest level have integrated video reviews to assist the on-the-field or court officials.

Officiating many sports requires that the official be in good physical condition and may require significant running. This incentive to maintain good physical condition is another benefit of sports officiating. An official who is out of shape may not be able to position himself or herself to be in the best position to make the right call. Many organizations require a physical conditioning test in order to move up to the highest level.

Aside from the many challenges that have already been discussed, sports officials must also be great managers of their time. The fan or administrator may see only the actual game action, but the sports official must travel to the games. At the highest levels this may involve long plane flights, and even at the high school level it may involve long drives. There is also a start-up cost to sports officiating, which includes buying the required officials' equipment for that sport (such as shoes, pants, shirt, and whistle), paying registration fees, paying officials' association dues, and paying for camps and training.

Charles H. Wilson, Jr.

See Also: Ethics in Sports; High School Sports; Intercollegiate Sports; Professional Sports.

Further Readings

Grunska, Jerry. *Successful Sports Officiating.* Champaign, IL: Human Kinetics, 1999.

Major League Baseball. "How to Become an Umpire." http://www.mlb.mlb.com/mlb/official_info/umpires/how-to-become.jsp (Accessed October 2014).

National Basketball Association. "Welcome to NBA Officials.com." https://www.nbaofficials.com (Accessed October 2014).

National Football League. "Officiating." http://www.nflofficiating.com (Accessed October 2014).

National Hockey League Officials Association. "How to Become a Referee." http://www.nhlofficials.com/howtobecomeareferee.asp (Accessed October, 2014).

Submissive Coaching Style

From the moment one starts a career as a coach, there are many things to take into consideration in order to ensure success during the process. One of the most important things that coaches need to do is to determine the kind of coaching style that they prefer to use to achieve the results that they desire. The coaching style that a coach chooses will often depend on many things, including the type of coaching that the coach had during their younger years and most important the style that they believe will be highly effective in delivering the results that they require. Generally there are three important coaching styles that coaches can put into practice from time to time. Coaches can either choose submissive coaching, cooperative coaching, or the command style of coaching. All of these methods have different angles and will certainly deliver different results in the long run.

Submissive coaching requires coaches to make as few decisions as possible. Most of the time, the coach is basically going to allow the athletes to take their time and make their own decisions. At this point, the coach will take an observatory role.

The coach is therefore going to provide a little bit of instruction to the athletes, perhaps guide them but in a minimalist capacity, and help the athletes organize their activities out of their own free will. The only time when the coach will get involved in the activities that are being carried out by the athletes is when the coach feels that it is absolutely necessary.

Submissive coaching is also referred to as the babysitter coaching style. There are certain situations where this approach can be considered a lazy attempt by the coach, especially in the event that the coach is either inexperienced about the coaching process or about the individuals that he or she is required to coach.

One of the most important things that coaches need to learn is the character of their athletes. It does not matter whether coaches are dealing with children, youth, or adults; it is still critical to understand athletes better to be able to structure an appropriate training mechanism for them.

There are athletes that have low motivation and at the same time low skill levels. These are the kind of clients who tend to be shy and quiet and in most cases they lack the self-esteem or confidence that would make them compete competitively with their counterparts. For these athletes, it is close to impossible to get successful results in training using excitable coaching techniques. When dealing with these athletes, it is important that the coach takes on a personal and careful approach, dealing with the athletes in a way that they are able to feel like that the coach is taking a keen interest in making sure they are able to overcome the challenges they are facing.

The core concept here is to make sure that the athletes does not feel like he or she is being targeted, or that his or her weaknesses are being exploited. Another thing all coaches contend with is the fact that in dealing with all athletes, it is important to be as patient as possible with them in order to achieve the appropriate results. Patience is critical because not all athletes will be highly gifted, and patience is needed to devise successful strategies for all athletes.

While at the same time focusing on the coaching style that should be applicable to the athletes, the level of motivation and the nature of the skills that the individuals possess are also important factors to take into consideration as a coach. There are individuals who have a low sense of motivation but at the same time can also be highly skilled. The role of a coach using the submissive approach to coaching is to make sure to pay attention to the athletes, their level of motivation, and their skill sets so that in the long run the coach is able to help them be the best they can.

In the submissive coaching approach, the moment a coach allows the athletes to make their own decisions, the coach is also allowing them a chance to develop personally. Personal development is a key element of personal training, something that a lot of people seem to take for granted. It shows the athletes that the coach believes in their ability to take things into their own hands, to make their own sound choices, and to develop into critical thinkers. If a coach starts with an athletes at an early age, he or she ends up with athletes that are proactive in nature because they have given athletes the power to express their thoughts freely.

Athletes usually seek motivation from their coaches and it is therefore the coach's role as the trainer to make sure that they not only provide this but they also encourage the athletes to believe that they can do it on their own. A little encouragement often goes a long way in ensuring success in training.

Michael Fox

See Also: Coaching Teenagers; Coaching Women; Coaching Youth; Command Coaching Style; Cooperative Coaching Style.

Further Readings

Calipari, John, and Michael Sokolove. *Players First: Coaching From the Inside Out*. New York: Penguin Press, 2014.

Morelli, Jason A., and Oscar D. Velez, eds. *Coaching and Management Techniques in Athletics*. New York: Nova Science Publishers, 2011.

Schinke, Robert, and Stephanie J. Hanrahan, eds. *Cultural Sport Psychology*. Champaign, IL: Human Kinetics, 2009.

T

Team Building

Team building is a skill that resonates throughout sports, business, education, and virtually every facet of life. From youth sports through professional sports, the ability to build teams is an essential part of any successful organization. Talent, brains, and money alone will not lead to sustained success. The ability to build teams includes, but is not limited to factors such as culture, environment, credibility, authenticity, diversity, ownership, and most important, the leadership ability of individuals within an organization. The business of sport is played out every day across all media. The very culture of sports provides a scoreboard for the world to see. How an organization creates, builds, and develops the team is quite literally the difference between winning and losing. Determining how to effectively build teams is up to the respective individuals and organizations.

Culture and Environment

Not every organization determines success based on the traditional measurements of win/loses, financial gain, or both. When discussing sports teams and athletes the leadership goals with regard to team building will vary based on the level of the competition. Is it more important to win games at the youth level or is winning based on the development of skills a child learns while playing a sport? Are wins more important than developing confidence, compassion, and class among youth? Those questions

need to be answered by the adults in charge. Most will argue that the development of youth is more vital to a community, school, region, and state than the actual wins and losses. However, many of those same people also believe that keeping score is an important part of the development process. Life is not always fair. People win and people lose; it is a fact of life. Determining how the score is kept can be determined at the earliest levels of development.

Many believe that wins and losses truly start to matter at the school level or at the seventh- and eighth-grade level. How those teams are built is based on the culture or a community. Do teams get built based on the fact that everyone who wants to play gets to play, or is this the start of the selection process that will follow athletes, coaches, and parents throughout their time in sports? And what are the factors that contribute to the decision making process; should the best athletes, the best students or the students with the best character make the team? Or is it the child of the most influential parent who should make the team? Once the decision is made it is time to put the best team builder in place to meet the goals of that particular environment.

The same cultural/environmental question is at the forefront of any business in general, but particularly in sports. Determining how a team will be built will always be influenced by the culture in which that team needs to operate and perform. When it comes to athletic teams, particularly as the athletes get older, winning is often used as the most important measurement of success. However, there are times that winning will not supersede the culture of an organization. Family-owned franchises in professional sports often value the culture of their organization over wins and losses. The same can be said for college teams as well. The reputation of an organization will trump everything else, particularly as one works back from the professional level down to the high school level.

This should not be taken to mean that winning does not matter. Quite the opposite is true; winning still matters as much as anything. Winning brings the revenue, the recognition, the development, and the chance for future success. The end game is to find the correct team builders that can provide both. There is a good reason why the average tenure of a head coach in all four major professional sports is less than four years; owners may be concerned about the culture of their teams, but they are just as concerned about the wins and losses. The key is to build the team to address both issues.

With regard to the sports businesses that are not played in professional stadiums and on college campuses across the country, but rather in office buildings, factories, and boardrooms around the world, the same influences determine who the team builders are within individual organizations. The culture of an organization will be determined by the individuals at the top of the organization chart, and it is up to those individuals to determine the culture of the organization and then empower the decision makers to hire, train, and develop the team builders. There are vast differences in the cultures of businesses that may not be readily recognized by the average consumer. Depending on whether or not an organization is family-owned, privately owned, or publicly traded makes a tremendous difference on how the teams are developed and built. Winning does not mean the same thing to everyone when it comes to business. For example, a privately owned American organization such as New Balance athletic shoes in some cases prefers domestic manufacturing, as opposed to overseas manufacturing at a higher profit, to preserve jobs in the United States. That is a cultural decision made at the very top of the organization. Another example can be seen when one looks at the advertising done by companies in the world of sports. Nike once used the slogan, "You Don't Win Silver, You Lose Gold,"

or as Reebok used at the same time, "Life is Short, Play Hard." These are two subtle, yet powerful distinctions that reflect the culture of two successful organizations in the world of sports manufacturing.

Leaders and Team Building

Building teams is an extremely important component for any organization, not just the teams that are made up of athletes and coaches. The higher one ascends in business is much like the path of an athlete. There is a certain amount of skill necessary to reach the top levels of one's profession regardless of whether one is an athlete or not. Less than 1 percent of athletes that play a sport ever achieve the level of professional participation in the four major sports. Over time one's talent either peaks for an individual or the individual simply stops improving at the rate necessary to remain competitive. The same is true for individuals tasked with building teams that do not perform for the public. There is a certain amount of skill necessary to build a team, but for the most part certain factors will contribute to one's ability to build teams within a desired organization and that organization's culture. An individual's authenticity, personality, commitment, and leadership style will determine one's success. Corporate executives and human resource professionals have found that, just like athletes at some point, not everyone is going to make it to the very top of their profession, and that is fine. Successful organizations are made

A squad at the U.S. Naval Academy participates in a team building exercise. The event places them in a physically- and mentally-demanding environment that instills values such as good leadership, teamwork, and perseverance. (U.S. Navy/Damon J. Moritz)

up of multiple team builders all working together to meet the overall goals of the organization.

Characteristics

Every player on a National Basketball Association (NBA) basketball team knows how to shoot a basketball and how to dribble. However, not every NBA player is expected to be the leading scorer or bring the ball up the floor; there is only one ball. Yet every player on the team knows the ultimate goal of the organization is to win a championship by doing things the correct way within the organization's stated culture. The players need to be on board with their individual role in order for the team to be successful.

Authenticity is often mentioned first when people discuss the role of building a team. Did the individual "pay his/her dues"? Did the person earn the position, or is the appointment of the individual viewed as a political move or a situation where the members of the team do not believe the leader has the authenticity to be in charge? Did the person ever play the game is another way to present this scenario. Bringing someone in without authenticity will in most cases inevitably fail simply because the members of the team do not have faith in the leader. Furthermore, if the team members or the department view the hire as a bad choice, then their faith in upper management also takes a credibility hit, so that multiple departments and employees question the strength of the team and the organization as a whole. Since senior management often oversees multiple departments, poor judgment with regard to team building in one area will most likely affect other departments as well because the decision can be viewed as weakness at the senior level.

The sports industry is filled with people who are competitive; this is why individuals seek positions in sports organizations and the sport industry. Bringing in someone from the outside, particularly from an industry competitor, can deflate a team almost immediately unless that person shows authenticity and credibility from the very beginning or has earned a reputation in the industry as a strong team builder in the eyes of his/her teammates. A successful team often depends on a leader's style. Some leaders like to lead with force or intimidation that does not work long term. That style may get results, but it does not build a team. Teams are best built by individuals who

involve members of the team in the decision making process and the strategic planning. The leader is ultimately responsible for the final decision. If leaders are honest and forthcoming to their teammates, the team will be more responsive to the manager's direction. Employees understand that not all decisions in an organization are determined by their direct supervisor, thus honesty and responsiveness are two major factors with regard to team building.

When building a team, diversity is an important factor with regard to the individuals who make up the team. Diversity in this case does not simply mean race and gender; it also refers to skill set. When building a professional sports team one wants to build the team with athletes who possess the skill to be professional athletes in a particular sport. That being said, Major League Baseball teams are not composed of 22 pitchers and National Hockey League teams are not comprised of only goalies. Each player on professional athletic teams is a professional athlete, yet they are not the same type of athlete.

Areas such as athlete endorsements, athlete compliance, and grassroots marketing are not often accounted for in other departments within a manufacturing organization. For example, if one was to build a team for the purpose of selling and servicing athletic teams, a successful strategy is to have males and females, a former athletic administrator, a person with a product background, an individual from an urban area, as well as an individual from an area where certain sports like lacrosse are culturally relevant. Furthermore if one can build that same team and account for numerous factors, such as advanced skills in social media, a strong computer person, and an individual who knows how to manage relationships, the team now has a diverse background covering a multitude of needed strengths without having to hire additional people, which will cause a drain on the budget and profitability of the company. Not only does this type team building make strong financial sense, but it also creates an environment/culture reliant on strong team building to be successful.

Conclusion

Team building is an essential part of the success of any organization, no matter what the size. The key to building strong teams involves various factors that are all important. Understanding the organization's stated goals, working within the established culture, having faith in the strengths of individual team members, and managing in a way that allows one to be honest and realistic, yet always maintaining the type of responsiveness and commitment to keep the team focused and motivated, are powerful elements in a team building equation.

Lawrence Brady

See Also: Comparative Models of Leadership; Leadership Models in Sports; Organizational Behavior; Organizational Culture; Organizational Leadership.

Further Readings
Lorinkova, N. M., M. J. Pearsall, and H. P. Sims. "Examining the Differential Longitudinal Performance of Directive Versus Empowering Leadership in Teams." *Academy of Management Journal*, v.56/2 (2013).
Darling, J. K., and V. Heller. "Effective Organizational Consulting Across Cultural Boundaries." *Organizational Development Journal*, v.30/4 (2012).
Smith, M. J., et al. "Transformational Leadership and Task Cohesion in Sport." *Psychology of Sport and Exercise*, v.14 (2013).

Team Culture

Teams can be viewed as organizations or collective groups of individuals. According to P. Chelladurai, organizations contain four common elements: (1) more than one person is involved, (2) members' contributions are specialized, (3) these specialized functions are coordinated, and (4) a common goal is being sought. The whole of an organization is more than the sum of its parts. Its complexity is revealed in the following attributions common to organizations: identity, instrumentality, program of activity, membership, boundaries, permanency, division of labor, hierarchy of authority, and rules and procedures. As an organization, a team develops and maintains a culture. Organizational culture is a pattern of norms that evolve as an organization integrates internal thinking and acclimates to the external environment. Like any organization, the values, beliefs, and customs of a team determine its culture.

Sport teams can also be viewed as open systems influenced by both internal and external circumstances. These consist of task environments, which include the customer, competition, labor, and supplier subcomponents, as well as general environments, which include economic, social, political, legal, and technological subcomponents. Influenced by these environments, Chelladurai described organizational systems as inputs, throughputs, and outputs. P. Senge alleged that each system is perfectly created to yield the results that are seen. Examining teams and organizations as systems focuses on the interaction of subsystems, stakeholders, and environments. The system approach enables leaders, members, and teams to be significant and contributing learners within the organization. Within a team system, the cultural components exist as inputs, throughputs, and outputs.

A group comprises two or more persons interacting in such a manner that each person influences and is influenced by each other person. People form groups that vary in size and complexity but have common features. According to A. V. Carron, groups exhibit common characteristics: (1) collective identity, (2) shared purposes, and (3) structured communication. A group typically develops through the following stages: forming, storming, norming, and performing. In forming, the group assembles, commonly with some level of formality. In storming, members engage in competition for status and influence, resulting in increased tension. In norming, members settle upon rules and standards. In performing, members work together within a mature team environment. Team culture is the expression of values and dispositions, a team's way of life. The culture facilitates and conveys standards of behavior to members. These expectations guide how members communicate, cooperate, and resolve conflict. When clear norms are established, everyone on a team is more likely to abide by them. Pervasive team culture fosters the environment that shapes members' experience. Culture impacts how the team functions, how the members and team perform, and the outcomes that result. When all members understand the culture, there is implicit, positive pressure to support the standards and meet the expectations of the culture.

Team culture is both perpetual and evolutionary. Changes in team culture are inevitable, and should not be feared or unilaterally resisted, but rather embraced as routine. E. H. Schein notes that change is often consensus-based and concentrated on mission, goals, resources, assessments, and strategies. Integrative leaders who empower members to be innovative in changing team culture are more likely to be successful. J. Collins and J. L. Porras propose that a vision based on core values enhances a team's ability to adapt to changing environments. M. Fullan suggests fundamental elements for leading change: (1) love for the teammates, (2) connect peers with team purpose, (3) enhance capacity, (4) embrace and promote learning, (5) be transparent, and (6) teams are systems that learn. Fullan goes on to offer these strategies: (1) cultivate team chemistry, (2) expect the unexpected in planning, (3) develop all team members, (4) structure learning opportunities, (5) develop in-team leaders, and (6) apply unavoidable productive pressure. If team members are committed individually, and to the team, successful change will result. Fullan further recommends that leaders must be guided by a purpose and understand the process of change as they develop relationships, create and share knowledge, and build unity.

Group Dynamics and Cohesion

Leadership is impacted by, and impacts, group dynamics and cohesion. Cohesion impacts performance, making it significant in group settings, according to Carron and colleagues. Cohesion is associated with togetherness and is commonly viewed as a dynamic process that reflects the inclination of a group to stay together in pursuit of its goals. Cohesion is defined as a "dynamic process that is often reflected in the tendency for a group to stick together and remain united in the pursuit of goals and objectives." There are several factors that affect cohesion: stability, similarity, size, support, and satisfaction. The duration of time that a group is together composes the stability that influences cohesion. The number of members in the group, and their similarity or diversity also affect cohesion. Leaders' support and encouragement enhances cohesion; and, cohesion is enhanced when members are satisfied with the level of commitment and conformity.

There are two forms of cohesion: social and task cohesion. Social cohesion involves social interaction and reflects the degree of attraction individual members have to one another. Task cohesion revolves around members' commitment to common group goals and refers to the degree to which members work together to achieve these goals. Just as these two types of cohesion can operate independently, groups have varying levels of interdependence. Coactive dependence occurs in groups where tasks have a common external connection, such as a wrestling team. Interactive dependence requires interactions among group members in order to complete the task. As group tasks, interdependence, and cohesion varies, leadership must vary as well.

Leaders should take an active, but not dominating, role in the creation of a team culture. Leaders, and members, should discuss culture and what the team wants as a culture, attending to the foundational values, attitudes and beliefs, individual and team goals, and expectations for behaviors. Developing a group identity in an environment where there is member commitment to common goals fosters pervasive unity. There are many aspects to group dynamics, one being cohesion. Attending to team chemistry fosters cohesion and can yield positive outcomes. The dynamic relationships within the group are important consideration in building group cohesion. Group dynamics reveal the processes within the group. Successful groups have chemistry, which depends on factors such as member characteristics and leadership. Establishing clear goals and attending to each individual member enhances the dynamic of a group, stimulating social and task cohesion, and a shared ethos aids in team building.

Symbolism is a reflection of team culture. Symbolism influences team culture and is manifested through stories and legends, symbols, ceremonies and rites, physical settings, and language. L. G. Bolman and T. E. Deal reframed organizations to include symbolism, which perpetuates culture through purposeful actions that yield common beliefs built through myths, heroes, rituals, architecture, jargon, and sagas that generate pride among team members. For example, the story of a legendary member or achievement can inspire cohesion. A logo or mascot can symbolize and help form a group's identity. A ritual or a specific way of doing an activity may reflect a "superstition" but may also be the ceremonious collective behaviors of a cohesive group. A physical setting (e.g., a stadium) specifically identified with a team can support cohesion. Language such as specific team terminology provides commonality and promotes team culture. There are many strategies that leaders can utilize to address team culture and build cohesion. Leaders must do the following:

- Facilitate open communication among members, seek input in decisions, recognize accomplishments, and actively manage conflicts.
- Include members in developing team goals, thus enhancing collective pride.
- Clarify common behavioral expectations.
- Address each individual's role and acknowledge their importance.
- Meet with members individually and collectively, and foster informal leaders among members.
- Be inclusive in pursuing change.
- Create opportunities for success to build evidence.
- Address the formation of cliques by facilitating both social and task-oriented interaction among members.
- Develop members' perception of ownership in the group by ensuring shared responsibilities for the members in pursuit of team goals.
- Employ leadership styles appropriate for members and situations.
- Build trust and respect among team members.
- Actively attend to task and social cohesion.
- Support member motives.
- Use constructive criticism and avoid personal criticism.
- Get to know the members.
- Assist members in setting appropriate individual goals.
- Include members in the development of rules and procedures.

The more cohesive a team is, the more likely the members will achieve peak performance and the team will reach its potential. Contrary to noncohesive teams, cohesive teams have clearly defined roles and behavioral expectations. They also differ from less cohesive teams through collective goals, cooperative relationships, shared responsibility, respect and trust, commitment to the team, positive communication, pride in membership, and collaboration.

Ensuring that members are aware of their teammates individual goals, and subsequently creating a transparent environment, allows members to support and assist one another, thereby enhancing chemistry. Transparent collaboration diminishes the likelihood of hidden agendas and enhances the alignment of individual and team goals. Pursuit of individual goals should support pursuit of team goals, making actions that are positive for the team, good for the member, and vice versa.

Evaluation of aspects of team chemistry by the members is an accurate way to determine how cohesive a team is. Players' perceptions are their reality and provide insights into the dynamics of the team. Ultimately, successful performance provides evidence that will enhance cohesion and contribute to a positive team culture. Cohesion contributes to increased satisfaction. If members on a cohesive team do not achieve satisfaction as a result of an unsuccessful performance, their cohesion will enhance their ongoing commitment to the group. Cohesion is a dynamic process supporting the development, preservation, and dissemination of team culture. A team's culture is shaped by its dynamics and cohesion, which have the capacity to adapt, change, grow, and improve. Team culture provides the framework for individual or team success. Leaders, members, and teams are simultaneously determinants and beneficiaries of team culture.

Robert E. Baker

See Also: Coaching for Character; Organizational Culture; Team Building.

Further Readings
Bolman, L. G., and T. E. Deal. *Reframing Organizations: Artistry, Choice and Leadership.* San Francisco: Jossey-Bass, 2008.
Carron, A. V. "Cohesiveness in Sport Groups: Interpretations and Considerations." *Journal of Sport Psychology*, v.4 (1982).
Carron, A. V., and P. Chelladurai. "Cohesiveness as a Factor in Sport Performance." *International Review of Sport Sociology*, v.2/16 (1981).
Carron, A. V., M. M. Colman, J. Wheeler, and D. Stevens. "Cohesion and Performance in Sport: A Meta Analysis." *Journal of Sport & Exercise Psychology*, v.24/2 (2002).

Chelladurai, P. *Managing Organizations for Sport and Physical Activity: A Systems Approach.* Scottsdale, AZ: Holcomb-Hathaway, 2009.

Collins, J., and J. L. Porras. *Built to Last: Successful Habits of Visionary Companies.* New York: Harper Business Essentials, 2004.

Fullan, M. *The Six Secrets of Change.* San Francisco: Jossey-Bass, 2008.

Schein, E. H. *Organizational Culture and Leadership.* San Francisco: Jossey-Bass, 2004.

Senge. P. *The Fifth Discipline: The Art and Practice of the Learning Organization.* New York: Doubleday, 1990.

Ticket Operations

Ticket operations is more than just selling tickets to sporting events; it is a year-round operation that requires outstanding leadership. There are a multitude of services offered to season ticket holders and premium seat customers in order to provide a superior level of customer service throughout the year. Some of these services include season ticket and premium seat renewals, seat relocations, ticket transfers, season ticket and premium seat sales, single game and group sales, and allocating and distributing postseason tickets when applicable. In addition, there are a variety of annual challenges experienced by ticket operations leadership, including adequate staffing in-season and during the off-season and enforcing policies and procedures fairly and consistently.

Season Ticket and Premium Seat Renewals

The renewal process for season ticket or premium seat accounts usually begins right after the end of the season. This is done for several reasons. First, ticket offices must know which seats are going to be renewed for the following season before seat relocations, ticket transfers, and single game sales can take place. Second, the sooner the renewal process takes place, the earlier sport organizations have revenue flowing into the organization. Season ticket and premium seat accounts often utilize multiple ticket invoices. Early notification of renewal and multiple invoices allow the annual payment, which is sometimes significant, to be broken down into payments that are more financially manageable. Ticket offices

usually accept a variety of payment methods, sometimes including the establishment of payment plans. Such flexibility is appreciated by fans and helps to increase the annual rate of account renewal.

Seat Relocations

Most sport organizations allow fans to upgrade their seat locations annually at the conclusion of the season ticket renewal process. Available seat locations and nonrenewed seats in the facility inventory are used to allow fans to relocate to areas of their choosing. Fans relocate seats for a variety of reasons, including improved sight lines, seats closer to friends and family, or away from an unfavorable situation. This process can be challenging depending on the number of seats being relocated. The more seats that need to be relocated, the more difficult the relocation process becomes. The order of seat relocations is based on account priority, which is determined by the age of the account. Fans who have been consistent account holders the longest have preference in the seat improvement process. When sport organizations have high renewal rates, fewer seats are available in open inventory. This limits options in the seat relocation process, which can create frustration among fans. Recently, the logistical process of moving seats within a facility has become more user-friendly due to the impact of technology. Once done manually and taking several months, the seat relocation process can now be done in several weeks online. The same software also allows fans to select and secure parking when applicable to the account on land controlled by the sport organization.

Ticket Transfers

Ticket transfers are also completed in the off-season. Unlike many of the other ticketing functions, transfers are not dependent on the renewal process. Transfers are based on existing seats moved from one season ticket account to another, and sometimes to multiple accounts. Seat transfers are typically limited to immediate family members including parents, grandparents, children, and siblings. When transfers include all existing seats going to multiple ticket accounts, it is important to remember that any priority, defined as seniority based on account longevity, associated with the account transferring the seats may be applied to only one account. Any additional accounts involved in the transfer receive new priority on the transferred seats, regardless of seat location. From a leadership perspective, enforcing such a policy is very important. This transfer policy ensures that all account holders are rewarded with a consistent and fair process for managing account priority.

Season Ticket and Premium Seat Sales

When season ticket sales begin, there is a specific process that needs to be utilized to maximize efficiency and be fair to all fans. All new season ticket seat locations should begin in the least desirable sections currently available at the facility. This ensures that any seats open the next year in better locations may be used for the seat relocation process. If this is not done, and fans purchasing new accounts can secure better seats than those with some account seniority, some fans may feel the process is unfair. This process means that new account holders must sometimes start at a higher level of facility and work their way down to better seat locations with the annual seat relocation process.

Individual Games Sales

Leadership is also very important when deciding how to distribute individual game tickets. Single game tickets are defined as all remaining tickets after season ticket sales have taken place and the seat relocation process has been completed. In markets where season ticket sales are below average, creativity may be needed to sell single game tickets. In situations such as this, a variety of promotions may be employed in order to make tickets more attractive to fans. Group sales are a great strategy to sell single game tickets. Less popular games may be paired with games considered "in demand" to boost overall sales. In situations where season ticket sales are strong and single game tickets are scarce, tickets may be distributed in-house or through a secondary ticket agent such as Ticketmaster. In some cases, a guaranteed number of game day tickets must be made available as part of the facility financing agreement between the team and the local city. Such an agreement ensures that all tickets do not end up in the hands of season ticket holders and ticket brokers on the secondary market. Having a guaranteed number of game day tickets available allows the average blue-collar fan, which may not be able to afford season tickets or tickets on the secondary market, an opportunity to purchase event tickets at face value.

Distributing Postseason Tickets

When applicable, the distribution of postseason tickets can be a significant challenge. When held at the respective home arena, the process is relatively simple. However, the process becomes challenging when a limited number of tickets exist for an event held at a different facility. When this happens, seats are typically limited to two tickets per account holder, regardless of the number of seats in the season ticket account. This is done to maximize the number of different account holders who have a chance to attend the event. Account priority dictates who has the best chance of receiving tickets. When demand outweighs the available supply of tickets, a lottery is used to select those who will receive tickets. The older the season ticket account, the better the chance of receiving tickets in the lottery.

Staffing

One of the staffing challenges in ticket operations is the seasonal nature of the business. Ticket offices typically operate with a handful of full-time staff supplemented with part-time workers as needed. While in season or during busy off-season situations, part-time staff may receive a significant number of hours per week. During the rest of the off-season full-time staff can typically handle the workload. This creates a difficult challenge for ticketing leadership. In professional sports, recruiting staff becomes easier due to the lure of being associated with a professional sports team. This can be a double-edged sword since hiring candidates who are "fans" of the team may lead to a lack of productivity. Employees who are fans of the team may spend too much time following the team at the expense of production in the workplace. In general, seasonal staff typically consists of retirees, local college students, and family members looking for a secondary income but with limited hours.

Enforcing Policies and Procedures

Another challenge for ticket office leadership is the enforcement of the organization's policies and procedures in a fair and consistent manner. Ticket operations policies and procedures are not created on a whim, but rather in response to the actions and behavior of fans. The consistent enforcement of policies and procedures by staff protects the sport organization and ensures that all fans are treated fairly, with none having preferential treatment. Sport is a very social activity and fans communicate with each other, especially their frustrations. This is especially true in the current age of social media. The inconsistent application of policies and/or procedures could lead to a backlash by fans, creating a difficult situation for the organization. However, there are times when the appropriate action is to make an exception to policies and procedures. This response is usually based on factors such as safety, circumstances, or intent. Leadership should empower either select staff to make exceptions to policies or procedures when the situation is appropriate.

James T. Reese

See Also: Professional Sports; Ticket Sales: Primary; Ticket Sales: Secondary Market.

Further Readings
Johnson, T. F., and J. T. Reese. "Ticketing." In *Encyclopedia of Sports Management and Marketing*, L. E. Swayne and M. Dodds, eds. Thousand Oaks, CA: Sage, 2011.
Reese, J. T., ed. *Ticket Operations and Sales Management in Sport*. Morgantown, WV: Fitness Information Technology, 2013.
Reese, J. T., M. A. Dodds, and D. L. Snyder. "Fans Apply Full-Court Press Over Reseating Policy." *College Athletics and the Law*, v.6/8 (2009).
Reese, J. T., M. S. Nagel, and R. M. Southall. "Marketing Implications of Ticket Transfers in the National Football League." *Sport Marketing Quarterly*, v.12/4 (2003)..
Reese, J. T., et al. "National Football League Ticket Transfer Policies: Legal and Policy Issues." *Journal of Legal Aspects of Sport*, v.14/2 (2004).

Ticket Sales: Primary

Primary ticket sales refer to those tickets sold by sport organizations and other authorized agents directly to the sport consumer. Authorized agents may include, but are not limited to, retail ticket locations, official team Web sites, or ticket agents such as Ticketmaster, Paciolan, and Turnstyles Ticketing. Primary sales do not include the resale of tickets by brokers, scalpers, or fans in the secondary market. The successful sale and distribution of tickets to sporting events takes more than just opening doors to allow fans to enter facilities; it requires strong planning and leadership.

There are benefits and drawbacks of selling tickets directly through a sport organization, as well as utilizing an authorized ticket agent. Whether tickets are sold in house or through an agent depend on the structure and needs of a sport organization. For example, though season ticket and premium seat sales are still processed in house, many professional sports teams and university athletic departments are beginning to outsource single game ticket sales rather than hiring and training additional employees. One of the benefits of outsourcing single game ticket sales is the efficiency in selling tickets. For example, by outsourcing to an authorized ticket agent, hundreds of phone representatives may be available to process individual orders simultaneously. From a staffing perspective, this is much more financially efficient than having in-house employees working the phones and sales windows at the organization's ticket office. However, there are drawbacks to outsourcing ticket sales. First, the sport organization must pay a fee to the ticket agent for each ticket sold. Second, and most important, the sport organization loses a certain amount of control over customer service since authorized ticket agents are not hired and trained by the sport organization. This can impact the "experience" fans have when purchasing tickets.

Reselling of Tickets by Professional Sports Teams
Many professional sports teams now allow season ticket holders to resell their tickets on the organization's Web site. These sales are not considered transactions in the primary ticket market. Some organizations limit the sale of tickets to face value, while others allow the open market to set the prices. Teams collect a fee or percentage of each transaction for offering the service. By profiting from each sale, the teams have entered, and are now participating, in the secondary ticket market.

Recruiting Sales Associates

Recruiting full-time sales staff is similar to recruiting college athletes or selecting athletes in a professional draft. It is an inexact science. However, just as coaches have metrics to rank athletic talent, sport sales professionals have qualities they look for when recruiting sales staff. Some of those qualities include displaying confidence, the ability to think on one's feet, being personable, and being receptive to sales training techniques, to name a few. Sport sales professionals search for sales talent in a variety of ways. For example, some college and university sport management programs work with professional sports teams and college athletic departments to sell ticket packages as part of the program's curriculum. This provides sport sales professionals an opportunity to evaluate talent before they become employees.

Some professional sports teams, such as the Philadelphia 76ers, have initiated a night sales program to boost ticket sales and prospect for candidates to fill entry sales positions. The 76ers work with local sport management programs, such as Drexel University and Temple University, to recruit undergraduate juniors and seniors interested in breaking into the sport industry through ticket sales. The candidates selected for the opportunity commit to working in the evening several nights per week to sell single game tickets at the 76ers sales office at the Wells Fargo Center. At the conclusion of the trial period,

A ticket for the 2009 Seattle Sounders inaugural soccer match, along with a scarf and pin badge. There are a number of primary ticket outlets around the world where tickets are sold by organizations contracting directly with these outlets to promote their event. (Wikimedia Commons/Dave Nakayama)

those students who perform the best or who show the most potential may be offered at full-time position upon graduation.

Another great location for ticket sales professionals to recruit talent is at the annual University of Mt. Union Sport Sales Workshop in Cleveland, Ohio. The conference is limited to approximately 80 students who travel from across the country to participate. Dozens of sports sales professionals from major league organizations travel to Cleveland and donate their time to interact with and evaluate prospective employees. Students have an opportunity to learn from industry professionals and participate in role-playing exercises designed to evaluate current sales skills as well as sales potential. Many students leave the event with offers for internships or entry-level sales positions in professional sports.

Finally, several secondary training sites such as the Sport Sales Combine or Sport Management Worldwide provide in-depth sales training for those who have completed college but are still interested in breaking into the sport industry through ticket sales. Participants pay a fee to complete the sales training program, which is up to eight weeks in duration and provided by sports sales professionals and other experts with a variety of experience in the sport industry. Many use these training programs as a stepping stool to a ticket sales position in the sport industry.

Sales Training and Motivating Staff

For those that sell tickets in house, proper sales training and employee motivation is crucial to the success of the sport organization. In addition to inside training programs, some leagues, such as the National Basketball Association, provide supplemental sales training support to each of the league's teams. Regardless, being successful in ticket sales takes an incredible amount of commitment, confidence, maturity, and perseverance. Most days are spent on the phone making a minimum of 100 sales calls per day. Sales staff spends the rest of the time with potential clients and role-playing to refine their craft. Sport ticket sales is a very competitive business. Those who generate results are able to move up the corporate ladder quickly with unlimited earning potential.

Due to the repetitive nature of ticket sales it is important for sport leaders to recognize that burnout may also play a factor in employee turnover. Subsequently, sport organizations provide a number of incentives to boost the morale of ticket sales staff and bring out their competitive nature. Incentives include financial rewards, gift certificates, and time off work, to name a few. In 2012 the Philadelphia 76ers purchased the historic hardwood floor from Hershey Park Arena in Hershey, Pennsylvania. On this floor, Wilt Chamberlain scored 100 points for the Philadelphia Warriors on March 2, 1962. The 76ers divided part of the floor into 2-inch-by-2-inch sections, mounted the pieces, and used them to distribute to sales staff that achieved sales goals throughout the year. This is just one of many examples of ways sport organizations can inspire and motivate sales staff.

Pricing Tickets

In no area of direct ticket sales is leadership more important than in ticket pricing. For the most part, gone are the days of uniform, fixed prices for all games in a season. The ticket pricing landscape now includes variable pricing, which includes higher prices for more popular games, and dynamic pricing, which is real-time pricing, similar to what has been used for years by the hotel and airline industries. These new pricing strategies are in response to the need for additional team revenue, as well as the desire to capture a share of the secondary ticket market, an estimated $5 billion industry annually. The key to these new pricing strategies is to maximize revenue based on what the industry will support without alienating fans in the process.

James T. Reese

See Also: Community Engagement for Sports Teams; Ticket Operations; Ticket Sales:Secondary Market.

Further Readings

Paul, R. J., and A. P. Weinbach. "Determinants of Dynamic Pricing Premiums in Major League Baseball." *Sport Marketing Quarterly*, v.22/3 (September 2013).

Reese, J. T. "Sports Organizations Want to Know if You've Got Personality." *SportsBusiness Journal*, v.11/32 (December 8, 2008).

Shapiro, S. L., and J. Drayer. "A New Age Of Demand-Based Pricing: An Examination of Dynamic Ticket Pricing and Secondary Market Prices in Major League Baseball." *Journal of Sport Management*, v.26/6 (November 2012).

Ticket Sales: Secondary Market

There are many different avenues that create the secondary ticket market and it is up to the fan to decide how to go about obtaining the tickets. Whether a father and son grab tickets from a scalper outside of the stadium, a group of friends purchase them on a Web site, or a person buys tickets from a coworker, it all falls under the term *secondary market*. There is a constant battle between the venue and the secondary market because ticket sales bring in a majority of the revenue in the sports industry.

The person-to-person market or the person-to-person style of reselling is exactly how it sounds; a person who possesses tickets and resells them to another. This style dates back to the Roman Empire. Fans who use this form of reselling may or may not know the person, but the end result is to get a good deal. There are times when money is not even exchanged in this style. Businesses who have ticket packages can reward employees with tickets to the big game. Very often one will find ticket scalpers outside of venues claiming that they need tickets even though they possess them. The reason they shout that they need tickets is because it is illegal to say they have tickets they intend to resell within a certain distance.

Forms of Secondary Market Ticket Sales

This style of reselling has exploded in recent years. Avid sports fans can name three or four different Web sites from which they have purchased tickets. A big advantage of this style is the number of Web sites to find tickets. Fans can do their research and check out the prices on StubHub, SeatGeek, Vivid Sports, TicketsNow, TicketCity, Craigslist, and eBay, to name a few. A large part of an account executive's position is visiting fans during game day and discussing how they obtained their tickets. More often than not if they did not purchase directly from the team, they purchase online. These Web sites have become even more dynamic than in the past because they can show users what other sites charge for similar seats. One of the biggest advantages of the online resell is being able to purchase tickets to an event that is sold out.

Ticket brokers are people whose business is the secondary market. Some ticket brokers work directly with sales offices to help them move larger quantities of tickets to games. The benefit for the sales offices is that it is able to hit its numbers, and the broker is able to get good deals and is able to turn a profit. The sports industry is seeing a growing number of teams who use exclusive ticket brokers to help move their inventory to less competitive games. A driving force behind why a ticket broker wants to become exclusive to a team is to work with a franchise, team, or school that does very well in a given sport, meaning the tickets can be priced high.

Advantages and Disadvantages

The secondary market can be very convenient for the fan, which is very important to the buyers. One of the convenient aspects of this market is that the fans can have the tickets right away. Whether they purchase face-to-face or online, they have the tickets immediately following the transaction. Alongside that advantage is the fact that the buyers are able to get event tickets below face value, or get tickets to a previously sold-out event. Even with the size of the secondary market business, there are still fears when using it. Fans will usually pay above face value for the tickets on the secondary market. Another monetary disadvantage would be fees. Buying online sites like StubHub will charge a certain percentage, usually around 30 percent. One of the biggest fears that fans have with the secondary market is the existence of counterfeit tickets. Scalpers are notorious for copying tickets and selling the same seats over and over again—they make money and the fans are denied at the door. Scalpers also purchase youth tickets, which are cheaper to buy and sell them as adult tickets. Venues will allow you to take the ticket and purchase the difference between youth and adult, but it is very inconvenient for the buyer.

Combating the Secondary Market

The secondary market is a $4 billion business; what this means is $4 billion is not being spent at the team box office every year. One of the strategic moves that teams have now made is variable pricing. Variable pricing is the process in which teams set the prices on their games before the season starts based on opponents and days of the week. Dynamic pricing is the in-season version of variable pricing. This is when teams change the prices based on winning or losing streaks, weather, and the opponent's current strength. These are some of the ways to get the dollars that fans spend online and have them spent directly at the box offices. Fans are now taking notice and with the proper research, they will know if they are getting the best deals.

Daniel R. Bartlett

See Also: Economics of Sports; Ticket Operations; Ticket Sales: Primary.

Further Readings

Burgess, Chad. "Guide to the Secondary Ticketing Market." SeatGeak. (August 1, 2012).

George, John. "How The Secondary Ticket Market Earned Legitimacy." *Philadelphia Business Journal* (December 20, 2013).

Servantes, Dan. "Ticketmaster and the Business of Scalping." *Music Business Journal* (October 2013).

Title IX

Title IX of the Education Amendments of 1972 prohibits discrimination on the basis of sex by any educational program or activity receiving federal funding. It was adopted to protect the underrepresented gender and it applies to all levels of education, including primary, secondary, and postsecondary. It also applies to all programs at an educational institution; if any part of the institution receives federal funding, all aspects and programs of the institution must comply with Title IX. Title IX is under the purview of the U.S. Department of Education. Title IX requires that institutions ensure their athletics programs both equally accommodate and equally treat their athletes. Equal accommodation measures whether the athletic participation opportunities at the institution reflect the interests and abilities of both sexes. It looks at both the selection of sports and the levels of competition available. Equal treatment covers the remaining aspects of an athletics program, such as practice time, facilities, and coaching.

Equal Accommodation

Title IX allows an institution to sponsor separate teams for each sex, as long as the team selection is based on competitive skill or the activity involved is a contact sport. The regulations define a contact sport as a sport whose major activity or purpose involves bodily contact. For a noncontact sport, if a school only sponsors a team for the over-represented gender, it may be required to allow members of the underrepresented gender to try out or it may be required to field a team for the underrepresented gender.

In 1979, the U.S. Department of Education released a policy interpretation, which introduced the Three Prong Test. A "Dear Colleague" letter issued by the assistant secretary for civil rights in 1996 furthered clarified the test. An institution does not need to meet all three prongs; as long as they meet one prong, they are in compliance with Title IX.

The first prong states that participation opportunities available to men and women must be substantially proportionate to their respective enrollment in the general student body. If the general student body is 60 percent female and 40 percent male, females must account for 60 percent of athletics participation while males must account for 40 percent. Participation opportunities mean the actual number of student-athletes participating and do not include unfilled roster spots. The Department of Education will consider substantial proportionality to allow for yearly fluctuations in both enrollment figures and in athletics participation. The department will also consider if the number of roster spots needed to achieve proportionality is sufficient to field a team. If they are not, the department will still consider the school in compliance with the first prong.

The second prong requires that an institution show a history and continuing practice of program expansion for the historically underrepresented gender. This expansion should be responsive to the interests and abilities of that gender. The Department of Education will look at the institution's record of expansion and its responsiveness to requests of the underrepresented gender. The agency will also determine if the institution has a plan in place

to continue such expansion in the future. The cutting of an underrepresented gender's team without a plan in place to expand other opportunities will cause the institution to fail this prong.

The third prong states that if an institution cannot comply with the second prong, it must show that it is fully and effectively accommodating the interests and abilities of the underrepresented gender. The Department of Education will look at the interest in a sport, the ability to sustain a team, and the availability of competition in that particular sport. However, the cutting of an under-represented gender's team is generally not allowed. The mere existence of the team can be evidence of the interest and ability. This is the hardest prong to meet; as of 2014, the Department of Education has not given direction on how an institution can determine if it is in compliance with the third prong.

Equal Treatment

Equal treatment of athletes has not received as much attention as equal accommodation, but it is the other main component of Title IX compliance. For equal treatment, the remaining aspects of an athletics program must also be equal. These include the scheduling of games and practices; the provision of facilities, including competition and practice facilities and locker rooms; the opportunity to receive coaching and tutoring; the assignment of coaches and academic tutors; the provision of equipment and supplies, travel and per diem allowance; provision of medical and training facilities and services; provision of housing and dining facilities; and publicity. The Department of Education will compare the treatment received by both genders and an institution will be in compliance with equal treatment if the treatment is equivalent. The department will take into account unique aspects of certain sports, namely football, and if sport-specific needs are met on an equitable basis, the institution will still comply with the equal treatment portion of Title IX.

Impact of Title IX

In the 1971 to 1972 academic year, the last academic year before Title IX, women accounted for 41.8 percent of students enrolled full time at a postsecondary degree-granting institution while men accounted for 58.2 percent. These percentages include students pursuing all levels of postsecondary degrees. In that same year, women accounted for 15 percent of the students participating in sport and recreation programs at colleges, while men accounted for 85 percent. These percentages include students participating in both intercollegiate programs and recreation programs. In the 2012 to 2013 academic year, the latest year for which statistics are available, women accounted for 54 percent of the full-time undergraduate students while men accounted for 46 percent of these students. In that same year, women accounted for 40.9 percent of intercollegiate student-athletes while men accounted for 59.1 percent of intercollegiate student-athletes. These data include information from both two-year and four-year institutions that sponsor intercollegiate athletics.

While the number of women participating in intercollegiate athletics has risen significantly, many college athletic departments are not in compliance with Title IX. Many of these institutions are struggling to meet the needs of the student body and the requirements of Title IX while balancing ever-growing budgetary issues. The easiest prong of the three-prong test to meet is the first prong. Many institutions appear to rely on cutting men's teams, rather than adding women's teams, to meet substantial proportionality. The sport of wrestling has been the hardest hit. Since the 1988 to 1989 academic year, wrestling has suffered a net loss of 108 teams across all three National Collegiate Athletic Association (NCAA) divisions. The statistics do not state the reason the institutions gave for cutting the wrestling teams, but opponents of the legislation blame Title IX. Opponents argue that the economic realities of intercollegiate athletics force a department to choose between men's and women's sports and something has to give and that something is nonrevenue men's sports. Proponents of the legislation argue that the point of Title IX is to raise women's sports to the level of men's sports, not lower the men's sports to the level of women's sports. They also argue that the legislation is not to blame; it is the increased amount spent on football and men's basketball that makes it more difficult to support other men's sports and all women's sports.

An issue intertwined with budget reasons is the role of football in an athletics department. Football is the largest revenue sport and the largest expenditure. It also has the most scholarships and uses the most roster spots. There is no equivalent female sport. Critics of Title IX argue that football should not be included when counting participation opportunities for these reasons. Proponents of Title IX argue that if teams in the National Football League can get by with 53 roster spots, college football teams do not need 85 football players on the roster.

In 2012, the United States celebrated the 40th anniversary of Title IX. In 2014, a women was named a National Basketball Association (NBA) assistant coach and a 13-year-old female baseball player was on the cover of *Sports Illustrated*. While society has come a long way toward gender equality in athletics, sport leaders will need to take it the rest of the way.

Kerri Cebula

See Also: Athletic Directors; Discrimination in Sports; High School Sports; Intercollegiate Sports; National Association of Intercollegiate Athletics; National Collegiate Athletic Association; Sports Law.

Further Readings
Barr, Kerensa E. "Comment: How the 'Boys of Fall' are Failing Title IX." *UMKC Law Review*, v.82 (Fall 2013).
Mitten, Matthew, et al. *Sports Law and Regulation Cases, Materials, and Problems*, 3rd ed. New York: Wolters Kluwer Law & Business, 2013.
U.S. Department of Education. "Clarification of Intercollegiate Athletics Policy Guidance: The Three-Part Test." http://www2.ed.gov/about/offices/list/ocr/docs/clarific.html (Accessed August 2014).
Zimmerman, Jonathan. "Blame Football, not Title IX." *Los Angeles Times* (January 9, 2014).

Top Rank Boxing

Boxing has been considered one of the best sporting alternatives for those who want to improve their coordination. Boxing is not just about becoming the next Muhammad Ali, it can also help athletes become fit.

Top Rank, Inc.

Top Rank, Inc. is a boxing promotion entity based in Nevada that was formed as a partnership between Bob Arum and Jabir Herbert Muhammad. The partnership was incorporated in 1973 and since then has have been at the helm of promoting some of the world's most popular boxers to date. Some of the boxers that have been promoted through Top Rank, Inc. include Muhammad Ali, Oscar De La Hoya, Manny Pacquiao, Floyd Mayweather, Jr., and Sugar Ray Leonard. These are just but some of the popular players who have been represented by the company and the list of boxers is very long.

Top rank boxing once partnered with ESPN Sports, at the time a struggling television network, which enabled boxing enthusiasts to get a weekly dose of boxing entertainment at home. Since then, the cable network built on this and ended up with the most widely and regularly televised boxing series seen on TV since 1964. *Top Rank Boxing on ESPN*, now defunct, was the longest-running cable TV series in the boxing medium.

Robert "Bob" Arum, an American businessman, went on to become one of the founding partners of Top Rank, Inc. By profession, Arum is a lawyer and a boxing promoter. In his career he has served in the tax division of the U.S. Attorney's Office in New York, after which he would venture into boxing. He was more interested in his legal profession and had little interest in boxing until after 1963.

Through his education and business savvy, he became a leading boxing promoter, and in the 1990s his profile became larger after he successfully represented Oscar De La Hoya, Julio Caesar Chavez, and Michael Carbajal. During this time, he became one of the leaders within the sport, rivaling the likes of Don King. Some of the superfights organized under his tenure include Marvin Hagler versus Roberto Duran and Hagler versus Thomas Hearns.

For someone of Arum's profile, controversy never seems to be far away. The first notable controversy in his boxing promotion career was in 1986, when he pitted Hagler versus John Mugabi and Hearns versus James Shuler as a double-header event in Las Vegas. Shuler lost the match in the first round, and later went to Arum's room to thank him for the opportunity to get a bout with Hearns. A few days later, Shuler would be found dead in a motorcycle accident. This would not stop Arum from promoting boxing events, for which he was becoming popular and a force in the industry. He kept building his reputation and with time he would go on to become a leader in the industry. Arum has been more interested in the promotion of Hispanic fights and fighters over the past few years. This is in light of the fact that boxing is considered the most popular sport in the Hispanic community. Most of the events that are hosted by his company are usually concentrated in the southwestern part of the country, with a significant emphasis on the regions that have large numbers of Spanish speakers. He has also diversified to promote events on Telefutura, a Spanish-language network in Spain. For his efforts in championing and promoting sporting events through the years, Arum has been indicted into the International Boxing Hall of Fame.

Recognition of Head Injuries

Top Rank has been supportive of the need to protect its athletes in order to control the threat of injuries caused by head trauma. Top Rank joined fellow boxing promotions group Golden Boy, Viacom media and the UFC mixed martial arts organization to pledge $600,000 to the government and the Cleveland Clinic to study the effects of head trauma on athletes in boxing and related sports. This comes amid concerns over boxers being at risk of developing serious mental conditions and brain deterioration. Top Rank is hoping to use its support of research on head injuries as a means of acknowledging this threat and to take a closer look at what can be done to make the sport safer.

International Boxing Hall of Fame

Many of the boxers who have been promoted by Top Rank have made it into boxing's top hall of fame. The International Boxing Hall of Fame (IBHOF) is a body mandated with honoring boxers, trainers and other individuals who have been significant contributors to the sport of boxing all over the world. Together with the World Boxing Hall of Fame, these are the only bodies that are recognized worldwide in appreciating the efforts of the industry players who are involved in championing the success of boxing.

Every other year ceremonies are held to honor all the members that have been inducted into the hall of fame. Such ceremonies are usually graced by the attendance of former world boxing champions among a host of other luminaries, including Hollywood superstars and boxing celebrities, and at times even political figures.

For professional boxers, it takes five years after they have retired from the sport to be considered as eligible to enter the hall of fame. There are five different categories under which inductees are selected every other year. According to rules that became effective in 2015, the five categories include the following:

- *Modern.* Boxers who have retired and whose last bout took place no earlier than 1989.
- *Old Timers.* The procedures instituted in 2015 divided this category into two subsections: early era, for boxers whose last bout was no earlier than 1893 and no later than 1943; and late era, for those whose last bout was no earlier than 1941 and no later than 1988.
- *Pioneers.* Boxers whose last fight was before 1892.
- *Observers.* Historians, artists, writers, and journalists who have promoted the sport through their line of work.
- *Nonparticipants.* Individuals whose contributions to boxing have been commendable.

The election process is carried out by members of the Boxing Writers Association of America and a host of other international boxing historians. Votes are drawn from Japan, Canada, England, Germany, South Africa, Mexico, the United States, and Puerto Rico. The votes are tabulated by an independent accounting firm, after which the results are presented to the hall. A news conference is held every year in December to announce the new inductees and the induction ceremony is held every year in June.

Michael Fox

See Also: Injury; Media Portrayals, Cable TV; Ranking Athletes.

Further Readings
Heiskanen, Benita. *The Urban Geography of Boxing: Race Class, and Gender in the Ring.* Abingdon, UK: Routledge, 2012.
Iole, Kevin. "Boxing Controversy: Top Rank Dismisses Matchmaker." *Las Vegas Review Journal,* (January 2004).
Margolick, David. *Beyond Glory: Joe Louis vs. Max Schmeling and a World on the Brink.* New York: Vintage, 2006.

Trait Leadership Theory

Effective leadership has been and continues to be a coveted established skill set by practicing leaders throughout history. In an effort to develop effective leadership skills, various leaders and their leadership styles have been examined for decades by a plethora of academics. Unfortunately, the findings of these studies frequently resulted in a vexing conclusion that it was not a simple task to define successful leadership. Researchers often unveiled numerous variables that impacted the leadership scenarios and outcomes. In an effort to offer direction to those seeking leadership advice, researchers throughout the past century have examined leaders from an assortment of approaches. Resulting information has led to development of a number of leadership approaches such as the Trait Approach, Behavioral Leadership, Situational Approach, and a more recently explored methodology of Transformational Leadership. The focus of this article is on the only approach that focuses on the leader and not the followers: the Trait Approach.

Dating back to the 1930s, the Trait Approach was one of the original approaches found in leadership research and literature. The Trait Approach identified the traits that often uniquely defined great leaders when compared to the general population. Because of this, the Trait Approach was often referred to as the Great Man theory. The Trait Approach focused on the qualities that leaders exhibited. Academics interested in these qualities scrutinized people who demonstrated these traits. Distinctly identified leadership traits included intelligence, extraversion, adjustment, dominance, and self-confidence, along with others that referred to a person's physical, intellectual, and personality traits. These characteristics were believed to be those with which a person was born, not traits that that were developed. Many early leadership scholars believed that no matter what the situation, there existed a defined set of characteristics that were found in a successful leader. The general theory behind the Trait Approach was that there existed a causal relationship between personality traits and leadership effectiveness.

Although the Trait Approach initially dominated leadership ideals, it has since experienced a long but inconsistent supportive history by scholars. With an increase of leadership investigations in the mid-1900s, academics studied leadership and expanded on the original Trait Theory Approach. Scholars analyzed the Trait Approach. After further investigation the list of traits was altered to include qualities such as alertness, insight, responsibility, initiative, persistence, self-confidence, and sociability. Other leadership intellectuals modified the list of traits and offered consideration into how each unique trait may be effectively applied within different situations.

A notable 1960s Trait Leadership Approach investigation by Gordon Lippett determined that an individual leader readily employed the methods of confrontation, search, and coping to effectively deal with a prevailing situation. Confrontation involved using a direct method with the people and with the situation necessitating leadership intervention. Effective leaders were not afraid to deal with a situational challenge and the people involved with it. Being able to do this meant commissioning good communication. Second, the method of searching involved leaders who sought an understanding of the people, the situation, and the causes behind the situation. Searching was described as the practice of determining the causes and treating them. Effective leadership research recommendations included examining issues deeper than just the superficial issue symptoms to deeper-rooted causes. This process involved utilizing the five senses while tuning in to others. This highly sensitized practice brought a leader into the situation with constituents and built trust among the parties.

Coping was the third method detailed and it involved realistic leadership, wherein, the leader honestly told people what to do, but did not control or manipulate them. Within the course of coping, problem-solving skills were used along with flexibility and openness to risk-taking. Based on these determinations, Lippett defined traits that were found associated with effective leaders that included the ability to research challenges as they occur (confrontation), communicate and build trust among team members (searching), and determine and employ the necessary decisions for managing tough situations (coping).

Following numerous trait studies completed in the mid-1900s, the ideal trait list was modified to include the following traits: physical vitality and stamina, intelligence and action-oriented judgment, eagerness to accept responsibility, task competence, understanding of followers and their needs, skill in dealing with people, need for achievement, capacity to motivate people, courage and resolution, trustworthiness, decisiveness, self-confidence, assertiveness, and adaptability and flexibility. The 1900s were an eventful time for academics investigating the Trait Approach. These studies resulted in voluminous modifications to the original concepts of the Trait Approach.

Over the last decade researchers have continued to question the leadership trait categories as being too definitive and chose to incorporate the new ideas of an assessment-centered approach and managerial competencies. A proposed multistage model by Janneke Oostrom and colleagues identified specific leader traits that influenced leadership processes and performance more than others and those traits that were easily influenced by the situation. Additionally, the relationships among traits were measured for leadership skills, personality scale scores, leadership experience, and leadership behavior. This research reflected on previous studies that also measured leadership skills. Similar work described the traits of a successful leader to be dependent on the time and the context and to incorporate personal values.

The history behind the evolution of the Trait Approach provided confirmation of continuous scrutiny and transformation. Today the Trait Approach is often supported by the general idea that leaders are gifted people who can do extraordinary things. Contemporary researchers such as Peter

Northouse acknowledge the value of specific traits in an effective leader such as those identified to be intelligence, self-confidence, determination, integrity, and sociability. Interestingly, within this list intelligence is the only trait noted that is innate. Therefore, when striving to develop into a successful leader, one need only to be born intelligent; then, over time, he or she will need to cultivate the other key characteristics. Taking into consideration the lengthiness of this Trait Approach analysis, continued investigation and refinement is recommended. The changing world and expectations on leaders also add to the challenge of defining the Trait Approach.

Conclusion

The Trait Approach, developed in the early 1900s, was considered revolutionary among scholars interested in defining effective leadership. Since that time, academics have continued to examine traits that contribute to the success of leaders. The Trait Approach continues to be referenced in leadership texts and studies today. It is noteworthy to say that there have not been any conclusive findings to support the usefulness of purely focusing on the items involved in the original Trait Approach when establishing oneself as an effective leader. Multiple studies have determined that successful leadership entails being able to effectively meet the needs of the individual and the situation.

Dependent upon the particular situation and the person in charge, the Trait Approach may or may not identify the key characteristics necessary for successful leaders in each unique situation. Researchers have shied away from referring to their conclusions as the Trait Approach. Instead researchers have developed new approaches with which to examine leaders such as transformational leadership and situational leadership. These researchers often defined specific traits as important to effective leadership but included other elements within the context. One can conclude from these findings that the Trait Approach is still a valid approach today, but exactly what traits are on "the list" are being continuously examined, analyzed, and recomposed.

Lana L. Huberty

See Also: Behavioral Leadership Theory; Leadership Skills for Coaches (Amateur Sport); Leadership Skills for Coaches (Professional Sport); Situational Leadership Theory.

Further Readings

Lippitt, G. "The President's Page: Looking at Leadership." *Training and Development Journal* (1969).

Mumford, M. D. *Leadership 101.* Upper Saddle River, NJ: Springer, 2010.

Oostrom, J., et al. "Implicit Trait Policies in Multimedia Situational Judgment Tests for Leadership Skills." *Human Performance*, v.25 (2012).

Zaccaro, S. J. "Trait-Based Perspectives of Leadership." *American Psychologist*, v.62/1 (2007).

Transformational Leadership

Transformational leadership is a process that transforms individuals' commitment to change and improvement in pursuit of organizational goals. It is a style of leadership that can inspire positive changes in members' motivation, morale, and performance. S. R. Covey notes:

> The goal of transformational leadership is to 'transform' people and organizations in a literal sense—to change them in mind and heart; enlarge vision, insight, and understanding; clarify purposes; make behavior congruent with beliefs, principles, or values; and bring about changes that are permanent, self-perpetuating, and momentum building.

Transformational leaders are concerned with organizational outcomes, involved in the process to achieve desired results, and attentive to the needs and success of each group member. They are generally charismatic, visionary, and ardent in inspiring members to evolve in pursuit of common goals. S. Somila, J. Barling, and N. Turner describe the transformational leadership style as framing stakeholder relationships "around a collective purpose in ways that transform, motivate, and enhance the actions and ethical aspirations of followers." Through their personality and shared vision, transformational leaders are able to encourage members' trust and respect and motivate them to alter their expectations and perceptions, resulting in increased commitment to the shared purpose. Transformational leaders offer a vision and promote a purpose that addresses members' intrinsic needs.

Transformational leadership involves weighing members' motives, satisfying their needs, and appreciating their contributions, according to P. G. Northouse. Because leadership is a complex process, it takes mindful determination to employ a transformational style. While there is no single strategy to become a transformational leader, Northouse suggests a transformational leader will (1) empower followers to act to advance the organization, (2) serve as a role model with strong character and values, (3) listen to all viewpoints in developing a spirit of cooperation, (4) create a shared vision in the organization, (5) serve as a change agent by modeling the initiation and implementation of change, and (6) facilitate others' contributions to the organization.

As a pioneer in the conceptualization of transformational leadership, James McGregor Burns did not describe transforming leadership as a set of behaviors, but rather noted that it is a process that "occurs when leaders and their followers raise one another to higher levels of morality and motivation." Bernard M. Bass further developed the concept of transformational leadership, observing that transformational leadership can be measured via the trust, respect, and loyalty that followers have for the leader and its impact on followers' motivation, performance, and satisfaction. Due to followers' trust and respect for the leader, they work harder and perform better. Transformational leaders inspire followers to identify with a shared vision and work toward a common goal that goes beyond their own self-interests. Bass suggested that leaders influence followers by attending to followers' needs, promoting awareness of the significance of their contributions, and fostering their commitment to organizational goals.

While Bass has noted that transformational leadership might be directed toward nefarious ends, Burns suggested that transformational leaders cultivate followers to accomplish these outcomes through processes that are grounded in

fairness. By setting clear goals and aligning individual needs within those goals, transformational leaders guide people toward a broader perspective beyond their own interests. Leaders maintain high expectations. They support and encourage followers and recognize the followers' contributions toward the organizational mission. They inspire and rouse the emotions of followers. In essence, they transform followers through idealized influence, inspirational motivation, intellectual stimulation, and individual consideration, according to Bass. Idealized influence, also known as charisma, is the degree to which followers identify with the leader as a result of the leader's behaviors and personality. Charismatic transformational leaders exhibit conviction in their actions and appeal to followers' emotions. This is related to Covey's concept of principle-centered leadership, wherein the leader articulates strong values and embodies them in actions. The leader serves as a role model and builds bidirectional trust with followers.

Inspirational motivation reflects the degree to which the leader's vision inspires followers. Leaders offering high inspirational motivation have high expectations and challenge followers to achieve. These leaders are optimistic and employ positive communication endorsing future goals. They provide followers with a sense of purpose that enhances their motivation and commitment to act. It is essential that transformational leaders motivating followers through a compelling inspirational vision are effective in being precise, persuasive, inspiring, and empowering in their communication with followers.

Intellectual stimulation occurs when a transformational leader challenges conventional wisdom, encourages follower creativity, and solicits followers' thoughts. These leaders take calculated risks and allow followers to do the same. The transformational leader encourages followers to be innovative in challenging the status quo. These leaders alter the organizational environment to support followers' success. The leaders' vision is the framework through which the followers connect with the leader, the organizational goals, and each other. Followers are likely to be motivated, creative, and committed to achieving the desired ends if they are privy to the big picture and are given the freedom to navigate through and around any roadblocks in pursuit of the vision.

Individualized consideration, or individualized attention, reflects the leader's attentiveness to each follower's needs. Transformational leaders serve as a mentor to the follower, coaching and listening to the follower's concerns. These leaders attempt to meet followers' needs. They respect their followers, which inspires mutual respect. They provide recognition for the contributions of each follower that allows for diversity in followers to be an accepted organizational strength. These leaders meet a variety of followers' needs, including self-actualization. They also encourage the development of leadership among their followers, which stimulates followers' growth and results in high levels of achievement.

Effective transformational leadership, through idealized influence, inspirational motivation, intellectual stimulation, and individual consideration, results in improved performance and satisfaction. Transformational leadership can be contrasted with transactional leadership.

Transactional leadership is based on an exchange process that implies reciprocity much in the way the N. C. Burbules characterized power relationships. Bass noted that transactional leadership is characterized by four characteristics: contingent rewards, active management by exception, passive management by exception, and laissez-faire. The use of contingent rewards is a common element in transactional leadership. Transactional leaders reward efforts, recognize achievements of followers, and promise rewards for good performance. Management by exception can be actively employed to manage both processes and followers. Transactional leaders monitor followers' compliance established rules and standards. The leader pursues any deviation and takes corrective actions to safeguard followers' future acquiescence in following rules within the process. Management by exception can also be passively applied by transactional leaders, wherein the leader intercedes only when followers neither meet established standards nor achieve desired goals. Transactional leaders can also be characterized by laissez-faire tendencies. These leaders avoid making decisions and abdicate their responsibilities. Transactional leadership also differs from transformational leadership in that it is not centered on change. While transformational leaders engage in activities that promote individual and organizational change, transactional leaders act to preserve the existing organizational culture.

Despite the many contradictions that are apparent between the transformational and transactional leadership styles, transformational leadership exists in juxtaposition to transactional leadership. On one side, Burns posited that transformational and transactional leadership styles are mutually exclusive. In contrast, Bass suggested that leaders can simultaneously demonstrate both transformational and transactional styles. Followers' reactions to transactional and transformational leadership may best be understood as a continuum. In a transactional environment, followers are not provided with the purpose of their work, only the rules and standards of performance. They often pursue their work begrudgingly. They do not have a shared vision and are not inclined to be committed to the organizational goals. In contrast, a transformational environment allows followers to be privy to the vision of the leader and cognizant of their own contributions to achieving the goals of the organization. Reflecting their amplified commitment, the followers are willing, even eager, to pursue the shared vision.

Robert E. Baker

See Also: Captains; Command Coaching Style; Cooperative Coaching Style; Development of Leadership Skills; Leadership Models in Sports; Leadership Skills for Athletes; Locker Room Leadership; Trait Leadership Theory.

Further Readings

Baker, R. E. "Effective Strategies for Sport Leaders." Presented at the Meeting of the American Alliance of Health Physical Education Recreation and Dance. Philadelphia, 2013.

Bass, B. M. "From Transactional to Transformational Leadership." *Organizational Dynamics*, v.18/3 (1990).

Bass, B. M. *Leadership and Performance.* New York: Free Press, 1985.

U

U.S. Anti-Doping Agency

Doping and the fight against it are key elements in the sporting world. As pharmaceutical companies and athletes find new ways to enhance athletes' performances, sport organizations must continually find ways to combat the temptation to dope, as well as punish those who do. In the United States, the United States Anti-Doping Agency (USADA) is responsible for the administration and education of doping codes, the testing of athletes, and the enforcement of sanctions. Other countries have their own anti-doping agencies, similar to USADA. The goal is to create a level, fair playing field among all athletes, while protecting athlete rights through the process. To achieve these goals, the USADA has created structures for administration and testing that aim to provide athletes with due process but also address doping issues in as efficient a way as possible.

The United States Anti-Doping Agency (USADA) is the independent, nongovernmental agency responsible for anti-doping enforcement for the Olympic, Paralympic, Pan American, and Parapan American sport movements in the United States. USADA began operation in October 2000 in response to problems with the United States Olympic Committee's (USOC) doping regulation at the time. The USOC Select Task Force on Drug Externalization made the recommendation to create the USADA, with support from Congress and the Office of National Drug Control Policy (ONDCP).

The USADA's role and responsibilities were codified in 2006. The USADA is responsible for the implementation of the World Anti-Doping Code (WADC) and other international standards related to doping in sport within the United States. This implementation includes conducting all aspects of the United States' anti-doping program, including education, testing, adjudication, and the creation of programs, policies, and procedures related to those goals.

The USADA's education activities include providing athletes, coaches, trainers, administrators, and the general public with information about, but not limited to, doping procedures, prohibited substances, and dietary supplements. This information is disseminated in several ways, including in-person training, various written materials, and Webinars and online tutorials.

Board of Directors and Staff

Initially, the USADA board of directors had nine members: two selected by the Athlete Advisory Council (AAC), two selected by the National Governing Body (NGB) Council, and five from outside the Olympic arena. In 2003, the board began electing all of its members while still considering recommendations from the NGB and AAC. Since 2006, the USADA board of directors has consisted of 10 members whose purpose is to support and advise the USADA staff in furtherance of the organization's mission and goals. Members of the board have varied backgrounds, including law, medicine, and education. A number of them have experience with the Olympic and Paralympic movements.

Fifteen men and six women have served on the board of directors during its existence. The chairman of the board of directors in 2014 was Edwin C. Moses. He is the fifth chairman in the board's history and has served as chair since October 2012. Moses is a former Olympic champion and possesses a master's of business administration. He is also the second nonwhite individual to hold the position, having been preceded in this distinction by Lawrence S. Brown. The USADA staff is led by a chief executive officer (CEO) who reports directly to the board of directors. There are also a chief science officer and chief operating officer. Beneath these executive positions are six senior staffers running various departments, including business affairs and finance, communications, legal/results management, operations, science, and doping control officers. In total, over 70 people work for the USADA.

Since its creation, the USADA has had only two CEOs. Terry Madden served for seven years, from the organization's inception until October 2007. He was succeeded by Travis Tygart. Both men possess law degrees and worked as attorneys prior to heading the USADA. During his tenure as CEO, Tygart was responsible for investigating and addressing the Lance Armstrong doping scandal and eventually made the decision to strip Armstrong of all his Tour de France titles and imposed a lifetime ban on the cyclist. This action lead to death threats being made against Tygart in 2013. These threats were investigated by the Federal Bureau of Investigation and two men were ultimately arrested.

Athlete Testing and the Review Board

Testing is done by USADA's doping control officers (DCOs). The DCOs perform both in- and out-of-competition testing, and are involved in actual sampling, as well as the shipping of samples and assisting athletes with paperwork related to the testing. The samples are then sent to one of the 32 accredited laboratories for testing human doping samples. Two of those laboratories are located in the United States: in Los Angeles, California; and Salt Lake City, Utah.

Once an athlete provides a sample, it can take, on average, two to six weeks for the results to be known. If the result is a positive test, approximately another two weeks are needed to analyze the "B" sample. If this result is also adverse to the athlete, then the initial determination is by a review board. The board in each case consists of three members, selected by the USADA CEO from a pre-existing list created by the board of directors. All reviewers serve two-year terms. Each review board must be composed of one expert in each of the following areas: legal, expert, and technical. The review process can take up to a month.

Based on the findings and recommendation of the review board, the USADA will either pursue a doping charge against an athlete or not. If so, the athlete then has 10 days to either accept the sanction or challenge it. If the athlete challenges the finding or sanction, then an arbitration hearing will be held, a process that can take three months or more. Each arbitration panel consists of either one or three arbiters. The arbiters are selected from approved American Arbitration Association (AAA) arbiters who are also members of the Court of Arbitration for Sport (CAS). The losing party then has 20 days to appeal to the Court of Arbitration for Sport, which can also take months to conclude. Athletes may also request that the case go directly to CAS and bypass the first round of arbitration. In total, it can be approximately 11 months from the time an athlete provides a sample to when a final, unappealable decision is rendered.

Genevieve F. E. Birren

See Also: Drugs, Doping; United States Olympic Committee; World Anti-Doping Agency.

Further Readings

"Designation of the United States Anti-Doping Agency." 21 U.S.C. §2001-2003 (2006).

Dziewa, Brian A. "USADA the Unconquerable: The One-Sided Nature of the United States Anti-Doping Administration's Arbitration Process." *St. Louis University Law Journal.* v.58/1 (2014).

Koller, Dionne L. "Does the Constitution Apply to the Actions of the United States Anti-Doping Agency?" *St. Louis Law Journal,* v.50/1 (2005).

U.S. Anti-Doping Agency. "Protocol for Olympic and Paralympic Movement Testing." http://www.usada.org/wp-content/uploads/USADA_protocol.pdf (Accessed July 2014).

Unionization of College Athletes

Since the advent of college sport, athletes have sought to receive appropriate compensation for their labor and protections for the risks they take on the field that threaten their health and safety. With the burgeoning of 24/7 sports television and the expansive multibillion-dollar business opportunities that arise out of the digital age, the college sports of football and men's basketball have become increasingly commercial, lucrative, and open to the opinions of critics who allege that these leagues are part of an unsustainable business model that effectively sets the value of player labor at zero through restrictions on forms of compensation, most notably the athletic scholarship, in violation of U.S. antitrust law.

Defenders of the system as it exists, most particularly the National Collegiate Athletic Association (NCAA) and power conferences (Atlantic Coast Conference, Big Ten, Big Twelve, PAC-12, Southeastern Conference) have attempted to justify these practices by arguing the business may be professional but the players are not, that they are governed by a principle of amateurism, and play as a matter of avocation (a pastime, a recreational pursuit) rather than a vocation (a job). A recent challenge in *O'Bannon v. NCAA* (2014) resulted in a judge ruling that the NCAA's amateurism argument was not a sufficient justification for failing to compensate players in a limited way in accordance with market forces. While that case is currently on appeal, many believe that long-standing assertions that college sports are an amateur endeavor no longer have the resonance they once did and that the college sport industry must change. An issue that has the capacity to clarify how the college sport industry will run in the future is addressing the status of college athletes in the profit sports of football and men's basketball. Are they employees who have the right to organize and collectively bargain? In this article, the origin of the term *student-athlete* and its relevance to the unionization effort of college athletes is examined along with an overview of the Northwestern football team's efforts to unionize in *College Athlete Players Association (CAPA) v. Northwestern University* (2014) and its implications.

The "Student-Athlete"

Despite its familiarity, the term *student-athlete* does not have a benign history. According to Walter Byers, the first executive director of the NCAA, the term was developed to deflect attention away from the fact that college athletes were being paid to play football so as to avoid the consequences of favorable rulings in worker compensation cases. A form of propaganda, as Byers explained in *Unsportsmanlike Conduct: Exploiting College Athletes*, "We crafted the term student-athlete, and soon it was embedded in all NCAA rules and interpretations as a mandated substitute for such words as players and athletes." In effect, the term was adopted to deflect attention away from the fact that athletes were being paid for their athletic services and the relationship they had with programs and institutions was that of an employee.

In the fall of 2013, the quarterback of the Northwestern football team, Kain Colter, along with teammates and football players from Georgia Tech, the University of North Carolina-Chapel Hill, and the University of Georgia staged a series of quiet protests. A few dozen players wrote the initials for the All Players United movement, "A. P. U.," on their wrist tape, a sign of a campaign calling for college athletes to unite for the purpose of advocating for safe playing conditions, better health care coverage, better compensation, and educational considerations. By early January 2014, with college sport authorities offering little in the way of a response apart from a campaign pledging never to support a "pay for play" system, the All Players United movement took to the air, flying a banner that flew over the Rose Bowl in Pasadena during the Bowl Championship Series national championship game. Continuing inertia on the part of NCAA officials, conference commissioners, and institutional athletics administrators was met several weeks later with an announcement that football players at Northwestern University had signed union cards and had filed a petition with the National Labor Relations Board (NLRB) to access their rights to organize and collectively bargain under the College Athlete Players Association.

Upon reviewing the case, NLRB regional director, Peter Sung Ohr determined in March of 2014 that Northwestern University football players were employees under the National Labor Relations Act (NLRA) using the common law test. An employee as defined by the common law test is "a person who performs services for another under contract for hire, subject to the other's control or right of control and in return for payment." Aligning the criteria with the terms and conditions under which Northwestern football players worked, Ohr reached a conclusion that players (1) provided valuable services in support of a football program that generated $235 million for the university between the years 2003 through 2012; (2) were under "strict and exacting control by their employer throughout the entire year," putting in 40 to 60 hours per week at their jobs as football players while being required to follow rules and regulations that were imposed on them and that governed nearly every aspect of their lives; and (3) were sought after, recruited, and compensated because of their athletic talents. Within Ohr's analysis, athletic scholarships were found to serve as a means of economic transfer between the university and the player. The players were determined to be employees of Northwestern who had the right to organize and to collectively bargain the terms and conditions of their employment.

Northwestern University Challenged Ruling in Favor of Players

Northwestern University appealed the ruling with the NLRB National Office, agreeing that the request for review raised substantive issues that warranted closer examination. In response to an invitation for interested parties to submit briefs addressing issues raised in the case, 24 amici briefs were filed. Those supporting Northwestern University (American Council on Education, NCAA, Big Ten and other conferences, for example) took issue with several key aspects of the decision, arguing that athletes are primarily students and not employees. Those supporting the players (professional sport player associations, other labor groups, a group of sport management and sport economics scholars) maintained that NCAA rules have been designed with the express purpose of denying full scholarship athletes their status as workers in order to control player costs and the labor force overall.

Implications

Should the College Athlete Players Association prevail, schools would need to deal with the consequences. While opponents of the idea that college athletes on full scholarship who are connected to a viable market are employees argue that chaos would reign because the NLRA applies only to private institutions, it is likely that NCAA Division I rules would be modified to reflect the ruling.

That said, the path to progress is not as simple as a final ruling in this case. In Ohio, a bill was filed with the state legislature to prevent college athletes from being designated as public employees. In North Carolina, the State Employees Association of North Carolina's governing board voted to allow college athletes to become members of that union a few weeks after the NLRB ruling. And the question of whether all college athletes on scholarship would be considered employees is an open one as well. Samantha Sackos, a former soccer player who played from 2010 through 2014, has sued the University of Houston, claiming that she was owed back pay under the Fair Labor Standards Act. The NCAA appears to be responding to some of these lawsuits with slow adoption of additional compensation above the full cost of attendance and limited placement of athletes within the governance structure with the opportunity to have a voice and vote. Unlike classic employee–employer relationships, however, the absence of a collective bargaining unit has left players vulnerable and typically subject to the control of the power brokers, including coaches, athletics administrators, conference executives, and NCAA authorities.

Ellen J. Staurowsky

See Also: High School Sports; Intercollegiate Sports; National Association of Intercollegiate Athletics.

Further Readings
Byers, Walter. *Unsportsmanlike Conduct: Exploiting College Athletes.* Ann Arbor: University of Michigan Press, 1996.
Ohr, Peter Sung. "Northwestern (Employer) and College Athletes Players Association (Petitioner)." http://www .nlrb.gov/case/13-RC-121359?page=4 (Accessed October 2014).
Sack, Allen, and Ellen J. Staurowsky. *College Athletes for Hire: The Evolution & Legacy of the NCAA Amateur Myth.* Westport, CT: Praeger Press, 1998.
Staurowsky, Ellen J. "The Significance of College Athletes Signing Union Cards." *Huffington Post.* http://www

.huffingtonpost.com/ellen-j-staurowsky/the-significance-of-college-athletes_b_4701486.html (Accessed October 2014).

Staurowsky, Ellen J. "College Athletes in the Age of the Super Conference." *Journal of Intercollegiate Sport*, v.7/1 (2014).

United States Olympic Committee

The United States Olympic Committee (USOC) is one of the most important, if not the most important, sport organizations in the United States. Since 1894, it has overseen the development and promotion of physical fitness, sent athletes to the Olympic and Paralympic Games, and overseen national governing bodies (NGBs) of particular sports. Because of its significance not only in the United States but also worldwide, it is important to know the mechanisms within the organization: its leadership, structure, administration, financing, and operations. Awareness of those mechanisms will enable one to better understand the world of sport, sport organizations, and the culture within them. The fact that the United States does not have a sports ministry, as is often seen in other countries, makes the USOC an even more interesting organization.

The USOC was founded in 1894 as the American Olympic Association. In 1940, the name was changed to the United States of America Sports Federation, and five years later in 1945 the name was changed again to the U.S. Olympic Association. In 1950, the organization was awarded its nonprofit status and in 1961 the name was changed for the last time to its current name: the U.S. Olympic Committee. Interestingly, the USOC is one of the four National Olympic Committees that has a dual role and also serves as the National Paralympic Committee. In 1978, the Amateur Sports Act (revised in 1998 and now known as the Ted Stevens Olympic and Amateur Sports Act) appointed the USOC as the main body responsible for overseeing all Olympic-related athletic activities in the United States. Since then, the USOC has coordinated the sports included in the Olympic, Paralympic, PanAmerican and

ParapanAmerican Games programs, as well as promoting physical fitness and participation in sport activities. Another primary responsibility is generating resources to support its mission and supervising distribution and effective use of such resources. The act also granted the USOC the authority to recognize National Governing Bodies of particular sports (currently 46).

Currently, the USOC's headquarters is in Colorado Springs, Colorado. The organization manages three Olympic Training Centers located in Colorado Springs, Colorado, Chula Vista, California, and Lake Placid, New York. As of 2013, the training sites served an average of 22,000 athletes. The organization is also working with 16 National Training Sites, located in 13 states across the United States.

Leadership and Structure

The USOC is governed by the board of directors, consisting of 16 members, and professional staff under the guidance of the chief executive officer (CEO). There are three councils that provide opinions and advice to the board and the USOC staff: (1) the Athletes' Advisory Council, (2) the NGB Council, and (3) the Multi-Sport Organizations Council.

Although the USOC is now considered a model organization, this has not always been the case. A congressional hearing was held in 2003 regarding whether the organization's structure might be impeding its mission. This was closely related to the Salt Lake City and Atlanta Olympic Games bid scandals. Members of the USOC staff were also accused of mismanagement, lack of focus, wastefulness, and mistreating athletes. There was also an ethical concern regarding USOC's CEO Lloyd Ward, who allegedly lobbied for his brother's company to secure Olympic-related business. As a result, a major restructuration of the organization occurred. The organization's top executives resigned from their positions, such as CEO, chief operations officer, marketing director, president, and ethics compliance officer. The board of directors was also reduced from 124 to 11 members. The changes also included reducing expenses and increasing athletes' NGB funding, beginning the "Athletes First" philosophy.

More turmoil occurred in 2009, after the organization's CEO, Jim Sherr, resigned. It is believed that

Sherr's resignation came about as a result of Chicago's Olympic bid, as it failed to receive expected support. The relations between the USOC and the IOC begin to worsen. An emphasis was also put on the lack of Paralympic success. The USOC's board of directors appointed the advisory committee to evaluate the board. In its report in March 2010, the advisory committee suggested that the board of directors should increase the number of members from 11 to 15, which is what eventually happened in late 2010.

Budget, Finances, and Marketing

The USOC creates its budget in four-year increments, reflecting Olympic Games preparation period, called quadrennium (i.e., 2005–08, 2009–12). Olympic years see USOC's budget double compared to non-Olympic years (revenues of $140.7 million in 2011 compared to $338.3 million in 2012; expenses $185 million in 2011 compared to $247 million in 2012). According to the "Athletes First" philosophy, in 2013, the USOC devoted 93 percent ($182 million) of its expenditures to support Team USA athletes. Around 40 percent ($73 million) of those expenditures were athletes' direct grants ($22 million), as well as NGBs and Olympic and Paralympic movement support ($51 million). The rest of USOC's expenditures (7 percent) covered administrative costs.

The USOC has a very impressive portfolio of marketing partners. Besides 11 worldwide Olympic sponsors, the USOC is working with 25 domestic partners, among them 24 Hour Fitness, Adecco, Airweave, AT&T, BMW, BP, Budweiser, Chobani, City, Deloitte, DeVry University, Highmark, Hilton Hhonors, Jet Set Sports, Kellogg's, Liberty Mutual, Nike, Oakley, Ralph Lauren, Smucker's, Ameritrade, The Hartford, USG, and NBC as a broadcast partner.

Regarding its fundraising initiatives, the USOC has an excellent development program. Its famous slogan, "America does not send athletes to the Olympics, Americans do," is used to solicit both smaller donations and major gifts. In 2013, the USOC had 44 donors who donated $100,000 each. The U.S. Olympic and Paralympic Foundation was established in 2013. The U.S. Olympic Foundation, created after the 1984 Olympic Games in Los Angeles, oversaw the money raised in the 1980s, without raising new funds. Fundraising was therefore USOC's responsibility. The professional team of 20 employees was securing $17 million per year in donations. With the new foundation, the goal is to increase fund-raising to $50 million per year.

USOC in Community

The USOC is creating and engaging itself in many community initiatives, such as Olympic Day, Community Olympic Development Programs, Warrior Games, Team for Tomorrow, and more. The organization also puts an emphasis on education by offering a Safe Sport program. Its goal is to prevent misconduct in sport and enable the members of sport communities to recognize, reduce and respond to such behaviors. The USOC has recognized sexual abuse, bullying, harassment, hazing, and emotional, physical, and sexual misconduct as threats, and is devoted to fighting them by providing relevant information, resources, and training to reduce abuse in sport.

Kasia A. Michalska

See Also: International Olympic Committee; Organizational Culture; Organizational Leadership; U.S. Anti-Doping Agency.

Further Readings

Abrahamson, Alan. "USOC Waiting for the Other Shoe to Drop." *Los Angeles Times* (March 7, 2003). http://articles.latimes.com/2003/mar/07/sports/sp-usoc7 (Accessed August 2014).

Associated Press. "USOC Adds Five New Board Members." http://sports.espn.go.com/oly/news/story?id=5927631 (Accessed August 2014).

Hersh, Philip. "McCain Calls USOC Hearing." *Chicago Tribune* (January 24, 2003). http://articles.chicagotribune.com/2003-01-24/sports/030124 0390_1_usoc-general-counsel-energy-management-technologies-lloyd-ward (Accessed August 2014).

Mickle, Tripp. "USOC Plans Foundation for Fundraising." http://www.sportsbusinessdaily.com/Journal/Issues/2013/04/08/Olympics/USOC.aspx (Accessed August 2012).

U.S. Olympic Committee. "Report of the United States Olympic Committee's Independent Advisory Committee on Governance." (March 26, 2010).

Women: Equal Pay

Sport is but one occupation in America where women do not receive compensation equal to that of their male peers. Over the course of the last 60 years, there have been several attempts to increase the level of equality related to pay in the workplace. There have been several pieces of legislation aimed at enhancing diversity and equity in pay including Title VII of the Civil Rights Act of 1964, The Equal Pay Act (1963), Title IX of the Educational Amendments of 1972, and the Lilly Ledbetter Equal Pay Act of 2009.

- Title VII of the Civil Rights Act of 1964 prohibits the discrimination of applicants and employees on the basis of race, color, religion, sex, and national origin. The law also prohibits employers from retaliating against applicants or employees who asserts his or her rights under the law associated with job discrimination matters.
- The Equal Pay Act (1963) prohibits the payment of different wages to men and women when conducting equal work in the same worksite. This law also protects individuals form retaliative measures akin to the protections of Title VII.
- Title IX of the Educational Amendments of 1972 is landmark legislation that prohibits discrimination based on gender in school settings that receive federal funding—whether for academics or athletics. Title IX states: "No person in the U.S. shall, on the basis of sex be excluded from participation in, or denied the benefits of, or be subjected to discrimination under any educational program or activity receiving federal aid."
- The Lilly Ledbetter Equal Pay Act was signed into law by President Barack Obama in 2009. The aim of the legislation is to close the pay gap between men and women in the United States. Currently, women earn just 77 cents to the dollar as compared to men completing the same work.

While these pieces of legislation have helped decrease wage disparity in the workplace, progress still needs to be made to realize equality in the workforce.

Wage Disparity in Professional Sport

There have been a number of studies that have examined pay within professional sport to determine whether athlete pay is tied to winning percentages, overall team revenue, and other variables. While these studies have produced conflicting findings, it is possible to draw broad conclusions about the lack of pay equality within professional sport in connection with gender.

With smaller roster sizes than those in the National Football League (NFL) or Major League Baseball (MLB), players in the National Basketball Association (NBA) typically earn high salaries. There are, however, significant inequalities in the salaries paid to players within the NBA. The distribution of wealth became more extreme following the collective bargaining agreement (CBA) introduced in 1995. The CBA increased the team payroll cap by 45 percent and restricted free agency. Various modifications have been made to the CBA since 1999. The result has been that teams recognizing the power of a star player to sell tickets and garner media attention have chosen to spend lucratively on one high-profile athlete and filled remaining roster spots with less talented, more affordable athletes. The result of the CBA was more lucrative salaries for the top 15 percent of star players in the league, and a larger number of men earning the league minimum. Interestingly, studies have determined that teams with a greater level of salary disbursement do not win more games.

The female counterpart league for the NBA is the Women's National Basketball Association (WNBA). This league was started by the NBA and has continued its association since its development. While the WNBA has sustained itself longer than many naysayers thought it would, and has positioned some of its more notable stars to gain further media attention and recognition as visible sport personalities, the compensation of the league's athletes lag far behind that of their NBA counterparts. The minimum salary for a WNBA player is $37,950, with an average player salary of approximately $72,000. Brittney Griner, the first overall draft pick for the WNBA in 2013, signed a contract worth just over $49,000. As a point of comparison, an NBA veteran with a few years of tenure would have a guaranteed minimal contract that would be equal to an entire team payroll for a WNBA squad. Many stars in the WNBA elect to compete abroad, where salaries are lucrative in comparison. For example, Griner earns over $600,000 to compete in China during the WNBA off-season.

Professional Tennis

The aforementioned examples of pay inequality focused primarily on men's teams. This is due primarily to the financial viability of men's professional sport and the importance each league plays in society. Women's professional sport has not been nearly as successful. The majority of professional leagues established for women over the course of history have failed. However, an area of interest to look at is meritocratic sports. Meritocratic sports are those in which earning status is determined by achievements. This notion is particularly relevant in the sport of women's tennis. Women's tennis has proved to be the most profitable professional sport, primarily due to its commercial appeal, global marketability, and established history. In 2007, arguably the most high-profile Grand Slam tennis event, Wimbledon, offered equal prize money to men and women, a first in modern sport history. Further, of the top earners in women's sport, four of the top five come from the sport of tennis.

Despite the financial success of women's tennis, there is room for improvement. Men still earn approximately $200,000 more than their female counterparts in annual prize money. Top earners in men's tennis earn on average $2.5 million more over the course of their careers. Scholars attribute the discrepancy to the fact that men's tennis players have to "work" more because they play seven sets compared to five played by women. Another popular argument in support of the skewed prize money is that men's tennis attracts more television viewers and thus more commercial sponsorship dollars. This defense has been refuted by studies documenting that for many tournaments, television ratings for women's events are actually stronger than men's.

Women competing at the professional level in golf in the Ladies Professional Golf Association (LPGA) are also paid far less than their male counterparts playing in the Professional Golf Association (PGA) tour. Total prize money for LPGA events totaled approximately $50 million, whereas men on the PGA tour competed for purses totaling $256 million, more than five times the total prize money available to women.

Gender and Wage Inequality in the National Collegiate Athletic Association

The previously mentioned examples shed light on the comparative platform for compensation in major professional sports. The subsequent section will address aspects associated with intercollegiate athletics. The battle over gender and wage equality has been fought in various forms. This has included female coaches suing over disparate compensation (i.e., the pay levels of a male Division I men's basketball coach compared to that of a male Division I women's basketball coach). For example, top-paid men's collegiate coaches are paid several-million dollars under annual contacts, and literally dozens of Division I coaches in major college football and major college basketball earn more than $1 million per year. At the same time, the average salary of coach for a women's team is commonly a fraction of the top-earning male coaches. It is important to note that salaries paid to Division I head coaches can far outweigh the compensation of other high-ranking officials such as university presidents and head athletic directors.

Elizabeth A. Gregg
Jason W. Lee

See Also: Discrimination in Sports; Economics of Sports; Gender and Sports Leadership.

Further Readings
Berri, David J., and R. Todd Jewell. "Wage Inequality and Firm Performance: Professional Basketball's Natural Experiment." *Atlantic Economic Journal*, v.32/2 (2004).
Borghesi, Richard. "Allocation of Scarce Resources: Insight From the NFL Salary Cap." *Journal of Economics & Business*, v.60/6 (2008).
Eitzen, D. Stanley. *Fair and Foul: Beyond the Myths and Paradoxes of Sport*, 5th ed. Lanham, MD: Rowman & Littlefield, 2012.
Flake, Colin R., et al. "Advantage Men: The Sex Pay Gap in Professional Tennis." *International Review for the Sociology of Sport*, v.48/3 (2012).
Hattery, Angela J. "They Play Like Girls: Gender and Race (In) Equity in NCAA Sports. *Wake Forest Journal of Law & Policy*, v.2/1(2012).
Simmons, Rob, and David J. Berri. "Mixing the Princes and the Paupers: Pay and Performance in the National Basketball Association." *Labour Economics*, v.18/3 (2011).

Women's Leadership in Sport

Although women have always played a role in sport, historically it was often a very limited role. Women's participation in sport increased dramatically and steadily with the implementation of Title IX in 1972, but growth has been much slower for women in leadership positions. Although some organizations, like the Women's National Basketball Association (WNBA), have included a significant number of women in leadership positions, other sport settings like college athletics include relatively few women at the decision-making levels. It is important to consider women's contribution to sport leadership because women and girls now make up almost 50 percent of the athletes at many levels.

Historical Perspective: The 1800s
In the mid-1800s, concern was raised over the lack of physical activity afforded to women and the potential impact this was having on their health. In response, several women's educational institutions began to prioritize exercise. Catherine Beecher, founder of the Hartford Female Seminary in Connecticut, was one of the earliest and most influential women in this regard. Beecher not only implemented a rigorous program of exercise and sport for her students, she also authored a book, *Physiology and Calisthenics for Families* (1856), that was then used at several other premier women's institutions of the day including Mount Holyoke Seminary in Massachusetts. In 1892, Senda Berenson, an instructor at Smith College in Massachusetts, brought basketball to women as the first women's team sport to be played in the United States. Berenson proceeded to alter the original rules of basketball to better suit women; she is known as the Mother of Women's Basketball and was admitted to the Basketball Hall of Fame in 1985. Berenson is also credited with bringing field hockey to American women from Europe and adapting volleyball for women.

By the 1890s, women were employed to be physical education instructors in most U.S. high schools and universitie,s but the role included working only with female students. During this same time period women's basketball games between universities began to occur, with female physical education instructors serving as coaches.

The 1900s
By the 1920s, women's physical education departments grew significantly and were led by women who gave instruction in sport and led intercollegiate

contests. "Play days" with three or more schools were a popular event for girls in both high school and college. During play days, instead of competing for one's school, the athletes were split up and played on mixed teams. Popular sports were basketball, golf, tennis, gymnastics, and swimming. However, as female athletes increasingly sought out more competition, many women physical educators were concerned about the masculine nature of what they felt to be a "male model" of athletics. The Committee on Women's Athletics (CWA), which was founded to exercise control over school and college sport for females, was determined to prevent women's sport from taking on the negative characteristics they associated with men's sport. To this end, the CWA fought to limit travel, publicity, and awards. Instead of focusing only on elite athletes, the CWA advocated for more opportunities for the majority of women and girls. During this time, however, the Amateur Athletic Union (AAU) attempted to collaborate with the CWA in order to expand its offerings to female athletes. The CWA refused because they felt they could better prevent women's athletics from going in a negative direction like men's sport. Additionally, the AAU was run by men and the CWA strongly felt that women should remain in control of sport for females. However, the AAU represented the United States in international sport at that time and female athletes were beginning to show strong interest in international and Olympic competition. By the 1940s, the AAU successfully claimed jurisdiction over several women's sports that expanded regional, national, and international competition for women in these sports but took some control away from women leaders.

From 1940 to 1960, attitudes began to shift regarding the appropriateness of serious sport for women and competitive varsity sport steadily overtook the "play day" model in many high schools and universities. However, the Division for Girls and Women's Sports (DGWS), which was formerly the CWA, insisted that women remained in the coaching and officiating roles. In the 1960s, a motivated group of women physical educators sought to develop competitive intercollegiate sport for women, but there was still a desire to maintain separation from the men and the commercialization that had already infiltrated men's college athletics. This

group formed a sub-unit of the DGWS to oversee women's college sport: the Association for Intercollegiate Athletics for Women (AIAW).

In 1971, the AIAW began to oversee women's college sport and the first college athletic scholarships were given to women shortly thereafter, but women's athletic departments continued to operate separately from men's athletic departments. Because of this separation, women held 90 percent of the coaching and administrative positions in women's athletic departments. The AIAW membership quickly grew to more than 900 universities, and there were championships in 19 different sports for women. However, the National Collegiate Athletic Association (NCAA), which had been governing men's college sport since the 1920s, soon questioned the necessity for a separate governing body for women's sport. By 1982, the NCAA was successful in taking over women's collegiate sport and the AIAW was disbanded. This takeover was the result of two factors: (1) the NCAA had greater resources for providing television coverage of championships, and (2) the passage of Title IX necessitated men's and women's collegiate athletic departments to merge. Although these events led to many more opportunities for female college athletes, women would no longer be in the majority in the leadership roles.

Impact of Title IX

Title IX of the Educational Amendments was passed in 1972 and mandated that women and girls be given equal access and equivalent treatment in sport. This legislation led to a massive expansion in women's athletic teams and a huge increase in participation by female athletes; in 2014, there were 200,000 female intercollegiate athletes compared to only 32,000 in 1970. High school sport participation increased from 294,000 female athletes in 1970 to 3.2 million in 2014.

However, it is important to note that Title IX applies only to participants and not to employees. Shortly after Title IX was enacted, many of the existing female leaders lost significant power in sport. Because Title IX mandates gender equity in all educational activities (including sport), physical education classes and athletic departments became coeducational and in many cases the male coaches and administrators took charge of the newly joined departments. The women who previously led the women's departments were relegated to lower-level positions. Even though there were many new women's teams created, female coaches now had to compete with men for these positions; men's interest in coaching women's teams was much greater than it had been before Title IX, when women's athletic departments were separate from men's. As a result, while women coached and oversaw 90 percent of women's teams in 1970, this number has rapidly declined and has been low ever since.

Modern Leadership

College. In 2014, only 22 percent of athletic directors were women, which is important to consider because women now make up 57 percent of the students on college campuses. Division III schools are more likely to have female athletic directors (30 percent) but they are also smaller, less prestigious athletic programs. Athletic departments that compete at the highest level, the Football Bowl Championship Series (BCS), have the fewest women athletic directors at only 6 percent in 2013. In an attempt to involve more women at the decision-making level of college athletics, in 1992 the NCAA began requiring that each athletic department create a senior woman administrator (SWA) position. The SWA was designated as the highest-ranking woman in the department but it was not intended for the SWA to oversee only women's sports. The SWA position has not proven effective at increasing the overall number of women in athletic administrative positions. However, from 2013 to 2014, several women become athletic directors for major Division I athletic programs for the first time.

Currently, 43 percent of collegiate head coaches are women. Women's college basketball is the most popular sport for women and it is also more likely to have a female head coach at 60 percent—other sports with higher percentages of female coaches are field hockey, lacrosse, and softball. Along with having more female athletic directors, Division III schools also tend to employ more women coaches, with 47 percent of their women's teams having female coaches. Today, the largest group of women employed in college athletics works as assistant coaches at 7,503. In 2014, this represented 56 percent of the assistant coaches for women's teams. The

high numbers of female assistant coaches seem to be encouraging because head coaches most often rise from the rank of assistant coach.

High School. Overall, the statistics for women coaching in high school are similar to college coaching. Across the United States in 2010 women coached 40 percent of girls' high school teams, however in basketball only 28 percent of the coaches are women. Because basketball is the most popular sport for women, it is also the most prestigious girls' sport and thus problematic that so few women are involved in its leadership. Additionally, while the overall percentage of female high school coaches is 40 percent, there are currently 12 states where only 20 percent of the coaches are women.

Pro Sport. In the United States and Canada professional sports teams generally involve very few women in leadership positions. The Women's Basketball Association (WNBA) includes the most women in decision-making positions with 40 percent female head coaches in 2014. In administrative leadership the WNBA had a female league president in 2014 and four teams had female general managers. Among men's professional sports, baseball and basketball lead the way in regard to employing women in decision-making roles. While there are no women in head coaching positions in Major League Baseball (MLB), there are 24 female vice presidents, one female head athletic trainer, and one female strength and conditioning coach. The National Basketball Association (NBA) employs two women as team presidents and 18 women as vice presidents. The NBA has also employed four different women as officials since 1997, with one female official remaining as a regular season referee in 2014.

Women also hold leadership positions with individual professional sport organizations. In tennis, Billie Jean King was a leader in pursuing gender equality in sport. In the 1970s, King's efforts started the first women's professional tennis tour in the United States and she founded the Women's Tennis Association (WTA), the international organizing body for women's professional tennis. Additionally, King insisted that tennis tournaments provide equal prize money to both male and female winners; today, tennis is one of only two sports (the other is running) to pay male and female athletes equally. Today however, while the WTA's chief executive officer (CEO) is a woman, only two other women sit on the WTA's 10 member board of directors. In golf, the Ladies Professional Golf Association (LPGA) was founded in 1950 by a group of 13 women golfers. In 2014, the LPGA was led by a male commissioner, with three women on the six-member board of directors.

Olympics. Even though women have been included as participants in the Olympic Games since 1900, the Olympic movement has been slow to include women in leadership roles. Initially women made up only 2 percent of the participants in the Olympics, but this rose steadily and in the 2012 London Olympics women composed 44 percent of the athletes. The International Olympic Committee (IOC), however, remained a male-only organization for nearly 100 years. The first women to serve on the IOC were Flor Isava-Fonseca of Venezuela and Pirjo Haeggman of Norway in 1981. As of 2014, this number increased to 24 but this represents only 22 percent of the IOC membership. Additionally, it was not until 1990 that a woman served on the IOC executive board (Isava-Fonseca), and in 2013 there were only four women serving on the 15-member executive board of the IOC. In an attempt to remedy the low representation of women in the Olympic movement, the IOC has mandated that all sport bodies involved in the Olympic movement (e.g., National Olympic Committees [NOC], International Sport Federations [IF]) include at least 20 percent women in decision-making positions. Small progress has been made through this IOC initiative, and in 2014 there were 11 NOCs (out of 204) with female presidents. Overall though, this objective has not been met, but the IOC is dedicated to improving gender equity in sport leadership and continues to make this a point of emphasis.

Women Coaching Men

Even though it is customary to see male coaches of women's teams, female coaches of men's teams remain extremely rare, at about 3 percent. When women do coach male athletes they are often in sports where the men and women train together like cross-country, track and field, swimming and diving, and tennis. On the other hand, many men coach women's teams, including coaches Geno Auriemma of the University of Connecticut women's basketball team and Anson Dorrance of the University of North Carolina women's soccer team. While there are currently no women who are head coaches of any high-profile men's teams, in 2014 the San Antonio Spurs of the NBA hired Becky Hammon, a former WNBA player, to be the league's first female assistant coach. In addition, in 2014 the NBA players' association hired their first female director, Michele Roberts.

Important Organizations in Women's Sport Leadership

Listed below are organizations that are important in advocating for women's representation in sport leadership. Web sites are also listed for each organization.

- The National Collegiate Athletic Association (NCAA): The NCAA mandates that each member school designate a female administrator in the SWA role. The NCAA also encourages member schools to achieve gender equity and publishes gender equity reports. *www.ncaa.org*
- The National Association of Collegiate Women Athletic Administrators (NACWAA) is dedicated to empowering, developing, and advancing the success of women in college athletics. NACWAA provides education, training, and networking for women who desire careers as college athletics administrators. *www.nacwaa.org*
- The National Women's Law Center provides education on Title IX, information on recent Title IX court cases, as well as support for filing such claims. *www.nwlc.org/our-issues/ education-%2526-title-ix/athletics*
- The Women's Sports Foundation (WSF) was founded in 1974 by tennis legend Billie Jean King. The WSF is an educational organization dedicated to "advancing the lives of girls and women through sport and physical activity." In order to encourage girls and women to be active, the WSF provides grants to programs that encourage activity among girls and celebrates the accomplishments of female athletes. *http://www.womenssportsfoundation.org*

- The American Association of University Women (AAUW) analyzes issues of gender equity on college campuses and provides education programs to assist women in becoming leaders on college campuses. *www.aauw.org*

In addition, many women's sports have associations for coaches that provide education, support, and networking. Examples include the following:

- Women's College Basketball Coaches Association (WBCA) *www.wbca.org*
- Intercollegiate Women's Lacrosse Coaches Association (IWLCA) *www.iwlca.org*
- National Fastpitch Coaches Association (softball) *www.nfca.org*
- National Field Hockey Coaches Association (NFHCA) *www.eteamz.com/nfhca*
- Women's Golf Coaches Association (WGCA) *www.wgcagolf.com*

Rachel M. Madsen

See Also: Athletic Directors; Coaching Women; Gender and Sports Leadership; High School Sports; Intercollegiate Sports; Sociology of Sport; Title IX; United States Olympic Committee (USOC), Women: Equal Pay.

Further Readings

Acosta, R. V. and L. J. Carpenter. "Women and Intercollegiate Sport, a Longitudinal,

Costa, S. D. and S. R. Guthrie. *Women and Sport: Interdisciplinary Perspectives.* Human Kinetics: Champaign, IL, 1994.

Lavoi, N. M. "One Sport Voice: A Critical Commentary on All Things Sport" (2013). http://www.nicolemlavoi.com (Accessed August 2014).

National Study: Thirty-Seven Year Update." West Brookfield, MA: The Project on Women and Social Change of Smith College and Brooklyn College of the City University of New York, 2014.

Title IX of the Educational Amendments, 20 U.S.C. §1681 (1972).

University of Central Florida Institute for Diversity and Ethics in Sport. "Racial and Gender Report Card" (2013). http://www.bus.ucf.edu/sportbusiness/?page=1445 (Accessed August 2014).

World Anti-Doping Agency

The challenge of athlete doping and how to detect it has plagued sports for many years. In recent years, pharmaceutical companies and athletes have found new ways to enhance athleteic performances, and in response sport organizations must continually find ways to combat the temptation to dope, as well as punish those who do.

The World Anti-Doping Agency (WADA) was created to address this specific issue in sport. WADA established the World Anti-Doping Code and other international doping standards, and currently provides the procedures that national anti-doping organizations (NADOs) must follow. It also provides education regarding doping to both athletes and sport organizations, as well as performing research into doping. The agency also performs investigations and address issues involving the trafficking of doping items and paraphernalia. Last, WADA manages anti-doping activities on a global scale and oversees the accredited doping laboratories.

WADA History and Purpose

The World Anti-Doping Agency is an independent, nongovernmental agency responsible for anti-doping enforcement and management for the Olympic and Paralympic movements, as well as other sport entities. It began operation in November of 2001, a result of the International Olympic Committee (IOC) convening the First World Conference on Doping in Sport in February 1999. This conference was convened after a doping scandal emerged in the 1998 Tour de France and consensus began to build that an independent body with uniform standards was needed to oversee doping on a global scale. WADA adopted the World Anti-Doping Code (WADC) in 2003 and it went into effect in 2004.

WADA is responsible for the implementation of the World Anti-Doping Code and for updating other international doping policies, such as the Banned Substance List. This implementation includes monitoring code compliance, cooperating with law enforcement, anti-doping development and coordination, education, athlete outreach, and science and medicine.

Foundation Board and Executive Committee

The foundation board is the top decision-making authority for WADA. It consists of 38 members, with 18 representatives each from governments and the Olympic movement. The governmental members are selected by the governments within each of five Olympic regions per the International Intergovernmental Consultative Group on Anti-Doping in Sport Meeting in May 2001. The five regions and their respective number of members on the Foundation Board are the Americas and Asia (with four members each); Europe (five members); and Oceania (two members), and Africa (three members).

The Olympic members are appointed from a variety of groups. The IOC, the Association of National Olympic Committees (ANOC), and the IOC Athletes Commission each appoint four members. The Association of Summer Olympic International Federations (ASOIF) appoints three members and the Association of International Olympic Winter Sports Federations (AIOWSF), International Paralympic Committee (IPC), and SportAccord (an association of international sport federations) each appoint one member. The final two members of the foundation board are the president and vice president of the board, selected by the board members. The president and vice president cannot both be Olympic or governmental and the roles are alternated between the two groups.

The WADA executive committee has 12 members, also composed equally between government and Olympic representatives and generally selected from foundation board members. The Olympic representatives are one each from the IOC, ANOC, ASOIF, SportAccord, and the IOC Athletes Commission. The governmental members each represent one of the five Olympic regions. The president and vice president of the foundation board serve the same positions for the executive committee.

WADA Leadership

WADA is established under the laws of Switzerland, but it is headquartered in Montreal, Quebec, Canada. Additionally, there are four regional offices run by regional directors. These offices are located in Cape Town, South Africa; Tokyo, Japan; Lausanne, Switzerland; and Montevideo, Uruguay. These offices are intended to allow WADA to better identify and address the needs in their respective regions. Regional directors report to the executive committee.

Since its creation, the WADA has had three presidents: Richard Pound, John Fahey, and Sir Craig Reedie. Pound was the first president of the WADA, serving in the role for over eight years, from its inception through 2007. He is considered the architect of WADA, having been charged by IOC then president Juan Antonio Samaranch with devising a solution for doping issues after the 1998 Tour de France scandal. Pound oversaw the creation and adoption of the WADC. He was criticized during his tenure as WADA president for his confrontational approach toward athletes who tested positive and would often issue preliminary rulings in those cases. Additionally, some athletes did not believe that they could get a genuinely fair hearing under Pound and that he would use these cases to gain publicity for himself. Prior to being elected WADA president, Pound was a member of the Canadian Olympic Committee (1968 to 1982), serving as the president the last five years, the IOC (1978 to present), serving as vice-president twice and was considered for IOC president. He also served on several other sport organizations, including the Canadian Squash Rackets Association and the Pan-American Sports Organization.

Fahey served as president from 2008 through 2013. He continued Pound's assertive hunt for doping violators. Additionally, his time as president was marked by several high-profile doping scandals, including a Jamaican track scandal, the Lance Armstrong revelations, and a doping scandal in his native Australia. However, unlike his predecessor, Fahey would rarely comment publicly on cases until they were concluded. Prior to being elected to the WADA presidency, Fahey served in elected office at various level of the Australian government (1984 to 2001). Fahey had no background in anti-doping efforts; however, he was a leader in bringing the 2000 Summer Olympic Games to Sydney.

Reedie was elected WADA president in November 2013, assuming the post for a three-year term on January 1, 2014. Prior to being elected WADA president, he had served as the president of the International Badminton Association (1981–84), chairman of the British Olympic Committee

(1992–2005), a member of the IOC (1994 to present), and the IOC Executive Committee (2009 to present).

The backgrounds of these presidents reveal that those coming from the Olympic movement maintain their roles and connections within that movement during their time as WADA president. These dual roles, serving both the Olympics and WADA, along with the strong interconnectedness between WADA and the Olympic movement, has raised questions regarding WADA's independence.

All three of the WADA presidents have been white males from Western countries (from Canada, Australia, and the United Kingdom). Additionally, until 2013 all vice presidents were also Western, and were white males (from Sweden and Denmark). In 2013, a black male from South Arica was elected as vice president. There is no specific information on the exact number of women who have served on the foundation board and executive committee, but as of July 2014, there are five women among the 38 members of the foundation board (two of which were athlete representatives) and two on the executive committee.

The limited representation into top-level roles by women in general and of men from non-Western countries is not unique to WADA. Only 24 of the IOC's 106 members are women, only five women have ever been elected to the IOC's executive board (with three being elected vice president), and all seven of the IOC presidents have been white males, six from Europe and one from the United States.

WADA Involvement in Doping Procedures

WADA does not actually test athletes. WADA's role is to make sure that proper procedures are followed and may on occasion involve itself in the postsanction appeal processes. All testing is done by national anti-doping agencies, who oversee doping control officers (DCOs). The DCOs perform both in- and out-of-competition testing, and perform the sample taking and the shipping of samples. The samples are then sent to one of the 32 WADA-accredited laboratories for testing human doping samples. Six of these are located in Asia, 18 in Europe, six in the Americas, and one each in Africa and Oceania.

Genevieve F. E. Birren

See Also: Drugs, Doping; International Olympic Committee; U.S. Anti-Doping Agency.

Further Readings
Cooper, Chris. *Run, Swim, Throw, Cheat: The Science Behind Drugs in Sport.* New York: Oxford University Press, 2012.
Hanstad, Dag Vidar, et al. "The Establishment of the World Anti-Doping Agency." *International Review for the Sociology of Sport*, v.43/3 (2008).
Mottram, David R. *Drugs in Sport.* New York: Routledge, 2010.
Nafziger, James A. R., and Stephen F. Ross, eds. *Handbook on International Sports Law.* Northampton, MA: Edward Elgar, 2011.
Sandvoss, Cornel, Michael Real, and Alina Bernstein, eds. *Bodies of Discourse: Sports Stars, Media, and the Global Public.* New York: Peter Lang, 2012.
World Anti-Doping Agency. "Constitutive Instrument of Foundation of the World Anti-Doping Agency." http://www.wada-ama.org/Documents/About_WADA/Statutes/WADA_Statutes_2009_EN.pdf (Accessed July 2014).

World Tennis

Tennis is an individual sport that is played today by millions of players at all levels of society and at all ages. The early origins of the game date back to the 12th century, while the origins of the modern games go back to the end of the 19th century.

On January 1, 1924, the International Lawn Tennis Federation (later the ITF) first adopted the Rules of Tennis. Although tennis was one of the original sports at the Athens Games in 1896—the first modern Olympics—it withdrew from the Olympics after the 1924 Games. Sixty years later, tennis returned to the Olympic Games, and as a result of efforts and support from the ITF and International Olympic Committee (IOC) executives, tennis was finally reinstated as a medal sport at Seoul in 1988.

The early professional tennis tour began during the 1920s, when tennis players playing exhibition games for paying audiences created a separation between the amateur and professional tennis ranks.

The open era began at the end of 1960s as a result of the commercialization of sport. The open era removed the distinction between amateur and professional tennis players and enabled top players to make their livings from tennis. The open era of tennis also established an international professional-tennis circuit, which attracts fans from all over the world and creates revenue from the sales of sponsorship and television rights. Today, tennis is considered one of the most popular sports globally.

Managing Organizations

There are three governing bodies for global tennis: the International Tennis Federation (ITF) is the world governing body, the Association of Tennis Professionals (ATP) is the leading governing body for men's professional tennis, and the Women Tennis Association (WTA) stands as the leading governing body for women's professional tennis.

International Tennis Federation (ITF). The International Lawn Tennis Federation (ILTF) was founded in Paris in 1913 when the four Grand Slam tournaments and the Davis Cup competition were already in existence. Because of the prominence of lawn as a surface at that time, the organization was called the International Lawn Tennis Federation until 1977, and then it dropped the word *lawn* to become the International Tennis Federation (ITF). In the 1970s, the ITF started a development program and a competitive circuit to motivate more active and broader participation among young players. During that time, the ITF strategically focused on different levels of participants; besides formulating the Davis Cup to reach a wider scope, it established an international junior and senior circuit. Additionally, it focused on an education program for coaches, as well as anti-doping programs to keep the sport clean. The ITF later established a certification process for officials and a wheelchair tennis department.

In 2013, the ITF celebrated its 100th year. Currently, the ITF is one of the largest international federations, with 210 member nations. The ITF administers and regulates tennis through over 200 affiliated national associations, along with six regional associations, and is the organization responsible for the Rules of Tennis. The ITF controls the major international team events for all age groups as well as for wheelchair tennis. It also controls the world's two largest annual international team competitions in sport, the Davis Cup by BNP Paribas for men and the Fed Cup by BNP Paribas for women. Other organizational responsibilities of the ITF include tennis in the Olympic Games and supporting its official championships, Grand Slam Tournaments, with administrative, officiating, and media services.

Association of Tennis Professionals (ATP). The ATP, the governing body of the men's professional tennis circuits, was formed in 1972. The rationale for the ATP's establishment was to protect the interests of male professional tennis players. Before the ATP, between 1974 and 1989 professional tennis was administered by the Men's International Professional Tennis Council (MIPTC), which consisted of representatives of the ATP, ILTF, and tournament directors. In 1988, the ATP created a plan for players to form a new tour in which they would play a major role and bear greater responsibility for the future of the sport. The ATP withdrew from the MIPTC and announced the creation of its own ATP Tour beginning in 1990. Within the next year, ATP made a broadcast deal, which resulted in spreading tennis around the world and increasing its popularity. The good governance and marketing of the sport brought international sponsors, extension of global reach and, of course, an increase in prize money. Within only seven years, the ATP broadcasts extended their reach to more than 200 countries.

In 2009, the organization was rebranded as the ATP World Tour and launched a new logo. In the same year, the ATP featured three new tournament categories. Since that time, the ATP World Tour has been composed of the ATP World Tour Masters 1000, ATP World Tour 500 series, ATP World Tour 250 series, ATP Challenger Tour, and the ATP Champions Tour for seniors. The ATP also organizes the ATP World Tour Finals, which is the season-ending championship and features the top eight singles players and doubles teams of the ATP rankings. Currently, the ATP World Tour includes 61 tournaments in 30 countries. The ATP publishes weekly rankings of professional tennis players, which are used for determining qualifications for entry and seeding in all tournaments for both singles and doubles. The prize money in 2014, which is distributed to all participants of the respective tournaments, totaled $93,239,063.

Women Tennis Association (WTA). The WTA was founded with the goal of protecting female tennis players and uniting all of women's professional tennis in one tour. Before the existence of the WTA, the pay differential between men and women was an issue for female players. In 1973, the U.S. Open offered equal prize money to men and women for the first time. As with the ATP, after making the first broadcasting deal in 1974, the WTA attracted sponsors and gained financial power. By 1980, there were more than 250 professional female players who were participating in the WTA Tour. The WTA has consistently developed the tour and increased the attractiveness of women's tennis on a global scale. Currently, the WTA Tour involves 54 tournaments in 33 countries and reaches an attendance of 5.3 million fans globally. The tour is broadcast in 177 countries with a total broadcast of 62,204 hours, making the tour the most watched female sport in the world. There are 2,500 professional players from 92 countries attending the tour, and the tour is composed of some of the most recognizable female players. The new tournament structure (introduced in 2009) includes Premier and International Tournaments. At the end of the season, the top-ranked eight players of the tour participate in the WTA Championships. Additionally, since 2012, the WTA 125K series has been added to the tour, which involves six tournaments. The total prize money in 2013, which is distributed to all participants of the respective tournaments, amounted to $118 million.

Grand Slams

The Grand Slam tournaments are the biggest annual tennis events in the world. The tournaments are also called the Majors. There are four Grand Slam tournaments: the Australian Open (held in Melbourne, Australia, in mid-January), the French Open (held in Paris, France, in May and June), Wimbledon (held in London, England, in June and July), and the U.S. Open (held in New York City in August and September). The term *Grand Slam* also refers to the achievement of winning all four major championships.

Serena and Venus Williams pictured during a first-round doubles game at the 2013 U.S. Open in New York, part of the four Grand Slam tournament events. The Grand Slam contains categories for men, women, boys, and girls. (Flickr/Edwin Martinez)

Wimbledon is the oldest tournament, founded in 1877, followed by the U.S. Open in 1881, the French Open in 1891, and the Australian Open in 1905. In 1925, the International Lawn Tennis Federation designated the Australian, French, British, and American championship tournaments as the four Majors. The Australian and U.S. Open are played on hard courts, the French Open on clay, and Wimbledon on grass. The play categories in the Grand Slam tournaments include men's singles champion, women's singles, men's doubles, women's doubles, and mixed doubles. Additionally, there are boys' singles, boys' doubles, girls' singles, girls' doubles, and wheelchair tennis. The Grand Slam tournaments offer the most ranking points, prize money, and public and media attention.

Team Events

Team tennis refers to tennis tournaments that consist of matches between different groups of players. They can be played at the international, national, or regional level. The most prominent team events in tennis are the Davis Cup and Fed Cup. Additionally, the ATP offers the World Team Cup, and the ITF offers the Hopman Cup events. Founded in 1975, the World Team Cup was the international team championship of the ATP until it ended in 2012. The Hopman Cup is an annual, international team indoor hard-court tennis tournament held in western Australia each year, which plays mixed-gender teams on a country-by-country basis. There are also national-level events such as World Team Tennis, which is a coed professional tennis league played in the United States.

Davis Cup

The Davis Cup is the premier international team event in men's tennis. It is run by the ITF. The Davis Cup began in 1900 as a competition between the United States and Great Britain. The idea of the Davis Cup was conceived a year earlier by four members of the Harvard University tennis team, who wished to set up a match between the United States and Great Britain. In 1969, a year after the start of the open era in tennis, 50 nations competed in the Davis Cup for the first time. Then, in 1972, the competition underwent a major change of format as the challenge round was abolished, resulting in the reigning champion having to play in every round, rather than gaining a bye directly into the final. In 1981, the current Davis Cup format was introduced. In the same year, the signed sponsor deals allowed the Davis Cup to give prize money. Currently, the Davis Cup is structured with a 16-nation World Group played over four weekends during the year. The remaining countries are then divided into three regional zones, depending on their location. Each elimination round between competing nations is held in one of the countries and is played as best-of-five matches (four singles, one doubles).

The competition celebrated its 100th final in 2012. In 2014, 122 nations participated, making the Davis Cup the world's largest annual international team competition in sport.

Fed Cup

The women's equivalent of the Davis Cup is the Fed Cup. The Fed Cup is the premier team competition in women's tennis. It was launched in 1963 to celebrate the 50th anniversary of the ITF. From 1963 to 1995, the tournament was called the Federation Cup. During its earliest times, it was played over one week in a different venue each year. The rise in entries led to the creation of regional qualifying competitions in 1992; and in 1995, the Federation Cup shortened its name to the Fed Cup and adopted a new format so that women, as well as men, could play for their countries in front of their supporters. The format has been adjusted several times since 1995; however, the current format, introduced in 2005, incorporates an eight-nation World Group and eight-nation World Group II, playing both home and away games over three weekends throughout the year. In the World Groups, each tie is contested in a best-of-five matches format and is played across two days. On the first day, there are two singles matches, and then the reverse singles matches take place on the following day. The final match is a doubles. In Zonal Groups I, II and III, ties are played over best-of-three matches (two singles and a doubles). In 2013, 95 nations participated in the Fed Cup.

Cem Tinaz

See Also: Leadership Models in Sports; Leadership Skills for Coaches (Professional Sport); Ranking Teams.

Further Readings

Association of Tennis Professionals (ATP). "How It All Began." http://www.atpworldtour.com/Corporate/History.aspx (Accessed July 2014).

Association of Tennis Professionals (ATP). "2014 ATP Tour Media Guide." http://www.atpworldtour.com/Press/Media-Guide.aspx (Accessed August 2014).

International Tennis Federation (ITF). "Annual Report & Accounts." http://www.itftennis.com/about/publications/itf.aspx (Accessed July 2014).

International Tennis Federation (ITF). "Davis Cup by BNP Paribas." http://www.itftennis.com/about/itf-events/davis-cup.aspx (Accessed July 2014).

International Tennis Federation (ITF). "FED Cup by BNP Paribas." http://www.itftennis.com/about/itf-events/fed-cup.aspx (Accessed July 2014).

International Tennis Federation (ITF). "ITF Celebrates 100 Years." http://www.itftennis.com/about/news/articles/itf-celebrates-100-years.aspx (Accessed July 2014).

Women's Tennis Association (WTA). "2014 WTA Media Guide." http://www.wtatennis.com/SEWTATour-Archive/Archive/MediaInfo/mediaguide2014.pdf (Accessed August 2014).

Resource Guide

Books

Aamidor, Abraham. *Chuck Taylor, Converse All Star: The True Story of the Man Behind the Most Famous Athletic Shoe in History*. Bloomington: Indiana University Press, 2006.

Abrams, Rober I. *Playing Tough: The World of Sports and Politics*. Lebanon, NH: Northeastern University Press, 2013.

Alexander, Kate. *Children and Organised Sport*. Edinburgh, UK: Dunedin Academic Press, 2011.

Anderson, Eric. *In the Game: Gay Athletes and the Cult of Masculinity*. Albany: State University of New York Press, 2005.

Anderson, Eric, ed. *Sport, Masculinities and Sexualities*. New York: Routledge, 2013.

Andrews, David L, and Ben Carrington, eds. *A Companion to Sport*. Hoboken, NJ: Wiley-Blackwell, 2013.

Ashe, Arthur, and Arnold Rampersad. *Days of Grace: A Memoir*. New York: Alfred A. Knopf, 1993.

Atchinson, Cara Carmichael, ed. *Sport and Gender Identities: Masculinities, Femininities, and Sexualities*. New York: Routledge, 2007.

Banner, Stuart. *The Baseball Trust: A History of Baseball's Antitrust Exemption*. New York: Oxford University Press, 2013.

Benn, Tansin, Gertrud Pfister, and Haifaa Jawad, eds. *Muslim Women and Sport*. New York: Routledge, 2010.

Blackburn, Kevin. *The Sportsmen of Changi*. Sydney: New South Wales Press, 2012.

Bredemeier, Brenda Light, and David Light Shields. *Sports and Character Development*. Washington, DC: President's Council on Physical Fitness and Sport, 2006.

Bromber, Katrin, Birgit Krawletz, and Joseph Maguire, eds. *Sports Across Asia: Politics, Cultures, and Identities*. New York: Routledge, 2013.

Bryant, Paul W. *Bear Bryant on Winning Football*. Rev. and updated by Gene Stallings. Englewood Cliffs, NJ: Prentice-Hall, 1983.

Calipari, John, and Michael Sokolove. *Players First: Coaching From the Inside Out*. New York: Penguin Press, 2014.

Carlos, John, with Dave Zirin. *The John Carlos Story: The Sports Moment That Changed the World*. Chicago: Haymarket Books, 2011.

Carter, David M. *Money Games: Profiting From the Convergence of Sports and Entertainment*. Palo Alto, CA: Stanford Business Books, 2011.

Champion, Walter T., Kirk D. Willis, and Patrick K. Thornton. *Intellectual Property Law in the Sports and Entertainment Industries*. Westport, CT: Praeger, 2014.

Christesen, Paul. *Sport and Democracy in the Ancient and Modern Worlds.* New York: Cambridge University Press, 2012.

Connor, Steven. *A Philosophy of Sport.* London: Reaktion Books, 2011.

Cornwell, T. Bettina. *Sponsorship in Marketing: Effective Communication Through Sports, Arts and Events.* New York: Routledge, 2014.

Cottrell, Robert C. *Two Pioneers: How Hank Greenberg and Jackie Robinson Transformed Baseball—and America.* Washington, DC: Potomac Books, 2012.

Craig, Peter, and Paul Beedle, eds. *Sport Sociology*, 2nd ed. Exeter, UK: Learning Matters, 2010.

Cronin, Mie, and David Mayall, eds. *Sporting Nationalism: Identity, Ethnicity, Immigration, and Assimilation.* Portland, OR: F. Cass, 1998.

Culverhouse, Gay. *Throwaway Players: The Concussion Crisis, from Pee Wee Football to the NFL.* Lake Forest, CA: Behler Publications, 2012.

Day, Dave. *Professionals, Amateurs and Performance Sports Coaching in England, 1789–1914.* New York: Peter Lang, 2012.

Dine, Philip. *Sport and Identity in France: Practices, Locations, Representations.* New York: Peter Lang, 2012.

Doherty, Leanne. *Level Playing Field for All? Female Political Leadership and Athletics.* Lanham, MD: Lexington Books, 2011.

Dunning, Eric. *Sport Matters: Sociological Studies of Sport, Violence, and Civilization.* New York: Routledge, 1999.

Du Toit, Angelique. *Making Sense of Coaching.* Thousand Oaks, CA: Sage, 2014.

Edmondson, Jacqueline. *Jesse Owens: A Biography.* Westport, CT: Greenwood Press, 2007.

Elias, Norbert, and Eric Dunning. *Quest for Excitement: Sport and Leisure in the Civilising Process.* Rev. ed. Dublin: University College Dublin Press, 2008.

Embry, Wayne, with Mary Schmitt Boyer. *The Inside Game: Race, Power, and Politics in the NBA.* Akron, OH: University of Akron Press, 2004.

Epstein, Adam. *Sports Law.* Mason, OH: South-Western, 2013.

Erenberg, Lewis A. *The Greatest Fight of Our Generation: Louis vs. Schmeling.* New York: Oxford University Press, 2006.

Fogel, Curtis. *Game-Day Gangsters: Crime and Deviance in Canadian Football.* Edmonton, Alberta: AU Press, 2013.

Forsyth, Janice, and Audrey R. Giles, eds. *Aboriginal Peoples and Sport in Canada: Historical Foundations and Contemporary Issues.* Vancouver: University of British Columbia Press, 2012.

Friedman, Hilary Levey. *Playing to Win: Raising Children in a Competitive Culture.* Berkeley: University of California Press, 2013.

Gardiner, Simon. *Sports Law.* 4th ed. New York: Routledge, 2012.

Garlett, Kyle. *Heart of Iron: My Journey From Transplant Patient to Ironman Triathlete.* Chicago: Chicago Review Press, 2011.

Gerson, Richard F. *The Executive Athlete: How Sports Psychology Helps Business People Become World-Class Performers.* Amherst, MA: HRD Press, 2008.

Giulianotti, Richard, and Roland Robertson. *Globalization and Football: A Critical Sociology.* Thousand Oaks, CA: Sage, 2009.

Gordon, Dan. *Coaching Science.* Exeter, UK: Learning Matters, 2009.

Goudsouzian, Aram. *King of the Court: Bill Russell and the Basketball Revolution.*

Berkeley: University of California Press, 2010.

Green, Christopher D., and Ludy T. Benjamin, Jr., eds. *Psychology Gets in the Game: Sport, Mind, and Behavior, 1880–1960.* Lincoln: University of Nebraska Press, 2009.

Green, Ken, and Ken Hardman, eds. *Physical Education: Essential Issues.* Thousand Oaks, CA: Sage, 2005.

Greenspoon, Leonard J., ed. *Jews in the Gym: Judaism, Sports, and Athletics.* West Lafayette, IN: Purdue University Press, 2012.

Griffin, Pat. *Strong Women, Deep Closets: Lesbians and Homophobia in Sport.* Champaign, IL: Human Kinetics, 1998.

Guttmann, Allen. *Games and Empires: Modern Sports and Cultural Imperialism.* New York: Columbia University Press, 1994.

Hagger, Martin, and Nikos Chartzisarantis. *Social Psychology of Exercise and Sport.* New York: Open University Press, 2005.

Hallen, Cheryl, and Lorne Adams, eds. *Event Management in Sport, Recreation, and Tourism: Theoretical and Practical Dimensions.* New York: Routledge, 2013.

Hallinan, Chris, and Barry Judd, eds. *Native Games: Indigenous People and Sports in the Post-Colonial World.* Bingley, UK: Emerald Group Publishing, 2013.

Hanc, John. *The B. A. A. at 125: The Official History of the Boston Athletic Association, 1887–2012.* New York: Skyhorse Publishing, 2012.

Haney, Hank. *The Big Miss: My Years Coaching Tiger Woods.* New York: Crown Archetype, 2012.

Hardman, Ken, and Ken Green, eds. *Contemporary Issues in Physical Education: International Perspectives.* Maidenhead,

Berkshire, England: Meyer & Meyer Sport, 2011.

Harris, Cecil, and Larryette Kyle-DeBose. *Charging the Net: A History of Black in Tennis from Althea Gibson and Arthur Ashe to the Williams Sisters.* Chicago: Ivan R. Dee, 2007.

Henderson, Simon. *Sidelined: How American Sports Challenged the Black Freedom Struggle.* Lexington: University Press of Kentucky, 2013.

Hughson, John, Clive Palmer, and Fiona Skillen, eds. *The Role of Sports in the Formation of Personal Identities: Studies in Community Loyalties.* Lewiston, NY: Edwin Mellen Press, 2012.

Ingle, Zachary, and David M. Sutera. *Gender and Genre in Sports Documentaries: Critical Essays.* Lanham, MD: Scarecrow Press, 2013.

Ingle, Zachary, and David M. Sutera. *Identity and Myth in Sports Documentaries: Critical Essays.* Lanham, MD: Scarecrow Press, 2013.

Jackson, Phil, and Hugh Delehanty. *Eleven Rings: The Soul of Success.* New York: Penguin Press, 2013.

Johnson, Jay, and Marery Holman, eds. *Making the Team: Inside the World of Sport Initiations and Hazing.* Toronto: Canadian Scholars' Press, 2004.

Jordan, Leslie-Ann, ed. *Sports Event Management: The Caribbean Experience.* Burlington, VT: Ashgate, 2011.

Kahle, Lynn R., and Angeline G. Close, eds. *Consumer Behavior: Knowledge for Effective Sports and Event Marketing.* New York: Routledge, 2011.

Kassens, Eva. *Planning Olympic Legacies: Transport Dreams and Urban Realities.* New York: Routledge, 2012.

Kietlinski, Robin. *Japanese Women and Sport: Beyond Baseball and Sumo*. London: Bloomsbury Academic, 2011.

Kurlansky, Mark. *Hank Greenberg: The Hero Who Didn't Want to Be One*. New Haven, CT: Yale University Press, 2011.

LaFeber, Walter. *Michael Jordan and the New Global Capitalism*. New York: W. W. Norton, 1999.

Lefever, Katrien. *New Media and Sport: International Legal Aspects*. Hague, Netherlands: T. M. C. Asser Press, 2012.

Lenskyj, Helen Jefferson. *Inside the Olympic Industry: Power, Politics, and Activism*. Albany: State University of New York Press, 2000.

Lixey, Kevin, ed. *Sport and Christianity: A Sign of the Times in the Light of Faith*. Washington, DC: Catholic University of America Press, 2012.

Loongley, Neil. *An Absence of Competition: The Sustained Competitive Advantage of the Monopoly Sports Leagues*. New York: Springer, 2013.

Margolick, David. *Beyond Glory: Joe Louis vs. Max Schmeling and a World on the Brink*. New York: Vintage, 2006.

Markula, Pirkko, ed. *Olympic Women and the Media: International Perspectives*. New York: Palgrave Macmillan, 2009.

Martin, Simon. *Sport Italia: The Italian Love Affair With Sport*. New York: I. B. Tauris, 2011.

McLeod, Ken. *We Are the Champions: The Politics of Sports and Popular Music*. Burlington, VT: Ashgate, 2011.

McNutt, Kevin. *Hooked on Hoops: Understanding Black Youths' Blind Devotion to Basketball*. Chicago: African American Images, 2002.

Meehan Williamm P., III. *Kids, Sports, and Concussion: A Guide for Coaches and Parents*. Westport, CT: Praeger, 2011.

Miller, Saul. *Performing Under Pressure: Gaining the Mental Edge in Business and Sport*. Toronto: J. Wiley & Sons Canada, 2010.

Morelli, Jason A., and Oscar D. Velez, eds. *Coaching and Management Techniques in Athletics*. New York: Nova Science Publishers, 2011.

Moser, Rosemarie Scolaro. *Ahead of the Game: The Parents' Guide to Youth Sport Concussion*. Hanover, NH: Dartmouth College Press, 2012.

Moskowitz, Tobias J., and L. Jon Wertheim. *Scorecasting: The Hidden Influences Behind How Sports are Played and Games are Won*. New York: Crowd Archetype, 2011.

Muza, Ghazzli, and Kay Dimmock, eds. *Scuba Diving Tourism*. New York: Routledge, 2013.

Myler, Patrick. *Ring of Hate: The Brown Bomber and Hitler's Hero: Joe Louis vs. Max Schmeling and the Bitter Propaganda War*. Edinburgh, UK: Mainstream, 2006.

Nafziger, James A. R., and Stephen F. Ross, eds. *Handbook on International Sports Law*. Northampton, MA: Edward Elgar, 2011.

Nathan, Daniel A., ed. *Rooting for the Home Team: Sport, Community, and Identity*. Urbana: University of Illinois Press, 2013.

Nauright, John, and Charles Parrish, eds. *Sports Around the World: History, Culture, and Practice*. Santa Barbara, CA: ABC-CLIO, 2012.

Ogden, David C., and Josel Nathan Rosen, eds. *A Locker Room of Her Own: Celebrity, Sexuality, and Female Athletes*. Jackson: University Press of Mississippi, 2013.

Overman, Steven J. *Living Out of Bounds: The Male Athlete's Everyday Life.* Westport, CT: Praeger, 2009.

Overman, Steven J., and Kelly Boyer Sagert. *Icons of Women's Sport.* Westport, CT: Greenwood, 2012.

Pitts, Adrian, and Hanwen Liao. *Sustainable Olympic Design and Urban Development.* New York: Routledge, 2009.

Potter, David. *The Victor's Crown: A History of Ancient Sport from Homer to Byzantium.* New York: Oxford University Press, 2012.

Pritchard, David. *Sport, Democracy, and War in Classical Athens.* New York: Cambridge University Press, 2013.

Preuss, Holger. *The Economics of Staging the Olympics: A Comparison of the Games, 1997–2008.* Northampton, MA: E. Elgar, 2004.

Roberts, Glyn, ed. *Advances in Motivation in Sport and Exercise.* Champaign, IL: Human Kinetics, 2001.

Rondinone, Troy. *Friday Night Fighter: Gaspar "Indio" Ortega and the Golden Age of Television Boxing.* Urbana: University of Illinois Press, 2013.

Rowe, David. *Global Media Sport: Flows, Forms and Futures.* London: Bloomsbury Academic, 2011.

Russell, Gordon W. *Aggression in the Sports World: A Social Psychological Perspective.* New York: Oxford University Press, 2008.

Salamone, Frank A., ed. *The Native American Identity in Sports: Creating and Preserving a Culture.* Lanham, MD: Scarecrow Press, 2013.

Salmon, Paul M. *Human Factors Methods and Sports Science: A Practical Guide.* Boca Raton, FL: CRC Press/Taylor & Francis Group, 2010.

Sandvoss, Cornel, Michael Real, and Alina Bernstein, eds. *Bodies of Discourse: Sports Stars, Media, and the Global Public.* New York: Peter Lang, 2012.

Scambler, Graham. *Sport and Society: History, Power and Culture.* Maidenhead, UK: Open University Press, 2005.

Schinke, Robert, and Stephanie J. Hanrahan, eds. *Cultural Sport Psychology.* Champaign, IL: Human Kinetics, 2009.

Shihade, Magid. *Not Just a Soccer Game: Colonialism and Conflict Among Palestinians in Israel.* Syracuse, NY: Syracuse University Press, 2011.

Siekman, Robert C. R. *Introduction to International and European Sports Law: Capita Selecta.* New York: Springer, 2012.

Siekmann, Robert C. R., and Janwillem Soek, eds. *Lex Sportiva: What is Sports Law.* Berlin: Springer, 2012.

Sion, Scott. *Jackie Robinson and the Integration of Baseball.* Hoboken, NJ: J. Wiley & Sons, 2002.

Smart, Barry. *The Sport Star: Modern Sport and the Cultural Economy of Sporting Celebrity.* Thousand Oaks, CA: Sage, 2005.

Smith, Tommie, with David Steele. *Silent Gesture: The Autobiography of Tommie Smith.* Philadelphia: Temple University Press, 2007.

Sulayem, Mohammed Be, Sean O'Connor, and David Hassan. *Sport Management in the Middle East: A Case Study Analysis.* New York: Routledge, 2013.

Surdam, David D. *Wins, Losses and Empty Seats: How Baseball Outlasted the Great Depression.* Lincoln: University of Nebraska Press, 2011.

Watts, Frank. *Coaching Kids: All Team Sports.* 2nd ed. Chicago: Price World Pub., 2011.

Wilson, John R. M. *Jackie Robinson and the American Dilemma.* New York: Longman, 2010.

Young, Kevin, and Kevin B. Wamsley, eds. *Global Olympics: Historical and Sociological Studies of the Modern Games.* Boston: Elsevier JAI, 2005.

Journals

American Physical Education Review
European Journal of Sports Studies
ICHPER-SD Journal of Research in Health, Physical Education, Recreation, Sport & Dance
International Sports Journal
Japanese Journal of Sport Psychology
Jeffrey S. Moorad Sports Law Journal Journal of Health and Physical Education
Journal of Leadership Education
Journal of Leadership Studies
Journal of Sport Behavior
Journal of Sport & Exercise Psychology
Journal of Strength and Conditioning Research
Leadership & Organization Development Journal
Leadership Excellence
Leadership in Action Leadership Quarterly
Open Sports Sciences Journal
Psychology and Sociology of Sport
Research Quarterly for Exercise and Sport
Scandinavian Sport Studies Forum
Scholastic Coach
Seton Hall Journal of Sports and Entertainment Law
Sport, Education and Society
Sports Illustrated
Strategic Leadership Review
Villanova Sports & Entertainment Law Journal

Internet

American Football Coaches Association
http://www.afca.com
Association for Applied Sport Psychology
http://www.appliedsportpsych.org
Exercise and Sport Psychology
(American Psychological Association)
http://www.apa.org/about/division/div47.aspx
International Olympic Committee
http://www.olympic.org/ioc
National Association of Basketball Coaches
http://www.nabc.org/landing/index
National Association of Collegiate Directors of Athletics
http://www.nacda.com
National Consortium for Academics and Sports
http://www.ncasports.org
National Interscholastic Athletic Administrators Association
http://www.niaaa.org
National Soccer Coaches Association
http://www.nscaa.com
National Sports Marketing Network
http://www.sportsmarketingnetwork.com
National Sportscasters and Sportswriters Association
http://nssafame.com
North American Society for Sport Management
http://www.nassm.com
North American Society for the Sociology of Sport
http://www.nasss.org
Society of Health and Physical Educators
http://www.shapeamerica.org
Sports & Society (Aspen Institute)
http://www.aspeninstitute.org/policy-work/sports-society

Sports Journalists' Association (UK)
  http://www.sportsjournalists.co.uk
Sports Lawyers Association
  http://www.sportslaw.org
Sport Marketing Association
  http://www.sportmarketingassociation.com

United States Olympic Committee
  http://www.teamusa.org
Women's Sports Foundation
  http://www.womenssportsfoundation.org

Index

Index note: Article titles and their page numbers are in **boldface**.

amateur sports, 3–7. *See also* International Amateur
    Athletic Federation (IAAF); **leadership skills for**
    coaches (amateur sport); professional sports
  adult, 5
  club sport and intramural sports, 5
  competitive intercollegiate sport, 4–5
  competitive youth sport, 4
  high school, 4
  individual level adult, 5–6
  NAAF, 31
  NCAA and, 151–152
  ranking athletes, 193
  recreational youth sport, 3–4
  team level adult sport, 6
  youth amateur sport, 3
ambassador, 140, A6
American Alpine Club, xix
American Association of University Women (AAUW),
    281
American Junior Golf Association (AJGA), 182
American Sport Education Program (ASEP), 41
Americans with Disabilities Act of 1990, 24
America's Cup, xxiv
anabolic steroids, 52, 65
  Major League Baseball steroid era, 123
  scandal, 191
anchoring, A7
appeasement, 129, A8
argument, 14, 116, 138, 238–239
Aristotle, 138, A9
Armstrong, Lance, 53, 212, 282
Arum, Robert, 263
ASEP (American Sport Education Program), 41
asociality, A10
assertiveness, 79, 265, A10
Association of Intercollegiate Athletics for Women
    (AIAW), 31, 150
Association of Tennis Professionals (ATP), 284–285
Athenian Model, 138
Athlete Learning Program about Health and Anti-
    Doping (ALPHA), 54
athletes, 54. *See also* **leadership skills for athletes;**
    National Collegiate Athletic Association
    (NCAA); players; **ranking athletes; social**
    media, players and athletes; unionization of
    college athletes
  athletic performance, 139
  attitude, 183
  autonomy, 41, 140

  as employees, 93
  equality of, 66–67
  psychology of, 85
  on radio, 131–132
  sports officiating and, 245–246
  USDA and, 270
athletics director, 7–8
  coaches as, 7–8
  control of coaches, 7
  divisional differences, 8
  financial, business, managerial education, 7–8
  NCAA relationships, 7
  past versus present, 7–8
  pay, 8
  vision, 42
Atlanta Hawks, 148
ATP (Association of Tennis Professionals), 284–285
attitude, 103, A11
  athlete, 183
  change, A11
  consumer, 11
  fan attitude, 55–56, 199
  leader, 38
  measuring, 201
  my way or highway, 34
  participant, 197, 221
  player, 112
  recreational, 196
  spare the rod, spoil the child attitude, 177
audience culture, 48
Auerbach, Red, xxii, xxv
Auriemma, Geno, 280
Australian Open, xxii
authentic leadership, A11
authenticity, A12
authoritarianism, A12
authority, 17, A12
  coaching, 112
  command coaching, 34
  compliance, 10
  hierarchy, 252
  reassigning, 102
auto racing, xxiv. *See also* **Formula One auto racing;**
    NASCAR
autonomy, 101, 205–206, A13
  athlete, 41, 140
  franchise owners, 57
  team, 152
Avolio, Bruce, A13

B

Bach, Thomas, 94
badminton, 6, 105, 283
Baillet-Latour, Henri de, 94
balanced processing, A13
Ballmer, Steve, 149
Baltimore Black Sox Colored Girls, xix
Baltimore Colts, 156
Bannister, Roger, xxii
bar debate, 193
Barclays English Premier League, 37
Barling, J., 267
baseball. *See also* Little League Baseball; **Major League Baseball**; **Minor League Baseball**
    African American players, xxi
    American Association, xix
    America's Pastime, 191
    Black Sox Scandal, 122, 191, 242
    catcher's mask design, xix
    commissioners, xx
    culture, 147
    first African American player, xix
    March Madness, 27, 91, 147
    Northwestern League, xix
    recreational youth sport, 3
    trades, xxiii
    U.S. Supreme Court on, 123
    women teams, xix
Baseball at Trotwood, LLC v. Dayton Professional Baseball Club, 117
basketball. *See also* **National Basketball Association**; Women's National Basketball Association (WNBA)
    invention of, xix, 143
    recreational youth sport, 3
    team level adult sport, 6
    WCBCA, 281
Bass, Bernard, 267–268, A14
Bauer, Alice, 97
BCS (Football Bowl Championship), 279
Beecher, Catherine, 277
behavioral leadership theory, **9–10**, A15.
    See also **organizational behavior**
    consideration and initiating structure in, 9
    employee orientation and production orientation in, 9
    Leadership Grid in, 9–10
    relationship and task behaviors in, 10
Belichick, Bill, 20, 174

Belmont Stakes, xx, xxiv
Beltran, Carlos, 37
Benjamin, Walter, 219
Berenson, Senda, 277
Berg, Patty, 97, 182
Berwanger, Jay, 49
best practice, 54, 146, 240, A16
Beta-2 Agonists, 52
Bettman, Gary, 160, 187–188
bicycling
    Boston Bicycle Club, xix
    competitive amateur, 5
    cyclocross, 5
    first factory, xix
    Midwest Flyover Omnium Race Series, 5
    racing, xx
    Tour de France, xxiv, 53
    Union Cycliste Internationale, 53
    U.S.A. Cycling, 5
Big Boards, 193
Big Brothers Big Sisters of America, A17
Big 12 Conference, 92
Big East Conference, 92
Big Four, 116
Big Ten Conference, 92
Bird, Larry, 148
Black Panther Party, 48
Black Sox Scandal, 122, 191, 242
blackmail, 19
Blake, Robert, 9
Blanchard, Kenneth, 102, 173, 208–210, A124, A161
Blank, Arthur, 117
Blatter, Joseph S., 74
Bledsoe, Drew, 174
BMI (body mass index), 52
body mass index (BMI), 52
Bolman, L. G., 253
Bonds, Barry, 123, 191
bonus baby system, 49
Borland, John, 1, 224–225
Boston Bicycle Club, xix
Boston Bruins, xxiii, 188
Boston Celtics, xxii, xxiii, xxv, 148, 215
Boston Red Sox, 37, 129–130, 191
Bountygate, 21
Bourdieu, Pierre, 218
Bowie, Sam, 50
Bowl Championship Series (BSC), 92, 271
boxing, 130, 183–185. *See also* **top rank boxing**

enforcing rules and subjectivity, 21
ethics in sports and, 66
intentional fouls, 20–21
NBA and, 20–21
NFL and, 19–20
organizational and institutional, 19–20
philosophical gray areas, 21
types of individual, 19
Chelladurai, P., 103, 106–107, 252
Cheyne, George, 81
Chicago Bulls, xxv, 50, 148, 190
Chicago Cubs, xxiii, 227
Chicago National League Ball Club v. Vincent, 116
Chicago White Sox, 20, 122, 191, 242
chief executive officer (CEO), 1, 61, 142, 270
Cho, Simon, 19
Churchill, Winston, A26
Cincinnati Bengals, 157, 212
Cincinnati Reds, 20
civic engagement, A27
civic leadership, A27
Civil Rights Act of 1964, 275
Clarett, Maurice, 50
Clemente, Roberto, 192
Clemson University, 15
Cleveland Browns, 156
Cleveland Cavaliers, 148
Cleveland Indians, xxiv
club sport, 5
coaching, A28. *See also* **command coaching style;
    cooperative coaching style; leadership skills
    for coaches (amateur sport); leadership
    skills for coaches (professional sport); legal
    responsibilities for coaches; submissive
    coaching style**
    athletics directors and, 7–8
    authority, 112
    football, xxii
    hierarchy, 196
    life coach, A101
    MLB, xxiii
    Situational Leadership Theory in, 209–210
coaching and sexual abuse, 21–23
    civil rights and, 22
    lack of reporting, 22
    prevention, 23
coaching inclusive sport and disability, 23–25
    Dear Colleague letter, 23–25
    recommendations, 24–25

coaching for character, 25–27
    evaluation, 26–27
    selecting values, 26
    teaching and defining, 26
    teaching values, 25
    walking the walk, 26
coaching philosophy for college athletics, 27–30
    adjusting, 29
    challenges, 29
    development of, 28–29
    dictated by coaching levels, 27
    incorporating, 29
    teams mirroring coaches, 28
    winning versus process of championship level
        program, 27–28
coaching teenagers, 30
coaching women, 31–32
    advice in, 32
    current state of, 31–32
    mentorship as, 32
    strategies for improvement, 32
    Title IX and, 31
    WCBCA, 281
coaching youth, 33–34
    being a role model, 34
    constructive criticism and, 33–34
    mental toughness and, 33
Coakley, J., 79
Cobb, Ty, 191
coercion, A28
    coercive diplomacy, A28
    coercive power, A28
    positive discipline and, 175–176
cognitive ancestral leader prototypes, A29
Coleman, Ronnie, 52
Coles, Robert, 218
collective bargaining agreements (CBAs), 50, 116, 122
collective cultures, 81
collective goals, 101
collective identity, A31
collective intelligence, A31
collective responsibility, A31
college amateur sports, 4
*College Athlete Players Association (CAPA) v.
    Northwestern University*, 271
Collins, J., 253
Color Run, 5
Colorado State University, xxv
Colter, Kain, 271

critical reflection, A40
critical thinking, A40
Croly, Herbert, A41
croquet, xx
Crosby, Sidney, 162
Crow, Brian, 13
Cruyff, Johan, 69
Cuban, Mark, 62–63
cultural change, 220
culture, 32. *See also* **organizational culture; team culture**
    audience, 48
    baseball, 147
    of bullying and hazing, 14, 119
    collective, 81
    constitution of, 138
    drug culture, 65, 190
    entrepreneurship, 61, 63
    Formula One auto racing, 76
    history of, 218
    inclusivity and, 198
    of locker room pools, 19
    metropolitan, 219
    patriarchy, 132–133
    religious, 183
    sport culture, 78, 132, 144, 196
    sporting, 6
    subcultures, 219
    winning, 120
Cyclops computer system, xxiv
CYO (Catholic Youth Organization), 3

D
Dallas Cowboys, 173–174, 188
Dallas Mavericks, 62, 148
Daly, Trevor, 188
Danoff, Bettye Mims, 97
Davis, Al, 189
Davis, Ernie, xxiii
Davis Cup, 286
DCOs (Doping Control Officers), 283
de Coubertin, Pierre, 94
De La Hoya, Oscar, 263
Deal, Terrence, 167, 253
Dear Colleague letter, 23–25, 261
deceit, 19
decision making, A44
    decision-making model of leadership, A44
    employee, 173

leadership skills for coaches (amateur sport), 111
    shared, 111
Deford, Frank, 128–129
DeFrantz, Anita, xxiv
deliberate play, 136
deliberate practice, 136
deliberative democracy, A46
Delta Topco, 76
Denison, Daniel, 167
Denver Broncos, 188
Denver Nuggets, 148
descriptive representation, A47
design by committee, A47
designated hitter (DH), 121
Detroit Pistons, 148
Dettweiler, Helen, 97
development of leadership skills, 45–46. *See also* **leadership skills for athletes; models of athlete development; sport-based youth development**
    Academy for Educational Development/Center for Youth Development and Policy Research, 230
    customized programs, 46
    NIAAA and, 163
    progressive programs, 45–46
    systematic programs, 45
DH (designated hitter), 121
Didrikson, Mildred ("Babe"), xxi, xxii, 182
DiMaggio, Joe, 191
2, 4 Dinitrophenol (DNP), 52
diplomacy, A49
discrimination in sports, 46–49. *See also* **bullying and hazing; Title IX; women: equal pay**
    current situation, 48–49
    gender discrimination, xxv
    Olympic games, 47–48
    overview, 46–47
    practitioners and social movements, 47–48
    sexism and derivatives, 48
dispute system, A50
DNP (2, 4 Dinitrophenol), 52
Doby, Larry, 62, 192
Donaghy, Tim, 20, 245
Dooley, Derek, 7
Dooley, Vince, 7
Doping Control Officers (DCOs), 283
Dorrance, Anson, 280
draft system, 49–51
    lottery system, 50–51
    MLB and, 49–50

NBA, 49–51
NFL and, 49–51
NHL and, 49–50
requirements and rights, 50
Dreikurs, Rudolf, 176
Drew Brees Foundation, 37
drugs, doping, 51–55. *See also* **U.S. Anti-Doping Agency (USADA)**; **World Anti-Doping Agency (WADA)**
drug culture, 65, 190
future of anti-doping, 54
high-profile sports examples, 53
NBA and, 190
NFL and, 53
organizations and actions, 53–54
Duke University, 28
Dunning, Eric, 220
Duran, Roberto, 263
Durkheim, Émile, 218, 220

E
EAP. *See* **Emergency Action Plan (EAP)**
early adopters, 12, A52
Eastern College Athletic Conference (ECAC), 24
ECAC. *See* Eastern College Athletic Conference (ECAC)
Ecclestone, Bernie, 76
economics of sports, 55–59. *See also* **sponsorship sales**; **ticket operations**; **ticket sales: primary**; **ticket sales: secondary market**
business of sports, 58–59
professional leagues, 57
sport consumption, 55–56
sports market, 56–57
teams, 57
Ederle, Gertrude, xxi
Edstrom, J. Sigfrid, 94
Eichberg, Henning, 218
Eitzen, D., 78
Elias, Norbert, 220
Emergency Action Plan (EAP), 43, **59–60**
creating the plan, 59
forms, 60
necessary information, 59–60
emotional intelligence, 103, 111, 112, A56
empathy, 26, 112, A57
employee, xxv, A58
appreciation, 168
athletes as, 93

decision-making, 173
fulfilled and dissatisfied, 10
motivation, 221
orientation, 9
student, 100
well-being, 38–39
empowerment, 10, 17, 103, 198, A59
entrepreneurship, 61–64, A59
advice in, 62
CEOs and, 61
charitable involvement, 63
culture, 61
entrepreneurial leadership, A60
establishing culture, 63
identification, 61–62
innovation in, 62–64
inspiration in, 62–64
environmental consciousness, 36
EPO (Erythropoietin), 52
Epstein, Charlotte, xx
equal accommodation, 261
Equal Pay Act of 1963, 275
Erving, Julius, 190
Erythropoietin (EPO), 52
ESPN, 126–128, 189, 190, 193
ethics in sports, 64–68, A61. *See also* **morality of professional sports**
cheating and, 65–66
in college athletics, 67
equality of athletes, 66–67
injury and, 87–88
overview, 64
PEDs and, 64–65
violence and, 65–66
winning and, 64–65
evaluation, A62
in coaching for character, 26–27
evaluating leadership, A61
legal responsibilities for coaches, 114–115
self-evaluation maintenance theory, A157
Ewing, Patrick, 50
expert mastery, 137
extraversion, 265, A64

F
Facebook, 212–213, 215
facilitators, A65
leaders as, 102
offensive, 210

sport as, 139
trained, 100
Fahey, John, 282
fairness, 244–245
fan attitude, 55–56, 199
Fed Cup, 286
Federal Baseball Club v. National League, 123
Fédération Internationale de Football Association
(FIFA)
ban on doping, 53
goal-line technology, xxv
investigations, 19
law suits, xxv
Fédération Sportive Féminine Internationale (FSFI), 48
feedback
in comparative models of sports leadership, 39–40
in positive discipline, 177
fencing, electrical scoring system, xxi
Ferguson, Missouri, A66
Fiedler, Fred, 101–102, A66
field hockey, 133, 186, 277, 279, 281
FIFA. *See* Fédération Internationale de Football
Association (FIFA)
FIFA World Cup, 69–75
FIFA leadership on sport and cultural issues, 69
history, 70–75
1906 international competition, Athens, 70
1908 Olympic Games, London, 70
1912 Olympic Games, Stockholm, 70
1920 Olympic Games, Belgium, 70
1924 Olympic Games, Paris, 70–71
1928 Olympic Games, Amsterdam, 71
1930 Uruguay, 71
1934 Italy, 71
1938 France, 71
1950 Brazil, 71
1954 Switzerland, 71–72
1958 Sweden, 72
1962 Chile, 72
1966 England, 72
1970 Mexico, 72
1974 West Germany, 72
1978 Argentina, 73
1982 Spain, 73
1986 Mexico, 73
1990 Italy, 73
1991 Women's World Cup, China, 73
1994 United States, 73
1995 Women's World Cup, Sweden, 73–74

1998 France, 73–74
1999 Women's World Cup, United States, 74
2002 Korea/Japan, 74
2003 Women's World Cup, United States, 74
2006 Germany, 74
2007 Women's World Cup, China, 74
2010 South Africa, 74–75
2011 Women's World Cup, Germany, 75
2014 Brazil, 75
2015 Women's World Cup, Canada, 75
2018 Russia, 75
2019 Women's World Cup, 75
2022 Qatar, 75
organizational structure, 70
Finley v. Kuhn, 116
First Tee, 232
Fischer, Bobby, xxiii
Five C Model, 103
Flood, Curt, xxiii
Flood v. Kuhn, 117
Foley, Jeremy, 8
football, xxv. *See also* **National Football League**;
Super Bowl
coaching, xxii
Heisman Trophy, xxiii, 49, 137
Intercollegiate Athletic Association, xx
Pop Warner Football, 3
recreational youth sport, 3
tackling dummy, xix
University Pittsburgh uniforms, xx
Football Bowl Championship (BCS), 279
Footer, Alyson, 15
Formula One auto racing, 75–78. *See also* **NASCAR**
culture, 76
latest developments, 76–77
management structure, 76
origins and global reach, 75–76
Foucault, Michel, 218
Four Horsemen, 128
Fowler, Susan, 209
FOX sports, 126–128, 143, 189, 193
France, Bill, 141
franchises
MLB, 192
owner autonomy, 57
Francis, Charles, 53
Frankfurt School, 219
Fraser v. Major League Soccer, 117
freeze frame footage, 21

Professional Golf Association, 179–183
    amateur and professional golf, 181
    golf as Olympic sport, 180
    golf as university sport, 180–181
    golf associations, 181–182
    golf participation, 180
    LPGA tour, 182
    members, 182
    PGA tour, 182
professional identification, A142
professional sports, 183–186. *See also* **amateur sports; leadership skills for coaches (professional sport); morality of professional sports**
    bullying and hazing and, 15
    controversy in collegiate sport, 185
    current trends, 185–186
    history, 183–184
    sports media and rise in popularity, 184–185
psychological safety, A144
psychology, 1
    of athletes, 85
    characteristics, 22
    social psychology, 219, A165
Ptah Hotep, A144
public interest, 36, A145
public leadership, A145
public–private partnership, A146
pyramid of success, 42

Q
qualitative research methodologies, 200–201, 223
quantitative research methodologies, 199–200, 223
Quebec Bulldogs, 187

R
race/ethnicity and sports leadership, 187–192
    in MLB, 191–192
    in NBA, 190–191
    in NFL, 188
    in NHL, 187–188
racquetball, 126
Rankin, Thomas L., xix
ranking athletes, 192–194
    amateur athletes, 193
    by popular media, 192–193
ranking teams, 194–195
    collegiate sports, 194–195
    high school sports, 195

    international soccer, 195
    professional sports, 194
Reagan, Ronald, 131
recreational attitude, 196
recreational versus competitive sport, 195–197
    participant attitude, 197
    sport participation history, 196–197
recreational youth sport, 3–4
Reedie, Craig, 282
reference class forecasting, A148
reference groups, 12
Rehabilitation Act of 1973, 23–24
Reichardt, Rick, 49
Reicher, Steve, 86
Relational Model of Leadership, 197–199, A149
    features, 198–199
    inclusivity, 198
    key assumption, 199
    shift in thinking, 197–198
relationship behavior, 10
relationship-oriented leadership, A149
religious culture, 183
reputation management, A150
research methods in sports leadership, 199–202
    academic journals and conferences, 201
    Academy for Educational Development/Center for Youth Development and Policy Research, 230
    gender and sports leadership, 79
    organizational culture, 167
    qualitative research methodologies, 200–201, 223
    quantitative research methodologies, 199–200, 223
    sponsorship sales, 223
resilience, A150
reward authority, A150
reward dependence, A150
reward power, A151
Rheume, Manon, xxiv
Rhode, Kimberly, xxv
Rice, Grantland, 128
Rice, Raven Ray, 158
Rice, Ray, 116
Rickey, Branch, 130, 191–192
Riggs, Bobby, xxiii
Riley, Pat, xxii
Rimet, Jules, 70
ripple down effect, 15
risk management process, 202–204, A151
    organization assessment, 202
    policy assessment, 202

Leadership
GLOSSARY

Essential Terms for the 21st Century

Jeni McRay, Editor

MISSION BELL MEDIA

Glossary Contents

Glossary Introduction

Leadership is one of the earliest subjects of study in the social sciences, with ancients such as Plato and Confucius devoting much of their work to studying the question of how to lead, and the earliest historians focused largely on accounts of kings' reigns or the mythological origins of the state. Long before there was a formal science of psychology, the question of what separated a leader from others was one that fascinated many writers and thinkers. In the Middle Ages, a self-help genre with roots in antiquity reached full flower with "Mirrors for Princes," guides written not for the self-improvement of the everyman but to improve the governance and conduct of the leader. Fields such as management, political science, and education all originated with a top-down view that principally considered the role of the leader, and even the field of biography originated as the life accounts of "Great Men."

We can formally date the birth of contemporary leadership studies to some point in between the Ohio State Leadership Studies of the 1940s, which focused on identifying behaviors associated with successful leadership, and the establishment of the first leadership studies doctoral program in 1979 (at the University of San Diego). The field has especially seen growth since the establishment in 1992 of the first undergraduate leadership studies school, the University of Richmond's Jepson School of Leadership Studies. But these developments had several important antecedents.

After the Industrial Revolution and urbanization changed American work life, 20th century business culture became engrossed in the study of management. The spread of compulsory public schooling led to the professionalization of teachers and the formal study of teaching methods, while the Progressive movement simultaneously began a similar study of parenting, leading to a flood of "how-to" parenting books that has not yet abated. As the size, scope, and responsibility of the federal government expanded during the New Deal era and World War II, the academic disciplines of public policy and public administration began to form.

Early theories of leadership focused on behavior, much as the Great Men biographies had focused on personality traits. As leadership studies matured, contingency theories were developed, like Robert Blake and Jane Mouton's managerial grid model, Robert House's path-goal theory, Paul Hersey and Ken Blanchard's situational leadership theory, and Fred Fiedler's contingency model, later reconceptualized as cognitive resource theory. More recent work has focused on transformational leadership, charisma, authenticity, servant leadership, adaptive leadership, and leadership's complement, followership.

Leadership studies is a still-developing field, one applicable to and drawing from numerous disciplines. Our glossary includes not only the terminology native to the field but also terms from the related areas of political science, education and pedagogy, organizational psychology, management, and the social sciences. The Asch conformity experiments, for instance, which measured the frequency with which test subjects offer an incorrect answer in order to conform with the majority opinion, were not conducted with leadership in mind, but they nevertheless have informed our understanding of individual and group behavior in leadership situations. In the most basic terms, understanding leadership entails understanding individual minds and group behaviors.

The headwords for this glossary were generated as an intriguing series of trees: an initial list was created by reading through various papers in the field and highlighting those terms a layman would need explained. Major studies and concepts from the history of leadership studies are included, from the Michigan Studies of Leadership to Patrick J. Montana and Bruce H. Charnov's varieties of power. Each of those terms then led to other terms for context or explication, a process that continued until we felt that we had carved the thing down to the bone. Fundamental ideas from psychology, sociology, and political science are thus included in order to provide proper context for the leadership theories that depend on them. In covering the history of leadership studies, we include not only the path that led directly to today's interdisciplinary field but also intertwined paths, such as the study of management, where we find Frederick Winslow Taylor and Peter Drucker.

Ideas and terminology are drawn not only from areas like governance and management but also from less obvious types of leadership, such as parenting, activism, diplomacy, and education, and from informal leader types, such

as "early adopters." These areas often include leadership scenarios similar in broad strokes to those of the worlds of business or politics but with important differences. Classroom management, for instance, offers specific leadership challenges given the student-to-teacher ratio (usually much higher than the employee-to-supervisor ratio in a workplace) and the different power dynamics in the teacher–student relationship compared to the supervisor–worker relationship.

Other terms, such as "critical thinking," "decision making," and "self-awareness," are included because of their relationship to certain leadership skills or practices or to the many aspects of communication. Because leadership often entails a degree of persuasion, terms germane to persuasion, influence, and argumentation are examined, from "bullying" to the "cognitive biases" that impair our perceptions. Likewise, because leaders so often preside over change, we include various concepts related to perceptions or experiences of change and transition, such as creeping normality.

In discussing real-world leadership practices, we have included terms related to different organizational structures, government institutions, and political ideologies. A small number of historical leaders are included as illustrative examples, from Alexander the Great to Charles Coughlin, as are the recent events of the Arab Spring and the Occupy movement. We also include a few examples of leadership actions (successful and otherwise) from modern history, such as Roosevelt's court-packing plan, the Cold War–era deterrence theory, and Lyndon Johnson's "Daisy" campaign ad.

It is our hope that this volume will not only help newcomers to leadership studies navigate the field but also suggest further areas of study.

About the Glossary Editor

Dr. Jeni McRay, commonly known to her students as "Dr. J," is an assistant professor of leadership studies at Fort Hays State University (FHSU) in Kansas. Her current responsibilities include developing and teaching undergraduate courses as part of unique cross-border partnerships with SIAS University and Shenyang Normal University in China. In this program, Chinese students earn dual degrees, one from their home institution and one from FHSU. This requires a unique blend of curriculum development, distance delivery, and intercultural knowledge and communication. Dr. McRay oversees all instructional materials and lectures/presentations and works closely with cooperating instructors who are employed by the Chinese institutions. In addition, she develops and teaches in the virtual online graduate program at FHSU and consults with a variety of organizations. Prior to this, Dr. McRay served in faculty and administrative roles at Southwestern College in Winfield, Kansas, including as a chief academic officer of its Professional Studies programs, and she was the recipient of the Affiliate Faculty Member of the Year award in 2004.

Dr. McRay earned her master's degree through Newman University in Wichita, Kansas, and her Ph.D. through the College of Educational Leadership at Kansas State University, with an emphasis in Adult and Continuing Education. Her primary areas of expertise and research include leadership development training, faculty development, higher education administration, online instructional design and delivery, adult and professional programs, learning/teaching styles, communication skills, and emotional intelligence.

Leadership
GLOSSARY

16PF Questionnaire

The 16PF or Sixteen Personality Factor Questionnaire was developed by Raymond Cattell in the 1940s and measures 16 primary personality traits: warmth, reasoning, emotional stability, dominance, liveliness, rule-consciousness, social boldness, sensitivity, vigilance, abstractedness, privateness, apprehension, openness to change, self-reliance, perfectionism, and tension. Later versions of the questionnaire were adapted to measure the Big Five (cf.).

The 48 Laws of Power

Robert Greene's *The 48 Laws of Power* was published in 1998 and details similarities Greene perceived between historical leaders and the powerful figures of the contemporary world, and 48 rules of behavior he distilled from his observations. Law 18, for instance, is "Do not build fortresses to defend yourself—isolation is dangerous." The law is illustrated with a story about a Chinese emperor who

Robert Greene, the author of The 48 Laws of Power. (Flickr/Robert Greene)

was so focused on hiding from his enemies that he lost touch with his subjects. Critics have pointed out that Greene's historical research was superficial and scattershot, and that he subjected none of his laws to experimental testing. But it was a runaway hit nonetheless, not only in the business world (American Apparel founder Dov Charney was a fan and appointed Greene to the board of directors), but the most-requested book in prison libraries. Greene co-wrote a follow-up, *The 50th Law*, with rapper Curtis "50 Cent" Jackson.

Abilene paradox

The Abilene paradox is a phenomenon in group decision making, wherein the group selects an option that is no one person's first choice, and often contrary to the desire of most members of the group. Jerry Harvey coined the term in his 1974 article of the same name, drawn from an anecdote about a family that takes a hot summer drive to Abilene, each dreading the trip but thinking the rest want to take it. Unlike groupthink, in which a poor decision is made that group members are at least initially (before the consequences are reaped) happy with, members party to an Abilene paradox are aware of their discomfort, unaware only that the other members share it. Harvey theorized that the Watergate scandal could have originated similarly. Like groupthink, the Abilene paradox can be prevented by effective leadership.

Absenteeism

Absenteeism is the level or pattern of absence from work, school, or some other obligation, and is used as a measure of performance, and in some cases as a predictor of performance quality or indicator of wellness in the relationship between the absentee and his obligation.

Absorption

In psychology, absorption is a personality trait measuring the tendency of an individual to become absorbed by his/her fantasies, dreams, and other mental imagery. It is measured by asking the subject questions about several sub-areas, including vivid memories, imagistic thought, altered states of consciousness, and responsiveness to engaging or inductive stimuli. Absorption is strongly correlated to openness to experience and impacts the strength of both positive experiences (such as daydreaming and the enjoyment of stimuli like music or art) and negative experiences. When absorption amplifies the strength of negative experiences, it can lead to a hypersensitivity that develops into a panic disorder or somatoform disorder.

Abusive supervision

Behavior from a leader or manager toward followers and subordinates that goes beyond using criticism or punishment as an incentive into belittling, verbal attacks, or other mistreatment may be considered abusive supervision. Abusive supervision has a tendency to create an atmosphere among employees in which social undermining is common and attention may be diverted away from achieving organizational goals and toward surviving or succeeding in a socially competitive atmosphere.

Academic freedom

Academic freedom is an ideological tenet that says that the teachers and scholars who make up "the academy" should be granted full freedom of inquiry and expression, without being subject to censorship or being threatened with loss of employment, imprisonment, or other repercussions. Academic tenure is widely adopted as a means of preserving academic freedom by protecting teachers from being fired without sufficient provable cause. Most Americans espouse a commitment to academic freedom in the abstract, but in practice it is considerably limited. The famous Scopes "monkey trial," for instance, debated the merits of evolution more than the merits of academic freedom, even though it is the most famous academic freedom case in American history. In the 21st century, "academic freedom" has become a euphemism for anti-evolution bills introduced in state legislatures to allow, or even require, the teaching of intelligent design or creationism.

Accommodating style

One of the leadership styles plotted on the managerial grid model, the accommodating style was originally called the country club style. Accommodating managers have a high concern for people and low concern for production, and so tend to the comfort and security of workers in the hope that a friendly and safe atmosphere will lead to better performance.

Adaptive expectations

In economics, adaptive expectations is the process by which consumers' experience in or knowledge of the past impacts their model of future events. Adaptive expectations are especially discussed in reference to price expectations and consumers' expectations of future trends like inflation, the value of their home, their wages, or the cost of various goods as a percentage of their income.

Adaptive leadership

Adaptive leadership is a leadership framework developed in the 1990s by Ronald Heifetz, one of the cofounders of the Center for Public Leadership. Adaptive leadership teaches individuals and organizations to deal with changing conditions through specific processes. This approach focuses not on traits or other characteristics of a leader but on actions of leading. For instance, in an organization, the core practices of the organization are identified, while well-designed experiments test new practices, which are then integrated into the organization.

Adaptive performance

Adaptive performance is an employee's capacity to adjust to changes in the work environment. In a 2000 journal article, E. D. Pulakos et al. presented a taxonomy of eight dimensions of adaptive performance: handling emergencies and crises; handling stress in the workforce; creative problem solving; dealing with uncertainty and unpredictability; learning new technology and procedures; demonstrating interpersonal adaptability; demonstrating cultural adaptability; and demonstrating physically oriented adaptability.

Adhocracy culture

One of four organizational cultures identified by Robert Quinn's Competing Values Framework, adhocracy culture is externally focused on the well-being of the organization as a whole and favors a flexible organization structure. Adhocracies value innovation in the workplace.

Adultism

Adultism is a system of beliefs resulting from the power adults inevitably have over children and the abuse of that power. The need for children to have less autonomy than adults does not automatically justify the belief that children have less worth than adults nor that every adult has authority or moral superiority over every child. Adultism can influence the approaches taken by parents, teachers, and other authority figures over children; it can lead to the problems and abuses of children being taken less seriously than those of adults; and it can be extended into ageism against young adults, by linking worth to age. Further, the inconsistent definition of de facto adulthood—with the voting age, drinking age, age of consent, working age, and age of candidacy being set to different ages in most American jurisdictions—creates an underclass of young adults with only a partial set of adult rights. The term in this sense was coined in a 1978 journal article in *Adolescence* by J. Flasher.

Adversarial process

An adversarial process is one that pits (usually) two sides against each other in order to resolve a situation. The legal system, for instance, determines an accused party's guilt or innocence (or the winning side in a civil suit) through an adversarial process in which each side is represented by an attorney who presents their case to a judge and sometimes a jury. Decision makers like presidents (like Lincoln, as portrayed in Doris Kearns Goodwin's *Team of Rivals*) and business leaders sometimes surround themselves with adversarial advisers, both to ensure that they hear all sides of an issue passionately presented and to make sure no one adviser's voice goes unchallenged.

Advice

In the social sciences, the study of advice is a subset of the study of decision making. Advice is a recommendation made to the decision maker. R. S. Dalal and S. Bonaccio's 2010 article "What Types of Advice Do Decision-Makers Prefer?" lists four kinds of advice: recommendation supporting an action; recommendation against an action; the provision of relevant information without advocating an action; and recommendation of a decision-making process. While the first type has been the subject of most advice research, Dalal and Bonaccio's finding was that the third type is the best-received by decision-makers. Advice may be professional or come from personal acquaintances.

Advice utilization

Advice utilization is the degree to which a decision-maker (or "judge," as the role is often called in social psychological experiments) takes an adviser's recommendation into account in making a decision. Zero or negative advice utilization is often called advice discounting.

Affect

In psychology, affect (as a noun) is the experience of emotion, though the term often refers to affect display, the external indicators of that experience, such as facial expression, tone of voice, and body language. Flat or blunted affect—limited experience or display of emotion—may be a sign of post-traumatic stress disorder, a personality or mood disorder, or brain damage, and in some cases is a symptom of shock. Flat affect is distinguishable in brain scans, with neural activity varying from that of healthy subjects. Affect is sometimes described as positive or negative, indicating the general type of emotion being experienced.

Affective forecasting

Affective forecasting is an individual's prediction of his future emotional state. Beliefs about one's future emotional state have an impact on decision making for obvious reasons—people are reluctant to make decisions whose outcomes will cause them negative emotions—and yet research since the 1990s has found that people are very poor at predicting these future states. Certain cognitive biases like the hot-cold empathy gap play a part in reducing their accuracy, but given the impact affective forecasting has on decision making, it is maybe as important that people are not aware of what poor predictors they are. Duration and intensity of emotion are the areas most likely to be erroneously predicted, usually in the direction of overestimation—people expect that hurts will last longer and positive events will buoy them longer than actually occurs.

Agency

Agency is individual action, along with its motivations and results. When an individual is said to "have agency," the term is being used more or less as a synonym for autonomy, meaning that the individual is able to act on his/her motivations and beliefs. Many social conflicts, explicit and unconscious, develop over disagreements as to the extent of agency. It can be difficult to explicitly establish the extent of an employee's agency in his work, for instance, and a worker often faces the possibility either for being criticized for not taking initiative and acting on his/her own to resolve a situation, or for overstepping and not consulting with a superior. The interplay between structure and agency is what shapes human behavior. In the example of the aforementioned worker, the social structure of his workplace and past work experiences impact whether he is more likely to err on the side of lacking initiative or of overstepping.

Agent of influence

In psychology, an agent of influence is a person who exerts power on another in order to change their behavior, attitudes, or beliefs. Either the agent or the target may be unaware of the influence.

Agentic leadership

An agentic leader is one who is assertive, competitive, and independent.

Agreeableness

Agreeableness is one of the "Big Five" dimensions of personality, reflecting the individual's investment in social harmony. Individuals with high scores of agreeableness are usually described as kind, generous, or helpful by others, and agreeableness correlates with the health of an individual's relationships with his team members in a workplace context. Among leaders, high agreeableness scores correlate with transformational leadership scores, but in a military environment are negatively correlated with transactional leadership.

Akrasia

An ancient Greek term meaning "lacking command," akrasia is the state of acting against one's best judgment. The question of how it is possible to act against one's best judgment is an old one and is important in forming expectations of how people will behave—a person cannot always be expected to do the thing he or she knows is the best choice. One explanation blames weakness of will, pointing out smokers who choose not to quit, but this does not satisfy scenarios that lack an analogue to nicotine addiction.

Alexander the Great

Alexander III or Alexander the Great was a 4th-century king of Maceon who came to the throne at age 20, and in the next 10 years expanded his empire to include much of the known world of his era, encompassing a stretch from Egypt in the west to the western edge of the Indian subcontinent in the east. It was one of the largest empires of the ancient world and perhaps more importantly, the fastest expansion of such scope. He was not only among the best military leaders in history—albeit benefiting from an experienced and skilled army—he was the student of the philosopher Aristotle and has long served as a symbol of a certain

Alexancder the Great, a student of Greek philosopher Aristotle, became known for his unconventional method of cutting the Gordian knot with his sword rather than join the ranks who unsuccessfully tried unknotting it. (Public Domain)

kind of wisdom, demonstrated in his "solution" to the Gordian knot. The knot was a complex tangle that had foiled many attempts to unknot it; Alexander cut through it with his sword. When he died at age 33, he had not yet executed his plan to invade Arabia. Civil wars among his generals and heirs fractured his empire after his death, but his legacy was considerable, resulting in the spread of Greek culture throughout his conquered territory and beyond.

Alpha

The first letter of the Greek alphabet, alpha also refers to an individual with the first (that is, dominant) social position in a group. The term originated in studies of animals, where the alpha is (for example) a pack leader, shown deference by other members of the group, with preferential access to food and other resources, and sometimes first choice of mates. Superior physical abilities are usually the prerequisite for being the alpha, though duties toward the group must be fulfilled in order to retain one's status and the health of the group. Alpha-led groups are distinct from family groups; though gray wolf packs were originally considered alpha-led groups, the terminology was disavowed by its coiner Rudolph Schenkel when he realized that most packs consisted of a pair of parents and their offspring, which provided a different explanation for the pack leader's exclusive sexual access to the elder female. Alpha leadership seems most common among primates, and "alpha male" is used figuratively in human society to refer to swaggering aggressive behavior aimed at dominance.

Ambassador

An ambassador is an officially recognized envoy from one sovereign state or international organization to another, to whom special diplomatic powers are granted. An ambassador is the highest ranked diplomat of his delegation and oversees his country's diplomatic business in the country to which he has been appointed.

Ambiguity effect

The ambiguity effect is a cognitive bias at play in decision-making scenarios in which some of the information relevant to the decision is unknown—and the decision maker is aware of the gap in his/her knowledge. As a result, the decision maker is more likely to select the option with known odds rather than gamble on one with unknown odds. There are many results of the ambiguity effect, many of which might be grouped under the rubric "better the devil you know," including the tendency to reelect incumbents and the resistance people show in altering work practices.

Ambiguity tolerance

In psychology, ambiguity tolerance is the capacity of an individual to deal with ambiguity without responding to it as a threat, and even to perceive ambiguity as desirable. Intolerance of ambiguity manifests in a need for categorization and certainty, a black-and-white view of the world, a preference for the familiar and rejection of the unusual, and difficulty in perceiving that one person can have both positive and negative traits or behaviors. Ambiguity-intolerant people may be authoritarian, closed-minded, prejudiced, anxious, or aggressive.

"The American Dream and the Popular Novel"

"The American Dream and the Popular Novel" is a 1985 study by sociologist Elizabeth Long. Examining American best sellers from 1945 to 1975, Long argued that these books collectively reflected the middle-class construction of the American Dream during that period.

American system of manufacturing

The American system of manufacturing was a distinct set of manufacturing practices that developed in the United States in the 19th century and by the end of that century had spread throughout the industrialized world. Key elements of the system included the use of interchangeable parts, division of labor along an assembly line, and semi-skilled labor that allowed for mass production on a previously unheard of scale. The American system provided the context in which scientific management developed toward the end of the century, dominating American industry by the time the Great Depression began.

Anarchism

Anarchism is a political ideology advocating anti-statism and self-governance, with significant variation beyond the disdain for the state. Anarchism may be individualist, referring to the anarchist ideologies that prize the individual and his autonomy, or social, which includes the many anarchist ideologies motivated by social equality and committed to stateless community.

Anchoring

Anchoring is a cognitive bias impacting decision making, in which the first piece of information introduced is consequently given too high a priority in the decision-making process. Even before the bias was formally studied, the effect had been observed in various circumstances. For instance, during negotiations, from salary negotiations with a potential new hire to the sale of a car, the initial figure that is named impacts the negotiations, regardless of how it was derived or how close it is to the preferred and acceptable figures of either party. Anchoring is a subset of a broader cognitive bias called

focusing, in which an individual's ability to make a decision or prediction is negatively affected because he assigns too much importance to a single factor or aspect of the scenario. Moving from the coastal south to New England to reduce one's exposure to hurricane risk, for instance, overlooks the aggregate inconvenience and cost of other inclement weather such as blizzards and ice storms.

Andorra

The small country of Andorra, landlocked between Spain and France, is the only country in the world with two ruling monarchs. A co-principality, Andorra is jointly ruled by the president of France and the bishop of Urgell (in the Spanish autonomous community of Catalonia). Andorra is a constitutional monarchy, in which these two monarchs exercise little practical power; political power is instead vested in the head of government, who is chosen from among the members of the General Council (the parliament) who are elected by the people. Andorra's monarchy has been shared since 1278, initially between the bishop of Urgell and the count of Foix, a county of southern France; the count's title was passed to the French king in 1607 when the last count of Foix, Henry of Navarre, became King Henry IV.

Anti-authoritarianism

Anti-authoritarianism is the ideological opposition to authoritarianism. While many ideologies advocate a limit to the power of the ruling authority—and a strong belief in civil liberties, popular sovereignty, and freethought is sufficient to characterize an ideology as anti-authoritarian, the term is especially associated with various schools of anarchist thought and the opposition to any institution of authority. Anti-authoritarian movements, anarchist and otherwise, arose after World War II in both Europe and North America in response to the fascist regimes that had been defeated in the war and the fascist regime that continued to rule in Spain. In the United States and United Kingdom, such movements have been associated with radical politics and the counterculture—the Beats, hippies, and punks, chronologically—but this has much to do with the concurrent rise in those countries of institutions of authority and conformity.

Anti-intellectualism

Anti-intellectualism is distrust of, hostility toward, or dislike of intellectuals and intellectual pursuits, including the liberal arts, the arts, and social sciences, especially coupled with a characterization of such pursuits as impractical, abstracted, elitist, or out of touch. There are strains of anti-intellectualism aimed at narrower targets, even within these fields and pursuits, such as a prejudice against performance art, postmodernism, or political theory. Though often used as a pejorative characterization, populists sometimes proudly present themselves as anti-intellectual.

Appeasement

Appeasement is the diplomatic policy of making concessions to an enemy nation as a means of avoiding or forestalling conflict. The term is sometimes avoided today because of its association with British Prime Minister Neville Chamberlain's handling of Nazi Germany in the late 1930s and Winston Churchill's subsequent blaming appeasement for necessitating World War II.

Applied psychology

Applied psychology is the application of psychological theories and thinking to real-life problems, not only in mental health counseling and therapy, but in management, education, sports coaching, the law, and other areas.

Appreciative inquiry

Appreciative inquiry (AI) is a decision-making approach that, instead of focusing on solving "problems," encourages the collective envisioning of possibilities followed by a dialogue aimed at identifying the best of those possibilities and the implementation of a design that realizes that best possibility. The developers of AI at Case Western in the 1980s and 1990s believed that problem-solving methodologies were flawed because they focused on the idea of a problem and the solution to that problem rather than on realizing an ideal model.

Arab Spring

The Arab Spring is one of the most significant leadership crises of the 21st century, consisting of a series of demonstrations, protests, and civil wars in the Arab world from 2010 to 2012. It began with the self-immolation of Mohamed Bouazizi in Tunisia in December 2010 as a protest against economic and political conditions. Bouazizi inspired a widespread protest

Thousands of demonstrators gather in Bayda, Libya, for support of Tripoli and Az Zawiyah. The Arab Spring protests continued from 2010 to 2012. (Wikimedia Commons)

movement in Tunisia that led to President Ben Ali's removal from power the following month, days after Bouazizi's death. Similar demonstrations followed in Egypt, Libya, Yemen, Syria, and Bahrain, as well as much of the Middle East and North Africa, resulting in widespread regime changes. Numerous long-time rulers were removed from power, while in Syria a civil war began that continues to the present. Complaints were numerous and varied, but economic policies and political freedoms were high among them.

Architectures of control

Architectures of control are approaches to architecture aimed at influencing behavior in a given space, either through physical barriers (fences, gates, and other movement restrictions) or psychological effects. The most obvious or overt examples are the designs of prisons and other facilities where criminals are held, but in some cities, public spaces may be designed to discourage use by the homeless (card-access ATM vestibules, anti-homeless spikes to prevent sleeping on benches), skateboarders, or graffiti artists. Workplaces are also designed to influence employee behavior, with the open-plan office a recently popular example.

Archontology

Archontology is the study of the chronologies of various political and religious leaders, such as kings or other heads of state, popes and other religious leaders, and the heads of government offices, agencies, and ministries. Archontology was among the earliest forms of history; texts listing the chronology of Sumerian kings, for instance, date to the 3rd millennium B.C.E.

Argument from authority

The argument from authority is a typical approach to arguments that often constitutes a logical fallacy. The basic form of the argument says that because X is an authority on a topic and X says Y about that topic, Y must be true. While this may seem reasonable, the problem is that no authority is infallible, and further, simply citing X's position on a topic does not, for instance, refute evidence that has been provided against Y.

Argumentation theory

Argumentation theory is the study of how arguments are constructed and how logical reasoning is used to support a conclusion. The interdisciplinary field includes studies of persuasion, rules of logic and inference, social linguistics, and formal argument contexts like debate and government body proceedings.

Aristotle

The ancient Greek philosopher Aristotle was a student of Plato's, and educated at his Academy, which historians believe served as a sort of leadership training center. Aristotle studied with Plato for 20 years, leaving to found his own school, the Lyceum, when Plato died. One of the earliest writers on psychology, Aristotle was also a serious political philosopher who wrote of the city (the political unit of his world) as a community partnership in which the potential for greater happiness is the main motive for membership. Aristotle was also the teacher of Alexander the Great, who governed more of the known world of his time than any head of state since.

The Art of War

The Art of War is an ancient Chinese military manual, one of China's Seven Military Classics, and has been an influence on both Eastern and Western strategic thinking, having first been translated into English in 1905. Attributed to

6th century B.C.E. general Sun Tzu, the text was probably revised and redacted several times in later centuries. It may have originated as several different texts later edited into a whole. In any event, the book approaches war as a necessary evil, with the goal of a fast victory in order to avoid significant economic losses. Strategy is treated as a combination of careful positioning of forces based on the physical environment of the battleground, and fast responses to changing conditions. Today, the book is commonly assigned in officer and military intelligence training, and numerous books have adapted its points to management, legal trials, and professional sports.

Arthashastra

The *Arthashastra* is an ancient Indian book on leadership, in the form of economic policy, statecraft, and military strategy. Dating to about the 4th century B.C.E. and ascribed to the scholar Chanayaka, the *Arthashastra* is realist in its ideology and exceptionally detailed in its prescriptions, which range from a complete outline of a bureaucratic government and legal system to a system of collectivist ethics that call for a redistribution of food and wealth during a famine to a list of the qualities required for a virtuous leader. A Rajarshi, or virtuous king, is characterized by his self-control, intellect (cultivated by learning from his elders), use of spies, promotion of public security, setting a good example, self-discipline, benevolence, groundedness, and nonviolence toward all living things. The *Arthashastra* even provides a schedule of how the leader's day should progress, broken into 16 periods of 90 minutes each (the leader is expected to wake up at 3 a.m. and meditate on the coming day before meeting with counselors at 4:30 a.m. and starting his work day). In training a future leader, self-discipline is important, the prerequisite for everything else.

Asch conformity experiments

In the 1950s, psychologist Solomon Asch conducted a series of experiments on the impact of the majority opinion on the individual opinion. Participants were shown a card with a line on it, and a second card with three lines of different length, labeled A, B, and C. Participants were asked to identify which labeled line was the same length as the line on the first card. Unbeknownst to them, the other participants in the room were confederates, instructed to give the correct answer in six out of 18 rounds, including the first two, and the same incorrect answer in the remaining 12. The goal was to see in how many of those 12 "critical trials" did the participant give the incorrect answer, matching the majority opinion. Seventy-five percent of participants conformed in a critical trial at least once (compared to a less than 1 percent error rate in the control group).

Asociality

In psychology, asociality, nonsociality, unsociality, or social disinterest all refer to a lack of interest in social interaction, as distinct from anti-social behavior, which is active hostility toward social interaction or other people. Introverts are considered mildly to moderately asocial, which may impact their work life and the management strategies that are the most effective in overseeing them, while extremes of asociality are usually the result of a clinical condition or disorder.

Assertiveness orientation

One of the global leadership cultural competencies identified by the GLOBE Project, assertiveness orientation is the extent to which individuals in an organization or a culture exhibit assertiveness or aggression in their interpersonal relationships or become confrontational.

Aston Group
The Aston Group were a group of organizational researchers working at England's Aston University from 1961 to 1970 who were instrumental in furthering the statistical analysis of organizations. Among the work done by the group is Diane Pheysey, Kerr Inkson, and Roy Payne's work on organizational climate; Derek Pugh, David Hickson, and Bob Hinings' work on the influence of technology, size, and environment on organizational structures; and an analysis of bureaucratization in organizations that found larger organizations are more likely to be standardized, formalized, and specialized, and that decision making decentralizes as organizations increase in size.

Atlas Shrugged
Atlas Shrugged is a 1957 dystopian novel by Ayn Rand, dramatizing her philosophy of objectivism. While socialism and communism, which Rand reviled, are political systems based on the importance of the worker, Rand's sympathies were with wealthy capitalist industrialists, who in this novel react to stricter regulations by abandoning their industries, leaving them to collapse. It has remained popular among American libertarians.

Attachment theory
Attachment theory is a psychological theory dealing with a specific area of human relationships: the response to threats, hurt, or separation from loved ones. Attachment theory explores how attachment to other people forms a fundamental human motivation, and in some areas of psychology and psychiatry, has displaced A.

Maslow's hierarchy of needs in explaining the source of human motivations. By the end of the 1970s, attachment theory had become the dominant psychological theory of the motivation of children; in the 1980s it was extended with application to adults' romantic relationships.

Attitude
An attitude is a measurable, mutable positive or negative feeling toward an attitude object (a person or group, thing, event, experience, or idea). Carl Jung referred to attitude as the psyche's "readiness . . . to act or react in a certain way."

Attitude change
Attitude change is the process or phenomenon of an individual's attitude toward an object changing. Attitudes are one of the most mutable aspects of personality, subject to change by social influence, new experience or new knowledge, and changes in emotion. Persuasion aimed at changing attitudes will often appeal to emotions: political campaign ads and public health ads often seek to use emotion to affect attitude, such as by associating a political viewpoint with a response of fear (the threat of war or terrorism) or disapproval (allegations of corruption or misconduct), or associating tobacco smoking with the ugliness of its health effects to counter the romanticized image of smoking in movies.

Attributional bias
An attributional bias is a cognitive bias consisting of the errors made when people attempt to assign reasons—make attributions—to behaviors, whether their own or others.

Authentic leadership
Authentic leaders are those who are self-aware enough to be true to themselves in their roles as leaders. Authentic leadership, especially as has

been discussed in recent scholarship (a resurgence of which began with Bill George's 2003 *Authentic Leadership*), is a leadership style that emphasizes sincerity and genuineness. Rather than treating leadership as playing a role, as some schools of thought suggest, authentic leaders are open with their followers and do not fear seeming imperfect.

Authentic Leadership Inventory

The Authentic Leadership Inventory (ALI) was developed by L. L. Neider and C. A. Schriesheim and published in *Leadership Quarterly* in 2011. Building on an earlier effort to measure authentic leadership based on followers' survey answers, the Authentic Leadership Questionnaire, the ALI consists of a 16-item inventory.

Authenticity

In psychology and philosophy, authenticity is the state of the conscious self staying true to one's own character and personality in the face of external pressures. It is by extension of this meaning that one might, more familiarly, refer to one's grandmother's cooking as "authentic," implying it is closer to the cuisine of her ancestral homeland and has not been Americanized. Authenticity is usually referred to only in the positive, as distinct from mere stubborn resistance to change.

Authoritarianism

Authoritarianism is a form of leadership or governance that expects absolute obedience from followers. Spanish political scientist Juan Linz, writing during the Francisco Franco regime, defined four traits of authoritarian governments: restrictions on political institutions (such as political parties, lobbying groups, and even legislatures); an emotional appeal used as the regime's claim to legitimacy, such as claiming that the government is the only thing keeping the people safe from some threat; restrictions on political mobilization, often including the repression of opposition; and vague definitions of the powers bestowed on the executive branch, which avoids well-defined limits on those powers.

Authority

The English word *authority* is derived from the Latin *auctoritas*, which in ancient Rome was the prestige and influence an individual enjoyed, which extended to political power and the ability to command. In English, authority has two distinct but related usages: it can refer both to the power of the state, as exercised by the government or those to whom it delegates power (police officers, for instance) and to the possession of significant knowledge on a subject, in the sense that a history professor may be an authority on ancient Roman politics. In the first usage, authority differs from mere power in that it implies legitimacy and sanction; an insurgent may challenge the authority of a totalitarian regime without questioning its power to enforce its will. The social sciences have extended this type of authority to refer to nonpolitical groups, including business leadership or the authority of parents over their children. "Authority figure" is commonly used to refer to individuals with authority over others, outside government contexts.

Authority problem

An authority problem is a conflict experienced by an individual who has difficulty coping with authority figures such as parents and teachers as an adolescent, or supervisors at work, police officers, and government figures as an adult. This can result in acting out, underperforming, or sabotaging efforts, even when the authority figure's goals align with the individual's.

Autocracy

An autocracy is a form of government in which a single person holds control, without legal restraints. The term *autocrat* was often used in Europe, for instance, to differentiate some rulers from constitutional monarchs, whose political powers were restricted. In practice, the line between an autocracy and an oligarchy—rule by the few—is blurry, since the practical mechanisms of governance require assistance from others and de facto power is necessarily delegated to them.

Autonomy

Autonomy, from the ancient Greek for "self-law," is the ability of a rational individual to make an informed decision, free from coercive external pressures. Employees tend to be more engaged when they are allowed to be autonomous, provided they also have access to the correct resources to do their work, but autonomy must be balanced against the need to meet organizational goals and retain well-defined roles. In social psychology, autonomy is a personal characteristic, the capacity to benefit and derive pleasure from independence, as opposed to sociotropy, which prizes interpersonal relationships. Each responds to a different style of leadership and a different type of workplace.

Autonomous work group

An autonomous work group is self-managed and is left to manage its own projects and develop its own practices and norms, including the distribution of labor and responsibilities among members.

Avolio, Bruce

Bruce Avolio is a leadership scholar, influenced by James MacGregor Burns and particularly active in work on transformational leadership and authentic leadership. Along with Bernard Bass, he has been one of the most prominent transformational leadership scholars, and together in the late 1990s they developed the full range leadership model, measured by the Multifactor Leadership Questionnaire. He is the executive director of the Center for Leadership and Strategic Thinking at the University of Washington's Michael G. Foster School of Business.

Bakunin, Mikhail

19th-century Russian anarchist Mikhail Bakunin is one of the leading figures in the history of anarchism, and founded collectivist anarchism, which advocates eliminating both the state and private ownership of the means of production, with production being controlled collectively by workers. "Does it follow that I reject all authority?" he wrote. "In the matter of boots, I refer to the authority of the bootmaker; concerning houses, canals, or railroads, I consult that of the architect or the engineer. . . . But I allow neither the bootmaker nor the architect nor savant to impose his authority upon me. I listen to them freely and with all the respect merited by their intelligence, their character, their knowledge, reserving always my incontestable right of criticism and censure. . . . I recognize no infallible authority, even in special questions . . . I have no absolute faith in any person."

Balanced processing

Balanced processing is one of the qualities of authentic leadership, and refers to the leader's request to hear opposing viewpoints during the decision-making process, and his even-handed response to opposition and disagreement.

Basking in reflected glory

Basking in reflected glory is a common psychological phenomenon in which an individual celebrates the success of another as though they are a part of it. There is an often-observed fine line between a parent's pride in their child's performance and their basking in the child's reflected glory, for instance, and in the workplace, it is not uncommon to find supervisors or team members celebrating the success of a worker's idea that they not only did not contribute to but actively opposed until it proved successful. Other examples of basking in reflected glory are found in sports fandom and Olympic Games watching, bragging about famous ancestors, and displays of school affiliation. In recent years, research has focused on the role of brand loyalty in basking in reflected glory, particularly with the capacity social media has provided to associate oneself with certain brands via likes, hashtags, and other means.

Bass, Bernard

Bernard Bass was a leadership studies scholar known for his work on transformational leadership, sometimes working with Bruce Avolio and building on the work of James MacGregor Burns. Bass coined the term *transformational leadership*, in 1985, for what Burns had called transforming leadership, and articulated the psychological underpinnings of the theory and transformational leadership's impact on follower motivation. Bass authored the *Bass Handbook of Leadership*, the fourth edition of which was being completed when he died in 2007, which was translated into numerous languages.

Batten School of Leadership and Public Policy

The Frank Batten School of Leadership and Public Policy was established at the University of Virginia in 2007 with a gift from Weather Channel co-founder Frank Batten Sr. The school teaches leadership studies with an emphasis on public policy and political science, offering both undergraduate and graduate degrees, including a number of dual-degree options.

"Bear in the woods"

The "bear in the woods" campaign advertisement for Ronald Reagan's 1984 reelection as president is one of the most famous campaign ads. It depicts a grizzly bear in a forest, who stops his advance when a man appears in the final scene. "There is a bear in the woods," the narrator intones over the footage. ". . . Some say the bear is tame. Others say it's vicious and dangerous. Since no one can really be sure who's right, isn't it smart to be as strong as the bear?" Neither Reagan's opponent Walter Mondale nor the Soviet Union, represented by the bear, was explicitly mentioned, but Reagan's leadership appeal was aptly summed up: while no one could know if the Cold War would ever heat up into direct armed conflict, Reagan was the president who, more than any other, had directed defense spending to prepare for the possibility. It was the sort of fear-mongering that had not been seen in a presidential campaign since "Daisy" (cf.) and was deliberately echoed in the less graceful "Wolves," a George W. Bush reelection campaign ad that specifically called out opponent John Kerry as less able to cope with the wolves of international terrorism.

Behavioral complexity

Behavioral complexity is the capacity of a leader to credibly engage in a wide variety of behaviors. A leader with high behavioral complexity can engage in contrary or opposing behaviors as the situation warrants, without compromising his integrity, making him more flexible in his choices. Much of the work on behavior complexity focuses on paradox, and the competing and sometimes opposing needs of organizational life, and by extension the capacity of skilled leaders to transcend that paradox.

Behavioral script

In behaviorist psychology, a behavioral script is not a literal deliberately composed script, but a description of the behaviors implicitly expected of participants in a given situation. Empirical studies have found that these standardized routines—like the sequence of events when one goes to the doctor for a checkup, or is interviewed for a job—are easily recognized, and that, for instance, when test subjects are read narratives presenting these scenarios, they are better able to recall "on-script" information directly related to the behavioral script than unrelated information, and may even fill in aspects of the script that were not provided. A scenario may describe a patient being weighed and measured by a nurse at his physical, for instance, and the test subject may add the detail of the patient removing shoes before his height measurement is taken, without realizing that detail was not included in the scenario.

Behavioral theories of leadership

Unlike trait-based theories of leadership, which presuppose that leaders come from the ranks of those who possess specific traits, behavioral theories of leadership see leadership as a system of behaviors—and as with other behaviors, leadership thus becomes something anyone can learn, whether through training or their own trial and error. The Ohio State University and University of Michigan leadership studies of the 1940s and 1950s, respectively, were the first major behavioral studies of leadership.

A Behavioral Theory of the Firm

Written by Richard M. Cyert and James G. March of Carnegie Mellon, *A Behavioral Theory of the Firm* was published in 1963, and challenged the mainstream theory of the firm that assumed perfect knowledge and profit maximization. Large corporations were portrayed as coalitions of individuals or groups, who set goals and make decisions both formally and informally, with different and potentially conflicting goals and information resources. The work popularized the idea of satisficing: achieving goals that are "good enough" rather than ideal.

Bell Telephone Company

The Bell Telephone Company was the telephone provider that originally formed as a holder of Alexander Graham Bell's telephone patents, and which is the predecessor of AT&T. Bell was long a center of innovation and ingenuity. In the post-World War II years, Bell's top executives became concerned with developing leadership among its management. Many of the junior executives came from technical backgrounds, either as technical school graduates or having learned on the job; few had four-year degrees from liberal arts institutions. The Institute of Humanistic Studies for Executives was formed in collaboration with the University of Pennsylvania, with a 10-month immersive liberal arts program for executives, constituting 550 hours of classroom work and an intensive reading load emphasizing literature and the humanities. Bell sunk considerable resources into the program: David Riesman discussed his groundbreaking sociological study *The Lonely Crowd* with the class, while a visiting Harvard lecturer addressed the poetry of Ezra Pound. Twenty-four hours of seminar time were devoted to James Joyce's controversial *Ulysses*, still considered obscene by many Americans. Follow-up surveys found that executives graduating from the course read more, were more engaged with current events, and were better able to see multiple sides of a conflict.

A small infant, mother, grandmother, and great-grandmother represent a group that satisfies the emotional need to belong. Belongingness is a powerful human need, such that Abraham Maslow listed the need to belong on his hierarchy of needs. (Flickr)

Belongingness

Belongingness is the human need to belong to a group, and is considered one of the most fundamental human motivations. Belonging to a group is more than just having a friendly relationship with group members; acceptance as a member impacts self-image and identity, and lack of belonging has significant emotional consequences. Belongingness is one of the motivations behind not only family unity and the formation of social groups of friends, but also involved participation in fandom of sports teams, comic books, and science fiction movies, to name a few. It impacts self-presentation by motivating individuals to highlight or conceal different aspects of their selves according to how they believe group members will receive them. Abraham Maslow listed the need to belong on his famous hierarchy of needs, and some psychologists argue that belongingness is one of the major motivations behind the formation of human culture, in contrast with Freud's view that the major psychological forces driving human behavior are aggression and sexuality.

Benchmarking

Benchmarking is a business practice of comparing performance metrics or business processes to extrinsic standards, such as the performance of competitors, or industry-set or regulatory standards. Typically, benchmark comparisons encompass comparisons of performance/quality, cost, and time. Best practice or process benchmarking has become more common in management practices, comparing not simply the final product but each process involved in bringing it to market.

Benevolent authoritative

One of Rensis Likert's management systems, in the benevolent authoritative system, most decision making is conducted at the top of the hierarchy by upper-level management, with little communication from the lower levels to the uppers. Employees at lower levels feel little responsibility for the organization's goals, and motivation is provided by both rewards and punishments.

Bennis, Warren

Warren Bennis was an organizational consultant and author whose work helped to shape the leadership studies field, especially with his 1961 *Harvard Business Review* article "The Revisionist Theory of Leadership." In the 1980s and 1990s he was one of the most sought public speakers on leadership and management.

Best practice

In business and management, a "best practice" is a method for performing a task or organizing a set of information that has been developed for use by multiple unrelated organizations, and is believed to produce the best results. Best practice templates are a product developed and sold by consulting firms.

Bet-the-company culture

One of four corporate cultures identified by T. E. Deal and A. A. Kennedy, characterized by slow reward and high risk. Stress in jobs in these cultures comes mainly from the risks associated with the business, such as in industries with a tremendous cost of entry, like the oil industry or automobile manufacturers.

Big Brothers Big Sisters of America

Founded in 1904, Big Brothers Big Sisters of America is one of the oldest mentorship programs in the country. Volunteer-run, BBBSA pairs children ("Little Brothers" and "Little Sisters") with mentors who spend time with them on a one-on-one basis. One of the most highly rated charities by institutes like Charity Navigator (which rates the organizational efficiency of charities), Forbes, the Better Business Bureau, and the American Institute of Philanthropy, BBBSA has had a profound effect on at-risk children. Children in the program are only half as likely to skip school or use illegal drugs, and report fewer conflicts in school and at home.

Big Five

The "Big Five" personality traits are traits that describe adult personality, sometimes abbreviated as OCEAN: Openness, Conscientiousness, Extraversion, Agreeableness, and Neuroticism. Each of the Big Five includes a number of smaller traits that may or may not be displayed; Extraversion includes both assertiveness and warmth, but not every extrovert exhibits both traits. Several independent teams constructed the Big Five model, the initial work having been done in 1961 by Ernest Tupes and Raymond Christal. The traits are assessed through lexical measures or self-assessing sentences, common measures for many personality tests. Some researchers have suggested that leaders demonstrate high levels of openness, low levels of neuroticism, and balanced levels of extraversion and conscientiousness, and administer personality tests as part of the interview process or when considering a promotion to a leadership position. One of the primary criticisms of the Big Five model is the number of traits it does not account for: conservativeness, gender identity (especially in the sense of the display of stereotypically masculine or feminine traits and behaviors), egotism, honesty, sense of humor, religiosity, and attitude toward risk, among others. Proponents argue that these traits can be correlated to the Big Five: for instance, research indicates that low levels of openness correlate to political conservatism.

Big Man

As used in anthropology with specific reference to the tribes of Melanesia and Polynesia, the Big Man is an individual who exerts influence on the tribe as a result of the respect they command or their persuasive skills, without possessing a formal source of authority. More than just a respected opinion-holder, the Big Man actively supports his followers through economic or physical assistance, in order to maintain his status. This role may be more figuratively perceived in other social groupings, and the presence of a leader without formal authority to lead is an important consideration for formal leaders.

Big Stick

President Theodore Roosevelt famously described his foreign policy in 1901 as "Speak softly and carry a big stick," the combination of negotiations with the implicit threat of military action.

Bobo Doll experiment

In 1961 and 1963, psychologist Albert Bandura conducted experiments in which children watched an adult hitting and verbally assaulting a Bobo doll, a person-sized inflatable toy with a weighted bottom giving it a low center of mass so that it bobs back up to an upright position after being struck. Children who had seen the adult acting aggressively with the doll were more likely to do so themselves; boys were more likely to be aggressive than girls, and those who had seen the adult scolded for being aggressive were less likely. The experiment was designed to demonstrate social cognition theory and the importance of replicating behavior in knowledge acquisition.

Bonaparte, Napoleon

Napoleon Bonaparte was a French military leader who took control of France in a coup d'etat in 1799, overthrowing the Directory that had taken control through the French Revolution, and soon establishing the First French Empire. Napoleon spent most of his time as emperor at war against a series of European coalitions, as he attempted to expand France's borders. He defeated five out of seven of the coalitions, repeatedly defeating opponents by manipulating them into positions of tactical disadvantage, often followed by a surprise attack by reserve troops. The French army was often smaller, but proved almost impossible to defeat, especially after the 1807 introduction of artillery units. Napoleon was eventually defeated at Waterloo in 1815, and spent the remainder of his life in exile on the island of St. Helena, despite numerous plans (many farfetched) to rescue him and restore his rule.

Boreout

Swiss business consultants Peter Werder and Philippe Rothlin introduced the idea of boreout in their 2007 book *Diagnose Boreout*. Boreout is an idea in management theory that proposes that the combination of boredom, lack of work, and lack of engagement—boreout—are a common problem in modern white-collar work, and that consequently, a manager's job is to prevent this from happening.

Boundary spanning

The term *boundary spanning* was coined by Michael Tushman in 1977 to refer to a concept that had been examined in the social sciences since the 1950s—the activity of individuals in an organization who connect that organization's inner workings with external information sources. In the technological ramp-up after World War II, many organizations operated large research and development labs. The manner in which these labs acquired and integrated information from the wider world of research outside the company was of considerable interest, in helping to make commercial research more effective and efficient.

Bradley effect

The Bradley effect is a phenomenon in which an individual's statement of future behavior differs from his actual behavior because of his self-consciousness in reporting his preference to a pollster: specifically, the phenomenon whereby a non-white candidate performs better in polls against a white candidate than in the actual election, due to the number of individuals unwilling to tell a pollster they prefer the white candidate. There is no consensus as to whether the Bradley effect remains a persistent phenomenon in the aftermath of President Barack Obama's reelection, but in either case it is an example of a broader effect in which individuals select a performance prediction to present that represents them in what they feel is a better light than their actual performance.

Brainstorming

Brainstorming is the process of generating spontaneous ideas by an individual or a group, especially the process of doing so without evaluating their value (which is reserved for a separate process later). The term originally referred to temporary insanity as used in legal defenses, but was (perhaps unknowingly) repurposed in the 1960s by advertising executive Alex Faickney Osborn, whose 1963 book *Applied Imagination* claimed that groups were better at generating ideas than individuals.

Bread and Circuses

"Bread and circuses," from the Latin *panem et circenses*, is a metaphor used to describe leaders who appease their followers or the public by superficial means, such as with pleasant distractions or the satisfaction of short-term and superficial requests. These actions are intended to draw attention away from more serious causes of concern. In the workplace, for instance, adding new vending machines or renovating the break area while continuing to ignore employee complaints about workplace safety or the bonus structure would be a bread and circuses maneuver.

Broaden and build theory of positive emotions

The broaden and build theory of positive emotions was first articulated by positive psychologist Barbara Fredrickson in 1998. According to the theory, positive emotions like joy, happiness, and interest or "engagedness" increase one's awareness and allow for a broader range of thinking and more innovative, creative, exploratory mental activity. Negative emotions, by driving the mind toward fight or flight responses, constrict possibilities and lead to narrow manners of thinking.

Brute fact

In philosophy, a brute fact is one that cannot be explained. Some schools of contemporary philosophy argue that at the most fundamental level, behind many or most phenomena are brute facts: the question of why someone likes their coffee with lots of sugar may be explained initially with reference to the individual's tastes and past experiences with coffee, which may then be explained further with a discussion of the neurobiology of taste and the cognitive science of food preferences, and an evolutionary biology discussion of the sweet tooth, just as a chemical explanation for the effect of sugar on the taste profile of coffee can be offered, with discussion of roasting and the evolution of the coffee plant, but either exploration will eventually land on brute facts, if only "why is there something instead of nothing," or why did the coffee plant evolve in the first place, or why did the practice of grinding a plant to make a beverage develop? Some things "just are." Not every school of thought accepts this.

Bullying

Bullying is the use of abuse—physical, emotional, or social—or the threat thereof to intimidate and cause harm to others, especially in such a way as to assert dominance or superiority over the target. Bullying is often characterized by behavior that skirts a perceived line. For instance, a bully may not punch his target, instead repeatedly lightly tapping him in a way that cannot do

A Bully-Free Zone sign hangs in a school in Berea, Ohio. In the United States, new attention has been brought to the issue of bullying as a culture-wide issue. (Flickr)

damage, implicitly or explicitly suggesting that complaining about a touch that is not painful makes the target weak. Classical bullying behaviors are those that are hard for authorities to punish because they seem, on the surface, less serious than an outright assault, or do no obvious "damage." We now know that the psychological effect can be severe even when the physical is not, and online bullying—which lacks a physical element—particularly of students and young people, and in some cases by parents or other authorities, has brought new attention to bullying as a culture-wide problem in the United States.

Bureaucracy

Bureaucracy consists of the non-elected government officials, especially those organized into various agencies and other groups, that oversee much of the policy-making, policy implementation, policy advising, and policy enforcement activity of a government. The word is sometimes used in a more figurative sense to refer to the administrative groups of a large nongovernment institution, and sometimes has a negative connotation, associated with the generation of red tape, unnecessary paperwork and micromanagement policies, and rules-bound stubbornness. Max Weber, though, believed bureaucracy, which delegates policy tasks to different groups of individuals with specialized skills and narrow areas of focus, was the most efficient method of administration, approaching the division of administrative labor in much the same way as the division of manufacturing labor.

Burnout

In social psychology, burnout refers to a state of exhaustion and disinterest in work that persists in the long term. The term was coined from Graham Greene's novel *A Burnt-Out Case*, about an architect who has ceased to enjoy either his work or his life. Burnout has pronounced negative effects both on an employee's work (productivity, quality, focus, engagement) and health (contributing to depression, stress, and the likelihood of coronary heart disease). Theories differ about the causes and remedies of burnout, but strategies for avoiding or coping with it are common products of social and occupational psychology.

Burns, James MacGregor

A Pulitzer Prize winner for his biography of Franklin Delano Roosevelt, James MacGregor Burns is one of the parents of modern leadership studies, thanks to his 1978 book *Leadership*. Later in his career he assembled a group of scholars to attempt a Grand Theory of Leadership, but in this early volume he offered one of the most succinct models of leadership: leadership as "the governance of change." Burns considered leadership not simply in terms of heads of governments and businesses, but as a process by which social change is enacted at many scales.

Business continuity planning

Business continuity planning is planning for the continuation of business operations after an interruption as a result of unpredictable extrinsic factors, such as a natural disaster, burglary, or accident. For instance, if a data center is destroyed, a business continuity plan includes information for restoring data from backups, ideally including designating which workers are responsible for responding to the event. If an office building is made unavailable for a period of time while spraying for bedbugs or recovering from storm damage, arrangements can be made for certain workers to work from home, others to take days off, and still others to work from an alternate temporary site. Business continuity planning is important to how a leader is perceived by others, as his response to change and his ability to manage the business through the change will be seen to reflect on his overall abilities and suitability. Plans can be tested in advance through drills, tabletop exercises, computer simulations, and other means.

Business decision mapping

Business decision mapping is an organizational decision-making tool in which diagrams illustrate the problem in a structured framework with visual language, overlapping in approach with techniques like mind mapping and dialogue mapping. Design theorist Horst Rittel developed IBIS (Issue-Based Information System) in 1968, as a visual language framework that has been adapted to business decision mapping and used in decision-mapping software packages.

Business education

Business education includes high school level business courses as well as college programs, and covers the theory and practice of business, including areas like accounting, marketing, management, and business administration. Common degrees include the Bachelor of Business Administration, the Bachelor of Business Management, the Bachelor of Accountancy, and the Master of Business Administration, but numerous schools have idiosyncratic programs reflecting a special emphasis or commitment to a particular approach or sector. Doctoral degrees are research-focused and less common. At the college level (and sometimes in high school), business education usually relies on the case method.

Business fable

A business fable is a fable or parable that is written to illustrate, sometimes allegorically, lessons about management, salesmanship, or other business practices. *The Greatest Salesman in the World* and *Who Moved My Cheese* are perhaps the best-known examples.

Business game

A business game is a simulation game used to teach business and management skills, ranging from finance and accounting to supply chain management and organizational behavior. Business games developed out of the war games used to teach strategy and tactics in the military, and thus developed alongside an increasing interest in game theory coming out of World War II. Business and war games are a subset of what is now called "serious games," though the term was applied retroactively. Some business games were developed not specifically for education, but as recreation, including the "Tycoon" line of games like Railroad and Roller Coaster Tycoon, or Sim Tower, from the makers of Civilization and the Sims. These games tend to emphasize micromanagement, however, often putting the player in a role that does not have an exact analogue outside of the game situation.

Business magnate

A business magnate, tycoon, or industrialist is a wealthy innovator in a particular industry, who has risen to a dominant position, often by pioneering a young technology or practice. The word *magnate* is derived from the Latin for "great man," reflecting the "great man leadership" model underlying the rhetoric that has historically surrounded discussion of these businesses. The 19th century saw a rise of magnates in the United States, including Andrew Carnegie and John D. Rockefeller, who pioneered the steel and oil industries. Often the best-known magnates are those presiding over the industries that seem to define their eras: Cornelius Vanderbilt in the age of the great railroads, William

Randolph Hearst as nationwide newspaper distribution became a serious cultural and political force, Bill Gates and Ted Turner in the age of the personal computing boom and the spread of cable television. Another term common in the 19th century was "captain of industry," a laudatory term used to refer to those whose businesses had contributed to the well-being of the country, in contrast with the "robber baron" derogatory label that referenced the tactics by which they sometimes built those businesses. Thomas Carlyle, a Great Man historian and early proponent of trait-based leadership theory, coined the "captain of industry" term in 1843.

Business process
A business process is a collection or series of tasks related to the production of a specific product or other aspect of the business's operations.

Business process outsourcing
Business process outsourcing is the contracting of specific business processes to third-party providers; the term is especially associated with the outsourcing of processes to overseas firms, as with the outsourcing of customer or technical support hotlines to India. The Philippines and India are the two largest hosts of outsourced business processes. In addition to customer service outsourcing, many back office functions like finance, human resources, and accounting are outsourced.

Business process reengineering
Dating from the 1990s, business process reengineering is a process of streamlining the processes of an organization in order to improve competitiveness, through better-designed workflow that, ideally, better serves customers while improving efficiency and reducing operational costs. Two reasons business process reengineering emerged

when it did were the increased reliance on and availability of information technology, as many businesses began to alter their processes anyway in order to keep up with or make use of the Internet and related technologies, and the rise of outsourcing. Though new ideas initially propelled BPR, the term was also used by some companies to relabel downsizing and other restructurings that had little to do with new methods of streamlining.

Business school
A business school is an institute of higher education that offers business-related degrees, such as in management, accounting, or business administration. Most business schools are programs within a larger university and the students typically take some required and elective courses from programs outside the business school. Other business schools are privately operated.

Business speak
Business speak, usually used pejoratively, is the unwieldy English associated with the business world, bureaucracies, and the business/management consulting industry. Features include argot specific to the work at hand, terms borrowed from other fields and repurposed, a heavy and often unnecessary use of portmanteaus and neologisms, and often confusing syntax.

Buzzword driven development
A management or project development method that focuses on novel, popular, or trendy practices or technologies, with little consideration for their appropriateness either for the work at hand or with one another.

Bystander apathy
In social psychology, bystander apathy refers to a tendency of individuals to fail to offer to help

a victim when other people are present, with the probability of any one individual offering help inversely proportional to the number of bystanders present. Interest in bystander apathy began after the murder of Kitty Genovese in 1964, though it was later discovered that media reports of neighbors witnessing her attack without reporting it were inaccurate.

Cadillac management

A management or development approach that treats the most expensive resources—including infrastructure and staff—as the safest route to successful completion.

Caesaropapism

A term popularized by Max Weber, caesaropapism is a form of political leadership in which the secular leader of a government is also the supreme religious leader, or in which the government otherwise has direct control over the relevant spiritual authority. It is not the opposite of theocracy, in that like theocracy there is no separation of church and state, and religious institutions have more political power than in other systems; however, in caesaropapism, it is the state that drives the church, rather than the other way around. The term combines "Caesar" or "emperor" and "pope." Historically, at various periods the Byzantine emperors held caesaropapist power over the Church of Constantinople, while King Henry VIII and Elizabeth I held power of the Church of England which Henry VIII created. (Today, the British monarch's leadership of the Church of England is purely ceremonial, practical power having been ceded to a legislative body.)

Roman Emperor Constantine, center, with bishops of the Roman Church. In caesaropapism, it is the state that drives the church. The Church of Constantine was ruled by the Byzantine emperors during various time periods. (Public Domain)

Carlyle, Thomas

A 19th century Scottish philosopher and historian, Thomas Carlyle is perhaps best remembered for his history of the French Revolution (Dickens's source for *A Tale of Two Cities*) and his description of economics as "the dismal science." He was also an early adherent of trait-based theories of leadership, cataloguing in his 1841 *Heroes and Hero Worship* the physical and mental characteristics of leaders from history.

Cascading failure

In a sufficiently interconnected system, a failure of one part can trigger the failure of successive parts or processes dependent on it, resulting in a cascading failure. Because the initial failure is not necessarily the first failure to be noticed, cascading failures can make problem solving difficult. Vulnerability to, and safeguards against, cascading failure is an important consideration in the design of any system, including organizations.

Case method

The case method is an approach to education in which students and an instructor discuss decisions to be made in a case that has been presented to the students, consisting of background material on a company, its industry, its competitors, and a key decision it needs to make. These case studies are prepared by various publishers, and some of the top business schools (including Harvard) have become known for their output in writing cases. The case method is one that relies on narrative to discuss and explore decision-making processes. The case method began in part because of a lack of existing textbooks when some of the earliest American business schools began operations.

Case study

A case study is a descriptive text of a specific case selected to illustrate a principle, event, phenomenon, or process. The most familiar form is the retrospective case study, which selects a real event in history and describes it in terms used to explore the underlying factors behind what happened, for the purposes of study in the social sciences, business school, or some other discipline. A prospective case study, on the other hand, describes the criteria of a case that's sought. The concepts of case study and the case method are related, but the case study is more than a teaching method, and is a key component of professional-level social sciences research, while the needs of the teaching cases used in the case method are not met by all case studies.

Catholic Church, leadership in

The Catholic Church is among the oldest institutions in the world, and has developed a hierarchy of leadership to oversee its activities. Authority stems from God, in the form of revealed scripture, the body of Catholic canon law, and the leadership of the pope, the Bishop of Rome who has for most of the Church's history held authority over other bishops. Bishops oversee the Church's nearly three thousand dioceses, which represent geographic territories, and within those dioceses priests oversee individual communities (parishes), assisted by deacons. Most duties can be performed by any of those clergy, with the sacrament of Holy Orders reserved for bishops alone, and those of the Eucharist, penance, confirmation, and annointing of the sick reserved for bishops and priests. Additionally, cardinals are priests or bishops who have special responsibilities, among them the election of a new pope when the office is vacated.

CAVE dwellers, CAVE people

CAVE (Citizens Against Virtually Everything) dwellers are neighborhood activists who oppose any change to the community, especially those who do not stand to benefit from such changes (such as two-car households who oppose public transportation expansion, empty nest homes who oppose building a new school). The term dates to at least the 1980s and is typically used in reference to activists who are regular fixtures at town meetings, zoning board hearings, and other municipal government sessions.

Center for Congressional and Presidential Studies

The Center for Congressional and Presidential Studies (CCPS) is operated by the American University School of Public Affairs and conducts both research and study programs on the U.S. Congress, the office of the president, and the relationship between them. The Public Affairs and Advocacy Institute offers an intensive course on lobbying, while the Campaign Management Institute is one of the few nationally recognized programs training students to work on political campaigns.

Center for Creative Leadership

The Center for Creative Leadership (CCL) is a non-profit organization founded in 1970 in Greensboro, North Carolina, to provide executive education and leadership training. Today it publishes a variety of leadership books, including the *CCL Handbook of Leadership Development*, which entered its third edition in 2010. Its offices include training facilities in Greensboro, Colorado Springs, and San Diego, and foreign offices in Brussels, Moscow, and Singapore.

Center for Ethical Leadership

The Center for Ethical Leadership was founded in 1991 by leadership studies professor Bill Grace, in order to offer ethical leadership development programs for neighborhood, business, government, religious, and youth leaders. In the 2000s, the Center evaluated its efforts and determined that training individuals had not been sufficient to meet its goals, and so has shifted focus toward team and community development. The Gracious Space program, for instance, teaches groups to work better together, through training, books, and customized consultations.

Center for Public Leadership

The Center for Public Leadership was established in 2000 at the John F. Kennedy School of Government at Harvard. An academic research center, it focuses on practical leadership skills for business, non-profit, and government leadership roles. Every year it publishes the *National Leadership Index*, quantifying American confidence in key leaders of various sectors.

David Gergen, director of the Center for Public Leadership, speaks at the World Economic Forum annual meeting in Davos, Switzerland, in 2013. (Flickr/World Economic Forum)

Chakravartin

An ancient Indian word, a Chakravartin is an ideal leader who is qualified to rule over the entire world. Similar concepts are found throughout the dharmic religions, sometimes representing rulers who practice ascetism.

Change management

Change management is the oversight of transitions in or throughout an organization, and may be either one element of a manager's duties, or the specialization of a particular type of manager. For example, large retail chains like Dollar General treat store-opening as a specialized skill, employing a number of itinerant team leaders whose job it is to oversee the opening of a new location, but who have no involvement in the normal day-to-day operations of a retail location after that initial transition. In other organizations, consultants may be hired to oversee changes in the work environment and corporate hierarchy that result from a merger, significant downsizing, expansion, or other reorganization.

Chargé d'affaires

In diplomacy, the leader of a diplomatic mission not led by an ambassador is called a charge d'affaires.

Charisma

Charisma is the vital and compelling personal charm possessed by some people. The modern conception of charisma is deeply influenced by American ideals of individualism, having developed in the 1950s across numerous spheres—the social sciences, the Christian community, entertainment media—whereas earlier usages reflected not a personal quality of character but the state of having been gifted with the grace of God, or favored by fate. Even in this earlier meaning, however, charisma did not mean quite the same thing as luck, and both usages reflected a quality that in some way set the individual apart from his peers in a manner that inspired people to be more likely to follow him. Charisma is related to many other concepts of markedness: photographers may consider one subject more photogenic than another, independent from their relative attractiveness; an actor may have screen presence, while two actors together may have chemistry.

Charismatic leadership or charismatic domination

One of Weber's ideal types of political leadership, charismatic leadership (sometimes translated as charismatic domination) is a form of leadership that commands obedience on the basis of the exemplary character of the leader. In some cases, that charismatic authority can be passed on from the original leader to a chosen successor, as in the case of Joseph Stalin's succession of Vladimir Lenin. Barring this, it is difficult for an organization's leadership style to survive beyond the original charismatic leader.

Len Oakes and other psychologists have argued that charismatic leaders are more likely to suffer from narcisissim.

Chauvinism

Chauvinism originally referred to a belligerent form of patriotism and partisanship, supposedly coined for a French soldier who remained loyal to Napoleon after his abdication. "Male chauvinism" was coined by the feminist movement to refer to men who were similarly unreasonably convinced of the superiority of men—or of the appropriateness of the status quo in which women occupied an inferior position—and in time, this became the most common usage of the word in English, especially in the United States. Today, chauvinism nearly always refers to male chauvinism. Chauvinism is a problem in the workplace for both men and women; many men, even avowed feminists, have unexamined chauvinistic beliefs or have developed a habit of learned helplessness. Psychoanalytic studies have found that challenging chauvinist beliefs can induce anxiety, and have implied that there are different psychological explanations for sexism than for racism and other forms of intolerance.

Checkbook diplomacy

Checkbook diplomacy is the use of economic aid or investments as a diplomatic tool.

Cherry picking

The act of selecting for presentation or consideration only the data that supports one's argument or a particular conclusion, especially if done deliberately.

Churchill, Winston

Winston Churchill was the prime minister of the United Kingdom for two noncoterminal

Winston Churchill, prime minister of the United Kingdom from 1940 to 1945 and 1951 to 1955, flashing his famous "V" for victory sign while appearing on Downing Street in London. (British Government Photo)

terms, from 1940 to 1945 and from 1951 to 1955. For his part in World War II, he became the first person made an honorary citizen of the United States—and remains the only person other than Mother Teresa to receive that honor while still living. As a young man, he rose to fame as a war correspondent, after which he held a number of political positions. In the 1930s, as a writer estranged from his Conservative party, he spoke out about Nazi Germany, and his criticism of Prime Minister Neville Chamberlain's appeasement toward Hitler was instrumental in his rise to succeed Chamberlain after World War II broke out. (To be fair, Chamberlain himself, upon resigning, recommended Churchill as his successor, in an unusual move.) He is today remembered for his oratory, including his promise before the Battle of Britain that "we shall fight on the beaches, we shall fight on the landing grounds, we shall fight in the fields and in the streets, we shall fight in the hills; we shall never surrender." After the war, Churchill was the Leader of the Opposition and a prominent figure in world affairs—coining the term *Iron Curtain* in reference to the creation of the communist Eastern Bloc—before returning to government in the 1950s as Britain dealt with its postwar economic crisis.

Civic engagement

Civic engagement is individual or collective participation in the community, especially at the local level and especially where government engagement is somehow involved. Civic engagement might include mobilizing members of the community to oppose the building of a gas pipeline through a conservation area, for instance; volunteering to help remove underwater hazards from a local swimming hole; conducting a voter registration drive; or participating in a town meeting.

Civic intelligence

Civic intelligence, which John Dewey called cooperative intelligence, is the intelligence of individuals, groups, and institutions with regard to civil society and citizenship.

Civic leadership

Civic leadership is leadership by local citizens, or in municipal matters, not necessarily through or as part of the local government. "Civic" means "relating to a town or city," and is synonymous with municipal. Civic leadership studies and training programs are predicated on the belief that every person is a potential leader. The University of South Dakota is one school that offers a civic leadership studies minor, while Fort Hays State University is home to the Center for Civic Leadership, which offers programs in citizen leadership development.

Clan culture

One of four organizational cultures identified by Robert Quinn's Competing Values Framework, clan culture is internally focused on the well-being of the people in the organization and favors a flexible organization structure. Leaders in these organizations act like parental figures. Communication throughout the organization is open and encouraged.

Classics

Classics or classical studies is the study of the culture of Greece and Rome, especially during the era of Classical Antiquity, and of their languages and literature. Interest in classics was revived during the Renaissance, when classical literature was rediscovered and a new appreciation developed for Greek and Latin, ancestors of most of the languages of western Europe. The classics provided the foundation of western culture and civilization, and as such offer a wealth of material for leadership studies, from the antecedents of Western political philosophy to histories of wise and foolish leaders.

Classroom management

Classroom management is the process of overseeing the activity and environment of a classroom, and the challenges it presents are heavily implicated in teacher job dissatisfaction. Classroom management differs from workplace management in several critical ways: most students are minors, which affects a teacher's disciplinary options, as well as impacting the students' emotional and social skills; the student to teacher ratio is often higher than the employee to supervisor ratio; students have few options for dealing with dissatisfaction, compared with employees who are present by choice; the overall goals of a classroom differ from those of other workplaces.

Coaching

A form of teaching, mentoring, or leadership, coaching is a guided development process led by a coach. Though associated today principally with sports and life coaches, the mentorship meaning of "coach" developed in the mid-19th century as slang for a tutor, though the usage of the word in the sports world began only a few years later.

Coercion

Coercion is the use of threats, force, or other pressure to make a party act against their will. While used by bullies and criminals, coercion is also the means by which some government regimes and other leaders have accomplished their ends, and can be found in the workplace, usually in more subtle forms than the threat of physical violence.

Coercive diplomacy

Coercive diplomacy is diplomacy conducted in conjunction with the threat of military force, in order to motivate the other party to acquiesce to a proposal.

Coercive power

Coercive power is one of John R. P. French and Bertram Raven's bases of power, and one of Patrick J. Montana and Bruce H. Charnov's varieties of organizational power. Coercion is the use of force to make the target comply against their wishes, though the target may not realize they are being coerced, and the force may not be physical; an employee who performs a task under threat of their job being at risk is an example of coercion, for instance, and personal coercion uses the threat of disapproval, which is dependent on the coercive party's approval being highly valued by the target.

Co-evolution of genes and culture
One of the hypotheses explaining cultural differences in decision making, as supported for instance by Lesley Newson, is the idea that biological and cultural differences evolved together. As behaviors were passed down from one generation to the next within a culture group, cultural variants developed, shaped by forces similar to those that shape the evolution of genes.

Cognitive ancestral leader prototypes
One theory in evolutionary leadership theory proposes the cognitive ancestral leader prototypes: specific types of leaders whom humans are inclined to choose (when choice is possible) in specific situations. Strong, physically vigorous, risk-taking leaders, especially young and male, are common in times of war, and by extension in times of crisis; older leaders, especially those perceived as nurturing or socially savvy, are preferred in times of peace.

Cognitive bias
A cognitive bias is a pattern in perception, interpretation, or judgment that consistently leads to the individual misunderstanding something about himself or his social environment, making a poor choice, or otherwise acting irrationally. Several hundred cognitive biases affecting judgment, perception, self-evaluation, and memory have been identified by researchers since the middle of the 20th century, and an awareness of cognitive biases is important not only in psychology and management, but in behavioral economics. While cognitive biases show that people cannot be expected to behave rationally at all times, their irrationality can nevertheless be predictable and follow specific patterns.

Cognitive bias mitigation
A number of tools and frameworks have been developed to try to reduce the effects of cognitive biases. Just as the human hand is shaky and may be guided in its drawing efforts by a ruler and compass, so too do such tools as reference class forecasting attempt to guide and render methodical human thinking. In already-methodical contexts, such as formal decision-making processes, this is more easily done. The real problem facing cognitive bias mitigation is the impact of cognitive biases on short-term decision making, from the behavior of people in social situations to the responses of victims, bystanders, and responders in emergencies. One of the best ways to mitigate the harm of cognitive biases on an individual level may simply be to be aware of and on guard against them.

Cognitive complexity
Cognitive complexity is a measure of the complexity of a person's perceptual skills and related faculties. High cognitive complexity allows a person to see nuances, shadings, and subtleties that escape the attention of others. In interpersonal relationships, high cognitive complexity allows one to better perceive the subtle differences between people, their attitudes, wants, and needs, rather than dealing with them with a one-size-fits-all approach.

Cognitive development
Cognitive development is the study of the cognitive skills—including language learning, perceptual skills, and information processing—of children, and the development of these skills

into those of adults. The modern field encompasses neuroscience as well as psychology, and grows out of Jean Piaget's work on the developmental psychology of children.

Cognitive resource theory

A reconceptualization of the Fiedler contingency model, developed in 1987 by Fred Fiedler and Joe Garcia. Rather than focusing on the three dimensions of the Fiedler contingency model, cognitive resource theory focuses on the leader's response to stress, on the belief that poor handling of stress impairs the leader's ability to make full use of his reason and the facts available to him when making decisions. Both intelligence and relevant experience assist in handling stress.

U.S. Air Force aircraft unloading in Berlin during the Berlin Blockade, one of the first major crises of the Cold War. From June 1948 to May 1949, the Soviet Union blocked access to Berlin, even though it was under Allied control. (U.S. Air Force)

The Cold War

The Cold War lasted, in most historians' approximations, from 1945 to 1991, and consisted of a period of formal hostility, strategic alliances, and proxy wars, without direct military conflict, between the United States and the Soviet Union. Further, during this period most international affairs, at least in the West, were tinged by this conflict, which served to elevate each country, as well as secure for the United States its preeminent position as the capitalist superpower. Proxy wars had the unintended consequences of setting up future conflicts, as the American and Soviet involvement in the Middle East helped inspire the rise of politicized Islamic fundamentalism, and provided weapons and training for future American enemies, including Saddam Hussein and the Afghani mujahideen who formed al-Qaeda. The necessity of this conflict was never universally accepted, especially once Eastern European communism ceased spreading and the boundaries between capitalist and communist spheres of control became essentially fixed. But it was a conflict that fueled the United States' military buildup in the 1950s, as well as the space race, and thus proved critical, at least for a time, to the country's manufacturing base, technological competence, and economy. It also proved an ongoing leadership challenge for American presidents, from Dwight Eisenhower warning about the power of the military-industrial complex to George H. W. Bush being condemned as a "wimp."

Collaborative governance

Collaborative governance is a form of governance in which representatives of various interests collaborate in the decision-making process, though typically one group has the official final authority to make the decision. Government groups and agencies may invite representatives from industry and advocacy groups to offer their input in a problem-solving discussion, for instance.

Collaborative leadership

Collaborative leadership is an approach to leadership that is most common in public–private partnerships, online projects such as Wikipedia and other open-source works, and that is often advocated as a solution to complex global issues like climate change. Collaborative leadership involves inputs from multiple sources, with the titular leader or leaders acting as facilitators as well as managers, and often involves cooperation between different groups.

Collective identity

Collective identity is the sense of belonging to a group, and the traits, behaviors, and other elements that members associate with that group, as opposed to their perception of themselves in relation to the group. Social psychologist George Mead noted that while social conditions and structures shape the identity of members, collective identity in turn shapes those structures. The idea of collective identity is at the heart of identity politics, an approach to political activity informed and motivated by one's group associations.

Collective intelligence

Collective intelligence is intelligence that results from the collective and collaborative efforts of many individuals, such as through voting, crowdsourcing, or consensus decision making, as well as less formal means.

Collective responsibility

Collective responsibility is the responsibility borne by individuals for other peoples' actions and behaviors, as a result of tolerating or ignoring them. In the workplace, this extends to employees being held responsible for the overall performance of the organization.

Collectivism

Collectivism puts a priority on the interdependence of people, in contrast with individualism's concern for each individual's independence. Neither is an ideology as such, but rather describes an element an ideology may possess. Most cultures include both collectivist and individualist elements but may incorporate one over the other into its collective self-image. The United States, even more than other Western countries, is a deeply individualist culture, for instance, but within the narrative of American identity are many stories evincing collectivist ideals, like the many stories of communities banding together to aid one of its members (or an outsider), from Amish barn raisings to crowdsourced good deeds or fund-raising by members of Reddit. Collectivism is widely associated with the Soviet Union, but some socialists argue that Western capitalism is actually a collectivist system, in which the freedom of the individual is constrained by economic choices he is forced to make and the social forces that result from capitalist structures.

Command responsibility

The doctrine of command responsibility was first applied in 1921 during the war crimes trials that followed World War I, and states that superior officers are responsible for the war crimes (or crimes against humanity or peace) of their subordinates. The exact interpretation of this doctrine has varied over time and circumstance. Notably, Lieutenant Ehren Watada refused in 2006 to be deployed to Iraq on the basis of the doctrine, claiming that the war was illegal.

Communal reinforcement

In psychology, communal reinforcement refers to the strengthening of peoples' belief in a concept as a result of it being repeatedly asserted in their community, regardless of the evidence or lack thereof. This is one of the mechanisms by which both urban legends and political propaganda propagate.

Communicative rationality

A set of theories, especially espoused by Jurgen Habermas and Karl-Otto Apel, proposing that rationality results from successful communication. Leadership scholars are interested in communicative rationality because of the way it describes the processes by which people reach agreement and make decisions in a group.

Comparative leadership studies

Comparative leadership studies approach leadership studies from a perspective informed by anthropology and the other social sciences, in examining leadership and leadership behaviors across different cultures.

Competence, four stages of

The four stages of competence is a model of learning that developed out of the work of psychologist Abraham Maslow in the 1970s, and describes the stages of learning a skill. The first stage is unconscious incompetence, the state of lacking a skill but not necessarily recognizing the importance of the skill—or believing that one possesses it, despite a lack of training or other means of acquisition. People in this stage may have difficulty recognizing competence in other people. The second stage is conscious incompetence, in which the individual still does not possess competence, but recognizes that fact, enabling them to learn from their mistakes. In the third stage, conscious competence, performance of the skill is possible but requires concentration, like when children use a mnemonic to help them tie their shoes. In the fourth and final stage, unconscious competence, skill has been attained and can be accessed automatically.

Competency

In leadership studies, competencies are the skills and behaviors that determine performance. Different models of leadership propose different lists and groups of competencies, though with significant overlap. For instance, many agencies of the U.S. federal government look for 28 leadership competencies in their leadership development. The Coast Guard groups these into Leading Self, Leading Others, Leading Performance and Change, and Leading the Coast Guard, while the Farm Service Agency (FSA) groups them as Managing Self, Managing Projects, Managing People, Managing Programs, and Leading Organizations. Both list largely similar competencies, though they may call them different things or list them in different groups. The Coast Guard's Leading Self group, for example, consists of competencies in Accountability and Responsibility, Followership, Self-Awareness and Learning, Aligning Values, Health and Well-Being, Personal Conduct, and Technical Proficiency. The FSAs Managing Self group includes Integrity/Honesty, Interpersonal Skills, Continual Learning, Resilience, Oral Communication, Written Communication, Flexibility, and Problem Solving—almost a completely different list. Many of the FSA's Managing Self competencies, however, are grouped by the Coast Guard under Leading Others, which combines Oral and Written Communication into Effective Communications, while dividing Interpersonal Skills into Influencing Others, Respect for Others and Diversity Management, Mentoring, Taking Care of People, and Team Building.

Competing Values Framework

Robert Quinn's Competing Values Framework (CVF) developed out of his studies of organizational effectiveness with John Rohrbaugh in

1983. The name represents the apparent conflict between the traits valued in organizations and leaders—flexibility and stability, for instance. Earlier models of leadership had tended to sort these traits or behaviors into dichotomies, as with Theory X versus Theory Y, or transformational versus transactional leadership. Quinn instead looked at the possibility and benefits of balancing different, even seemingly conflicting, styles of leadership. The CVF is a spatial model created by juxtaposing two value dimensions—internal versus external organizational focus, and stable controlled organizational structure versus flexibility—resulting in four quadrants representing four types of organizational culture. The Organizational Culture Assessment Instrument developed by Quinn and Kim Cameron in 1999 distinguishes these four types as clan culture (internal/flexible), adhocracy (external/flexible), market (external/controlled), and hierarchy (internal/controlled).

Complaint system

A complaint system in an organization is the set of procedures and mechanisms by which workers can report complaints and expect to have them addressed. Originally instituted by or at the request of labor unions, complaint systems underwent an evolution in the late 20th century as the study of conflict management became more sophisticated. Most large organizations now have integrated conflict management systems, with the goal of the organization learning from the conflicts that arise.

Complexity leadership theory

Complexity leadership theory draws on complexity science and complex adaptive systems theory in its investigation of polyarchic leadership (leadership by the many of the many, rather than by the few as in oligarchies). Leadership under this theory is not a skill that can be learned or engineered through training, but a phenomenon that arises through the interaction of individuals in an organization. One of the newer areas of inquiry in leadership studies, complexity leadership theory comes primarily out of studies of medical leadership in the 2000s, and Nick Obolensky's 2010 book *Complex Adaptive Leadership*.

Complexity theory

Complexity theory is a body of theory surrounding complex systems, which are organized but unpredictable. Examples of complex systems are easily observed in nature: the movement of leaves on a tree in response to the breeze, or the motion of ocean waves against the beach, either of which may be an easily explained phenomenon in broad terms, but so complex as to defy making predictions about exactly what shape the water will take as it reaches the shore, or exactly which direction any given leaf will twist or turn. Complex systems involve many interconnected components resulting in these phenomena, and like the leaves or the waves, they may not appear complex at first glance. There is considerable interest in adapting complexity theory to the leadership and management of organizations, and to organizational studies. Organizations are systems made up of numerous components, business processes, and interpersonal interactions, and can be studied like complex adaptive systems that self-organize and evince emergent properties.

Compliance

Compliance is acquiescence to a request. The reasons why people comply are a major area of study in social psychology, and the attempt to gain compliance is called persuasion.

Confidence-building measures

In international relations, confidence-building measures (CBMs) are actions taken to reduce tensions between states and specifically the suspicion or fear of attack between two or more states. Such measures usually involve exchanges and disclosures of information. During the Cold War, for instance, it was common for the United States and the Soviet Union to each inform the other party when war games or alert exercises were being held, or when aircraft or naval operations would be held outside of the usual locations. The importance of these information exchanges cannot be overstated: during NATO's Able Archer 83 exercise in November 1983, members of the Soviet leadership were convinced the exercise was a genuine preparation for war, leading to the Soviet nuclear forces being put on alert. As a feedback model, CBMs have relevance beyond international relations, and are a significant strategy in communication, in which two sides in a potential conflict or tense situation share information in order to prevent anyone acting aggressively.

Confirmation bias

Confirmation bias is a cognitive bias describing the tendency to weight more heavily information that confirms beliefs one already holds or a hypothesis one is testing. As long ago as the 5th century B.C.E., Thucydides wrote of humanity's tendency "to entrust to careless hope what they long for, and to use sovereign reason to thrust aside what they do not fancy." The fact that the bias is measurably more pronounced when in emotionally intense contexts and when the beliefs in question are an important part of one's self-concept is one that has received considerable attention by researchers. It also indicates something about the difficulty of finding consensus in disagreements where both sides are deeply entrenched and emotionally invested, insofar as each side literally perceives the corpus of evidence differently.

Conflict resolution

The facilitation of a fair and agreeable ending to a conflict. Conflict resolution is a process that can transpire on a scale ranging from an interpersonal conflict between two people to international diplomacy and peacemaking, and there are relevant methodological similarities at all scales in between. In academic study, conflict resolution focuses especially on regional and national conflicts and on peace-building work in conflict-impacted communities. Prominent schools in the field include Cornell University, home to the Scheinman Institute on Conflict Resolution; George Mason University, the first school to offer a Ph.D. program in conflict resolution; and Tel Aviv University, which offers an International Program in Conflict Resolution and Mediation, in English.

Conformity

Conformity is the action of an individual matching his beliefs, actions, or attitudes to match those of his group, whether voluntarily or under coercion. The desire to conform has been well demonstrated in experiments, notably those of Solomon Asch. Psychologist Herbert Kelman differentiated in a 1958 article between three kinds of conformity: compliance, which is a public face of conformity while maintaining one's own conflicting position internally; identification is conforming not to a group position (or at least not because it is a group position) but to a position held by a specific individual because of specific attitudes the individual holds toward that individual, and a desire to be more like them, such as a beloved celebrity; and internalization, in which the group position is adopted by the individual to a great enough degree that he accepts it as his own and will be loathe to abandon it.

Confucius

A 6th-century B.C.E. Chinese philosopher, Confucius established the school (Confucianism) responsible for the Five Classics of Chinese literature and taught a code of ethics and conduct grounded in traditional Chinese beliefs. His system of ethics was based on the cultivation of good judgment rather than an explicit code of behavior; virtuous actions are made by virtuous thinkers. His political philosophy developed out of this, and he emphasized that a virtuous leader is one that rules not through either coercion or bribery but through morality, such that his followers will feel a deep sense of duty to be led by him. Much of what he prescribed for kings and other rulers would be compatible today with authentic leadership.

Conscientiousness

Conscientiousness is one of the "Big Five" personality traits, characterized by thoroughness, efficiency, and systematic organization. High levels of conscientiousness characterize workplace perfectionists and "workaholics," who may become compulsive enough in their behavior that striving for efficiency actually results in inefficiency. Conscientiousness is related to impulse control and work ethic, and so those with low conscientiousness scores may exhibit antisocial or criminal behavior, or may simply be prone to procrastination. (As with most such statements, the tie between low conscientiousness and criminal behavior must be taken with a grain of salt; white-collar crime is actually moderately correlated with high levels of conscientiousness.)

Consensus

Consensus is a general agreement among a group, whether concerning a course of action or a sentiment held by the members of the group. Often it represents the decision or resolution that faces the least objection, rather than representing the first preference of a majority of the group. Various decision-making processes seek to find or build consensus, even if the final authority for the decision lies elsewhere (with a leader or group of leaders, for instance, or as determined by a vote). Building consensus may also be seen as minimizing dissent, which explains its appeal even when it is not required to take action, as dissent can lead to lingering resentment, frictions, and ongoing problems.

Consensus decision making

Group decision making sometimes seeks to find a consensus of the group, rather than an adversarial decision-making process like a majority vote that overrules the minority. In some cases this may be required of or by the group, as with a jury or the decision-making meetings held by the Occupy Wall Street movement. In other cases it may simply be the group's preference, whether explicitly expressed or not. Consensus does not mean that the decision made by the group is the preferred option of all group members, or even of any member, and may simply be the option that was the least objectionable. Each member "consents," but does not necessarily "agree." Decision-making processes that require a supermajority vote to pick an option are sometimes considered consensus processes, even though they do include dissenting votes.

Consent of the governed

The consent of the governed is a concept reflecting a particular view of political legitimacy, which argues that the only legitimate regime is one that has the popular support of the people, in contrast with the divine right of kings or the Mandate of Heaven. The first major historical example of such a regime is that of 5th-century B.C.E. Athens, though the political idea of the consent of the governed was not developed until the Enlightenment—in fact, ancient Greek philosophy like that of Plato was more frequently concerned with arguing against the Athenian model. John Locke in particular, in his Second Treatise on Government, argued that only a government operating with the consent of the governed would be able to satisfy the fundamental needs of the nation. This concept was reflected in the Declaration of Independence, and Jean-Jacques Rousseau later developed it as part of his social contract theory.

Consequential strangers

Consequential strangers are personal connections who are neither family nor close friends, and so include many work connections, as well as professionals with whom one interacts on a recurring basis, such as doormen or security guards, the receptionist in one's doctor's office, one's dentist, or the wait staff at a favorite restaurant. They may also include social acquaintances with whom one has not had much one-on-one contact, such as friends-of-friends who are often invited to the same parties, or the neighbors of relatives whom one regularly visits. Sociological and social psychological work has become increasingly interested in these peripheral, secondary, or weak relationships, because of the sheer bulk of social "space" that they occupy in our lives. For instance, social interactions at work may be superficial beyond the interactions that focus on work itself, but they can nevertheless be crucial to one's emotional health.

Considerate style of leadership

As described by Fred Fiedler, a considerate style of leadership is one that focuses on relationships among co-workers, typified by a leader who derives satisfaction from healthy and positive interpersonal dynamics. This is particularly appropriate to work environments in which workers need or want autonomy in determining the course of their work, such as in research groups or college faculty, as opposed to work that benefits from or requires a high degree of task structure, such as factory work, emergency or disaster response, or a political campaign.

Consideration

One of two factors identified by the Ohio State Leadership Studies, consideration is the level of concern a leader displays for the well-being of his followers. Leaders who focus on this factor make themselves accessible and approachable to their followers, treat everyone as equal without strict concern for a hierarchy of roles, and foster employee engagement in the workplace. *See also* authenticity

Constitutional monarchy

A constitutional monarchy is not simply a monarchy in which the monarch's powers are limited by a written constitution but rather a form of democracy in which the monarch is a head of state whose actual political powers are limited. Most political powers are instead held by other bodies or by an executive branch of government that coexists with the monarch. In the United Kingdom, for instance, the prime minister holds most of the executive political power and is determined through election. Most constitutional monarchies are in western Europe, though Japan and Thailand are notable exceptions.

Constructivism

Constructivism is a theory of epistemology that posits that knowledge and meaning are created—constructed—in the human mind by the interaction between the individual's ideas and his experiences, a process that begins in infancy. Constructivists tend to put greater emphasis on the learner's role in the process of learning. At Phillips Exeter Academy, for instance, the Harkness method was developed, named for the circular Harkness table (named for a donor) at which students would sit for a discussion they guide themselves.

Consultative system

One of Renis Likert's management systems, in the consultative system, upper management controls decision making impacting the whole organization and general policies, while lower level employees are given a degree of decision-making power over their own work. Lower levels are consulted as part of the decision-making process at the upper levels, while both rewards and punishments are used to motivate behavior.

Consumer confidence

An economic indicator measuring consumers' feelings about the national economy in general and their personal financial situation specifically, as a factor impacting their future spending activity.

Contagious shooting

In military and police experiences, in which multiple armed officers or soldiers are present in a potentially threatening scenario, "contagious shooting" is an observed phenomenon in which one person in the group shooting leads to the others doing so. Though there is no scientific study confirming the phenomenon, it has been used to explain situations in which a number of shots are fired that are disproportionate to the threat level, such as many instances in which dozens of shots are fired by multiple officers at a single armed suspect, even when this requires reloading.

Contingency theory

The contingency theory school of behavioral theory says that the best system of leadership or decision making is contingent on internal and external factors specific to the situation, and that there is no universal "best" system. This has been used to explain why approaches that were successful in one set of circumstances did not translate to success for a leader or business in a different set of circumstances.

Continuous improvement

Continuous improvement (CI) is an effort in management to constantly improve products, services, or the processes involved in their production. Incremental continuous improvement, for instance, is a key feature of Japanese manufacturing. Though many point out that "continual improvement" is preferred grammatically, "continuous improvement" is nevertheless the term that has been adopted in the management world.

Control freak

A control freak is someone who is too invested in controlling the circumstances around them and the actions of people working under or with them. The phrase was coined in the 1960s in contrast with the loosening of social and cultural mores at the time and is not a formal psychological term, but there is considerable overlap between the idea of the control freak, the disorder of the antisocial personality, and the behaviors of micromanagement and perfectionism.

Corporate climate

Corporate climate is closely related to corporate culture, and consists of an organization's employees' perceptions of properties in the work environment (physical, social, organizational, and so on) that influence employee behavior. Corporate climate has a significant effect on employee retention and absenteeism.

Corporate governance

Corporate governance consists of the entities, processes, and mechanisms that direct and control the operations and activities of a corporation. Duties of corporate governance include the equitable treatment of shareholders and non-shareholder stakeholders, integrity on the part of corporate leadership and the organization as a whole, and transparency in the roles and responsibilities of corporate leadership. The "Anglo-American" model of corporate governance, practiced in most American and British companies, uses a system of corporate officers overseen by a single-tiered board of directors, while much of the rest of Europe uses a two-tiered board, one made up of executives and the other of non-executive members representing shareholders.

Corporation for National and Community Service

A U.S. federal agency formed after the 1990 National and Community Service Act, responsible for operating several programs aimed at supporting "the American culture of citizenship, service, and responsibility." Corporation for National and Community Service is the largest provider of grants for service and volunteer work, and operates the intensive community service program AmeriCorps, which provides staff for public agencies and non-profit community organizations; Senior Corps, which provides aid to senior citizens through community programs; and Learn and Serve America, which provides service learning programs for students.

Coughlin, Charles

Father Charles Coughlin is one of the better-known modern examples of a demagogue who was not himself a politician. The Catholic priest was an early adopter of mass media, addressing an audience in the Detroit, Michigan, area in 1926, on a radio program that was picked up nationally

Father Charles Coughlin delivered frequent radio addresses while leading the Christian Front group. (Library of Congress)

in 1930. His pre-Depression addresses covered mainly religious topics, and he was a staunch opponent of the Ku Klux Klan, which had adopted an anti-Catholic stance in its second incarnation. After the Depression, Coughlin became increasingly political, supporting the populist Huey Long and many of Roosevelt's New Deal reforms, but by the mid-1930s becoming known for his support of fascism, his anti-Semitism, and his claims that Jewish bankers had caused the Russian Revolution, while a "cash famine" had caused the Great Depression.

Counter-insurgency

The attempt by an incumbent government to resist and defeat an armed rebellion (or insurgency).

Court-packing plan

The court-packing plan was a strategy of President Franklin D. Roosevelt's, culminating in the failed Judicial Procedures Reform Bill of 1937. Because FDR's New Deal bills so drastically changed the scope of the federal government's powers and activities, he had faced difficulty with the Supreme Court, which heard several cases alleging that New Deal reforms were unconstitutional. Most were found in FDR's favor, but the experience soured his opinion of the judiciary branch, and he sought the power to increase the size of the court so that he could appoint enough new justices. Given the reverence the public possesses for the Constitution, and the widespread perception at the time of the court as guardians of that Constitution, it is a testament to Roosevelt's own popularity that his presidency was not more tarnished by this fairly clear overstep. The legislation failed, though notably while the bill was under discussion, the court ruled in favor on three New Deal cases Roosevelt had been concerned about. The fight over court-packing drifted from a conflict between FDR and the court into one between the president and factions within his own party; had World War II not brought many recalcitrants and resignees back to the fold, he might have permanently lost the support he enjoyed for the first half of his presidency.

Cowboy diplomacy

A disparaging term for foreign policy actions that involve heavy risk or provocation, especially with the implication that the cowboy diplomat in question lacks a mature and nuanced view of international relations.

Craft analogy

The ancient Greek philosopher Plato introduced the "craft analogy" of leadership in his attack on democracy (as practiced in Athens, where most public officials were selected by lottery). Plato wrote of the value of specialized training: physicians receive specialized training in order to be able to tend to the body's ailments, experienced sailors train new sailors in order to pass

on technical skills and accumulated knowledge of the sea, and so on. Leadership in Plato's view similarly benefited from, even required, specialized training, and was a true craft (that is, skill-based and teachable), rather than something that simply emerged from the would-be leader's personality and character.

Cravath system

The Cravath system is a law firm management system developed at Cravath, Swaine, and Moore, a New York City law firm, in the 19th century. It has since been adopted by many firms. The system encourages partners—who are the only tenured employees—to work together rather than in cliques, and adopts an "up or out" policy such that associates who are not made partner within ten years are dismissed. Similarly, partners are only hired from within the office, except when expertise is required that is unavailable in that pool. The partners lead the firm with a firm hand. The Cravath system also uses a lockstep compensation system for pay.

Creative class

The creative class as a socioeconomic class consisting of about 30 percent of the workforce was proposed by economics professor Richard Florida in 2002. Florida divided the creative class into the super-creatives, who are fully engaged in creative work for a living, and creative professionals, knowledge workers who solve specific types of problems in fields like healthcare, finance, and the legal sector. Florida's work was concerned in large part with predictions about the growth of the creative class, which were made before the 2008 financial crisis changed many of the important variables, and he has been criticized for not providing a clear definition of "creative." It dovetails with the rise of the term *quaternary sector* to refer to a fourth sector of the economy, based on information, knowledge, and knowledge-based services, and thus including media and culture businesses.

Creative industries

Creative industries, sometimes classed as part of the "quaternary sector" of the economy, include advertising, architecture, art, crafts, design, fashion, film, music, performing arts, publishing, research and development, toys, broadcasting, and video games. The more common European term is cultural industries, while some economic literature uses the term *creative economy*. The creative industries have risen in prominence in recent decades, as well as producing vital American exports at a time when manufacturing has declined. Richard Caves has proposed a list of properties characterizing the creative industries, including demand uncertainty as a result of the difficulty of ascertaining consumer reaction, much less predicting it, and "art for art's sake"—the fact that creative workers will work for lower wages and fewer rewards because the work itself is fulfilling.

Credentialism

Credentialism is the preferential status accorded to professional or academic credentials such as licenses, certificates, degrees, or organizational memberships, especially in hiring practices. The class effects of credentialism are well documented, since college degrees, for instance, are more easily available to the upper and middle class, and a college graduate will often be hired over a non-graduate even when the two candidates are equal in merit.

Creeping normality

Creeping normality is a phenomenon whereby a radical change, introduced incrementally, is accepted as normal because each increment is in of itself too small to inspire serious objection. It is often used in reference to climate change, for instance, in which any given change year to year is fairly small until accumulated changes cause a "sudden" disaster, or to the disappearance of the wetlands in coastal regions, the suburbanization and development of former farm towns, or the increase in cost of certain services and utilities.

Critical mass

In nuclear physics, critical mass is the level of fissile material mass needed for a nuclear chain reaction to sustain itself. In social dynamics, critical mass is achieved when an innovation has been adopted by a sufficient number of members of a social system that the rate of adoption can sustain itself.

Critical reflection

Critical reflection is a critical thinking process in which the individual examines and assesses the assumptions, presuppositions, and biases that inform his understanding of the world. S. D. Brookfield identified three phases of critical reflection: the identification of assumptions, the assessment of their validity, and the transformation of the individual's body of assumptions into something more appropriate. In some schools of thought in education, concepts similar to critical reflection are called reflective practice, reflective thinking, or reflexivity. In cooperative education, many educators recommend critical reflection assignments for students, in order to better guide the development of their understanding.

Critical thinking

"A well-trained man knows how to answer questions," sociologist E. Digby Baltzell wrote in

Harper's in 1955, "An educated man knows what questions are worth asking." He was addressing the goals of Bell Telephone's new liberal arts program for its executives, founded in order to develop leadership within the organization among managers who had primarily technical backgrounds. The curriculum focused on none of the technical issues their work addressed, but rather on developing their intellects and their critical thinking faculties. Critical thinking is disciplined thinking, by a rational agent who is able to evaluate the information available to them and the relationships among pieces of that information, and analyze and synthesize the results in the process of developing their views. Key to critical thinking is the awareness of the process, of one's own biases and the biases of others, and the ability to see multiple sides of a scenario, rather than responding from emotion or "going by the gut."

Croly, Herbert

One of the intellectual leaders of the late-19th- and early-20th-century Progressive movement, Herbert Croly co-founded the liberal magazine *The New Republic*. His books *The Promise of American Life* (1909) and *Progressive Democracy* (1914) were among the most most influential books on American liberalism, calling for stronger and more effective federal institutions, commercial reforms including the adoption of workplace democracy, and constituting the strongest articulation of an American liberalism that is neither anti-capitalist nor pacifist, advocating the protection of democracy abroad and an economic system that both respects the worker and encourages American ingenuity. His works were a strong influence on the New Deal, though he died shortly after the Great Depression began, without seeing his ideas adopted as policy.

Cross-cultural communication

Cross-cultural communication is a discipline that studies the ways people from different cultural backgrounds communicate, both among themselves and with one another, and the different types and strategies of communication found in cultures. It developed during the Cold War, when both the private sector and governments found that foreign language training alone was not sufficient preparation for expanding their operations internationally.

Crowd manipulation

Crowd manipulation is the attempt to influence or control a crowd's behavior or beliefs, in contexts ranging from sales pitches to large crowds to political campaign rallies.

Crystallized intelligence

Crystallized intelligence is one of two factors of general intelligence, representing the ability to use previously acquired skills and knowledge in order to solve problems or perform tasks. Crystallized intelligence is the ability to use and apply one's knowledge, whereas its counterpart, fluid knowledge, is the ability to perform in new situations based on methodologies like inductive or deductive reasoning.

Crystallized self

In contrast with the idea—prevalent in self-help books and the popular imagination, somewhat less dominant in psychology—that each individual has a single true and authentic self, the idea of the "crystallized self" is that of a faceted individual capable of showing multiple equally true selves. Notions of what constitutes the true self are particularly key to discussions of authenticity and authentic leadership, and more broadly to the idea of identity as explored by the social sciences.

Cult of personality

The "cult of personality" is the phenomenon that arises around a particular leader to create an idealized and heroic image. The term is especially associated with the state-sponsored idealization of such leaders, through propaganda, media influence, and even policy issues, and so the classic modern-day examples are Kim Il-Sung and Kim Jong-Il of North Korea, and Joseph Stalin of the Soviet Union. The term is sometimes used—though rarely by political scientists—more loosely to refer to the lionization of a leader or the glorification of a leader, and in this sense has been used in reference to people like Gandhi and Martin Luther King, Jr.

Cultural determinism

Cultural determinism states that key elements of an individual's psychological makeup, including aspects of behavior and emotional responses, are determined by the culture in which they are raised. Not every aspect is culturally determined, and the extent of variation in any given aspect varies from culture to culture as well. For instance, rural New Englanders are certainly not all identical in behavior or psychology, but most would agree their stoicism is a behavior common to the culture. Because culture is itself the collective product of individuals, cultural determinism paints a picture of individuals collectively creating a structure that perpetuates certain values and behaviors.

Cultural diplomacy

Cultural diplomacy is diplomacy conducted through the exchange of cultural products of the nation, as a way of encouraging understanding of and even emotional investment in one's own country on the part of the targeted country. The United States, as the chief exporter of culture for much of the 20th century, essentially stumbled into cultural diplomacy without a plan; South Korea, on the other hand, has engaged in a specific program of cultural diplomacy in recent years, called Hallyu.

Cultural diversity

Cultural diversity is the presence of multiple cultures, especially the healthy coexistence and mutual respect of such cultures. Just as biodiversity, the wide variety of life on Earth, is thought to be necessary for and an indicator of the quality of the health of the planet's ecosystem, so too have organizations like UNESCO argued that cultural diversity is necessary for the health of humanity. By extension, cultural diversity can be valuable for an organization in introducing a greater variety of viewpoints and competencies. Ideally, diversity is integrated into the organization, rather than grafted onto it through a separate program.

Cultural heritage hypothesis

The cultural heritage hypothesis is one attempt to explain the origin of cultural differences in decision making. The hypothesis explains these and other cultural differences with reference to the major philosophies and values forming the basis of a culture—Confucian thought, for instance, for much of Asia, and Aristotelian thought for much of the West. The differences between these philosophical systems trickle down into differences in behavior, values, and priorities. This seems to discount the relevance of philosophical developments since, or at least to subordinate their relevance to that of the earlier schools of thought.

Cultural schema

Cultural schema are schema that exist throughout a culture rather than just for the individual. While an individual's schema are formed by experience, cultural schema are formed by shared experiences and represent norms, expectations, and shared knowledge. There are basic schema consisting of facts, like what the capital of the United States is, and more complex schema representing information individuals might have trouble explaining the origin of, like the toppings that could potentially taste good on a pizza, a schema that differs significantly by country and sometimes region. Other schema deal with social situations, social roles, etiquette, and values attached to certain behaviors or traits.

Culture and affect display

The expression and display of emotion varies considerably by culture, and seems to be most noticeable in the difference between Eastern and Western displays (very little work has been done on affect display or emotions in the cultures of sub-Saharan Africa or the indigenous cultures of Australia or the Americas). Generally speaking, affect display is subtler and more moderate in Asia than in Europe and the Americas. This difference is sometimes chalked up to the Eastern tendency toward collectivist cultures, compared to the Western sacralizing of individualism, with the implication that in an individualist culture, broader displays of emotion are encouraged and accepted. The relative stoicism of Eastern cultures historically contributed to the Western caricature of Asians as "inscrutable" or "mysterious." There are notable exceptions to these generalizations, and Finland in particular is noted for cultural norms discouraging broad affect display in public. Differences in affect display can lead to cross-cultural misunderstandings, as well as impact the extent to which an individual interacting with members of another culture is able to put his putative charisma and social skills to work.

Culture trust and distrust

Any culture may be thought of as a culture of trust or distrust. Cultures of trust are associated with greater well-being and economic growth, and members are better able to manage insecure situations. Individuals in cultures of distrust tend to perceive trusting individuals as naive or weak, and live in a culture of cynicism, exploitation, and corruption.

Cyber-harassment in the workplace

The sociological work on the effect of the Internet as a communication medium on the inhibitions and empathy of communicators is considerable, and at least some of this disinhibiting effect seems to hold even when the medium is not anonymizing—when the conversation is between people who know each other. Cyber-harassment and cyber-bullying are serious problems in modern culture, and the workplace is not immune to them. Messages sent by e-mail, messenger programs, or over social networks may bully their targets directly or may include sexist, racist, or otherwise offensive material that constitutes harassment. Further, the use of social networks, which are mediated outside the workplace, raises questions about the proper interaction between co-workers online, outside of work hours.

"Daisy"

"Daisy" was the most famous piece of Lyndon B. Johnson's 1964 presidential campaign against ultraconservative hawk Barry Goldwater. While its descendant in fear-mongering campaign ads, "Bear in the woods," positioned Ronald Reagan as the only president prepared for (presumably nuclear) conflict with Russia, "Daisy" warned against such conflict, and implied it would be much more likely under Goldwater. The ad depicts a 2-year-old girl picking the petals of a daisy while counting, fading into a missile launch countdown and a nuclear explosion. The final voiceover says, "Vote for President Johnson on November 3. The stakes are too high for you to stay home."

Dalai Lama

The Dalai Lama is a religious and sometimes political leader in Tibetan Buddhism, whose teachers are titled "lama." Certain lamas called tulkus are considered the reincarnations of enlightened beings of the past (before the Chinese invasion of 1950, there were thousands of tulkus in Tibet; there are now roughly 500). Tulkus, nearly all of whom are male, have specific lineages of reincarnation, and the current Dalai Lama is the fourteenth in the lineage, believed to be the manifestation of Avalokitesvara, the bodhisattva (enlightened being) who is the universal manifestation of compassion. At various times from the 1600s until the Chinese invasion, several Dalai Lamas served as the head of the Tibetan government. The 14th Dalai Lama has lived in exile since fleeing to India in 1959, and retired as head of the Tibetan government in exile in 2011. Though he mentioned in

Tenzin Gyatso, His Holiness The 14th Dalai Lama of Tibet (left), won the Nobel Peace Prize in 1989. The Dalai Lama is the longest-living incumbent. (Seattle Municipal Archives)

a 1970s interview that he expected to be the last Dalai Lama, he announced at the time of his retirement that the decision of whether or not to reincarnate would be made following discussions with other lamas and comment from the public of the Tibetan diaspora.

Decentralized decision making

Decision-making processes that are distributed across a group are called decentralized decision making, especially in large organizations where decision-making processes and authority can be distributed across multiple layers, so that workers have some amount of decision-making power over their own work, managers over the aims of the groups they manage, department heads over the purview of their departments, and so on.

Decision engineering

Decision engineering approaches organizational decision making from an engineering perspective, by incorporating best practices in order to provide a structured decision-making framework that is informed by complexity theory and systems thinking.

Decision making

The process of selecting a choice from multiple possibilities is one of the oldest areas of study in philosophy and the social sciences, and has been an important area of study in disciplines from political science and ethics to psychology and neuroscience. Studies may be, broadly, either descriptive—illustrating how individuals and groups make decisions—or prescriptive, presenting or justifying a preferred method.

Decision-making model of leadership

The decision-making model of leadership posits that leadership is fundamentally a decision-making activity (more than it is a relationship with followers, for instance). Like Situational Leadership Theory, this model is well-suited to leadership training because it supposes that leaders *can* be trained, and that leadership is a teachable skill.

Decision theory

Decision theory is the study of the underlying factors involved in making a decision, and of the optimality and rationality of the resulting decision. Decision theory is similar to game theory—and to a game theorist may simply appear to be a special case of game theory—and plays an important role in economics, philosophy, and the social sciences. It is correct both to speak of "decision theory," as in the field, and "a decision theory," as in the specific theoretical underpinnings of a decision-making methodology.

Deep blue sea

Wilfred Drath used the metaphor of the deep blue sea to explain the difference between leaders and leadership in leadership studies: leaders are the white caps of ocean waves, but they cannot be understood without understanding the mechanics of the deep blue sea below them. Drath differentiated these approaches as personal leadership (the Great Man–influenced study of the character and attributes of individual leaders) and relational leadership, the study of the deep blue sea, in the form of the system of relationships in which leadership takes place.

Defensive realism

An application of realism (cf.) in its international relations sense, defensive realism says that because survival is the main motivator of states and states act rationally, states will always act to maximize their own security and defenses.

Definition of the situation

In sociology, the definition of the situation consists of the characteristics of a given social situation, including the roles assumed by the participants, the norms and values governing or guiding their actions, and other elements. Successful social interaction requires agreeing to the definition of the situation, which is rarely explicit; in fact, in some situations, attempting to explicitly define the situation may be counterproductive or met with resistance.

Defense mechanism

In psychology, a defense mechanism is an unconscious coping strategy for dealing with anxiety. Common defense mechanisms discussed in Freudian psychoanalysis, for instance, include rationalization, in which the individual justifies his own bad behavior or impulses by concocting valid reasons to support it, turning it into "good" behavior and avoiding the anxiety of guilt; and repression, in which the individual buries an impulse or the feelings about a behavior rather than deal with them. Defense mechanisms are not inherently unhealthy, and become unhealthy only when they lead to unhealthy behavior or cause emotional damage. The presence of the defense mechanism is one of the factors explaining how people are able to behave in a way that is contrary to their stated beliefs and values. Defense mechanisms in the workplace can result in challenges for leaders. Workers may have developed unrealistic views of the quality of their work or their relationships with other people as the result of pathological defense mechanisms like the superiority complex, for instance, or may respond to stress in the workplace with passive aggression.

Healthy defense mechanisms include forgiveness—which relieves the individual of the anxiety of continuing to think about the wrong done against them—as well as emotional self-regulation.

Deformation professionnelle

The French phrase *deformation professionnelle* translates literally as "professional deformation," but might be better called "conditioning" or "socialization." The phrase captures the idea that one's profession, in part because it takes up so many waking hours and so many hours of concentration and engagement, shapes the way one views the world—not simply in positive ways by exposing one to valuable information about the workings of the world, but by distorting one's view. A common worry, for instance, is that police officers begin to see the world as one filled with criminals and victims, while the views of divorce lawyers on the virtues of marriage are the subject matter of a number of romantic comedies.

Deindividuation

Deindividuation is the phenomenon of diminished self-awareness and self-evaluation when in groups, often leading to a diminution of inhibitions.

Deliberative democracy

Deliberative democracy is a term coined by Joseph M. Bessette in his 1980 book of the same name, and refers to democratic government in which the decision-making process is committed to deliberation, not in lieu of voting but as a key component of the process. In the United States, the Green Party is the only party specifically committed to deliberative democracy, but various government and non-profit groups have encouraged deliberation in the run-up to specific legislative issues, notably health care reform.

Demagogue

The word *demagogue* originally meant a leader of the common people, with no specific connotation beyond that. The word comes from the ancient Greek, and in Athens the word came to be used to refer to violent and trouble-making lower-class citizens who were elected to office, usually after a campaign of emotional appeal, lies, and unkept promises. Demagogue has since come to mean a political leader who gains power by exploiting the fears, prejudices, and other negative emotions of the working class. Their political rhetoric is often marked by extremism, a call to action, and positions that eschew deliberation, compromise, and moderation in favor of decisiveness and easy to understand sound bites.

Demand control model

A model from positive psychology that promotes a workplace design of high demand and high control, in order to encourage employee learning and autonomy. Social support between managers and employees is important in this model, in order to place workers in positions that keep them active and interested in seeking out challenging situations.

Deming, W. Edwards

W. Edwards Deming introduced the Effiency movement to Japan after World War II, as part of the larger effort to modernize and Westernize aspects of Japanese industry. When Japan's postwar economy rebounded in the Japanese "economic miracle" of the 1950s, Deming was given much of the credit, especially by the United States, and he eventually returned to the United States to work as a consultant.

During the late 1970s and early 1980s, when economic competition with Japan's manufacturing sector was of chief concern to Americans, his expert opinion was sought to increase the efficiency of American industries, leading to a consultancy position with Ford (which in turn led to the launch of the Ford Taurus) and the publication of his book *Quality, Productivity, and Competitive Position*, later republished as *Out of the Crisis*. The book was the primary inspiration for the Total Quality Management movement, a revival of the Efficiency movement.

Democratic peace theory

Democratic peace theory, interdemocracy nonaggression theory, or mutual democratic pacifism are all terms to refer to the idea that democratic states are less likely to go to war with other democratic states. Explanations of the theory include the effect of war on reelection, the possibility of successful diplomatic institutions to resolve conflicts instead, and the inclination to view other democratic states favorably. Advocates of the theory sometimes conflict with the realist view that the world is in a constant state of war; on the other hand, critics of democratic peace theory point to the lack of a well-defined model of causality and the possibility that it is only an irrelevant correlation. Often relevant to the discussion is the much discussed fact that there have been no major European general wars since the end of World War II, an unprecedented period of peace that might be explained by the advent of the European Union or factors related to the Cold War and its dissipation. There have been some well-known wars between democracies, notably the Spanish–American and Mexican–American wars, the Boer wars, and the American Revolutionary War.

Depersonalization

In normal psychological context, depersonalization is the experience of watching oneself act with no sense of control, often accompanied with the feeling of being less real. It can be experienced by anyone and is often a response to trauma, but chronic depersonalization is associated with a variety of disorders. In social psychology, however, depersonalization is the perception of the self as the embodiment of a social stereotype rather than as a unique individual.

Descriptive

There is a divide in philosophy and many of the social sciences between the descriptive and the prescriptive. Descriptive work and research seeks to describe the world—descriptive approaches to sociology, for instance, model how people and institutions behave, while descriptive linguistic describes how people use language. Prescriptivism, in contrast, is occupied with defending the right way to do something, rather than showing the various ways people do that thing. Descriptive models of leadership focus not on recommending leadership approaches, but identifying what real-world leaders actually do (and, often, the effects of what they do).

Descriptive representation

Descriptive representation is the mathematical proportion of members of a given group who are elected or appointed to a given government body, such as the number of women in Congress. *See also* substantive representation

Design by committee

"Design by committee" is a pejorative term referring to a project that has been designed or managed with the input of multiple parties and has suffered for it. The pejorative dimension of an otherwise neutral-sounding, descriptive phrase may be a reference to the description of a camel as a "horse designed by committee," attributed to the automobile designer Alec Issigonis.

Deterrence theory

Deterrence theory was a military strategy used during the Cold War and was best articulated in Thomas Schelling's 1966 *Diplomacy of Violence*. The essence of the theory states that military strategy in the Cold War, because of the consequences of going to war, needed to be concerned with not just victory but with dissuading the other side from engaging in hostilities. Though Americans and Soviets spent most of the Cold War anticipating the beginnings of war, almost five decades passed from the end of their World War II alliance to the dissolution of communism without a single missile launched (though several proxy wars were fought, to neither side's satisfaction). Deterrence theory is essentially synonymous with nuclear deterrence: the amassing of a well-distributed and well-protected nuclear arms stockpile (though both of these adjectives have been questioned in hindsight) sufficient to dissuade the other party from attempting war due to the realities of Mutually Assured Destruction. Sixteen years after the end of the Cold War, several architects of deterrence theory—notably Henry Kissinger and George Shultz—disavowed it in a *Wall Street Journal* article in which they expressed their concerns about the threats posed by decades of nuclear weapons proliferation.

Dictatorial style

One of the leadership styles plotted on the managerial grid model, the dictatorial style was originally called the produce or perish style. Dictatorial managers have a high concern for production and low concern for people, and

expect employees' pay to be sufficient motive to ensure performance and loyalty, or they risk being replaced. This is the same leadership style as Theory X (cf).

Dictatorship of the proletariat

In the works of Karl Marx, Friedrich Engels, and their followers, a dictatorship of the proletariat, in which the working class has seized political power, is a transitional step between capitalism—in which the capitalists possess the power—and communism, in which power is commonly owned. "Dictatorship" here means simply "rule," and modern translations of Marx sometimes reflect this, but the phrase entered the English language and fossilized before "dictatorship" became synonymous with "autocracy."

Differential psychology

Differential psychology is the psychological study of the ways and reasons that individuals exhibit different behaviors, including personality, intelligence and other mental capacities, skills and abilities, interests, self-concept and esteem, and morals.

Diffusion of innovations

Communications studies professor Everett Rogers introduced the theory of the diffusion of innovations in his 1962 book of the same name, which has remained in print and an important contribution in the study of ideas and technology. Innovations—new technologies or ideas—are, according to this theory, passed along through channels of communication by participants in the social system in which they have been introduced. Rogers helped popularize the term *early adopter*, in reference to opinion leaders who are among the first to adopt an innovation.

Diffusion of responsibility

Diffusion of responsibility is a phenomenon that occurs in groups, wherein any given individual is less likely to take the initiative to perform an action or resolve a problem if other people are present who could do so. In the workplace, this is one justification for the explicit division of labor and duties. In situations where someone needs help, this phenomenon is called the bystander effect, the most famous example of which is the typical portrayal of the Kitty Genovese murder. As it happens, that portrayal is inaccurate, but the idea of a woman having been murdered in full view of her neighbors, who did nothing to intervene or report the crime to the police, was the catalyst for much of the research into the diffusion of responsibility.

Dilbert Principle

The Dilbert Principle, introduced in the Dilbert comic strip by Scott Adams, states that the least competent people are promoted to management positions in order to shift them away from roles that actually perform work.

Diplomacy

Diplomacy is the art of negotiations that transpire between representatives of states, including trade and economics issues, human rights and environmental concerns, war and peace-making, as well as the everyday business of maintaining diplomatic relationships between states. In the modern world, diplomacy has arisen as a professional field, and ambassadors and their staffs are significant players in international affairs, largely unnoticed by the public. While the focus of history is often on the diplomats of the largest or most aggressive states, the role of small state diplomacy is slowly being recognized, as smaller states are so affected by the actions of larger states that diplomacy is one of the most vital tools available to ensure the protection of their interests. Diplomats act in accordance to policies over which they have no control—set by the executive and legislative branches—but nevertheless frequently take on leadership positions, negotiating terms of treaties, finding means of gaining strategic advantage over other states, and acting to avoid armed conflicts. Because of their importance, diplomats and their communication have long been considered untouchable by foreign powers, either by convention or—in the modern world—by international agreement.

Diplomat

See diplomacy

Diplomatic history

The history of international relations between countries, diplomatic history tends to focus specifically on the relevant foreign policy and trade relations of the countries involved, and the official negotiations between states, rather than cultural exchanges and informal contact between citizens. Diplomatic histories tend to focus on leaders, having been influenced by the Great Man histories, though some focus on the important role played by individual diplomats and the choices they make. Diplomatic histories go back as far as the ancient Greek Thucydides, but are especially associated with the 19th and 20th centuries; the 19th-century German historian Leopold von Ranke considered diplomatic history the most important field in history. Winston Churchill's 1948 history *The Gathering Storm* set the tone for even non-diplomatic histories of World War II in its portrayal of appeasement policies.

Direct democracy

Direct democracy is a form of democratic governance in which actions and policies are determined by the group, whether through voting, consensus building, or other means, rather than by elected representatives, as in representative democracy. Direct democracy invites the danger of the tyranny of the majority, concerns over which led to the framing of the U.S. government as a representative democracy. However, direct democracy practices are used in many American communities, as well as for specific kinds of laws and policies in every state (proposed constitutional amendments, for instance, and referred to the legislature by a vote of the people in almost every state, while 19 states give the people the power to recall an elected official through popular vote). Concerns with the electoral college, even before the controversial 2000 presidential election, have motivated a push for direct elections of the president, and technological advances have led some to advocate electronic direct democracy, facilitating participation in policy votes through computers.

Disney method

A problem-solving and idea-generating strategy developed by neuro-linguistic programming pioneer and motivational speaker Robert Dilts, the Disney method calls for the use of four different thinking styles, undertaken in sequence as the group adopts different roles: that of outsiders, to gain an external objective perspective; that of dreamers, to brainstorm creative solutions; that of realists, to examine the brainstormed ideas and their possible implementations; and that of critics, to evaluate the plan of the realists. Key to Dilts's method is that the same people perform these four roles, rather than distributing them to different people.

Dispositional affect

In psychology, dispositional affect is the personality trait that reflects an individual's general tendency toward positive or negative views and responses. It is not the same as optimism versus pessimism, though that is a convenient comparison. An individual with a high positive affectivity will tend toward optimism but also experiences positive moods more often and in a larger variety of circumstances, while experiencing generally high energy. Someone with high negative affectivity may be a pessimist but is also more easily upset, tends toward low self-esteem, becomes distressed when challenged, and tends to exhibit high levels of negative moods like nervousness, annoyance, fear, or melancholy. Dispositional affect is sometimes called the lens through which the individual sees the world—pink (as in rose-colored glasses) or black—and has a clear effect on the individual's interpersonal relationships and presence. Dispositional affect has experimentally demonstrated effects on both decision making and negotiation, as well—high-positive individuals are more open to cooperation, flexibility, and "outside the box" suggestions. Contrary to expectation of some researchers, risk aversion does not seem to be affected.

Dispute system

See complaint system

Dissanayake, Ellen

In her 1995 book *Homo Aestheticus*, anthropologist Ellen Dissanayake argues that there is an innate human need to "make special," and that accordingly, artistic activities should be considered in the same light as rituals and festivals, as ways in which humans approach aspects of their experience to "make special." The singling out of individuals as leaders is similarly "making special."

Dissident

A dissident actively opposes the power of a particular status quo. Although the term originally referred to those who separated from the Church of England, since the 1940s it has been used in political contexts, first to refer to critics of communism in eastern Europe. More recently it has been applied to Americans acting in opposition to key activities of the American government, such as Edward Snowden.

Divide and conquer

To "divide and conquer" is to break a group into smaller parts over which power can be maintained, or obtained, more easily than the whole, and to continue to prevent those smaller groups from consolidating. It is especially associated with imperialism, beginning with ancient Rome and practiced by the colonial powers during the 18th and 19th century, when European powers would create or encourage social divisions in African and Asian nations over which they held sway.

Divine right of kings

The doctrine of the divine right of kings states that the monarch receives his authority and legitimacy directly from God, and is thus bound by no earthly authority. This was the justification for absolute monarchy in Europe, though Catholics and Protestants tended to differ on the role of the church in such an arrangement, with the Catholic Church tending to favor a view of the pope as possessing an authority greater than those of any king (which created a check against the power of monarchs), as the representative of God, while Protestants were more likely to favor treating the church as an institution that answered to, or operated completely independent from, the state. The alliance between the pope and various monarchs of western Europe was an important one; the pope's endorsement of a monarch as chosen by God validated the power of each of them.

In Asia, a similar concept was the Mandate of Heaven.

Dollar diplomacy

Dollar diplomacy began as an American foreign policy in the late 19th and early 20th centuries, in which guaranteed loans were extended to foreign governments as enticement to get them to agree to American requests. It was especially key in American relations with Latin America.

Dominant minority

A dominant minority is a minority group that is sufficiently powerful to be politically or economically dominant in a country. This usually refers to ethnic minorities who, often for historical reasons, control the political or economic institutions of a country, such as the Russian-speaking Ukrainians of Ukraine, the Basque-Chileans of Chile, and the Americo-Liberians of Liberia. In the age of imperialism, it was also true of whites in South Africa and Rhodesia, the Dutch in the Dutch East Indies, and the French in Vietnam. On a smaller scale, dominant minorities may be found in cities where most of the key leadership and law enforcement positions are filled by the same ethnic minority, such as the whites of Ferguson, Missouri.

Draft

The draft is an informal U.S. term for the practice of military conscription—the compulsory enlistment of young men (almost exclusively) in the military, one of the oldest methods for populating an army. Since the political, cultural, and military failures of the Vietnam War, reviving the draft has been perceived as a political impossibility, but it was a driving force in the culture of young American men for over a century.

Dramaturgy

Dramaturgy is a framework in sociology, introduced by Erving Goffman in his 1959 *Presentation of Self in Everyday Life*, which describes social interactions in theatrical terms, and constructs them as dependent on time, setting, and audience. In particular, individual identity in dramaturgical sociology is presented as fluid, shaped in response to interactions with others, and scenes that are played out.

Drive theory

Drive theory is one of the "four psychologies" forming the foundation of modern psychology. Building on the work of Sigmund Freud, it studies psychological drives—the drive to meet a psychological need—and the phenomena that arise from the tension of unmet needs and the manner by which the individual meets those needs.

Drucker, Peter

Peter Drucker was a management consultant and author best known for his development of management by objectives, or management by results. His first major work, 1946's *Concept of the Corporation*, is an examination of General Motors and its relationship to society. His delineation of the interpersonal interactions within the company, the political environment, decision-making processes, and power structures, provided a new way to look at a business, arguably the most significant change in approaches to management since scientific management. He wrote 39 books in addition to running his management consulting firm, and his work became popular enough in Japan that a 2009 best-selling novel, *What if the Female Manager of a High-School Baseball Team Read Drucker's Management*, was adapted into both animated and live-action films. The Global Peter Drucker Forum is an annual international management conference devoted to his philosophy.

Dunning-Kruger effect

The Dunning-Kruger (DK) effect is a cognitive bias whereby an individual who is unskilled in a given area not only overestimates his ability in that area, but has difficulty recognizing the genuine ability of others in that area. It is named for David Dunning and Justin Kruger, Cornell University researchers who first conducted experiments testing it in 1999. Experiments also demonstrated that the bias is not permanent—learning the skill in question leads to recognition of one's previous incompetence. Media coverage of the DK effect focused on the tendency of people to overrate their abilities in areas where they lack skills and training, but equally interesting—and differentiating the cognitive bias from a superiority complex or the overconfidence effect—is the inability to recognize skill in others. The combination easily leads to circumstances in which someone continues to make poor choices informed by their own incompetence even when they have been advised otherwise by competent people, because they lack the grounding in the relevant area to recognize competence when they see it.

Dyad

In sociology, a dyad is the smallest possible social group, consisting of two people. Any two people who interact in some way constitute a dyad, and the strength and stability of the dyad is the result of their efforts, intensity, and the amount of time they spend together, as well as the relative rewards and costs that are incurred.

Early adopter

The term *early adopter* was introduced in Everett Rogers' 1962 book *Diffusion of Innovations* and has become well-known in the 21st century. Early adopters are among the first individuals who either (in the original coinage) become customers of a new product or (in the recent broader sense) adopt a new technology, process, approach, or idea. One may speak both of an individual being an early adopter of an iPhone and of a business being an early adopter of pay-by-smartphone-app technologies. Rogers described a bell curve, consisting (in order of adoption) of innovators, early adopters, early majority, late majority, and laggards. In this bell curve, it is important to note that early adopters are the second group to adopt an innovation; they are characterized by being choosier than the innovators (who are attracted to novelty), but still tend to be wealthier and more technologically literature than the majority. Their choosiness makes them important opinion leaders. In some cases, early adopters are an important part of the business model behind a new product: their purchases at higher prices, before the mass release of a cheaper model, essentially subsidize the cost of the product for later adopters; in other cases, the product they purchase is buggier or lacks key features introduced in the later version the majority will adopt, and their user experiences and feedback help to improve the product's design (which is not to say that they are acknowledged as beta testers).

Eating your own dog food

Eating your own dog food is the practice of a company using its own products as evidence of their faith in those products. In 1981, for instance, Apple Computer eliminated the use of typewriters in their offices, in favor of Apple computers for all word processing, spreadsheets, etc. In contrast, the adoption of AOL e-mail by Time Warner after the 2001 merger of the two companies was seen as disastrous, because there was no way to import old e-mails, which were lost as a result.

Economic history

Economic history uses both historical and statistic methods to study historical events, trends, and institutions from the perspective of modern economic theory. This may encompass areas of labor history or international relations. Often a goal is to demonstrate the validity of economic theories with reference to the past, or to increase understanding of economic theory through an economic understanding of the past.

Educational psychology

Educational psychology is the branch of psychology that studies learning, especially but not limited to the study of formal educational settings and the ways to optimize the experience. The study of learning encompasses individual, group, and organizational learning and experiences, memory, cognition and conceptualization, instruction, and the impact on the learning experience of other psychological factors. For instance, developmental psychology and educational psychology share an interest in how young children learn.

Efficiency movement

The Eficciency movement was a decentralized movement in business practices, especially in the industry and the public sector, in the late 19th and early 20th centuries. In the United States, the Efficiency movement (which had the support of many of the age's business tycoons, like Andrew Carnegie) was part of the larger Progressive movement which was inspired by the scientific and technological advances of the 19th century to seek scientifically informed improvements to as many aspects of life

A PRACTICAL FORESTER
(A subject that had attention all through Mr.
Roosevelt's Presidency.)

A 1908 editorial cartoon featuring Theodore Roosevelt, who was staunchly committed to conserving natural resources. The conservation movement came to prominence during the Progressive era. (Public Domain)

Division in 1910, examining city employees' performance and standardizing procedures for maximum efficiency. Schools of business administration offered management training programs for both the public and private sector, and Efficiency spread even to the use of natural resources, thanks to Theodore Roosevelt's staunch commitment to conservationism. The Efficiency movement finally fell out of favor due to Herbert Hoover's failure to adequately deal with the Great Depression of 1929; Hoover was the president most strongly associated with the movement, in part due to his background as an engineer.

Effort heuristic

The effort heuristic is an idea in psychology saying that people assign a value to a thing based on their perceptions of the effort that went into it, rather than simply its quality or function. This also affects the efforts people put into their work: if the goal does not seem valuable, their efforts will be diminished. Similarly, people observing their work will undervalue it if they believe it came easily, independent of their performance quality.

Ego psychology

Ego psychology is one of the "four psychologies" forming the foundation of modern psychology. It consists of the study and elaboration of Sigmund Freud's model of the mind as being divided into id, ego, and superego: instinct (id), judgment (superego), and the mediator between them (ego).

Egocentric advice discounting

In the social science study of advice, egocentric advice discounting is the tendency of a decision-maker to prioritize advice they receive that is closely aligned to the preconceptions

as possible. One of the most far-ranging social movements in the United States, Progressivism encompassed efforts as varied as modernizing facilities for the mentally ill in light of the new psychological science, improving services to the poor and sick in order to reduce poverty, creating state- or nation-wide standards for free public education, increasing the rights of workers and women, and creating professional standards and governing bodies for roles like doctors and lawyers. The Efficiency movement sought to maximize the utility of the advances of the Industrial Revolution, by making factory work as efficient as possible through scientific management (cf.), and to create a class of trained bureaucrats. Chicago, for instance, was the first of several cities to create an Efficiency and opinions they had formed before seeking advice. This is functionally similar to confirmation bias.

Elites

In political science, the elites or power elite are a small group of people with disproportionate political power or wealth. Leadership studies in political science have typically focused on members of this group, including heads of state, government officials, and leaders of political movements. C. Wright Mills's 1957 book *The Power Elite* discussed elites in America as primarily a group of prep school and Ivy League educated–WASPs from well-established wealthy families, from which group a disproportionate number of political and military leaders have come. Mills distinguishes the power elite from the more British idea of a ruling class because its power is consolidated through association with wealth-generating and -preserving organizations rather than through the British class system, which is more concerned with social ties and family prominence than with wealth.

Elitism

Elitism is the belief that a particular group of people, because of a particular kind of superiority (usually based on class, wealth, or education), generates opinions and judgments that should be lent greater weight than those of others. It is compatible with ideas like Plato's philosopher kings, but when the elite group is defined broadly enough, it is also at the heart of such things as literacy tests for voter registration.

Elizabeth I

The Queen of England from 1558 until 1603, Elizabeth I was the last monarch of the Tudor dynasty, and the daughter of Henry VIII. She came to the throne as a young woman in a tumultuous time, the third monarch in a five-year span, succeeding her half-brother Edward VI and half-sister Mary, the latter of whom had attempted to remarry the Church of England back to Rome after Henry had severed its ties, and had imprisoned Elizabeth for suspected conspiring with Protestants. Despite or because of this, Elizabeth was a moderate both politically and religiously, reestablishing the Church of England, reducing factionalism in her government, and playing it safe in foreign affairs. She never married and was believed to remain a virgin all her life. The Elizabethan era now named for her included the dramas and poetry of William Shakespeare and Christopher Marlowe, the voyages of Francis Drake, the first English settlements in the New World, and the music of composers like William Byrd and Thomas Campion. It is still considered a golden age for the country.

Emerson, Harrington

Inspired by Frederick Winslow Taylor, management consultant Harrington Emerson adopted scientific management principles—originally developed for factory labor—for the Santa Fe Railway, creating a division between staff employees, who worked as managers, and line employees, who did most of the labor. Bonuses were paid for better-than-average work, as well as to foremen, and time studies were performed in order to set standards for each task (after first standardizing equipment throughout the railway).

Emotional aperture

Emotional aperture is the ability to perceive group emotions, rather than focusing only on the affect display of a single person. Leaders skilled at emotional aperture are able to perceive the affective diversity of their group and the relative high positives and low negatives of the moods in play, in addition to "taking the temperature of the room" and determining the most common emotion in the group. This is an aspect of emotional intelligence, but most tests and studies of emotional intelligence have focused on one-on-one interactions.

Emotional competence
Emotional competence is related to emotional intelligence, and consists of the ability to express and vent one's emotions, rather than suppressing or ignoring them. Psychologists believe emotional competence is an important component of well-being.

Emotional contagion
Emotional contagion is the unintentional emulation or reflection of one person's emotions by another person, especially beginning with mimicry of their emotional expressions, followed by reflections of the emotions themselves. Emotional contagion has been subject to extensive research that has found people's emotions are heavily influenced by the nonverbal emotion-indicating cues of others, such that they can reflect emotions they are not even aware the other person is feeling. Neuroscientists have theorized that mirror neurons may be implicated in the mechanism of emotional contagion. Emotional contagion received considerable press in 2014 after the revelation that Facebook had carried out an experiment on over half a million users by manipulating their news feed to measure the extent to which exposure to negative emotions in others' status feeds would result in posting similar emotional statuses.

Emotional intelligence
Emotional intelligence is the capacity to perceive, understand, and manage emotions. The concept was developed in the 1990s, and various attempts have been made to quantify emotional intelligence in individuals, as well as to link high scores to leadership ability. There is disagreement as to whether emotional intelligence measures something distinct from existing personality tests and metrics, or if it represents something already described by models like the Big Five. The term was first coined by Daniel Goleman, in whose formulation it consists of five components: self-awareness, self-regulation, internal motivation, empathy, and social skills.

Emotional self-regulation
Emotional self-regulation is the ability to have emotional responses to changing circumstances that are honest and authentic while at the same time remaining within the bounds of social norms and continuing to function in one's life. Although to some degree this means keeping an even keel—not giving in to drastic sways in mood or wallowing in emotional extremes—it also entails modulating behavior even when internal emotions are strong. For instance, upon hearing of a death in the family, an individual may wait until they are home, or at least no longer in a public setting, before bursting into tears. And tears or no, emotional self-regulation allows that individual to deal with the pragmatic post-mortem processes like funeral arrangements, notifying friends and family and employers, dealing with the will, and so on, without simply repressing grief and anger. In leaders, emotional self-regulation is an important part of professionalism.

Emotional tyranny
Communication Studies professor Vincent Waldron coined the term *emotional tyranny* in 2000 to refer to the use of emotions and emotional displays by leaders and influential

members of a group in ways that are cruel, damaging, or are motivated by seeking control. Tactics of such tyranny include using emotional language to describe employees, rather than describing their behavior or the results of their work; using emotional displays as a punishment or threat, such as subjecting workers to angry tirades or displays of disappointment, especially as a way to manipulate their behavior; and including emotional language in workplace communications. Emotional tyranny is especially associated with aggressive displays of emotion, but Waldron's description would also be consistent with a manipulative form of passive aggression in a supervisor whose employees work not under threat of an enraged outburst, but the threat of crying, guilt, or panic at the prospect of goals not being met.

Emotions in the workplace

The importance of the emotional states of the workplace and the emotional impact of events and processes at work has enjoyed greater attention in research since the publication of Arlie Hochschild's 1983 *The Managed Heart*. Emotions of individuals and groups play a role in the social health of the workplace and the engagement, absenteeism, and satisfaction of individual workers, while the negative use or expression of emotions is consistently associated with poor leadership.

Empathic accuracy

Empathic accuracy is a specific measure of empathy, measuring the accuracy with which an individual can determine the feelings and emotional state (and possibly the causes and contexts thereof) of another person. The term was coined in 1988 and has been the subject of neuroscience research, which has shown that the two areas of the brain most associated with it are (1)

affect sharing, the ability to share the emotion the other person is feeling; and (2) mentalizing, the ability to think about and label that emotion. The increased public awareness of autism spectrum disorders and Asperger's syndrome in the 21st century has, in turn, increased awareness of how fundamental processes like empathy are to the everyday social interactions of people who are not on the spectrum.

Empathy

Empathy is the human ability to recognize and understand the emotions felt by another, and to be influenced by them—to feel happy because of another person's joy, for instance, or be moved to anger by another person's rage. It includes the ability to emotionally engage in fiction or other representations (including movies, music, nonfictional biographies, and other works in which individuals' emotions are portrayed). Empathy is not an all-or-nothing capacity—we may sometimes perceive that someone is feeling a negative emotion, but have difficulty, especially if we lack the context of what has brought them to this state, pinpointing whether it is anger, guilt, or sadness. Empathy is not the same as sympathy—recognizing emotion, even understanding its sources, does not require feeling tender toward them or perceiving them as in need. It is the precursor to emotional contagion, however. Empathy is a significant factor in interpersonal interactions, one that has been extensively studied but for which extensive study yet remains. It is key to certain forms of intelligence, and likely to charismatic and authentic leadership styles.

"The Emperor's New Clothes"

"The Emperor's New Clothes" is one of Hans Christian Andersen's fairy tales, first published in 1837 as the third booklet in his *Fairy*

Tales Told for Children series, along with "The Little Mermaid." The story is perhaps his most familiar today: the Emperor, motivated by his vanity, purchases new clothes from con men who convince him that they are invisible only to the stupid and incompetent. Though they present him with nothing at all, the Emperor pretends to be impressed by them so as not to seem stupid; his ministers do likewise, as do the townsfolk when the Emperor parades before them. Only a naive child who does not understand the desire to conform cries out that the Emperor is naked. Often told today as a parable about groupthink, in its time it was likely also a criticism of the growing bureaucracy and the hopeless leaders who were led by their advisers.

Empire building

Empire building is the acquisition of resources outside a country's borders for the purpose of expanding that country's size, power, or influence, and is used figuratively to refer to the territorial expansion of individuals and groups in a corporate culture by exerting control over increasing numbers of projects.

Employee

An employee provides labor to a business on an ongoing basis, almost always in a specific job role. In American labor law, "employee" has legal dimensions of meaning that are more specific than "worker," bearing on certain protections and rights as well as the taxes paid by an employer, compared to the situation faced by, for instance, independent contractors, who receive pay but not benefits, and are technically operating their own business which sells labor to the client business. Nevertheless, in this volume "employee" and "worker" are used synonymously except when otherwise noted.

"Employee engagement," for instance, describes a concept frequently relevant to independent contractors as well, but is more commonly found in the literature than the more inclusively phrased "worker engagement."

Employee engagement

Employee engagement is a positive outcome of a healthy relationship between an organization and its employees, resulting in employees who are interested in their work and feel a sense of satisfaction when it is done well or achieves positive results. Employee engagement requires a good match between the employee's role in the organization and their self-image, as well as between their beliefs about their role and the actual day-to-day work they do. That is, they should intuitively understand not only why the work is being done, but why they are the ones doing it.

Employee morale

Employee morale is the well-being and satisfaction of an employee and is a significant contributor to productivity, while low morale is correlated with absenteeism and turnover.

Employee silence

Employee silence is the withholding of information relevant to an organization by its employees, either by choice or because proper communication channels have not been established nor use of them encouraged.

Employee survey

An employee survey is one distributed to employees throughout an organization and is used to monitor employee feelings about their compensation, their job role, their working environment, and any problems in the course of their work. Employee surveys are a valuable diagnostic tool but also a source of resentment if they do not lead to a satisfying response when problems are reported.

Employeeship

Employeeship is a Swedish management philosophy in which a partnership between managers and employees replaces the traditional leadership hierarchy, in order to cultivate a supportive work environment in which managers act as facilitators for employees' skills and ideas.

Empowerment

Empowerment is the process of increasing the strength and engagement of a group or individual. In the last few decades, employee empowerment has become an increasingly popular concept in management theory, and empowerment is often considered one of the leadership competencies. Increasing the strength of employees means giving them greater authority, responsibility, and autonomy in the performance of their jobs, without overburdening them with tasks for which they are not prepared. Communication is important, as are clear boundaries so that the employee does not feel adrift rather than empowered. Many people stress the importance of mentoring here as well. Medical leadership researcher C. A. Rajotte, in the 1996 *The Kansas Nurse* article "Empowerment as a Leadership Theory," listed educating, leading, structuring, providing, mentoring, and actualizing as the methods of empowering, in combination with team-building and power-sharing.

Engineering management

Engineering management is an approach to management that brings an engineering mindset to business management. While there is overlap with industrial engineering, industrial engineers are not always managers, whereas engineering managers are typically trained in both engineering and business, often earning a degree in each. (A small number of programs teach engineering management as its own discipline, including Rensselaer Polytechnic Institute, George Washington University, and West Point.)

Enhancers

In substitutes for leadership theory, enhancers are workplace factors that increase the effectiveness of leadership. These include experienced followers, non-routine tasks, group norms that encourage cooperation, and leaders who have the ability to reward followers with a reward that is relevant and valuable to them.

Entrepreneur

An entrepreneur is a person who starts a business and bears responsibility for its success or failure. Economic studies of entrepreneurship are among the antecedents to modern leadership studies, as there have been debates and theories about the traits, qualities, and behaviors of entrepreneurs, and the effects of these factors on the success of their businesses since at least the 18th century, when Richard Cantillon described the entrepreneur as a risk-taker who made his fortune by identifying and taking advantage of new opportunities despite their uncertain outcome. Similarly, in the 1960s, Peter Drucker described the entrepreneur as one who looks for changes in the marketplace or available technologies and develops them into profitable ventures. Many economists have described entrepreneurs as necessary to or healthy for the economy, as they pioneer new areas of business that can later be entered by more risk-averse organizations. Barriers to entrepreneurship have thus largely been viewed as unhealthy restrictions.

Entrepreneurial leadership

Entrepreneurial leadership consists of using the skills of an entrepreneur in order to lead an organization, and when advocated, is often contrasted with a "corporate mind-set" that has become stagnant through risk aversion and hidebound fixation on procedure. Entrepreneurs, in contrast, are risk-friendly, innovative, and adept at managing change. The classic example is Apple's Steve Jobs, who led his company from the early days of personal computing when not everyone in the industry was even convinced of the long-term demand for personal computers to an age of mobile devices that his company virtually created.

Environmental psychology

Environmental psychology is an interdisciplinary branch of applied psychology that examines the relationship between individuals and their surrounding environment, including the natural and built environments as well as the social world. Environmental psychologists are concerned with improving built environment design, especially workplaces, housing, and public spaces, in order to improve human well-being.

Episcopal ordination

Episcopal ordination in the Catholic Church is the process of elevating a priest to the position of bishop, a role conferring greater responsibilities and duties, notably the administration of the Catholic community in specific bishopric regions (called dioceses in the Roman Catholic Church and eparchies in the Eastern Catholic Churches). Less numerous than priests, more numerous than cardinals, bishops constitute an important part of Catholic leadership, and a shortage of bishops at various times and places (such as during the colonizing of North America) has been considered a serious concern.

Equal consideration of interests

The principle of equal consideration of interests states that the interests of all involved or affected parties should be considered equally when determining the correct course of action in a situation. Though the concept dates back at least as far as utilitarianism, the principle was coined by Peter Singer in his 1979 *Practical Ethics*, which explores the ramifications of the principle in dealing with equality, disability, embryo experimentation, euthanasia, political violence, overseas aid, refugees, and (in the third edition) climate change, as well as addressing whether there is a moral obligation to help others.

ERG theory

Existence, Relatedness, and Growth (ERG) is a psychological theory formulated by Clayton Paul Alderfer and based on Abraham Maslow's hierarchy of needs. ERG theory reclassifies Maslow's five-tiered hierarchy into three groups. The Existence group of needs consists of those things needed for basic material existence, such as a safe environment in which to live, food, sleep, and security, and so includes Maslow's Physiological and Safety tiers. The Relatedness group combines Belongingness and Esteem, and includes the human needs related to social interaction. The Growth group overlaps with Maslow's Esteem tier and includes his Self-Actualization tier, and includes the needs that address the human desire for personal growth.

Escalation of commitment

Escalation commitment or irrational escalation is the phenomenon whereby decision-makers continue to pursue a course of action despite new evidence suggesting it should be abandoned or re-evaluated, as in the proverb of throwing good money after bad. The phenomenon often results from cognitive biases like the overconfidence effect, overplacement, and the Dunning-Kruger effect, all of which cause people to put too much faith in their own judgment and skills. Gambling is a common example of escalation of commitment, as are the American government's commitments to the Vietnam and Iraq wars, but the phenomenon is seen in numerous areas.

Ethical leadership

Ethical leadership is leadership that is guided by a moral code that both informs the decisions they make and their approach to leading, in their interactions with and treatment of followers, colleagues, superiors, and others. While other theories of leadership do not specifically advocate immorality, many approaches to leadership have been essentially amoral, focused on the bottom line—which is one source of the "Hitler problem" (cf.), as it complicates the evaluation of a leader who meets goals but is morally abhorrent, or one whose goals themselves are morally abhorrent. The tendency toward a people-focused approach to leadership naturally leads to the advocacy of ethics in leadership, which is compatible with many different leadership models. The founder of the Center for Ethical Leadership, Bill Grace, proposed the 4-V Model of Ethical Leadership, consisting of Values, Vision, Voice, and Virtue, with additional elements including Service (connecting Vision and Values), Polis (political engagement, connecting Vision and Voice), and Renewal (the reevaluation of one's actions, connecting Voice and Values).

Ethics

Ethics, ethical theory, or moral theory is the branch of philosophy that addresses moral values of conduct. Unlike most areas of philosophical inquiry, most ethics work is normative or applied—devoted to determining the best way to determine the right course of action, and the right course of action for a given situation—whereas most philosophy is more concerned with theory than its applications. Ethics is not a school or approach to philosophy, but rather an area of inquiry; it is more important to some philosophers and schools than others.

Ethology

Ethology is the study of animal behavior under natural conditions (as opposed to behaviorism, which studies the behavioral responses of animals in controlled studies, such as the famous example of Ivan Pavlov's dogs). Since E. O. Wilson's 1975 *Sociobiology: The New Synthesis*, especially, ethology has been concerned with the behavior of and within animal social groups, rather than of individuals. This trend in ethology occasionally dovetails with the rise of evolutionary psychology, which seeks evolutionary explanations for human social behavior, and serious attention is given to parallels between human and animal behaviors. Recent work such as that of Roberto Bonanni's group finds commonality in leadership behavior among humans and free-ranging dogs.

Evaluating leadership

Lewis Edinger, in a 1975 article in *Comparative Politics*, categorized evaluations of leadership as using two kinds of criteria: intrinsic and extrinsic. Intrinsic criteria examine how the leader's group performed relative to its objectives, and perhaps measures like profit, cost, efficiency, customer or employee satisfaction, and so forth. Extrinsic criteria compare the leader's performance to the observer's own values and ideas of how leading should be conducted.

Evaluation

An evaluation is an assessment of an employee's, group's, department's, or project's performance relative to goals, along with feedback and other details.

Evolutionary leadership theory

At the intersection of evolutionary psychology and organizational psychology is evolutionary leadership theory, which presumes that significant traits related to the leader–follower relationship are evolved adaptations. Parallels between human leadership relationships and leadership in the animal world, especially primates, are important, but so is the distinction between leadership and simple social dominance, which is typically motivated by competition for limited resources. In its prescriptive mode, evolutionary leadership theory focuses on the importance of developing followers rather than subordinates.

Evolutionary psychology

Evolutionary psychology is an interdisciplinary intersection of basic psychology and evolutionary biology, concerned with the role of human evolution in mental and psychological traits, from personality to the functions of memory and language. Evolutionary psychology does not propose that all psychological traits within humanity are evolved adaptations, but rather seeks to uncover which traits are. Most evolutionary biologists are adaptationists, meaning that they consider natural selection to have exerted considerable power on the development of human psychology, through psychological traits that are the products of adaptation.

Executive

"Executive," "leader," and "manager" are used quasi-synonymously, but when distinctions are made, "executive" typically refers to someone in upper-level management at a tier consisting of the top 10 percent (or less) of an organization. Executives often have roles with greater autonomy than lower-level managers, and include department heads and vice presidents.

Executive development

Executive development is any activity aimed at fostering and developing the skills and behaviors of the executives of an organization, or those who are on track to be appointed to such positions. Many larger organizations have a dedicated executive development process or team, which may include training seminars, training in skills such as processes and operations of the company, or team building and communication exercises.

Executive education

Executive education programs are operated for business executives and high-level managers. Usually offered by a graduate school arm of a business school, they are rarely degree-granting or credit-bearing, but teach skills for upper-level management, ranging from leadership and communication skills to corporate finance and management theory. The fastest-growing sector of the market is customized executive education programs, which are constructed for a single company's executives as part of their executive development activity.

Expectancy theory

Expectancy theory, first proposed by management professor Victor Vroom in 1964, says that an individual's behavior is motivated by their expectations of the outcome of that behavior, especially as compared to alternatives. (A lottery ticket buyer does not expect that purchasing a ticket will lead to winning, for instance, but *does* expect that purchasing a ticket increases their odds of winning, compared to not buying a ticket.) Vroom proposed this theory in order to point out the need for organizations to directly tie worker rewards to performance, and to ensure that they are of a type appropriate to motivate the worker. The basic variables involved in expectancy theory are valence, the desirability of a given outcome; expectancy, the individual's belief that his effort at attempting a task will be successful; and instrumentality, the individual's belief that succeeding at a task will lead to the given outcome. Difficult goals like winning the lottery or setting a sales record have a low expectancy, which lowers the individual's motivation even when the valence is very high.

Expectancy violations theory

Expectancy violations theory (EVT) is a communications theory explaining peoples' reactions to unexpected behavior from other people. Violation refers to the transgression of a rule or norm, possibly explicit but more often implicit and sometimes specific to the individuals involved, as when a friend suddenly seems to act out of character. EVT originated in communication research on reactions to violations of personal space, such as in Judee Burgoon's 1976 Nonverbal Expectancy Violations Model. Like expectancy theory, EVT focuses on expectancy and valence. Violation valence is the positive or negative value the individual assigns to another person's breach of expectations, while communicator reward valence is the value the individual assigns to the person himself, based on their ability to bring value to the individual in the future. For instance, a loved one, who is valued by the individual and has great power to reward the individual in the future through ongoing displays of love, is typically accorded greater access to personal space than a casual friend.

Expert authority

Expert authority is authority that a leader enjoys when his team respects his skills or knowledge in a given area and is confident in his use of those skills.

Expert power

Expert power is one of John R. P. French and Bertram Raven's bases of power, and one of Patrick J. Montana and Bruce H. Charnov's varieties of organizational power. Expert power is influence that can be exerted because of one's special skills or knowledge, especially as proven by credentials or reputation.

Experiential education

Experiential education is an approach to education that emphasizes the importance of experiential learning. Experiential education is a common approach to job training, and has become increasingly important in management training and organizational development. Several learning games have been developed for experiential education.

Experiential learning

Experiential learning is learning through direct experience and subsequent reflection on the experience. Building on the work of developmental psychologist Jean Piaget and educational reformer John Dewey, educational theorist David Kolb popularized experiential learning, and introduced a four-element model with Ron Fry: concrete experience, observation of and reflection on that experience, abstraction and conceptualization following reflection, and testing of new concepts.

Experimental political science

Experimental political science—the use of experiments for discovery in political science—is a newer area of political science than theory is, and even today many political scientists are skeptical about the utility of experimentation over analysis of existing data. Typically, experimental political science focuses on voter psychology, including polling methodology, effects of media coverage, and impacts on voter turnout, and the effects of different voting systems, both by the electorate and by legislators.

Exploitative authoritative

One of Rensis Likert's management systems, in the exploitative authoritative system, leaders motivate their workers through negative incentives like threats and punishment. Decision-making power is not well distributed through the hierarchy, with most decisions made at the top levels and most communication conducted one way from the top down.

Extra-role behavior

Extra-role behavior (ERB) was defined in 1995 by Linn Van Dyne, L. L. Cummings, and Judi Mclean Parks, building on the work of Dennis Organ and others on Organizational Citizenship Behavior. Both concepts refer to employee behavior that benefits the organization, but lies outside the behavior that is explicitly asked of the employee by organizational policies or the definition of his duties. Since the 1960s, studies have shown that these behaviors are key to an organization's overall effectiveness and well-being. However, ERB encompasses behavior that not only is not requested by the employee's role definition or policies but actually dissents. Principled organizational dissent, for instance, protests injustice in the organization, while whistle blowing reports wrongdoing within or by the organization, both of which are held to be for the good of the organization by correcting its behavior.

Extraversion

Extraversion is one of the "Big Five" personality traits, characterized by the individual's engagement with the outside world. Extraverts are perceived by others as full of energy or "the life of the party," and feel positive about their interactions with other people in social situations, including strangers. Extraversion and its opposite, introversion, exist on a continuum, though individuals because of their past experiences or other personality traits may feel more or less extraverted in specific types of social environments.

Extrinsic motivation

Extrinsic motivation is motivation to perform a behavior that is introduced from outside the individual. Both rewards and punishments are extrinsic motivations, whether explicit and agreed upon in advance (grades and detention for students) or implicit and assumed (the reaction of the crowd to sports or other performances). Certain approaches to education, parenting, and management favor extrinsic motivation as a way to condition individuals' behavior, and extrinsic factors can provide motivation in cases where no intrinsic motivation exists.

Eye contact

Eye contact is an important part of nonverbal communication, typically seen in Western cultures as a sign of confidence and honesty during conversation, as well as a way to direct another person's attention. Aversion to eye contact is often interpreted as insecurity or deviousness, which leads to misunderstandings due not only to cultural differences but different levels of social comfort among individuals within a culture.

Fa

In Chinese philosophy, fa is a concept sometimes translated as "law" or "model," as in a

Eye contact is thought to have a large influence on social behavior, and is often a sign of confidence and social communication, while a lack of eye contact can give the impression of insecurity or dishonesty. (Wikimedia Commons/Bild Bundersarachiv)

model for behavior. It originated in the Mohist school (cf. Mozi), in which fa were required to pass the "three tests" (or criteria): they must have precedence in the sage kings, who represented a Golden Age of the Chinese past; they must be logically sound; and they must benefit the people and the state. Though Confucianism displaced the Mohist school, the concept of fa remained important in Chinese thought and political philosophy.

Facial expression

Facial expressions are one of the major forms of nonverbal communication, and carry much of the weight of social information in face-to-face human conversation. Facial expressions carry so much meaning that according to some studies, a small percentage (less than 1 percent) of the population can detect lying based on facial expression without special training.

Facilitator

The role of the facilitator emerged in the business world in the 1980s, though it has been an important role in Quaker decision-making meetings since the 18th century, and in various protest movements for much of the 20th century. A facilitator runs a meeting but is not a chief decision-maker the way a department chair or business head is, and is not interested in presenting or persuading people to support a specific plan. Impartiality is part of their goal, and they simply guide the conversation, sometimes according to a specific predetermined protocol. Facilitators set the agenda for the meeting, call on those who are to speak and ensure that they have the space to do so, and moderate the discussion without commenting on its merits.

Family as model for the state

Since the ancient Greek philosophers, various thinkers have proposed an understanding of the operations and structure of the state with reference to analogous structures in the family unit. By extension this has meant a model of the leader as a parental figure—usually explicitly a father. Some models have focused on the family as a model of the relationship between the leader and his subjects, while others have used it to explain relationships within the state's leadership, such as between a monarch and the aristocracy.

Fayolism

Fayolism was a management theory developed by French mining engineer Henri Fayol, similar to but developed independently from scientific management, around 1900. Fayolism's key distinction compared to Frederick W. Taylor's work in scientific management is in its focus on management rather than on the task. The five principles of Fayolist management are planning, organizing, command (the implementation of the plan, with proper allocation of resources and motivation of employees), coordination (the harmonizing of activities among managers, and communication between elements of the organization), and control (the evaluation and improvement of performance and communication). Fayol also staunchly advocated face-to-face communication over written communication, contrary to the conventional wisdom at the time, which favored the formality of letter writing.

Fear mongering

The use of fear to influence the feelings or behaviors of others. While fear mongering could capitalize on reasonable levels of fear of legitimate dangers, it is more commonly associated with the creation or inspiration of hyperbolic fear. The most famous modern examples are found in political campaign advertisements, especially "Daisy" and "Bear in the woods" (cf.), but there are many cases of leaders and authority figures using fear as a motivator, from parents and educators exaggerating the effects of drug use or poor grades to influence their childrens' behavior to managers who keep employees in a state of fear for their jobs.

Ferguson, Missouri

Ferguson, Missouri, is a small predominantly black city in the Greater St. Louis metropolitan area. In August 2014, it became the first American site to which Amnesty International sent delegates to witness and gather testimony about human rights abuses, during protests following the fatal shooting of unarmed black teenager Michael Brown by local police. The police response to the protests, including the use of military equipment, widespread tear-gassing of nonviolent protesters, arrests of journalists, refusal by officers to provide their own names or badge numbers, and numerous incidents of police officers pointing loaded weapons at unarmed protesters and journalists even when

they knew they were on camera, was widely held as a critical failure of leadership. Governor Jay Nixon and President Barack Obama both faced criticism for not responding more decisively in the first two weeks; Nixon in particular was berated for issuing a curfew rather than publicly taking disciplinary action against the various police officers and authorities at fault. The protests raised important issues about the continuing problem of personal and institutional racism in the United States, disparate treatment of blacks and whites by the justice system, the militarization of local and state police, and the proper limits on police power. In the aftermath, among the investigations launched by local, state, and federal authorities, the U.S. Commission on Civil Rights requested a Justice Department investigation into the racial makeup (nearly all white) of the Ferguson city council and police force.

Fiedler, Fred

Fred Fiedler is an influential organizational psychologist who introduced the contingency theory of leadership. Contingency theory is a behaviorist approach to decision making that says the optimum decision is contingent on situation specifics. Fiedler built on the work of the Ohio State and Michigan leadership studies, and used contingency theory to explain the failures of scientific management, which took a "one size fits all" approach to leadership. Fiedler was also instrumental in focusing on the role of stress in leadership and the way interpersonal dynamics can drive decision making as much or more than rationally perceived pros and cons.

Fiedler contingency model

The contingency model of leadership developed by Fred Fiedler describes the relationship between a leader and the favorableness of the situation in which he is leading, as determined by the relationship between the leader and his followers, the degree to which the group's tasks are structured, and the inherent power of the leader's role. Powerful leaders with healthy relationships with their followers, overseeing highly structured activities, are the most successful in Fiedler's model.

Figurehead

A figurehead is an individual with a title implying a leadership role, who exercises little to no actual power of authority—either by convention or due to structural limits on this exercise. The monarch of the United Kingdom is arguably a figurehead, possessing power that is principally ceremonial; then again, the financial resources of the royal family and the cost of maintaining their household is just as arguably a passive use of significant power, especially in the eyes of anti-monarchists. The term *figurehead* is also used as an insult to refer to a leader who could exercise power but is largely controlled by another figure.

"First they came . . ."

An untitled poem by Martin Niemoller deals with the blindness of Germans to the effects of the Nazis' rise to power. Niemoller delivered the poem as a speech in many variant forms in his career as a pastor, and so there is no official version. The familiar version reads:

> First they came for the Communists, and I did not speak out—because I was not a communist. Then they came for the Trade Unionists, and I did not speak out—because I was not a trade unionist. Then they came for the Jews, and I did not speak out—because I was not a Jew. Then

they came for me—and there was no one left to speak for me."

Flat organization

A flat organization is one with little to no middle management, which in a sufficiently large organization results in more decentralized decision making, as there are fewer supervisory layers between upper management and the workers. This is typically accomplished with self-managing teams, a model that has become common in software companies where it may help that most of the labor required is highly skilled labor. Flat organizations overlap with but are distinct from cooperatives, in which not only decision making but ownership is decentralized.

Flow

In psychology, flow is a mental state in which the subject is completely immersed in his activity: focused, energized, engaged, and perhaps most importantly, enjoying the immersion, in a way that is not necessarily true of the similar concept of hyperfocus. Flow is commonly described as "being in the zone," and is in many ways the opposite of the "autopilot effect" of performing a task expertly but without engagement as a result of frequent repetition, as often happens to commuters on their drive home. One of the goals of positive psychology is to increase the experience of flow for workers. Owen Schaffer listed seven conditions for flow: knowing what to do, how to do it, how well you're doing it, and were to go, with difficult challenges, well-developed skills, and sufficient lack of distractions. In a workplace context, flow is related to employee engagement: mere competence is not enough; flow responds to a reasonable challenge and the pleasure of mastering it. The idea of flow is well developed in eastern religions but new to Western psychology.

Fluid intelligence

Fluid intelligence is a factor of general intelligence, representing the capacity to solve problems in new situations, independent of knowledge. Inductive and deductive reasoning and logic skills are part of fluid intelligence, as opposed to crystallized intelligence, which is the use of already acquired skills and knowledge.

Follett, Mary Parker

Mary Parker Follett was a management consultant and one of the pioneers in management theory in the early 20th century. Her work focused on employee participation, negotiation, reciprocal relationships in a professional context, and the noncoercive power-sharing approach to leadership that she called "integration." She was a great critic of micromanagement, which she called "bossism."

Followership

Followership is the complement to leadership, the social process of and capacity to follow a leader or leaders. Robert Kelley's work has been at the forefront of the academic study of followership. In 1988's *Harvard Business Review* article "In Praise of Followers," he identifies four qualities of followership: self-management (including independence, critical thinking, self-awareness, and self-evaluation), commitment to the group goal, competence in the areas relevant to the follower's role, and the courage to be candid with superiors.

Followership patterns

Robert Kelley identified five patterns of followership, based on two behavioral dimensions: whether the follower is active or passive, and whether or not he is a critical thinker. Sheep are passive followers who require constant supervision in their work. Yes-People (or Conformists) are committed to their work, but do not question the leader or act on their own initiative. Pragmatics are not as devoted to the leader's directions as Yes-People, but neither will they pursue an action or idea until it has the support of the majority, which may make them slow to react in response to a change in information or circumstances. The Alienated resent the leader and constantly question his decisions or authority, and may try to slow down the group's progress. Star Followers (or Exemplary Followers) require little supervision and are engaged critical thinkers, sharing the leader's goals but evaluating courses of action before following them.

Fordism

Named for automobile tycoon Henry Ford, Fordism is an industrialized and standardized system of mass production, encompassing both economic and social dimensions. Fordism is sometimes compared to Frederick W. Taylor's scientific management, and Taylor himself apparently thought Ford had adopted his techniques, but many of Ford's practices were independently formulated. Fordism is most associated with the standardization of products and the tools and processes used to make them, which is the aspect most consistent with scientific management and the one that was eventually adopted by nearly all of American manufacturing, at least those industries that use assembly lines. But Fordism also called for higher wages for workers, specifically for the purpose of ensuring that they could afford the products they were making—in this case, automobiles. Ford was far more concerned than Taylor with absenteeism and employee turnover, which in a Taylorist system are solvable by hiring different employees. Of course, Fordism was tailored specifically for the automobile industry, a novel product that, however revolutionary, was more expensive than most manufactured household goods. Ford's success has been tied in large part to his workers' wages, because he was able to turn his employees into customers.

Forer effect

The Forer effect (named for psychologist Bertram Forer) is the tendency of individuals to perceive vague, general statements that could apply to most people as highly accurate if they are told the statements are tailored specifically to them. For instance, most descriptions of personality derived from various forms of divination—handwriting analysis, fortune telling, palm reading, astrology, etc.—contain multiple statements, often vague, so that the individual will identify with at least some of them. In his initial experiment, Forer used statements including "You have a tendency to be critical of yourself" and "At times you are extroverted, affable, sociable, while at other times you are introverted, wary, reserved." Avoiding the Forer effect is a criterion of well-constructed personality tests. Similar phenomena are seen in the workplace, such as when feedback is presented in general enough terms that it could apply to most situations or individuals.

Founder's syndrome

Founder's syndrome is a system of difficulties faced by an organization as a result of one or more of its founders retaining disproportionate influence on the organization. Especially in the cases of organizations that have grown much larger than when the founder first instituted them, there may not be a well-considered management hierarchy in place, or one of the founders may routinely ignore the hierarchy and its norms. Decision-making processes may seem opaque even to other members of upper management, and key employees and board members may have been selected for their support or connection to a founder and so serve the founder's interest rather than the organization's.

Four Frames

Lee Bolman and Terrence Deal introduced the Four Frames model in 1984's *Reframing Organizations: Artistry, Choice, and Leadership.* Each of the four frames represents a way people view the world, which influences their approach to organization and leadership. The Structural frame views organizations as machine-like and favors rules, policies, and technology, and leadership's task as providing social architecture suited to the organization's goals. The Human Resource frame views organizations as family-like, based on relationships, skills, and needs, and leadership's task as empowering employees and keeping organizational needs in line with human ones. The Political frame views organizations as jungles full of conflict and competition, where leaders need to support and advocate an agenda and consolidate a power base around it. And the Symbolic frame views organizations in theatrical or temple-like terms, responding favorably to narrative, ritual, and ceremony, and requiring their leaders to inspire them. Although individuals tend to favor one or two frames, most people adopt different frames in different situations, as no one frame is suitable for all situations. Each frame favors slightly different approaches to basic organizational activities like strategic planning (which the Political frame treats as an opportunity for conflicting views to be expressed, while the Human Resources frame treats it as an opportunity to encourage participation in the process), decision making, goal setting, communication, team meetings, and conflict resolution. These different frames also produce different types of leaders, whether effective or not: Structural leaders tend to be architects or tyrants; Human Resources leaders, catalysts or pushovers; Political leaders, negotiators or con artists; and Symbolic leaders, prophets or fanatics.

Four psychologies

The "four psychologies" are the areas of psychology that provide the foundation of modern psychology on which both therapists and theorists draw. They consist of self psychology, the school of psychoanalysis that focuses on empathy, mirroring, the disruption of developmental needs, and other areas as developed in Chicago by Heinz Kohut; drive theory, the analysis of different psychological drives and needs and the phenomena that result from them; ego psychology, which builds on Sigmund Freud's model of the mind as consisting of id, ego, and superego; and object relations, which proposes that family experiences in infancy shape the future adult's relationships with other people.

Freethought

Freethought is an ideological position that favors reason and empiricism over authority and dogma. Though sometimes associated with atheism or agnosticism today, "free-thinkers" originated in 17th-century England as people who rejected the authority of the Church of England in favor of their own personal study of the Bible, though the term quickly spread to encompass those who rejected the authority of the Catholic Church and of religious traditions in general. Over the 19th century, freethought became associated with humanism, a rejection of nationalism and ethnocentrism, and

especially a rejection of preserving traditional institutions on the basis of their traditional authority, and an insistence that traditional beliefs and values must be supportable by objective reason. In the United States, the Free Thought movement began in the early 19th century, supporting philosophical skepticism, humanism, and freedom of speech and expression, and played a major role in the development of utopian communities.

French and Raven's bases of power

Social psychologists John R. P. French and Bertram Raven studied power in social influence settings in 1959, resulting in a model proposing five bases of power (with a sixth added by Raven in 1965) representing the different forms it can take. Power in this sense refers to social influence—the ability to change another person's behavior, attitudes, or beliefs—which is fundamental to an understanding of leadership. The bases of power they identified are Coercion, Reward, Legitimacy, Expert, Reference, and Informational (added by Raven).

Freud, Sigmund

The founder of psychoanalysis and one of the founders of psychology, Sigmund Freud began his work in the late 19th century, helped to spread psychoanalysis in the early 20th century even as some of his earliest followers began to develop their independent psychological theories, and continued to publish until his death in the 1930s. The defining feature of his work was the treating of psychological conditions through dialogue between the patient and the psychoanalyst, combined with his revolutionary theories of the mind, including the scientific analysis of dreams, his theory of the unconscious and the importance of the unconscious mind, the use of free association as a therapeutic technique, the existence of a sex drive and a death drive, and the mechanism of repression. While few outside the humanities continue to adopt Freud's ideas without alteration—he has been deeply influential on literary criticism in that respect—much of modern psychology is still defined by reactions to Freud or refinements to his ideas. He was among the first to study the decision-making habits and patterns of ordinary people, as opposed to commenting on the wisdom of the decisions of powerful leaders, and notable in seeing little mechanical or cognitive difference between the processes of one man debating whether to ask for a raise and another man debating whether to lead his nation to war.

The friendship paradox and centrality

The friendship paradox is the fact that most people have fewer friends than their friends have, on average. This is true for other forms of social connection as well: most people have had fewer sexual partners than their sexual partners have had. The reason for this is the same regardless of the type of social connection: the people with the greatest number of connections have an increased probability of being among one's own connections. Those people are in an interesting position, as the exceptions to the friendship paradox's generalization: they have more friends than most of their friends have, and have greater than average centrality, referring to their position in a map of their social networks. Further, the greater their centrality, the more it influences their access to certain kinds of social information. One well-publicized study found that highly central people are aware of flu outbreaks two weeks before professional surveillance methods are, because their information access is superior to the sampling methods used.

Fuhrerprinzip

The Fuhrerprinzip (German for "leader principle") is a term from German political science, referring to a principle upon which a government can be founded, stating that the leader's will supersedes other sources of law. The term was introduced by social Darwinist Hermann Keyserling, who believed that certain individuals were born to rule, and that their followers should not restrict their freedom to do so. The Fuhrerprinzip was the foundation of Adolf Hitler's Third Reich, and was invoked in the post–World War II Nuremberg Trials to support the claim that those charged with war crimes were simply following orders.

Full Range Leadership Model

Developed by leadership scholars Bernie Bass and Bruce Avolio in the late 1990s, the Full Range Leadership Model describes six lower-order factors and three higher-order factors of laissez-faire, transactional, and transformational leadership. The model describes transformational leadership in terms of idealized influence, inspirational motivation, intellectual stimulation, and individualized consideration, and is measured by the Multifactor Leadership Questionnaire developed by Bass.

Functional leadership theory

Functional leadership theory is a behavior-based theory of leadership that focuses on the functions that leaders perform or are responsible for. Rather than focusing on what leaders are like, as with trait-based theories, functional leadership theory focuses on what leading is. Functional leadership studies often extend their focus beyond the titular leader to look at what leadership functions are being performed in an organization, regardless of the title or formal role of the individuals performing them. John Adair's work lists eight leadership functions: task definition, planning, team briefing, controlling production, evaluating results, motivating individuals, organizing groups, and setting an example. Functional leadership is influential in leadership training because it implies a set of leadership skills that can be taught.

Future orientation

One of the global leadership cultural competencies identified by the GLOBE Project, future orientation is the extent to which individuals in an organization, group, or culture keep the future in mind through behaviors like saving and investing, planning, or constructing long-term strategies, which likewise influences their ability to delay gratification. Projects like climate change mitigation, for instance, have substantial short-term costs, with very long-term benefits, and have proven politically and practically difficult because of the level of future orientation required of supporters (and because of the number of supporters required for a project of such scope and breadth).

Galbraith's *Anatomy of Power*

Economist and diplomat John Kenneth Galbraith is best known for his trilogy on economics: *American Capitalism* (1952), *The Affluent Society* (1958), and *The New Industrial State* (1967). In 1983's *Anatomy of Power*, he classified power into three types: condign power, gained through use or threat of force; compensatory power, in which obedience is bought; and conditioned power, attained through persuasion. Further, power stems from one of three sources: leadership or personality, wealth, or organization (by being the organization's leader).

Game theory

Game theory is the study of mathematical models to represent conflict, cooperation, and decision making by intelligent and rational decision makers. Integral to economics, game theory has also become important in biology and the social sciences. It began in the middle of the 20th century with John von Neumann's 1944 *Theory of Games and Economic Behavior*, which demonstrated the way economic activity could be modeled and studied by treating it as a game with strategies, rules, and rewards. Organizational psychology, political science, peace studies, and political economy make heavy use of game theory, and game theory has been used to explain the stability of government forms, candidates' performance in primaries and elections, and group behavior in cooperative or competitive settings. In biology, game theory frequently focuses not only on evolutionary game theory but on communication games, to explain and model both animal and human communication.

Gandhi, Mahatma Mohandas

Mahatma Gandhi was the most prominent leader of the Indian nationalist movement in the early 20th century, seeking freedom from British rule, and is generally considered the father of the modern country of India. He led nonviolent protest movements against British rule both in India and in the Indian community in South Africa, and became the leader of the Indian National Congress in 1921, where he worked for women's rights, religious pluralism, and the end of poverty, in addition to his overarching quest for Indian independence. When independence was finally granted in 1947, in the form of separate Hindu (India) and Muslim (Pakistan) states, Gandhi traveled to the regions affected by religiously motivated violence among the displaced, rather than partake in the official celebrations of independence. He undertook several fasts in the attempt to promote

Mahatma Gandhi (right) employed nonviolent civil disobedience to lead India to independence, inspiring movements for freedom and civil rights around the world. (Wikimedia Commons/Dave Davis for Acme Newspictures)

religious pluralism, and having attained independence at last, some Hindu Indians were offended by his support of Muslims. He was assassinated by a Hindu nationalist in 1948, less than half a year after independence.

Gantt chart

Henry Gantt was an engineer and management consultant who learned scientific management from Frederick Winslow Taylor in the 1880s and developed the Gantt chart in the 1910s. The Gantt chart is a bar chart illustrating a project schedule from start to finish, with a work breakdown of the various stages and processes of the project. Later additions to the Gantt chart included the use of shading to demonstrate completion percentage of various stages, and a precedence network showing the relationships

between different processes. Gantt charts were adopted by the American military beginning with World War I, and today are commonly used in Web-based collaborative groupware.

Gardner, Howard

A professor of cognition and education at the Harvard Graduate School of Education, Howard Gardner is best known for his theory of multiple intelligences, and also published an analysis of leadership, *Leading Minds: An Anatomy of Leadership*, in 1995. In it, he argues that humans' expectation of being led is inherited from our evolutionary forebears among the primates. Gardner also focuses on leaders as storytellers, presenting and embodying a particular narrative.

Gemeinschaft and Gesellschaft

Gemeinschaft and gesellschaft are German terms for "community" and "society" and were used by German sociologists to name two opposed categories of social ties—those based on Gemeinschaft, or community, which are derived from personal social experiences and the values and beliefs that are developed as a result of those experiences; and those based on Gesellschaft, or society, which are derived from indirect interactions and formal values.

Gender and leadership

Leadership has historically been a male role in most human cultures, and women remain extremely underrepresented in both political and business leadership today: only about 16 percent of the directors of Fortune 500 companies are women, which is about the same percentage of delegates to the 2013 World Economic Forum who were women. There is no evidence to suggest that women are less effective business leaders—in fact, the less than 5 percent of

Fortune 500 companies with female CEOs outperformed the S&P 500 in a 2014 *Fortune* magazine study, returning an average of 103.4 percent compared to 69.5 percent. The research is inconclusive on the impact of gender on leadership style or effectiveness, with some studies finding no difference and others finding small but nontrivial differences.

Gender egalitarianism

One of the global leadership cultural competencies identified by the GLOBE Project, gender egalitarianism is the extent to which an organization or culture avoids, prevents, or works to stop gender-based discrimination and gender role differences.

Generation gap

The generation gap is a term in use since the 1960s to refer to the cultural differences between older and younger people, traditionally between parents and their college-age children; in discussions of voting trends, the gap discussed is sometimes wider, as in the gay marriage debate, in which the broadest support is found in the youngest tier of voters, and the least support in the oldest tier. But traditionally, it has referred to the tendency of young people to be more socially liberal than their parents (and by implication, to become more conservative with age), and more experimental in their lifestyle and fashion choices. Increasingly, the generation gap is also relevant when it comes to social media competence, as trends can live and die in a four- or five-year span.

Gesture

Gestures are bodily movements communicating specific information (as opposed to body language that is simply expressive). The use of gesture in language seems to be universal, but the extent to which gesture is relied upon varies considerably from culture to culture; Italians are notorious for their heavy use of it compared to Americans.

Gilbreth, Frank, Sr.

Frank Gilbreth was an early pioneer in the Efficiency movement, who extended the principles of scientific management first developed by Frederick Winslow Taylor by adding the concept of the motion study—a study of the physical process of performing a discrete task constituting part of a company's operations, in order to optimize that process for maximum efficiency. Frank's wife, Lillian, was the first organizational psychologist, and the two used their large family to conduct efficiency experiments, as later recounted in *Cheaper by the Dozen*, a book by two of their children, adapted into a film with Myrna Loy, and its sequel *Belles on Their Toes*.

Gilbreth, Lillian

Lillian Gilbreth was one of the first female engineers and is considered the first organizational psychologist. Her Ph.D. from Brown University was the first degree granted in industrial psychology, and she was the first engineer to bring psychological principles to scientific management by suggesting changes to Frederick Winslow Taylor's original work that were better-informed about human character and motivation. Gilbreth also worked as a consultant and marketing

Lillian Gilbreth, one of the first women to become an engineer, is best known for the management and efficiency techniques she and her husband devised. (Flickr/Smithsonian)

researcher, using psychology to craft marketing campaigns during the Great Depression, and created the modern "work triangle" kitchen design (still common today) as a way of applying scientific management to household work.

Global leadership

Global leadership is the interdisciplinary study of leadership throughout the world and in the context of globalization, with an emphasis on determining the competencies, skills, and knowledges that leaders in a globalized world should possess. The Institute for Global Leadership at Tufts University, for instance, is an incubator for innovative approaches to global issues. Social psychologist Geert Hofstede's 1980 research identified several global leadership dimensions: individualism vs collectivism, long-term orientation, masculinity, power distance index, and uncertainty avoidance index.

GLOBE Project

The Global Leadership and Organizational Behavior Effectiveness Research (GLOBE) Project began in 1991 under the leadership of scholar Robert House at the Wharton School and continued Geert Hofstede's work on cultural dimensions of global leadership. Researchers, including co-investigators in 62 different cultures, collected data from 17,300 managers in 951 organizations. The cultures were grouped into Anglo Cultures, Arab Cultures, Confucian Asia, Eastern Europe, Germanic Europe, Latin America, Latin Europe, Nordic Europe, Southern Asia, and Sub-Sahara Africa. When the data was analyzed, the group identified six dimensions of culturally endorsed implicit leadership (CLT): charismatic/value-based; team-oriented; self-protective; participative; human orientation; and autonomous. Further, they identified nine cultural competencies:

performance orientation (the extent to which excellence is rewarded), assertiveness orientation (the extent to which individuals are assertive in their social relationships), future orientation (the degree to which individuals plan for the future), human orientation (the extent to which individuals are encouraged to be altruistic, friendly, or kind), institutional collectivism, in-group collectivism, gender egalitarianism, power distance, and uncertainty avoidance.

Goffman, Erving

One of the most cited sociologists, Erving Goffman's work is central to American sociology in the 20th century, and largely concerned the sociology of everyday life, the self, and social interaction. His seminal work, 1959's *The Presentation of Self in Everyday Life*, uses the allegory of the theater to portray humans as in a state of constant performance, in which certain social practices are adopted to avoid embarrassment of the self or others, while private thoughts remain "backstage." Every person is both an actor and an audience. One of the key elements of the book is the necessity of actors agreeing to the definition of the situation (cf.).

"Good enough"

In software and systems design, the "good enough" principle says that products do not need to be optimal, they only need to be good enough to meet consumer needs. A product that's "too good" may wind up being too expensive, or simply fail to find sufficient consumers who have a use for its additional capacities. Though coined in a software design context, the principle has broad applicability. In some cases, as with basic point-and-shoot digital cameras, the Chromebook bare-bones laptop, and cell phones marketed at seniors, "just good enough" is even a marketing talking point.

Good Manufacturing Practices
Good Manufacturing Practices (GMP) are the manufacturing practices guidelines recommended by a regulatory agency in order to meet a minimum level of quality and to minimize safety risks. "Good X Practices (GxP)" exist in many fields, including Good Clinical Practices for clinical drug studies, Good Laboratory Practices for laboratory experiments, and other GxP recommendations or regulations.

Grand theory of leadership
The grand or general theory of leadership is a hypothetical theory that would represent the unified findings of scholars in the multidisciplinary field of leadership studies: a set of universal principles related to leadership–subordinate relationships. Leadership scholar James MacGregor Burns convened a group of scholars at the Jepson School of Leadership Studies in 2001 with the intent of developing such a theory. Some scholars in the field rejected the idea of a unified theory outright, but Burns and others believed that leadership studies was a fragmented field and risked being trivialized. The group never produced such a theory, but the attempt to do so constituted an energetic and lengthy discussion of leadership studies, its findings, and its methodologies.

Great Men
In the 18th and especially the 19th century, scholars treated history as the work of "Great Men"—often heroic, virtuous, or especially competent men, especially when history was considered from their point of view, but sometimes simply men of great influence or charisma. Though the Great Men approach was particularly popular in the United States (and lives on in the form of popular mammoth biographies like Robert Caro's multivolume work on Lyndon B. Johnson), and was perhaps influenced by the American fascination with individualism and with the role individuals played in the independence and industrialization of the nation, Scotsman Thomas Carlyle actually was the first to formalize the idea, when he said "The history of the world is but the biography of great men." In contrast, Herbert Spencer argued that these great men were products of larger social forces, while Leo Tolstoy argued that Great Men "are but labels that serve to give a name to an event."

Scottish philosopher, Thomas Carlyle, who popularized the Great Man theory when he said that the world's history "is but the biography of great men." (Public Domain)

The Greatest Sa lesman in the World
First published in 1968, Og Mandino's *Greatest Salesman in the World* became a best-seller translated into 25 languages. An insurance salesman who attributed his success and recovery from alcoholism and suicidal feelings to self-help and motivation books, he wrote his own, consisting of elaborations of ten declarative statements: "Today I begin a new life. I will greet this day with love in my heart. I will persist until I succeed. I am nature's greatest miracle. I will live this day as if it is my last. Today I will be the master of my emotions. I will laugh at the world. Today I will multiply my value a hundredfold. I will act now. I will pray for guidance." The book praises the value of work, and uses incidents from a life as a salesman to illustrate its points.

Group affective tone

An aggregate of the moods of the members of a group is called the group affective tone. Not all groups have an affective tone, if members do not share similar moods, but common social experiences, common experiences with the work environment, emotional contagion, and the stability of group membership all conspire to make mood similarity likely.

Group cohesiveness

Group cohesiveness is the nature and strength of the bonds linking members of a group to one another and to the group as a whole, and consists of their perceptions of unity in a joint effort, the social relationships among them, the task-related relationships among them, and members of the group's feelings about each other and the group. There are many schools of thought about how to achieve healthy group cohesiveness and whether certain types of group makeup are more inclined toward cohesion.

Group conflict

Group conflict is a conflict either between groups or within a group. Intragroup conflicts may result from disagreement over goals or the means of achieving those goals, or from personality conflicts between members. Some studies have suggested that a plurality of intragroup conflicts among upper management are personality-driven rather than based on issues related to the work of the group.

Group decision making

Group decision making is the process of making a decision collectively, sharing participation in the process and responsibility for the outcome. Studies have found that groups often make very different decisions than individuals do, the reasons for which are the subject of ongoing study.

While groupthink is the best-known phenomenon, in part because of the fame of the Bay of Pigs invasion, which was used to illustrate it in Irving Janis's work, there are others that impact group decision making, which is not to say that they always make it worse. Common problems include time management (Parkinson's law applies here, stating that "A task will expand to fill the time available for its completion"); difficulty in setting discussion priorities and getting bogged down in trivialities, nuances, side discussions that will not affect the final outcome or represent a single member's hobby horse; and the possibility of rushing through the process and allowing the most passionate or charismatic members to sway the rest of the group. On the other hand, a group can avoid the individual biases of any one of its members, and can contribute greater information and relevant experience to inform the decision-making process. *See also* Consensus decision making, satisficing

Group emotion

Group emotion is the collection of emotions and moods experienced by members of a group. Experiments have shown that people are affected by the moods of those around them; Facebook famously even experimented with the status updates Facebook users see, to demonstrate the impact on their own status updates. Group emotion can and often is discussed in terms of the aggregation of the moods and emotions of individuals, but it can also be looked at from the group-as-a-whole perspective, which posits the group dynamic as having an impact on the moods of the members, especially with reference to their interactions with one another.

Group narcissism

Group narcissism is excessive love of one's own group, be it a work group, ethnic group, national identity, or any other group. It is related to, or can be an expression of, ethnocentrism, nationalism, chauvinism, and elitism, and can lead to cronyism and nepotism. Some psychologists believe it is an extension of personal or individual narcissism: "I am fantastic; my membership in this group is important to my conception of the 'I' that is fantastic; therefore, membership in this group is evidence of being fantastic." However, there are certainly cases where group narcissism can coexist with a personal low self-esteem, as can sometimes be found with white supremacists or nationalists. Group narcissism can also be the narcissism of a group, that is, the feeling and view that emerges from a group made up of individual narcissists, as discussed in the work of Jerrold Post.

Group polarization

Group polarization is the tendency of individuals to voice stronger opinions in a group situation than in individual situations. As a result, decisions made by a group have a tendency to be more extreme or involve more drastic change than if an individual group member had made a decision. Group polarization is frequently used to explain the decisions of groups as diverse as juries, terrorist and hate groups, political parties, and committees.

Groupthink

Groupthink is a phenomenon that can emerge in a group of people making a decision, in which the desire to avoid conflict leads to a superficial consensus that is achieved without due consideration of other options. Despite this, members of the group may be as devoted in their advocacy of the decision as one reached through more rational means. When William Whyte Jr. coined the term in a 1952 *Fortune* magazine article, he called it "a rationalized conformity—an open,

articulate philosophy that holds that group values are not only expedient but right and good as well." Many different group dynamics can result in groupthink, but common among them are dynamics that encourage or enforce conformity, and groups that value group harmony over rational action and accuracy. Groupthink occurs in myriad situations both trivial and dangerous, from a group of friends deciding on where to go for dinner and arriving at a restaurant that was no one's preference (cf. Abilene paradox) to the mass suicides of cults. The John F. Kennedy administration's decision to invade the Bay of Pigs in 1961, based on a plan put together by the Dwight D. Eisenhower administration, was used as an example by psychologist Irving Janis in his early work on the concept.

Groupware

Groupware is software that assists people in collaborating through the creation and maintenance of a collaborative working environment in which files can be worked on and annotated by multiple members of the group, often with the addition of project management capacities like group calendars, messaging, and task assignment sheets. Though collaborative computing applications were envisioned early on, the first widespread applications were actually recreational—Colossal Cave Adventure and other MUDs (Multi-User Dungeons) allowed multiple users to play the same dungeon video game together from different computer terminals, in an antecedent to today's massively multiplayer online roleplaying games. PARC's Pavel Curtis, who had adapted the MUD concept to the online social environment—a sort of massively multiplayer chat room—of LambdaMOO in the early 1990s, later developed groupware that simulated an auditorium, which became the basis for a commercial package sold to the military. Key to MUDs, LambdaMOO, and modern groupware, as opposed to other early multiuser software packages like IRC, is persistence of data: information about each user and their activities is saved and restored in each session.

Guru

In the religions of the Indian subcontinent (Buddhism, Hinduism, Jainism, Sikhism), "guru" means "teacher," especially a mentor who passes on religious teachings as well as practical knowledge. In the United States, it has typically referred to a Hindu teacher who leads his pupils toward enlightenment, but "guru" often refers to a teacher of individuals or organizations in a specialized field. Management consultants, marketing researchers, and other outsiders brought in to advise an organization may, if they have made a name for themselves in their cottage industry, be referred to as a "management guru" or similar term. Likewise, "leadership gurus" have developed their own industry, offering leadership development services to organizations or operating leadership training seminars for individuals.

Habermas, Jurgen

Jurgen Habermas is a German philosopher of the Frankfurt school. He has written on the rule of law, social theory and epistemology, democracy, capitalism, and German politics, and is perhaps best known for his theory of communicative rationality. He participated in a famous published dialogue with Cardinal Joseph Ratzinger, a year before his election to the papacy, on philosophy, religion, and reason, and has spoken of the emergence of post-secular civilization and the need for the secular to be tolerant of the religious just as the religious must be tolerant of the secular.

Hallyu

Hallyu or the Korean Wave is a South Korean term for its increased export of culture since the 1990s. The South Korean government has made loans and credit available to entertainment and food companies in order to increase exports, and established a Presidential Council on Nation Branding in 2009. Many parts of the world—even those, like the United States, that already had a well-established Korean community—have seen a marked increase in recent years in the popularity or prevalence of Korean cuisine, Korean music, and Korean entertainment, while pop star Psy ("Gangnam Style") became an international sensation. Hallyu is an exercise of soft power or public diplomacy—an attempt to influence worldwide perceptions of Korea and of Koreans (who have been treated poorly throughout much of their immigration diaspora).

Halo effect

A cognitive bias by which an individual's feelings about a person influence their evaluation of that person's behaviors and competencies. Often this is used to refer to the Warren G. Harding effect—assuming that a physically attractive person is also competent—but the halo effect is a broader phenomenon that is not limited to leadership competency.

Hansei

One of the Japanese cultural terms introduced to the United States through cross-pollination of Japanese and American business practices, hansei means "self-reflection," and refers to making clear what one's errors were and planning to improve in the future. At Toyota and some other Japanese companies, a hansei meeting is held after each project's completion, even if it is considered a success, in order to critically evaluate and discuss one's own work on the project. An important aspect of hansei is the belief that a point will never be reached when there is nothing that could have been improved upon.

Happiness

In the workplace, positive psychology has repeatedly found correlations between happiness and productivity, as well as employee engagement and job satisfaction, and a negative correlation with absenteeism. Nevertheless, most management approaches treat happiness as a side effect rather than a goal. There is a growing movement to change this.

Haptics

Haptics is a form of nonverbal communication conducted by touch. While some forms of haptic communication are both easily noticeable and clear in their meaning—a kiss on the cheek or a handshake (whether in greeting or to denote agreement to a deal), for instance—other forms are more subtle and often conducted unconsciously, such as lightly touching the listener while speaking in order to underline a point, or squeezing the speaker's hand while listening to indicate support. Norms of haptic communication vary by culture, and because touch involves entering personal space, there are often different sets of unspoken norms based on gender and level of intimacy.

Hard power

Hard power is, in Joseph Nye's phrase, "the ability to use the carrots and sticks of economic and military might to make others follow your will." While "carrots" are positive rewards and the "stick" is the threat of violent punishment, such overt and tangible displays of power are considered "hard" in contrast with soft power, a term Nye coined to refer to forms of diplomacy.

Harvard Business Review

Harvard Business Review is a management magazine published monthly by Harvard Business Publishing, a subsidiary of Harvard University. Founded in 1922 and made more accessible to a general audience in the 1980s, it was one of the first venues to introduce concepts like the glass ceiling, globalization, and core competence, and has published many of the luminaries of the management and leadership studies world.

Hawthorne studies

The Hawthorne studies were a series of 1924 to 1932 psychological experiments conducted by Elton Mayo at the Hawthorne Works, a Chicago area factory. The studies initially suggested that improving lighting in the workplace improved productivity, but a later investigation by Henry A. Landsberger in 1950 pointed out that the productivity increases ended when the study did. Landsberger's belief was that the fact of a change, and the awareness of a study being conducted, was actually the driving factor behind the workers' increased productivity, rather than the specifics of the change. Novelty, in other words, caused a temporary increase, which has since been called the Hawthorne effect.

Hazing

A ritual of harassment and humiliation used to initiate a person into a group, hazing is especially associated with college fraternities, but similar behavior is evinced by other close-knit and particularly male groups, including sports teams, private schools, gangs, and military units. Rituals range from the lengthy pledge week of fraternities to the old practice of painting a printer's apprentice's genitals with ink, and proponents say that the shared experience of hazing creates close bonds among initiates.

Similar rituals are sometimes adopted in the workplace, though they rarely involve the sort of physical harassment common elsewhere.

The hedgehog's dilemma

The hedgehog's (porcupine's) dilemma is that he needs to huddle close to the other hedgehogs in the group to stay warm in the winter, and yet cannot get too close to them lest they hurt one another with their spines. They remain apart despite mutual intentions to be close. The image was first invoked by German philosopher Arthur Schopenhauer to illustrate the life of the individual in human society: intimacy is not possible without mutual harm, despite intentions, and knowledge of this (or the first brush against those spikes) causes people to engage in shallow relationships. Sigmund Freud later quoted and helped to popularize Schopenhauer's analogy in his work on group psychology. A common rejoinder to Schopenhauer is that he has supplied his own solution: the hedgehogs need to huddle close, but not *too* close; it is his own pessimism that supposes the distance dictated by the spines is sufficient to prevent warmth and intimacy.

Hedonistic relevance

Hedonistic relevance is an attributional bias whereby an individual explains a person's behavior, when that behavior negatively affects the observing individual, with reference to the person's character and disposition rather than external factors. The classic example is to assign motive and intent to someone who has accidentally bumped into you, dropped or broken something of yours, or spilled something on you.

Heifetz, Ronald

The co-founder of the Center for Public Leadership at the John F. Kennedy School of Government (Harvard), Ronald Heifetz is a leading leadership studies scholar who has promoted adaptive leadership in the education field. His best-known book, *Leadership Without Easy Answers*, was first published in 1994 and focuses on the difference between technical problems solvable through expertise and problems requiring adaptive leadership.

Herd behavior

Herd behavior is the behavior of people as a group without direction or planning. While common in the animal world, among humans herd behavior is a marked category because of our usual reliance on communication. In some instances, stock market bubbles and riots have been blamed on herd behavior.

Here Comes Everybody

Here Comes Everybody: The Power of Organizing Without Organizations is a 2008 book by Clay Shirky on group dynamics in the age of social media, crowdfunding, filesharing, and Wikipedia.

Heterarchy

A heterarchy is one of the major ways to structure an organization. Unlike a hierarchy, in which different elements of the organization are ranked in static tiers, the elements of a heterarchy are unranked or can be re-ranked in different configurations. Sociologist David Stark has explored heterarchies, their distributed intelligence, their emergence in post-socialist economies in eastern Europe, and their applicability to Western organizations.

Hierarchy

A hierarchy is one of the major ways to structure an organization, in which elements of the organization are arranged in static tiers ranked with respect to one another. The hierarchy is the form of the typical bureaucracy, with executive leadership at the top, followed by department heads who oversee tiers of middle managers and supervisors overseeing work groups and teams. In most business and government organizations, as well as in the Catholic Church, every entity in the organization except the topmost is subordinate to a single other entity, which is usually visualized as either a pyramid or a tree. The hierarchy is a common enough form of organization that the other two major forms defined by triarchy theory are little known, especially in the business world.

Hierarchy culture

One of four organizational cultures identified by Robert Quinn's Competing Values Framework, hierarchy culture is focused on the well-being of people in the organization and favors a controlled organization structure. Hierarchical organizations tend to be bureaucratic, with clearly defined policies, procedures, and roles.

Hinduism

The dominant religion of India, Hinduism developed as a synthesis of Indian religious traditions in the 1st millennium B.C.E., shortly after Buddhism. Hinduism encompasses religious, philosophical, and cultural dimensions, and is intertwined with India's caste system, though non-Hindus in India are also part of the system. Brahmans, the highest of the castes, are the Hindu priests and religious leaders, responsible for leading rituals and ceremonies and running religious buildings and institutions. Another traditional Brahman role is that of the guru, a teacher who imparts knowledge to his disciple through a close spiritual relationship. Gurus are not exclusively religious in nature and are found in the arts and practical studies. Hinduism stresses authenticity, sincerity, and self-knowledge as keys to a guru's ability to work with disciples.

History

History is the study of the human past (while historiography is the study of how history has been written). Historical methodologies vary considerably with the area and era of study; the differences in documentation available for 1950s America compared to ancient Sumer necessitate differences in method. As a formal discipline, history grows out of the work of the ancient Greeks (beginning with Herodotus), most of whom focused on the recent past and its impact on or relevance to the present. The modern discipline and its commitment to objectivity begins more or less in the Enlightenment, as epitomized by the works of Edward Gibbon and Thomas Carlyle. Historiographical trends have varied over time: "Great Man" histories dominated the 19th and 20th centuries, while the last decades have seen a rise in social history, multi- and interdisciplinary approaches, and cultural studies.

The Hitler Problem

"The Hitler Problem" is Joanne Ciulla's term for a conundrum in leadership studies: the dichotomy between an effective leader (as Adolf Hitler could be considered) and an ethical one. The layman is familiar with the dichotomy in the form of the old saying about Hitler's fellow fascist dictator Benito Mussolini "making the trains run on time," and the implication that a tyrannical ruler can nevertheless get things done; this overstates Mussolini's actual effectiveness, however, not to mention the state of the Italian railways. The Hitler Problem can be used in support of defining leadership in a way that is at least broadly prescriptive.

Hofstede, Geert

Dutch psychologist Geert Hofstede is best known for his work on cultural dimensions and global leadership. Much of his work deals with cultural differences or cross-cultural studies, an interest inspired by his travels as a young man after World War II, including a voyage to Indonesia and an extended trip to England, both of which left him struck by culture shock. Before his work in psychology, he worked in management, with a background in engineering. Later he founded the Personnel Research Department at IBM, conducting opinion surveys of IBM employees throughout the world. He published his first major work on cross-cultural studies, *Culture's Consequences*, in 1980, the same year he co-founded the Institute for Research on Intercultural Cooperation. Critics of Hofstede's work focus principally on the level of cultural determinism that he assumes.

Hoshin Kanri

A Japanese management method, hoshin kanri ("direction management") is a strategic planning concept in which a group of employees contribute their own ideas, expertise, and experience to developing a strategy. The method is influenced by the work of W. Edwards Deming, who worked as a consultant in Japan after World War II, and systematizes the strategic planning process. One of its key elements is the use of quality storyboards: after a policy statement has been defined, each manager draws a storyboard illustrating their understanding of it, with managers discussing their storyboards with each manager above and below them in the hierarchy in order to smooth out differences and align approaches.

Hostile media effect

The hostile media effect is an error in perception in which one who is a strong partisan of an issue perceives media coverage of the issue as biased against them. Studies of the effect have been conducted since 1982.

Hostile work environment

A hostile work environment is one in which workers are reluctant or afraid to come to the workplace because of harassment or factors that create a deeply unpleasant environment.

Hot-cold empathy gap

The term *hot-cold empathy gap* was coined by psychologist George Loewenstein, and refers to a cognitive bias in peoples' perceptions of behavior. The gap represents the inability to empathize with and truly understand the effects of emotions one is not oneself currently experiencing. Further, the gap is such that the individual often underestimates its extent and may not realize it is there at all (in contrast with situations in which individuals who have trouble relating to a given situation are well aware of their difficulty). Not being aware of the gap results in ascribing others' behavior to factors other than the emotion or circumstance with which the individual is unable to empathize. While some of the most important ramifications of this gap impinge on interactions with other people—in the workplace, for instance, an employer may not understand the impact of emotional or physical trauma on an employee, and so may not approve a request for leave or a reduction in performance quality—the gap applies even to predicting one's own behavior. Loewenstein, for instance, wrote of a study showing that young men were unable to predict the level of risky sexual behavior they would accept while aroused. The empathy gap is also implicated in the tensions and frictions that result from members of an unmarked category being unable to relate to the effects of membership on members of a marked category, such as racial minority status, addiction, or disability. Social psychology experiments have found that those in power experience difficulty understanding or predicting the behavior of the comparatively powerless, but again, are largely unaware of the gap.

How to Win Friends and Influence People

How to Win Friends and Influence People by Dale Carnegie was published in 1936, based on self-improvement courses Carnegie had offered for some years. It became the first self-help best seller, incorporating elements of business books—the book promised to help readers become better salesmen or executives, win new clients, and increase their earning power, among other pragmatic goals—as well as books of moral instruction and pop psychology. The book was especially influential in its advice on influencing other people by flattering them and avoiding direct criticism. One of Carnegie's pieces of advice has virtually become standard behavior: making a request by asking "do me a favor" rather than explicitly asking for something, in order to make the target feel important and benevolent.

Human microphone

A method for delivering a speech, the human microphone involves the participation of a group of people who cooperate with the speaker. The speaker speaks a phrase at a time, pausing to allow the group to repeat the phrase in unison in order to amplify it. This can be repeated for several waves, with groups at the edge of earshot repeating what the first group said in order to carry the speech, a phrase at a time, farther out. The method was associated with the anti-nuclear protest movement in the 1970s and 1980s but became better known when used by Occupy Wall Street.

Human orientation

One of the global leadership cultural competencies identified by the GLOBE Project, human orientation is the measure of the friendliness, altruism, and compassion of the individuals in an organization, group, or society.

Human relations theory

Human relations theory is an area of organizational psychology that studies the behavior of people in groups, and the role of the worker in his organization in terms of his individual psychology rather than simply his defined duties and relationship to other workers.

Human resource management

Human resource management (HR) is an activity within an organization devoted to putting the organization's human resources—its employees—to best use in order to meet organizational goals. In large enough organizations, HR is typically its own department, and activities include recruitment and development, performance appraisal, and the pay and benefit system, as well as the handling of disputes and conflicts.

Human Resources frame

In L. Bolman and T. Deal's Four Frame model, the Human Resources frame is one of the distinctive frames through which people view the world. This frame is concerned with individuals, feelings, understanding others and one's own need to be understood, personal expression, and the view of the organization as a family.

Hundred Flowers Campaign

The Hundred Flowers Campaign was a 1956 initiative by the Communist government of China to entrap dissidents and counter-revolutionaries by inviting citizens to speak openly about their feelings about the communist regime, which

Mao Zedong and the Chinese Communist government enacted the Hundred Flowers Campaign, designed to entrap citizens with anti-communist views. (Public Domain)

was still young but had come to power through a decade-long civil war. Identified dissidents faced punishments ranging from the relatively minor to labor camp sentences and executions.

Hunter-gatherer societies

Before the Neolithic age—characterized by the development of agriculture—human societies depended on hunting and gathering in order to acquire food. Evolutionary leadership theory describes several means by which leaders in such societies (which tended not to develop the long-term institutions of Neolithic and later societies) had their power checked. The most extreme was murder, especially of a violent leader. But leaders could simply have their power limited through disobedience, departure of subgroups within the group, criticism to undercut the leader, and gossip to deplete the leader's prestige.

Identity negotiation

In sociology, identity negotiation is the process by which people reach implicit and unspoken agreements about the roles they assume in their relationships, which roles, once formulated, they are expected to maintain or violate the expectations of the other people in the relationship. Erving Goffman's work, such as in *The Presentation of Self in Everyday Life*, pioneered this view of identity in the mid-20th century, a time when many women were entering the workforce and implicitly "violating" the housewife role they had been consigned to, while young people reaching adulthood began to challenge the roles assigned to them or from which they were asked to choose.

Identity shift effect

The mechanism by which peer pressure works has been called the identity shift effect by psychologist Wendy Traynor, building on the work of social psychologist Leon Festinger. In Treynor's model, the individual experiences distress at the prospect of social rejection as a result of not conforming to the social norm of his peers, resulting in a change in behavior. This change in behavior causes a new source of distress as a result of having compromised one's standards, leading to a change in self-image (or shift in identity) in which the peer norm is adopted as a personal norm, eliminating the conflict.

Idiosyncrasy credits

In social psychology, idiosyncrasy credits are a concept representing the ability of a member of a group to violate the social norms of that group without exceeding the threshold of the group's tolerance for deviation. Edwin Hollander first coined the term in the 1950s to represent the affect of accumulated positive feelings from the group, allowing for deviation from the norm for members who have in essence "proven themselves" and whose deviation therefore is not sufficient to call into question whether they belong in the group. Idiosyncrasy credits can also be used to explain how one member's deviation can be punished while another's deviation—even a deviation from the same norm—can be rewarded, and the way minority views can become influential within a group. Hollander argued that idiosyncrasy credits are particularly important in American corporate culture, in which the accumulation of such credits is necessary for leaders to climb the corporate ladder to positions of ever-greater responsibility, at which point they are given the leeway to behave idiosyncratically, changing the very norms they were promoted for honoring.

"If it ain't broke, don't fix it"

This maxim was popularized by Bert Lance, the banker who served as President Jimmy Carter's director of the Office of Management and Budget. In a 1977 article in the U.S. Chamber of Commerce's newsletter *Nation's Business*, Lance said the United States needed to take the "if it ain't broke, don't fix it" approach in order to cut spending. The maxim has since become associated less with frugality and more with the implication that introducing change to a working system may stop it from working.

Ignoratio elenchi

The ignoratio elenchi, or irrelevant conclusion, is a fallacy of relevance in which the arguer presents an argument that is irrelevant to the issue at hand. Closely related is the straw man, which presents an argument that refutes a point the other side has not actually attempted to make. Both fallacies are a type of informal fallacy—arguments that are fallacious for failing to support the conclusion.

Immune neglect

Immune neglect is a cognitive bias affecting an individual's ability to predict the emotional impact an event or decision will have on him. Specifically, it is the inability to properly account for the psychological immune system, which works to help people recover from negative emotions. As a result, people predict that they will feel badly for much longer than they actually do.

Impact bias

The impact bias is a cognitive bias affecting peoples' ability to predict their future emotional states (affective forecasting). Specifically, it is the tendency to overestimate the intensity or duration of these states, despite their previous experience with the same or similar emotional states. This affects decision making, since it seems to weight more heavily the emotional impact of outcomes.

Impeachment

Impeachment is the legal process of accusing a public official of illegal activity, possibly followed by civil or criminal proceedings or the removal of the official from office. In the United States, for instance, the Constitution defines federal impeachments as concerning "the President, Vice President, and all civil officers of the United States," and their impeachable crimes as "treason, bribery, or other high crimes and misdemeanors." The power to impeach is given to the House of Representatives, while the Senate tries the impeachment. Neither "other high crimes" nor "civil officers" is defined in the Constitution, and so many specifics of federal impeachment are unclear, including whether members of Congress are impeachable; the sole attempt to impeach a member of Congress (Senator William Blount in 1798) did not resolve the issue, though it did famously cause a fistfight to break out between two congressmen. The Senate dismissed the impeachment on the grounds that senators were not impeachable, but expelled Blount from the Senate anyway, and the ruling is not considered final.

In-group

In-group refers to a social group with which an individual identifies.

In-group collectivism

One of the global leadership cultural competencies identified by the GLOBE Project, in-group collectivism is a measure of the extent to which individuals feel pride in their group membership.

Inclusive management

In public administration, inclusive management is a management style that is similar to participatory management in the private sector. Under this approach, managers involve not only members of their organization but members of the public, politicians representing the relevant constituency, and experts in relevant fields, in the process of making decisions about policy or actions taken by the organization, and in addressing public problems within the organization's scope. Inclusive management is especially associated with the public managers of Grand Rapids, Michigan, who coined the "50/50 rule," stating that the process of making a decision or addressing a problem is equally important to public satisfaction as the outcome.

Inclusivity

Inclusivity is the organizational goal of ensuring that members feel they belong. Belongingness has been recognized as one of the most fundamenal human motivations, and as leadership and management have become more people-focused, the value has become clear of making group members feel accepted by and engaged in the operations of the group. Inclusivity in the workplace borrows practices from and reflects similar values to political inclusivity (which seeks to encourage the participation and inclusion of all citizens in politics and policy), in making sure members do not feel excluded because of their age, gender, sexual orientation, race or ethnicity, religion, disability, or other identity traits. Common to most organizational inclusivity programs is the goal of making employees feel valued and creating a supportive environment that benefits the quality of work and employee engagement of everyone.

Inattentional blindness

Inattentional blindness is caused not by a vision defect but by inattention and may be impacted by mental workload and attentional capacity.

Incrementalism

Incrementalism is a work method in which incremental changes are made to a project rather than large additions. Typically, incrementalist work is not as thoroughly planned as in traditional methods. Instead, the most pressing problem of the moment is dealt with. Though often criticized in American business culture, Denmark's wind energy industry was built incrementally from an agricultural origin as opposed to the smaller American wind energy industry, which developed out of the aerospace industry with heavy research institute involvement, and required significant up-front capital investment. Incrementalism is also popular in product design divisions of Japanese businesses.

Indifferent style

One of the leadership styles plotted on the managerial grid model, the style was originally called the impoverished style. Indifferent managers have a low concern for both production and people and are primarily interested in staying out of trouble and preserving their position.

Individualism

Individualism is an ideology that attaches significant value to the individual. Independence, self-reliance, personal freedom, and self-expression are all highly valued and receive precedence over concerns of a larger group like the state, and within reason need to be protected from interference by larger groups. Liberalism is founded on individualism, as are anarchism and libertarianism, and John Locke provided a motto for individualism when he wrote, "No one ought to harm another in his life, health, liberty, or possessions." Individualism is contrasted with collectivism and other ideologies that put the interests of the group or groups above those of individuals.

Individualism versus collectivism
One of the cultural dimensions of organizations identified by Geert Hofstede, individualism versus collectivism represents the organization's position on a spectrum with individualism at one extreme, as seen in the United States, and collectivism, in which members are emotionally dependent on and invested in their organization, at the other.

Industrial engineering
Industrial engineering is the branch of engineering dealing with complex systems of equipment, materials, information, and people. The term originated in the manufacturing sector, but industrial engineers are found in all kinds of organizations, including the health care industry, the military, theme parks, and publishing. Industrial engineering involves systems thinking and a holistic, top-down view of a business or organization, followed by an examination and streamlining of the processes of its operations.

Industrial psychology or I/O psychology
See Organizational psychology

Industrial sociology
Industrial sociology is the branch of sociology engaged in an examination and critique of ongoing trends in labor, employment, management practices, and related issues like globalization, the impacts of international trade, and outsourcing and offshoring.

Influence
Influence is the formal or informal, overt or covert, ability to affect the behaviors, decisions, or emotions of others, or the behavior or decisions of organizations. Influence is wielded in numerous ways, not always consciously and not always in ways that serve the influencer's interests—making a poor impression in a job interview enacts a negative influence on the organization's likelihood of hiring you, for instance. At a greater extreme, reactance is the psychological term for the motivation of someone responding to an attempt to influence them by adopting the opposite of the behavior or viewpoint toward which the influencer is pushing them.

Informal fallacy
An informal fallacy is an argument that fails to support its conclusion due to a flaw in reasoning, but unlike a formal fallacy, it is not the result of a flaw in logic.

Informational power
Informational power is one of John R. P. French and Bertram Raven's bases of power, and one of Patrick J. Montana and Bruce H. Charnov's varieties of organizational power. It was the sixth base, identified separately by Raven several years after he and French identified the first five. Informational power is power exerted by providing the target with information that results in a change in their attitudes or behavior.

Informational social influence
Informational social influence, or social proof, is a conformity-enforcing phenomenon in

which individuals mimic the observed behavior of others in their attempt to behave correctly in a given situation. It is especially pronounced in ambiguous social situations in which the individual does not already possess a "script" for the appropriate behavior and has not already developed his own norms or habits. The effect may be conscious or unconscious and can lead to a large group confidently making an incorrect choice as a behavior or attitude cascades through it. This form of social influence is also sometimes blamed for the phenomenon of copycat suicide.

Initiating structure
One of two factors identified by the Ohio State Leadership Studies, the "initiating structure" factor refers to the way a leader organizes and defines roles within the group, delegates tasks among those roles, and organizes activities for the group. Setting specific performance metrics both for the group and for individual roles, establishing rules and procedures, and focusing on maintaining a schedule are behaviors associated with initiating structure.

Institutional economics
Institutional economics, beginning with Thorstein Veblen's work in the late 19th century, is the study of the role of institutions in economic behavior, incorporating in its classical form an evolutionary perspective, Veblen having been influenced by the work of Charles Darwin.

Institutional collectivism
One of the global leadership cultural competencies identified by the GLOBE Project, institutional collectivism is the extent to which the institutional culture of an organization or institutional cultures throughout a society encourage collective action and distribution of resources.

Instrumentality
In Victor Vroom's expectancy theory, instrumentality is an individual's belief that he will be rewarded if he performs a particular task. Instrumentality is affected by past history, trust in and consistency on the part of the source of the reward, and faith in the fairness or neutrality of the reward system.

Intelligence
Intelligence is a trait that is difficult to adequately define, as a mental capability that encompasses knowledge, memory, reasoning, creativity, capacity for abstract thought and synthesizing information, communication, learning, problem solving, logic, and critical thinking. Intelligence tests are widespread but generally measure only certain applications of intelligence and reasoning skills. The difficulty in defining intelligence in turn makes it difficult to establish the extent to which non-humans are intelligent, with some researchers distinguishing between animal instinct and the capacity for abstract thought, an understanding of consequences, and the ability to plan for the future based on past experiences, while other researchers ascribe intelligence or intelligence-like capacities not only to many animal species but to some plants. (Two common criteria for intelligence in a species are the ability to set goals and the ability to learn from past experiences.) Numerous studies have indicated that successful leaders have above-average intelligence.

International Leadership Association
The International Leadership Association was founded in 1999 and has a membership of about 2,000. Established with a grant from the W. K. Kellogg Foundation, it is headquartered at the University of Maryland, College Park, and is the principal member association for leadership

studies. The annual conference is held in the fall and alternates between North American and non–North American host cities.

Instructional theory

An instructional theory is a framework describing methods of instruction: ways to help people acquire skills and knowledge.

Intellectual history

Intellectual history is the subfield of the history discipline that studies major ideas, the context in which they were developed and by whom they were developed, the social and cultural institutions relevant to their development, and the factors affecting these ideas' adoption or abandonment. Intellectual history has supplanted the earlier history of ideas, and is differentiated principally by its insistence that those ideas cannot be studied in historical context without reference to the individuals who formulated, popularized, and discussed them. Intellectual history includes and overlaps with many subfields, including the history of political thought, the history of philosophy, and historiography itself.

Internalized moral perspective

One of the qualities of authentic leadership, "internalized moral perspective" refers to the leader's possession of a strong sense of ethics that is well developed and resists external pressures.

Intrinsic motivation

Intrinsic motivation is motivation that is driven by factors within the individual, such as an enjoyment or personal interest in the behavior or task in question. Studies find, for instance, that students who are interested in increasing their knowledge or mastery of a subject perform better than those interested in earning a grade (or,

in younger students, a gold star, sticker, et cetera). Of course, there are cases where no intrinsic motivation exists and only extrinsic motivation will bring a behavior about.

Intuition

Intuition is a perceptive or cognitive capacity that does not rely on reason or inference, though it may draw on knowledge through processes inaudible to the conscious mind. Intuition has been studied extensively in psychology and cognitive science, and is associated with creative capacities and scientific innovation, but is not well understood even by the standards of cognitive science. The extent to which one relies on intuition over or instead of reason is one of the measures taken in many personality tests, and empathy is often treated as an aspect of intuition, at least insofar as its role in anticipating or sensing the emotions of others.

Iroquois Confederacy Grand Council

The Grand Council is the ruling assembly of the Iroquois Confederacy, a group of Native American nations in the northeast that historically included the Mohawk, Oneida, Onondaga, Cayuga, and Seneca, with the Tuscarora joining in 1722. Long before European contact, as early as the 12th century and no later than the 15th, the Grand Council made its decisions through consensus represented by a 75 percent super majority of its delegates. This system of government was a significant influence both on early New England colonies and later on the Articles of Confederacy and the Constitution.

Jepson School of Leadership Studies

The Jepson School of Leadership Studies in Virginia was founded in 1992 at the University of Richmond, with a donation from Robert S. Jepson Jr. Co-founder Joanna B. Ciulla has described

Jepson as "a liberal arts school with an explicit focus on the study of leadership," and its commitment to liberal arts is a distinct one, resulting in students studying history, philosophy, and literature as part of their growing understanding of leadership. This was a significant statement about the school's position on leadership studies, as at the time most of the literature in the field came from management and psychology. This characterization is also meant to differentiate Jepson from leadership training schools, the founders having decided to avoid that route.

Jesus as leader

Jesus of Nazareth is often used as an illustrative example of exemplary leadership, though the exact lessons to be drawn from his example vary from usage to usage. German sociologist Max Weber used him as an example of a charismatic leader with un-everyday-ness (cf.), one who repeatedly used the formula, in reference to the scripture that came before him, "It has been written . . . but I say unto you . . .," asserting his authority as the source of the law.

Joan of Arc

Joan of Arc is a Roman Catholic saint who was born to a French peasant family in the early 15th century. As a teenager, she claimed to experience visions of Saints Margaret and Catherine and the Archangel Michael, telling her to support Charles VII, the king of France whose legitimacy was questioned by England, a conflict forming part of the Hundred Years' War. When Joan's participation in the siege of Orleans led to a fast and decisive victory, she rose quickly to fame, and Charles was crowned not long after. When she was captured by the English, she was tried and burned at the stake for her claims of visions, at the age of 19. A Catholic court later debunked the trial and declared her

a martyr; she was canonized in the 20th century, becoming one of France's patron saints.

Job Characteristics Model

The Job Characteristics Model (JCM) is a work design theory that has influenced workplace-based positive psychology. Designed to create personally enriching jobs, in its original formulation it addressed five job characteristics (autonomy, feedback, skill variety, task identity, and task significance) and five work-driven outcomes (absenteeism, motivation, performance, satisfaction, and turnover). Though related in some ways to the old theories of scientific management that emphasized efficiency, versions of JCM have more recently been proposed that emphasize workplace happiness as a route to productivity.

Job enrichment

Job enrichment is a strategy to motivate employees by defining their job to include a variety of tasks and responsibilities, coupled with feedback, encouragement, and sufficient communication to make their tasks feel meaningful and contextualized.

Job rotation

Job rotation is the practice of assigning a worker to different roles within the organization in succession, often over a period of several years. Job rotation is used to train employees and help locate their ideal role, especially young employees fresh from college who have academic credentials but little relevant previous work experience. Job rotation can also be used to alleviate boredom or to reduce the risk of injuries resulting from repetitive task performance. A similar practice is used in the training of medical students, wherein the last two years of their four-year education are spent rotating through multiple medical specialties, in which they work full-time jobs under supervising physicians. Often they are required to rotate through internal medicine, pediatrics, obstetrics and gynecology, family medicine, radiology, neurology, emergency medicine, and surgery, as well as a sub-internship in their chosen specialty.

John F. Kennedy School of Government

The John F. Kennedy School of Government is a public policy graduate school at Harvard University, offering graduate degrees in public policy, public administration, and international development. Approaches to public policy studies vary considerably by school, and Harvard Kennedy School (HKS) is characterized by its leadership-based approach.

Judge-adviser system

A judge-adviser system is an advice structure studied in the social sciences, in which the judge is the individual with decision-making power in a situation, while the adviser is a second individual providing a recommendation or relevant information. Experimental studies of advice usually focus on the judge-adviser structure, with participants taking randomly assigned roles.

Judicial activism

Judicial activism is a usually pejorative term referring to judges whose rulings are motivated not wholly by interpretations of the relevant body of law, but by personal considerations, including political, ethical, moral, and religious beliefs. The term is especially used in reference to Supreme Court decisions with wide-ranging effects, from those upholding or banning segregation to recent decisions like *Bush v. Gore* and *Citizens United v. FEC*. Though the term is associated with complaints about the Court overstepping its authority, judicial activism

Seated in the front row are Sigmund Freud, G. Stanley Hall, and Carl Jung. Abraham A. Brill, Ernest Jones, and Sandor Ferenczi stand in the back row, in a 1909 photograph. (Public Domain)

need not be constructed as a wrong, and there are defenders of such activism who see it as a valid aspect of judicial review. Right or wrong, judicial activism amounts to a sort of leadership from the bench.

Jung, Carl

The Swiss psychiatrist Carl Jung was an early colleague of Sigmund Freud, though the two had a falling-out over their conceptions of the libido. Dismissed by Freud as too mystical, the more mystical and stranger elements of his work and his interest in alchemy and astrology did prove influential to the New Age movement and the new religious movements of the 1960s—but he also introduced the ideas of the archetype, the collective unconscious, and synchronicity, and his work on personality types was the basis for the Myers-Briggs Type Indicator, as well as influencing much of personality psychology and trait-based theories of leadership.

Juran, Joseph

One of the American engineers who traveled to Japan after World War II to help restore and modernize Japanese manufacturing, Joseph Juran became an influential management consultant, especially in the area of quality management. He was the first to apply the Pareto principle to quality control issues and among the first to draw attention to the cost of poor quality, a concept referring to the costs an organization could save by improving the quality of its performance.

Jus ad bellum

The Latin phrase for "right to war," jus ad bellum refers to the criteria that determine (in advance of engagement) whether a war is a just war.

Jus in bello

Latin for "right in war," jus in bello refers to the criteria of a justly conducted war.

Just war

A just war is one that is morally defensible, as defined by meeting at least two sets of traditional criteria: those showing that there is a moral reason to go to war, and those showing that conduct during the war is moral. Jus post bellum refers to a third set of criteria more recently proposed: the moral nature of postwar actions like reconstruction. The idea of a just war assumes that war is not always the worst possible choice, an assumption that is rejected by some pacifists. The pacifist Ben Salmon, for instance, was sentenced to death for desertion during World War I, writing to President Woodrow Wilson that there was no such thing as a just war. (His sentence was later commuted to 25 years hard labor, and along with other conscientious objectors, he was pardoned in 1920 in response to public demand.)

Juvenal

The 2nd-century Roman poet Juvenal was a satirist of ancient Roman society. He is best remembered for contributing two phrases to Western culture, which have survived across many languages: "bread and circuses," in the sense of the appeasement offered by a ruling power (in the form of food to nourish their bodies and entertainment to occupy their minds) to the populace as distraction from tyranny and injustice; and "quis custodiet ipsos custodes," "who will guard the guardians themselves," often translated into English as "who watches the watchmen?" This latter question is asked as a criticism of dictatorships and oligarchies, even the benevolent ones such as proposed by the philosopher Plato: without a system in check by which rulers can be removed from office, such as in a democracy, what means is there to ensure that rulers will abide by the law and rule justly?

Kaizen

"Good change" in Japanese, kaizen is a term with slightly different connotations in many areas of life, from banking to psychotherapy. It was introduced to Americans via Japanese management practices, in which kaizen refers to the continual reassessment and, when possible, improvement of business processes and job functions. The key difference between kaizen in this usage and other forms of structural change to an organization's business processes is the sense that kaizen is a continuous process rather than a one-time event. More drastic change is called "kaikaku."

Kellerman, Barbara

One of the founders of the International Leadership Association, Barbara Kellerman is a professor of public leadership at the Kennedy School of Government at Harvard University. Her work focuses on followership as well as the leadership styles of women.

Keynesian Revolution

After the publication of John Maynard Keynes's *General Theory* in 1936, inspired by his study of the factors leading to the Great Depression, the orthodox view in the field of economics shifted quickly from the neoclassical economics that had prevailed to the new Keynesian view. The key difference was Keynes's insistence that the driving factor behind employment levels was demand, not supply, whereas prior to the unemployment crisis of the Great Depression, economists believed that in an unregulated free market, full employment equilibrium would naturally occur. After Keynes, regulation of the market was seen as necessary for the safety of the economy. Keynesian economics lost much of its influence on policy in the late 1970s as a result of that decade's economic travails and the rise of the deregulation-happy Ronald Reagan Republicans, but saw a resurgence after the 2008 financial crisis. Keynes's Biercean definition of capitalism remains important: "the astounding belief that the most wicked of men will do the most wicked of things for the greatest good of everyone."

Kinesics

Kinesics is the area of nonverbal communication related to movements of the body, including gestures, posture, and facial expressions, and the study of that area. The term was coined by anthropologist Ray Birdwhistell, who considered the term *body language* inaccurate. Examples of kinesic communication range from a nod of the head meaning "yes" (or "I am listening") to a student shifting in their seat indicating a wandering attention. Kinesic communication varies greatly from culture to culture.

King, Martin Luther, Jr.

The Reverend Martin Luther King, Jr., was one of the most prominent leaders of the African American Civil Rights movement in the 1950s and 1960s. A Baptist minister, he helped found the Southern Christian Leadership Conference in 1957 after organizing the Montgomery bus boycott after the arrest of Rosa Parks. A famously powerful speaker, he was considered a radical by J. Edgar Hoover and the Federal Bureau of Investigation, though today he is often contrasted with other civil rights leaders like Malcolm X who were less moderate in their views of how equality was to be achieved. For 13 years, King was one of the most prominent figures in the country, leading marches and other demonstrations, affirming his commitment to nonviolence, and speaking out against the Vietnam War. He was assassinated in 1968 by James Earl Ray; in 1999, Loyd Jowers, who owned a restaurant near the site of the attack, was found responsible by a Memphis jury for a conspiracy to murder King, but the details remain vague.

Knew-it-all-along

The knew-it-all-along effect is a cognitive bias in which people misremember and overestimate the extent of their past knowledge, such that they project backward onto their conception of their past self the understanding that they currently possess.

Knowledge

Knowledge is information and understanding that is acquired through experience or education. Knowledge includes both practical understanding—usually acquired through hands-on experience—and theoretical understanding. Knowledge must be acquired, which requires exposure to new information (though existing knowledge can be preserved or strengthened through repeated exposure, and connections between pieces of acquired knowledge can be discovered). The philosophical study of the nature of knowledge is called epistemology, while cognitive science, neuroscience, and psychology all approach the mechanisms and processes of knowledge acquisition and retention.

Kritarchy

Kritarchy is rulership by judges, as for example in ancient Israel as depicted in the Old Testament Book of Judges in the era before the appointment of Saul as the first king.

Lacan, Jacques

The most significant figure in psychoanalysis after Sigmund Freud, Jacques Lacan was one of the principal French intellectuals of the 1950s, 1960s, and 1970s. He held annual seminars in Paris from 1953 to 1981, which helped spread his ideas. Chief among them was his interrogation of ego psychology and rereading of Freud in light of the developments of the last half-century, and his extension of Freud's work on drives (psychological motivations that are inherently unsatisfiable and thus account for much of human behavior).

Laissez-Faire

Laissez-faire, "let them do/let them be," is perhaps the best-known French phrase in economics. It represents an approach to economic policy that calls for avoiding restrictions, regulations, tariffs, and subsidies as much as possible, limiting the government's involvement to the protection of ownership rights and, in most formulations, protection from fraud and other basic crimes. (Some do not even call for fraud protection, arguing that market forces are sufficient to disincentivize it.)

Lateral communication

Lateral communication in an organization transpires among participants at the same organizational level, such as between members of the same department. Lateral communication is more direct and effective, and studies have found that when members of an organization need to rely on lateral communication to solve a problem, information sharing and task coordination are easier than when vertical communication (between participants on different levels of the hierarchy) is required. On the other hand, it can invoke its own special pitfalls, notably territoriality as departments and teams work to protect their respective turfs.

Lateral thinking

Lateral thinking is a problem-solving approach that applies creative thinking and indirect reasoning rather than "vertical" step-by-step logic or "horizontal" brainstorming. Maltese physician and author Edward de Bono introduced the term in 1967. One of its methods is called "disproving" (or "the black hat," in de Bono's later *Six Thinking Hats*), in which statements accepted as common knowledge or obviously true are challenged and assumed to be wrong.

Law of the instrument

The law of the instrument is a maxim first stated by philosopher Abraham Kaplan in 1964 and rephrased by psychologist Abraham Maslow, more famously, in 1966. Kaplan's "law of the instrument" stated, "Give a small boy a hammer, and he will find everything he encounters needs pounding." Maslow rephrased this as, "If the only tool you have is a hammer, it is tempting to treat everything as if it were a nail." The popular adage derived from this is "If all you have is a hammer, everything looks like a nail," which naturally has been widely attributed to Mark Twain, who said no such thing. In any formulation, the maxim reflects a certain common and dangerous narrow-mindedness that views the

American prisoners captured in Ardennes, Germany, in 1944. The law of war concerns acceptable wartime conduct, including the treatment of prisoners. (German Federal Archives)

world in terms defined by one's own capabilities and competencies, and so insists on solutions that make use of those capabilities.

Law of war

The area of international law concerning acceptable actions in war and justifications for going to war, including issues like the treatment of prisoners, civilian casualties and civilian targets, prohibited weapons, proportionality, and the acceptance of surrender.

Leader Authenticity Scale

The Leader Authenticity Scale (LAS) was the first method developed to measure authentic leadership, and was introduced in 1983 by education researchers James E. Henderson and Wayne K. Hoy. The three areas most closely examined were accountability, avoiding manipulation of followers, and "salience of self over role"—the leader's ability to behave the same regardless of his job title, rather than assuming a role.

Leader–member exchange theory

Leader–member exchange or LMX theory is a leadership theory that is concerned with the dyadic relationship between leaders and followers, called leader–member exchanges. Each of these exchange relationships influences factors that impact the follower's work, including their resource access, influence on the decision-making process, and overall performance. Thus, healthy relationships with followers leads to better organizational performance. LMX theory grew out of role theory in the 1960s and 1970s, and posits three stages of the leader–member relationship: role-taking, role-making, and routinization. Role-taking occurs when a member first joins the group. Role-making occurs as new members take on tasks, and as a result of their performance at work, are subconsciously perceived by their supervisors as either in-group (a "team player" who fits in with the group) or out-group (as a result of lack of motivation or work quality). Routinization is the stage in which routines and habits develop in the relationship between a team member and a supervisor, with in-group members developing a healthier relationship with their supervisor while out-group members may have trouble earning trust back. One prescription growing out of LMX theory is for managers to identify the workers they have subconsciously treated as out-group, and reevaluate whether they still deserve that classification or have simply become alienated as a result of the unhealthy leader–member exchange.

Leadership

The act of being in charge of the decisions and actions of a group, of setting its goals, of issuing instructions to its members or to delegated go-betweens, and of evaluating the outcome of decisions. Leaders may be formal or informal, chosen by the group or appointed by an outside party, even selected at random, as with the jury foreman in some jurisdictions. The duties and powers of a leader naturally vary as well. When undertaken deliberately and skillfully, leadership can be seen as both an art and a science, and studied from either perspective.

Leadership (journal)

Published by Sage since 2005, *Leadership* is a scholarly journal of leadership studies. It is distinct in its solidly interdisciplinary approach, whereas the leadership studies journals preceding it were grounded primarily in psychology and management.

Leadership accountability movement

In the 21st century, there has been a loosely connected movement or trend to hold leaders of various institutions accountable for the harm caused by their actions or inaction. Clear examples include the growing dissent over the Catholic Church's handling of priestly sexual abuse, and the role that dissent may have played in the retirement of Pope Benedict; the establishment of the International Criminal Court and the United Nations Convention Against Corruption; protests greeting G8 meetings; the Arab Spring protests, and similarly motivated protests in Europe and Africa; and possible changes in the American demeanor toward Israel's treatment of Palestinians.

Leadership Behavior Description Questionnaire

A questionnaire designed by the Ohio State Leadership Studies team in the 1940s to measure nine different areas of leader behavior. Questionnaires were distributed to various groups whose members were asked to identify how frequently their leader engaged in each of 150 different behaviors. The two areas that showed the most variation were labeled

Consideration and Initiating Structure, which provided a framework for early leadership studies that moved away from a focus on leader personality in favor of leader behavior.

The Leadership Challenge

The Leadership Challenge is a 1987 book by James Kouzes and Barry Posner, which introduced their model of "the five practices of exemplary leadership," as supported by case studies. Their studies began with surveys of leaders, asking what practices they associated with their personal best performance. Rejecting trait-based models of leadership, they present a number of common personality traits and explain how people with these personalities can learn leadership skills and practices. The five practices they identified were labeled "Model the Way," "Inspire a Shared Vision," "Challenge the Process," "Enable Others to Act," and "Encourage the Heart," the least common of the five in their studies. "Encourage the Heart" combines authentic leadership, inclusivity, and taking pains to recognize employee successes and contributions. One of the most influential leadership books, *The Leadership Challenge* has been published in several editions (the 5th was released in 2012 on its 25th anniversary) and 20 languages, and Kouzes and Posner have become more prescriptive over time, developing self-assessment tools based on their book that have been adopted by government agencies and the Red Cross.

Leadership development

Leadership development is the attempt to improve leadership behaviors and abilities in individuals. This may take the form of a college program, such as some offered at business schools, or smaller-scale events like weekend seminars or executive retreats.

Leadership Institute at Harvard College

The Leadership Institute at Harvard College was founded in 2005 by four undergraduates. It is a student-run leadership development program, offering workshops, forums, and speaking engagements through the Leadership Development Initiative and the Presidents' Forum.

Leadership presence

Leadership presence is a concept that shows up in many discussions of leadership, and may at least in some cases be the same as charisma. In his *Three Levels of Leadership*, James Scouller uses the term to refer to a "something" that the most effective leaders have that allows them to command attention and trust, a "something" that varies from leader to leader—which in Scouller's view accounts for the failures of trait-based leadership theories.

Leadership pedagogy

Leadership pedagogy is the science of teaching leadership or leadership studies, which involves an introduction to various theories and models of leadership, group psychology, management theory, and other areas.

Leadership philosophy versus leadership theory

The distinction between a leadership philosophy and a leadership theory is sometimes useful. Though both may be normative, the former advocates specific values, as in ethical leadership or servant leadership, while the latter focuses on maximizing effectiveness. This should not be confused with the difference between normative (or prescriptive) leadership theory, which advocates a specific approach to leadership, and descriptive leadership theory, which merely describes how leadership is performed in the world.

Leadership psychology

A cross-disciplinary field, leadership psychology examines leadership as something that occurs in a complex system of individual and group behaviors. It is influenced both by positive psychology and by adaptive leadership, and studies the ways leaders work with followers to identify goals, assign roles, build consensus, and collaborate on projects. Leadership in introducing or adapting to necessary changes is also an area of interest.

Leadership Quarterly

The *Leadership Quarterly* (LQ) is the oldest scholarly journal for leadership studies, having been published in affiliation with the International Leadership Association since 1990. One of the highest-ranked journals in management and applied psychology, it primarily publishes scholars from those fields, though it is interdisciplinary in scope and open to submissions from other disciplines. In 2014, amid complaints about the quality of research in the leadership studies field and the increase in articles of specious quality, LQ retracted five articles from a Florida International University researcher whose work had been met with a flurry of reader complaints.

Leadership Series

Since 2003, the central event of India's Symbiosis Institute of International Business has been the Leadership Series, a three-day series of events attended by prominent speakers and participants from the worlds of business, politics, and international affairs.

Leadership studies

Leadership studies is a multidisciplinary field examining the phenomenon of leadership, the roles of leaders and followers, and the many styles of leadership. Leadership studies grew out of psychology and management, but history, philosophy, and the social sciences have long addressed leadership issues, while questions raised in education, public policy, and international relations have often had relevance to leadership. Today the field draws on numerous disciplines and includes researchers from diverse academic backgrounds.

Lean

Lean, short for "lean production" or "lean manufacturing," is an approach to production that builds on Frederick W. Taylor's scientific management from the early 20th century and Toyota Production System developed mid-century in focusing on the elimination of any resource expenditure that is not represented by added value for the end customer. Lean government takes a similar approach to the provision of government services, seeking to eliminate waste and inefficiency in public programs. Lean government had been implemented in Cape Coral, Florida; Grand Rapids, Michigan; and Fort Wayne, Indiana, among other cities.

Learning by doing

Learning by doing refers to experiential learning, and in economics, it refers to an organization or its employees learning to improve productivity as a result of performing its work, and in the course of that performance, streamlining or improving certain processes or becoming more adept through practice.

Learning by teaching

Learning by teaching is a method of education in which students are selected to teach part of a class's lesson, choosing their own methodology and approach (rather than simply making an oral presentation within a rigid didactic formula). This has long been practiced to deal with labor shortages: in early European schools, older students sometimes taught younger ones, passing on what they had learned only a few years earlier, while today in American universities much of the labor burden in the teaching of introductory courses is borne by graduate students. The emphasis of learning by teaching, though, is the benefit to the student-as-teacher and the way it engages them with the material.

Learning theory

A learning theory is a framework describing the absorption and handling of information during learning processes, and forms the underpinning of an educational, instructional, or management approach.

Least preferred coworker

In Fiedler's contingency theory of leadership, the least preferred co-worker (LPC) is the co-worker with whom the leader has had the least success in work relationships. The importance of the LPC measurement is not how it reflects on the individual the leader considers their LPC, but rather on how they rate and describe their LPC, which in Fred Fiedler's view indicates their approach to work. Those who are motivated mostly by interpersonal dynamics will view an LPC less favorably regardless of that co-worker's productivity, while someone with a more "bottom line" orientation will forgive interpersonal frictions if the co-worker contributes something to the work group's productivity.

Legalism

In Chinese philosophy, the legalist school was a 1st millennium B.C.E. philosophical movement concerned with advocating the running of the state according to a strictly followed system of laws. Legalism was essentially pragmatic, but heavily influenced by the values promoted by both Confucianism and Mohism (though those schools differed strongly in some important areas). A key aspect of legalism was the *shi*, or mystery of authority, with which the emperor was imbued, and which entitled him to the unquestioning obedience of his people. The leader, in turn, was not supposed to be too showy or overt in his demands—a leader who needs to make threats is one who is not confident he will be obeyed, which calls into question his possession of *shi*. Because the emperor was supposed to remain mysterious and low profile, this also necessitated an elaborate bureaucracy, which in turn helped to justify the necessity of an elaborate system of rules for its operations.

Legitimacy

Legitimacy literally means "lawfulness," but in politics refers to the general acceptance of a ruling authority by the populace. Many regimes may be legal but considered illegitimate, especially if free elections were not held to put the regime in power; even in such cases when elections were held, if there are concerns about voter access, restrictions on the right to vote, or the vote-counting process, the elected regime may be considered illegitimate. The controversy over the 2000 U.S. presidential election is an obvious example of this. In the political philosophy of John Locke, the source of legitimacy is the consent of the governed.

Legitimacy (French and Raven)

Legitimacy is one of John R. P. French and Bertram Raven's bases of power, and one of Patrick J. Montana and Bruce H. Charnov's varieties of organizational power. Legitimate power originates from being elected, appointed, or otherwise put in a position of power by means that accord to social norms and expectations, or from being put in a position in which social norms say that they are entitled to power (though saying so explicitly may be unfamiliar). Influence is exerted because the target feels obligated. This includes not only the power of elected or appointed officials, for instance, but the influence on an individual's actions when they see someone in need and feel obligated to offer assistance because the values they have taken in from the social norms of their surroundings tell them to.

Leveling

In the work of existential philosopher Soren Kierkegaard, leveling is a social phenomenon in which all human activities are assigned equal value, smoothing out the complexities and whorls and grooves of individual experience until abstraction overtakes the uniqueness of the individual. Leveling is a communication process that occurs during organizational socialization. Idle talk and gossip leads to creating secondhand needs and definitions of selfhood, an abstract concept of "the public" with which the individual compares himself and loses his individual definition of the self in the process, adopting the societal definition in its place. This in turn leads to the individual renouncing responsibility, which instead rests with the crowd. Similarly, adopting organizational beliefs and values as part of organizational socialization distances the individual from his authentic beliefs, and in so doing, reduces his feelings of personal responsibility. Kierkegaard condemns leveling because it reduces personal responsibility, self-reflection, and individual authenticity—the basic requirements of authentic leadership— and so condemns the idle talk and gossiping that he feels create the process. Self-reflection and introspection act as checks against the effects of leveling.

Lexical hypothesis

One of the key hypotheses in the psychology of personality, the lexical hypothesis was first proposed by English psychologist Francis Galton in the 19th century. The lexical hypothesis states that because our encounters with personality traits are such an important part of our experience, major personality traits are inevitably reflected in our language—that is, a natural language always develops the capacity to discuss these personality traits—and the most important or prominent personality traits may be referred to with a single word. Numerous theories and methodologies in the psychology of personality depend on the lexical hypothesis, including most personality tests and metrics, which depend on description (by the self or other) and therefore take as a postulate the capacity of language to accurately discuss personality traits. There are many criticisms of the hypothesis, despite its widespread use. It seems predicated on a more precise use of language than laymen apply to personality-descriptive terms, for one thing. For another, there has been considerable debate throughout the history of philosophy as to whether language is sufficient to fully describe human experience. What's more, language does not account for the whole of human communication, and by extension even a rephrasing of the lexical hypothesis itself could suggest that while all major personality traits are reflected in human communication, some of them could be indicated only by body language, vocal tone, and other paralinguistic cues.

Liberal arts

The concept of the liberal arts is inherited from classical Greek education, in which Aristotle believed they represented the disciplines and areas of knowledge necessary for free people. In medieval Europe, this developed into the trivium (logic, grammar, and rhetoric—the verbal arts) and the quadrivium (mathematics and its three classical applications: music, astronomy, and geometry). Much of what we now associate with the liberal arts—history, the social sciences, the study of literature—did not yet exist as a formal field of study. This focus on education as individual development, as distinct from job training (the purpose to which the liberal arts have been shoehorned today), in many ways presages the development of leadership studies and explains the identification of leadership studies institutes like the Jepson School with the liberal arts.

Liberum veto

The Liberum veto was a unique feature of the Polish-Lithuanian Sejm (the legislature) in the 16th through 18th centuries. It allowed any legislator to end the session and nullify the legislation that had already passed by shouting out his veto. The legislature operated on the principle that if nobles were all equal, the legislation they passed could only be passed unanimously. In later years the Liberum veto was held up as an emblem of an ineffective system.

Life coach

A life coach works one-on-one with clients (though they may also publish work detailing their views and methodology, or offer seminars) in an attempt to help them develop and pursue their personal and professional goals. Unlike a therapist or analyst, the life coach does not offer counseling or psychological analysis but may recommend seeking out such services as a step in realizing a goal. Nevertheless, they occupy a similar cultural niche occupied by analysts and encounter groups in the 1960s through the 1980s and have not coincidentally become popular as the therapy field has shifted away from long-term relationships in favor of short-term crisis interventions. In most states, life coaches are not subject to licensing or other restrictions, though in some they are classed as mental health professionals and bound by relevant regulation.

Lifestyle guru

A type of life coach that developed in the 1990s, a lifestyle guru is an individual who combines religious advising with hands-on guidance to change one's lifestyle. Like life coaches and personal trainers, lifestyle gurus primarily work one-on-one with clients, and are especially associated with the idle rich, but may also air their views in books, magazine articles, or Web sites.

Likert, Rensis

A University of Michigan professor in the Institute for Social Research, Rensis Likert (1903–81) was an early pioneer in leadership studies. He led Michigan's Leadership Studies group in the 1950s and developed Likert's Management Systems—four broad descriptive styles of management he had observed in his work, which he later expanded to describe educational institutions as well as business organizations. Likert also developed the Likert scale, which is still used in social science and marketing surveys. Instead of asking respondents to answer "agree" or "disagree" to various statements, the Likert scale uses a five point scale of agreement from "strongly agree" to "strongly disagree" in order to weight response according to strength of feeling.

Likert's management systems

Leadership studies pioneer Rensis Likert identified and described four management systems, originally based on the management styles he found in his studies of supervisors of an insurance company and later revised to apply to educational settings as well. Each system assigns roles to leaders and their followers and defines the relationships between them: exploitative authoritative, benevolent authoritative, consultive system, and participative system.

Lincoln, Abraham, as leader

When Barack Obama ran for president in 2008, he named *Team of Rivals: The Political Genius of Abraham Lincoln*, Doris Kearns Goodwin's 2005 book about President Abraham Lincoln's leadership, as the one book other than the Bible that he would bring to the White House, in answer to a question journalists ask of presidential candidates to elicit answers that symbolize their values and views of the presidency. But although there is widespread consensus among historians that Lincoln was an exceptionally capable leader, there is little agreement on what lessons can be drawn from his leadership. Goodwin's study, which won the Pulitzer Prize, stressed Lincoln's desire to hear multiple points of view before making a decision and his choice of political rivals as his cabinet

Abraham Lincoln was a highly capable leader, aided by his strong communication and persuasion skills. (Library of Congress)

members. In 2008 Goodwin presented a keynote address to the Society for Human and Resource Management titled "The 10 Qualities that Made Lincoln Great," applying Lincoln thinking to modern management. Others have pointed to the relationship between the presidency and the Constitution, which defines and limits its powers, and Lincoln's recognition that leading a constitutional government was a unique challenge that required self-restraint. Still others pointed to his performance in the Lincoln–Douglas debates, and drew attention to his skills of communication and persuasion and his ability to regulate his emotions.

Lockstep compensation

A compensation system associated with the legal profession, lockstep compensation determines an employee's salary based on their seniority in the organization, regardless of merit or other considerations. In legal firms, this may be true of all attorneys (with separate base pay levels for associates and partners), just partners, or just partners and partner-track associates.

The Lonely Crowd

David Riesman, Nathan Glazer, and Reuel Denney's *The Lonely Crowd*, published in 1950, is one of the most influential sociological studies of the United States, and is particularly focused on the position of the country in the middle of the 20th century, when the middle class that had arisen after the Industrial Revolution began to dominate the country with its "other-directed" culture. The third of three cultural types analyzed in American history by Riesman, other-directed individuals define themselves in relation to others, and are accommodating and malleable as a result. It was this type that proved necessary for the rise of corporations and large organizations in the post–World War II years. *The Lonely Crowd* functions as an unintended perfect companion to *White Collar* and *The Organization Man*.

Long- versus short-term orientation

One of the cultural dimensions of organizations identified by Geert Hofstede, organizations and other cultures tend to be primarily concerned with either the short term or the long term. Long-term-oriented cultures are more able to adapt to changing conditions, as well as being more inclined toward perseverance; short-term cultures are more invested in their current values as representing absolute truth, and more likely to believe that a current practice is the best practice.

Lucretius

The Roman philosopher Lucretius, writing in the 1st century B.C.E., is best known for his epic poem "De Rerum Natura" ("On the Nature of Things"), which argued that belief in the gods was the source of human unhappiness, because humans conceived of bitter and wrathful gods; that the universe was governed by material laws, not supernatural whims; and that death is neither good nor bad for the deceased, representing a simple and complete cessation of being, without the continuation of consciousness in an afterlife. In ancient Rome, this was not necessarily revolutionary, as philosophers explored a wide variety of ideas; when the poem was rediscovered, translated, and circulated in Europe in the 15th and 16th centuries, it played a key role in catalyzing the humanistic revolution of the Renaissance.

Lyndon B. Johnson School of Public Affairs

The Lyndon B. Johnson (LBJ) School of Public Affairs is a graduate school at the University of Texas at Austin (UTA), offering master's and doctoral degrees in public affairs and related fields (as well as dual-degree programs in conjunction with other UTA schools). The LBJ School includes the Center for Politics and Governance, devoted to leadership development in the political sphere.

The Man in the Gray Flannel Suit

In many ways the fictional companion to *The Organization Man*, 1955's *The Man in the Gray Flannel Suit*, by Sloan Wilson, captured much of the zeitgeist of the 1950s. In the novel, Tom Rath and his wife Betsy struggle to find meaning in a business-dominated world.

Management consulting

Management consulting is the business of improving an organization's performance by introducing changes to its management practices. Organizations may hire a management consulting firm to deal with a specific problem or concern, or simply seek an evaluation of their performance and the ways it can be improved. Management consulting dates to Arthur D. Little Inc., which formed as a partnership in 1886, and experienced periods of significant growth in the 1930s (due to the changes introduced by the Glass-Steagall Act) and the 1980s. Many consulting firms specialize in specific industries or specific areas, such as human resource consulting or information technology consulting. Around the turn of the 21st century, the management consulting industry shifted from a time-and-materials-based pricing model to results-based pricing, with some consultants working for a fixed price based on specific deliverables and others working for a fraction of the value of the performance improvement that is introduced. Some corporations instead hire internal management consultants, who work on a full-time rather than project basis.

Management development

Management development is the increase of competence in managers by various means, including training, seminars, executive education programs, mentoring, self-evaluations, and other possibilities.

Management fad

"Management fad" is a pejorative term for a change introduced by management, with the implication being that the change has not been well considered or is not well suited to the organization, or that it will be replaced by a newer incompatible change when the next fad sweeps through the industry. Management fads are generally associated with changes to terminology, including new or rephrased job titles and new terms for existing business processes and practices, and a cottage industry of consultants whose job is to implement the fad. Similar fads are found in education, though the relatively greater organizational inertia of the education industry slows their adoption and consequently reduces their population.

Management by objectives

See Management by results

Management by perkele

A Finnish style of authoritarian leadership ("perkele" is a Finnish deity whose name is shouted in roughly the same contexts as "frak!" or "dang it!") originally associated with the Finnish army, in which no dissent is tolerated, but now used especially by the Swedish to refer to the use of such authoritarian approaches in the private sector where they are less appropriate.

Management by results

Management by results is an approach to management that focuses on defining an organization's goals through participation by both management and workers and setting policies and practices that are clearly appropriate to those goals, such that employees have an understanding of the results that are intended by their labors.

Management by wandering around

In the Japanese business world, the *genba* or *gemba* is the shop floor or wherever most of the organization's production takes place, and "going to the genba" means managers walking through the production area to observe and interact. In the United States, "management by wandering around" similarly calls for managers to physically interact at the site of production, not simply visiting in response to a problem or at appointed times, but at random impromptu points, in order to experience a random sampling of the production process.

Managerial grid model

Developed in 1964 by Robert Blake and Jane Mouton, the managerial grid model is a model of situational leadership, influenced by Theory X and Theory Y (cf.). The model portrays a grid with two axes, concern for production and concern for people, with a range from one to nine, and five styles of leadership plotted on the resulting graph: indifferent (or impoverished), accommodating (or country club), dictatorial (or produce or perish), status quo (or middle of the road), and sound (or team). Two other styles were later added: the paternalistic style, which discourages dissent and supports followers through praise; and the opportunistic style, which adopts whichever position on the grid suits its purposes.

Mandate of Heaven

The Mandate of Heaven is a concept in Chinese political philosophy that derives the legitimacy of an emperor's rule from the will of Heaven. The mandate is bestowed upon a just ruler, but may be withdrawn if he ceases to be just, resulting in an overthrow by rivals. Therefore, calamities experienced by the people of ancient China, including natural disasters and famines, were taken as signs that the Mandate of Heaven had been withdrawn. The principle was first used to justify the overthrow of the Shang dynasty by the Zhou dynasty and was invoked thereafter as a way to discourage abuses of power.

Mandela, Nelson

Nelson Mandela was one of the leaders of the anti-apartheid movement in South Africa, and the first black President of South Africa, elected in 1994 in the country's first fully multiracial election. A lawyer and activist in the 1940s and 1950s, he was imprisoned in 1962 for his campaign of sabotage against South Africa's apartheid regime. The apartheid policy, a system of legally classified racial groups segregated into specific residential areas, had been formally instituted in 1948, though racial segregation in general dated to the colonial era. While Mandela was in prison, apartheid was strengthened; basic services like education and health care were segregated, and blacks were denied South African citizenship and assigned citizenship to one of 10 tribes instead. Mandela became the public face of anti-apartheid resistance and was released in 1990 after international pressures. His negotiations with South African President F. W. de Klerk saved face for the latter and led to the abolition of apartheid and the first multiracial elections. As president, Mandela worked to undo apartheid and address its damages, while expanding health care. He declined a second term and instead became an international activist working against poverty and AIDS until his death in 2013.

Market culture

One of four organizational cultures identified by Robert Quinn's Competing Values Framework, market culture is externally focused on the well-being of the organization as a whole and favors a controlled organization structure. Leaders in market culture organizations motivate employees with rewards contingent on performance.

Martin, John Levi

University of Chicago sociology professor John Levi Martin's work suggests microscale cultural institutions result in the emergence of macroscale social structures.

Maryland School of Public Policy

Part of the University of Maryland, the Maryland School of Public Policy is located inside the Capital Beltway and is one of the highest-ranked policy schools in the country. It offers master's programs in public policy and public management, including a specialization in management and leadership in which students study the relationship of government to the private and nonprofit sectors, as well as theories of leadership.

Marxism

Marxism is an ideology founded on historical materialism and Marxist dialectics, concerned with class struggle and a critique of capitalism. It may be more accurate to speak of Marxisms, or of Marxist ideologies, than a single interpretation of Marxism, which began with the work of German philosophers Karl Marx and Friedrich Engels in the mid-19th century. It is especially concerned with the development of society around the means by which people provide for their material needs, and thus an economic basis for the discussion of cultural, social, legal, and political institutions and phenomena. Marx's view of an ideal society is best summed up by the maxim often erroneously attributed to him, but which was actually coined by Louis Blanc: "From each according to his ability, to each according to his need." In this way, maximum value is created, and everyone's needs are attended.

Masculinity versus femininity

One of the cultural dimensions proposed by Geert Hofstede, masculinity versus femininity represents the way emotional roles are distributed between the genders. In masculine cultures, gender role differences are drastic and there is little flexibility, as in parts of the Arab world. In feminine cultures, men and women play similar roles and hold similar values.

Maslow's hierarchy of needs

Maslow's hierarchy of needs is a theory of human motivation proposed by psychologist Abraham Maslow in a 1943 paper, and later expanded. It is often represented as a pyramid, with the most basic human needs at the base level. From the most to least basic, the hierarchy of needs consists of physiological needs (air, food, water, sleep, etc.), safety (including the physical safety of the body from harm or ill health as well as safety of the family, access to resources, and employment), belongingness, esteem (including the needs for self-respect and respect by others), and self-actualization and self-transcendence (including the need for creative outlets, moral systems, and intellectual pursuits). The model provides a way to think of human needs that acknowledges the psychological need for things like self-respect or creative outlets while also explaining why these things may be sacrificed in the service of more fundamental needs. Maslow was also instrumental in the work recognizing the importance of belongingness as a human motivation. Though Maslow's work is less prominent in modern psychology than attachment theory, it remains influential and well-known in sociology, management, and leadership studies. Geert Hofstede has criticized the hierarchy for being culture-specific, arguing that the arrangement of needs actually differs from culture to culture, and that in particular the Maslow hierarchy reflects the values of an especially individualistic society.

Maternalism

Maternalism is an ideology that promotes a particular model of femininity and femaleness, and based on that model promotes the involvement of women in specifically female-appropriate roles in society. Arguably, maternalism helped involve women in roles outside the home in the 19th century, when women were prominent in the leadership of social reform movements, but the notion of there being male- and female-appropriate roles in working life is at odds with the goals of second-wave feminism and gender equality, and is at least in part responsible for the underrepresentation of women in leadership roles in nearly every industry.

Matriarchy

A matriarchy is a social, political, or cultural system in which women occupy all or most of the leadership roles. Unlike a patriarchial society, there is no real historical evidence for the existence of true matriarchal cultures, the 19th century theories about prehistoric matriarchal cultures having long since been discredited. The prevalence of matrilineal systems—systems in which descent or membership is traced through the mother's lineage, as with Jewishness today and numerous cultures throughout the world in the pre-modern

An elderly Hopi matriarch. The Hopi Native American tribe in northeastern Arizona had a gender ideology based on female superiority, with women central to the institutions of clan and household. (Public Domain)

era—strongly suggests that egalitarian cultures were once more common.

Maxwell School

The Maxwell School of Citizenship and Public Affairs, in Syracuse, New York, was founded in 1924 and was the first school to offer a graduate degree in public administration.

Mayo, Elton

Elton Mayo was an Australian psychologist whose work influenced the young field of organizational psychology in the early 20th century. Mayo pioneered human relations theory and innovative studies of productivity, including the impact of workplace lighting choices on employee productivity, and conducted the Hawthorne Studies. One of the key findings of Mayo's work was that the desire to feel a sense of belonging in the group impacted workers more than financial incentives or working conditions.

MBA

The master of business administration (MBA) is a graduate degree in business administration, which was introduced in the United States in the early 20th century against the background of scientific management. The first graduate degree in business was the Master of Science in Commerce, offered by the Tuck School of Business at Dartmouth, the first graduate business school in the United States, in 1900. The

Harvard Business School opened in 1908 with an MBA program. The prestige of the MBA, especially in American institutions, was seriously damaged by the financial crisis of 2008 and the role played by the worlds of finance, management, and academia.

Men's rights movement

The men's rights movement originated in the 1970s as a countermovement to second-wave feminism. Early men's rights groups in the 1920s opposed the entrance of women into the labor market, in part because it was another group with which white male workers would have to compete; labor parties and unions had previously opposed immigration and child labor for the same reason, to preserve the value of white male labor. With that battle essentially lost, the 1970s men's rights movement instead opposed other initiatives of feminists, both real and imagined, especially the alleged "feminization" of American culture.

Mentoring

Mentoring is a relationship between two people, in which the more experienced or knowledgeable of the two helps to guide the other and develop good habits. Mentoring is distinct from tutoring in that it typically differs substantially from teaching, as mentoring tends to be not only less formal but as concerned with the transmission of norms, social capital, traditions, and frames of reference as with knowledge. Where once the terms *protege* and *protegee* were used to refer to the less experienced member of the relationship, today "mentee" has become more common. Mentoring has enjoyed healthy growth since the 1970s in the business world, and is a standard part of the academic world, in which graduate students work with a thesis or dissertation adviser who typically acts to introduce the student to the world of professional academia and the norms and behaviors thereof, in addition to helping shape the thesis or dissertation.

Mentoring techniques

A 1995 survey of mentoring in the business world by Bob Aubrey and Paul Cohen found that most mentoring activities were represented by five techniques. In "accompanying," the mentor takes part in the learning process with the mentee. In "sowing," the mentee is given information that they are not ready to put to use or understand yet, in anticipation of the situation in which it will finally become clear. In "catalyzing," the mentor drops the mentee into the deep end of the pool, so to speak, forcing them to work and learn under pressure. In "showing," the mentor demonstrates the thing they are teaching. And in "harvesting," the mentor asks the mentee questions about their progress so far, especially with the intent of guiding the conversation so that the mentee makes connections they had not been able to articulate previously.

Metamotivation

Metamotivation is a psychological concept from the work of Abraham Maslow, best known for Maslow's hierarchy of needs. In that hierarchy, the highest tier—the least pressing of the basic needs—is devoted to self-actualization, such as creative outlets. In Maslow's framework, "motivation" describes any drive concerned with meeting the basic needs of the hierarchy, while "metamotivation" is the motivation of individuals who have met their basic needs, including self-actualization, and are now striving to transcend that hierarchy in order to fulfill their potential as humans. The "metaneeds" beyond the hierarchy include

Wholeness, Perfection, Completion, Justice, Richness, Simplicity, Liveliness, Beauty, Goodness, Uniqueness, Playfulness, Truth, Autonomy, and Meaningfulness.

Mexican standoff

"Mexican standoff" is a term, first coined in the 19th century, for a confrontation among three parties, each of whom is hostile toward the other two. Originally coined to refer to armed conflicts in the age of revolvers, this scenario meant that any one party who acted on his aggression—fired his weapon—would be left vulnerable to attack by a minimum of one of the other two parties. From the perspective of any given participant, A, the most advantageous possibility is for B to kill C, freeing A to kill B. Because all three are in this identical position, it is not safe for any of the three to act, nor is there a means of safely withdrawing.

Michigan Studies of Leadership

A series of leadership studies by Rensis Likert at the University of Michigan in the 1950s, the Michigan studies focused on identifying which leadership styles most benefited job satisfaction and productivity. Likert's team sorted leaders into two broad styles (employee-oriented and production-oriented), of which an employee-oriented approach without close supervision led to the best results. Likert's team also identified task-oriented behavior, relationship-oriented behavior, and participative leadership as critical characteristics of effective leadership.

Micromanagement

Micromanagement is a management style conducted through close observation of employees' work coupled with frequent input or intervention. Micromanagement results when supervisors are unable to commit to delegating the workload, instead assigning duties to employees without trusting them to carry those duties out. A manager and an employee may not always agree on the line between attention to detail and micromanagement, of course, but even the perception of being micromanaged interferes with employee engagement, satisfaction, and security.

Milgram, Stanley

Yale professor Stanley Milgram is best known for his 1961 experiment in which participants were asked to administer electrical shocks to subjects answering test questions incorrectly. In actuality no shocks were administered, and the test centered on participants' willingness to follow orders. Milgram wanted to use the test to answer moral questions raised by the war crimes trials of Nazi participants in the Holocaust in the aftermath of World War II (Adolf Eichmann's trial began shortly before the experiment), and whether there was anything unusually immoral about those participants or if it could be surmised that anyone in their position would have been just as willing to follow orders. Milgram is also known for the "small world experiment," which examined the path length of social networks and led to the concept "six degrees of separation."

Milgram experiment

The Milgram experiment, named for Yale professor Stanley Milgram, is one of the most famous experiments in social psychology. First conducted in 1961, the experiment was published in 1963, with further detail in a 1974 book. The experiment put participants in a position in which an authority figure ordered them to administer mild (but increasingly less mild) electrical shocks to another subject after each wrong answer in a simple test. In actuality no shocks were administered; the recipient of the imagined shocks was a confederate. What the experiment really tested was participants' willingness to follow orders, with the result that 65 percent of participants continued through the end of the experiment (administering an imaginary 450-volt shock, sufficient to be fatal), though every single participant paused at some point and did not continue until being told to. The ethics of the experiment have been called into question, with some critics predicting long-lasting psychological trauma to the participants.

Minority influence

Minority influence is social influence wielded by a minority group over the majority—sometimes constructed as the opposite of conformity. Minority influence requires that the group itself be unified in its viewpoint, which can lead to infighting between factions of the minority group. Latane and Wolf's social impact model states that the influence of a minority decreases as the size of the minority increases. In a group decision-making scenario, a minority of one wields considerable influence over the majority. Solomon Asch's experiments demonstrated "the magical number three," showing that although a minority of three wields drastically less influence than a minority of one, increasing the size of the group beyond that decreases influence only small amounts.

Mintzberg, Henry

Henry Mintzberg is a Canadian professor of management studies who is critical of both management education and the management consulting industry. He is best known for his organizational configurations model, which describes possible organizational configurations: the simple structure (associated with entrepreneurs), the bureaucracy, the professional organization, the diversified organization, and the innovative organization or "adhocracy."

Mirror neuron

A mirror neuron is a neuron (nerve cell) that activates or "fires" both when an action is performed and when that same action is observed being performed by another. Mirror neurons are present in both humans and animals, and their discovery has led to numerous theories of human behavior and social cognition. However, it is likely that more claims have been made about mirror neurons than will find support in further research; there is as yet no explanation for how mirror neurons could "feed into" cognitive functions like imitation and mimicry, for instance.

Mirrors for Princes

A genre of instructional political writing in Europe in the Middle Ages and the Renaissance, mirrors for princes were books on governance. Most were written as textbooks, but some were written as histories with pointed references to what historical figures had done right or wrong, in order to use them as instructive examples. Some were written for specific rulers: *John of Ireland's Mirror of Wisdom* was written for King James IV of Scotland, for instance, while *Erasmus's Education of a Christian Prince* was written for King Charles V of Spain. When composed for a specific ruler, the work was usually presented to him either in anticipation of his coronation or not long thereafter.

Mirroring

Mirroring is the mimicking of one person's behavior by another, especially while interacting with them, including the copying of body language and gestures, word choice, tone of voice, facial expressions, accent, and affect. Mirroring frequently occurs even between casual acquaintances or strangers, as listeners often mirror the smiles, frowns, and other expressions of the speaker. In most cases mirroring is unconscious and unnoticed by the speaker. It may help to build rapport and trust between people.

Mismatch hypothesis

In evolutionary psychology, the mismatch hypothesis says that some problems in human groups and human society are the result of a mismatch between our current needs and the needs for which certain psychological traits were developed. The chance of such a mismatch increases in inverse proportion to the amount of significant change the brain has undergone since the development of those traits, and so this hypothesis depends on a reasonably slow-evolving brain and reasonably early dates for the development of the relevant traits. A common example is the observed preference for young, physically vital leaders, despite the fact that leaders are no longer expected to exert physical power over either the group's enemies or their subordinates, and in fact will be less effective leaders if they do so.

Mission Accomplished speech

In 2003, President George W. Bush's televised address from the USS *Abraham Lincoln* aircraft carrier, in front of a banner reading "Mission Accomplished," declared an end to major combat in the Iraq War. The sentiment was considered premature and over-the-top posturing even at the time, and the Iraqi insurgency soon offered the proof, as U.S. troops did not withdraw for another eight years (during which time an Iraqi civil war was fought), with the insurgency continuing even after that. Like Bush's father, President George H. W. Bush, his words were used against him as evidence of incompetent leadership. In the elder Bush's case,

Sailors returning to port on the USS Abraham Lincoln, *sporting the* Mission Accomplished *banner that President George W. Bush was photographed in front of.* (U.S. Navy)

his famous campaign promise "Read my lips: no new taxes," made after an eight-year period of significant tax decreases under Reagan and against the inevitability of raising taxes to make up for the resulting budget deficits, was abandoned two years into his presidency.

Mission creep

Mission creep is the undesirable expansion of a project beyond its original goals or scope, and is especially used in cases where there is a perceived danger of failing as a result of the project's reach exceeding its grasp. Coined in reference to the United Nations peacekeeping mission in Somalia in 1993, the term has since itself expanded its mission to encompass nonmilitary projects (both public and private sector), and has been retroactively applied to the Korean War.

MIT Sloan School of Management

Established in 1914 as the engineering administration program, the Sloan School of Management is the business school of the Massachusetts Institute of Technology. Like its parent institution, MIT Sloan emphasizes innovation, and its faculty has contributed some of the best-known theories in finance and management, including Theory X and Theory Y, System Dynamics, the Black-Scholes model of derivative markets, and the random walk hypothesis of stock market prices. MIT Sloan is also home to the MIT Leadership Center.

Modes of leadership

Psychologist David Wilkinson developed his "modes of leadership" in 2006's *Ambiguity Advantage*, describing leaders' responses to ambiguity. Wilkinson discussed four modes, each a different viewpoint and way of thinking: technical leadership, favored by dictatorial and risk-averse leaders, who deal with ambiguity by denying it and acting with certainty; cooperative leadership, which seeks to reduce uncertainty and mitigate risk through the distribution of power to teams; collaborative leadership, which seeks agreement from followers and deals with ambiguity through group discussion; and generative leadership, which seeks opportunity in ambiguity.

Monarch

A monarch is a head of state, usually one who inherits their rulership or is selected from among a number of potential heirs, and who typically rules for life. Today, most monarchs have limited powers or act as ceremonial heads of state while elected officials serve as heads of government, but historically monarchs controlled the national government in conjunction with regional leaders, religious authorities, and parliamentary bodies. Common titles for monarchs include emperor, king, queen, grand duke, sultan, emir, caliph, raja, khan, and pharaoh.

Monitoring competence

Monitoring competence is the process of remaining aware of the extent of one's knowledge and skills. More self-aware people are generally also aware of their skills and limitations.

Monopoly on violence

The monopoly on violence, from the German *Gewaltmonopol* ("Violence-Monopoly"), is Max Weber's term for the idea that the state is in sole possession of—has a monopoly on—the legitimate use of physical force, which it delegates to instruments like the police force, the military, and the institution of capital punishment. This concept is the basis for criminalizing other uses of violence without implying any guilt on the part of the state for its own violence, or any hypocrisy in the case of the state executing a murderer. The existence of the monopoly does not itself absolve the state of its responsibilities in the use of physical force or the need to have strict regulations on the type and extent of force used in specific circumstances; the use of force by the police, for instance, is strictly bound by law and behavioral codes, and even war against other countries abides by international law.

Monterey Institute of International Studies

The Monterey Institute of International Studies in California is a graduate school of Middlebury College (Vermont), offering programs in international policy, international business, translation and interpretation, and environmental policy, as well as operating five research centers. The institute specializes in training leaders for the cross-cultural, multi-lingual world of international affairs. One of its research centers is the Center for the Blue Economy, training future leaders in the sustainable management of the oceans.

Moral development

Moral development is the study of the emergence of morality in children and through adulthood, and of the beliefs, attitudes, emotions, and behaviors that make up moral understanding. Sigmund Freud, for instance, believed morality developed as the child learns to repress his selfishness and is socialized by his parents. Jean Piaget, in his work on the psychological development of children, posited that children shift from focus mainly on obeying authority to developing their own moral beliefs. Lawrence Kohlberg expanded on Piaget's work, beginning as a graduate student in 1958. In Kohlberg's work, moral reasoning develops over the course of six stages as the individual becomes more adept at handling moral dilemmas. The first two stages, the pre-conventional level, are obedience and punishment orientation, and self-interest orientation. At this level, individuals are focused mainly on the consequences of their actions on themselves—avoiding punishment, in the first stage, and gaining a reward in the second stage. The conventional level consists of conformity, and social-order-maintaining orientation. This level represents the moral reasoning of adolescents and many adults, who derive morality from their understanding of society's expectations of them. Stage three, for instance, seeks to conform with expectations, while stage four focuses on the need to abide by laws and conventions in order for society to function. Finally, the post-conventional level consists of social contract orientation and universal ethical principles. At this level, the individuals truly own their own morals, and are better able to perceive the difference between law-abiding behavior and moral behavior and to advocate for changes in the law in order to better reflect their moral understanding. Kohlberg sometimes noted moral stage regression in individuals, in which case he may note them as "stage five and a half," possessing characteristics of both stage five and the abandoned stage six.

Moral hazard

Moral hazard is the problem that results when a party is protected from the consequences of risk taking to a sufficient degree to make them likelier to take risks. The classic example of moral hazard is in the insurance industry, in which insurers have to deal with the possibility that the possession of insurance will lead the insured to risk-taking behaviors. In recent years, the impact of moral hazard on the financial sector has become obvious. But on a smaller scale, the concept has bearing in many leadership situations, from parenting—many parents having to weigh the pros and cons of bailing a child out of a difficulty versus letting them learn from their errors—to management. Nepotism and other managerial biases in favor of certain employees create a condition of moral hazard; so does the security of an employee's position due to factors other than the quality of his work, whether this means tenure in an academic setting or internal political factors. Above all else, when the corporate culture of a workplace does not hold each worker and manager accountable for the consequences of their work, moral hazard is invited. In some cases the problem may be simply that there are so many steps between the worker and the negative outcome of their work that there is no easy path for the consequences to take.

Motivation

Motivation is the force driving an action. Exploring the roots of human motivation has been a large part of the focus of psychology, from Sigmund Freud's discussion of the sex drive to Abraham Maslow's hierarchy of needs. Motivation may be intrinsic—driven by an appreciation of the task itself—or extrinsic, in which the task is less important than the outcome resulting from performing the task. Most theories of motivation are pluralistic, and may differentiate between conscious and unconscious motivations. The understanding of motivation is important in predicting and modeling human behavior, especially given that self-interest alone is not enough to explain behaviors, nor do humans act with perfect rationality.

Motivation crowding theory

According to motivation crowding theory, the addition of extrinsic motivations related to a behavior can diminish or negate existing intrinsic motivations. "Overjustification effect" is the term for when this happens by an extrinsic reward being offered for a behavior, removing the intrinsic motivation so that the reward becomes necessary to motivate the behavior. But it is true of punishments as well, and punishing a given behavior can result in removing the intrinsic motivation to avoid that behavior.

Motivation-hygiene theory

Motivation-hygiene theory is a psychological theory developed by Frederick Herzberg and influenced by Abraham Maslow's hierarchy of needs. According to the theory, one set of workplace factors is associated with job satisfaction, while a separate set is associated with job dissatisfaction, and the two phenomena are independent of one another. In other words, increasing job satisfaction does not decrease job dissatisfaction—the two do not represent different ranges on the same metaphorical thermometer, but are rather two completely separate measures. This idea grew out of Herzberg's initial work on the insufficiency of lower-level needs (like salary and job security) in providing job satisfaction. The name of the theory comes from the separation between *motivators*, intrinsic conditions of a job that provide job satisfaction, such as being given responsibility or engaging in a challenge, and *hygiene* factors that do not provide job satisfaction but do cause job dissatisfaction if they are absent, such as job security, salary and benefits, social status benefits, and working conditions.

Mozi

Mozi or Mo Tzu was a 5th-century B.C.E. Chinese philosopher in the early Warring States period. Mohism, the school of thought he developed, fell out of favor when both legalism and Confucianism gained more influence, but some Mohist concepts remained embedded in classical Chinese philosophy. Authenticity and self-knowledge were crucial to Mozi, and he argued against obedience to ritual and the traditional attachment to family and clan, contrasting in this respect with Confucius. Much of what Mozi proposed amounts to a model of enlightened self-interest, one that demanded equal respect and love for all, not just those to whom one had a personal bond. His system of ethics was similar to Western utilitarianism, except that the goal was not happiness but public goods in the form of wealth, population growth (a concern in a civilization accustomed to periodic famine), and domestic tranquility.

Multifactor Leadership Questionnaire

The Multifactor Leadership Questionnaire (MLQ) was developed by Bernard Bass in 1985, as part of his work extending the theories of James MacGregor Burns on transformational and transactional leadership. The MLQ has gone through several revisions, and measures leadership behaviors as perceived both by the leader himself and his followers. Bass later developed the Full Range Leadership Model to complement the MLQ.

Multiple Constituency Framework

Anne Tsui's Multiple Constituency Framework is a behavioral complexity model of leadership that examines the way managers deal with multiple constituencies, both internal (subordinates, peers, and superiors) and external (investors, customers, competitors), with different and possibly conflicting demands. Key to the framework and others like it is the premise that organizational effectiveness is measured not by the pursuit of a single goal but by serving multiple interests represented by the relevant constituencies. Tsui built on the work of multiple theorists, dating back to Eric Rhenman's introduction of constituencies (referred to as stakeholders) in his work on industrial demography in 1968. Different subunits of the organization have different sets of constituencies; the human resources and materials management departments of a manufacturing plant, for instance, serve different constituencies and pursue different goals in their activities. In Tsui's approach, the effectiveness of the organization is measured by the subjective perceptions of the constituencies served.

Munsterberg, Hugo

Hugo Munsterberg was a pioneer in applied psychology in the early 20th century. Initially influenced by William James, he rejected James's acceptance of mysticism and psychoanalysis and focused more on practical aims. He became interested in Frederick W. Taylor's scientific management, and applied himself to adding a psychological dimension to the approach, including guides to the types of employees to hire for various roles, and psychological methods for increasing motivation and performance or improving advertising and marketing efforts.

Murray, Henry

Henry Murray was a Harvard psychology professor and one of the first to teach psychoanalysis at Harvard. His work focused on the theory of personality he called Personology, according to which people are driven by both latent and manifest needs, as well as extrinsic factors in the form of "press" (discrete external influences) and "thema" (patterns of press and need).

Mushroom management

Mushroom management is the phenomenon of management doing a poor job of communicating with employees, who are expected to thrive while "being kept in the dark and fed manure."

Mutually assured destruction

Mutually assured destruction (MAD) is a nuclear deterrence doctrine that prevailed for much of the Cold War. Grounded in game theory, the doctrine states that once both sides of a conflict are armed with sufficiently destructive weapons, neither side has an incentive to initiate armed conflict because of the assurance of the level of damage both sides would take. Though the American government has since said that MAD was only one element of its strategy, the doctrine can be seen at work in the nuclear arms race, as well as in the expensive development of a sea-based nuclear force that would survive an attack on land targets.

My Lai Massacre

The My Lai Massacre was the mass killing of 300 to 500 unarmed Vietnamese civilians in U.S.-allied South Vietnam by U.S. Army soldiers, in 1968. Initially reported as a firefight with Viet Cong soldiers, it was discovered that American troops had not been fired upon, nor did they show any interest in ceasing their killing of civilians they had forced into a ditch when an American helicopter crew intervened in an attempt to stop them. When an attempted cover-up failed, 14 officers were court-martialed for suppressing evidence (largely to have the charges dropped), while Lieutenant William Calley, the ranking officer on-site of the massacre, was convicted to life in prison. Calley claimed to be following orders of his commanding officer, but no sufficient evidence of this was found, and the commanding officer was acquitted. Though not as broad in scope as the war crimes that were the subject of the Nuremberg Trials, the My Lai Massacre has a place in discussions of rank, authority, and responsibility.

Myers-Briggs Type Indicator

The Myers-Briggs Type Indicator (MBTI) was developed by mother and daughter Katharine Cook Briggs and Isabel Briggs Myers, based on the work of Carl Jung. The MBTI is a psychometric questionnaire intended to reveal the ways the respondent makes decisions and sees the world. From Jung it took the idea that four major functions—sensing, intuition, feeling, and thinking—provide our experience of the world, and that at any given time, one of them is dominant. The MBTI sorts respondents into one of 16 categories based on four dichotomies: Extraversion (E) or Introversion (I); Sensing (S) or Intuition (N); Thinking (T) or Feeling (F); and Judgment (J) or Perception (P). About 5 percent of the population are an INFP, for instance, characterized by sensitivity to criticism, low assertiveness, a strong sense of right and wrong, and a creative drive. About 10 percent of the population are an ESTJ, characterized as being matter-of-fact and pragmatic, good at and enjoying organizing and administration.

Narcissism

Narcissism is obsessive or preoccupying vanity, named for the Greek myth of Narcissus, a young man who became obsessed with his own reflection. Narcissism has been an area of study of psychology since Sigmund Freud, who devoted a book to the trait. Many modern psychologists consider some amount of healthy narcissism—which pursues self-interest but balances aggression, and is truthful about the self's traits—to be a necessary component of a healthy life, and even unhealthy levels of narcissism are not necessarily the same as Narcissistic Personality Disorder, which tends to feature grandiosity, self-obsession, and the pursuit of behaviors that validate one's sense of self.

Narcissistic defense

A narcissistic defense is a defense mechanism that acts to preserve an idealized self-perception. All people, especially as children, are susceptible to narcissistic defenses, not just narcissists. They usually operate unconsciously, and deal with information that reflects negatively on the self and could cause feelings of shame, guilt, or anxiety. In addition to defenses that simply bury the facts in question—unconscious repression, for instance, or conscious denial—there are defenses that construct a new narrative around the facts. The significance of an individual's failure or wrongdoing may be minimized, for instance, or justified through rationalization. Alternately, the individual may see someone else as bearing the blame for what is actually the individual's failing. In the workplace, narcissistic defenses make it difficult for people to accurately self-evaluate their own competence and performance, even when they believe they are being honest. Similarly, they complicate identifying the problem in a dysfunctional or unproductive work team or work environment.

Narcissistic parent

A narcissistic parent, whether it is highly developed enough to constitute Narcissistic Personality Disorder or not, poses an emotional danger to their children. Such parents may feel threatened by their children's eventual independence, and their lack of empathy may cause them to treat their child as a person who exists for the parent's benefit. These children often grow up narcissistic themselves, both to defend themselves from the manipulation of their parent and because they have learned from observing their parents that selfishness leads to getting one's needs met.

Narcissistic Personality Disorder

Narcissistic Personality Disorder (NPD) is a personality disorder classified in 1968, and known in earlier psychological literature as megalomania. The disorder involves an obsession and preoccupation with one's personal virtues, especially outwardly perceptible virtues like power, influence, prestige, and appearance. While the *Diagnostic and Statistical Manual of Mental Disorders* does not recognize official subtypes, many psychologists differentiate between exhibitionist narcissists who tend toward unsafe sexual behaviors and pathological deception, charlatan types who exploit others, narcissists compensating for low self-esteem, and so on. Many believe NPD is associated with charismatic leadership.

NASA Academy

Founded in 1993, the National Aeronautics and Space Administration (NASA) and NASA Academy is a leadership training program for college students, consisting of a 10-week summer program at a NASA center (including Ames Research Center, Marshall Space Flight Center, and Glenn Research Center). The program consists of research, team-building activities, visits to NASA labs and centers, and lectures by and socializing with aerospace industry leaders, across a long workday scheduled from 7:30 A.M. until 9 P.M. Eric Anderson, chairman of the Commercial Spaceflight Federation, is an alumnus.

National Youth Leadership Council

The National Youth Leadership Council (NYLC) is a national non-profit group formed in 1983 and based in Saint Paul, Minnesota. The NYLC promotes service learning in the United States through workshops, service projects, research publications, and hosting of the annual National Service Learning Conference.

"The Nature of the Firm"

A 1937 article in the journal *Economica* by British economist Ronald Coase (only 27 at the time), "The Nature of the Firm" was an exploration of the economic reasons individuals form partnerships and companies, notably the transaction costs of using the market.

Need for achievement

A term introduced by Henry Murray's Personology theory, need for achievement is a motivation driven by the desire for mastery of skill, accomplishment, or victory, and is rewarded by recognition of this achievement. This motivation is moderately risk-friendly and interested in innovation, but needs goals precisely defined.

Need for affiliation

A term introduced by Henry Murray's Personology theory, need for affiliation is a motivation driven by belongingness, the desire to feel involved with a group. People with a high level of this motivation do not always make effective leaders but are engaged team members, and require regular approval from and interaction with their co-workers and supervisors.

Need for cognition

In psychology, the need for cognition (NFC) is a personality factor that makes people seek challenging cognitive activities like problem solving, engaging debates over ideas, and activities that involve evaluating ideas (which includes many leadership roles). People with a low NFC score are more susceptible to believing stereotypes and broad generalizations, but those with high NFC scores have been found to be more susceptible to the creation of false memories.

Need for power

A term introduced by Henry Murray's Personology theory, need for power is a motivation driven by the desire to influence and dominate others. The motivation is associated with risk-friendliness, aggression, and competitiveness.

Negative selection

Negative selection is a phenomenon seen in certain kinds of leaders (including both political and business leaders) in which incompetent subordinates are deliberately selected in order to prevent them from presenting a threat to the leader's power.

Negativity effect

The negativity effect is a set of attributional biases that cause an individual, when considering the behavior of someone they do not like, to blame that person for any negative behaviors or outcomes associated with them, while explaining away any positive behaviors as the result of the environment or other external factors.

Negotiation theory

Negotiation theory is the formal study of negotiations, a special class of conflict resolution, using decision analysis, game theory, and other frameworks. Negotiation theory defines negotiation as the process that is engaged in when one party requires the other party's agreement in order to take action or accomplish a goal, such as when negotiating the terms of a treaty, which does not exist unless all parties agree to the same terms, or negotiating the salary for a potential new employee. Different theories of negotiation describe the negotiation process differently. Strategic analysis uses game theory and describes it as a series of games. Integrative analysis describes it as a series of procedural stages. Structural analysis examines the distribution and use of power between the negotiating parties.

Nemawashi

The Japanese term *nemawashi*, introduced to Americans mainly via the Toyota Production System, refers to the preparations for an upcoming change in an organization, including the beginning of a new project. Such preparations include collecting comments and feedback, getting "the lay of the land" and discovering what response to the change will be, and—particularly important in Japanese business culture—informing highly placed members in the organization of the proposed change, regardless whether it will affect them or their work. In Japan, one of the privileges of rank is the expectation of being consulted on any change being considered.

Nepotism

Favoritism in hiring or appointment practices, especially toward relatives or people known through family connections. Nepotism was coined to refer to the appointment of cardinals who were the nephews (*nepos* in Latin) of bishops or popes, a widespread practice in the Catholic Church, but has application in politics and the private sector. In many contexts it is considered a form of corruption—a serious one, if it is suspected that the appointment is a way for the appointee to make money from the position—while in other contexts it may be frowned upon or mocked but does not constitute an ethical breach.

Neuromanagement

Neuromanagement is the study of management, leadership, and economics from a neuroscience perspective, and overlaps with the similar science of neuroeconomics in its reference to neurological explanations of behavior. It is particularly concerned with discovering the brain activities and processes implicated in decision making, the neural basis of preferences and game modeling, and the modeling of decision making. Zhejiang University in China founded the Neuromanagement Lab in 2006.

Neuroticism

Neuroticism is one of the "Big Five" personality traits, characterized by feelings of envy, anxiety, and moodiness, and a poor ability to cope with stress. While neuroticism is not the same as neurosis, high scores of neuroticism are a risk factor for the panic and anxiety disorders which have historically been labeled neuroses.

Neutralizers

In substitutes for leadership theory, neutralizers are factors in the work environment that reduce the effectiveness of leadership. These include the leader not having the power to reward subordinates for performance, and subordinates being indifferent to the reward.

NIMBY

NIMBY stands for "Not In My Back Yard," used to characterize an individual's position on a project when the individual supports the project's necessity or desirability but wants it located someplace where he or she will not be exposed to its negative side effects. It is especially associated with discussions of chemical plants and waste dumps, which historically are more likely to end up located in or near poor neighborhoods whose residents lack the influence to

This tower in Washington, D.C., was later removed due to complaints from residents of the neighborhood. Local citizens had adopted a "Not In My Back Yard" position regarding the structure. (Wikimedia Commons/Kate Mereand)

prevent it, but is also used in reference to the placement of infrastructure and services ranging from homeless shelters and institutional housing to highways, airports, and strip malls, and is sometimes used more figuratively to refer to financial sacrifices like layoffs or budget cuts. Executives who speak of the necessity of belt-tightening due to a financial crisis, leading to layoffs, canceled bonuses, or other negative effects felt by the lower levels of a company, while receiving bonuses themselves for reducing expenses, are an example of the latter.

Nirvana fallacy

The nirvana fallacy is an informal fallacy identified in 1969, in which the individual focuses on an idealized but unrealistic solution to a problem to such a degree that the realistic and adequate alternatives available seem unacceptable. Rather than choose between real available options, they thus perceive any choice as a choice between the perfect and the adequate, and reject the adequate.

Noble lie

The noble lie is an untruth propagated by the ruling class to maintain harmony and civil peace. As originally described in Plato's *Republic*, it often takes the form of a religious belief—Plato's example is a myth explaining the origins and justifying the continued existence of the social stratification of ancient Greece in such a way as to preserve the hierarchy of the classes and discourage class revolt, while inspiring devotion to the nation. Since the Enlightenment, some thinkers have considered religion itself as a noble lie—a fictional story told for the purposes of social control, in order to encourage belief in specific values.

Non-concurrence

IBM, which pioneered the computer industry, developed a decision-making tradition called "non-concurring," according to which any department head had the power to veto a proposed company strategy or policy if it was not aligned with his department's needs or strategy. When Lou Gerstner became the new chief executive officer in the 1990s, he saw non-concurrence as part of IBM's "Culture of 'no,'" in which too much energy was spent blocking changes rather than moving forward, and that this had contributed to the company's losing ground to competitors. He ended the non-concurrence policy quickly.

Nonverbal influence

Nonverbal influence is the influence one person wields over another through means other than verbal communication, such as through cues imparted by tone of voice, facial expression, or body language. This influence may take the form of intimidation—which includes not only physical intimidation but the threat of anger, disappointment, or tears—or may appeal to attraction or similarity. For instance, some studies of mirroring have found that people tend to mirror each others' body language and tone of voice, even accent, which increases the sympathy accorded to them. Nonverbal displays of power and status include accent, demeanor, clothes and accessories, and may also factor into influence.

Normative model of decision making

The normative model of decision making was developed by Yale leadership studies professor Victor Vroom, beginning in the 1970s. The model proposes to predict the effectiveness of a given decision-making process, and identifies five types of such processes, in order from most to least level of leader participation: Decide (in which the leader alone decides), Individual Consultation (in which members are individually consulted for input), Group Consultation, Facilitation (in which the decision is made by group consensus, with the leader leading the discussion), and Delegation.

Normative social influence

Normative social influence is a conformity-enforcing phenomenon in which the individual is influenced by the desire to be accepted, respected, liked, and approved of by other people, and so adjusts his behavior or attitudes accordingly. Belongingness is a powerful human motivation, universal throughout cultures, and the desire to belong to a group influences the individual's behaviors and attitudes in order to help him fit in with his group, or find one with which he fits.

Northouse, Peter

Peter Northouse is a leadership studies scholar and the author of *Leadership: Theory and Practice*, now in its sixth edition. His work has covered ethical leadership, leadership assessment, and leadership and group dynamics, as well as work on contingency theories of leadership and path-goal theory.

Not invented here

"Not invented here" is a shorthand phrase referring to the tendency in institutional and corporate cultures to avoid the adoption, use, purchase, or reliance on products, standards, or practices that were developed elsewhere. Sometimes the external costs associated with such adoption are the primary reason, particularly if adopting the product means purchasing or licensing it from a competitor. But the phrase is especially associated with the form of tribalism that rejects such products and practices not for pragmatic reasons but out of spite or fear.

Novelty seeking

Novelty seeking is a personality trait that drives the individual to seek out new experiences, leading to impulsive decision making and associated with a quick temper. Novelty seeking is correlated with extraversion, and inversely correlated with conscientiousness.

Nut Island effect

As coined by Paul Levy in a 2001 article on Boston Harbor pollution, the Nut Island effect is an organizational phenomenon in which a group experiences a catastrophic loss of their task-completion ability because the organization's skilled assets—the employees necessary to complete the task—have become isolated from the leadership overseeing the project. This is typically the result of leadership that is primarily engaged with activities other than seeing the task through to completion. Forced into autonomy, the employees may lack key resources or situational knowledge required to do their work.

Oakes, Len

An Australian psychologist and former cult member, Len Oakes used an "adjective checklist" of 300 items in his dissertation on charismatic leaders of new religious movements, seeking patterns in the responses. Published in 1997 as *Prophetic Charisma*, the study proposed two types of cult leaders: messianic prophets and charismatic prophets. Oakes ascribes some similarities in leaders with otherwise dissimilar backgrounds and beliefs to narcissistic personality disorder.

Obedience

Obedience is the following of instructions from an authority due to social pressures. Psychology has shown that people have a natural tendency toward obedience, whether this is socialized in them or somehow present in our biology, and the instinct is believed to have been necessary to make communal life among early humans possible. There is significant debate over the effect of obedience on the ethics of our behavior: that is, when one does something on the orders of a formal authority, how is the responsibility for that action distributed between the authority and the follower?

Object relations theory

One of the "four psychologies" constituting modern psychology, object relations theory is a model in psychoanalytic psychology according to which experiences with family and other caregivers as an infant shape the way the individual interacts with others as an adult. The theory builds on Sigmund Freud's concept of the object relation, the specific object that bodily drives seek in order to satisfy their needs.

Occupational health psychology

Occupational health psychology is the applied psychology field that focuses on the well-being and safety of workers, having emerged from organizational psychology in the late 20th century. Though areas of study include physical factors of occupational stress, especially those contributing to cardiovascular disease, much of OHP is concerned with psychological distress caused by the work environment or work-related economic factors, behavioral issues with health ramifications, psychosocial conflicts in the workplace from bullying to violence, and psychological factors in workplace accidents.

Occupy movement hand signals

Occupy Wall Street and the larger Occupy movement developed a system of hand signals, some of which have been used in Quaker meetings and by other protest movements, in order to silently express positions during consensus-building meetings. Twinkling fingers—both hands raised with wiggling fingers—indicate strong agreement, for instance, as does a thumbs-up gesture. Other hand gestures indicate having a question for the speaker, believing important information has been left out by the speaker, asking the speaker to return to the topic at hand, a break from consensus, or that the speaker needs to speak up.

Occupy Wall Street

Occupy Wall Street (OWS) is a protest movement that began in Zucotti Park on Wall Street in New York City on September 17, 2011. Beginning with the peaceful occupation of the park in order to bring attention to—among other things—economic inequality and the largely unpunished role of Wall Street's finance industry in the 2008 financial crisis, OWS inspired the Occupy movement in other parts of the country and of the world. The protest was initiated by the Canadian anti-consumerist

magazine *Adbusters*, inspired by the Arab Spring, but was considered leaderless once set in motion. Its specific concerns or impact aside, OWS was notable for its anti-hierarchical structure and consensus-based approach to decision making. The OWS assembly draws on practices from the anti-nuclear movement, feminist protests, and Quaker practices, holding decision-making meetings in which all viewpoints are allowed time for expression, with facilitators calling on speakers waiting in line in a "stack," in which white men waited at the back of the line while marginalized groups like racial minorities were asked to cut to the front. Meetings attempted to reach consensus, with the bar lowered to a 90 percent majority vote if consensus proved impossible. Though formally leaderless, informal leaders emerged in the larger cities—in New York, more than 70 working groups were responsible for organizing and making decisions about Occupy Wall Street's activities at the height of its growth—as certain facilitators proved more or less adept at managing the crowd and encouraging participation in the most crowded or contentious assemblies.

Beginning on September 17, 2011, Zuccotti Park was occupied by hundreds of protestors during the Occupy Wall Street protest movement. (Wikimedia Commons/David Shankbone)

Offensive realism

Offensive realism is a variant of political realism, according to which because the main motive of states is survival, and because the world is in a constant state of aggression, the state rationally acts to maximize its ability to go to war. Arms races such as those of the Cold War are a natural result.

Office of the future

The "office of the future" is a concept dating from shortly after the construction of the first computers in the 1940s, which percolated through the popular imagination quickly and thoroughly enough to be satirized in comic strips and cartoons decades before most offices even phased out typewriters in favor of personal computers. The technological changes of the early Cold War years and the rise of the "organization man" painted a picture of what we now call a paperless office, with computers mediating most interactions among employees or between employees and management.

Ohio State Leadership Studies

The leadership studies conducted from 1945 through the 1950s at Ohio State University focused on identifying observable behaviors in successful leaders, in contrast with earlier studies that focused on trying to under personality traits common to effective leaders. The resulting Leaders Behavior Description Questionnaire in many ways constitutes the birth of modern leadership studies. Ohio State continues to run a strong leadership studies program, and in 1990 opened the OSU Leadership Center in the College of Food, Agricultural, and Environmental Sciences.

Old boys' club

The old boys' club or old boy network is a metaphor referring to social connections among members of male-only or traditionally male-dominated groups, and especially the way that these social connections ease the way to professional success. Common examples are fraternity membership or alumnus status with a private school or prestigious college. For instance, for many years, the bulk of the writing staff at *Saturday Night Live* was made up of former writers for the *Harvard Lampoon*, and the "white shoe" or prestigious and century-old law firms and banks of Boston and New York have a long tradition of hiring WASPs with Ivy League educations. The old boys' club also consists of family connections, as when someone gets a job interview with a company whose vice president went to the same school as one's father, or who summered at the same lake as one's grandfather. The old boys' club is for many reasons typically associated with not only maleness but whiteness and old money.

Old Testament

In the Old Testament (or Hebrew Tanakh), leadership is a trait bestowed by God to various individuals, and the relative worth of leaders is a frequent theme. While Moses is chosen to lead the children of Israel out of bondage in Egypt, for instance, and to receive the Ten Commandments, his brother Aaron speaks on his behalf and establishes the priesthood. Later, once the nations of Israel and Judah are established, Israel is without a monarch until the people demand one, leading to God's anointing of Saul, who is succeeded by the complex figure of David—guilty of some of the worst behavior of any Biblical protagonist but revered as one of the greatest kings. The Nevi'im, or books of the prophets, are characterized by their repeated warnings to Israel and other nations that their good fortunes are inextricably linked with their obedience to God and their reaffirmation that God is the source of worldly authority.

The One Minute Manager

The One Minute Manager is a best-selling business book published in 1982, and written by Ken Blanchard and Spencer Johnson. In keeping with the early 1980s climate of efficiency-obsession and competition with the management culture of Japan, *The One Minute Manager* prescribes three techniques for managers: one-minute goals, one-minute praisings, and one-minute reprimands, in order to maximize managerial effectiveness while minimizing time commitment. Blanchard later developed situational leadership theory with professor Paul Hersey, while Johnson wrote the best-selling book *Who Moved My Cheese?*

One-upmanship

One-upmanship is the practice of repeatedly outperforming a competitor, particular in response to his outperformance of you; arms races are one example, as is the idea of "keeping up with the Joneses." Dr. Seuss's work references one-upmanship several times, notably in the *Butter Battle Book* and *The Sneetches*.

Openness

Openness is one of the "Big Five" personality traits, and some studies of leadership personality traits have suggested that leaders should have a higher than average level of openness. It is sometimes called "openness to experience," and includes the following facets: active imagination, aesthetic sensitivity, attentiveness to inner feelings, preference for variety, and intellectual curiosity, traits that research indicates are strongly correlated with one another. Studies show that openness has a normal distribution in the population, with few people scoring very high or very low. Openness tends to correlate with creativity, general knowledge, the need for cognition, happiness, and positive affect, but has no correlation to life satisfaction. There is no significant difference between the scores of men and women.

Opinion leader

Opinion leaders exert a greater than average amount of influence when it comes to shaping the opinions of those around them. They may be perceived as experts or as possessing a cache that makes others want to be aligned with their tastes. Early adopters (cf.) tend to be opinion leaders, especially insofar as a sufficient number of them must adopt an innovation for it to thrive. Advertising and marketing researchers have done considerable work on opinion leadership in the quest to spend advertising dollars most effectively, and social media has offered a new wealth of data to be analyzed. Although opinion leaders can include professional reviewers and other members of the media, the importance of opinion leaders is principally that they have more influence on the formation of opinions than the professional media do.

Opportunity cost

In microeconomics, an opportunity cost is, in a decision-making situation, the value of the choice that is not selected: specifically, it is the value of the next-best possibility, not the sum or average of all rejected choices. In a simple example, a game show contestant choosing between the mystery prizes behind doors number one and two loses the value of door number two as an opportunity cost of selecting door number one. Every decision involves opportunity costs; inexperienced leaders or insecure decision-makers sometimes fixate on opportunity costs rather than weighing them against the gains of the choice selected. Similarly, pundits and politicians may discredit an opponent's choice by focusing not on the benefits gained but on the opportunity costs exacted.

The Organization Man

The Organization Man, published in 1956, is one of the most influential books published on management. Written by William H. Whyte—who later coined the term *groupthink*—it was based on in-depth interviews of the executives of the preeminent American corporations. Throughout the book, Whyte explored the idea that despite the overt idealization of individualism espoused in American rhetoric and entertainment, Americans were actually deeply collectivist, and more likely to trust organizations to make sound decisions than individuals. By extension, working for an organization made more sense than striking out on one's own. Whyte also discussed the commonality of risk-aversion among executives, and the ease of remaining an executive once attaining the position.

Organizational behavior

Organizational behavior is the study of the behavior of organizations and the individuals within those organizations, as well as the relationship between human behavior and the behavior, structure, and environment of the organization. Organizational behavior draws on the many tools of social science, including qualitative and quantitative research and statistical modeling. Where modern organizational behavior studies differ from earlier work in related fields is in their heavy reliance on computer simulation for both the macro- and micro-level of behavior in organizations. Studies often focus on specific behavioral problems like sexual harassment, workplace bullying and

abuse by superiors, decision-making problems, and counterproductive work.

Organizational citizenship behavior

Organizational citizenship behavior (OCB) is individual behavior that helps to promote the well-being of the organization but occurs outside the set of behaviors that are explicitly rewarded by the organization, such as those that are rewarded by performance incentives or specifically requested by supervisors or policies. Since the 1960s, work on organizational citizenship behavior has illustrated how important this kind of employee behavior is to the effectiveness and well-being of an organization. The standard definition was articulated by Dennis Organ in the 1970s, but Organ's work has been challenged because of the difficulty of clearly identifying OCB in the workplace. Organ himself has noted that the definition was more useful when jobs had clearly defined tasks, and that the influence of management theory on the workplace, and the increase in ambiguously defined work roles, has blurred the lines between reward-motivated or rule-driven behavior and OCB. A similar, more recently articulated, concept is extra-role behavior.

Organizational culture

Organizational culture is the culture of an organization, both as a result of policies and practices adopted by management and as it emerges from the social interactions among workers. Google's organizational culture, for instance, includes its use of "Innovation Time Off" to motivate employees by allowing them to spend 20 percent of their time on their own projects, its internal slogans like "don't be evil" and "you can be serious without a suit," and the considerable amenities available to workers in the Mountain

View, California, "Googleplex." Like other types of culture, organizational culture includes both behaviors and values, and long-time employees may become attached to elements of corporate culture to a degree unexplained by those elements' practical value to them.

Organizational dissent

Organizational dissent is disagreement with the practices of an organization. Typically shown little tolerance by leadership, dissent may nevertheless be an important force, acting as a check against authority that oversteps, policies and practices that are unethical or immoral, or other problems.

Organizational identification

Organizational identification is the extent of an individual's identification with the organization, and the extent to which he shares its goals and values, participates in its culture, and engages emotionally with its work. Organizational identification is above all else the individual's perception of an "us" that includes the individual and an organization as contrasted with an external "them" that may include competitors, regulators, etc.

Organizational intelligence

Organizational intelligence is the ability of an organization to accumulate and use knowledge related to its goals, to learn from its experiences, and to make sense of complex situations in order to adequately make informed decisions.

Organizational justice

Organizational justice, injustice, or fairness is the treatment by an organization of its workers, and the workers' feelings about that treatment. While the law, industry regulations, and labor union agreements govern what an organization has the power to do, not everything in its power will be seen as fair by the workers; at the same time, not every action by leadership that is negatively received by employees will be negatively received because of perceived unfairness. Rather, organizational justice is the appropriate treatment of employees in their work roles, collectively and as individuals, and a commensurate response to changes or behavior. (cf. Perceived Psychological Contract Violation.)

Organizational psychology

Organizational psychology is the field of applied psychology focusing on human behavior in the workplace, as well as the behavior of organizations. It is one of the most widely recognized specialties in applied psychology, also known as industrial and organizational psychology, I/O psychology, occupational psychology, and work psychology. Organizational psychologists work to improve organizational health by improving the satisfaction and well-being of its employees and developing the organization's interpersonal relationships.

Organizational socialization

Organizational socialization or onboarding refers to the processes by which new employees become socialized to the organization, acquiring not only skills and knowledge but behaviors and organizational social norms. Some aspects of organizational socialization are formal, as with job training, new employee orientation, seminars for new members, and the freshman orientation activities of many American colleges. But many are informal, as new workers absorb "unwritten rules" of behavior and other norms, technical jargon and terms of art, informal slang endemic to the industry or the organization, and other elements. Studies have found that organizational socialization plays an important role in productivity and employee engagement, and employees may be more receptive to learning the preferred way to perform a task when they first begin a job than to being corrected later. Picking up the norms of a new workplace also helps with employee morale and feelings of acceptance and belongingness. However, at least one study (N. J. Allen and J. P. Meyer, 1990) found that organizational socialization increased employee commitment but actually reduced role clarity, presumably by delaying the new employee's engagement with his role-specific duties. There is also concern for the effects of what Soren Kierkegaard called leveling, which can result as the new employee's individuality is eclipsed by his adoption of organizational norms.

Organizational storytelling

An interdisciplinary field incorporating management and organization studies, organizational storytelling is an approach to understanding organizational culture and behavior. Organizational storytelling uses narrative in order to uncover the root and meaning of organizational behavior.

Organizational Studies

Organizational studies is the study of the structures, processes, and practices of organizations, their construction, and their social, cultural, and economic impacts. Organizational studies has usually been approached from a functionalist framework, which is interested in society as a complex system of interrelated parts, of which organizations are one kind. Functionalism studies the large social structures of society, their role in shaping society, and the way that parts of a large stable system work together. Functionalism is out of favor in the social sciences in favor of frameworks (like critical theory) that draw attention to contradictions, conflicts, and inequalities rather than assuming the premise of stability, but its methodology is still common in many disciplines.

Out of the Crisis

W. Edwards Deming's 1982 book *Out of the Crisis*, originally published as *Quality, Productivity, and Competitive Position* but reissued in 1986 to capitalize on Deming's fame as the consultant to Ford who inspired the development of the Taurus, was an influential work on management. Deming had introduced the Efficiency movement to postwar Japan and was credited with its economic miracle before returning to the United States as a management consultant. *Out of the Crisis* offered 14 efficiency-minded principles, inspiring a revival of the Efficiency movement called the Total Quality Management movement:

1. Constancy of purpose in improving products and services.
2. Recognize the need for change and commit to it.
3. Do the job right the first time, and minimize reliance on inspection.
4. Minimize total cost and seek a single long-term supplier for any one item.
5. Constantly improve the system of production.
6. On-the-job training.
7. Supervisors must be leaders.
8. Reduce fear that interferes with employee engagement.
9. Reduce interdepartmental barriers to teamwork.
10. Eliminate target goals and slogans that put the burden of productivity and quality on the employee, instead acknowledging

management's responsibility to lead employees to these goals.

11. Make supervisors responsible for quality, not numbers.
12. Eliminate management by objectives, which is contrary to good leadership practices.
13. Adopt a program of self-improvement.
14. Involve every employee in changing the organization.

Outgroup

A social group with which an individual does not identify. (cf. In-group).

Outside the box

The image of an idea originating from "outside the box" is a metaphor that has become popular in management to illustrate the idea of the paradigm. A paradigm is a conceptual framework, a pattern of reasoning about a given thing, which has developed over time. When information is incomplete, paradigms may be faulty, and work reaches a point where improvements can only be made by going "outside the box" and introducing ideas that contradict the accepted paradigm. This is an important phenomenon in Thomas Kuhn's *The Structure of Scientific Revolutions*, for instance, but has also been adopted as the way to improve management and business practices by challenging the presumption that the status quo represents the best solution. It is also used to support the usefulness of management consultants, who have not worked in the organizational culture of the businesses for whom they consult and have not absorbed the same assumptions. A typical example of "outside the box" thinking is the legend of the Gordian knot, in which Alexander the Great "solved" the problem of how to untie an impossibly tangled knot that had foiled others—by drawing his sword and slicing through it.

Overconfidence effect

The overconfidence effect is a cognitive bias whereby an individual's confidence in his skill or judgment is consistently higher than his accuracy or objective skill level. In many tests demonstrating the effects, for instance, people are asked a number of general knowledge questions in which they both provide an answer and rate the confidence they have in that answer. Subjects consistently rated their confidence much more highly than their performance warranted. This remains true in experiments in which the subject cannot possibly know the answer for certain, due to its obscure and trivial nature—in the Marc Alpert and Howard Raiffa study in 1982, one question asked how many eggs were produced by the American egg industry every year—and even in experiments in which subjects have the overconfidence effect explained to them ahead of time.

Overjustification effect

The overjustification effect causes intrinsic motivation for an activity to decrease in response to a reward being offered for the activity, which puts the focus on reward seeking and requires that rewards continue to be offered for the activity. This is a concern in parenting, for instance, when tying allowance directly to a chore can prevent the child from developing an intrinsic motivation to perform the chore (which may influence their attitudes toward housework, yard work, or other activities in young adulthood when allowance is no longer disbursed). Likewise, in the workplace, rewarding employees for specific tasks may help assure those tasks are performed but interferes with the employees' intrinsic motivations for performing them. When the reward is discontinued, no motivation exists to continue the activity. This runs counter to the school of thought prescribing positive reinforcement in order to encourage specific behaviors. The overjustification effect has been experimentally demonstrated since Edward Deci's first experiments in 1971.

Overplacement

Related to the Dunning-Kruger effect, the overconfidence effect, and narcissism is overplacement, the belief that one is better than one's peers. Overplacement is often less obvious than narcissism, and experimental evidence suggests it is more common. The most famous example is the 1981 study in which 93 percent of American drivers considered themselves better than the median.

Overton window

Joseph P. Overton of the Mackinac Center for Public Policy proposed the idea that there is a narrow range of possibilities—a "window"—that the public will accept in any given situation, and that the success or failure of any political proposition depends in part on fitting this window. The history of the Affordable Care Act, and its antecedents in the Clinton health care plan, makes an interesting study of an attempt to fit a wide-reaching reform into a narrow window.

Panda diplomacy

Panda diplomacy is a term for the long tradition in China of presenting other countries with gifts of giant pandas, beginning with the 7th century Empress Wu Zetian's gift of two pandas to the Emperor of Japan. The People's Republic of China has been especially active in panda diplomacy, making gifts of two dozen pandas from 1958 to 1982. So strongly were panda gifts associated with Chinese diplomacy that the offer of two pandas to Taiwan was debated for several years before it was accepted, in part due to concerns over the international trade of endangered species and in part because of Taiwanese fears about the implications of accepting a gift from China.

Papal conclave

The papal conclave is the method used by the Catholic Church for selecting a new bishop of Rome, more popularly known as the pope, the leader of the Church and successor to Peter. Since 1059, the College of Cardinals has served as the sole electoral body in papal conclaves, and since 1970 participating cardinals have been limited to those under 80 years old. A cardinal is a Catholic priest or bishop who has been selected to join the College of Cardinals, and usually has special duties beyond ordinary clergyman. The conclave holds a series of anonymous votes, typically interspersed with significant discussion both within conclave as a whole and in small groups (usually supporting one cause or another, such as liberal Catholics pooling their votes behind a common candidate). Proceedings are secret, and each day a fire is lit in St Peter's Basilica, with dark smoke indicating to the public that no pope has been elected or white smoke heralding the arrival of a new pope. (The color of the smoke is chemically manipulated; in the past, damp tinder was added to produce black smoke.)

Parental responsibility

The extent and effect of parents' responsibility for their minor childrens' action is a sometimes vague area of law. It is generally true that parents bear responsibility for their childrens' actions in civil cases, for instance, though this is often a moot point since children cannot consent to contracts without a parent co-signing and thus consenting to liability anyway. In criminal cases, parents are usually responsible for making restitution payments necessitated by crimes their children commit, but in most states, implicit in the criminal code as it bears on children is the assumption that most crimes they commit will not be of the most serious kind. The role and responsibility of parents whose children commit violent crimes is thus a largely unaddressed issue, and there is a movement to more strongly criminalize parental neglect in such cases as it leads to allowing these crimes to occur. As in many areas of law, California has led the way, with the 1988 Street Terrorism and Prevention Act, which allows parents to face prison sentences for "gross deviation from normal standards of supervision."

Parentification

Parentification is a role reversal phenomenon in which a child is forced to take the authoritarian, caregiving, or otherwise parent-like role in dealing with their own parent. This is distinct from children who "raise themselves" or self-parent, and is similarly not typically used to describe normal events of a parent–child relationship at the end of the parent's life, such as caregiving or financial assistance by a child to a sick or dying parent. More commonly it refers to the child providing emotional support, such as by mediating between the parent and other family members or friends, or by acting as a confidant or recipient of "venting." It can also refer to instrumental parentification, in which the child performs the practical tasks that would normally be considered the parent's purview, including bill paying and other household management, caring for sick family members, and taking care of siblings to an extent that clearly goes beyond the bounds of babysitting.

Parenting

Parenting is one of the most basic forms of leadership, as parents guide their children through their development, bear responsibility for their children's actions and behavior, and are required to adapt to changing circumstances as their children grow. As with business and political leadership, a significant amount of literature has been devoted to the promotion of different parenting styles. The leadership studies field has not ignored parenting either. Micha Popper and Ofra Mayseless have written about the lessons transformational leadership can take from parenting, while Franklin Kudo conducted a study in 2012 on the impact of authoritative parenting of adolescents on their development of transformational leadership skills.

Parenting style

A parenting style is an approach to or theory of parenting. Developmental psychologist Diana Baumrind has developed parenting styles into three general types: authoritative, in which the parent is both demanding and responsive, with a high expectation of the growing child's maturity and a focus on the child's feelings—not to indulge them but rather to teach the child emotional self-regulation and problem-solving skills; authoritarian, in which the parent is demanding but not responsive, with high expectations of the child's obedience to parental rules and a tendency to use punishment as a motivator; and indulgent, which is responsive but not demanding, with few specific expectations for the child and a dislike or outright rejection of punishment.

Pareto principle

The Pareto principle states that 80 percent of effects stem from 20 percent of causes. The term was coined and applied by management consultant Joseph Juran, and named for economist Vilfredo Pareto, who had written about 80 percent of Italian land being owned by 20 percent of the population, and that 80 percent of the peas in his garden came from 20 percent of the pods. Juran applied this formulation to quality control—80 percent of problems come from 20 percent of sources—but there have been numerous other management applications since, including the rule of thumb that 80 percent of sales come from 20 percent of customers, 80 percent of complaints come from 20 percent of customers, 80 percent of sales come from 20 percent of the product line, 80 percent of profits are made in 20 percent of the time spent, and 80 percent of workplace injuries come from 20 percent of potential hazards. The Pareto principle is an important one in setting priorities, illustrating that not every problem or activity is of equal concern or impact.

Participative system

One of Rensis Likert's management systems, the participative system is the one that most involves employees in decision-making processes, and was advocated by Likert as the most effective. Communication flows freely among all levels, rather than being directed mainly from the top of the hierarchy to lower levels, and managers are kept well-versed in events and problems at the lower levels. Employees as a group participate in setting policy and organizational goals.

Participatory management

In the 1920s, work in human relations theory led to recommendations by management researchers that organizations adopt a participatory management style: a management approach in which employees participate in some level of organizational decision making. Typically, upper management retains the final authority and responsibility for making decisions, but employees are engaged with the process and offer their input.

Passing the buck

"Passing the buck" is a phrase dating at least to the 19th century to refer to disavowing responsibility or explicitly assigning responsibility for one's own actions to someone else. Leaders are sometimes able to shield themselves from taking responsibility by letting subordinates fall on their swords; President Harry Truman explicitly distanced himself from such tactics with the sign on his desk in the Oval Office, reading "The buck stops here."

President Harry Truman famously had a sign on his desk that read "the buck stops here." (NARA)

Passive-aggressive behavior

Passive-aggressive behavior is the expression of hostility and negative emotions through passive methods rather than explicit aggression, such as through body language, tone of voice, deliberately poor or slow performance of work, insincerity or sarcasm, victim-playing, feigned helplessness in order to avoid performing a task, or other means. In the workplace, employee behavior like lateness or procrastination may be taken as passive aggressive, while managers may exhibit passive aggressive behavior through destructively negative attitudes or feigned helplessness that forces subordinates to perform menial tasks for them that they claim they cannot do themselves.

Pater familias

The oldest male in the household, the pater familias was the legal head of the family in ancient Rome, given legal power over his family's property and dependents (including his wife, children, adopted relatives, freedmen, and slaves), as well as legal responsibilities to see after their welfare, maintain his household's moral standing, and perform the duties of a good citizen, including political and civic engagement and honoring his ancestral gods. Legally, he had the power of life or death over any member of his family, though this right is invoked more often in historical fiction set in ancient Rome than it was actually seen in history, apart from the practice (widespread, legally mandated, but not universal) of putting to death infants with significant birth defects.

Paternalism

Paternalism is a style of leadership in which, just as parents limit the freedom of their children as part of their responsibility as parents, leaders limit the freedom and autonomy of those they lead. Paternalism is especially associated with governments, and with laws that limit individual choice in circumstances where those choices affect only the individual (the common examples being laws mandating seatbelt or motorcycle helmet usage), and the term tends to be used derogatorily. There is often disagreement about whether a requirement really is paternalistic: for instance, opponents of vaccination oppose vaccination requirements as paternalistic, while proponents point out that herd immunity and the existence of immunocompromised people means that whether an individual is vaccinated or not has a public health impact beyond the impact on the individual. In the workplace, a paternalistic approach to leadership might more frequently be styled micro-management.

Path-goal theory

The path-goal theory or model was developed by Robert House in 1971, and says that a leader's role is to guide followers to choose the paths that will meet their individual and organizational goals, which will require the leader to engage in different kinds of leadership behaviors as the situation demands. When followers are successful in meeting their goals, they will perceive this behavior positively. This model describes flexibility on the part of the leader, rather than adhering to a narrowly defined leadership style. Both environmental factors and the characteristics and needs of followers will impact leader behavior.

Patriarchy

Patriarchy is a social, political, or cultural system in which men occupy all or most of the leadership roles, especially one in which fathers are given authority over their households. In the modern world, few countries are legal patriarchies—the perpetuation of the patriarchy is rather a matter of tradition and norms, sometimes with laws supporting or informed by a patriarchal view without explicitly invoking it. For instance, in much of the world, marital rape—rape of a spouse by the other spouse—was not illegal, which is to say not legally recognized as rape, until the 19th or 20th century, and in jurisdictions where it is not explicitly criminalized, it is often impossible to prosecute. This legal fact does not make specific mention of a patriarchy, but it reflects the idea that the husband has a right to sex with his wife that exceeds his wife's right to say no. Outside of legal structures, patriarchy is perpetuated by unequal pay and unequal access to jobs, by unequal treatment due to gender, by the politicization of birth control and other women's health issues, by the perpetuation of the idea of women as homemakers and fathers as breadwinners, and other factors. In contrast with this, anthropologists generally believe that prehistoric human communities were egalitarian, leaving open the question of when patriarchal structures were developed.

PDCA

PDCA is a management method for continuous improvement, standing for Plan-Do-Check-Act: Plan, by establishing objectives, expectations, and the processes necessary to achieve them; Do, by implementing the plan; Check, by studying the differences between the plan and the results; Act, by correcting the plan. The method was popularized by management consultant W. Edwards Deming, who sometimes formulated it as PDSA, substituting Study for Check.

Peace through strength

Peace through strength is a phrase dating to at least as early as Emperor Hadrian of 1st-century Rome, and was likely old when he used it. It is a leadership strategy that seeks to avoid conflict by amassing such strength that one's opponents will not risk the losses they would face. This was also the strategy of both the Soviet Union and especially the United States during the Cold War, and was turned into virtually the defining feature of Ronald Reagan's campaigns and presidency.

Peak experience

A peak experience is an ecstatic state characterized by euphoria and feelings of interconnectedness. The term is particularly associated with psychologist Abraham Maslow, who may have used it in an attempt to find a term more neutral than religious or mystical experience. Though peak experiences do not appear on Maslow's hierarchy of needs, he considers them the next level, the goal of those who have satisfied and transcended the basic needs.

Pecking order

A term in both English and German for a stratified social hierarchy preserved by expressions of dominance, figuratively referring to the dominant pecking of hens, and the idea of each hen being pecked by the hen above it in the hierarchy and pecking the hen below it. This pecking need not actually occur to establish the hierarchy: the hierarchy represents each hen's relative ability to dominate, but that ability may be estimated based on size and the deference of other hens. Similarly, when pecking order refers to non-hen social systems, dominance may be maintained not through outright conflict but the mutually understood outcome of hypothetical conflict.

Pedagogy leaders

Pedagogy is the science of education. Most graduate programs in the humanities and social sciences, for instance, include a pedagogy course to impart skills to future professors. Pedagogy leaders are teachers and other educators who spread good teaching practices through a workforce. At Canons High School in the United Kingdom, for instance, pedagogy leaders were hired in 2012 in order to introduce top-down reforms to the teaching practices of the school. The best teachers in the school were selected to teach their methods to their colleagues in seminars.

Peer mentoring

Peer mentoring is mentoring among peers rather than between a mentor and a significantly younger mentee. Primarily associated with education, peer mentoring is sometimes found in the workplace with lateral colleagues rather than superiors who perform the mentoring, which has the potential to form bonds between the co-workers. Mentoring has been found to have a positive correlation with employee retention.

Peer pressure

The influence of a peer group on an individual's attitudes or behaviors. Generally, peer pressure exerts an influence that drives the individual's choices toward the group norm, although in some cases it may be a perceived group norm. Studies of undergraduate binge drinking, for instance, have found that discomfort with binge drinking is high even among participants, many of whom seem to believe they are alone in participating in a behavior that makes them uncomfortable and that the rest of the group finds normal. Peer pressure is a particularly valuable concept in sociology and psychology when it refers to pressures exerted accidentally or unconsciously, rather than acts of persuasion. The behaviors encouraged by peer pressure need not be negative, and some public health campaigns and leadership strategies have focused on using peer pressure to encourage good habits and behavior.

Penalty authority

Penalty authority is authority that a leader retains by creating an atmosphere of fear of punishment, such that he enjoys obedience because his followers fear they will suffer a loss of status, bonuses, or their jobs.

People's history

A "people's history" or "history from below" is an account of history from the perspective of "the people," rather than the from the perspective of the leaders, in contrast with the Great Man approach of the 19th and 20th centuries. Such histories tend to focus on class conflicts or conflicts between the oppressed and their oppressors, and share concerns with postcolonialism, Marxist history, feminist history, and new labor history.

People skills

The term *people skills* overlaps considerably with "soft skills," in consisting of skills concerned with interpersonal relationships, including not only communication skills, but empathy, emotional intelligence, and the ability to persuade and inculcate trust and respect. The difference is mainly in how they are talked about, "soft skills" being contrasted with the "hard skills" that bear directly on a person's job role.

Perceived psychological contract violation

The idea of the perceived psychological contract violation (PPCV) has been explored in organizational psychology since the 1990s, and refers to an employee's negative feelings about an employer's behavior when the employee believes the employer has betrayed a promise or agreement. The PPCV especially refers to breaches of implicit agreement rather than explicit breaches of contract, and usually refers to situations in which the employer has not overstepped their legal rights. Some studies have suggested that an employee's probability of feeling PPCV is inversely proportional to his identification with the organization.

Performance improvement

Performance improvement is a measurement of the improvement in a business process or procedure at the organizational, team, or employee level. It can be measured in a number of ways, including hard measurements like profits, costs, and output, and soft measurements like customer satisfaction surveys and other feedback. Quality control processes are responsible for measuring and improving performance.

Performance orientation

One of the global leadership cultural competencies identified by the GLOBE Project, performance orientation is the degree to which a group, organization, or society encourages excellence in its members by rewarding excellent or improved performance.

Pericles

A 5th-century B.C.E. general in ancient Greece, Pericles ruled Athens during its golden age, the internecine period between the Persian and Peloponnesian Wars. Historian Thucydides called him "the first citizen of Athens," and Herodotus based his political philosophy on the democratic system that the city-state enjoyed under Pericles. Among Pericles' initiatives were paying jurors for their time, so that poor Athenians could participate in jury service, and the promotion of the arts, education, and beautification of public spaces. He was celebrated both as a military leader and an inspiring orator.

Person culture

One of four types of corporate culture identified by Charles Handy and Roger Harrison. In a person culture, each member considers himself superior to the organization. This tends to be untenable for large organizations, but small partnerships can function from this perspective, especially when each partner has a distinct set of skills or resources that he contributes.

Person/situation debate

In psychology, the person/situation debate is the disagreement in the field over whether behavior is primarily the result of the individual's personality traits or the situation in which their behavior is enacted.

Personal branding

The term *personal branding* was first coined by business management writer Tom Peters in 1997, though as a practice it is much older and was a key part of self-improvement books like *Think and Grow Rich* as early as the 1930s. Personal branding is the marketing by the individual of himself and his professional identity, especially through techniques that distinguish his "brand identity" in the same way one would market that of a business.

Personal leadership

The study of leadership in terms of the characteristics of leaders, especially their skills, actions, decision-making strategies, and personality traits. Leadership gurus and the self-help industry traditionally focus on personal leadership, because this is a view of leadership that implies leadership can be taught.

Personality clash

A personality clash is a conflict that transpires not because of disagreement over a contested issue but because of an incompatibility in the personalities of the people involved. Personality conflicts have been the subject of psychological study since at least Carl Jung, who looked at the problems between opposed traits like thinking and feeling or extraversion and introversion and saw in them the root causes of many ostensibly intellectual disputes. Just as those intellectual disputes were not, in their time, acknowledged as personality clashes, so too today a conflict may develop between two people that is ostensibly waged over a particular issue or decision, but is really motivated by the personality difference between them and the different values or perceptions that they hold as a result. These underlying differences may not be expressed, which can make resolving the work at hand difficult.

Personality theories of leadership

Personality theories of leadership are those founded on the idea that someone can be a "natural" leader—that good leadership is a product of specific personality types, not specific skills (which is not the same as saying that skills are not important). The Great Man approach to history and leadership was the dominant view until the 20th century, and early leadership studies in the post–World War II years focused on personality traits possessed by leaders.

Peter Principle

The Peter Principle, named for Laurence J. Peter who introduced the concept in his 1969 humorous book of the same name, states that employees and managers are promoted based on their performance in their current role rather than demonstrated suitability for the new role, and that people are therefore promoted until they arrive in a job at which they are incompetent, while competent people are regularly shifted away from the roles at which they excel.

Philosopher

From the ancient Greek for "lover of wisdom," a philosopher is an intellectual engaged in developing and supporting claims of truth, especially with truth as an end in itself rather than, as in psychology, for the purpose of treatment of an individual. This does not mean philosophers are impractical, though; many branches of philosophy are engaged with specific practical issues, like political philosophy and ethics. Other branches like metaphysics and epistemology are admittedly more abstract.

Philosopher Kings

The ancient Greek philosopher Plato was a staunch critic of democracy as practiced in Athens (cf. Sortition and Craft analogy), and proposed instead that society should be ruled by "Philosopher Kings." Such leaders would be selected for their capacity to be trained for the role, and in being thoroughly trained—not only in leadership but in what we now call the liberal arts, with a thorough practical education as well—they would have the skills necessary to govern justly and effectively. In comparison, Plato found democracy to be little more than mob rule.

Piaget, Jean

The 20th century Swiss psychologist Jean Piaget contributed greatly to developmental psychology. Today he is best known for defining four developmental stages: the sensorimotor stage from birth to age 2, the preoperational stage from age 2 to 7, the concrete operational stage from age 7 to 11, and the formal operational stage as abstract reasoning develops. Even when psychologists disagree with some of the specifics of Piaget's theories, he was instrumental in introducing the idea that adult cognitive processes and abilities do not arrive in an instant.

Ping pong diplomacy

Ping pong diplomacy is a common term for the visits to China and the United States by ping pong players from the other country, at a time when few American citizens were permitted to enter China. The U.S. Table Tennis team, in fact, were the first Americans (along with the journalists accompanying them) to enter Beijing in 22 years, when they arrived in April 1971. The event led to the first real improvement in Chinese/U.S. relations in years, and was followed up by President Richard Nixon's visit to China in 1972, and that of a Chinese ping pong delegation to the U.S. several months later. China's attempt to invite similar delegations from other countries proved to have little success.

Planning fallacy

The term *planning fallacy* was introduced in 1979 by psychologists Daniel Kahneman and Amos Tversky, who also developed reference class forecasting. The fallacy refers to an observed pattern of individuals underestimating the time they will need to complete a task, even when they have previously had similar tasks run overtime. The effect is true for multiple kinds of tasks, both mental and physical, individual and group, but only when predicting one's own work.

Plato's Academy

The ancient Greek philosopher Plato, a generation after Pericles, founded his Academy in Athens in 387 B.C.E. Plato had studied with Socrates, Pericles's contemporary, who had argued for the good of teaching politics and ethics. Plato went one step further and argued that education, rather than aristocratic birth, could and should produce leaders. The complete curriculum is unknown, but mathematics and philosophy would have been included, and perhaps "natural philosophy," or what we now call the hard sciences. The academy attracted students from all over ancient Greece, and the traditional view of historians has been that it served as a leadership training center; it is difficult to say how much practical governance formed part of the curriculum, as opposed to more abstract political philosophy.

Pluralistic ignorance

Pluralistic ignorance is a phenomenon found in social groups, wherein the majority of members privately believe one thing but publicly espouse a conflicting thing, motivated by the belief that their real opinion is not shared by the others. The classic example is that of excessive drinking on college campuses. Numerous studies show that a large number of heavy drinkers in college drink more than they are comfortable with in the belief that they need to keep up with the others around them and that they are the only ones uncomfortable with it. "The Emperor's New Clothes" is often used as an illustration of the same effect.

Plutarch

The 1st-century Greek historian Plutarch is today best known for his work *Parallel Lives*. Like most historians of his era, he was concerned less with historical accuracy and context and more with the lessons that could be illustrated with reference to historical events or personages. *Parallel Lives* presents 50 short biographies, 46 of them arranged in pairs of one Greek life and one Roman life. The complete text has not survived, and some of the surviving text has been changed by a later editor, but the gist of it is clear. Plutarch was concerned with illustrating the moral character of his subjects, and the bulk of his energy was spent demonstrating the parallels between physical characteristics of his subjects and their moral and psychological characteristics—a tendency that persists in everything from phrenology to handwriting analysis to palm reading. He is a clear antecedent to the "Great Man" school of biography, which had been inspired in part by the revived interest in Plutarch during the Renaissance and subsequent strains of thought that developed throughout the Enlightenment.

Political frame

In L. Bolman and T. Deal's Four Frame model, the Political frame is one of the distinctive frames from which people approach the world. It perceives the world in terms of power, resources, and competition, highlighting differences in perspectives, needs, or lifestyles. It tends to approach things in terms of negotiation, coercion, or power alliances.

Political philosophy

The philosophical field devoted to the study of politics, law, justice, liberty, and authority.

Political science

A social science focused on the study of politics, the state and government, and political behavior. Political science has its roots in the work of Plato and Aristotle, and draws on numerous fields, overlapping with most of the social sciences.

Popular sovereignty

Popular sovereignty is the idea that the authority of the government originates with and is sustained by the consent of the people, which is the basis for social contract theories.

Populism

Populism is an approach to political thought that favors those things that will appeal to the people—it is not a specific ideology so much as it is a behavior. In the United States, it is a term rarely used reflexively, but this was not always the case. Up through the New Deal era, many politicians and activists referred to themselves as populist. Agrarian and farmers' movements of the 19th century were explicitly populist, and the Populist Party wielded some power in the presidential election of 1896. Since the 1930s, however, "populist" has more often become a pejorative term, one especially associated with preying on popular fears or misconceptions in order to garner votes. A number of candidates and officials have done their part to blacken the name. Populist governor and senator Huey P. Long was famous for his manipulation of public sentiment to amass power and wealth, and in the south after the civil rights movement, populism meant white peoples' populism: the Populist Party name was revived for the presidential campaigns of former

Ku Klux Klan leaders Willis Carto and David Duke. In the 21st century, several new populist parties have formed, while the Tea Party and the Occupy movement have been true populist phenomena.

Positive psychological capital

Positive psychological capital (PsyCap) is a state in which an individual experiences hope, optimism, resilience, and high self-efficacy. Helping employees achieve PsyCap in the workplace is one of the goals of positive psychology as implemented by organizational psychologists.

Positive Psychology

A school of psychology, developed in the late 1990s that emphasizes applications of psychological understanding to the improvement of normal life rather than simply the treatment of mental illness, crisis, or trauma. Like humanistic philosophy, positive psychology focuses on happiness. In the workplace, positive psychology focuses on employee engagement, emotional intelligence, and avoiding burnout.

Post, Jerrold

Psychologist Jerrold Post has theorized that collective or group narcissism emerges when a narcissistic charismatic leader is paired with individually narcissistic followers. The leader plays to their individual narcissism by praising the qualities of the group as a whole and its superiority to others; the leader–follower relationship that emerges is thus deeply narcissistic, with a leader who needs to be admired and followers dazzled by their leader's force of personality as a reflection on their own group identity. Hitler is the obvious example here, a charismatic leader who constantly invoked national and racial pride, contrasted with his condemnation of so-called weaker peoples.

Post-Fordism

Post-Fordism is a term often used to refer to the standard system of production in the industrialized world since the late 20th century, and the cultural, social, political, and economic institutions and phenomena associated with it. The name is coined in reference to Fordism, Henry Ford's approach to automobile manufacturing in the early 20th century. Post-Fordism is characterized by the increased participation of women in the workforce compared to previous eras, increasing specialization of businesses and jobs, and the rise of information technology, but beyond this there is considerable disagreement over what constitutes a post-Fordist business, and whether or not post-Fordism coexists alongside a changed Fordism or if it has supplanted Fordism entirely.

Power

In the social sciences, power is the ability to influence others. It may be exerted consciously or unconsciously. The term *agent of influence* is often used to refer to the person exerting power. The target—the person being influenced—may or may not be aware that they are being influenced, and even if they are aware that the agent of influence is responsible for the change, they may not think of the scenario in terms of a power dynamic. For instance, a history teacher may assign a textbook or give a lecture that changes a student's views of a political issue, but the student may not think of this as the history teacher having wielded power over him. In the 21st century, psychological experiments have suggested that those who have more power also have less empathy, and that this effect is causative: as they gain power, they become less interested in or less able to see circumstances from the viewpoints of other people. However, research also shows that those

with greater power are more likely to be proactive; one study found that powerful people were three times more likely to offer to help a person in distress. The use of power in interpersonal or professional relationships is increasingly an area studied with game theory.

Power culture

One of four types of corporate culture identified by Charles Handy and Roger Harrison. In a power culture, culture is concentrated in a central figure or small group, with little bureaucracy.

Power distance

One of the cultural dimensions identified by Geert Hofstede, power distance is the difference in power between an executive and a given subordinate, or in a society, between the most and least powerful. The power distance index is the greatest difference in power between the most and least powerful that is acceptable to the least powerful.

Pragmatism

A philosophical school of thought originating in the United States, pragmatism began with the work of Charles Sanders Peirce, William James, and John Dewey in the late 19th century. It is best represented by the pragmatist maxim, which calls for examining a hypothesis in light of its practical consequences. Though pragmatism encompasses metaphysical, epistemological, and empiricist dimensions, in common usage it means a concern for practical ends. A pragmatic approach to management, for instance, is one that is less concerned with the implications of managerial practices and more concerned with their impact on meeting organizational goals. Similarly, pragmatic ethics focus less on the inherent moral value of a given action and more on the morality of its consequences. Classical pragmatism was actually not as ends-focused as it seems—John Dewey disparaged work and education being treated only as means to their respective ends, and thought each should be rewarding in itself—but has perhaps had its greatest impact on the public administration profession, in which administrators are principally concerned with evaluating potential programs and plans in terms of their practical consequences.

Pre-attentive processing

Pre-attentive processing is the gathering of information from an individual's surroundings by his unconscious mind, and the processing of that information by the unconscious before it is given over to conscious processing—before it is "noticed," in other words. Pre-attentive processing is the mechanism that is responsible for what an individual notices first about the stimuli in his environment, and which characteristics of a stimulus stand out. Does the model on the billboard stand out the most, the brand logo behind her, the tiger she is posed with, or the fact that a different billboard was there yesterday, thwarting his expectations? Poor sleep or lack of sleep slows down the process of pre-attentive processing, which is one of the specific phenomena making up the "grogginess" we feel when we first get up in the morning, or if we are suddenly wakened in the middle of the night. This is also one reason sleep is so important to mental or emotional work and decision making.

Precautionary principle

The precautionary principle is a concept in public policy, stating that in circumstances in which there is scientific uncertainty as to whether a given action poses a risk to the public or to the environment, the correct response is to avoid the action unless it can be shown that it is harmless. More a guiding principle of policy than an element thereof, it is in large part a reaction to the numerous practices of the past that were later learned to be harmful as science improved, including the public health impact of pesticides and the environmental impact of chlorofluorocarbons.

Prescriptive

There is a divide in philosophy and most of the social sciences between the descriptive and the prescriptive. While the descriptive simply models an aspect of the world as it is—descriptive linguistics describes how people use language, while descriptive leadership studies identify the things real-world leaders do or the traits they have—the prescriptive approach is concerned with identifying, defending, and advocating the best way to do something. Prescriptive grammar is the familiar rules-based grammar exemplified by William Strunk and E. B. White's *Elements of Style*; prescriptive leadership studies identifies the most successful model of leadership. Prescriptive works on leadership go back thousands of years, to ancient wisdom literature such as that of Ptah Hotep; descriptive works are essentially introduced by the social sciences and the study of management in the 20th century.

Presentism

Presentism is the depiction, construction, or response to the past that is inflected by anachronistic present-day perspectives. In discussing history and literature, this is problematic; as Pulitzer-winning historian John Lewis Gaddis wrote, "the times impose their values upon lives; there's no point in condemning individuals for the circumstances in which they find themselves." There is no way to usefully address the effectiveness of historical leaders without considering their actions in the context of their times. In philosophy, presentism also refers to a model of time that says that only events in the present are real.

Preventive diplomacy

Preventive diplomacy is practiced in order to prevent disputes from occurring or escalating, as opposed to diplomatic measures taken to control the damage of disputes already escalated.

Priming

In psychology, priming is a memory effect that influences the individual's response to a stimulus as a result of previous exposure to another stimulus. A simple experimental example is showing people strings of letters to see how quickly they can identify which strings are gibberish and which are real words. Words are identified more quickly when preceded by related words—yellow will be recognized more quickly after purple than after jalapeno, for instance.

The Prince

The most famous of the "mirrors for princes," Niccolo Machiavelli's Il Principe was first circulated in 1513 and officially published in 1532, after Machiavelli's death. Machiavelli had worked in the government of Florence from 1498 to 1512, while the Medici family was out of power, and wrote The Prince when they returned and the government was replaced. The Prince presents instructions for governance, and its apparent amorality is the inspiration for the term Machiavellian. Both the Catholic Church and the humanists of the Renaissance condemned The Prince, though Enlightenment philosopher Jean-Jacques Rousseau, in the 18th century, interpreted the work as a satire of ruthlessness rather than a celebration thereof. Though this view has been echoed by more recent political philosophers, the questions of where Machiavelli stood and how exactly The Prince was meant to be received have not been satisfactorily resolved.

Private leadership

One of the Three Levels of Leadership, private leadership is James Scouller's term for the 14 behaviors (9 related to "maintenance," 5 related to the individual's task) that leaders use in one-on-one interactions with individuals. Private leadership is focused on increasing the confidence and performance of the individual with respect to the goal at hand.

Problem-solving courts

Problem-solving courts are those that seek a resolution to the issues brought before them other than simple punishment for crimes. In the United States, they began with the efforts of judges in the 1990s to divert drug addicts to treatment programs rather than sentence them to prison, in order to reduce recidivism, on the theory that their addiction had motivated their criminal behavior and would continue to do so until they had the means to overcome it. Drug courts have become increasingly common, in which judges have considerable leeway in the way they handle the cases brought before them.

Problem statement

A problem statement is a device used in problem solving, which concisely defines the problem, whose problem it is, the limitations (in resources like time or money) on possible solutions, and the form that the resolution can take. Problem statements are normally simply tools to get the problem-solving process going, but sometimes highlight issues that need to be addressed, such as an inability to clearly articulate what the problem is (which reduces the odds of finding a satisfactory solution) or the discovery that there are actually separate problems that can be dealt with independently.

Procedural justice
Procedural justice is fairness in the processes used by a group, organization, or government to distribute resources and address and resolve conflicts, a concept also known as due process when used in reference to U.S. law. Procedural justice implies some impartiality about what constitutes a fair outcome of a procedure, and perhaps some system of evaluating or contesting an outcome (such as the institution of the court of appeals, in the American legal system). High levels of procedural justice tend to be associated with group members feeling a high level of belongingness.

Process culture
One of four corporate cultures identified by T. E. Deal and A. A. Kennedy, characterized by slow feedback and low risk. Jobs in these cultures are generally low stress and secure, with the biggest sources of stress coming from interpersonal conflicts, incompetent co-workers or poorly designed work procedures, or in the case of public-facing roles, dealing with the public. Typical examples include the retail business, the hospitality industry, and banks.

Professional identification
Professional identification is the degree to which an individual defines himself as a member of his profession, as measured by a scale developed by Blake E. Ashforth and Fred Mael

in 1989. Work on the impact of professional identification has uncovered two clear phenomena: employees with a high degree of professional identification are more likely to perceive administrators as outsiders, restricting their degree of organizational identification; and professional identification is strongly associated with the perception that accords status to a high quality of work more than to a high salary or profit-making potential. (Much of the work on professional identification has been done on doctors, though, who have a high average salary.)

Professional network service
Professional network services are social networks that are intended for professional connections, interactions, and networking. LinkedIn is the most popular example, but there are numerous other networks, including some specific to industries or job types, and some focused more explicitly on connecting contractors with work.

Project engineer
A project engineer either works with or works as a project manager, depending on the needs of the company, in overseeing the planning, resource management, and execution of a technical project.

Project manager
A project manager is tasked with the planning, execution, and completion of a project. They are a specialized professional common in certain fields, notably the technology and construction industries. Professional certification exists, though it is not required by all firms, and although some graduate programs in project management are offered, the field's formalization is still young.

Promoting adversaries

When both sides in a conflict can benefit in some way from maintaining the conflict, this behavior or relationship is called "promoting adversaries." In the private sector, the "cola wars" of Pepsi and Coca-Cola in the 1980s led both companies to innovate and continue to develop their products. In international relations, a sustained conflict like the Cold War helps keep regimes in power and favors certain areas of government spending.

A button from the "cola wars" between Pepsi and Coca-Cola proclaims that the consumer picked Coke during a blind taste test. (Wikimedia Commons)

Proxemics

The term *proxemics* was coined by cultural anthropologist Edward T. Hall in 1963, to refer to an area in the study of nonverbal communication, specifically the use of space. While kinesics and haptics refer to nonverbal communication conducted by body language and touch, the way space is used for communication includes the distance people put between themselves and others, and the way people's posture and body positioning changes (along with changes in the pitch of their voice) as other people approach. The bounds of personal space and reactions to violations thereof are of particular concern.

Psychoanalysis

Psychoanalysis is a set of psychological theories and therapeutic mechanisms dealing with human behavior, the mind, human motivation, and the treatment of psychological problems. Popularized and largely formulated by Sigmund Freud, psychoanalysis was further developed by his colleagues Alfred Adler and Carl Jung, and later followers like Jacques Lacan. Psychoanalysis is one of the most influential theories on the layman's understanding of human behavior, and psychoanalytical concepts like free association, ego, Freudian slips, and the symbolism of dreams have trickled down into the popular imagining. As one of the first scientific approaches to understanding human behavior, psychoanalysis has provided numerous tools both to analyze leadership and to help leaders better understand their followers' needs.

Psychodynamic approaches to leadership

Psychodynamic approaches to leadership are theories or models of leadership that are influenced by psychodynamics, the area of psychology that systematizes and studies the motives, drives, and emotions underlying human behavior. Psychodynamic theories draw on Sigmund Freud, Carl Jung, and their successors, and are related to psychohistory, the branch of psychodynamics that explains the behavior of historical figures through reference to modern psychology. While many theories of leadership draw heavily on sociology or political science, psychodynamic approaches draw on concepts from psychology like individuation, regression, and the shadow self.

Psychology of reasoning

The psychology of reasoning incorporates psychology, cognitive science, linguistics, probability theory, and neuroscience to study the way people reason, solve problems, and make decisions. The relationship between emotion and reasoning, the development of reasoning, the impact of completeness or incompleteness of knowledge on reasoning, and the differences in individual versus group reasoning are all important areas of study. Psychology of reasoning studies both the processes of reasoning that occur internally—both consciously and otherwise—and the way people articulate their reasoning using natural language, which is especially important in decision making and attempts to persuade or influence others.

Psychological contract

The psychological contract is the set of perceptions, beliefs, and obligations held mutually by an employee and his employer. The term contrasts with an explicit written contract, and includes those elements of the relationship not included in the contract, whether implicit or explicit. For instance, an unspoken agreement between workers and a supervisor may say that employees will work productively, and in return the supervisor will not hover over them or micromanage, will safeguard the security of their jobs, and will be reasonable in responding to requests for vacation time. Psychological contracts became more important and arguably more detailed over the course of the 20th century, as the growing prosperity of the United States led Americans to develop a greater expectation of pleasure from their jobs and an adequate work–life balance.

Psychological immune system

The psychological immune system is a metaphor for the many mechanisms that protect an individual from negative emotions, and which work to reduce their intensity and duration. Because these mechanisms do not operate in view of the conscious mind, they are not accounted for in affective forecasting.

Psychological safety

Psychological safety is a condition in a group dynamic such that members of the team feel safe with one another—not simply physically safe, but rather, able to raise concerns or express honest opinions about the work at hand and other issues of concern to the group without fear of judgment or reprisals. Adept leadership inculcates psychological safety in the group, especially when group members are involved in the operations and decision-making procedures of the group and roles are clearly understood.

Psychometrics

Psychometrics is the area of psychology concerned with the creation of objective measurement tools for psychological qualities like skills, attitudes, moods, and personality traits, and with statistical research related to those tools. Like modern psychology itself, psychometrics arose in the 19th century and has been subject to numerous trends as well as changes brought on by technological advances. The foundational concepts to psychometrics are validity and reliability. Reliability is the easiest to test: the same measurement taken multiple times should have consistent results. Validity requires reliability, as well as statistical evidence that the test measures what it is intended to measure.

Ptah Hotep

The ancient Egyptian vizier Ptah Hotep lived in the 5th Dynasty period of Egypt, probably during the 25th century B.C.E., and is buried at Saqqara along with his descendents. Viziers were advisers to the pharaohs (Djedkare Isesi in this case) as well as overseeing much of the bureaucracy of the government. Ptah Hotep authored one of the oldest known books, *The Maxims of Ptah Hotep*, consisting of the wisdom he had accumulated in his lifetime and wished to pass on to the younger generation. Many of the maxims deal with leadership, including this simple one encouraging good works: "If you are a man who leads, who controls the affairs of the many, seek out every beneficent deed, that your conduct may be blameless."

Public administration

An interdisciplinary academic discipline, public administration studies the implementation of government policy and best practices for managing public programs. A somewhat older discipline than leadership studies, it followed a similar course in its development, originating as an area of common interest for academics in various fields (political science, economics, law, business administration, and sociology, primarily) a generation or so after the creation of New Deal programs contributed to the professionalization of civil service. Eventually it emerged as its own discipline, with dedicated studies and degree programs.

Public diplomacy

Public diplomacy is diplomacy conducted with the public of a foreign nation rather than with its leadership. Cultural diplomacy is sometimes discussed as a form of public diplomacy, but a different form of public diplomacy has been an important part of American foreign policy since the end of World War II, as the American government has sought to encourage foreign populaces to become disillusioned first with communist regimes and later with various regimes in the Middle East and North Africa. International broadcasting is a key element of public diplomacy efforts, and Radio Free Europe (RFE) has broadcast U.S.-sponsored news and propaganda since 1949. While European broadcasts cover a smaller range than they did during the Cold War, RFE (which formally merged with the similar Radio Liberty) now broadcasts in the Middle East as well.

Public interest

Public interest or the public good is the well-being of the general public. While government policy decisions need to take public interest into account, the private sector is not always required to do so, nor motivated to do so in such cases where working against the public interest will have no impact on profits nor on the private lives of the decision-makers (as in the case of outsourcing labor to a cheaper county). The regulatory framework of many industries is a compromise between bowing to the public interest and honoring the American ideal of a free market.

Public leadership

One of the Three Levels of Leadership, public leadership is James Scouller's term for the 34 leadership behaviors that leaders use when influencing a group of two or more people, such as in meetings. Scouller divides the 34 behaviors into groups: group building and maintenance (12 behaviors), ideation, problemsolving, and decisionmaking (10), executing the plan (6), setting the vision (4), and planning (2). Public leadership is concerned with driving collaborative and collective efforts and creating at atmosphere of trust that leads to high performance.

Public management

Public management is the administration of government and non-profit organizations, and especially the use of management tools borrowed from or analogous to those of the private sector in such administration. While the concerns and goals of the public sector differ from those of the private sector, many management approaches are goal-independent.

Public policy

As an academic discipline, public policy is the study of policies formulated and set by governments and their constituent parts, and of the decision-making processes behind such policies. It intersects with other social sciences, especially political science, economics, and sociology. Approaches to public policy vary considerably among the schools offering degree programs, with Indiana University focusing on multidisciplinary concentrations and non-profit management, the University of Illinois at Chicago focusing on decision-making processes, and the John F. Kennedy School of Government at Harvard taking a leadership-based approach grounded in political science.

Public–private partnership

A public–private partnership (PPP) is a venture conducted through a partnership of a government agency and one or more private businesses, often with the private business assuming all or most of the financial risk, in exchange for a high reward potential. PPPs are a way to shield taxpayers from the risks of certain ventures, while encouraging business opportunities. They range from public transit ventures to the privatization of emergency services in some jurisdictions.

Pygmalion effect

Named for the Greek myth of the statue given life, the Pygmalion effect results in individuals performing better as a result of higher expectations being set for them.

Quaker-based consensus

The Quaker model of consensus decision making is a method that has developed over time since about the 18th century, and that the Quakers introduced to anti-war protest movements in the 20th century. The process emphasizes allowing every interested party a chance to express their view, while a clerk or convenor acts as a facilitator. The facilitator prevents discussions from either spending too much time covering the areas where there is already general agreement or degenerating into arguments over trivialities; instead, they identify areas of disagreement, rephrase each side's viewpoint for clarification, and guide the discussion in order to attempt to resolve the conflict. The facilitator is not the decision maker, which is a key difference from decision-making processes in which the leader may attempt to facilitate discussion but nevertheless does not distance himself from his power. The facilitator has no more authority than anyone else. As the discussion develops, the facilitator continues to articulate the viewpoints as they come closer and closer to consensus. In the 21st century, large Quaker meetings are actually intentionally slowed down in order to moderate the tone of discussion. Volunteer runners bring wireless microphones to speakers waiting for their turn, and are asked to walk at a casual pace as an opportunity to slow the discussion.

Quality management

Quality management is the process of ensuring that an organization or the products and services it provides are consistent, and consists of both quality assurance and quality control, as well as planning elements and strategies for improvement.

Quality storyboard

A tool for quality management, a quality storyboard is a visual way to present a narrative about the quality control process.

Queen bee syndrome

Queen bee syndrome is a phenomenon wherein a female leader is more critical of her female subordinates than of males. Repeatedly found in the workplace since its coinage in 1973 by

Graham Staines, Toby Jayaratne, and Carol Tavris, queen bee syndrome has been observed and studied in high school and junior high in recent years, in response to an overall call in psychology and sociology to examine the problem of adolescent bullying. In the business world, queen bees tend to be older and politically conservative.

"Quest for causality"

James MacGregor Burns' evocative description of leadership studies. A Pulitzer Prize winner for his biography of Franklin Delano Roosevelt, Burns wrote one of the early major works in the field with his 1978 *Leadership*, which explored leadership from a historian's perspective, as the process of governance over social change. In investigating change, the work of the traditional historian is to determine cause. Burns thus saw leadership studies as a form of historical analysis.

Qui facet per alium facit per se

"He who acts through another does the act himself," says the Latin legal term, which assigns responsibility to an employer for the actions he hires an employee to do.

RAND Corporation

The RAND (Research ANd Development) Corporation is a non-profit policy think tank based in Santa Monica, California, and financed by a combination of private and public funding. Originally spun out of the Air Force in the early days of the Cold War to develop new weapons, it became famous for developing the doctrine of mutually assured destruction, and although about half of its work involved national security issues, it has expanded to include transportation policy, social welfare, and other areas. Its RAND Health Insurance Experiment was one of the largest health insurance studies. The RAND Corporation operates a small graduate school, the Frederick S. Pardee RAND Graduate School, for about 100 students seeking master's or doctorate degrees in policy analysis. Most classes are taught by RAND researchers, and include topics like economics, political science, arms control, criminology, and national security.

Random choice

A random choice is one that is arrived at without recourse to preference or reasons. Ideally, all possibilities are given an equal probability of selection. Random choice has sometimes been suggested as the best means to make certain decisions, including leader selection. The military draft, for instance, is considered most fair when it is random. Many augury techniques in the ancient world amount to random choice, and their popularity has been read by some anthropologists as indicating that, in the absence of the ability to determine the right choice based on evidence, a random choice may have a greater chance of being successful than a choice based on incomplete evidence or a faulty understanding. The random selection of public officials and other leaders is called sortition.

Ratchet effect

In sociology, the ratchet effect is the difficulty of reversing an activity or backtracking once a certain event has happened, thus "locking in place" a pattern or expectation. In business, this often refers to the effect on the expectations of higher-ups of a team achieving a performance benchmark; if the benchmark is exceeded, frequently this then becomes the minimum level expected for the next period's performance, which motivates managers to avoid exceeding target performance levels for fear of being "locked in" and committed to continually achieving that level.

Rational choice theory

Rational choice theory, sometimes just called choice theory, is used in the social sciences and economics as the framework for modeling human behavior. Originally used principally to model economic behavior, it has become much more widely used since the 1980s, in part due to Gary Becker's applications of rational choice theory to drug addiction, racial discrimination, crime, and family organization.

Rational-legal authority

Rational-legal authority is a concept from sociologist Max Weber's work on political leadership, and refers to political authority that is derived from and legitimized by a system of underlying laws. Further, the government has a monopoly on the enactment and enforcement of laws and on the use of physical force. The modern state as a rational-legal authority is almost universal now, but it emerged in the West from feudalism.

Reactivity

Reactivity is the change in behavior that an individual makes as the result of being observed. While important in psychological experiments, because the behavior of an individual knowingly participating in an experiment (as ethics regulations require) will not be exactly the same as in the real world, reactivity is important in management and leadership as well, in predicting and managing follower behavior.

Realism

In international relations, realism is a school of thought that developed in the early 20th century, building on the work of Niccolo Machiavelli and Thomas Hobbes. The realist view is predicated on four assumptions: the international system is anarchic, meaning that there is no entity above states that can govern them, and a state of constant antagonism prevails; states are the most important actors in the international system; all states are unitary and rational, meaning that they seek to attain resources and pursue self-interest; the primary concern of every state is survival. Realists, in contrast with earlier ideologies, see humans as inherently competitive and self-interested, and state behavior as growing from those influences.

Reference class forecasting

Reference class forecasting (RCF) plans for the future with reference to the outcome of past situations. It is a method developed by psychologists Daniel Kahneman and Amos Tversky, the former of whom was awarded the Nobel Prize in Economics in part for his contributions to the theory. RCF is intended to correct for the effects of cognitive biases like overconfidence, by forecasting the future of an outcome of an event through a three-part process consisting of identifying the reference class of the project and past projects included in that class; establishing a probability distribution for the reference class; and comparing the future project to the reference class distribution in order to forecast the outcome.

Referent authority

Referent authority is authority enjoyed by a leader as a result of charm, personality, and an ability to influence others and command respect.

Referent power

Referent power is one of John R. P. French and Bertram Raven's bases of power, and one of Patrick J. Montana and Bruce H. Charnov's varieties of organizational power. It originates as a result of the group or organizational affiliations of the individual. This power may be either positive or negative. For instance, there was a time in the 1920s when membership in the second incarnation of the Ku Klux Klan conferred greater social influence—power—within the community, whereas by the end of that century, David Duke's association with the Klan put a well-defined ceiling on his political aspirations.

Reinvent the wheel

To reinvent the wheel is to sink energy and resources into the development of something that simply duplicates the functionality of something that already exists, and especially something that is already optimized. The phrase is used in a number of contexts, the most important of which refer not to a company's product line but to their internal processes and procedures, and the danger of creating a new procedure simply for the novelty of it, when an optimized procedure already exists.

Relational leadership

In Wilfred Drath's coinage, relational leadership is a study of leadership that goes beyond consideration of the traits and characteristics of individual leaders in order to take into account the whole context in which leadership occurs, and the network of relationships leaders are surrounded by.

Relational transparency

One of the qualities of authentic leadership (cf.), relational transparency refers to the leader's openness about his thoughts, beliefs, and feelings, without overstepping into matters that would be inappropriate or unprofessional.

Relationship-oriented leadership

Relationship-oriented leadership is a leadership approach that focuses on team members, especially keeping them motivated, matching them to the best role, and keeping communication open. Relationship-oriented leaders support, mentor, and develop their workers, encourage collaboration, and may be proactive in seeking resolutions to conflicts among team members. The terms *employee-oriented leadership* (or employee-oriented management) and *people-oriented leadership* are also used. Relationship-oriented leadership is sometimes contrasted with task-oriented leadership, and studies of their relative effectiveness led to the formulation of situational leadership theory.

Relevance paradox

In a relevance paradox, an attempt to gather information for a decision-making process fails when the set of information that is eliminated because of its irrelevance actually includes critical information. This is a typical problem in identifying which information is necessary to a decision-making process or discussion, because the relevance of information is not always clear until the full circumstances of the situation are clear, and the full circumstances are revealed only by assembling all relevant information. The "Seattle way," the political procedure generally followed in Seattle and King County, Washington, is often criticized as being slow moving and circular, but one of the strengths of the tortoise-like pace of its deliberations is that it can avoid this pitfall. Discussions of the relevance paradox can often sound like a jumble of double-speak, as with Secretary of Defense Donald Rumsfeld's 2002 statement in a news briefing that there are "known unknowns; that is to say we know there are some things we do not know. But there are also unknown unknowns, the ones we don't know we don't know."

Terrorist attacks like those that took place in New York at the World Trade Center on September 11, 2001, have made organizational resilience increasingly more valued. (Flickr)

Reputation management

In public relations, reputation management is the conscious oversight of a person or organization's reputation, and the actions taken to influence that reputation. In the 21st century, this has become particularly associated with overseeing the online presence of search engine results associated with the subject, and attempts to manipulate those results. Reputation management is an extension of personal branding.

Resilience

Resilience in an organization is the ability to anticipate and adapt to disruption. Resilience is necessary to the organization's creation of long-term value. In the 21st century, organizational resilience has become increasingly valued, in part due to the threat of terrorist attacks made more palpable by the 9/11 attacks and the impact of several highly publicized natural disasters and the ongoing effects of climate change.

Respondeat superior

"Let the master answer," in legal Latin. A legal doctrine of responsibility, also called the master-servant rule and applicable not only in the Anglo-American common law tradition but encoded as civil law in many states. The doctrine assigns responsibility to an employer for the actions employees commit in the course of their employment, with a few exceptions.

Responsible autonomy

Responsible autonomy is one of the major ways to structure an organization, in which the units making up an organization—either individual members or small groups—are given autonomy in their choices and activities, while bearing responsibility for the outcome of those actions. This is the common form of organization in research institutes, for instance, as well as many think tanks, investment funds, and the Sudbury schools (as well as some alternative colleges).

Reward authority

Reward authority is authority enjoyed by a leader because of their use of positive reinforcement and the rewards they offer their followers for performance.

Reward dependence

Reward dependence is a personality trait, which tends to remain a constant throughout a person's life, characterized by having a strong response to signaled rewards such as compliments and social approval, and the tendency to adjust one's behavior in order to continue receiving those rewards. Reward dependence involves, but is not synonymous with, dependence on the approval of others, and is substantially correlated with extraversion. It is believed that reward dependence may be implicated in some addictive behaviors, in which the addictive substance is a substitute for the approval of family or peers.

Reward power

Reward power is one of John R. P. French and Bertram Raven's bases of power, and one of Patrick J. Montana and Bruce H. Charnov's varieties of organizational power. Reward, despite the name, includes both positive and negative incentives. A teenager given use of the car for a weekend trip as a reward for making the honor roll is a positive example of reward power, but grounding that teenager for crashing the car is still reward power, using negative incentive. Reward power uses the agent of influence's ability to give or take tangible or emotional rewards.

Right-wing authoritarianism

In personality psychology, right-wing authoritarianism (RWA) is willingness to submit to legitimate authority, whether in the form of individual authority figures issuing orders or adherence to social norms and conventions. People with a high degree of RWA are, furthermore, hostile to those who deviate from these norms or make trouble by resisting authority. People with a high degree of RWA may also have trouble accepting as legitimate the leadership of leaders who are not, themselves, sufficiently authoritarian, or may shift their allegiance to other elements in the leadership hierarchy—as with the attitude toward the Democratic President Barack Obama on the part of many right-wing authoritarians who treated him as a threat to social conventions and pledged their commitment to the Republican elements in Congress instead. That said, despite the use of "right-wing" in this term, RWA is not itself a politically partisan trait, nor one found either exclusively in political conservatives or universally in political conservatives, though the Canadian psychologist who first identified it believed it was more likely to be found in American Republicans and Canadian Conservatives.

Ringelmann effect

The Ringelmann effect is named for French agricultural engineer Maxmilien Ringelmann, who found that individual group members become less productive as the size of the group increases. There are two main causes of the Ringelmann effect: larger groups are harder to coordinate, and so the organization of the group and its division of labor becomes less efficient; and motivation decreases, often unconsciously. Because much of the Ringelmann effect is unconscious, group members do not always accurately self-report productivity and may not be aware of the effect.

Risk management

Risk management is the handling of risk, through the perception and assessment of risks in a situation and their prioritization, followed by the actions necessary to monitor such risks, mitigate their effects, or minimize their occurrence. Risks range from the possibility of a debtor not making good on their debt to a natural disaster, and everything in between. In business, risk management especially involves those related to any aspect of the business plan not playing out in the expected manner, from higher costs being incurred to profits not reaching their necessary threshold.

Risk perception

Risk perception is an individual's capacity to recognize the presence, nature, and severity of risk. Theories about how risk perception develops come from both psychology and sociology, with some focusing on the mechanics of the mind and others on the influence of culture on risk heuristics. Risk perception is key in understanding decision making, since so many decisions involve some amount of risk.

Robert's Rules of Order

A book of rules of order to be used by organizations following parliamentary procedures, Brigadier General Henry Martyn *Robert's Rules of Order* is the most commonly used such guide in the United States. First published in 1876, it has been reissued continuously, the most recent (11th) edition dating from 2011. Based on procedures used in Congress in the 19th century, it is nevertheless not intended for use by legislative assemblies but rather assemblies ranging from church meetings to town zoning committees to groups in the corporate world.

Role congruity theory

Role congruity theory says that the degree to which members of a group are perceived positively accords to the degree to which they fit the social roles associated with that group. The typical examples given in role congruity theory are gender roles—role congruity theory originated as a model explaining prejudicial treatment of female leaders, because traits associated with stereotypical female gender roles (helpfulness, empathy) are at odds with stereotypical leadership traits (competitiveness, assertiveness, authoritativeness). Work has also been done to demonstrate the relevance of role congruity theory to race.

Role culture

One of four types of corporate culture identified by Charles Handy and Roger Harrison. In a role culture, the bureaucracy is elaborate and individual roles and their relationships to each other are well-defined. Established procedures guide activity more than the personalities of leaders do.

Role engulfment

Role engulfment is a phenomenon whereby an individual's identity becomes subjugated by a specific role or trait that the individual has made preeminent in his self-image, such as "parent," "depressed," or "class clown." Role engulfment can impact work experiences in numerous ways, among them the possibility that an employee's self-image is too tied up in a specific work role, making them resist change.

Romance of leadership

Social constructionist leadership scholar James R. Meindl introduced the concept of the "romance of leadership" in 1995. The romance of leadership theory suggests that leadership is given too much credit for the outcome of group actions—that because we are, as a culture or a species, enamored of the phenomenon of leadership, we are too inclined to use leadership to explain both positive and negative outcomes. Similarly, this view finds that examinations of leaders are often too interested in personality traits, attributing "leaderness" to traits that have nothing to do with the role.

Roosevelt, Franklin D., as leader

Franklin Delano Roosevelt was elected president of the United Sates in 1932 after the failure of Herbert Hoover to adequately respond to the Great Depression of 1929, and was reelected three times, serving a total of 12 years until his death in 1945. One of the foremost leaders in world affairs in the middle of the century, he was as significant a president for his foreign policy—leading the nation into World War II and overseeing all but its final months—as for his domestic policy, which reshaped the structure of the federal government and its relationship to the people. FDR was best known for his "New Deal" programs, which not only provided relief for the Great Depression but sought to create a system that would lessen the effects of income inequality and break the boom-and-bust cycle that had dominated the American economy for over a century. His programs were successful, but his critics called him both a fascist and a communist. Further, his tactics in retaining power were questioned even by his allies. His own vice president, "Cactus Jack" Garner, opposed his efforts in 1937 to increase the size of the Supreme Court in order to add more Roosevelt allies to the bench, and many considered his pursuit of a third and fourth term—however successful—to be unseemly in light of George Washington's self-imposed two-term limit.

Root cause analysis
Root cause analysis is a problem-solving approach that seeks out the root causes of problems rather than focusing on causal factors that are implicated in but not necessary to the problem's occurrence.

Rost, Joseph
Joseph Rost was a professor of leadership studies at the University of San Diego from 1976 to 1996, a founder of its Institute for the Advancement of Leadership, and a posthumous recipient of the International Leadership Association's 2008 Lifetime Achievement Award. In his seminal 1991 work *Leadership for the 21st Century*, he was one of the first to emphasize the multidisciplinary nature of leadership studies. In that work he also proposed settling on a definition of "leader" that would be used by the whole of the community, arguing that this was necessary for the leadership studies field to progress.

Rotation method
The rotation method is a concept from philosopher Soren Kierkegaard's *Either/Or*, his debut book which focused on aesthetic and ethical thinking. Analogous to the crop rotation practice in agriculture, the rotation method is the constant change from one activity or interest to another, used by aesthetes to avoid boredom. The mental anguish of boredom in performing repetitious tasks is one of the themes of Kierkegaard's work.

Rutgers University School of Public Affairs and Administration
The Rutgers University School of Public Affairs and Administration is one of the top programs in the country in public management, and offers both bachelor's and graduate degrees. The school focuses on best practices in public management, accountability, and transparency, and was one of the first to offer an undergraduate minor in public service.

Sabotage
Sabotage is an action taken to disrupt or weaken an organization or its projects. Labor unions have used workplace sabotage as a means of taking direct action against intolerable working conditions, the most common forms of which are the labor strike and the slowdown, though the sick-out (essentially a one-day strike) is common as well. All these methods purposefully reduce productivity, and have been adopted by non-union groups of workers as well.

Sage kings
The sage kings, or five emperors, were mythological or semi-mythological leaders of ancient China in the 3rd millennium B.C.E. who were exemplars of moral leadership. Not every source agrees about which five emperors are included among the sage kings—often grouped with the "three sovereigns," rulers like the Yellow Emperor who possessed divine powers that

aided in their rule—but they were used as a reference point in Chinese philosophy, a standard against which later rulers were measured.

Salesman

The 1969 documentary *Salesman*, directed by Albert and David Maysles and Charlotte Zwerin, follows four salesmen in New England and Florida as they try to sell Bibles door-to-door in low-income neighborhoods. The film was inspired by Truman Capote's *In Cold Blood*—not its subject matter, but rather Capote's description of it as a nonfiction novel. *Salesman*, similarly, is a documentary constructed as a narrative. One of the most critically acclaimed movies of the year, and later released as part of the Criterion Collection, it was both an important social document and an intimate look at the mood, personality, and business of sales, the pursuit of which had become so important in American capitalism.

Sarbanes-Oxley Act of 2002

Sarbanes-Oxley is an American federal law named for Senator Paul Sarbanes and Representative Michael G. Oxley. In response to significant corporate and accounting scandals in the preceding years, sufficient to injure public confidence in the securities markets and cost investors billions of dollars, the act strengthened corporate board responsibilities, increased transparency and disclosure requirements, created the quasi-public Public Company Accounting Oversight Board, and created new criminal penalties for various actions associated with corporate fraud. The act passed with almost unanimous support in both houses, though it has since faced criticism by far-right Republicans, several of whom continued to oppose it after the 2008 financial crisis, arguing that Sarbanes-Oxley slowed recovery.

Satisficing

Political theorist and economist Herbert Simon introduced the term *satisficing* as a portmanteau of "satisfy" and "suffice." Satisficing is a decision-making approach that, instead of seeking the best possible outcome, explores options until the first reasonably acceptable outcome is found. This is best understood not as an alternative to seeking the best possible outcome but a description of behavior in circumstances where the choice leading to the best possible outcome cannot be determined. Simon was one of the first to describe the behavior of businesses in terms of the behavior of individuals, and in doing so, pointed out that that behavior is constrained by human limitations; individuals are not machines that sort through options and possibilities until the optimal route is determined. Satisficing is important both in understanding others' behavior and in evaluating decision-making processes when leading a group.

Savanna principle

Originally proposed by Satoshi Kanazawa, the savanna principle is a concept from evolutionary psychology that calls for understanding the development of the human brain, and the fundamentals of human psychology, in the context of its development as an optimal adaptation for a specific environment: the African savanna the human race once called home. The savanna principle presumes that there has been no significant evolutionary development of the brain in the last 10,000 years or more, which not all biologists accept.

Scenario planning

Scenario planning is a technique used in long-term planning, by developing possible future scenarios an organization may face and planning an appropriate response to them.

Originally part of the simulation games used by military intelligence and public policy makers, the private sector has adopted scenario planning as well. Royal Dutch Shell, for instance, engaged in scenario planning after the energy crisis of the 1970s.

Schema

In psychology and related fields, a schema is a mental framework organizing pieces or groups of information and the relationships between them. A given social role like "father" involves a schema, for instance, as does a stereotype about a given thing—neither is a single piece or list of information, but a structure consisting of multiple pieces of interrelated information.

Scientific management

Scientific management was developed in the late 19th century when Frederick Winslow Taylor studied the work being done in factories with the aim of improving their productivity by eliminating unnecessary elements of processes and allocating labor for maximum efficiency. Scientific management's heyday came in the 1910s as factory output increased, standardized parts became available in almost every industry, and Henry Ford began his assembly line. Scientific management was a response both to the new labor conditions of the Industrial Revolution and the birth of the social sciences, and was one of many instances in a larger turn of the century phenomenon of applying scientific thinking and methodologies to reorganizing various aspects of human life.

Scope creep

When a project is poorly defined, scope creep can result, as the scope of the project continually expands or changes.

Seagull management

A management style in which managers communicate with lower-level employees only in response to their perception that a problem has arisen, and especially one in which managers respond to problems hastily and impulsively, lacking the context to make an informed decision.

Secession

Secession is the act of withdrawing from a group entity, especially a political union (withdrawing from a treaty organization like the World Trade Organization is rarely expressed as a secession in English). Because secession involves repudiating the authority of the state, there has been debate over whether there is a right to secession, either inherent or in specific political circumstances. There remains disagreement, for instance, over whether the Confederate states had the right to secede from the United States—which is a question independent of the merits of their rationale for doing so. Certain formulations of the consent of the governed imply a right to secession, based on the idea that membership in the political union is voluntary and the product of continued consent. The pragmatics of secession raise other questions, when those who wish to secede do not own or otherwise control contiguous territory: though a right to secession would imply otherwise, in practical terms the secession of 5 percent of the voters in each state is less plausible and perhaps less defensible than the secession of all the residents of a single state.

Second-term curse

"Second-term curse" refers to a tendency of second presidential terms to be less successful than the first, and especially for them to suffer from failures that cannot simply be ascribed to the fact that the incumbent does not need to worry about reelection. Nate Silver, the statistician behind FiveThirtyEight.com, has confirmed that approval ratings are lower in second terms. Classic examples include presidents who faced scandals about their own conduct—Nixon, Reagan, and Clinton—as well as those who oversaw unpopular or failed wars, like Truman and Johnson. Franklin D. Roosevelt's second term began with his failed "court-packing plan," though he recovered and was re-elected to third and fourth terms.

Second-wave feminism

While first-wave feminism, as it is now called, focused on obtaining basic rights for women, second-wave feminism, beginning in the 1960s in the United States, broadened its focus to include legal challenges like the laws surrounding spousal rape, cultural challenges with the treatment and portrayal of women, reproductive rights, and the same de facto inequalities faced by racial minorities. It ended in the early 1980s after the ratification deadline for the Equal Rights Amendment, making equal rights for women a Constitutional requirement,

A 1970 Women's Liberation March protest in Washington, D.C. Second-wave feminism continued until the passage of the Equal Rights Amendment in the early 1980s. (Wikimeida Commons/ Warren K. Leffler)

passed without successful ratification. Second-wave feminism was the first movement to address the role of women in the workplace, the fight for equal pay, and the need for women to have equal access to leadership roles as men do, a fight that continues in the 21st century.

Security dilemma

An important concept in international relations especially during the Cold War, the security dilemma is a phenomenon whereby one state takes actions intended to increase its security, resulting in other states taking similar measures. This is the basic foundation of defensive realism, and is a popular theory with scholars who see war as resulting from communication problems.

Self-awareness

Self-awareness is one of numerous concepts dealing with the self and personal identity, consisting of the capacity to identify one's consciousness with one's body (a capacity that may be lacking in some animals with no sense of self, for instance), distinct from other individuals: a being possessing one's thoughts, emotions, and memories, and directing one's actions. Self-awareness is a function or prerequisite of intelligence, at least as we usually conceive it, and while in biology it is treated largely as a binary (an animal is or is not self-aware), in psychology we may speak of degrees of self-awareness, such that one individual is more self-aware than another if he is possessed of an accurate sense of his abilities, competencies, and knowledge.

Self-concept

Self-concept is similar to the more familiar idea of self-image, but where self-image might be conceived of as a photograph (or "selfie"), self-concept is a portfolio, consisting of a system of beliefs about oneself, including identity traits like ethnic and sexual identity, social role information such as that related to gender, age, class, or employment, as well as knowledge, skills, and competencies.

Self-conscious emotions

Self-conscious emotions are those that are triggered by other people's reactions, or projections and fantasizing about those reactions, and include both positive emotions like pride and negative emotions like embarrassment, envy, shame, and guilt. The negative self-conscious emotions especially can play a restrictive role in people's participation in social settings and decision-making processes, discouraging them from showing dissent, contributing novel ideas, or sharing relevant information.

Self-consciousness

Self-consciousness is preoccupying self-awareness, especially in response to observation or a feeling of being observed. It is associated with unpleasant feelings arising in conjunction with a hyperawareness of one's appearance to others.

Self-determination theory

A theory of human personality and motivation, self-determination theory focuses on the individual's psychological needs and the extent to which the individual's behavior is driven by intrinsic or extrinsic motivations. Key to self-determination theory is the idea of the internalization of a motive: the attempt to take an extrinsic motivating factor like a reward or external pressures and internalize it, turning it into an internal motivation by adjusting personal values. Self-determination theory also categorizes goals according to whether they are intrinsic (furthering personal development) or extrinsic (attaining externally

provided rewards like wealth or the attention of the opposite sex).

Self-efficacy

Self-efficacy is one's belief in one's skills, capacities, and ability to achieve goals.

Self-esteem

Self-esteem is similar to self-concept or self-image but consists of the evaluation of the self rather than specific information about the perceived self. While a self-evaluation involves the individual's feelings about their traits, behavior, performance, or abilities in specifically defined areas, self-esteem is the individual's overall feelings about themselves, including basic statements ("I am a good person"; "I am weak-willed") and positive or negative emotions like pride or shame. Self-esteem is important in psychology and management due to its implication in well-being and emotional health, its impact on things like employee engagement and assertiveness, and its presence on Maslow's hierarchy of needs. Many leadership studies scholars believe that effective leaders have strong self-esteem.

Self-evaluation maintenance theory

Self-evaluation maintenance theory is a psychological theory of interpersonal relationships. It posits that two people who know each other will each attempt to make themselves feel good through comparison to the other person. Some people, as a result, deliberately surround themselves with less intelligent, attractive, or successful people, which keeps their self-evaluation positive. Others seek out people who approximate their own capabilities in order to constantly challenge themselves to improve. One of the suppositions of self-evaluation maintenance theory is that people are more threatened by the success of friends than that of strangers.

Self-image

Self-image is an individual's mental picture of himself. Though not limited to a single picture, it represents more limited information than the self-concept, and includes information both about how the individual sees himself and how he believes he is perceived by others.

Self-management

Self-management or labor management is the management of an organization by its workers, which has been advocated by many socialists. This may take the form of direct democracy via meetings of workers to make decisions, or the election of managers in a form of representative democracy. In either case, workers retain a high degree of autonomy in the performance of their job roles. The goal is to eliminate the exploitation of labor. For instance, self-managed farms flourished during the Great Depression to the point that half of American farmers worked for a self-managed farm (often now called a "co-op"). The rise of industrial agriculture after World War II changed this, though self-managed farms did not entirely disappear.

Self-monitoring

In psychology, self-monitoring is a behavior related to impression management and dramaturgy, consisting of paying close attention to one's self-presentation in terms of how others are likely to perceive it and making adjustments as appropriate. People with low self-monitoring activity tend to dislike the idea of playing a role or of presenting an outward self that contrasts with their self-image, while people with high self-monitoring activity tend to be more concerned with manners, etiquette, social conventions, and other artificial constructs governing social interactions. Low self-monitors may also have difficulty compromising or experiencing empathy for others. Self-monitoring is important in organizational psychology and the sociology of work, because of the necessity in many workplaces to adapt to social circumstances and modulate one's expression of inward feelings.

Self-perception theory

Psychologist Daryl Bem's self-perception theory is a model of attitude formation in which, in cases where there is no relevant previous experience leading to the development of an attitude, people develop attitudes by monitoring their own behaviors and deriving the attitudes they believe to be the cause of those behaviors.

Semmelweis effect

The Semmelweis effect is the phenomenon in which new evidence is rejected because it contradicts an established paradigm or way of doing things. It was coined in the 20th century in reference to Ignaz Semmelweis, the doctor who discovered that childbed fever mortality rates could be decimated if doctors would wash their hands with an antiseptic solution but who was unable to convince his colleagues to follow his recommendations (often because the suggestion that a doctor's hands could be the source of contamination was seen as crass).

Sensation seeking

The personality trait of sensation seeking leads the individual to seek out experiences and sensations and to be open to risk-taking behaviors in search thereof, though risk-taking is not necessary for satisfying the itch. Sensation seekers may gravitate toward thrill-seeking like skydiving and scuba diving may seek new sensory experiences through drug use, meditation or mysticism, or various arts, or may be drawn to disinhibiting environments where heavy drinking or unrestricted sex are the norm. Sensation seekers tend to be easily bored and restless.

Serious games

Serious games are simply those that are designed and played for a purpose other than play, or which incorporate play as a learning tool. Many simulation games are employed as serious games, and the military has a long history of using war games to teach strategy.

Servant leadership

Servant leadership is an approach to leadership that puts the needs of others first and shares power rather than wielding it from the top of a hierarchy. The term was coined by management theorist Robert Greenleaf in his 1970 essay "The Servant as Leader," having founded the Center for Applied Ethics in 1964 (since renamed the Greenleaf Center for Servant Leadership) to develop his leadership theories. Servant leadership has ancient roots, especially in the *Tao te Ching*, and Greenleaf's articulation of the theory was inspired in part by his reading Herman Hesse's 1932 novel *Journey to the East*, in which the servant of a religious sect that includes a range of figures from Pythagoras and Mozart to Tristram Shandy and Puss in Boots is revealed to be the sect's leader. Greenleaf's prescription is for leaders to similarly view themselves as servants first, working to realize the goals of their followers, which involves participation by followers in goal-setting and decision-making processes, as well as open communication. Greenleaf's work lists 10 characteristics of servant leaders: listening, empathy, healing, awareness, persuasion, conceptualization, foresight,

stewardship, commitment to the growth of others, and building community. The idea of servant leadership has since been further explored by others, including Kent Keith, James Sipe, and Don Frick.

Service learning

A presentational mode of liberal arts education in which students are engaged in community service as part of their learning experience. Service learning prioritizes both personal reflection and community investment, and may be part of a program or course within a college curriculum or built into the institution's approach and expectations. Hampshire College, for instance, has a service learning component in the form of its Third World Expectation, which requires students to engage in a substantial project or program benefiting the third world, whether abroad or in the United States (traditionally through direct action, not simply fund-raising or raising awareness).

The Seven Habits of Highly Effective People

One of the most successful management or self-help books, Stephen Covey's *Seven Habits of Highly Effective People* was published in 1989. The seven habits Covey explores are proactivity, beginning with the end in mind, putting first things first, thinking "win-win," empathic listening, synergy, and spiritual renewal. The book also contrasts "abundance mentality," the belief that there is enough success to go around, with "scarcity mentality," which leads to competition for perceived scarce resources.

Shared information bias

Shared information bias is a cognitive bias that affects group decision making. It is the tendency of groups to spend most of their time, or a disproportionate amount of time, reviewing and discussing the information that every member of the group is already familiar with, rather than bringing members up to speed on information known to only some members. This does not have to result from the desire to actually hide that information from the other members, it simply has that effect. When the unshared information would lead the group to making a different, and more optimal, decision, the phenomenon is also known as hidden profiles. One of the reasons information remains unshared is because groups are often more motivated to reach a consensus than to make the best decision, and this can simply be more easily accomplished by focusing on information known to all. Further, because unnecessary time is spent reviewing shared information, a member with information that is new to the others may feel that sharing it would be a time burden, or would make them uncomfortable by putting them in the position of disagreeing, or seeming to disagree, with the proto-consensus.

Shunning
Shunning is an act of social rejection by a group, consisting of the group members avoiding contact or association with the shunned individual. Used as a formal punishment in some legal systems and religious groups, it is used by informal social groups to inflict shame on the subject, especially for transgressing some social norm.

Shyness
Shyness is characterized by mildly unpleasant feelings like fidgetiness, awkwardness, or nervousness when interacting with, in proximity to, or being observed by other people; in some shy people, this is more pronounced when the other people are strangers. Shyness is often associated with low self-esteem or social inexperience, and is not the same as introversion: while some introverts may be shy, preferring limited social activity does not always mean being uncomfortable with social activity. Stronger forms of shyness constitute social anxiety. While on the surface, shyness seems like a hurdle for a leader to overcome, some people feel shy only in regard to one-on-one or unstructured social interaction and are more adept at impersonal contexts like public speaking or addressing a group from the comfort of a defined social role. Such shy leaders, however, would have difficulty being authentic leaders (cf.).

Simon, Herbert A.
Twentieth-century economist and political scientist Herbert A. Simon was a major contributor to the behavioral theory of the firm in the 1950s. Simon's work examined the behavior of decision makers within companies in uncertain situations, in which bounded rationality resulted in their "satisficing": aiming for realistic goals rather than maximized profit or utility. Prior to the behavioral theory of the firm, the theory of the firm treated companies as monoliths, without considering the behaviors of individual employees and leaders, or their conflicts and incomplete information access.

Simulation theory of empathy
The simulation theory of empathy is a theory in the philosophy of mind, stating that empathy works through the mirror neuron system by setting up mental processes that mirror the behavior of others to make sense of that behavior.

Situated cognition
In psychology, the theory of situated cognition says that knowing exists in situ—"in position" or "locally"—with doing, and that all knowledge has a context that includes activity, culture, language, and social elements.

Situational leadership theory

Situational leadership theory (SLT), originally called the Life Cycle Theory of Leadership, was developed by professor Paul Hersey and leadership guru Ken Blanchard in the 1970s. SLT is based on the idea that there is no one-size-fits-all approach to leadership, but rather that successful leaders are flexible and adapt their style to suit the situation. By the 1990s, SLT was wildly successful in the leadership training world, and had been adopted by most Fortune 500 companies. Little research affirmed the specific claims made in SLT literature, however, which sorted leadership styles into four types of behavior (telling, selling, participating, and delegating) and follower groups into four levels of maturity (representing their experience, skill level, and willingness to take responsibility).

Smith, Adam

Scottish philosopher Adam Smith was one of the central figures of the Enlightenment period, and his 1776 work *An Inquiry Into the Nature and Causes of the Wealth of Nations* is the first modern study of economics, introducing ideas of free market capitalism still influential today. One of Smith's key concepts was that of rational self-interest—the idea that well-informed economic actors in an unregulated market will take actions that, though motivated by self-interest, will benefit the economy as a whole. His view of management was simple and taken up by the Industrial Revolution: management should maximize productivity.

Social anxiety

Social anxiety is a very common state of discomfort felt by individuals during social interactions or at the prospect of social interactions, especially when encountering circumstances that are emotionally charged or unfamiliar. These feelings may be motivated or exacerbated by uncertainty about norms or how one's behavior will be received, or may be felt as a sense of being overwhelmed by social inputs. Social anxiety is a normal phenomenon in childhood and adolescence as part of social and emotional development, and is felt by most adults at some point in their lives. Very specific social anxiety, revolving around formal presentations or performances in front of others, is typically referred to as stage fright, while low-level social anxiety focused on interaction with strangers is often considered mere shyness, but about one-sixth of American adults suffer from an anxiety disorder, in which anxiety is chronic and impacts quality of life, as well as social skills and abilities. Anxiety is also one of the disorders most frequently treated with medication, which has become increasingly common and complex since the heyday of Quaaludes in the 1970s.

Social cognition

In psychology and cognitive science, social cognition refers to a group of social abilities involving cognition processes—the storage, retrieval, and processing of information by the brain. Such processes involve the use of schemas to organize information, and as a result, new information is handled in light of how easily it is integrated into existing schemas (it is generally thought that the more detailed a schema is, the harder it is to process information that contrasts with it). Someone who has unexamined biases about race or ethnicity may have mild difficulty absorbing information conflicting with the stereotypical views they hold; someone who is an active member of a racist organization, who devotes time and thought to propagating racist views, will face much greater difficulty. Culture, social environment, and personal experiences all impact the schema we develop. For instance, staying on the theme of stereotypes, Americans tend to have fewer schema dealing with members of Eastern religions than they do with members of Abrahamic religions, due in part to lack of frequent contact and in part due to lack of representation in the media.

Social cognitive theory

In psychology and education, social cognitive theory is the theory that some amount of a person's knowledge acquisition occurs during social interactions and the observation of others (including via media), and that a key element of knowledge acquisition has always involved replicating observed actions and behaviors rather than simple trial and error. This idea is important not simply in studying how people learn but how social norms are formed, how behaviors can be "contagious," how morality develops, and the influence of culture on the individual.

Social compensation

Social compensation is the tendency of individuals working in a group to work harder than they would if they were working alone.

Social competence

Social competence represents an individual's collection of skills and motivations that contribute to success in the social sphere. These include social and communication skills, as well as self-efficacy, cognitive skills, emotional intelligence and empathy, and many others.

Social desirability bias

Social desirability bias is the tendency of individuals in a survey or other setting to offer answers that they believe will be viewed favorably, even in circumstances where there is "no wrong answer," or responses are anonymous and the individual will be shielded from the consequences of their answers. This is especially a concern in social psychology studies of embarrassing, criminal, or unethical behavior, from sexual infidelity to drug use, and the manner in which the bias affects reporting is not always consistent: for instance, some people may underreport their past recreational drug use, while others who have not experimented with drugs may report having done so for fear of seeming prudish. Further, in the workplace, the bias can make it difficult for management or third parties to obtain an accurate picture of employee attitudes.

Social emotions

Social emotions are an area of study in behavioral neuroscience, the rise of functional imaging allowing a greater neurological investigation into the role of emotions in decision making. Social emotions are those that require the presence or imagined representation of other people. While sadness requires only a knowledge of one's own state, for instance, pride, embarrassment, guilt, and envy all require the knowledge of another person's state of mind. Social emotions develop later than the more basic emotions, with young children having difficulty understanding (and perhaps feeling) them. Social emotions develop as our social skills and awareness of other people do; our ability to feel embarrassed is in a sense an unfortunate side effect of our ability to empathize.

Social engineering

Social engineering is the attempt to influence social behaviors on a large scale, through scientific methods. Advertising and marketing are essentially profit-motivated social engineering, and when the term is used derogatorily, it is often in that context. However, the term also refers to the processes behind many public service announcements (PSAs) and public health campaigns, including campaigns against suicide, domestic violence, and rape. True social engineering involves more than just a public service announcement against littering; its techniques are backed by statistical analyses, and its aims focused on the areas where the most good can be done. In the 21st century, grassroots campaigns have engaged in social engineering via social media, in the form of propagated memes and Twitter hashtags.

Social entrepreneurship

Social entrepreneurship is entrepreneurship over a venture that seeks to solve some social problem or provide value to society. While this often transpires in the non-profit sector, it need not be limited to that, and there has been a rise of socially conscious businesses, from microfinance lending institutions to fair trade coffee microroasters.

Social exchange theory

Social exchange theory is a theory in sociology and psychology that views social behavior as resulting from an exchange process developed out of a cost-benefit analysis that individuals conduct in order to determine the risks and benefits of any given social relationship. Although the theory presupposes that most of this analysis is conducted unconsciously, it is also implicitly acknowledged in pop culture, from magazine quizzes on knowing when to break up with a romantic partner to sitcom characters who make pros-and-cons lists about potential girlfriends. Social exchange theory posits that this calculus occurs not just for romantic relationships, but friendships and professional relationships as well as the ephemeral

relationships that exist between people making small talk at a bus stop, exchanging words with a customer at the cash register, and so on. Any exchange of activity or conversation, between two or more people, involving some amount or kind of reward or cost, constitutes social exchange, as first discussed by sociologist George Homans in 1958. Homans focused specifically on dyadic exchanges—those between two people—and on mechanisms that reinforce behavior, while later theorists expanded the focus of social exchange theory to other social groups and mechanisms. "Rewards" in social exchanges can be seemingly trivial—a nod of acknowledgment, a smile, anything that contributes to positive feelings like a sense of acceptance or belongingness—while costs may be nothing more than the time it takes to interact with the other person, or the diversion of concentration from some other matter. The rules governing social exchanges, beyond reciprocity and negotiated agreements, have not yet received much attention from researchers, as Russell Cropanzano and Marie S. Mitchell pointed out in their 2005 *Journal of*

"Rewards" in social exchange in the business place include smiles, nods of acknowledgment, or anything that makes the employee feel that they are accepted and belong. (Photos.com)

Management article "Social Exchange Theory: An Interdisciplinary Review."

Social exclusion
Social exclusion is the exclusion of individuals or communities from resources accessible by most of society, resulting in alienation and de facto disenfranchisement. While many forms of such exclusion are illegal if they prevent a person from, for instance, obtaining a job or buying a house, not every social category is protected, and discrimination against even explicitly protected groups can transpire in contexts the law does not regulate, such as when members of such groups are excluded from socialization at or after work.

Social facilitation
Social facilitation is the theory that individuals perform tasks differently when in view of others: specifically, the sense of evaluation leads simple tasks to be performed more easily, familiar tasks to be performed better and faster, and unfamiliar tasks to be performed worse because of the imagined pressures the individual feels. Social facilitation is one of the oldest theories in social psychology, dating to the late 19th century. The phrase itself was coined in 1924 by Floyd Allport, the founder of social psychology, and various theories have explained the phenomenon through reference to social pressures or the impact of perceived observation on attention to the task.

Social inhibition
Social inhibition is the avoidance of social interactions or group social situations, whether conscious or unconscious. Consistently high levels of social inhibition are associated with disorders like social anxiety, but moderate levels of social inhibition can also affect work performance and the fit between a workplace culture and an individual worker.

Social integration
Social integration is the process by which an individual is integrated into a social group. Social integration in the workplace can be important in order to make workers feel like part of the organization, and to keep up employee engagement, though by the same token attempts to encourage social integration can easily seem artificial and forced.

Social intelligence
Social intelligence is similar in some respects to social skills or emotional intelligence, but represents competence in social environments and relationships, including politics and interpersonal conflicts, collaboration, reciprocity, and personal relationships (family, friendly, or romantic). Some scientists, notably archaeologist Steve Mithen and psychologist Nicholas Humphrey, hypothesize that social intelligence is the form of intelligence that differentiated humans from their ancestors and the rest of the animal kingdom. Daniel Goleman has described social intelligence as consisting of two major dimensions: social awareness (which includes empathy, emotional intelligence, and social cognition) and social facility ("people skills," as well as social influence and self-presentation).

Social intuitionism
The theory of social intuitionism says that moral judgments are derived from intuition rather than reason, in contrast with the traditional rationalist models of morality and moral judgment, which have largely prevailed. In social intuitionism, reason is still implicated, but its primary role is in its use to generate a justification for a decision dictated unconsciously by

intuition. In a sense, intuition points to a destination, and reason draws the map. As an explanatory framework, one of the strengths of social intuitionism is its ability to explain how an action can feel "inherently wrong." Its drawback, though unavoidable if it holds true, is that reasoning presents an easier model by which to convince others of one's moral conclusions.

Social justice

Social justice is the equitable distribution of resources and opportunities within society, and the capacity of members of that society to achieve their potential as individuals and to contribute to the society. Member enjoy such privileges regardless of background membership, such as gender or sexuality, religious or political affiliation, disability, race or ethnicity, or socioeconomic background. The term was coined in the 19th century to refer to a concept present in philosophy in some form or another since the classical era, but has especially gained traction since John Rawls' 1971 *Theory of Justice*, which integrated social justice into the idea of the social contract. "Justice denies that the loss of freedom for some is made right by a greater good shared by others," he argued. With this and other work, Rawls reinvigorated the field of political philosophy. Social justice has since become associated with various human rights movements, from liberation theology to the young socially progressive subculture of Tumblr, which has been influential in speaking out against transphobia and cultural appropriation.

Social loafing

One half of the Ringelmann effect, social loafing is the phenomenon of group members spending less effort on their work than they would as individuals, and reducing their effort as the size of the group grows.

Social norm

A social norm is a belief held by a social group about appropriate behaviors in a given context. While social groups may have explicit rules, norms are less formal, and in fact may even contradict explicit rules adopted by and binding the same group. Consider local speed limits, and the fact that a driver staying strictly within a posted 35-mile-per-hour speed limit will, if driving on a main thoroughfare, not only inevitably be passed by other drivers but may be treated as if they are holding up traffic. Norms within social groups may also contradict laws or rules of a larger group or culture to which the social group belongs, as in teen groups in which underage drinking is the norm. Norms may also be more subtle; speaking without affect or avoiding eye contact violates a common American social norm, for instance, but neither is a behavior many Americans would actually condemn. Norms are learned from one's social groups and arise from social interactions. Tolerance of deviance varies from group to group, and not all members within a group are accorded the same leeway.

Social proof

Social proof is the phenomenon of people checking and emulating the actions of the people around them in an attempt to exhibit the correct behavior for a given situation.

Social psychology

Social psychology is an interdisciplinary branch of psychology and sociology concerned with the way the behaviors and mental states of people are influenced by other people. Social psychology research is highly experiment-driven, with American research tending to focus on the effects felt on the individual, while European work tends to deal with group dynamics. The forms of social influence studied include not only those manifest in direct social interaction but those involving the presence of imagined people or implied people, such as watching movies or reading books, or represented by internalized social norms. Persuasion, influence, conformity, attraction, communication, self-concept, and social exchange theory are among the popular areas of study. Some of the best-known experiments in the social sciences come from social psychology, including the Milgram study, the Stanford prison study, and Asch's conformity experiments.

Social sciences

The social sciences are a group of academic disciplines that were formalized in the 19th century (to which many aspects of modern education can be dated), all of which concern society and the human condition. The social sciences include anthropology, economics, political science, psychology, and sociology, as well as interdisciplinary fields like area studies, environmental studies, and international studies. History is sometimes considered a social science (and certainly draws on all the social sciences), sometimes one of the humanities, just as management straddles the span between the social sciences and business.

Social skills

Social skills are those skills dealing with interaction with other people, whether one-on-one or in groups, and are often referred to as interpersonal skills in management literature. Social skills include the ability to empathize and to listen, to persuade or entertain others, to glean information from others' behavior, communication skills, and of course leadership. Social skill ability is curtailed by various disorders, most commonly including attention deficit, mood, personality, and autism spectrum disorders.

Social undermining

Social undermining is the activity of preventing a person from achieving a goal by directing negative emotions and statements toward them, whether to discourage them and undercut their motivation or to discredit them with peers and co-workers. It can be a problem in competitive workplaces in which employees evaluate their own success, performance, and potential to advance in comparison to that of those around them.

Socially distributed cognition

In psychology, the theory of socially distributed cognition as formulated in the 1980s by Edwin Hutchins says that an individual's knowledge exists not simply within him but in the social and physical environments surrounding him. In this framework, cognition is not a process simply performed by an individual but in conjunction with other individuals interacting with the environment. Hutchins built on work by John Milton Roberts, who argued that social organization could be seen as cognition performed by a community, and later sociologists who proposed models by which beliefs were distributed across a society. The importance of this theoretical framework is the way it underscores learning as a social phenomenon.

Sociotropy

Sociotropy is the personality trait of being overly invested in interpersonal relationships, both with individuals and with social groups, especially characterized by a need for acceptance and to maintain numerous close relationships. Sociotropy can lead to depression in the wake of a rift in these relationships, and has been linked experimentally both to low self-esteem and to identification with traditionally feminine gender roles.

Soft power

Soft power is a term coined by Joseph Nye to refer to certain approaches to diplomacy and persuasion, in contrast with the "hard power" represented by military threat and economic reward, or more broadly, by overt displays of reward or punishment. "Soft power" was first used in Nye's 1990 *Bound to Lead: The Changing Nature of American Power* and related journal articles, and expanded in the course of his work and others'. Soft power is now regularly acknowledged and discussed in foreign policy discussions. Pope John Paul II's work against the communist regimes of eastern Europe, especially his 1979 visit to his native Poland, is considered a key example of a successful use of soft power, though this is easier to say in hindsight than it would have been in the intervening decade in which the eommunists retained their position of power.

Pope John Paul II in Poland in June 1979. The trip sparked the formation of the Solidarity movement. (U.S. White House/Eric Draper)

Soft skills

Soft skills are those associated with feelings, insights, emotions, and relationships with other people, as opposed to the "hard skills" drawn upon to perform tasks in one's job role. Soft skills include communication, friendliness, empathy, and persuasion. Some jobs are noteworthy for the role soft skills play in an individual's overall success, more significantly than do hard skills, such as the law or social work; in some leadership theories this is true for leadership as well.

Soldiering

Soldiering was Frederick Winslow Taylor's term for the habit of workers performing at the slowest rate they could manage without being disciplined for it, also called malingering, loafing, goldbricking, or dogging. While many management approaches are discipline oriented, Taylor and Lillian Gilbreth recognized that the problem here was motivation and employees who were not sufficiently engaged or interested in their work, and that better motivating employees would both increase productivity and reduce the workload of supervisors.

Somebody Else's Problem

Originally named by humorist Douglas Adams, Somebody Else's Problem is a phenomenon that has been studied by psychologists and philosophers, in which individuals and groups distance themselves from the need to solve a problem or address an emergency. Climate change, especially as caused by controllable human behaviors, is sometimes used as an example.

Sortition

Sortition is the random selection of political decision makers. In ancient Athens, which pioneered democratic institutions, sortition as the method for appointing most public officials was considered a cornerstone of democracy. It is today used to select jurors, and in some cases to select a jury foreman from among a group of jurors. Sortition has been proposed by several political thinkers as a method for appointing legislators; it is less commonly recommended as a method for determining the executive official (for example, a president, governor, or mayor, among other positions).

Sound style

One of the leadership styles plotted on the managerial grid model, the sound style was originally called the team style. Sound managers have a high concern for both people and production, and have the same leadership style as Theory Y (cf.).

Spreadthink
Spreadthink is a measurable phenomenon in which a group is persistently unable to agree on a complex issue, typified by an inability to even agree on the prioritization of sub-issues or perhaps the relevant facts, and marked by the fact that this inability is not the result of faulty decision-making processes or a lack of organization.

Stability-instability paradox
The stability-instability paradox is a theory about nuclear weapons in international relations, stating that when two countries both possess nuclear weapons, although the probability of war between them decreases (cf. Mutually assured destruction), the probability of indirect conflicts between them increases, as seen in the many proxy wars and other conflicts of the Cold War, and between India and Pakistan today.

Stakeholder
Historically, a stakeholder was a neutral third party without an interest in the financial matter at stake, such as a person who holds gamblers' stakes and is responsible for distributing them to the winner. This original literal meaning was then broadened to encompass escrow agents and other figures who hold money or property while a transaction between other parties is conducted. As so often happens, the term was repurposed by the business world, and since the late 20th century it has become common to discuss "stakeholders" in the sense of "all those who have a stake in the issue at hand." In some decision-making processes it can be important to include all stakeholders in the discussion, not just those who have the authority to make the decision.

Standing on the shoulders of giants
A metaphor dating back at least as far as the 12th century and popularized by Isaac Newton in the 17th century, "standing on the shoulders of giants" illustrates the idea of one's work depending on the past work of others, and of achieving greatness by building on those earlier foundations. It is sometimes phrased in an accusatory sense, particularly if the subject standing on the shoulders is perceived as taking credit for the height of the giants.

Stanford prison experiment
The Stanford prison experiment was conducted in 1971 by Philip Zimbardo, and was funded by the U.S. Office of Naval Research, which sought a better understanding of the conflicts between military prisoners and their guards. The experiment has become one of the most famous psychological experiments, in which participants were randomly assigned roles of prisoners and guards. Prisoners were brought to their cells in a Stanford University basement, where guards worked in teams for eight-hour shifts. Over the course of the experiment, guards enacted authoritarian behaviors on their own initiative, treated prisoners cruelly, and pitted them against each other, while the prisoners passively accepted it, except for two who quit early. (The experiment as a whole was also ended early.) The experiment supported a model of behavior dictated by situation rather than personality traits, and Zimbardo himself was surprised by the extent to which participants became absorbed in their roles. The experiments received the publicity they did in part because of

high-profile prison riots at San Quentin and especially Attica shortly after the study's conclusion, and was back in headlines in 2004 when Zimbardo testified as an expert witness in the trial of one of the guards accused of prisoner torture at Abu Ghraib.

State within a state

The idea of a "state within a state" or imperium in imperio (the original state motto of Ohio, reflecting its influence on the early nation) is that of a faction within a country that acts outside the legitimate civilian government. Historically, the United Fruit Company in the Caribbean was one such example, operating independently of the Caribbean nations in which it operated and setting up "banana republics" in several countries. The American intelligence community is sometimes accused of being a modern example.

Statesmanship

A statesman is simply a politician or other public official, but the word usually refers to one with the benefit of a long career, and by extension statesmanship is governance or diplomacy that is conducted with wisdom and finesse. John Stuart Mill used the term in a fairly neutral sense—requiring the adjective preceding it—when he said "a great statesman is one who knows when to depart from traditions," while a century later on the Bicentennial of the United States, Britain's Queen Elizabeth II declared, "We lost the American colonies because we lacked that statesmanship to know the right time, and the manner of yielding, what is impossible to keep."

Status group

In Max Weber's sociology, status groups are social groups that are differentiated on non-economic bases, such as prestige or religion, in contrast with political groups or social class. Modern status groups are an analogue to the social importance of concepts like honor in earlier Western societies.

Status quo style

One of the leadership styles plotted on the managerial grid model, the status quo style was originally called the middle-of-the-road style. Status quo managers try to balance workers' needs with the company's goals, often with the result of doing an incomplete job of both.

Stereotype threat

One of the most intensely researched phenomena in social psychology, stereotype threat is the feeling an individual has that he faces the risk of confirming one or more negative stereotypes about a group of which he is a member. Performance-related stereotypes can result in poor performance precisely because the individual is undermined by the worry that his performance will not be good enough to overcome the stereotype.

Stewardship

Stewardship is an ethical concept named for the domestic steward, a household servant whose duties involved running the household of a noble or wealthy family: distributing labor among household staff, overseeing their work, administering disciplinary actions, and managing finances related to the staff and their expenses. As an ethical framework, stewardship implies a form of leadership or administration that entails responsible resource management and the idea that ownership resides elsewhere. In Christian theology, for instance, stewardship is the idea that humankind are the stewards of the Earth, with a moral duty to preserve and respect natural resources, which are only given to them to manage, not to own or deplete. In management, stewardship similarly calls for managers to responsibly manage the resources over which they are given control.

Stogdill, Ralph M.

Ralph M. Stogdill was an influential leadership studies scholar, whose 1948 article "Personal Factors Associated with Leadership: A Survey of the Literature" summed up many of the findings of trait-based leadership studies to that point. A member of the Ohio State University leadership studies, Stogdill initially did not believe that there were specific traits associated with leadership, but changed his views by the time he published his *Handbook of Leadership* in 1974, several years before his death. Stogdill's handbook presented his articulation of trait theory, identifying adaptability, alertness to the social environment, ambition, assertiveness, decisiveness, dependability, dominance, energy, persistence, self-confidence, and a willingness to take responsibility as critical for leaders, as well as social and communication skills, administrative ability, creativity, and knowledge specific to the group's work.

Strategic contingencies theory

One of the Aston Group of organizational researchers, David Hickson developed the strategic contingencies theory in 1971. The theory underscores the importance of social interaction and communications in order to maintain leadership, and positions power as, in part, the ability to deal with uncertainty and control contingencies. In this framework, leaders are principally problem solvers; personality traits and personal charisma are less important to their leadership effectiveness than their ability to solve the problem at hand.

Strategic management

Strategic management is the oversight, development, and implementation of a company's major goals, and is key to forming and preserving the company's core identity.

Strategic planning

Strategic planning is the process of formulating and elaborating an organization's strategy, and identifying the ways this strategy impacts priorities and other decision-making processes, as well as ensuring that the organization's strategy is appropriate for the resources it has access to.

Straw man

The straw man argument is an informal fallacy that misrepresents the opposing side, and so is structured to refute a point other than the one

This editorial cartoon from a 1990s issue of Harper's Weekly *shows President William McKinley shooting a cannon at a straw man and its constructors. The caption reads "SMASHED!" A straw man argument is structured to refute a point that one's opponent is making.* (Public Domain)

the opponent is actually making. This is a common tactic used to score a metaphorical point with the audience, because it allows the arguer to present an argument the audience will agree with. Experienced rhetoricians, while certainly aware of the fallacy, are able to use it to great effect, depending on the audience to react emotionally rather than to examine the logical underpinnings of the debate.

Strong versus weak governors

In the United States, while the executive of every state's government has the same title—governor—the powers of those executive offices vary greatly from state to state. Despite producing many nationally famous governors, Texas has been the classic example of a weak governor state. The governor of Texas has no cabinet, for instance, and limited influence on the boards and commissions of the executive branch, members of which cannot be fired, and two-thirds of whom serve terms of more than two years. This not only empowers the legislative branch, which is better able to exert influence on executive branch agencies through funding measures, but decentralizes the power of the executive branch, such that many agencies are basically self-run (and headed by elected officials). While the Texas governor has the power to veto legislation—a power all governors have, since North Carolina amended its constitution in the 1990s to allow it—he is not allowed a "pocket veto," and legislation he neither signs nor vetoes becomes law.

Structural frame

In Lee G. Bolman and Terrence E. Deal's Four Frame model, the Structural frame is one of the distinctive frames affecting the way people view the world. The structural frame is invested in rules, procedures, policies, hierarchies, specificity, and well-defined roles. It tends to see organizations as bureaucracies.

Structure

In history and the social sciences, "structure" refers to institutions and cultural elements that form the context in which people act. The social relationships in society, both formal and informal, both emerging from individual actions and determining those actions, constitute the social structure, from the micro scale of individual behavior in the context of social norms and etiquette to the macro scale of the socioeconomic class system and the roles played by attitudes toward gender, race, ethnicity, religion, sexuality, and language use. Different approaches model these structures differently. Marxist sociology, for instance, focuses on the economic effect of social structures, treating cultural effects as side effects.

Substantive representation

Substantive representation is a measure in political science, representing the effect that elected or appointed members of a government body who are members of a particular group have on its activity. This is a contrast with descriptive representation, which represents their simple mathematical proportion in that body. For instance, women may make up a particular proportion of the membership of a state legislature, but if they are not members or heads of the important committees within that legislature, or otherwise represented in the leadership of the legislature, their impact on legislation passed will not be proportional to their raw numbers.

Substitutes

In substitutes for leadership theory, substitutes are workplace factors that reduce the necessity of leadership. This includes subordinate skill and professional orientation; routine and unambiguous tasks, such as menial labor; satisfying tasks; clear job goals; and self-managed teams.

Substitutes for leadership theory

A leadership theory developed by Steven Kerr and John Jermier in 1978, substitutes for leadership theory deals with elements in the workplace that impact leader effectiveness: substitutes, neutralizers, and enhancers. Substitutes increase subordinate performance without the need for leadership; neutralizers reduce leader effectiveness; enhancers increase leader effectiveness. The theory received a lot of attention in the 1980s until the rise of transformational leadership.

Succession planning

Succession planning is the process of preparing individuals within an organization to take over leadership positions at some point in the future. While the emphasis is often on identifying "backups" for senior management positions in order to ensure a smooth transition in the event of a senior executive departing, succession planning also includes identifying and preparing viable candidates for middle-management and team leader positions. Succession planning can be assisted by internal leadership development. In smaller businesses, succession planning is key to the business's survival of the retirement, or even reduced participation, of the founders.

Sudbury school

A Sudbury school, named for the Sudbury Valley School founded in 1968 in Framingham, Massachusetts, is a school run by direct democracy in which both students and staff are enfranchised. The core principle of Sudbury

schools is that the only trait children lack that adults possess is experience, and so the role of teachers is to guide students to and through experiences. Students decide how to spend their time, and school governance and policy decisions are made through meetings modeled after New England town meetings. This includes even aspects of governance that town meetings usually delegate to an elected body or professional administrators, like hiring and firing decisions. The school day is only lightly structured, with no separation into age-based groups nor required courses. In some ways the Sudbury schools resemble the experimental and alternative liberal arts colleges founded in the same era, like Hampshire College in nearby Amherst, Massachusetts, but for younger students (Sudbury Valley is attended by students ages 4 to 19).

Superior orders

Superior orders or lawful orders is a defense used in the Nuremberg war crimes trials in the aftermath of World War II. The plea, based on the precedent of command responsibility established 20 years earlier, argues that an individual is not guilty when the actions he committed were ordered by a superior officer. The defense was not sufficient to avoid punishment, but did succeed in lessening it in many cases. Since Nuremberg, courts have been inconsistent in their opinions on the superior orders defense.

Supermajority

In voting systems, a supermajority is the requirement that a proposal pass only with a proportion of votes that is some specific amount fewer than a mere majority of the votes—such as the two-thirds supermajority vote required for Congress to override a veto, or the three-quarters supermajority required for states to ratify a Constitutional amendment.

Suppression of dissent

The act of suppressing disagreement with those in power, whether through punishment or silencing. Indirect suppression may take the form of social and economic pressures that make an individual unwilling to express dissent, or to continue expressing it, because of consequences either in the workplace or in his chances of being retained or promoted in the future.

Symbolic Frame

The Symbolic Frame is one of the distinctive frames affecting the way people see the world, and is based on Lee G. Bolman and Terrence E. Deal's Four Frame model. The Symbolic Frame echoes the viewpoint of Erving Goffman's *Presentation of Self in Everyday Life*, focusing on the dramaturgy of human interactions, the roles people assume, and the rituals and stories of human cultures.

Systems thinking

Systems thinking is concerned with the understanding of systems and their components and processes, such as the people, procedures, structures, and norms that make up an organization, with special regard for their linkages and interactions. Systems thinking involves a more holistic or "big picture" view of phenomena, which can help prevent unintended consequences. Developing a thorough understanding of an organization through systems thinking improves organizational communication and identifies problems before they become critical.

Tao te Ching

The *Tao te Ching* is the foundational text of the philosophical and religious system of Taoism, having been written in China by the sage Lao Tzu around the 6th century B.C.E. In it, several passages advocate what is now called servant

A Taoist priest (daoshi) in Macau, China, in 2006. The religious and philisophical system of Taoism is based on the Tao te Ching. (Wikimedia Commons)

leadership, including "When [the sage's] task is accomplished and things have been completed, all the people say, 'We ourselves have achieved it!'" and "The highest type of ruler is one of whose existence the people are barely aware."

Task culture

One of four types of corporate culture identified by Charles Handy and Roger Harrison. In a task culture, every group is formed to address a specific problem or decision and organization tends to be according to expertise, with highly skilled roles.

Task-oriented leadership

Task-oriented leadership is leadership that is focused on specific tasks necessary to the meeting of team goals, with an emphasis on process and procedure, structure, well-defined roles, and time management. Task-oriented leadership is sometimes contrasted with relationship-oriented leadership, and early work in leadership studies addressed the issue of whether task- or relationship-orientation was more effective. Situational leadership theory developed out of that work.

Taylor, Frederick Winslow

The father of scientific management, Frederick Winslow Taylor was a mechanical engineer who became one of the first management consultants during the Industrial Revolution. Before the word *productivity* even entered usage in its labor-output meaning, Taylor had devoted himself to increasing productivity in factories by increasing the efficiency of both machines and work processes. He helped to develop high-speed steel at Bethlehem Steel, but left his position in 1901 and promoted himself as a management consultant, writer, and lecturer. "Taylorism" consisted of four related principles: rule of thumb or traditional procedures were replaced with those derived from a scientific study of the task being performed; employees were trained rather than teaching themselves; each individual task to be performed by any employee was defined through detailed instruction; and managers were developed in order to better distribute the operations of the company into planning and supervision (managers) and the actual task performance (workers). One of the areas where he has faced the most criticism is in this fourth principle, since he had no interest in worker autonomy, and preferred as much control as possible to be in the hands of management. Adopting scientific management occasionally led to strikes as a result.

Team

Leadership studies, as well as psychology and management literature, use the terms *team*, *group*, *work team*, and *work group* interchangeably, to refer to formal or informal groups of workers engaged collaboratively in a task, project, or area of an organization's activities.

Team-based leadership

Leadership in team-based organizations is distributed more broadly than in hierarchical organizations, and is similar to horizontal or collective leadership. The defining factor is that leadership is performed by individuals other than (in addition to) the appointed leader, sometimes described (as in the work of Jay B. Carson, Paul E. Tesluck, and Jennifer A. Marrone)

as an emergent property of the team as a result of the distribution of influence throughout team members. Team leadership and teamwork are increasingly vital areas of study in the 21st century, but the research is fairly young. Areas of study include the use of social network analysis to reveal team leadership behaviors, factors and behaviors that facilitate team leadership, the role of external support or leadership, and the stages and life cycles of team-led groups.

Team composition

Team composition is the aspect of a team consisting of the collection of attributes of its members, which is a strong determining factor on other aspects of the team and its functions. There are conflicting schools of thought about what kind of team composition is most effective for a healthy and productive dynamic, as well as which member attributes are important. Being an outlier in a team—differing from the rest of the team in some attribute like type or quantity of experience, race, gender, age, or previous work background—can place a team member at a disadvantage, but many schools of thought suggest that neither should a team be too homogenous. A sufficiently large heterogenous team can be thought of as possessing a faultline dividing it into homogenous sub-teams as a result of the social roles team members adopt.

Terror Management Theory

Terror Management Theory stipulates that humans are uniquely predisposed toward existential terror, because they possess both the same self-preservation instinct as other animals as well as a unique capacity for abstract thinking and advanced cognition that makes them aware of their mortality. Many social and cultural institutions are thus developed to cope with this fear of death, including a belief in an afterlife, resurrection, reincarnation, and systems of morality and behavior that increase our happiness or feeling of self-worth, in order to offset that terror. Leaders naturally arise as individuals who affirm our terror-dampening social constructs are elevated.

Theory of constraints

In management, the theory of constraints says that a small number of constraints stand in the way of an organization's goals and that the organization should be restructured around them.

Theory of the firm

The theory of the firm is a system of economic theories describing the nature and behavior of the firm (a company or corporation) and its relationship to the market. In the 1960s, managerial and behavioral theories of the firm began to focus on the role of individuals (especially leaders and managers within the hierarchy) in determining traits and behavior of firms.

Theory Theory

Theory Theory is a psychological theory about people's psychological theories, in a sense. Theory Theory says that an individual's ability to empathize with other people and understand their behavior is connected to an internalized "folk psychology" that they have developed based on their experiences, observations, and the ideas to which they have been exposed. This internalized psychological theory begins developing when the individual is a young child, and so at first consists of very basic observations, many of which are undoubtedly false (the child has little sense of his parents' lives outside of childrearing). According to the Child Scientist theory, many child behaviors are explained as children testing out psychological theories in the world.

Theory X and Theory Y

Theory X and Theory Y are theories of management developed by MIT Sloan School of Management professor Douglas McGregor and presented in his 1960 book *The Human Side of Enterprise*. Each theory is based on a different attitude managers take toward their employees. In Theory X, management acts from the assumption that employees have an inherent dislike of work, which they will indulge if so allowed, and therefore prevent this by adopting a hierarchical system of management in order to closely supervise all levels of production and work within the organization. Because of the negative view of workers, negative incentives tend to be used to guide behavior instead of offering rewards for positive results. Similarly, job roles are highly structured because of the assumption that a dislike of work will prevent employees from taking initiative. Theory Y, on the other hand, assumes work is a natural pursuit that employees can enjoy, and that the conditions can be created in which employees will actively seek out tasks and responsibility. This is more likely than Theory X to lead to a climate of trust and open communication. Theory Y is an application to the workplace of much of the work of psychologist Abraham Maslow.

Theory Z

Theory Z is a term coined in reference to Theory X and Theory Y. Various "Theories Z" have been coined representing an approach to management that is neither Theory X nor Theory Y. Abraham Maslow, for instance, used it to refer to an even more positive view than Theory Y, one adopted by those who had transcended self-actualization, whom he alternately calls mystics or transcenders. Transcenders are those for whom "peak experiences and plateau experiences become the most important things in their lives," and who comfortably speak the language of poets and the profoundly religious. Everything is potentially sacred to them, and they perceive in everyone the potential for greatness. Maslow offered little guidance for the management applications of Theory Z, however. Hawaiian business professor William Ouchi offered a more pragmatically minded Theory Z, as part of his "Japanese management" style that he taught during the 1980s in response to the Asian economic boom and the often explicitly xenophobic American paranoia over Japanese economic competition. Ouchi's Theory Z focuses on the well-being of employees as Theory Y does, but ensures loyalty by providing a life-long job, so that the employee associates the organization's well-being with his own. Theory Z management prizes stability in the organization as well as high employee morale, and treats these as necessary preconditions to meeting organizational goals.

Think tank

A think tank is an organization devoted to research, whether in the sciences or related to public policy. Policy think tanks, often called policy institutes, are often but not always partisan in their design: for instance, the Cato Institute, Heritage Foundation, and Center for American Progress are American policy institutes promoting libertarianism, conservatism, and progressivism, respectively. Functionally, think tanks have some similarities with the role monasteries played in the intellectual development of medieval Europe, but in their modern form they date to the 19th century. Think tanks enjoyed two major periods of growth: the 1940s and early 1950s, due to the Cold War and rapid technological growth; and the 1980s through the early 21st century, when globalization motivated the creation of more than

half of today's think tanks. The oldest American think tanks—the Carnegie Endowment for International Peace, the Brookings Institution, the Hoover Institution, the National Bureau of Economic Research, and the Council on Foreign Relations—are devoted to public policy or economic policy. In 1946, the RAND Corporation was established by the Air Force, and its initial focus on weapons development broadened quickly, with RAND contributing to the space program and artificial intelligence, the technologies leading to the Internet, wargaming and game theory, and social choice theory.

Thomas, Kenneth

Kenneth Thomas identified five styles of negotiation in his work on conflict management in the mid-2000s: accommodating (in which the negotiator acts to solve the other party's problems, pays attention to the emotional and nonverbal signals from the other party, and may feel taken advantage of); avoiding (individuals who avoid negotiating if they can, and tend to be reserved and tactful, avoiding confrontations); collaborating (negotiatiors who enjoy problem solving and try to address all concerns, with the risk of overcomplicating an issue by introducing too many factors); competing (highly strategic negotiators who treat the process like a game and risk harming their relationship with the other party); and compromising (negotiators who want to reach a fair outcome but do not like to dally and spend too much time on the details).

Three Levels of Leadership

The Three Levels of Leadership model was presented in James Scouller's 2011 book by the same name, and is sometimes called the 3P model or Integrated Psychological model. Scouller's goal was to adapt the strengths of previous leadership theories while escaping their limitations. The

"3 Ps" of the model are public, private, and personal leadership. The first two refer to outward behaviors, of which Scouller enumerates 34 public leadership behaviors and 14 private (one-on-one) leadership behaviors. The third and innermost level is personal leadership, consisting of the leader's skills, emotions, competencies, and leadership presence. Effective leadership means harmony among these three levels and developing one's personal leadership traits while practicing effective outward leadership behaviors.

Time and motion study

Time and motion studies were introduced by the Efficiency movement that developed around scientific management. Time studies were originally developed to establish standard performance times for the tasks constituting a business's operations. Frank and Lillian Gilbreth later conducted motion studies that established the best series of motions for such tasks, by improving posture and eliminating unnecessary or inefficient movement. The purpose of each was the same: to standardize the work done in a company (originally in factories, with later scholars extending the idea to other types of businesses) in order to maximize efficiency.

Tombstone mentality

A term in the aviation industry that is useful in general discussions of organizations, "tombstone mentality" refers to the idea that aviation safety is improved only in response to a death, as a result of the insufficient economic motive of safety in the absence of specific market pressures.

Total Quality Management

Not to be confused with quality management (cf.), Total Quality Management (TQM) was a specific movement in the 1980s, inspired by W. Edwards Deming's *Out of the Crisis*, and was in many ways a revival of the Efficiency movement in American industry. In response to manufacturing competition from newly competitive countries like Japan, TQM sought to improve American competition by improving management practices and work processes. Beyond the manufacturing industry, it was adopted by many elements of the U.S. military.

Totalitarianism

Totalitarianism is an approach to governance in which the state is given the greatest possible control over society and its institutions. In Weimar Germany, totalitarianism was first developed as a positive possibility, one in which the state and society were ideologically unified. As practiced, totalitarianism in, for instance, Nazi Germany, fascist Italy, the Soviet Union, and North Korea, is a dictatorship in which the ruling group extends its influence beyond merely the political and economic, monopolizing cultural and social power as well, controlling art, education, and private life.

Paintings of dictators Kim Jong-il, Supreme Leader of the Democratic People's Republic of Korea (North Korea), and his predecessor and father, Kim Il-sung. Kim Jong-un succeeded his father, Kim Jong-il, in 2011. (Wikimedia Commons)

Tough-guy macho culture

One of four corporate cultures identified by Terence Deal and Allan Kennedy, characterized by rapid feedback and high risk. Jobs in these cultures are high stress as a result of the risk, the stakes, and the difficulty of the work, as in police work, professional sports, and jobs where the cost of failure is high, such as surgery.

Town meeting

The town meeting is a mechanism of direct democracy in which all adult members of the town are welcome in a discussion of a local policy issue, and to participate in the vote determining the course of action on that policy issue. Although the term is also sometimes used to refer to discussion-only sessions, in which the decision is made by some elected or appointed body after taking input from voters, the first meaning has special significance as a form of government rarely practiced anymore outside of New England. The town meeting and its participants essentially assume the legislative duties for the town, and in many cases the powers of the executive branch are significantly curtailed, beyond what is authorized or ordered by the ballot issues resolved at town meeting. Less common in cities, town meetings remain common in towns, suburbs, and unincorporated areas in Maine, New Hampshire, and Vermont, while slightly modified in Massachusetts and Connecticut. In most cases, day-to-day administrative duties are delegated to a body such as a board of selectmen, and at a minimum, an annual town meeting begins the business of the government for the year, discussing and voting on budget issues, changes to the law, regulations, or the tax rate, progress on long-term projects, the results of promises or concerns expressed the previous year, etc. Further meetings may be called in response to specific issues, and town meetings may also be held separately to determine courses of action for a school district, water district, or other special administrative district.

Toxic leader

A toxic leader is one whose management of a group worsens their work, group affective mood, employee engagement, or some other element of their situation as a direct consequence of their management style. There is no one style of toxic leadership; like being a "good leader," there are behaviors and styles associated with it, some combination of which aggregates to toxicity. Arrogance and condescension are commonly identified problems, but toxic leaders may go even further, competing with their followers, bullying them, exploiting them, playing mind games with them, or actively deceiving them.

Toxic workplace

Similar to a toxic leader, a toxic workplace is one whose social and procedural environment actively makes things worse for its workers, whether because of one or more toxic employees (a problem solved by their removal or rehabilitation) or because of corporate culture factors that harm employee engagement, productivity, satisfaction, or other measures, or which encourage an unsafe level of workplace stress. Even when policies and procedures are reasonable and no one individual is toxic, for instance, a workplace that is consistently understaffed or unprepared for some emergency circumstance may become toxic. Toxicity of this sort also leads to frictions among employees that can encourage bullying, distrust, and antisocial behavior.

Toynbee, Arnold J.

Arnold Toynbee was a 20th century British historian who is best known for his monumental

12-volume *A Study of History*, published from 1934 to 1961. The work combined the modern historical approach pioneered by Leopold von Ranke in the previous century and applied it to the early 20th century's fascination with "universal history" (which took as its subject the whole of human civilization, not just a single nation-state), tracing the development and decay of Toynbee's 19 major civilizations, four abortive civilizations, and five arrested civilizations, focusing in each case on the leaders who guided their civilizations through change to varying degrees of success.

Toyota Production System

The Toyota Production System (TPS) is a production system developed by Toyota, the Japanese automotive manufacturer, from the 1940s through the 1970s. TPS is designed to eliminate unnecessary waste and inefficiency in production, while at the same time encouraging teamwork, respect for others, and the ongoing improvement of business operations and organizational knowledge. TPS continues to be influential today, and is one of the influences on Lean.

Traditional domination

Traditional domination is one of Max Weber's three ideal types of leadership, and refers to leadership that is derived from tradition or custom. The traditional authority of a father/husband over the other members of his family for much of Western history is one such example, and on a larger scale, feudalism was based on leadership that is inherited or distributed according to traditional rules.

Trained incapacity

American economist and sociologist Thorstein Veblen coined the term *trained incapacity* in 1933, to refer to the phenomenon in which a trained, skilled individual's abilities are detrimental to their accurate view of the world.

Trait ascription bias

Trait ascription bias is a cognitive bias resulting in people seeing themselves as capable of a significant range of moods, behaviors, and personality, while other people are less complex and capable of a narrower, more predictable range of the same. As a result, the behavior of others is viewed as representative of their personality, while behaviors of oneself may be described as situational and not something one should fairly be judged by.

Trait-based theories of leadership

Personality and trait-based theories of leadership are among the oldest leadership theories, growing out of the Great Man approach to history. Such theories focus on the personality traits associated with effective leaders, rather than on behaviors or methodologies of leadership. Studies suggest leaders have above-average intelligence, for instance, though typically they are not too significantly more intelligent than their followers. Leaders also tend to be sociable, confident, and determined. However, not all people who possess the traits associated with leadership become leaders, and critics of trait-based theories say that they focus too much on what leaders are like rather than on what they do.

Transactional leadership

Transactional leadership is a leadership style that uses rewards and punishment to motivate followers. Typically, transactional leaders look for faults in followers' work in order to be corrected, and the style is generally reactive rather than proactive. It is characterized by dealing with followers in terms of appeals to their self-interest and by working within the organizational culture to maintain the status quo.

Transatlantic Policy Consortium

The Transatlantic Policy Consortium is a network of higher education institutions in the public policy and public administration fields, devoted to promoting dialogue and joint research on transatlantic public policy issues.

Transformational leadership

Transformational leadership is a leadership style that seeks to increase followers' motivation and performance through various means. The name alludes to the role of the leader in shaping—transforming—his followers, and was coined in part to differentiate from transactional leadership. The means by which transformational leaders mold their followers include intellectual stimulation, the individualized consideration they give each one, the leader's ability to inspire their followers, and the ability of the leader to act as a role model who influences their followers' choices and behavior.

Transpersonal business studies

Transpersonal business studies is the application of transpersonal psychology to the world of business and management: the study of the spiritual side of business, management, and work, as well as the application of transpersonal psychology to the act of management. Transpersonal management prioritizes the importance of emotional intelligence and transformational leadership, as well as creativity, innovation, and self-actualization.

Transpersonal psychology

Transpersonal psychology is an approach to modern psychology that has a special concern for the spiritual or transcendent spheres of the human condition, including peak experiences, religious practices, and spiritual self-development. It developed in the 1960s amid the backdrop of increased academic interest in altered states of consciousness and the mystical, the Fourth Great Awakening, and the human potential movement, though Abraham Maslow also pioneered the focus in psychology on peak experiences. Transpersonal psychology should not be confused with parapsychology, but is interested in understanding some of the same phenomena, notably near-death experiences and mystical experiences. Critics argue that the school sometimes offers a cloak of legitimacy to ideas or thinkers who are merely rehashing New Age philosophy without scholarly rigor, and some transpersonal psychologists have themselves chastised their colleagues for not being better at policing the fringe.

Triarchy theory

Triarchy theory suggests that there are three fundamental ways to structure an organization: hierarchy, the most familiar form; heterarchy, in which different elements of the organization are unranked; and responsible autonomy, in which individuals or groups act autonomously and bear the responsibility for the outcome of their actions.

Tridimensional personality questionnaire

The tridimensional personality questionnaire (TPQ) was developed by C. Robert Cloninger and measures three dimensions of personality: reward dependence, novelty seeking, and harm avoidance. The test consists of 100 questions the respondent answers with true/false. Cloninger has used the test as the basis for personality genetics research, correlating the three dimensions with low noradrenergic activity, low dopaminergic activity, and high serotonergic activity, respectively.

Trompenaars' model of national cultural differences

In the 1990s, management theorists Fons Trompenaars and Charles Hampden-Turner developed a model of seven cultural dimensions representing values and behaviors of a culture. The model is intended to assist with cross-cultural communication, especially in the world of international business. The seven dimensions are universalism (favoring broad general rules and using the best fit for a given situation) versus particularism (which considers each case on its own merits); individualism versus collectivism; neutral (or stoic) versus outwardly emotional; specific versus diffuse (the degree to which work and personal life are kept separate); achievement versus ascription (is the source of status personal achievement or something granted externally, such as according to seniority?); sequential (doing tasks one at a time) versus synchronic (juggling several tasks at once); and internal versus external control.

True self and false self

Mid-century psychoanalysis began to work with the concepts of the "true self" and "false self," building on the work of Donald W. Winnicott. The false self is a facade the individual constructs (initially as a child) and presents to the world, overlapping with but not identical to Carl Jung's concept of the persona. The true self is the real self beneath. James Masterson has argued that personality disorders have in common their conflict between the true and false self, while Alexander Lowen has emphasized the importance of the false self in analyses of narcissism and narcissistic personality disorder.

Trust management

In management sciences, trust management is the creation and maintenance of systems that allow parties to assess reliability, both of other parties and of potentially risky transactions, in the interest of developing trusting professional relationships.

Truthiness

Truthiness is the characteristic of an assertion or argument that "feels right," especially one that is made authoritatively, without considering the evidence or engaging with opposing views. The concept was introduced in the October 17, 2005, premiere episode of Stephen Colbert's *Colbert Report*, a satirical news show that especially focuses on the rhetoric of conservatives in the Bush and Tea Party eras. It became *Merriam-Webster*'s *Dictionary's* Word of the Year the following year, and appears in the *Oxford English Dictionary*. The concept resonated as much as it did because it attaches a vivid

First Lady Michelle Obama during an appearance on Stephen Colbert's The Colbert Report in 2012. Cobert introduced the concept of "truthiness" in 2005. (Wikimedia Commons)

descriptive name to an important phenomenon in rhetoric and leadership: the appeal to emotion, especially one framed in a way to cast aspersions on recourse to conflicting facts.

Turf war
A turf war is a struggle for control over territory, whether physical, cultural, in the market, or in some other sense. The term is originally associated with frontier livestock herders and later used in reference to struggles between criminal groups in the early 20th century, but today often refers to factions or individuals within companies or political entities.

Turnover
Turnover is the rate at which an organization loses and gains employees, the duration an average employee tends to remain. High turnover is associated with instability and inefficiency because it prevents the accumulation of job-specific knowledge by employees, although some businesses (particularly those relying on large amounts of unskilled low-paid labor) assume high turnover as a given in their business model (for this reason, when the Bureau of Labor Statistics reports turnover rates, farm labor is typically excluded). While the average turnover rate is about 3 or 4 percent over a year, businesses in some industries like hospitality can have normal turnover rates as high as 80 percent.

Twinkling fingers
A method of expressing agreement with a speaker during a discussion, without the interruption caused by clapping. Hands are raised with the fingers wiggling. If hands are pointed down, it indicates disagreement. Also known as spirit fingers. Associated mainly with consensus-based decision making.

Two-step flow of communication
According to the two-step flow of communication model, individuals' opinions are more influenced by the opinion leaders they come in contact with than by the media, though the opinion leaders themselves are influenced by the media. For some, this model illustrates the importance of opinion leaders, while for others, it simply points out opinion leaders' role as the means by which the media's influence is disseminated.

Typical intellectual engagement
Typical intellectual engagement is a personality factor that deals with an individual's enjoyment of or engagement with activities that are intellectually stimulating and challenging. Unlike intelligence quotient (IQ) tests, it is concerned not with an individual's maximum performance level, but their typical performance in intellectual domains. It has a moderate correlation to general knowledge and is significantly predictive of academic performance.

Tyranny of the majority
The "tyranny of the majority" is a problem in democratic systems in which a minority group suffers oppression at the hands of the ruling majority. The most common solution is that of the American federal government: constitutional limits on the power of the government over its people, including the Bill of Rights, which recognizes specific rights that a mere vote is insufficient to supersede. The danger of the tyranny of the majority is one reasons that the process of altering this foundational document of the government is more difficult than that of electing officials or passing laws in the legislature.

Uncertainty avoidance
One of the cultural dimensions identified by Geert Hofstede, uncertainty avoidance consists

of an organization's activities, both rational and irrational, that help it cope with the uncertainty of the future, including recordkeeping, aspects of accounting, and the organization's planning activities.

Unconscious cognition

Unconscious cognition consists of the mental processes of which the conscious mind is unaware, including learning, perception, memory, and thought. The role of the unconscious mind in various cognitive processes is not fully understood, but its presence in those processes is undeniable and has been at the center of psychological thought and research since Sigmund Freud and Carl Jung. One area where there seems to be the most agreement on the role of the unconscious is in data gathering; phenomena from optical illusions and hallucinations to subliminal messages have shown this. Unconscious attitudes about race, gender, and other traits have an impact on decision making, from the weight we give someone's input to hiring and firing decisions.

Unconscious thought theory

Unconscious thought theory (UTT) is the theory that the unconscious mind not only continues to work on problems and tasks initiated by the conscious mind but outperforms conscious effort in complex tasks with many variables, while underperforming in simpler tasks with few variables. The term was coined in 2006 but goes back at least to Sigmund Freud, who recommended that the most important decisions be made by the unconscious. The experimental data is, to be fair, unclear: until Ap Dijksterhuis's experiments in the 2000s, the bulk of experiments in the 1980s and 1990s suggested that the unconscious was suited only to simple problem solving. Among the points in UTT's

favor, however, are the unconscious mind's lack of certain cognitive biases that interfere with the utility of conscious thought: especially the problem of weighting, in which deliberation over a decision can warp one's reasoning, and the rule-based pattern of conscious decision making which sometimes results in poorer choices than the associative thinking of the unconscious.

Un-everyday-ness

German political scientist Max Weber coined the term *un-everyday-ness* to refer to the exceptional nature claimed by charismatic leaders. In religious contexts, this un-everyday-ness would be a divine calling, having been selected by God, perhaps even proven through the performance of miracles. Political candidates sometimes similarly position themselves as specially chosen subjects of destiny, especially if they have a parent or ancestor who was a beloved statesman. Specifics vary, but this un-everday-ness is a quality or characteristic other than mere skill that sets the leader apart from his followers.

University of Pittsburgh Graduate School of Public and International Affairs

A University of Pittsburgh school offering graduate programs in public administration, international development, and public and international affairs. The school is also home to the Johnson Institute for Responsible Leadership, which develops course material on accountability and ethics for the school's core curriculum.

Unschooling

Unschooling is an educational method that focuses on experiential learning over the trappings of compulsory education, and usually eschews standardized curricula or tests, traditional grading methods, and performance metrics like multiple-choice or short-answer tests. Unschooling is particularly associated with home schooling, but enjoys overlap with other educational approaches like those of some alternative schools and the Sudbury schools.

Up or out

"Up or out" is an approach to employee management, whereby any employee who is not promoted within a certain period of time (usually excepting those above a certain level) is fired. The U.S. military, for instance, discharges any officer twice passed over for promotion, while the Cravath system of law firm management gives associate lawyers 10 years to reach partner.

Valence

In Victor Vroom's expectancy theory, valence is the value of a specific reward for performing a task, as perceived by the individual who would receive it. It is affected by the individual's wants and needs and familiarity with the reward.

Varieties of Power (Montana and Charnov)

In their 2008 book *Management*, Patrick J. Montana and Bruce H. Charnov build on John R. P. French and Bertram Raven's *Bases of Social Power*, classifying seven types of organizational power available to a leader: legitimate power, reward power, coercive power, expert power, charisma power, referent power, and information power.

Veblen, Thorstein

Thorstein Veblen was an American sociologist and economist who developed institutional economics and coined the term *conspicuous consumption*, referring to the spending of money as a method of demonstrating wealth and especially social status. His less commonly known contribution was the phrase *conspicuous leisure*, referring to the display and use of leisure time to similarly denote social status and importance—one explanation for the vacations and golf days traditionally associated with doctors, for instance.

Vicarious liability

In common law, vicarious liability is a form of secondary liability carried by a third party who has the right, ability, or duty to control the actions of the violator who is primarily liable. The typical example is that of a superior who bears some responsibility for the actions of his subordinate, and it is part of the legal framework that makes a business liable for some of the actions of its employees when those actions are committed in the course of their employment (there are many exceptions, notably in the case of assaults committed by employees). Parents are generally held to bear vicarious liability for the actions of their minor children, though this is its own unique area of common law.

Victim playing

To play the victim is to play out the role of victim as a strategy for seeking attention, manipulating others, or calling attention from one's own abuse of others. It may be found in the workplace when the work environment is emotionally unhealthy, especially when the atmosphere is not a trusting one.

Villard, Henry

Henry Villard was a 19th century financier who made his fortune in the transportation industry. German sociologist Max Weber used him as an example of the power of charisma, as at one point Villard raised money from investors without telling them the nature of the investment—requiring them to evaluate their desire to invest based purely on their faith in his judgment, rather than on their own judgment of the specifics.

Vitality curve

A vitality curve is a method in which a workforce is evaluated according to the productivity of its individual workers. For instance, former General Electric CEO Jack Welch advocated the "rank and yank" method, in which a workforce is divided into its most productive 20 percent, the "vital 70 percent" in the middle, and the least productive 10 percent, who are fired. Similar systems have been used by IBM and Dow Chemical since the mid-2000s, by Motorola in the 1990s, and throughout the accounting and management consulting industries.

Voluntariness

Voluntariness is an important philosophical and legal concept, the state of making a choice according to one's free will, without coercion. Contracts in most legal systems require voluntary agreement by both parties at the time of signing, as does a guilty plea in a criminal court.

von Ranke, Leopold

The 19th century German historian Leopold von Ranke is one of the most important historians in the development of the field, and instituted the standards followed by modern historians today, notably its use of primary sources and attempt at objectivity. He favored narrative histories—history told as a story, especially chronologically—and was instrumental in the rise of diplomatic history and the continued dominance of Great Man histories, treating history largely as the product of the actions of significant leaders. It is because of von Ranke that nearly all historical analyses, especially those grounded in the methodologies of traditional history, are also studies of leadership.

Vroom-Yetton contingency model

Yale School of Management professor Victor Vroom and Phillip Yetton developed a contingency model of situational leadership in their 1973 work *Leadership and Decision-Making*, which Vroom later expanded in his 1988 collaboration with Arthur Yago, *The New Leadership*. The model identifies five types of leadership for different situations: Autocratic Type I, Autocratic Type II (with followers providing information for the decision-making process), Consultative Type I (leader meets with specific followers individually to seek their input), Consultative Type II (leader meets with specific followers for a group discussion to provide input), and Group-Based (in which the leader and followers work together to make a decision). Seven yes/no questions determine the best leadership style for the situation:

1. Is there a quality requirement or technical or rational grounds for selecting one solution above others?
2. Does the leader have sufficient information to make a quality decision?
3. Is the problem structured? Are there alternative courses of action?
4. Does implementing the solution require acceptance or cooperation by subordinates?
5. If the leader makes the decision himself, is it likely to be accepted by followers?
6. Do subordinates share the organizational goals relevant to the decision?
7. Are subordinates likely to conflict over choosing the right solution?

War as a metaphor

In American political discourse, "war" has often been used as the term for "a serious campaign by the government to eradicate a given thing." Federal Bureau of Investigation head

J. Edgar Hoover waged a "war on crime" in the 1930s, and since the 1960s, many presidents have defined a large part of their presidency by their metaphorical war of choice—even those who were also engaged in actual wars. Lyndon B. Johnson's (LBJ) "War on Poverty" set the precedent, followed by Richard Nixon's "War on Drugs," and Jimmy Carter did not explicitly adopt a "War on Overseas Oil Dependence" but did use the war metaphor in his discussions of the 1974 energy crisis. In the 21st century, the war metaphor has seen increased usage as an accusation rather than policy signaling; conservative Republicans have accused their opponents of waging a "War on Christmas," while Democrats have defended against the "War on Women." What this derogatory usage seems to lack, in contrast with the LBJ strain, is the implication that where there is a war, there are generals and heroes.

War's inefficiency puzzle

The question of why states that are otherwise rational actors would choose to fight wars is one that has long puzzled scholars. The costs of war vastly outweigh the benefits; only an invaded country given no choice can really claim that going to war is a better choice than not going to war, in terms of costs. This is in part because war is famously unpredictable; only in the most drastic power imbalances do wars proceed predictably. Most international relations scholars agree that there are three likely answers for war: an abundance of optimism leading decision makers to drastically overestimate the benefits of war and underestimate its costs; problems of commitment, which includes the decision to go to war by one side when the other side is slowly increasing power, because it means that a war now is less costly than a war later; and issue indivisibility, when the war is

fought over something that cannot be distributed among multiple parties, as with the Crusades' fight for control of Jerusalem or the disputes in a civil war.

Warren Harding Effect

Warren G. Harding was elected president of the United States in 1920 on the promise of a "return to normalcy" after World War I and a rise in American radicalism, his campaign being one of the first to rely heavily on advertising professionals. Though he won by the largest popular vote margins in presidential history, his presidency is widely considered the worst in history, including a staggering number of scandals (most of them events of genuine substance, not merely manufactured by political opponents), instances of corruption, and numerous extramarital affairs. The tendency to be blinded by a leader's attractiveness despite their lack of merit has been called the Warren Harding Effect.

Weber, Max

German philosopher Max Weber was, with Emile Durkheim and Karl Marx, one of the founders of sociology in the 19th and early 20th centuries, and was notable for his examination of the roles of religion and culture in the invention and rise of capitalism. In his political theory, he extensively studied styles of political leadership, and much of the early work on public administration was influenced by him.

Weber's ideal types of political leadership

Sociologist Max Weber defined three ideal types of political leadership or authority: charismatic domination, traditional domination, and legal domination, the last of which included the modern bureaucracy. Weber was the first to study bureaucracy, and considered it the most efficient form of governance.

Typically, controversial wedge issues that divide a social or political group have a populist theme, relating to matters such as national security, race, or gay marriage. (Wikimedia Commons/Max Halberstadt)

Wedge issue

A controversial social issue that divides a social or political group. In the 21st century, gay marriage and marijuana legalization have been wedge issues among American conservatives, with vastly different opinions held by the two increasingly powerful segments among conservatives: the libertarians and the Religious Right. Earlier in the century, the wars in Afghanistan and Iraq were similarly divisive among Democrats. Pushing a wedge issue can damage one's own party—though failing to resolve the conflict can similarly cause damage—and more commonly, members of one party are accused of leveraging the wedge to hurt the other.

Wharton School

The Wharton School of the University of Pennsylvania is an Ivy League business school within the University of Pennsylvania, and was the first university business school. Founded in 1881 by Philadelphia industrialist Joseph Wharton, it was intended to offer a means of attaining business knowledge other than the apprenticeship system, and to prepare corporate and public leaders for the rapid changes of the Industrial Revolution.

Whig history

A British term in origin, a Whig history is an approach to history that presents a narrative in which the past took an inevitable and inexorable path toward progress and enlightenment, especially one resulting in the development of modern-day Anglo-American political institutions. The term *Whiggish history* is sometimes preferred when not specifically referring to a political history of the United Kingdom; a Whiggish history of science, for instance, assumes modern scientific understanding in its specific formulation to be an inevitability and the history of science to be one of ever greater acquisition of knowledge, an accusation often leveled against historians of science.

Whistleblower

Someone who reports wrongdoing in an organization, especially an employee of that organization reporting the wrongdoing to a government or regulatory agency in the name of the public interest, is called a whistleblower. Whistleblower protection laws in the United States date to 1778, initially protecting whistleblowers from libel; more recent laws have attempted to protect whistleblowers from other reprisals.

White Collar: The American Middle Classes

Sociologist C. Wright Mills's 1951 *White Collar: The American Middle Classes* popularized the notion of the white-collar worker, a term coined 20 years earlier by Upton Sinclair, and chronicled the growth of this new class in growing American cities. Like other major works on corporate America in the 1950s—*The Man in the*

Gray Flannel Suit and *The Organization Man*—it focused on the alienation felt by the individual in the capitalist world of Cold War America.

Who Moved My Cheese?

Who Moved My Cheese? by Spencer Johnson is one of the most popular business fables, published in 1998. The story about mice and "little-people" hunting for cheese portrays responses to change, and gained popularity in an age of widespread corporate structural change in the form of mergers, downsizing, the dotcom boom and bust, and globalization, resulting in numerous cases of supervisors purchasing and distributing copies of the book to their employees. Johnson had previous success co-authoring *The One Minute Manager*.

Whuffie

In Cory Doctorow's science fiction novel *Down and Out in the Magic Kingdom*, set in a post-scarcity society in which most resources are free for everyone, Whuffie is a reputation-based currency transacted online. Popular or unpopular behavior leads to gaining or losing Whuffie, and certain social access is restricted to those with sufficient Whuffie scores. Though referred to as a currency, Whuffie does not transfer between individuals—giving someone Whuffie in response to one's approval of their actions does not deplete one's own Whuffie, just as "liking" a Facebook status does not expend a like from one's own status.

The Wire

One of the most critically acclaimed television dramas of all time, *The Wire* aired on HBO from 2002 to 2008, and was created by former police reporter David Simon. Though ostensibly focused on the efforts of city police to rein in the Baltimore drug trade, the scope of the series encompassed the labor unions of the seaport, the city government and its relationship to key civilian leadership groups, the school system, and the local newspaper. Several key themes emerged: the dysfunction of American institutions, and especially the similarities in their dysfunction despite drastic differences in their functions; phenomena, especially negative ones, resulting from poor communication between different levels in an organization's hierarchy, including but not limited to the top level's active disinterest in listening to the bottom level; the struggle of the individual against the inertia of the institution or organization with which he is affiliated; and the different styles and motivations of leaders of these institutions. One notable behavior shown in most of these institutions is "juking the stats": selectively classifying performance data for the sake of achieving specific benchmarks, even though the ability to do so thus renders those benchmarks meaningless.

Wisdom of the crowd

The wisdom of the crowd is a process of consulting a large group for answers to a question. For certain kinds of questions, this process, through averaging, cancels out individual biases and tendencies toward error. Studies have found that the collective opinion yielded by this process is as accurate or more accurate than the opinion of any one member of the group in several areas, including general world knowledge.

Woodward, Joan

An important scholar in leadership studies and contingency theory in the 1950s and 1960s, British sociologist Joan Woodward identified six types of contingency that impact an organization's decision making in any given scenario: technology, suppliers and distributors, consumer interest groups, customers and competitors, government factors, and union factors.

Workers' council

A workers' council is a governing body of a workplace, farm, school, or other enterprise that is self-managed by workers. While some self-managed organizations are run by meetings where decisions are made by vote, others hold elections to appoint delegates to a workers' council, usually with the requirement of a high turnover rate to avoid the creation of a managerial class.

Work-hard, play-hard culture

One of four corporate cultures identified by T. E. Deal and A. A. Kennedy, characterized by fast feedback and low risk. Typical of software companies and restaurants, jobs in these cultures involve large workloads with rapid follow-through required, but involve little uncertainty.

Workplace bullying

Bullying in the workplace is recurring mistreatment of an employee, whether by a superior or a co-worker. Bullying need not be physical, and can transpire within the rules of the workplace, taking forms like the belittling of an employee's opinions (work-related or otherwise), jokes at the employee's expense, teasing and insults, social isolation, belittling the employee's work or pointedly ignoring their work or its positive aspects, or in the case of bullying supervisors, assigning unfair or impossible workloads, deadlines, or other work conditions, or purposely setting the employee up to fail. It is easy for workplace bullying to change the culture of the workplace, and a personal conflict between two employees may lead to a culture of bullying within the organization. Several states have passed laws on abusive work environments, but none have focused specifically on bullying.

Workplace democracy

Workplace democracy is the adoption of democratic principles of leadership and decision making in the workplace, including voting, due process, and some form of power sharing. Some trade unions are committed to democratic structures in their function, for instance, and management science has investigated the use of democratic structuring in businesses.

Workplace friendship

Workplace friendship is simply a friendly relationship between co-workers, but studies have found that both job satisfaction and career success are related to the quality of workplace relationships, and that not all workplaces are equally conducive to such friendships.

Workplace gossip

Workplace gossip is rumor, innuendo, or confidences about third parties exchanged by co-workers. While generally unavoidable, when gossip pervades the workplace, it can have an unhealthy disinhibiting effect on conversation and composure, as well as undermining trust.

Workplace harassment

Workplace harassment is the offensive or aggressive behavior of a worker directed at one or more other workers. Workplace harassment causes significant work stress, even for those other than the workers targeted, and when the harasser is a manager or other superior, the effect on employee engagement, absenteeism, and turnover can be profound.

Workplace listening

The workplace requires active listening skills and an awareness of the importance of nonverbal communication in order to avoid misunderstandings and conflicts. This is particularly true for leaders, whose followers may feel ignored or unvalued if they do not feel they are being listened to.

Workplace politics

Workplace or office politics refers to the networks of power, influence, alliance, and social connections that exist in the workplace, and in some cases the ways in which individuals accrue intangible status that is not entirely derived from their rank or job role. Workplace politics may center around issues related to the work at hand or may be driven primarily by social factors.

Workplace wellness

Workplace wellness is the promotion of healthy behavior in the workplace and by employees, including health and wellness fairs, on-site fitness facilities, and any form of health or fitness education, weight mangement program, or medical screening offered to employees.

WYSE International

WYSE (World Youth Service and Enterprise) International is a charitable organization providing education and leadership development for young people in conjunction with the United Nations Department of Public Information. Established in 1989, it has offered courses to participants in 100 countries.

Xeer

Xeer is the legal system of Somalia, which for years provided the only stable governance of the essentially stateless society as a result of the civil war preventing the formation of an effective government. (Somalia has maintained a largely informal economy in the same period.) Xeer developed in the Horn of Africa in the 7th century, under no known outside influences, and was the only legal system in the region until Europeans arrived in the late 19th century. Under xeer, elder Somalis consult the precedent of previous cases in mediating disputes and criminal matters, and the law emerges from their collective decisions. Each head of an extended family, selected by its elder members after lengthy deliberation, is the judge for that family. A decentralized legal system, xeer is one reason Somalis have resisted ascribing legitimacy to any centralized government formed since its independence from colonial powers.

Zedong, Mao

Mao Zedong, transliterated as Mao Tsu-tung in older texts, was the founding father of the People's Republic of China, and served as the Chairman of the Communist Party of China from 1945 to his death in 1976. A young man during the Chinese revolutions of the early 20th century, Mao was exposed to Marxism and Leninism in college and founded the Communist Party of China (CPC) in 1921. The CPC based its ideology on that of Soviet premier Vladimir Lenin, who had been instrumental in the October Revolution that brought communists to power in Russia in 1917. Leninism focused on democratic decision making and discussion followed by total unity in commitment to the results of the decision-making process. When Mao came to power after the CPC overthrew the Chinese government following a 10-year civil war, he made China a single-party state, launched several initiatives against his "counter-revolutionary" enemies, and attempted to transform the Chinese economy into an industrial one, diverting resources away from agriculture and contributing to the deadliest famine in history. A cult of personality developed around him during the Great Leap Forward, his industrialization program, and there continues to be widespread disagreement over his legacy. The

Chinese Communist Party has rejected many of Mao's economic principles while officially considering him a national hero. Outside China, scholars point both to the terrible atrocities he ordered in the name of stamping out resistance to the revolution and to the possibility that his leadership created a communist state better able to survive than those of eastern Europe.

Zero Defects

Zero Defects was an approach to management in manufacturing in the 1960s and 1970s, which sought to eliminate defects from manufactured products as a means of eliminating waste and reducing cost. Zero Defects originated in the vastly expanding defense industry, in which defective products posed a concern even more significant than those in other industries. However, because of its reliance on costly inspections and quality management systems, Zero Defects was criticized as inefficient by later schools of thought, including that introduced in W. Deming's *Out of the Crisis*.